# ACCOUNTING
## FOR NON-ACCOUNTING STUDENTS

Visit the *Accounting for Non-Accounting Students, seventh edition* Companion Website at **www.pearsoned.co.uk/dyson** to find valuable **student** learning material including:

- Multiple choice questions to help test your learning
- Extra question material
- Links to relevant sites on the web
- Glossary explaining key terms mentioned in the book

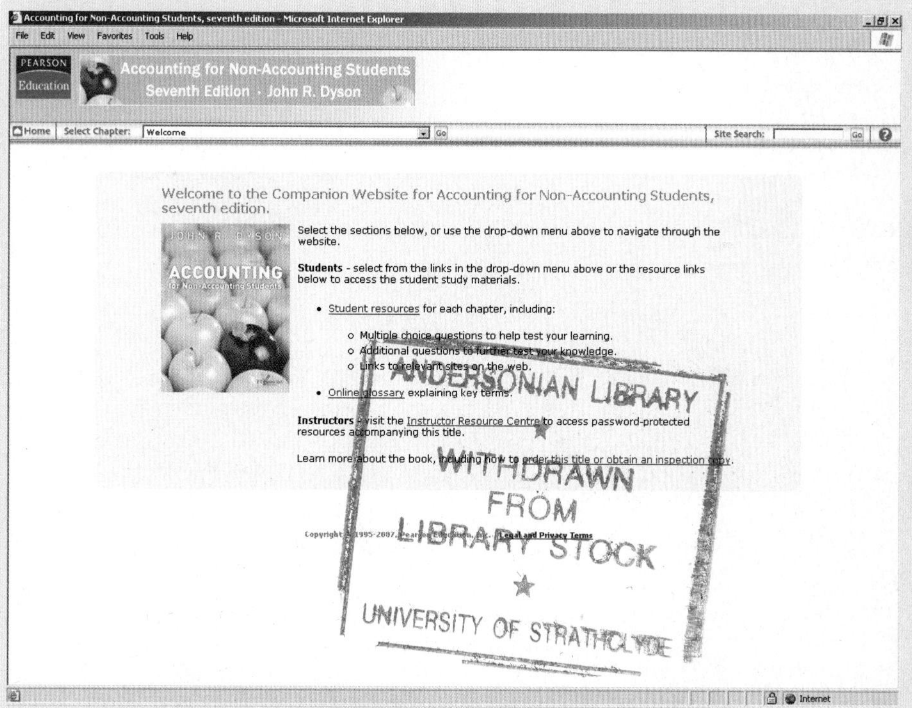

We work with leading authors to develop the strongest educational materials in Accounting, bringing cutting-edge thinking and best learning practice to a global market.

Under a range of well-known imprints, including Financial Times Prentice Hall, we craft high quality print and electronic publications which help readers to understand and apply their content, whether studying or at work.

To find out more about the complete range of our publishing please visit us on the World Wide Web at: **www.pearsoned.co.uk**

# ACCOUNTING
## FOR NON-ACCOUNTING STUDENTS

Seventh Edition

John R. Dyson

An imprint of Pearson Education
Harlow, England • London • New York • Boston • San Francisco • Toronto • Sydney • Singapore • Hong Kong
Tokyo • Seoul • Taipei • New Delhi • Cape Town • Madrid • Mexico City • Amsterdam • Munich • Paris • Milan

**Pearson Education Limited**

Edinburgh Gate
Harlow
Essex CM20 2JE
England

and Associated Companies throughout the world

*Visit us on the World Wide Web at*:
www.pearsoned.co.uk

First edition published in Great Britain under the Pitman Publishing imprint in 1987
Second edition 1991
Third edition 1994
Fourth edition published under the Financial Times Pitman Publishing imprint in 1997
Fifth edition 2001
Sixth edition 2004
**Seventh edition 2007**



ISBN: 978-0-273-70922-0

**British Library Cataloguing-in-Publication Data**
A catalogue record for this book is available from the British Library

10 9 8 7 6 5 4 3 2 1
10 09 08 07

Typeset in 10.5/13pt Minion by 30
Printed and bound by Mateu Cromo Artes Graficas, Spain

*The publisher's policy is to use paper manufactured from sustainable forests.*

# Brief contents

# Contents

## Supporting resources

Visit www.pearsoned.co.uk/dyson to find valuable online resources

**Companion Website for students**

- Multiple choice questions to help test your learning
- Extra question material
- Links to relevant sites on the web
- Glossary explaining key terms mentioned in the book

**For instructors**

- Complete, downloadable Lecturer's Guide
- PowerPoint slides that can be downloaded and used for presentations
- Multiple choice questions for use in class, together with answers
- Answers to extra question material in the Companion Website
- Extra case studies and guidelines on using them with students

**Also**: The Companion Website provides the following features:

- Search tool to help locate specific items of content
- E-mail results and profile tools to send results of quizzes to instructors
- Online help and support to assist with website usage and troubleshooting

For more information please contact your local Pearson Education sales representative or visit www.pearsoned.co.uk/dyson

# Preface

## Why study accounting?

This book provides a solid introduction to accounting for those students who are required to study it as part of a non-accounting course. It is also of benefit to those managers in business, government or industry whose work involves them in dealing with accounting information.

Non-accountants are often puzzled why they are required to take a course in accounting, and even more so when they have to take a demanding examination at the end of it. The fact is that these days, no matter what your job, you need to have some knowledge of accounting matters. The main reason for this is that for different specialists to talk to each other they have to speak in a language that everyone understands. In business (in its widest sense) that language is money and that happens to be the language that accountants are trained in. The use of a common language enables them to translate all the various activities that take place within a business and to report on them on the same basis. So if you need to know what is going on in other departments (as you almost certainly will) you will find it much easier if you speak the language of accounting.

## The book's purpose

The problem with many accounting textbooks is that they are written primarily for accounting students. As a result they go way beyond what a non-accountant needs. This book is different. The subject is not covered superficially but it avoids going into too much technical detail that is really only of relevance to accountants. Nevertheless, by the time you get to the end of the book you will have gained a perfectly adequate knowledge and understanding of accounting that will enable you to do your job much more effectively.

## Some guidance for lecturers

The book is divided into four parts. Part 1 introduces students to the world of accounting, Part 2 deals with financial accounting, Part 3 with financial reporting and Part 4 with management accounting.

As you will probably be aware, many further and higher education institutions now operate a modular structure for the delivery of their courses. This book is particularly useful if your own institution does the same. Some accounting syllabi for non-accounting students then combine both financial accounting and management accounting in one module while others split them between separate modules. The book is designed so that it can easily be adapted irrespective of whether you combine them or split them.

It is highly unlikely, of course, that the contents of the book will match precisely the syllabus requirements of your own course. There are bound to be topics to which you give more or less emphasis and there will be others that are not covered at all in the book. Nevertheless, the book has now been widely used throughout the UK for over 20 years and in many countries overseas. From the feedback that has been received the contents appear to meet the main requirements of most introductory accounting courses for non-accounting students.

There is one topic, however, that splits opinion right down the middle – double-entry book-keeping. Some lecturers are absolutely convinced that non-accounting students need to have a grounding in this topic if they are to understand where the information comes from, what problems there are with it and how it can be used. Other lecturers are adamant that it is totally unnecessary for non-accounting students.

As opinion is so evenly divided on this subject, we have decided to retain double-entry book-keeping in the main part of the book. If you do not include the topic in your syllabus it can be easily left out by skipping the whole of Chapter 3 (Recording data) and possibly even Chapter 4 (Sole trader accounts). You could then pick up the thread of the book in Chapter 5 (Last minute adjustments) provided you are sure that your students know something about a trial balance, a profit and loss account, and a balance sheet.

In this edition we have taken the opportunity to revise and to bring the sixth edition up to date. There have been no major structural changes. The most significant feature that has had to be accommodated is the switch, in 2005, to International Accounting Standards and International Financial Reporting Standards for European Union listed companies. This event has required some substantial changes to be made to Chapter 9 (Information disclosure), Chapter 10 (The annual report), Chapter 11 (The annual accounts) and Chapter 12 (Interpretation of accounts). By their very nature, both Chapter 13 (Contemporary issues) and Chapter 22 (Emerging issues) have also been subject to substantial revision.

Elsewhere, the news stories that begin every chapter and the real-life examples used throughout the book have been replaced with more recent ones. Similarly the various activities and tutorial questions have been re-dated in order to make them contemporary.

## Some guidance for college and university students

If you are using this book as part of a formal course, your lecturer should have provided you with a work scheme. The work scheme will outline just how much of the book you are expected to cover each week. In addition to the work done in your lecture, you will probably have to read each chapter at least twice.

As you work through a chapter you will come across a number of 'activities'. Most of them require you to do something or to find something out. The idea of these activities is to encourage you to stop your reading of the text at various points and to think about what you have just read.

There are few right and wrong answers in accounting so we want you to gain some experience in deciding for yourself what you would do if you were faced with the type of issues covered in the activities.

You are also recommended to attempt as many of the questions that follow each chapter as you can. The more questions that you do, the more confident you will be that you really do understand the subject matter. However, avoid looking at the answers (there are some at the back of the book) until you are absolutely certain that you do not know how to do the question. If the answer is not at the back of the book, ask your lecturer to download it for you from the *Lecturer's Guide*.

## Some guidance for students studying on their own

If you are studying accounting without having the opportunity of having face-to-face tuition, we suggest that you adopt the following study plan.

1 Organize your private study so that you have covered every topic in your syllabus at least two weeks before your examination. A proven method is to divide the number of weeks (or perhaps days!) you have available by the number of topics. This gives you the *average* time that you should spend on each topic. Allow for some topics requiring more time than others but don't rush though a topic just because you are behind your timetable. Instead, try to put in a few extra hours that week.
2 Read each chapter slowly. Be careful to do each activity and to work through each example. Don't worry if you do not understand each point immediately. Read on to the end of the chapter.
3 Read the chapter again, this time making sure that you understand each point. If necessary, go back and re-read and repeat until you do understand the point.
4 Attempt as many questions at the end of each chapter as you can, but do not look at the answers until you have completed the question or you are certain that you cannot do it. The questions are generally graded so the more difficult ones come towards the end. If you can do them all without too much difficulty then you can move on to the next chapter with great confidence. However, before you do it is not a bad idea to re-read the chapter again.

## More guidance for all students

At this early stage of your accounting career we want to emphasize that accounting involves much more than being good at doing simple arithmetic (contrary to popular opinion it is not highly mathematical). The solution to many accounting problems often calls for a considerable amount of personal judgement and this means that there is bound to be an element of subjectivity in whatever you decide to do.

The simplified examples used in this book illustrate some complicated issues and problems in the real world that are not easily solved. You should, therefore, treat the suggested answers with caution and use them as an opportunity to question the methodology adopted. This will mean that when you are presented with some accounting information in your job, you will automatically subject it (rightly) to a great deal of questioning. That is as it should be because, as you will shortly discover, if you were an accountant and you happened to be asked, '*What do 2 + 2 make?*', you might well reply by asking another question, '*What do you want it to make?*'.

Puzzled? Intrigued? Then read on – and good luck with your studies.

*An explanation*

In order to avoid tedious repetition and tortuous circumlocution, the masculine pronoun has generally been adopted throughout this book. No offence is intended to anyone, most of all to my female readers, and I hope none will be taken.

# Guided tour

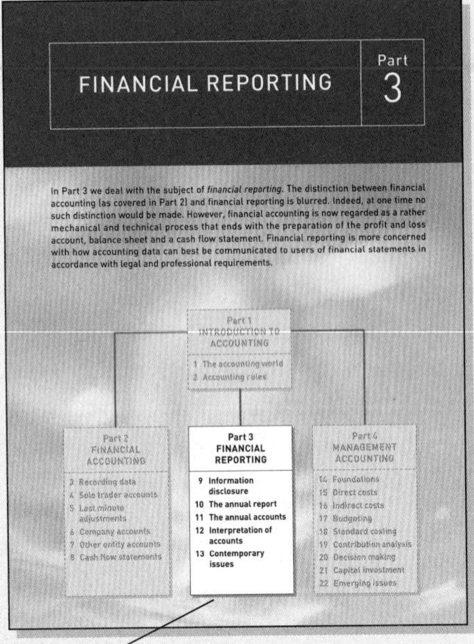

FINANCIAL REPORTING

Part 3

In Part 3 we deal with the subject of *financial reporting*. The distinction between financial accounting (as covered in Part 2) and financial reporting is blurred. Indeed, at one time no such distinction would be made. However, financial accounting is now regarded as a rather mechanical and technical process that ends with the preparation of the profit and loss account, balance sheet and a cash flow statement. Financial reporting is more concerned with how accounting data can best be communicated to users of financial statements in accordance with legal and professional requirements.



**Part openers** contain a diagram to help you find your way around the book

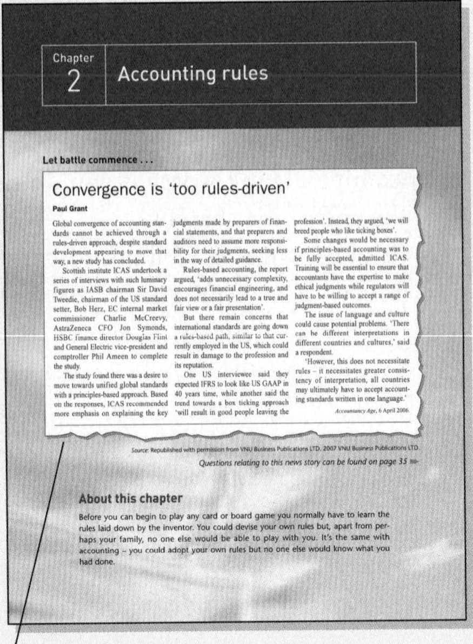

Chapter 2 Accounting rules

**Let battle commence . . .**

## Convergence is 'too rules-driven'

**Paul Grant**

Global convergence of accounting standards cannot be achieved through a rules-driven approach, despite standard development appearing to move that way, a new study has concluded.

Scottish institute ICAS undertook a series of interviews with such luminary figures as IASB chairman Sir David Tweedie, chairman of the US standard setter, Bob Herz, EC internal market commissioner Charlie McCreevy, AstraZeneca CFO Jon Symonds, HSBC finance director Douglas Flint and General Electric vice-president and comptroller Phil Ameen to complete the study.

The study found there was a desire to move towards unified global standards with a principles-based approach. Based on the responses, ICAS recommended more emphasis on explaining the key judgments made by preparers of financial statements, and that preparers and auditors need to assume more responsibility for their judgments, seeking less in the way of detailed guidance.

Rules-based accounting, the report argued, 'adds unnecessary complexity, encourages financial engineering, and does not necessarily lead to a true and fair view or a fair presentation'.

But there remain concerns that international standards are going down a rules-based path, similar to that currently employed in the US, which could result in damage to the profession and its reputation.

One US interviewee said they expected IFRS to look like US GAAP in 40 years time, while another said the trend towards a box ticking approach 'will result in good people leaving the profession'. Instead, they argued, 'we will breed people who like ticking boxes'.

Some changes would be necessary if principles-based accounting was to be fully accepted, admitted ICAS. Training will be essential to ensure that accountants have the expertise to make ethical judgments while regulators will have to be willing to accept a range of judgment-based outcomes.

The issue of language and culture could cause potential problems. 'There can be different interpretations in different countries and cultures,' said a respondent.

'However, this does not necessitate rules – it necessitates greater consistency of interpretation, all countries may ultimately have to accept accounting standards written in one language.'

*Accountancy Age*, 6 April 2006.

Source: Republished with permission from VNU Business Publications LTD. 2007 VNU Business Publications LTD.

*Questions relating to this news story can be found on page 35*

**About this chapter**

Before you can begin to play any card or board game you normally have to learn the rules laid down by the inventor. You could devise your own rules but, apart from perhaps your family, no one else would be able to play with you. It's the same with accounting – you could adopt your own rules but no one else would know what you had done.

**Chapter openers** feature a topical news article relating chapter content to the real world

CHAPTER 2 ACCOUNTING RULES 23

Unlike a card or a board game, however, no one actually sat down and devised a set of accounting rules that everyone else adopted. What happened was that over a long period of time a common procedure gradually evolved, so much so that now we can identify a number of generally accepted accounting practices.

In this book we will refer to such practices as *accounting rules*, although you will find a bewildering number of other terms used in practice, e.g. assumptions, axioms, concepts, conventions, objectives, policies, postulates, principles and procedures!

The main purpose of the chapter is to identify those accounting rules that underpin the contents of this book and that lie behind the type of financial statements you are likely to come across in your everyday life.

**Learning objectives**

By the end of this chapter you should be able to:

- trace the historical development of conventional accounting procedures;
- identify the main accounting rules used in preparing financial statements;
- classify them into three broad groupings;
- describe each accounting rule;
- explain why each of them is important.

**Why this chapter is important for non-accountants**

As a non-accountant, do you need to question the information that your accountants give you? Do you have to know where they have got it from? Does it matter if you just accept it? We think that the answer to all three questions is 'yes' because as a senior manager you are ultimately responsible for whatever your accountants do. If something goes wrong you just can't blame it on them (or on the computer for that matter). As the old cliché has it: *the buck stops with you.*

In order to satisfy yourself that the accountants *have* got it right, you need to be familiar with what procedures they have used in preparing any information that they give to you. Almost certainly they will have used a number of well-established rules that have evolved over many centuries. Unfortunately, many of them are capable of individual interpretation and some require a great deal of subjective judgement. This means that, within the rules, it is quite possible to obtain a number of solutions simply by interpreting the rules a little more rigorously, or by being less pessimistic about a possible outcome.

So it is your responsibility to check that you agree with your accountants' interpretation and judgement before you accept their recommendations. But you cannot really do that unless you understand what they have done and why they have done it. This chapter will give you that understanding by explaining the basis upon which financial statements are prepared.

Before we turn to it in some detail it would be helpful if we first gave you a brief outline of the historical development of accounting procedures.

**Learning objectives** are provided in each chapter

**Why this chapter is important for non-accountants** explores the applications and benefits of chapter content for the non-accountant

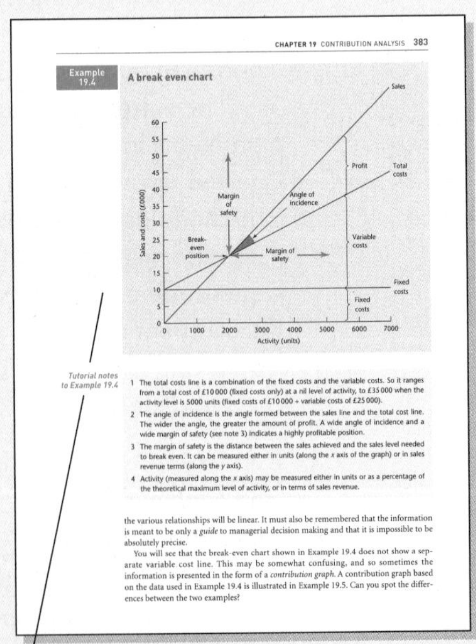

CHAPTER 19 CONTRIBUTION ANALYSIS 383

Example 19.4 **A break even chart**



*Tutorial notes to Example 19.4*

1 The total costs line is a combination of the fixed costs and the variable costs. So it ranges from a total cost of £10 000 (fixed costs only) at a nil level of activity, to £35 000 when the activity level is 5000 units (fixed costs of £10 000 + variable costs of £25 000).

2 The angle of incidence is the angle formed between the sales line and the total cost line. The wider the angle, the greater the amount of profit. A wide angle of incidence and a wide margin of safety (see note 3) indicates a highly profitable position.

3 The margin of safety is the distance between the sales achieved and the sales level needed to break even. It can be measured either in units (along the $x$ axis of the graph) or in sales revenue terms (along the $y$ axis).

4 Activity (measured along the $x$ axis) may be measured either in units or as a percentage of the theoretical maximum level of activity, or in terms of sales revenue.

the various relationships will be linear. It must also be remembered that the information is meant to be only a *guide* to managerial decision making and that it is impossible to be absolutely precise.

You will see that the break-even chart shown in Example 19.4 does not show a separate variable cost line. This may be somewhat confusing, and so sometimes the information is presented in the form of a *contribution graph*. A contribution graph based on the data used in Example 19.4 is illustrated in Example 19.5. Can you spot the differences between the two examples?

**Examples** are spread throughout the chapter

**Activities** test student understanding at regular intervals throughout the chapter

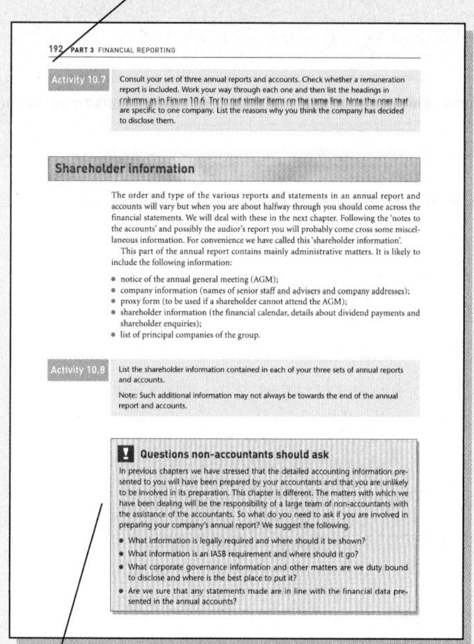

192 PART 3 FINANCIAL REPORTING

**Activity 10.7** Consult your set of three annual reports and accounts. Check whether a remuneration report is included. Work your way through each one and then list the headings in columns as in Figure 10.6. Try to put similar items on the same line. Note the ones that are specific to one company. List the reasons why you think the company has decided to disclose them.

## Shareholder information

The order and type of the various reports and statements in an annual report and accounts will vary but when you are about halfway through you should come across the financial statements. We will deal with these in the next chapter. Following the 'notes to the accounts' and possibly the audior's report you will probably come cross some miscellaneous information. For convenience we have called this 'shareholder information'.

This part of the annual report contains mainly administrative matters. It is likely to include the following information:

- notice of the annual general meeting (AGM);
- company information (names of senior staff and advisers and company addresses);
- proxy form (to be used if a shareholder cannot attend the AGM);
- shareholder information (the financial calendar, details about dividend payments and shareholder enquiries);
- list of principal companies of the group.

**Activity 10.8** List the shareholder information contained in each of your three sets of annual reports and accounts.

Note: Such additional information may not always be towards the end of the annual report and accounts.

**Questions non-accountants should ask**

In previous chapters we have stressed that the detailed accounting information presented to you will have been prepared by your accountants and that you are unlikely to be involved in its preparation. This chapter is different. The matters with which we have been dealing will be the responsibility of a large team of non-accountants with the assistance of the accountants. So what do you need to ask if you are involved in preparing your company's annual report? We suggest the following.

- What information is legally required and where should it be shown?
- What information is an IASB requirement and where should it go?
- What corporate governance information and other matters are we duty bound to disclose and where is the best place to put it?
- Are we sure that any statements made are in line with the financial data presented in the annual accounts?

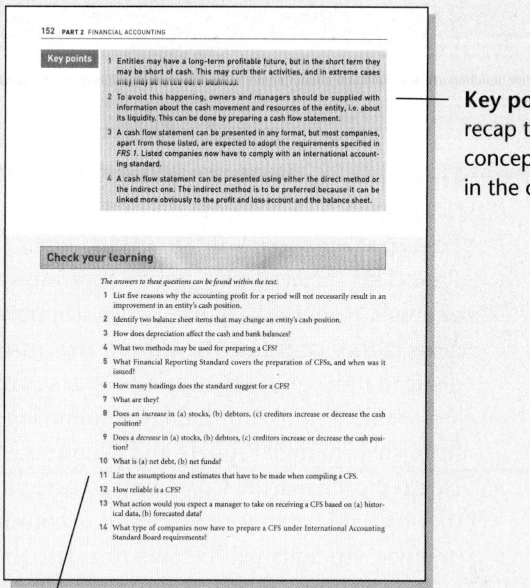

152 PART 2 FINANCIAL ACCOUNTING

**Key points**

1 Entities may have a long-term profitable future, but in the short term they may be short of cash. This may curb their activities, and in extreme cases they may be forced out of business.

2 To avoid this happening, owners and managers should be supplied with information about the cash movement and resources of the entity, i.e. about its liquidity. This can be done by preparing a cash flow statement.

3 A cash flow statement can be presented in any format, but most companies, apart from those listed, are expected to adopt the requirements specified in *FRS 1*. Listed companies now have to comply with an international accounting standard.

4 A cash flow statement can be presented using either the direct method or the indirect one. The indirect method is to be preferred because it can be linked more obviously to the profit and loss account and the balance sheet.

## Check your learning

*The answers to these questions can be found within the text.*

1 List five reasons why the accounting profit for a period will not necessarily result in an improvement in an entity's cash position.

2 Identify two balance sheet items that may change an entity's cash position.

3 How does depreciation affect the cash and bank balances?

4 What two methods may be used for preparing a CFS?

5 What Financial Reporting Standard covers the preparation of CFSs, and when was it issued?

6 How many headings does the standard suggest for a CFS?

7 What are they?

8 Does an *increase* in (a) stocks, (b) debtors, (c) creditors increase or decrease the cash position?

9 Does a *decrease* in (a) stocks, (b) debtors, (c) creditors increase or decrease the cash position?

10 What is (a) net debt, (b) net funds?

11 List the assumptions and estimates that have to be made when compiling a CFS.

12 How reliable is a CFS?

13 What action would you expect a manager to take on receiving a CFS based on (a) historical data, (b) forecasted data?

14 What type of companies now have to prepare a CFS under International Accounting Standard Board requirements?

**Key points** recap the main concepts studied in the chapter

**Questions non-accountants should ask** offer questions business managers might ask to assist in the decision-making process

**Check your learning** tests absorption of chapter content and offers a useful revision aid

**News story quizzes** provide thought-provoking questions relating to topical news articles

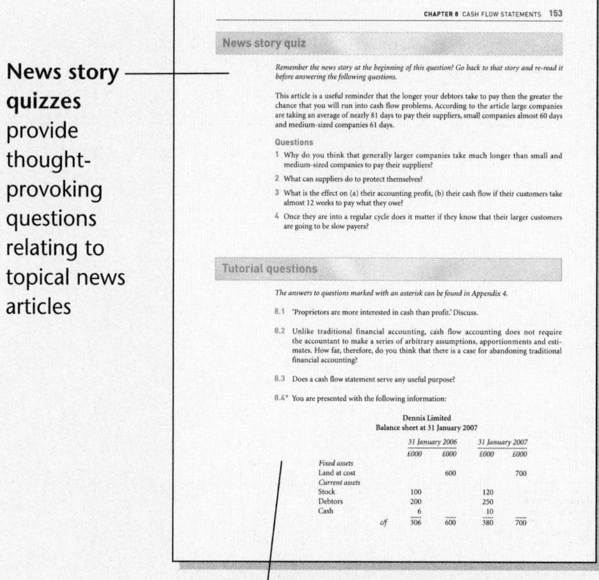

CHAPTER 8 CASH FLOW STATEMENTS 153

## News story quiz

*Remember the news story at the beginning of this question? Go back to that story and re-read it before answering the following questions.*

This article is a useful reminder that the longer your debtors take to pay then the greater the chance that you will run into cash flow problems. According to the article large companies are taking an average of nearly 81 days to pay their suppliers, small companies almost 60 days and medium-sized companies 61 days.

**Questions**

1 Why do you think that generally larger companies take much longer than small and medium-sized companies to pay their suppliers?

2 What can suppliers do to protect themselves?

3 What is the effect on (a) their accounting profit, (b) their cash flow if their customers take almost 12 weeks to pay what they owe?

4 Once they are into a regular cycle does it matter if they know that their larger customers are going to be slow payers?

## Tutorial questions

*The answers to questions marked with an asterisk can be found in Appendix 4.*

8.1 'Proprietors are more interested in cash than profit.' Discuss.

8.2 Unlike traditional financial accounting, cash flow accounting does not require the accountant to make a series of arbitrary assumptions, apportionments and estimates. How far, therefore, do you think that there is a case for abandoning traditional financial accounting?

8.3 Does a cash flow statement serve any useful purpose?

8.4* You are presented with the following information:

**Dennis Limited**
**Balance sheet at 31 January 2007**

| | *31 January 2006* | | *31 January 2007* | |
|---|---|---|---|---|
| | *£000* | *£000* | *£000* | *£000* |
| *Fixed assets* | | | | |
| Land at cost | | 600 | | 700 |
| *Current assets* | | | | |
| Stock | 100 | | 120 | |
| Debtors | 200 | | 250 | |
| Cash | 6 | | 10 | |
| c/f | 306 | 600 | 380 | 700 |

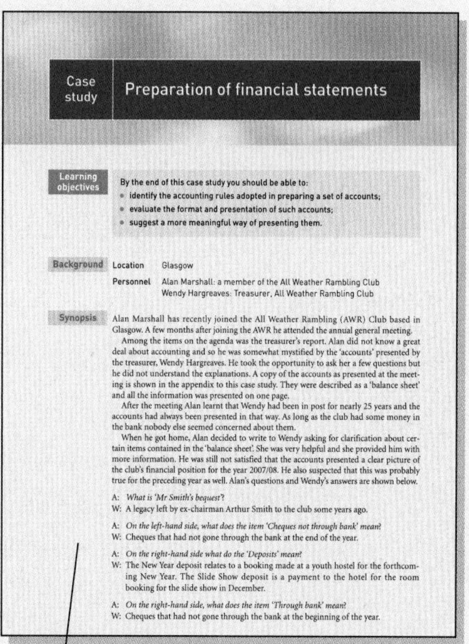

**Case study** Preparation of financial statements

**Learning objectives**

By the end of this case study you should be able to:

- identify the accounting rules adopted in preparing a set of accounts;
- evaluate the format and presentation of such accounts;
- suggest a more meaningful way of presenting them.

**Background**

Location Glasgow

Personnel Alan Marshall: a member of the All Weather Rambling Club
Wendy Hargreaves: Treasurer, All Weather Rambling Club

**Synopsis**

Alan Marshall has recently joined the All Weather Rambling (AWR) Club based in Glasgow. A few months after joining the AWR he attended the annual general meeting.

Among the items on the agenda was the treasurer's report. Alan did not know a great deal about accounting and so he was somewhat mystified by the 'accounts' presented by the treasurer, Wendy Hargreaves. He took the opportunity to ask her a few questions but he did not understand the explanations. A copy of the accounts as presented at the meeting is shown in the appendix to this case study. They were described as a 'balance sheet' and all the information was presented on one page.

After the meeting Alan learnt that Wendy had been in post for nearly 25 years and the accounts had always been presented in that way. As long as the club had some money in the bank nobody else seemed concerned about them.

When he got home, Alan decided to write to Wendy asking for clarification about certain items contained in the 'balance sheet'. She was very helpful and she provided him with more information. He was still not satisfied that the accounts presented a clear picture of the club's financial position for the year 2007/08. He also suspected that this was probably true for the preceding year as well. Alan's questions and Wendy's answers are shown below.

A: *What is 'Mr Smith's bequest'?*
W: A legacy left by ex-chairman Arthur Smith to the club some years ago.

A: *On the left-hand side, what does the item 'Cheques not through bank' mean?*
W: Cheques that had not gone through the bank at the end of the year.

A: *On the right-hand side what do the 'Deposits' mean?*
W: The New Year deposit relates to a booking made at a youth hostel for the forthcoming New Year. The Slide Show deposit is a payment to the hotel for the room booking for the slide show in December.

A: *On the right-hand side, what does the item 'Through bank' mean?*
W: Cheques that had not gone through the bank at the beginning of the year.

**Tutorial questions** offer ideas for assignments or class discussion

**Case studies** appear at the end of each part

Visit the Companion Website at **www.pearsoned.co.uk/dyson** to find further practice questions, study material and links to relevant sites on the World Wide Web. See page xi for full contents.

# Acknowledgements

My thanks are due to the editors of the following journals and newspapers for permission to reproduce copyright material: *Accountancy Age*, *Accountingnet*, *The Advertiser*, *Financial Management*, *Financial Times*, *The Guardian*, *The Herald and Lewis Virtual Press*. This material may not be reproduced or transmitted unless written permission is obtained from the original owner or publisher. I hope that the inclusion of some actual news stories continues to enliven the introduction to each chapter and encourages students to think about the various issues covered in the stories.

I would also like to thank the following companies for permission to extract material from their annual reports and accounts: Aggreko plc, A.G. Barr plc, Cairn Energy plc, Devro plc, J. Smart & Co. (Contractors) plc, and Robert Wiseman Dairies plc. It is hoped that by using actual reports and accounts to illustrate various aspects of accounting practice, students will be able to relate the textbook material more easily with the real world. I am particularly grateful to these companies, therefore, for enabling me to introduce non-accounting students to the real world, and I wish to acknowledge the valuable contribution that such companies have made to the contents of this book. The companies are, of course, not responsible for any comments made in the book about their respective annual reports and accounts.

# Publisher's acknowledgements

We are grateful to the following for permission to reproduce copyright material:

Figures 10.3 and 10.4 and material, from data extracted from the Annual Report and Accounts 2005, J. Smart & Co. (Contractors) PLC and Subsidiary Companies, by permission of J. Smart & Co. (Contractors) PLC; Figures 10.5 and 10.6 from data extracted from the Annual Report and Accounts 2005, by permission of Cairn Energy PLC; Data extracted from the Annual Report and Accounts 2005, by permission of Aggreko plc; Figure 11.3 and material, from data extracted from the Annual Report and Accounts 2006, A.G. Barr plc, by permission of Barr Soft Drinks; Figures 10.2, 10.5, 10.6 and 22.1 and material, from data extracted from the Annual Report and Accounts 2005, by permission of Devro plc; Data extracted from the Annual Report and Financial Statements for 2002, 2003, 2004, 2005 and 2006, by permission of Robert Wiseman Dairies PLC.

The Financial Times Limited for 'China struggles to overcome shortage of good accountants' © *Financial Times*, 6 June 2006; 'Convergence is "too rules-driven"' in *Accountancy Age*, 6 April, (Grant, P., 2006). Republished with permission from VNU Business Publications LTD. 2007 VNU Business Publications LTD; 'Accounting errors may happen again at NAB' in *The Advertiser*, 28 February, (Turnbull, J., 2006) © 2007 AAP.; 'Experts boot out football reforms' in *Accountancy Age*, 8 September, (Neveling, N., 2005). Republished with permission from VNU Business Publications LTD. 2007 VNU Business Publications LTD; 'Axle Group loses bearings' in *The Herald*, 12 January, Newsquest Media Group Ltd, (Rogerson, P., 2006). Reproduced with permission from The Herald (Glasgow) Newsquest (Herald & Times) Ltd © Newsquest Media Group Ltd; '£100m write-off for Cairn' in *Accountancy Age*, 26 January (Neveling, N., 2006). Republished with permission from VNU Business Publications LTD. 2007 VNU Business Publications LTD; 'Home Office pins Whitehall farce on IT implementation difficulties' in Financial Management (UK), March, (2006), by permission of CIMA; 'Larger companies taking longer to pay up' in *CRN*, 24 January, (Hailstone, L., 2006). Republished with permission from VNU Business Publications LTD. 2007 VNU Business Publications LTD; 'Spirent hit hard by IFRS rules' in *Accountancy Age*, 22 June, (Neveling, N., 2006). Republished with permission from VNU Business Publications LTD. 2007 VNU Business Publications LTD; 'An adequate replacement' in *Accountancy Age*, 12 January, (Copnell, T., 2006). Republished with permission from VNU Business Publications LTD. 2007 VNU Business Publications LTD; 'FDs and investors divided over IFRS' in *Accountancy Age*, 27 July, (Neveling, N., 2006). Republished with permission from VNU Business Publications LTD. 2007 VNU Business Publications LTD; 'Shell under fire as oil price boom results in UK's biggest ever profit' in *The Guardian*, 3 February (Macalister, T., 2006). Copyright Guardian News & Media Ltd 2006; 'ASB faces fierce opposition over approach to standards' in *Accountancy Age*, 26 January, (Grant, P., 2006). Republished with permission from VNU Business Publications LTD. 2007 VNU Business Publications LTD; 'NHS told to put finances ahead of medicine' in *Accountancy Age*, 23 January, (Reed, K., 2006). Republished with permission from VNU Business Publications LTD. 2007 VNU Business

Publications LTD; 'Drinks supplier improves supply chain efficiency' in *Computing*, 26 January, (Knights, M., 2006). Republished with permission from VNU Business Publications LTD. 2007 VNU Business Publications LTD; 'Rise in profit warnings blamed on poor sales' in *Accountancy Age*, 16 January, (Accountancyage.com, 2006). Republished with permission from VNU Business Publications LTD. 2007 VNU Business Publications LTD; 'Joseph Signs Up Cognos To Cut Out Spreadsheets', in *Lewis' Virtual Press Room*, 1 February, (www.cognos.com, 2006) by permission of Lewis PR/Cognos; 'Sage readies integrated software for SMEs', *Accountancy Age*, 21 February, (Howorth, R., 2006). Republished with permission from VNU Business Publications LTD. 2007 VNU Business Publications LTD; 'Queen's flight costs were "ten times higher"' in *Accountancy Age*, 21 April (Accountancyage.com, 2006). Republished with permission from VNU Business Publications LTD. 2007 VNU Business Publications LTD; 'Picture messaging is still too expensive' in *Accountancy Age*, 13 January, (Thomson, I., 2006). Republished with permission from VNU Business Publications LTD. 2007 VNU Business Publications LTD; 'Sage acquires US firm for £184m' in *Accountancy Age*, 9 January, (2006). Republished with permission from VNU Business Publications LTD. 2007 VNU Business Publications LTD; 'Health warning issued on fads in management accounting' in *Accountingnet.ie*, 31 January, (Heaphy, S., 2006) by permission of CIMA.

In some instances we have been unable to trace the owners of copyright material, and we would appreciate any information that would enable us to do so.

# INTRODUCTION TO ACCOUNTING

# Part 1

This book is divided into four main parts as shown below. Part 1 contains two chapters. In Chapter 1 we provide some background about accounting, the accountancy profession, and the organizations that accountants work for. In Chapter 2 we outline the conventional rules that accountants normally follow when preparing accounting statements.

**Part 1 INTRODUCTION TO ACCOUNTING**

1 The accounting world
2 Accounting rules

**Part 2 FINANCIAL ACCOUNTING**

3 Recording data
4 Sole trader accounts
5 Last minute adjustments
6 Company accounts
7 Other entity accounts
8 Cash flow statements

**Part 3 FINANCIAL REPORTING**

9 Information disclosure
10 The annual report
11 The annual accounts
12 Interpretation of accounts
13 Contemporary issues

**Part 4 MANAGEMENT ACCOUNTING**

14 Foundations
15 Direct costs
16 Indirect costs
17 Budgeting
18 Standard costing
19 Contribution analysis
20 Decision making
21 Capital investment
22 Emerging issues

# Chapter 1 The accounting world

## Accountants: even China wants them . . .

# China struggles to overcome shortage of good accountants

A lasting legacy of the Cultural Revolution is hampering business, writes Barney Jopson

The 40th anniversary of the start of the Cultural Revolution passed without ceremony last month in China, where the authorities continue to suppress memories of the decade of ultra-leftist turmoil.

But the legacy of the war waged against capitalist thinking is all too evident in one unlikely quarter: the accountancy profession.

For 10 years from 1966, accountants were among hundreds of thousands of professionals and intellectuals who were denounced, sent to internal exile, or even killed. The supply of graduate number-crunchers was cut off as accounting education at university was largely shut down.

Today, with the school leavers of the Cultural Revolution in their late 40s and 50s, the effects of that chaotic decade compound a deeper structural problem.

From 1949 to 1966, and for 15 more years after the launch of economic reforms in 1978, Chinese accountants used a Soviet book-keeping system designed for a centrally planned economy – a world apart from western accounting. The result: a void where China is desperate for senior accountants with know-how relevant to its modern economy.

Stephen Taylor, a partner at Deloitte, one of the big four international accountancy groups, in Hong Kong, says: 'Do we lack experienced, grey-haired people [in mainland China]? Yes. One of the biggest challenges we have is getting the right level of experience and oversight.'

The sector is not exceptional. Banks, businesses and the legal profession also suffer from a dearth of senior people with education and experience.

But the problem is acute in accountancy because demand for the services is rocketing.

The shortage is more than a personnel headache for the big four firms and their smaller local rivals. It has the potential to slow down – or even trip up – China's integration into the system of global capital markets.

The icons of that integration are former state-owned enterprises that have listed outside the mainland. Bank of China last week raised $9.7bn (€7.5bn, £5.2bn) from an initial public offering in Hong Kong, setting a record for a Chinese company.

The queue of groups seeking to follow in their footsteps is growing. But some have been held up by a struggle to secure big-four accountants, who are needed to make their books fit for foreign consumption.

'When you take a state-owned enterprise that has had weak internal controls, it can be enormously labour-intensive to come up with financials we can work with,' says one investment banker in Hong Kong. 'My impression is that the big four are stretched. I've seen cases where clients may have to delay a transaction because their auditors can't provide resources at short notice.'

The other dimension of China's integration into global markets is foreign investment on the Shanghai and Shenzhen stock exchanges – and, it, too is affected by the skills and capacity of Chinese accountants.

True, the appetite of some overseas fund managers is such that new money is likely to flood in the moment existing limits on A-share investment are loosened. But many others stay away. They harbour deep scepticism about the quality of Chinese accounting and governance, underscored by scandals over manipulated earnings, hidden debts and crooked auditors.

As part of a crackdown on wrong doing, the government announced in February that listed companies would be required to follow international standards on accounting and auditing.

Accountants at local firms are now racing to understand these rules. But for some it is a tall task. Beyond the technicalities, the bigger challenge is absorbing alien notions such as maintaining a dispassionate distance from audit clients.

Recalling the scrapping of Soviet accounting in 1993, Chen Yugui, secretary-general of the Chinese Institute of Certified Public Accountants, says: 'Over the past 10 years we have been transforming our thinking about accounting.'

But that has not solved staff problems for Chen Yonghong, chief partner of TZPA, China's seventh-biggest domestic accountancy firm. 'I don't think there is a lack of people per se, but there is a lack of good international people,' he says. 'We get many applicants but only a few are sufficiently professional.'

*Financial Times*, 6 June 2006.

*Questions relating to this news story can be found on page 20*

## About this chapter

This chapter sets the scene for the rest of the book.

The chapter begins with an explanation of why it is important for you as a non-accountant to study accounting. It then gives a brief explanation of the nature and purpose of accounting and of its historical development. This is followed by an outline of the main branches of accounting and a description of the accountancy profession. The last main section of the chapter gives a brief overview of the economic structure of the United Kingdom.

**Learning objectives**

**By the end of this chapter you should be able to:**

- **summarize the nature and purpose of accounting;**
- **outline its history;**
- **explain why non-accountants need to know something about accounting;**
- **identify the main branches of accounting;**
- **list the major accountancy bodies in the United Kingdom;**
- **outline the main types of public and private entities operating in the United Kingdom.**

## ! Why accounting is important for non-accountants

You've probably got hold of this book because you're a student. You're doing a certificate, degree or diploma course in perhaps business, engineering, languages, management, law or one of the sciences. And then you found to your horror that you have to do some accounting. Why?

OK, we'll try to explain. You probably have a vague idea that accounting has something to do with balance sheets and profits and tax and, er, *stuff* but you are certainly not sure what that has to do with the subject you're studying. And you resent it.

Right. Now accounting is basically about collecting information and letting people have it who need it, like shareholders and managers. Like you – or at least like you hope to be. 'So what?' you might well ask. 'If I need it or want it I'll just ask the accountants to get it for me.' That's fine but if you were a manager would you really be quite happy to accept *all* that the accountants gave you? Would you know what it meant, how reliable it was and what you were supposed to do with it? We suspect that if you really think about the repercussions of *not* questioning what your accountants gave you, you would be (to say the least) a little unhappy. Perhaps even a bit worried, especially if you were legally responsible for it all.

The point we are making is that accountants provide a service for other people. Most accountants are probably highly qualified, experienced and good at their job, but as accountants they should not take the *decisions*. That is the manager's job – maybe your job and you will know much more about your business than any accountant. And there is no doubt that you will be able to make even *better* decisions if you have some knowledge and some understanding of the nature of accounting information along with what it can and what it cannot do in helping you to plan and to control the running of a business.

So in a sentence – if you know something about accounting you will become a *better* manager. By the end of the book you will be well on the way to becoming one.

This first chapter sets the scene for the remaining chapters. It is important for you because it provides you with the necessary background information to enable you to become a better manager.

## Nature and purpose

We begin our accounting studies by giving a brief explanation of what accounting is and what it *does*. We will then tell you something of what it *doesn't* do. For our purposes we will use the following definition of accounting:

**Accounting is a service provided for those who need information about an entity's financial performance, its assets and its liabilities.**

This definition contains a number of features that require some explanation.

- *Service.* Accounting is of assistance to other people – if nobody wanted the service there would be no such thing as accounting.
- *Information.* The information traditionally collected by accountants is restricted to what can be quantified and translated into monetary terms.
- *Entity.* An entity is a jargon term used by accountants to describe any type of organization, e.g. an individual or a business organization such as a company. Usually there are two parties to any transaction: one entity gives and the other receives. In accounting we restrict the information we collect about the transaction to the entity that appointed us. Of course the other entity's accountants will be doing the same thing from *its* point of view.
- *Financial performance.* The financial performance is judged by matching incomes received with expenditure incurred over a period of time (usually one year).
- *Assets.* You may think of an asset as being something tangible that you *own*, such as a house or a car. In accounting it is regarded as being something that will result in a future economic benefit as a result of a past event. For example, the purchase of plant and machinery will provide a benefit over very many years and thereby help the entity generate income in those years.
- *Liabilities.* Again you may think a liability as something that you owe but in accounting it is defined as an obligation arising from a past event. For example, you may have bought some furniture but you don't have to start paying for it until next year. So for the time being, what you owe is an obligation, i.e. a liability.

The above summary shows that accounting information is somewhat restricted:

- It relates to only one entity.
- It has to be quantifiable.
- It must be capable of being converted into monetary terms.
- It relates to an arbitrary period of time.
- A distinction is made between economic benefits that relate to the current period, previous periods or future ones.

Non-accountants are often surprised when they realize that accounting information is restricted in such ways. This gives rise to what is sometimes called the *expectations gap*, i.e. when users expect more from accounting information than it is capable of providing. In the early 2000s there were a number of well-publicized accounting scandals in Europe and America, e.g. Enron and WorldCom. Such so-called scandals caused enormous embarrassment to the accountancy profession. Although some of them were brought about by fraud (a criminal offence in the UK), many of them arose because of the expectations gap.

We shall be returning to this subject later in the book but in the meantime we will provide you with a brief review of how accounting has developed over very many years.

**Activity 1.1**

Look up the definition of accounting in three well-known dictionaries (such as the *Oxford Dictionary*). Copy the definitions into your notebook. Then try to frame your own definition based on the definitions given in your three dictionaries.

## Historical development of accounting

The word *account* in everyday language is often used as a substitute for an *explanation* or a *report* of certain actions or events. If you are an employee, for example, you may have to explain to your employer just how you have been spending your time, or if you are a manager you may have to report to the owner on how the business is doing. In order to explain or to report, you will, of course, have to remember what you were doing or what happened. As it is not always easy to remember, you may need to keep some written record. In effect, such records can be said to provide the basis of a rudimentary accounting (or reporting) system.

In a primitive sense, man has always been involved in some form of accounting. It may have gone no further than a farmer (say) measuring his worth simply by counting the number of cows or sheep that he owned. However, the growth of a monetary system enabled a more sophisticated method to be developed. It then became possible to calculate the increase or decrease in individual wealth over a period of time, and to assess whether (say) a farmer with ten cows and fifty sheep was wealthier than one who had sixty pigs. Figure 1.1 illustrates just how difficult it would be to assess the wealth of a farmer in a non-monetary system.

| His possessions | A year ago | Now | Change |
|---|---|---|---|
| Cows | ●●●●●●●●●● | ●●●●●●●●●●●●●●● | +5 |
| Hens [● = 10] | ●●●●●●●●●● | ●●●●●●● | –30 |
| Pigs | ●●●●●● | ●●●● | –2 |
| Sheep [● = 10] | ●●●●● | ●●●●●●● | +20 |
| Land [● = 1 acre] | ●●●● | ●●●● | no change |
| Cottage | ● | ● | no change |
| Carts | ●●● | ● | –2 |
| Ploughs | ● | ●● | +1 |

**Figure 1.1 Accounting for a farmer's wealth**

Even with the growth of a monetary system, it took a very long time for formal documentary systems to become commonplace, although it is possible to trace the origins of modern book-keeping at least as far back as the twelfth century. We know that from about that time, traders began to adopt a system of recording information that we now refer to as *double-entry book-keeping*. By the end of the fifteenth century, double-entry book-keeping was widely used in Venice and the surrounding areas; indeed, the first-known book on the subject was published in 1494 by an Italian mathematician called Pacioli. Modern book-keeping systems are still based on principles established in the fifteenth century, although they have had to be adapted to suit modern conditions.

Why has a recording system devised in medieval times lasted for so long? There are two main reasons:

- it provides an accurate record of what has happened to a business over a specified period of time;
- information extracted from the system can help the owner or the manager to operate the business much more effectively.

In essence, the system provides the answers to three basic questions that owners (and managers) want to know. They are as follows (see also Figure 1.2):

- What profit has the business made?
- How much does the business owe?
- How much is owed to it?

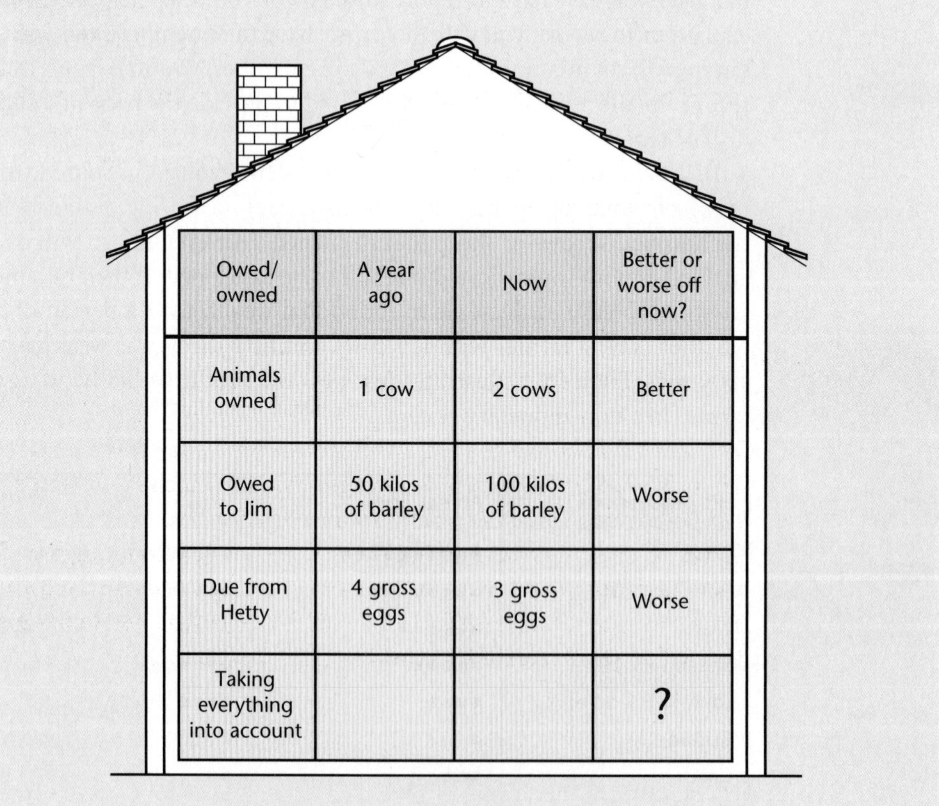


**Figure 1.2 An owner's vital questions**

The medieval system dealt largely with simple agricultural and trading entities. In the eighteenth century, however, the UK underwent what was called the *Industrial Revolution*. Economic activity gradually moved away from growing things to making or manufacturing them. In the early days of the Industrial Revolution managers had to depend upon the type of information supplied to the owners. The owners' need was for *financial* purposes, i.e. to calculate how much profit they had made. Financial information was prepared infrequently (perhaps only once a year) and then not in any great detail. Managers needed information largely for *costing* purposes, i.e. to work out the cost of making individual products. Such information was required more than once a year and in some considerable detail.

As a result of the different information needs of owners and managers, separate accounting systems were developed. However, as much of the basic data were common to both systems, they were gradually brought together. It would be rare now to find any entity that had a separate financial accounting system and a separate costing system.

Another change in more recent years is that it is possible to identify more than two user groups. Besides owners and managers, information may also now be required by creditors, customers, employees, government, investors, lenders and the public.

While accounting gradually evolved into two main branches in the nineteenth century (financial accounting and cost accounting), there were additional developments in the twentieth century. We examine the structure of accounting as it is today in the next section.

**Activity 1.2**

Complete the following sentences:

(a) The word _______ in everyday language means an explanation or a report.
(b) Traders in the fifteenth century began to adopt a system of _________ to record information.
(c) The owners of a business want to know how much _______ a business has made.
(d) An _______ is a term used to describe any type of organization.
(e) In the eighteenth century the United Kingdom underwent an _________ _________.

## Branches of accounting

The work that accountants now undertake ranges far beyond that of simply preparing financial and costing statements. It is possible to identify at least six main branches of accounting and a number of important sub-branches.

We will deal with each of the main branches of accounting broadly in the order that they have developed over the last 100 years, i.e. financial accounting, management accounting, auditing, taxation, financial management, and bankruptcy and liquidation. You will see from Figure 1.3 how they all fit together.

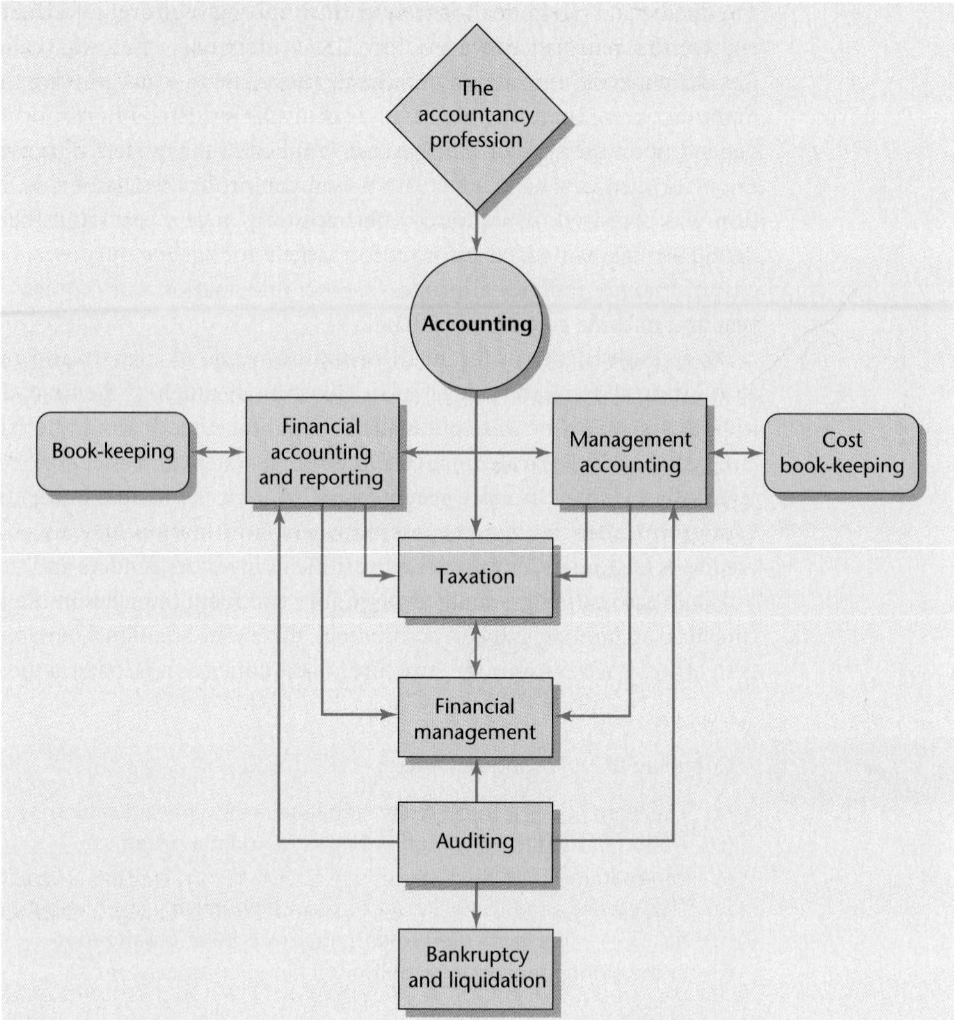


**Figure 1.3 The main branches of accounting**

## Financial accounting

We have already discussed in some detail the nature, purpose and development of financial accounting. We do not need to say much more except to give you the formal definition used by the Chartered Institute of Management Accountants (CIMA). It is as follows:

> *Classification and recording of the monetary transactions of an entity in accordance with established concepts, principles, accounting standards and legal requirements and their presentation, by means of income statements, balance sheets and cash flow statements, during and at the end of an accounting period. (CIMA, Official Terminology, 2005)*

We will explain what is meant by 'concepts, principles, accounting standards and legal requirements' in the next chapter.

A distinction can be made between *financial accounting* and *financial reporting* and we do so in this book mainly for practical reasons, in order to break the information down into manageable parts. *Financial accounting* may be regarded as being the accounting process that ends with the preparation of the financial statements, i.e. the profit and loss account, the balance sheet and the cash flow statement. *Financial reporting* then becomes the process of communicating financial accounting to users of such information. It involves supplying them with additional information along with a detailed quantitative and qualitative analysis of the underlying data.

### Book-keeping

An important sub-branch of financial accounting is book-keeping. Indeed, book-keeping may be regarded as the foundation on which the entire discipline of accounting is built.

Book-keeping is a mechanical task involving the collection of basic financial data. The data are entered in special records known as *books of account* and then extracted in the form of a *trial balance*. The trial balance enables a profit and loss account and a balance sheet to be prepared.

The CIMA definition of book-keeping is:

> *Recording of monetary transactions, appropriately classified, in the financial records of an entity. (op. cit., p. 60)*

## Management accounting

Management accounting has grown out of nineteenth century financial accounting and it may now be regarded as an all-embracing term. The CIMA definition is as follows:

> *Management accounting is the application of the principles of accounting and financial management to create, protect, preserve and increase value for the stakeholders of for-profit and not-for-profit enterprises in the public and private sectors. (CIMA, Official Terminology, 2005)*

This definition is immediately followed by a statement explaining that:

> *'Management accounting is an integral part of management. It requires the identification, generation, presentation, interpretation and use of relevant information to ...'*

There then follows a list of nine functions of management accounting. In summary these are: forming strategy; planning; determining capital structures and financing; designing reward strategies; informing about operational decisions; controlling operations and ensuring the efficient use of resources; measuring and reporting on performance; safeguarding assets; implementing corporate governance procedures, risk management and internal control.

Clearly, management accounting has come a long way since its *costing* days in the nineteenth century. In fact CIMA does not now recommend using the term 'costing' on its own unless it is accompanied by a qualifying adjective, e.g. *contract* costing or *job* costing. But it does give us a definition of cost accounting:

> *Gathering of cost information and its attachment to cost objects, the establishment of budgets, standard costs and actual costs of operations, processes, activities or products; and the analysis of variances, profitability or the social use of funds. (CIMA, Official Terminology, 2005)*

Interestingly, CIMA does not offer a specific definition of cost book-keeping but it does define the verb 'to cost':

> *To ascertain the cost of a specified thing or activity.*

It then points out that:

> *The word cost can rarely stand alone and should be qualified as to its nature and limitations.*

But by combining this definition of 'cost' with the definition of 'book-keeping' given above, we can arrive at a suitable working definition of cost book-keeping:

> *The recording of monetary transactions, appropriately classified, in the financial records of an entity in order to ascertain the cost of a specified thing or activity.*

And the development of this form of accounting in the nineteenth century was brought about because, with increasing industrialization, it soon became apparent that financial accounting was not capable of costing individual 'things' or 'activities'.

## Auditing

CIMA defines an audit as being:

> *Systematic examination of the activities and status of an entity, based primarily on investigation and analysis of its systems, controls and records. (CIMA, Official Terminology, 2005)*

So auditing is the process of carrying out that investigation.

Not all entities have their accounts audited but for some entities (such as large limited liability companies) it is a legal requirement.

Auditors are usually trained accountants who specialize in ascertaining whether the accounts are credible, i.e. whether they can be believed. There are two main types of auditors.

1 *External auditors.* External auditors are appointed by the owners of an entity. They are independent of the entity and they are not employed by it. They report to the owners and not to the managers of the entity. Large limited liability companies are required to have an external audit. External auditors report on whether the financial accounts represent what is called 'a true and fair view' of the entity's affairs for a certain period of time. They may do some detailed checking of its records in order to be able to come to such a view, but normally they would be selective. If they are then satisfied, they will be able to report their findings to the owners. The public often believe that the job of an auditor is to discover whether any fraud has taken place. This is not so. This misconceived perception forms part of the expectations gap discussed earlier in the chapter.
2 *Internal auditors.* Some entities employ internal auditors. Internal auditors are appointed by the managers of the entity; they are employees of the entity and they answer to its management. Internal auditors perform routine tasks and undertake some detailed checking of the entity's accounting procedures. Their task may also go beyond the financial accounts e.g. they may do some checking of the planning and control procedures and conduct 'value-for-money' tests.

External auditors and internal auditors usually work together very closely. Nevertheless, they do have separate roles and responsibilities. External auditors have always to remember that internal auditors are employees of the entity; they may be strongly influenced by the management of the entity and they may be subject to the same pressures as other employees, e.g. job security, pay and promotion prospects. But even external auditors are not completely independent. In the case of a large company, for example, the directors only recommend the appointment of the company's auditors to the shareholders. As the shareholders usually accept what the directors recommend, the directors are in a strong position if they want to dismiss the auditors. The auditors can then appeal directly to the shareholders but again the shareholders usually accept the directors' recommendation.

## Taxation

Taxation is a highly complex and technical branch of accounting. Those accountants who are involved in tax work are responsible for computing the amount of tax payable both by business entities and by individuals. It is not necessary for anybody or any entity to pay more tax than is required by the law. It is, therefore, perfectly legitimate to search out all legal means of minimizing the amount of tax that might be demanded by the government. This is known as *tax avoidance.* The non-declaration of sources of income on which tax might be payable is known as *tax evasion.* Tax evasion is a very serious offence and it can lead to a long prison sentence. The borderline between tax avoidance and tax evasion is a narrow one and tax accountants have to steer a fine line between what is lawful and what might not be acceptable.

## Financial management

Financial management is a relatively new branch of accounting. It has grown rapidly over the last 30 years. Financial managers are responsible for setting financial objectives, making plans based on those objectives, obtaining the finance needed to achieve the plans and generally safeguarding all the financial resources of the entity.

Financial managers are much more likely to be heavily involved in the *management* of an entity than is generally the case with other management accountants (although that is changing). It should also be noted that financial managers draw on a much wider range of disciplines (e.g. economics and mathematics) than does the more traditional accountant, and they also rely more heavily on non-financial and more qualitative data.

### Bankruptcy and liquidation

One other highly specialist branch of accounting that you may sometimes read about is that connected with *insolvency*, i.e. with bankruptcy or liquidation. This branch of accounting is extremely specialized. It has a long history but it is not one that most accountants will have had either anything to do with or indeed know much about.

*Bankruptcy* is a formal legal procedure. The term is applied to individuals when their financial affairs are so serious that they have to be given some form of legal protection from their creditors. The term *liquidation* is usually applied to a company when it also gets into serious financial difficulties and its affairs have to be 'wound up', i.e. arrangements made for it to go out of existence in an orderly fashion.

Companies do not necessarily go immediately into liquidation if they get into financial difficulties. An attempt will usually be made either to rescue them or to protect certain types of creditors. In these situations, accountants sometimes act as *administrators*. Their appointment freezes creditors' rights. This prevents the company from being put into liquidation during a period when the administrators are attempting to manage the company. By contrast, *receivers* may be appointed on behalf of loan creditors. The creditors' loans may be secured on certain property. The receivers will try to obtain the income from that property or they may attempt to sell it.

We hope that you never come into contact with insolvency practitioners and so we will move on swiftly to have a look at another topic, namely the structure of the accountancy profession.

**Activity 1.3**

State whether each of the following statements is true or false:

(a) An auditor's job is to find out whether a fraud has taken place. *True/false*
(b) Management accounts are required by law. *True/false*
(c) Tax avoidance is lawful. *True/false*
(d) A balance sheet is a list of assets and liabilities. *True/false*
(e) Companies have to go into liquidation if they get into financial difficulties. *True/false*

## The accountancy profession

There are six major accountancy bodies operating in the United Kingdom. They are:

- Institute of Chartered Accountants in England and Wales (ICAEW)
- Institute of Chartered Accountants in Ireland (ICAI)
- Institute of Chartered Accountants of Scotland (ICAS)
- Association of Chartered Certified Accountants (ACCA)
- Chartered Institute of Management Accountants (CIMA)
- Chartered Institute of Public Finance and Accountancy (CIPFA).

The Irish Institute (ICAI) is included in the list because it has a strong influence in Northern Ireland. The organization of the accountancy profession is also shown in Figure 1.4.

Although all six major professional accountancy bodies now have a Royal Charter, it is still customary to refer only to members of ICAEW, ICAI, and ICAS as *chartered accountants*. Such chartered accountants have usually had to undergo a period of training in a practising office, i.e. one that offers accounting services directly to the public. This distinguishes them from members of the other three accountancy bodies. Much practice work is involved in auditing and taxation but, after qualifying, many chartered accountants go to work in commerce or industry. ACCA members may also obtain their training in practice but relevant experience elsewhere counts towards their qualification. CIMA members usually train and work in industry, while CIPFA members specialize almost exclusively in central and local government.

Apart from the six major bodies, there are a number of important (although far less well-known) smaller accountancy associations and societies, e.g. the Association of Authorized Public Accountants, the Institute of Cost and Executive Accountants and the Institute of Financial Accountants. Such bodies offer some form of accountancy qualification but they have not yet managed to achieve the status or prestige attached to being a member of one of the six major bodies. They are usually referred to as *secondary bodies*.

There is also another very important accountancy body, the Association of Accounting Technicians. The association was formed in 1980 as a professional organization especially for those accountants who *assist* qualified accountants in preparing

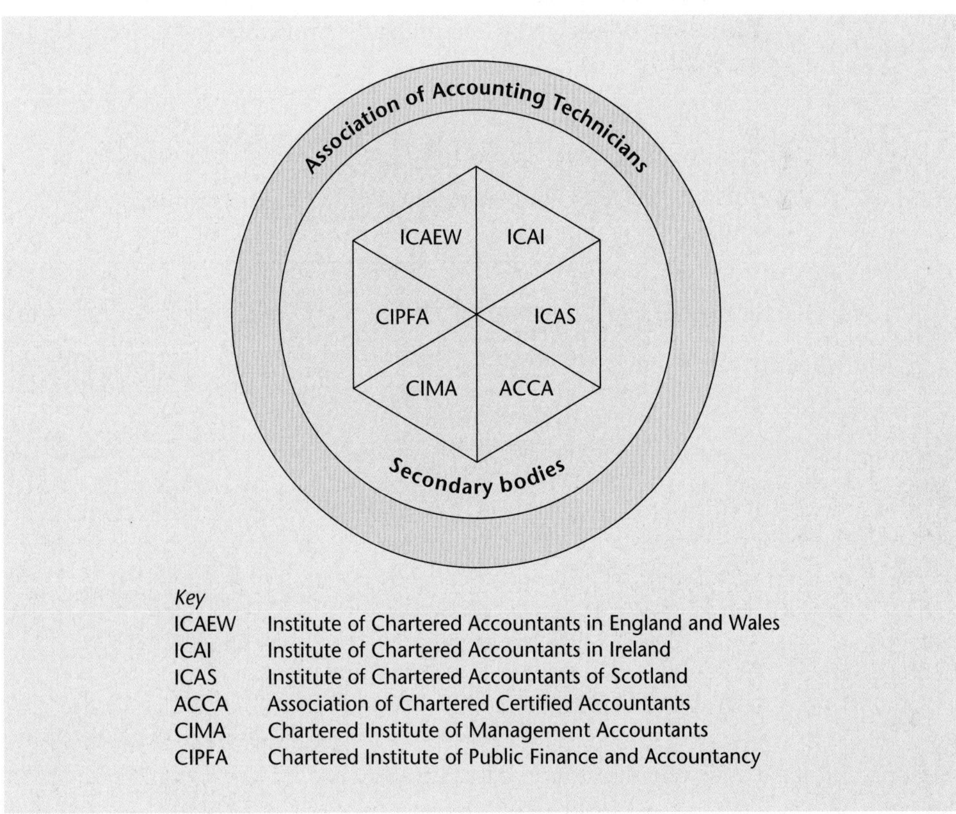


**Figure 1.4 Organization of the UK accountancy profession**

accounting information. In order to become an accounting technician, it is necessary to take (or be exempt from) the association's examinations. These are not easy, although they tend to be less technically demanding and more practical than those of the six major bodies.

**Activity 1.4**

Which is the odd one out among the following professional accountancy bodies? State your reasons for the one that you select.

(a) AAT
(b) CIMA
(c) CIPFA
(d) ICAEW

## Public and private entities

The main aim of this section is to introduce you to the two main types of entities with which we shall be primarily concerned in this book – *sole traders* and *companies.* Before we can do this we need to explain a little bit about the economic structure of the United Kingdom.

In order to simplify our analysis, we will classify the UK economy into two broad groupings – the *profit-making sector* and the *not-for-profit sector.* Within each of these sectors it is then possible to distinguish a number of different types of entities (see Figure 1.5). We begin by examining the profit-making sector.

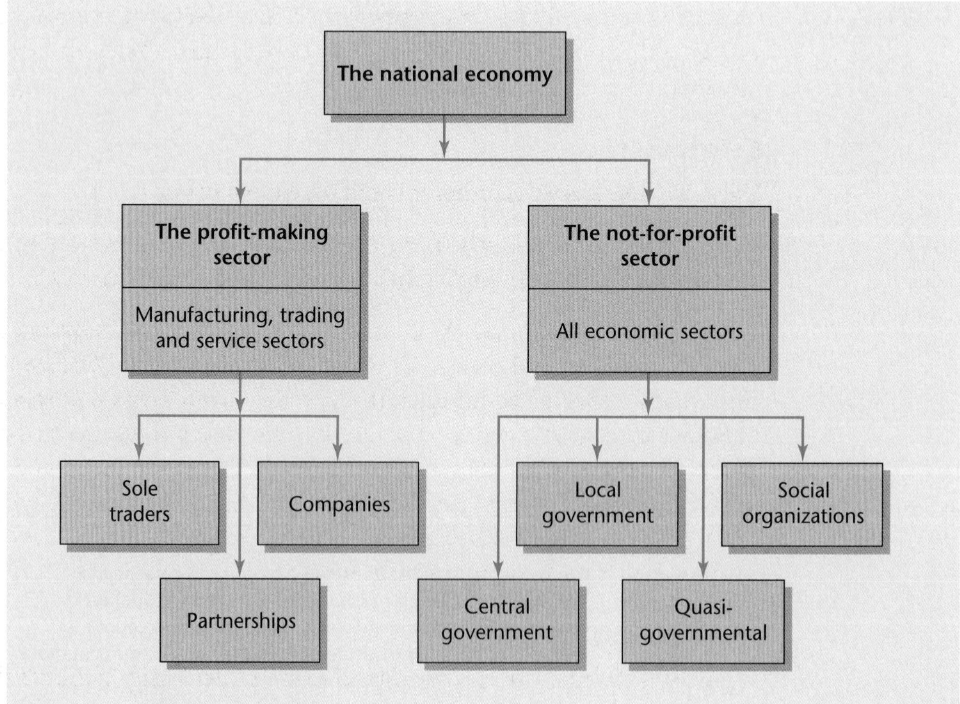


**Figure 1.5 Public and private entities**

## The profit-making sector

The profit-making sector is extremely diverse, but it is possible to recognize three major subdivisions. These are the manufacturing sector, the trading sector, and the service sector.

The *manufacturing sector* is involved in purchasing raw materials and component parts, converting (or incorporating) them into finished goods and then selling them to customers. Examples of manufacturing enterprises include the chemicals, glass, iron and steel, and textile industries.

The *trading sector* purchases finished goods and then sells them to their customers without any further major conversion work normally being done on them. Trading enterprises are found in the retailing and wholesaling sectors, such as shops, supermarkets and builders merchants.

The *service sector* provides advice or assistance to customers or clients, such as hairdressing, legal and travel services. Unlike the manufacturing and trading sectors, the service sector does not usually deal in physical or tangible goods. However, there are some exceptions – the hotel and restaurant trade, for example, is normally classed as part of the service sector even though it provides major tangible services such as the provision of accommodation, food and drink.

The accounting systems required of manufacturing, trading and service sector entities are all slightly different, although they are based on similar principles and procedures. Manufacturing entity accounts are the most complex, trading entity accounts are fairly straightforward, while service entity accounts are usually quite simple.

Until about 20 years ago the manufacturing sector was of major significance in the UK. It is now much less important and the service sector has largely taken its place.

The products or the services offered by the manufacturing, trading or service sectors may be different but the way that they are organized is still very similar. Within each sector you will find three main types of entities. These are *sole traders*, *partnerships* and *companies*. The basic distinction between such entities reflects who owns them, how they are financed and what the law requires of them.

### Sole traders

The term 'sole trader' is rather misleading for two reasons:

- 'sole' does not necessarily mean that only one person is involved in the entity;
- 'trader' may also encompass manufacturing and service entities.

The term really reflects the *ownership* of the entity, the main requirement being that only one individual should own it. The owner would normally also be the main source of finance and he would be expected to play a reasonably active part in its management.

Sole traders usually work on a very informal basis and some private matters relating to the owner are often indistinguishable from those of the business. Sole trader accounts are fairly straightforward and there is no specific legislation that covers the accounting arrangements. We shall be using sole trader accounts in Chapters 3 to 5 in order to demonstrate some basic accounting techniques.

### Partnerships

A partnership entity is very similar to a sole trader entity except that there must be at least *two owners* of the business. Partnerships sometimes grow out of a sole trader entity, perhaps because more money needs to be put into the business or because the sole trader needs some help in managing it. It is also quite common for a new business to start out as a partnership, e.g. when some friends get together to start a home-decorating service or to form a car-repair business.

The partners should agree among themselves how much money they will each put into the business, what jobs they will do, how many hours they will work, and how the profits and losses will be shared. In the absence of any agreement (whether formal or informal), partnerships in the United Kingdom are covered by the Partnership Act 1890.

There is also a new type of partnership. This was introduced in 2001. It is known as a *Limited Liability Partnership* (LLP). An LLP has a separate legal personality from that of its owners (like a company), and it protects the partners from personal bankruptcy.

Partnership accounts are very similar to those of sole traders and we shall not be dealing with them in this book.

### Companies

A company is another different type of business organization. There are many different forms of companies but basically a company is an entity that has a separate existence from that of its owners. We are going to be primarily concerned with *limited liability companies*. The term 'limited liability' means that the owners of such companies are only required to finance the business up to an agreed amount. Once they have contributed that amount, they cannot be called on to contribute any more, even if the company gets into financial difficulties.

As there is a risk that limited liability companies may not be able to pay off their debts, Parliament has had to give some legal protection to those parties who may become involved with them. The details are contained within the Companies Act 1985. We will be dealing with company accounts in some detail in Chapters 6 to 11.

**Activity 1.5**

Insert in the following table one advantage and one disadvantage of operating a business as (a) a sole trader, (b) a partnership, (c) as a limited liability company.

| Type of entity | Advantage | Disadvantage |
|---|---|---|
| (a) Sole trader | | |
| (b) Partnership | | |
| (c) Limited liability company | | |

## The not-for-profit sector

By 'not-for-profit' we mean those entities whose primary purpose is to provide a service to the public rather than to make a profit from their operations. We will consider this sector under four main headings: central government, local government, quasi-governmental bodies and social organizations.

Within the three governmental groups, there is a wide variety of different types of entities. Governmental accounting is extremely specialized and it would require a book of its own to deal with it. We shall also not be considering the accounts of social organizations in any great depth because their accounting procedures are similar to profit-making entities.

### Central government

Central government is responsible for services such as macro-economic policy, education, defence, foreign affairs, health and social security. These responsibilities are directly controlled by Cabinet ministers who answer to Parliament at Westminster for their actions. In 1999, some of these central government responsibilities were 'devolved', i.e. they became the direct responsibility of elected bodies in Northern Ireland, Scotland and Wales.

### Local government

For well over a century, central government has also devolved many of its responsibilities to local authorities, i.e. smaller units of authority that have some geographical and community coherence. Councillors are elected by the local community. They have responsibility for those services that central government has delegated, for example, the local administration of education, housing, the police and social services.

### Quasi-governmental bodies

Central government also operates indirectly through quasi-governmental bodies, such as the British Broadcasting Corporation (BBC), the Post Office, colleges and universities. Such bodies are nominally independent of central government, even though it normally provides their main funds and their senior managers may be appointed by government ministers.

### Social organizations

This category covers a wide range of cultural, educational, recreational and social bodies. Some are formally constituted and professionally managed, such as national and international charities, while others are local organizations run by volunteers on a part-time basis, e.g. bridge and rugby clubs.

**Activity 1.6**

Into which category may the following functions/services best be placed? Tick the appropriate column.

| Function/service | Central government | Local government | Quasi-governmental | Social organization |
|---|---|---|---|---|
| 1 Broadcasting | | | | |
| 2 Famine relief | | | | |
| 3 Postal deliveries | | | | |
| 4 Social services | | | | |
| 5 Work and pensions | | | | |

## Questions non-accountants should ask

This is an introductory chapter, so at this stage there are not many technical questions that you might be able to put to your accountants. Your questions, therefore, are more likely to be about the accountants themselves, the organization of the accounting function within the entity and the role that the accountants see themselves playing within the entity. The following is a sample of the types of general questions that as a non-accountant you might like to put to the accountants employed within your own entity.

- How many accountants do we employ?
- How many of them are members of one of the six main professional accounting bodies and what are they?
- How is the accounting function organized?
- What can the accountants do to help me do my job more effectively and efficiently?
- What information do the accountants want me to give to them and when is it wanted?
- What is it to be used for?
- What information are they going to give back to me?
- What am I supposed to do with it?
- How can all of us – managers and accountants in the entity – work together as a team?

## Conclusion

The main aim of this chapter has been to introduce the non-accountant to the world of accounting. We have emphasized that the main purpose of accounting is to provide financial information to those parties that need it.

Of course, information must be useful if it is to have any purpose, but as a non-accountant you may feel reluctant to question any accounting information that lands on your desk. You may also not understand why the accountant is always asking you what you might think are irrelevant questions, and so you respond with any old nonsense. You then perhaps feel a bit guilty and a little frustrated; you would like to know more, but you dare not ask. We hope that by the time you have worked your way through this book, you will have the confidence to ask and, furthermore, that you will understand the answer. Good luck!

Now that the world of accounting has been outlined, we can turn to more detailed subject matter. The first task is to learn the basic rules of accounting. These are covered in the next chapter.

## Key points

1 To account for something means to give an explanation or to report on it.

2 Owners of an entity want to know (a) how well it is doing, (b) what it owes, and (c) how much is owed to it.

3 Accounting is important for non-accountants because (a) they must make sure their own entity complies with any legal requirements, and (b) an accounting system can provide them with information that will help them do their jobs more effectively and efficiently.

4 The six main branches of accounting are auditing, financial accounting/reporting, financial management, management accounting, taxation, and bankruptcy and liquidation.

5 Sub-branches of accounting include book-keeping (a function of financial accounting) and cost book-keeping (a function of management accounting).

6 There are six major professional accountancy bodies in the UK: the Institute of Chartered Accountants in England and Wales, the Institute of Chartered Accountants in Ireland, the Institute of Chartered Accountants of Scotland, the Association of Chartered Certified Accountants, the Chartered Institute of Management Accountants and the Chartered Institute of Public Finance and Accountancy.

7 There are two economic sectors within the UK economy: the profit-making sector and the not-for-profit sector. Within the profit-making sector, business operations can be classified as being manufacturing, trading or servicing and they may be organized as sole trader entities, as partnerships or as companies.

8 The not-for-profit sector includes central government and local government operations, quasi-governmental bodies and social organizations. Governmental operations are extremely complex and the accounting requirements are highly specialized. Social organizations are also diverse. They include various associations, charities, clubs, societies and sundry voluntary organizations, and their accounting requirements are usually similar to those found in the profit-making sector.

## Check your learning

*The answers to these questions can be found within the text.*

1 What is accounting?

2 What is meant by an 'entity'?

3 Give three reasons why accounting is an important subject for non-accountants to study.

4 What is meant by the word 'account'?

5 What name is given to the system of recording information that evolved in medieval times?

6 What are the three basic questions that the owner of a business wants answering?

7 What economic event happened in the UK during the eighteenth century?

8 What happened to the ownership and management of businesses during the nineteenth century in the UK?

9 For what purpose did managers in nineteenth century industrial entities require more detailed information?

10 List three user groups of accounting information.

11 What are the six main branches of accounting?

12 Of which main branch of accounting does cost accounting form a part?

13 What is the difference between 'book-keeping' and 'cost book-keeping'?

14 Explain the difference between 'bankruptcy' and 'liquidation'.

15 List the six major UK professional accountancy bodies.

16 What function does the *Association of Accounting Technicians* fill?

17 Name three types of entities that fall within the profit-making sector of the UK economy.

18 What is meant by the concept of 'limited liability'?

19 What role do local authorities play in the not-for-profit sector of the economy?

20 Name one quasi-governmental body.

## News story quiz

*Remember the news story at the beginning of this chapter? Go back to that story and re-read it before answering the following questions.*

The pace and scale of change in China's economic and political life is staggering. This article reflects the movement away from a Soviet-style economy to much more of a Western approach. The news that China recognizes that it is short of accountants capable of supervising this change is truly remarkable.

### Questions

1 How far do you think that the article is exaggerating the importance of accountants in a Western-style economy?

2 Do you think that China's development really would be slowed down unless it gets more accountants?

3 What appears to be the most important task that accountants are expected to undertake in a Chinese enterprise?

4 What other tasks can you identify that accountants will be expected to do?

## Tutorial questions

*The answers to questions marked with an asterisk can be found in Appendix 4.*

1.1 'Accountants stifle managerial initiative and enterprise.' Discuss.

1.2 Do you think that auditors should be responsible for detecting fraud?

1.3 The following statement was made by a student: 'I cannot understand why accountants have such a high status and why they yield such power.' How would you respond to such an assertion?

1.4* Why should a non-accountant study accounting?

1.5* Describe two main purposes of accounting.

1.6* What statutory obligations require the preparation of management accounts in any kind of entity?

1.7 State briefly the main reasons why a company may employ a team of accountants.

1.8* What statutory obligations support the publication of financial accounts in respect of limited liability companies?

1.9 Why does a limited liability company have to engage a firm of external auditors, and for what purpose?

1.10 Assume that you are a personnel officer in a manufacturing company, and that one of your employees is a young engineering manager called Joseph Sykes. Joseph has been chosen to attend the local university's business school to study for a diploma in management. Joseph is reluctant to attend the course because he will have to study accounting. As an engineer, he thinks that it will be a waste of time for him to study such a subject.

*Required:*
Draft an internal memorandum addressed to Joseph explaining why it would be of benefit to him to study accounting.

1.11 Clare Wong spends a lot of her time working for a large local charity. The charity has grown enormously in recent years and the trustees have been advised to overhaul their accounting procedures. This would involve its workers (most of whom are voluntary) in more book-keeping, and there is a great deal of resistance to this move. The staff have said that they are there to help the needy and not to get involved in book-keeping.

*Required:*
As the financial consultant to the charity, prepare some notes that you could use in speaking to the voluntary workers in order to try to persuade them to accept the new proposals.

**Further practice questions, study material and links to relevant sites on the World Wide Web can be found on the website that accompanies this book. The site can be found at www.pearsoned.co.uk/dyson**

Chapter 2

# Accounting rules

## Let battle commence . . .

### Convergence is 'too rules-driven'

**Paul Grant**

Global convergence of accounting standards cannot be achieved through a rules-driven approach, despite standard development appearing to move that way, a new study has concluded.

Scottish institute ICAS undertook a series of interviews with such luminary figures as IASB chairman Sir David Tweedie, chairman of the US standard setter, Bob Herz, EC internal market commissioner Charlie McCreevy, AstraZeneca CFO Jon Symonds, HSBC finance director Douglas Flint and General Electric vice-president and comptroller Phil Ameen to complete the study.

The study found there was a desire to move towards unified global standards with a principles-based approach. Based on the responses, ICAS recommended more emphasis on explaining the key judgments made by preparers of financial statements, and that preparers and auditors need to assume more responsibility for their judgments, seeking less in the way of detailed guidance.

Rules-based accounting, the report argued, 'adds unnecessary complexity, encourages financial engineering, and does not necessarily lead to a true and fair view or a fair presentation'.

But there remain concerns that international standards are going down a rules-based path, similar to that currently employed in the US, which could result in damage to the profession and its reputation.

One US interviewee said they expected IFRS to look like US GAAP in 40 years time, while another said the trend towards a box ticking approach 'will result in good people leaving the profession'. Instead, they argued, 'we will breed people who like ticking boxes'.

Some changes would be necessary if principles-based accounting was to be fully accepted, admitted ICAS. Training will be essential to ensure that accountants have the expertise to make ethical judgments while regulators will have to be willing to accept a range of judgment-based outcomes.

The issue of language and culture could cause potential problems. 'There can be different interpretations in different countries and cultures,' said a respondent.

'However, this does not necessitate rules – it necessitates greater consistency of interpretation, all countries may ultimately have to accept accounting standards written in one language.'

*Accountancy Age*, 6 April 2006.



*Questions relating to this news story can be found on page 35*

## About this chapter

Before you can begin to play any card or board game you normally have to learn the rules laid down by the inventor. You could devise your own rules but, apart from perhaps your family, no one else would be able to play with you. It's the same with accounting – you could adopt your own rules but no one else would know what you had done.

Unlike a card or a board game, however, no one actually sat down and devised a set of accounting rules that everyone else adopted. What happened was that over a long period of time a common procedure gradually evolved, so much so that now we can identify a number of generally accepted accounting practices.

In this book we will refer to such practices as *accounting rules*, although you will find a bewildering number of other terms used in practice, e.g. assumptions, axioms, concepts, conventions, objectives, policies, postulates, principles and procedures!

The main purpose of the chapter is to identify those accounting rules that underpin the contents of this book and that lie behind the type of financial statements you are likely to come across in your everyday life.

**Learning objectives**

**By the end of this chapter you should be able to:**

- **trace the historical development of conventional accounting procedures;**
- **identify the main accounting rules used in preparing financial statements;**
- **classify them into three broad groupings;**
- **describe each accounting rule;**
- **explain why each of them is important.**

## Why this chapter is important for non-accountants

As a non-accountant, do you need to question the information that your accountants give you? Do you have to know where they have got it from? Does it matter if you just accept it? We think that the answer to all three questions is 'yes' because as a senior manager you are ultimately responsible for whatever your accountants do. If something goes wrong you just can't blame it on them (or on the computer for that matter). As the old cliché has it: *the buck stops with you.*

In order to satisfy yourself that the accountants *have* got it right, you need to be familiar with what procedures they have used in preparing any information that they give to you. Almost certainly they will have used a number of well-established rules that have evolved over many centuries. Unfortunately, many of them are capable of individual interpretation and some require a great deal of subjective judgement. This means that, within the rules, it is quite possible to obtain a number of solutions simply by interpreting the rules a little more rigorously, or by being less pessimistic about a possible outcome.

So it is your responsibility to check that you agree with your accountants' interpretation and judgement before you accept their recommendations. But you cannot really do that unless you understand what they have done and why they have done it. This chapter will give you that understanding by explaining the basis upon which financial statements are prepared.

Before we turn to it in some detail it would be helpful if we first gave you a brief outline of the historical development of accounting procedures.

## Historical development

The practice of accounting has evolved slowly over many centuries. Accounts were prepared originally for stewardship purposes and it is only in more recent times that they have become more widely used. This has meant that some of the traditional practices have had to be adapted to suit more recent requirements. The requirement to produce accounts on an annual basis, for example, means that a number of arbitrary decisions have to be taken to deal with some projects that last for more than one year, such as the building of a power plant.

Users of accounts are not always aware of such difficulties. They sometimes expect accounts to be prepared in a certain way and then they become upset when they find that this not the case. We referred to this phenomenon in the last chapter as the 'expectations gap'. It follows that in order to bridge the expectations gap users should be aware of the basis upon which accounts have been prepared, i.e. they have to know the rules.

Until the middle of the nineteenth century accounting rules were largely conventions that had gradually become accepted by custom and practice over many centuries. A number of laws were then introduced to regulate company accounting practices but it was not until 1948 that accounting became much more *rule* based. Nevertheless, accountants still had a great deal of discretion in how they prepared a set of financial statements for companies, and even more so for other types of entities.

A major change took place in 1971 when a number of the major accountancy bodies began to issue a series of guides called *Statements of Standard Accounting Practice* (SSAPs) through a body initially called the Accounting Standards Steering Committee (ASSC). Then in 1991 the responsibility for issuing accounting standards was passed over to yet another body called the Accounting Standards Board (ASB). The ASB began to phase out SSAPs and replace them with *Financial Reporting Standards* (FRSs).

SSAPs and FRSs lay down the way that financial statements must be prepared and presented. They are not absolutely prescriptive but many entities (especially companies) would have to have some good reasons for not adopting them. If they haven't, then there are some legal sanctions that could be enforced.

One of the main problems with SSAPs was they were not based on any conceptual or theoretical framework, i.e. no one framed them on the basis of what was the best way of doing something in theory and then applying it in practice. Instead, SSAPs just tended to incorporate generally accepted practice at the time, regardless of whether a fundamental rethink should first be undertaken. For years, academic accountants had tried to formulate a conceptual framework but with very little success in getting their ideas across.

Then in 1989 there was a breakthrough when the International Accounting Standards Committee (IASC) published a document called *Framework for the Preparation and Presentation of Financial Statements*. The IASC was responsible for issuing accounting standards on a worldwide basis. Such standards were generally more broad-based than UK ones and they tended to be less influential. The IASC later changed its name to the International Accounting Standards Board (IASB). Since 2005 it has become a much more influential body (but not because of its change of name) as EU-listed companies are now required to incorporate international financial standards into their published financial statements.

The IASC/B was ahead of the game and it was not until 1999 that the ASB produced its own framework of accounting principles in a document called *Statement of Principles For Financial Reporting*. This statement relied heavily on the IASC's earlier work. It is over 100 pages long and is quite a complex document. As a non-accountant, all you need to know at this stage is that its principles form the basis of any FRSs that the ASB issues and that they feature particularly prominently in *FRS 18* (which deals with accounting policies). We have, therefore, taken them very much into account in presenting our summary of the basic rules of accounting as outlined in this chapter.

We are going to discuss 14 of the most common accounting rules. These rules have evolved over the centuries and they are the most relevant as far as this book is concerned. In order to make the discussion a little easier to follow, we have grouped them into three broad categories: boundary rules, measurement rules and ethical rules. These are shown in a diagrammatic format in Figure 2.1.

We start with the boundary rules.

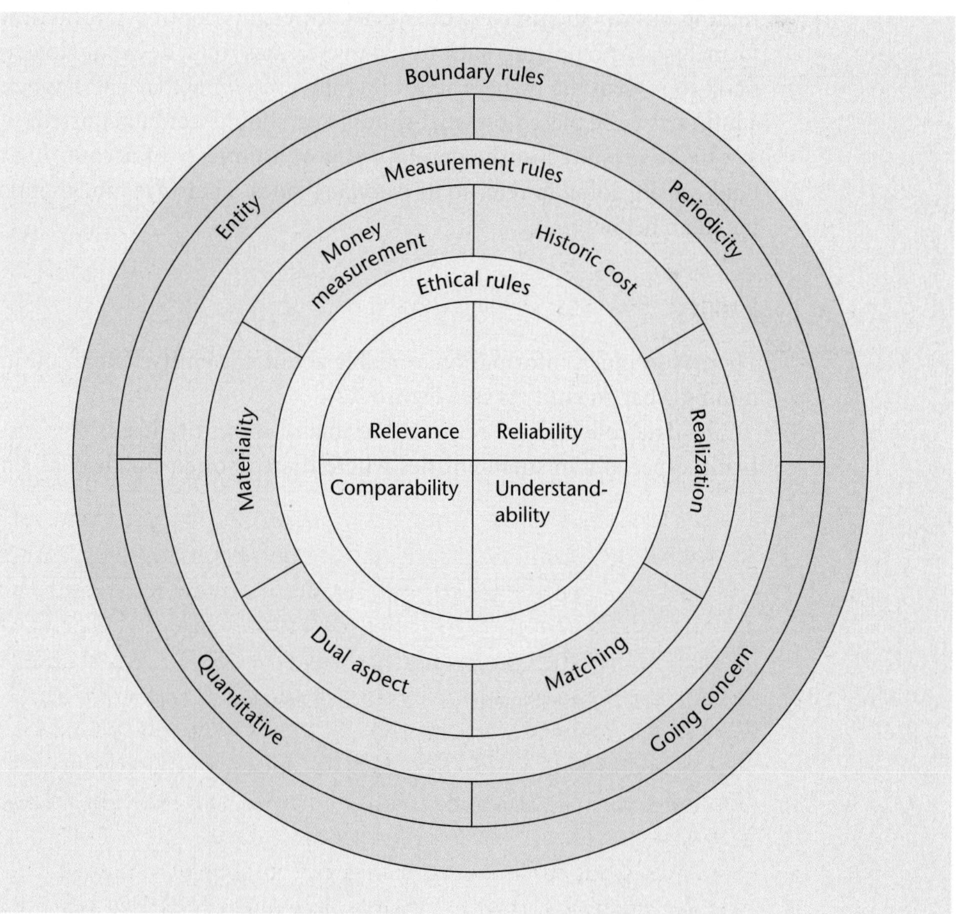


**Figure 2.1 The basic accounting rules**

**Activity 2.1**

Consult a reputable dictionary (such as the *Oxford Dictionary*) and write down the meaning of the following words. They may each have several meanings so extract the ones that relate more to fact or truth.

(a) assumptions
(b) axioms
(c) concepts
(d) conventions
(e) postulates
(f) principles
(g) procedures.

Consider carefully the definitions that you have extracted. Do they all have a similar meaning?

## Boundary rules

In small entities, the owners can probably obtain all the information that they need by finding out for themselves. In larger entities this is often impracticable, and so a more formal way of reporting back to the owners has to be devised. However, it would be difficult to inform the owners about literally *everything* that had happened to the entity so a limit has to be placed on what should and should not be reported.

This has resulted in the development of a number of accounting rules which in this book we are going to refer to as *boundary* rules. There are four main ones and we examine them below.

### Entity

There is so much information available about any entity that accountants start by determining what an entity is (see Figure 2.2).

The data collected are restricted to that of the entity itself. This is sometimes very difficult, especially in small entities where there is often no clear distinction between the

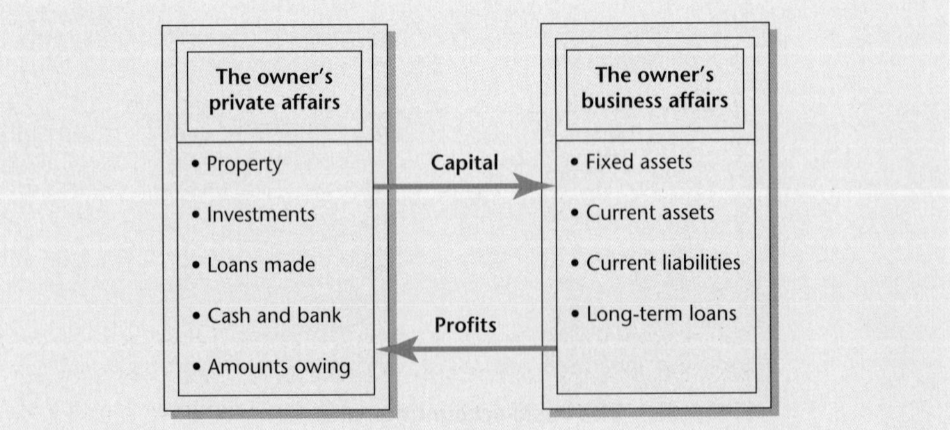


**Figure 2.2 The entity rule: separation of business and private affairs**

public affairs of the entity and the private affairs of the owner. In a profit-making business, for example, the owners sometimes charge their household expenditure to the business or use their private bank account to pay for goods and services meant for the business. In such situations, accountants have to decide where the business ends and the private affairs of the owners begin. They have then to establish exactly what the business owes the owner and what the owner owes the business. The accountants will, however, only be interested in recording in the books of the business the effect these various transactions have on the *business*: they are not interested in the effect that they have on the owner's private affairs. Indeed, it would be an entirely different exercise if the accountants were to deal with the owner's private affairs. This would mean that they were accounting for two different entities – one private and one public – although there may be a great deal of overlap between them.

## Periodicity

Most entities are usually started in the expectation that they will operate for an indeterminate period of time, so it is clearly unsatisfactory for an owner to have to wait years before any report is prepared on how the entity is doing. The owner almost certainly wishes to receive regular reports at frequent intervals.

It follows that if an entity has an unlimited life then any report must be prepared at the end of an arbitrary period of time. In practice, financial statements are usually prepared at the end of a calendar year. Such a time period has developed largely as a matter of custom, although it does reflect the agricultural cycle in Western Europe. In addition, there is a natural human tendency to compare what has happened this year with what happened last year – possibly again reflecting the seasons. Nevertheless, where entities have an unlimited life (as is usually the case with manufacturing organizations), the preparation of annual accounts presents considerable problems in relating specific events to appropriate accounting periods.

**Activity 2.2**

List three advantages and disadvantages of preparing financial accounts only once a year.

| Advantages | Disadvantages |
|---|---|
| 1 | 1 |
| 2 | 2 |
| 3 | 3 |

## Going concern

The periodicity rule requires a regular period of account to be established, regardless either of the life of the entity or of the arbitrary nature of such a period. The going concern rule arises out of the periodicity rule. It assumes that an entity will continue in existence for the foreseeable future unless there is some strong evidence to the contrary. It is important to make absolutely certain that this assumption is correct, because a different set of accounting rules needs to be adopted if an entity's immediate future is altogether uncertain.

### Quantitative

Accountants usually restrict the data that are collected to those that are easily quantifiable. For example, it is possible to count the number of people that an entity employs but it is difficult to quantify the *skill* of the employees. Such a concept is almost impossible to put into numbers and so it is not normally incorporated into a conventional accounting system.

## Measurement rules

The boundary rules determine *what* data should be included in an accounting system, whereas the measurement rules explain *how* those data should be recorded. There are six main measurement rules which we outline below.

### Money measurement

It would be very cumbersome to record information simply in terms of quantifiable amounts. It would also be impossible to make any fair comparisons between various types of assets (such as livestock and farm machinery) or different types of transactions (such as the sale of eggs and the purchase of corn). In order to make meaningful comparison, we need to convert the data into a common recognizable measure.

The monetary unit serves such a purpose and since most quantifiable information is capable of being translated into monetary terms there is usually no difficulty in adopting the monetary measurement rule.

### Historic cost

The historic cost rule is an extension of the money measurement rule. It requires transactions to be recorded at their *original* (i.e. their historic) cost and subsequent changes in prices or values are usually ignored. Increased costs may arise because of a combination of an improved product and through changes in the purchasing power of the monetary unit, i.e. through inflation.

Inflation tends to overstate the level of accounting profit as it is traditionally calculated. Over the last 40 years, there have been several attempts in the United Kingdom to change the method of accounting in order to allow for the effects of inflation. There has been so much disagreement on what should replace *historic cost accounting* (HCA) that the problem is now hardly ever debated. Throughout most of this book we shall be adopting the historic cost rule.

### Realization

One of the problems of applying the periodicity rule is that of determining in which period a particular transaction took place. The easiest way would be to recognize it only when cash had been exchanged, so a particular sale would only be treated as a sale when the debtor had paid for it. This form of accounting is known as *cash flow accounting* (CFA). It is not normally used in practice because the receipt and payment of cash in a particular period may be entirely accidental, e.g. one day can make all the difference between whether a sale goes into Period 1 or Period 2. This means that it is then difficult to make fair comparisons between different periods.

In order to allow for this problem, accountants treat a transaction as having taken place when the entity has either received the cash (or its equivalent) or it is pretty certain that it will do so. And that is the problem, because *you* might well be pretty certain and so you will include it in Period 1 while *I* might be more cautious and wait until Period 2.

We have explained the realization rule in terms of a *sales* transaction but *FRS 18* (which covers accounting policies) has a much wider context: it deals in terms of *profits*:

> *It is generally accepted that profits shall be treated as realized … only when realized* in the form either of cash or of other assets the ultimate cash realization of which can be assessed with reasonable certainty. [*In this context, 'realized' may also encompass profits relating to assets that are readily realizable.] (ASB, FRS 18, para. 28)*

What does this mean? In simple terms you can assume that when you are dealing with sales (or other incomes) include them in the period when you received the cash or in the period that you can be reasonably confident that you will do so. The same point applies to payments, although this is a less difficult decision because you can decide when you are going to make the payment. In practice it's the 'reasonably confident' bit that does it and the reason why so many companies have to restate their accounts because they have overestimated their income.

The realization rule can produce some rather misleading results. For example, a company may treat goods as having been sold in 2008. In 2009 it finds that the purchaser cannot pay for them. What can it do? Its accounts for 2008 have already been approved and it is too late to change them. Obviously the sales for that year were overstated (and so too, almost certainly, was the profit). But the customer defaults in 2009, and so how can the *bad debt* (as it is known) be dealt with in *that* year? We shall be explaining how in Chapter 5.

**Activity 2.3**

A contracting company divides each of its sales into five stages: (1) on order; (2) on despatch; (3) on installation; (4) on commissioning; and (5) on completion of a 12-month warranty period.

Assume that an order for Contract A (worth £100 000) is signed on 1 January 2008 and the warranty period ends on 31 December 2010. In which year or years would you treat the £100 000 as revenue (i.e. sales)?

## Matching

The matching rule (*FRS 18* refers to it as *accruals*) has a very close link with the realization rule. Once you have decided in which period to include a particular transaction then you should allow for the *non-cash effect* of particular transactions in order to be able to compare more fairly one period with another, i.e. match them. This means that when you are preparing the financial statements at the end of a period you have to allow for *accruals* and *prepayments.* An accrual is an amount that is owed by an entity at the end of an accounting period for services given during that period, e.g. electricity consumed in Period 1 and paid for in Period 2. A prepayment is an amount that is *owing* to the entity at the end of a period for services it has paid for in advance of a service being provided in a future period, e.g. insurance paid for in Period 1 for cover in Period 2.

When preparing financial statements, allowance has to be made not only for *closing* accruals and prepayments (i.e. those at the end of the period) but for opening accruals and prepayments (i.e. those at the beginning of the period). This can involve quite a lot of complicated arithmetical adjustment as you can see from Figure 2.3.

While an accruals and prepayments system of accounting does enable the incomes of one period to be matched much more fairly against the costs of the same period, it requires the accountant to estimate the level of both accruals and prepayments at the end of an accounting period. So a degree of subjectivity is automatically built into the system.

## Dual aspect

The dual aspect rule is a useful practical rule, although it really only reflects what is obvious. It is built round the fact that every time something is given, someone (or something) else receives it. In other words, every time a transaction take place there is always a twofold effect. If the entity buys a car for cash, for example, then the cash account goes down and the car account goes up.

We explained in Chapter 1 that this twofold effect was recognized many centuries ago. It gave rise to the system of recording information known as *double-entry book-keeping.* This system of book-keeping is still widely used, although most systems are now computerized. From long experience, it has been found that the system is a most convenient way of recording all sorts of useful information about the entity and of ensuring some form of control over its affairs.

There is no real need to adopt the dual aspect rule in recording information: it is entirely a practical rule that has proved itself over many centuries. Voluntary organizations (such as a drama club or a stamp collecting society) may not think that it is

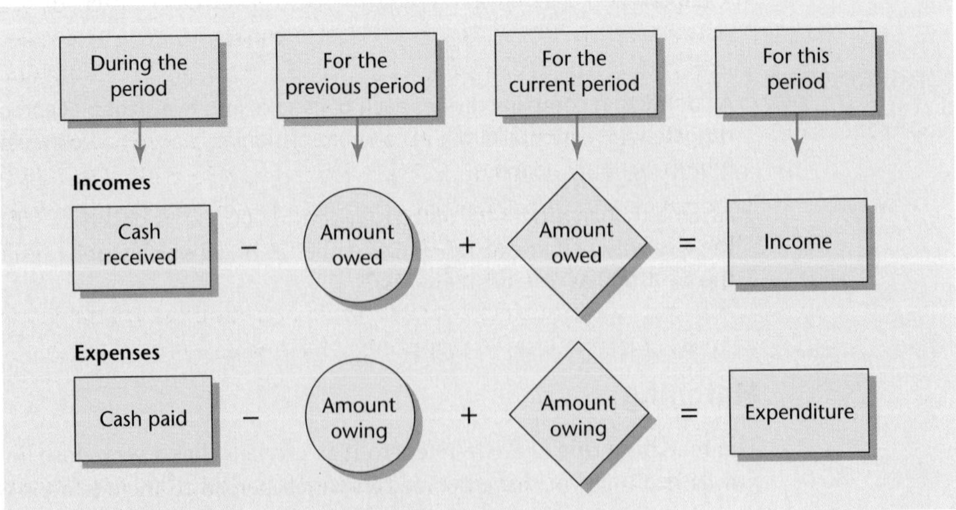


Figure 2.3 **Illustration of the matching rule**

worthwhile to adopt it, but you are strongly recommended to do so in any entity with which you are concerned. If you do, you will find that it gives you more control over the entity's affairs, besides providing you with a great deal more information.

Double-entry book-keeping will be examined in more detail in the next chapter.

### Materiality

Strict application of the various accounting rules may not always be practical. It could involve a considerable amount of work that may be out of all proportion to the information that is eventually obtained. The materiality rule permits other rules to be ignored if the effects are not considered to be *material*, i.e. if they are not significant.

The materiality rule avoids the necessity to follow other accounting rules to the point of absurdity. It would normally be considered unnecessary, for example, to value the closing stock of small amounts of stationery or to maintain detailed records of inexpensive items of office equipment. However, it should be borne in mind that what is immaterial for a large organization may not be so for a small one.

If you decide that a certain item is immaterial then it does not matter how you deal with it in the financial statements, because, by definition, it cannot possibly have any great effect on the results. But you have to remember that this is yet another example of an element of subjectivity being built into the results.

## Ethical rules

*FRS 18* identifies four ethical rules, although they are presented under the heading 'Objectives and constraints in selecting accounting policies'. There are four such 'objectives and constraints': relevance, reliability, comparability and understandability. We outline each of them below.

### Relevance

The amount of information that could be supplied to the users of financial information is practically unlimited. If too much information is supplied it becomes difficult to handle and to absorb. Indeed, often the best way to hide information is to provide too much of it.

So information must be *useful* if its purpose is either to judge the financial position of an entity or its performance. What is meant by 'useful'? *FRS 18* suggests that useful information has three qualities: it is presented in time to make decisions; it can influences the decisions being made; it either confirms what the users already think and/or it helps them predict what might happen.

The message here, then, is that it would be unprofessional for an accountant to supply you with information if it were not helpful to you.

### Reliability

*FRS 18* indicates that for financial information to be reliable it must meet five criteria.

- *Substantiality*: it must reflect the substance of what has taken place.
- *Neutrality*: it must be free from deliberate or systematic bias.

- *Error-free*: it must be free from material (i.e. significant) errors.
- *Complete*: it must include all significant information.
- *Prudence*: it must have been prepared with a degree of caution when conditions are uncertain.

In other words, when presenting financial information be realistic, be objective, don't make mistakes, include everything that is relevant and be prudent.

Sometimes there can be a conflict between these various criteria, especially between neutrality and prudence. When faced with an uncertain situation and you are not sure what to do, if you are a fairly conservative sort of person you may adopt a highly cautious approach. So you will adopt a policy that has the effect of understating profits. That way you avoid paying profits out of the business to the shareholders and then trying to recover them if your optimism was not justified. However, if you act too cautiously you are not being neutral or objective. You are not considering the problem coolly and putting to one side your own prejudices. You should consider the facts carefully and come to a judgement based on the balance of probability that a certain event will or will not take place.

## Comparability

Information contained in financial statements can be particularly useful if the financial results for one period can be compared fairly with another period (or for that matter, another entity). So the information needs to have been prepared on a similar basis and it should be consistent over a period of time. This means that you should not change your accounting methods from one period to another unless there is a good reason for doing so, e.g. when something is completely out of date. Comparability also requires the disclosure of information that is meaningful or useful so that users of financial statements can see what you have done, why you have done it and the effect of doing so.

## Understandability

It seems obvious that if financial statements are to be useful they should be understandable to those who are going to receive them. And yet there are many accountants who would argue that this does not mean that they should be made *simpler*. Simplifying things, they argue, may distort the information and make it less reliable and relevant. The ASB, to some extent, appears to support this argument because *FRS 18* maintains that financial statements need

> *'to be capable of being understood by users having a reasonable knowledge of business and economic activities and accounting and a willingness to study with reasonable diligence the information provided.' (para. 41)*

So now you know. If we did not convince you in the first chapter, the ASB is telling you bluntly *why* you need to have a *reasonable knowledge of accounting* and that you should be *willing to study it with reasonable diligence*.

Some people think that's like going to the doctor and being told what's wrong with you in complicated medical terms. When you ask to be told in simple terms, the reply is, 'Sorry, Mr Jones. It's too complicated to simplify. You'll have to study medicine if you want to know what I'm telling you and what you should do. But it's serious.'

**Activity 2.4**

Supermarket companies sometimes receive a discount from suppliers for meeting a specified sales target. Such discounts may be paid in advance. The accounting treatment of the discount could be dealt with in several ways:

- it could be included in the profit and loss account for the period in which it was received;
- it could be amortized (apportioned) over the span of the contract; and
- it could be included in the profit and loss account for the period in which the sales target is met.

To what extent is the accounting treatment of such discounts an ethical decision? Prepare some notes indicating how you think this problem should be dealt with.

### Questions non-accountants should ask

This is a most important chapter. Apart from preparing the foundation for what follows in the rest of the book, it provides you with a number of important accounting issues that are extremely relevant and important in the real world. While you may be advised by your accountants, ultimately you will be responsible for any action taken by the entity you work for. So it is important that you know what your accountants have done and why.

Some of the accounting rules outlined in this chapter are fairly non-controversial. The entity, periodicity, quantitative, money measurement, matching and dual aspect rules do not normally cause too much of a problem. The remaining rules may do so, so you must question the application of them. We suggest that you pose the following questions:

- What absolute assurances can you give me that the entity is a going concern?
- What justification is there for including all our transactions at their historic cost?
- Can we use more up-to-date costs for some items, e.g. property?
- How would we then value and depreciate such items?
- Is the method used for the determination of income absolutely cast-iron?
- What method have you used for determining what is an immaterial item?
- To what extent has the need to be neutral been overridden by the need to be prudent?
- Are there any items in the accounts that could be justifiably left out or presented in a different way without any problems?

## Conclusion

In this chapter we have identified 14 basic accounting rules that accountants usually adopt in the preparation of accounting statements. We have described four of these rules as boundary rules, six as measurement rules and four as ethical rules. We have argued that the boundary rules limit the amount and type of information that is traditionally collected and stored in an accounting system. The measurement rules provide some guidance on how that information should be recorded, and the ethical rules lay down a code of conduct on how all the other rules should be interpreted.

The exact number, classification and description of these various accounting rules is subject to much debate among accountants. Most entities can adopt what rules they like, although it would be most unusual if they did not accept the going concern, matching, and reliability rules.

## Key points

1. In preparing accounting statements, accountants adopt a number of rules that have evolved over a number of centuries.
2. There are four main boundary rules: entity, periodicity, going concern and quantitative.
3. Measurement rules include money measurement, historic cost, realization, matching, dual aspect and materiality.
4. Ethical rules include relevance, reliability, comparability, and understandability.

## Check your learning

*The answers to these questions can be found within the text.*

1. Name three other terms that mean the same as 'accounting rules'.
2. What do the following initials stand for: (a) SSAP, (b) FRS, (c) ASB?
3. List three categories of accounting rules.
4. What is meant by an 'entity'?
5. What accounting rule is used to describe a defined period of time?
6. What is a 'going concern'?
7. What types of qualitative information is normally included in financial statements?
8. Name three non-monetary items included in most financial statements.
9. Name one type of asset that may not be included at its historic cost in financial statements?
10. What is another term for 'matching'?
11. What does 'dual aspect' mean?
12. How do you decide whether or not a transaction is 'material'?
13. Are 'neutrality' and 'prudence' compatible?
14. What factors are used to determine whether any items included in financial statements are relevant?

## News story quiz

*Remember the news story at the beginning of this chapter? Go back to that story and re-read it before answering the following questions.*

This article reflects the contrast between the British and American approaches to the preparation of financial statements.

### Questions

1 What is meant by the phrases 'rules-driven' approach and 'principles-based' approach?

2 How do you think that preparers and auditors could assume more responsibility for their judgements?

3 How far do you agree with the four objections to rules-based accounting?

4 Do you think that even with rule-driven accounting there would still be a need for individual judgement?

## Tutorial questions

*The answers to questions marked with an asterisk can be found in Appendix 4.*

2.1 Do you think that when a set of financial accounts is being prepared, neutrality should override prudence?

2.2 'The law should lay down precise formats, contents and methods for the preparation of limited liability company accounts.' Discuss.

2.3 The Accounting Standards Board now bases its Financial Reporting Standards on what is sometimes called a 'conceptual framework'. How far do you think that this approach is likely to be successful?

In questions 2.4, 2.5 and 2.6 you are required to state which accounting rule the accountant would most probably adopt in dealing with the various problems.

2.4* (a) Electricity consumed in Period 1 and paid for in Period 2.
(b) Equipment originally purchased for £20 000 which would now cost £30 000.
(c) The company's good industrial relations record.
(d) A five-year construction contract.
(e) A customer with a poor credit record might go bankrupt owing the company £5000.
(f) The company's vehicles, which would only have a small scrap value if the company goes into liquidation.

2.5* (a) A demand by the company's chairman to include every detailed transaction in the presentation of the annual accounts.
(b) A sole-trader business which has paid the proprietor's income tax based on the business profits for the year.
(c) A proposed change in the methods of valuing stock.

(d) The valuation of a litre of petrol in one vehicle at the end of accounting Period 1.
(e) A vehicle which could be sold for more than its purchase price.
(f) Goods which were sold to a customer in Period 1, but for which the cash was only received in Period 2.

2.6* (a) The proprietor who has supplied the business capital out of his own private bank account.
(b) The sales manager who is always very optimistic about the creditworthiness of prospective customers.
(c) The managing director who does not want annual accounts prepared as the company operates a continuous 24-hour-a-day, 365-days-a-year process.
(d) At the end of Period 1, it is difficult to be certain whether the company will have to pay legal fees of £1000 or £3000.
(e) The proprietor who argues that the accountant has got a motor vehicle entered twice in the books of account.
(f) Some goods were purchased and entered into stock at the end of Period 1, but they were not paid for until Period 2.

2.7 The following is a list of problems which an accountant may well meet in practice.

(a) The transfer fee of a footballer.
(b) Goods are sold in one period, but the cash for them is received in a later period.
(c) The proprietor's personal dwelling house has been used as security for a loan which the bank has granted to the company.
(d) What profit to take in the third year of a five-year construction contract.
(e) Small stocks of stationery held at the accounting year end.
(f) Expenditure incurred in working on the improvement of a new drug.

*Required:*
(1) Which accounting rule the accountant would most probably adopt in dealing with each of the above problems?
(2) State the reasons for your choice.

2.8 *FRS 18* (accounting policies) states that profits shall be treated as realized and included in the profit and loss account only when the cash due 'can be assessed with reasonable certainty' (para. 28).
How far do you think that this requirement removes any difficulty in determining in which accounting period a sale has taken place?

2.9 The adoption of the realization and matching rules in preparing financial accounts requires a great deal of subjective judgement.

*Required:*
Write an essay examining whether it would be fairer, easier and more meaningful to prepare financial accounts on a cash received/cash paid basis.

**Further practice questions, study material and links to relevant sites on the World Wide Web can be found on the website that accompanies this book. The site can be found at www.pearsoned.co.uk/dyson**

# FINANCIAL ACCOUNTING

# Part 2

In Part 2 we outline the principles of double-entry book-keeping and explain how to prepare financial accounts for sole traders, companies and for some other types of entitites in the not-for-profit sector. The relationship of Part 2 to the rest of the book is shown below.

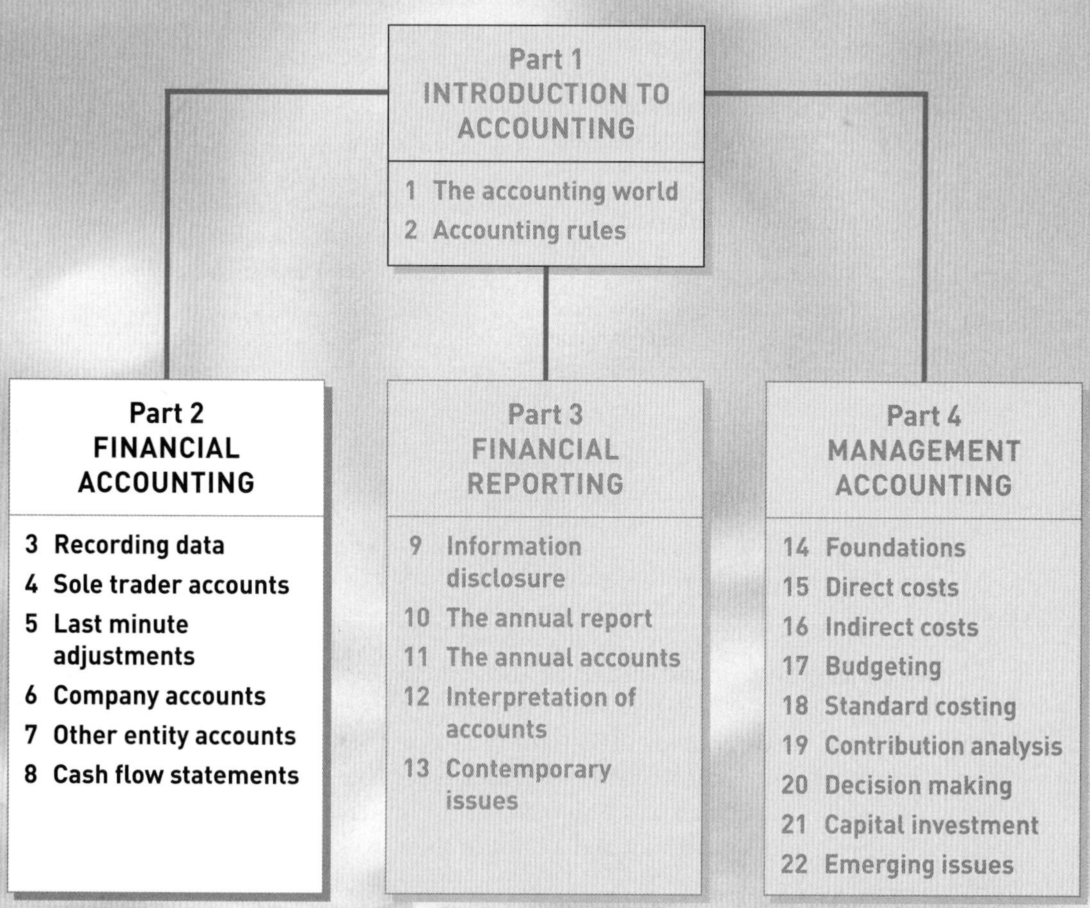

# Chapter 3 Recording data

**Even big companies can have problems in recording data . . .**

## Accounting errors may happen again at NAB

**Jeff Turnbull**

National Australia Bank chief executive John Stewart refused to give an assurance yesterday that no more errors would be unearthed in the bank's financial accounts.

Australia's biggest bank temporarily suspended trading in its shares yesterday morning after discovering its annual report contained classification errors resulting in mistakes in lending volume data.

The report overstated the bank's exposure to the real estate construction sector. The loans and advances for the sector actually totalled $1.6 billion in fiscal 2005, not $5.7 billion as originally stated.

The annual report also incorrectly stated instalment loans and other personal lending, including credit cards, totalled $21.6 billion instead of $15.4 billion because the original sum had wrongly included overdrafts.

The two blunders added up to $10.3 billion in miscalculations.

'We don't think there are any, other mistakes but we can't be sure,' Mr Stewart said.

'We will carry out a full investigation as to how it happened but I think this is probably a simple human error because people are having to work around the system.'

Shares were up 63c to $36.55.

*The Advertiser*, 28 February 2006.



*Questions relating to this news story can be found on page 58*

## About this chapter

A number of basic accounting rules were outlined in the previous chapter. One of these was the *dual aspect* rule. In this chapter we are going to examine this rule in much more detail.

We will explain how accountants use the dual aspect rule to record data and how periodically the system is checked to ensure that it is accurate. This is done by compiling what is known as a 'trial balance'. The trial balance is then used to prepare a trading account, a profit and loss account and a balance sheet, which we will deal with in the next chapter.

**Learning objectives**

By the end of this chapter you should be able to:

- explain what is meant by the 'accounting equation';
- define the terms 'debit' and 'credit';
- write up some simple ledger accounts;
- extract a trial balance;
- identify six errors not revealed in a trial balance.

## Why this chapter is important for non-accountants

This chapter is important for three main reasons.

**1** *To learn the language accountants use.* The chapter will enable you to become familiar with the language and terminology used by accountants. This means that it will then be much easier for you to discuss with them any issues arising from the reports that they prepare for you.

**2** *To check the reliability of information presented to you.* The chapter gives you a basic knowledge of the fundamental recording systems used by all types of entities throughout the world. You will then be able to assess the reliability of any accounting information based on the data that has been included in the system. You will also be more aware of what information has *not* been recorded. This will enable you to take into account what is missing from the accounts when considering the usefulness of any information presented to you by your accountants.

**3** *To debate with accountants on equal terms.* Accounting information is based on a considerable number of questionable assumptions. These may not always be valid. If you are familiar with the language and nuances of fundamental accounting procedures, you will be able to have a much more meaningful and relevant debate with your accountants about the type of information that is useful to you in your job.

## The accounting equation

The system that accountants use to record financial data is known as *double-entry book-keeping*. Double-entry book-keeping is based on the dual aspect rule, i.e. a recognition that every transaction has a twofold effect. So if I loan you £100, a twofold effect arises because: I give you some money and you receive it. But the transaction also has a twofold effect on *both of us*.

- *The effect on you:* (1) your cash goes up by £100 and (2) what you owe me also goes up by £100.
- *The effect on me*: (2) my cash goes down by £100 and (2) what I am owed by you goes up by £100.

If an entity (say) 'me' uses this twofold effect to record *twice* each of the transactions that take place between 'me' and another entity (say) 'you', then I am using some form of double-entry book-keeping. The most commonly used system has evolved over six hundred years and it is now used on a worldwide basis. Before we describe how it works, however, we must first introduce you to three important accounting terms. They are as follows:

- *Assets*: These are possessions or resources *owned* by an entity. They include physical or tangible possessions such as property, plant, machinery, stock, and cash and bank balances. They also include intangible assets, i.e. non-physical possessions such as copyright and patent rights, as well as debts owed to the entity, i.e. trade and other debtors.
- *Capital*: This is the term used to describe the amount that the owners have invested in an entity. In effect, their 'capital' is the amount owed by the entity to its owners.
- *Liabilities*: These are the opposite of assets. They are the amounts owed *by* an entity to outside parties. They include loans, bank overdrafts, creditors, i.e. amounts owing to parties for the supply of goods and services to the entity that have not yet been settled in cash.

There is a close relationship between assets, capital and liabilities. It is frequently presented in the form of what is called the 'accounting equation':

**Assets = capital + liabilities**

In other words, what the entity owns in terms of possessions has been financed by a combination of funds provided by the owners and by borrowing.

We will illustrate the use of the accounting equation with a simple example. Let us assume that you have decided to go into business. You do so by transferring £2000 in cash from your own private bank account. The entity rule means that we are not interested in your private affairs, so we only want to keep track of how the business deals with your £2000.

The business now has £2000 invested in it. This is its capital but it also has £2000 in cash. The cash is an asset. So the £2000 asset equals the £2000 of capital. This relationship between the assets and the capital can be expressed as an equation:

| Assets | | | Capital | |
|---|---|---|---|---|
| Cash | £2000 | = | Capital | £2000 |

The equation captures the twofold effect of the transaction: the assets of the business have been increased by the capital that has been contributed by the owner.

Now suppose that you then decide to transfer £1500 of the cash to a business bank account. The effect on the equation is:

| Assets | | | Capital | |
|---|---|---|---|---|
| | £ | | | £ |
| Bank | 1500 | = | Capital | 2000 |
| Cash | 500 | | | |
| | 2000 | | | 2000 |

As you can see, there has simply been a change on the *assets* side of the equation.

Suppose now that you borrow £500 in cash from one of your friends to provide further financial help to the business. The assets will be increased by an inflow of £500 in cash, but £500 will be owed to your friend. The £500 owed is a liability and your friend has become a creditor of the business. The business has total assets of £2500 (£1500 at the bank and £1000 in cash). Its capital is £2000 and it has a liability of £500. The equation then reads:

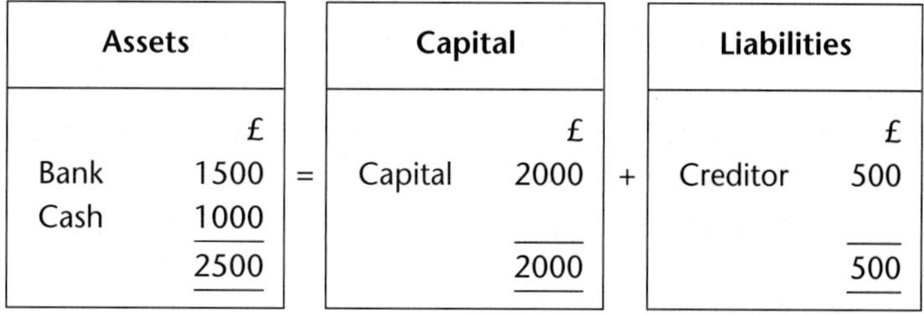

| **Assets** | | | **Capital** | | | **Liabilities** | |
|---|---|---|---|---|---|---|---|
| | £ | | | £ | | | £ |
| Bank | 1500 | = | Capital | 2000 | + | Creditor | 500 |
| Cash | 1000 | | | | | | |
| | 2500 | | | 2000 | | | 500 |

If £800 of goods were then purchased in cash for subsequent resale to the entity's customers, the equation would read:

| **Assets** | | | **Capital** | | | **Liabilities** | |
|---|---|---|---|---|---|---|---|
| | £ | | | £ | | | £ |
| Stocks | 800 | = | Capital | 2000 | + | Creditor | 500 |
| Bank | 1500 | | | | | | |
| Cash | 200 | | | 2000 | | | 500 |
| | 2500 | | | | | | |

Again there has been a change on the assets side of the equation when £800 of the cash (an asset) was used to purchase £800 of goods for resale (i.e. stocks), another asset.

The equation is becoming somewhat complicated but it does enable us to see the effect that *any* transaction has on the entity. The vital point to remember about the accounting equation is:

> **If an adjustment is made to one side of the equation, you *must* make an identical adjustment *either* to the other side of the equation or to the same side.**

This maxim reflects the basic rule of double-entry book-keeping:

> **Every transaction must be recorded twice.**

We will explain how this is done in the next section.

**Activity 3.1**

What are the missing words in the following statements?

(a) The accounting equation is represented by ______ = ______ + ________.
(b) Every transaction must be recorded _____.

## Double-entry book-keeping

We are going to explain how a *handwritten* double-entry book-keeping system works, even though these days most systems are computerized. We do so because both systems use the same accounting principles. The principles are, however, much easier to understand when they are applied to a simple handwritten system.

We now return to the accounting equation. It reflects the twofold effect of every transaction and a double-entry book-keeping system records that effect (whether it is handwritten or computerized). This means that, just as every transaction results in two adjustments being made to the accounting equation, two changes are also made to the accounting system. A change to the accounting system is called an *entry* and so we talk about making entries in the accounts. An *account* is simply a history or a record of a particular type of transaction. Accounts used to be kept in various bound books referred to as ledgers and all the *ledgers*, used in a particular accounting system are known collectively as the *books of account.*

The effect of entering a particular transaction once in one ledger account and again in another ledger account is to cause the balance on each of the two accounts either to go up or to go down (like the accounting equation). So a transaction can either *increase* or *decrease* the total amount held in an account. In other words, an account either *receives* (i.e. accepts) an additional amount or it *gives* (i.e. releases) it. This receiving and giving effect has given rise to two terms from Latin that are commonly used in accounting:

> ***debit****: meaning to receive, or value received;*
> ***credit****: meaning to give, or value given.*

Accountants judge the twofold effect of all transactions on particular accounts from a receiving and giving point of view and each transaction is recorded on that basis. So when a transaction takes place, it is necessary to ask the following two questions:

- Which account should *receive* this transaction, i.e. which account should be debited?
- Which account has *given* this amount, i.e. which account should be credited?

Accounts have been designed to keep the debit entries separate from the credit entries. This helps to emphasize the opposite, albeit equal, effect that each transaction has within the recording system. In a handwritten system the separation is achieved by recording the debit entries on the left-hand side of the page, and the credit entries on the right-hand side. Each account is normally kept on a separate page in a ledger (i.e. a book of account). A traditional handwritten ledger account is illustrated in Figure 3.1.

In the next section we will show you how particular transactions are recorded in ledger accounts.

**Activity 3.2**

In one sentence describe what is meant by each of the following terms:

(a) An account is ________________________________.
(b) A ledger is ________________________________.
(c) Debit is ________________________________.
(d) Credit is ________________________________.

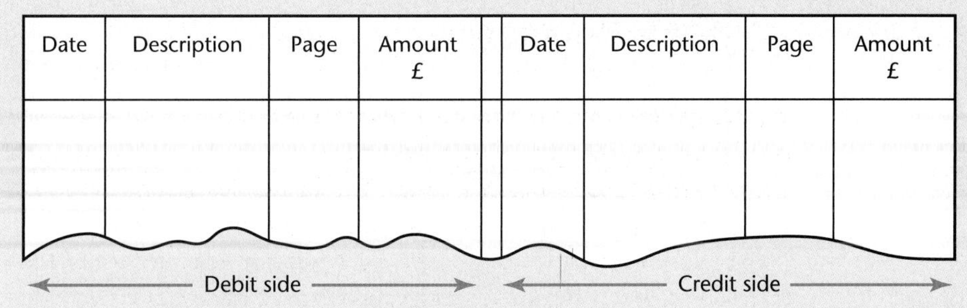


*Notes*
1 The columnar headings would normally be omitted.
2 The description of each entry is usually limited to the *title* of the corresponding account in which the equal entry and opposite entry may be found.
3 The page column is used to refer to the page number of the corresponding account.
4 This example of a ledger account may nowadays only be found in a fairly basic handwritten book-keeping system. The debit and credit columns in a computerized account would normally be side-by-side.

**Figure 3.1 Example of a ledger account**

## Working with accounts

There are four specific purposes behind this section:

- to outline what type of transactions are included in an account;
- to show how they are entered in an account;
- to explain what is meant by a debit balance and a credit balance;
- to demonstrate what happens at the end of an accounting period.

We should stress that we are not trying to turn you into a book-keeper. We just think that you need to know something about how accounting information is recorded and compiled before it is presented to you as a manager. If you do, then we believe that it will be much more useful to you in deciding what to do with it.

### Choice of accounts

There is no specified or statutory list of accounts that *must* be used. Much will depend on the size and nature of the entity, and whether it is in the private or public sector. Sometimes it is not clear, even to accountants, what account to use so they then adopt the maxim ***if in doubt, open another account.*** It really does not matter how many accounts are used – they can always be combined if some of them prove to be unnecessary.

We summarize below the meaning and purpose of some of the types of accounts that you are likely to come across in your career. Figure 3.2 also shows you how they are all so closely interlinked.

#### Capital

The *Capital Account* records what the owner has contributed (or given) to the entity out of private resources in order to start the business and keep it going. In other words, it shows what the business owes the owner.

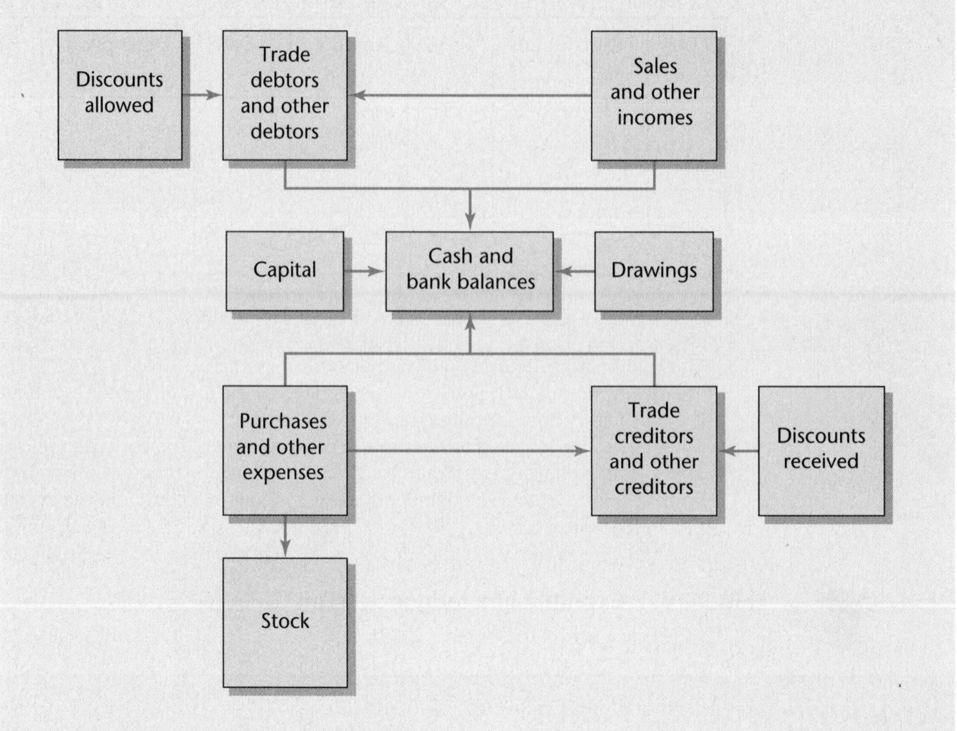


**Figure 3.2 Interlinking of accounts**

### Cash at bank

The *Bank Account* records what money the entity keeps at the bank. It shows what has been put in (usually in the form of cash and cheques) and what has been taken out (usually by cheque payments).

### Cash in hand

The *Cash Account* works on similar lines to the Bank Account, except that it records the physical cash received (such as notes, coins and cheques) before they are paid into the bank. The cash received may be used to purchase goods and services, or it may be paid straight into the bank. From a control point of view, it is best not to pay for purchases directly out of cash receipts, but to draw an amount out of the bank specifically for sundry cash purchases. Any large amount should be paid by cheque.

### Creditors

*Creditor Accounts* record what the entity owes its suppliers for goods or services purchased or supplied on credit (see also *trade creditors*).

### Debtors

*Debtor Accounts* record what is owed to the entity by its customers for goods or services sold to them on credit (see also *trade debtors*).

### Discounts allowed

*Discounts allowed* are cash discounts granted to the entity's customers for the prompt settlement of any debts due to the entity. The amount of cash received from debtors who claim a cash discount will then be less than the total amount for which they have been invoiced.

### Discounts received

*Discounts received* relate to cash discounts given by the entity's suppliers for the prompt payment of any amounts due to them. So, the amount paid to the entity's creditors will be less than the invoiced amount.

### Drawings

The term *drawings* has a special meaning in accounting. The *Drawings Account* is used to record what cash (or goods) the owner has withdrawn from the business for his personal use.

### Petty cash

The *Petty Cash Account* is similar to both the Bank Account and the Cash Account. It is usually limited to the recording of minor cash transactions, such as bus fares, or tea and coffee for the office. The cash used to finance this account will normally be transferred from the Bank Account.

### Sales

The *Sales Account* records the value of goods sold to customers during a particular accounting period. The account includes both cash and credit sales. It does not include receipts from (say) the sale of a motor car originally purchased for use within the business.

### Stock

Stock includes goods which have not been sold at the end of an accounting period. In accounting terminology, this would be referred to as *closing stock*. The closing stock at the end of one period becomes the *opening stock* at the beginning of the next period.

### Purchases

The term *purchases* has a restricted meaning in accounting. It relates to those goods that are bought primarily with the intention of selling them (normally at a profit). The purchase of some motor cars, for example, would not usually be recorded in the *Purchases Account* unless they have been bought with the intention of selling them to customers. Goods not intended for resale are usually recorded in separate accounts. Some purchases may also require further work to be done on them before they are eventually sold.

### Trade creditors

*Trade Creditor Accounts* are similar to Creditor Accounts except that they relate specifically to trading items, i.e. purchases.

### Trade debtors

*Trade Debtor Accounts* are similar to Debtor Accounts except that they also relate specifically to trading items, i.e. sales.

### Trade discounts

*Trade discounts* are a form of special discount. They may be given for placing a large order, for example, or for being a loyal customer. Trade discounts are deducted from the normal purchase or selling price. They are not recorded in the books of account and they will not appear on any invoice.

Once the book-keeper has chosen the accounts in which to record all the transactions for a particular accounting period, it is then necessary to decide which account should be debited and which account should be credited. We examine this problem in the next subsection.

**Activity 3.3**

Which two ledger accounts would you use in recording each of the following transactions?

(a) cash sales
(b) rent paid by cheque
(c) wages paid in cash
(d) a supplier of goods paid by cheque
(e) goods sold on credit to Ford.

## Entering transactions in accounts

There is one simple rule that should be followed when entering a transaction in an account:

**Debit the account which receives**

and

**Credit the account which gives.**

This rule is illustrated in Example 3.1, which contains some common ledger account entries.

**Example 3.1**

### Example of some common ledger account entries

**Entry 1**
The proprietor contributes some cash to the business.

*Debit*: Cash Account *Credit*: Capital Account

*Reason*: The Cash Account receives some cash given to the business by the owner. His Capital Account is the giving account and the Cash Account is the receiving account.

**Entry 2**
Some cash in the till is paid into the business bank account.

*Debit*: Bank Account *Credit*: Cash Account

*Reason*: The Cash Account is the giving account because it is releasing some cash to the Bank Account.

**Entry 3**
A van is purchased for use in the business; it is paid for by cheque.

*Debit*: Van Account *Credit*: Bank Account

*Reason*: The Bank Account is giving some money in order to pay for a van, so the Bank Account must be credited as it is the giving account.

**Entry 4**
Some goods are purchased for cash.

*Debit*: Purchases Account *Credit*: Cash Account

*Reason*: The Cash Account is giving up an amount of cash in order to pay for some purchases. The Cash Account is the giving account, so it must be credited.

**Entry 5**
Some goods are purchased on credit terms from Fred.

*Debit*: Purchases Account *Credit*: Fred's Account

*Reason*: Fred is supplying the goods on credit terms to the business. As he is the giver, his account must be credited.

**Entry 6**
Some goods are sold for cash.

*Debit*: Cash Account *Credit:* Sales Account

*Reason*: The Cash Account receives the cash from the sale of goods and the Sales Account is credited because it is the giving or supplying account.

**Entry 7**
Some goods are sold on credit terms to Sarah.

*Debit*: Sarah's Account *Credit:* Sales Account

*Reason*: Sarah's Account is debited because she is receiving the goods, and the Sales Account is credited because it is supplying (or giving) them.

**Activity 3.4**

Is there anything wrong with the following abbreviated bank account?

| *Debit* | | | *Credit* | | |
|---|---|---|---|---|---|
| | | *£000* | | | *£000* |
| 10.3.09 | Wages paid | 1000 | 6.6.09 | Interest received | 500 |

It is not always easy to think of the receiving and of the giving effect of each transaction. You will find that it is very easy to get them mixed up and to then reverse the entries. If we look at Entries 6 and 7 in Example 3.1, for example, it is difficult to understand why the Sales Account should be credited. Why is the Sales Account the giving account? Surely it is *receiving* an amount and not giving anything? In one sense, it is receiving something, but then that applies to any entry in any account. So, in the case of the sales account, regard it as a *supplying* account because it gives (or releases) something to another account.

If you find this concept difficult to understand, think of the effect on the opposite account. A cash sale, for example, results in cash being increased (not decreased). The cash account must, therefore, be the *receiving* account and it must be debited. Somebody (say Jones) must have given the cash, but as it is a cash sale, we credit it straight to the sales account as the *supplying* account.

If the sales had been sold to Jones on credit, his account would have been debited (because his account is the *receiving* account) and credited to sales (again because it is the *supplying* account).

**Activity 3.5**

State which account should be debited and which account should be credited in respect of each of the following terms:

(a) cash paid to a supplier
(b) office rent paid by cheque
(c) cash sales
(d) dividend received by cheque.

## A ledger account example

This section illustrates the procedure adopted in entering various transactions in ledger accounts. The section brings together the basic material covered in the earlier part of this chapter. It demonstrates the use of various accounts, and the debiting and crediting effect of different types of transactions.

**Example 3.2**

### Joe Simple: a sole trader

The following information relates to Joe Simple, who started a new business on 1 January 2008:

| | | |
|---|---|---|
| 1 | 1.1.08 | Joe started the business with £5000 in cash. |
| 2 | 3.1.08 | He paid £3000 of the cash into a business bank account. |
| 3 | 5.1.08 | Joe bought a van for £2000 paying by cheque. |
| 4 | 7.1.08 | He bought some goods, paying £1000 in cash. |
| 5 | 9.1.08 | Joe sold some of the goods, receiving £1500 in cash. |

*Required*:

Enter the above transactions in Joe's ledger accounts.

**Answer to Example 3.2**

**Joe Simple's books of account**

*Cash Account*

| | | £ | | | £ |
|---|---|---|---|---|---|
| 1.1.08 | Capital (1) | 5 000 | 3.1.08 | Bank (2) | 3 000 |
| 9.1.08 | Sales (5) | 1 500 | 7.1.08 | Purchases (4) | 1 000 |

*Capital Account*

| | | £ | | | £ |
|---|---|---|---|---|---|
| | | | 1.1.08 | Cash (1) | 5 000 |

*Bank Account*

| | | £ | | | £ |
|---|---|---|---|---|---|
| 3.1.08 | Cash (2) | 3 000 | 5.1.08 | Van (3) | 2 000 |

*Van Account*

| | | £ | | | £ |
|---|---|---|---|---|---|
| 5.1.08 | Bank (3) | 2 000 | | | |

*Purchases Account*

| | | £ | | | £ |
|---|---|---|---|---|---|
| 7.1.08 | Cash (4) | 1 000 | | | |

*Sales Account*

| | | £ | | | £ |
|---|---|---|---|---|---|
| | | | 9.1.08 | Cash (5) | 1 500 |

*Tutorial notes*

1 The numbers in brackets after each entry refer to the example notes; they have been inserted for tutorial guidance only.

2 The narration relates to that account in which the equal and opposite entry may be found.

After entering all the transactions for a particular period in appropriate ledger accounts, the next stage in the exercise is to calculate the balance on each account as at the end of each accounting period. We show you how to do this in the next section.

## Balancing the accounts

During a particular accounting period, some accounts (such as the bank and cash accounts) will contain a great many debit and credit entries. Some accounts may contain either mainly debit entries (e.g. the purchases account), or largely credit entries (e.g. the sales account). It would be somewhat inconvenient to allow the entries (whether mainly debits, credits or a mixture of both) to build up without occasionally striking a balance. Indeed, the owner will almost certainly want to know not just what is in each account, but also what its overall, or *net* balance is (i.e. the total of all the debit entries less the total of all the credit entries). So on occasions it will be necessary to calculate the balance on each account.

Balancing an account requires the book-keeper to add up all the respective debit and credit entries, take one total away from the other, and arrive at the net balance.

Accounts may be balanced fairly frequently, e.g. once a week or once a month, but some entities may only do so when they prepare their annual accounts. In order to keep a tight control on the management of the business, it is advisable to balance the accounts at reasonably short intervals. The frequency will depend on the nature and the size of the entity but once a month is probably sufficient for most entities.

The balancing of the accounts is part of the double-entry procedure, and the method is quite formal. In Example 3.3 overleaf we show how to balance an account with a *debit* balance on it (i.e. when its total debit entries exceed its total credit entries).

Example 3.3

## Balancing an account with a debit balance

*Cash Account*

| | | £ | | | £ |
|---|---|---|---|---|---|
| 1.1.08 | Sales (1) | 2 000 | 10.1.08 | Jones (1) | 3 000 |
| 15.1.08 | Rent received (1) | 1 000 | 25.1.08 | Davies (1) | 5 000 |
| 20.1.08 | Smith (1) | 4 000 | | | |
| 31.1.08 | Sales (1) | 8 000 | 31.1.08 | Balance c/d (2) | 7 000 |
| | (3) | 15 000 | | (3) | 15 000 |
| 1.2.08 | Balance b/d (4) | 7 000 | | | |

*Note*: The number shown after each narration relates to the tutorial notes below.

*Tutorial notes*

1 The total debit entries equal £15 000 (2000 + 1000 + 4000 + 8000). The total credit entries equal £8000 (3000 + 5000). The net balance on this account, therefore, at 31 January 2008 is a *debit balance* of £7000 (15 000 – 8000). Until both the debit entries and the credit entries have been totalled, of course, it will not usually be apparent whether the balance is a debit one or a credit one. However, it should be noted that there can never be a credit balance in a cash account, because it is impossible to pay out more cash than has been received.

2 The debit balance of £7000 is inserted on the *credit* side of the account at the time that the account is balanced (in the case of Example 3.3, at 31 January 2008). This then enables the total of the credit column to be balanced so that it agrees with the total of the debit column. The abbreviation 'c/d' means carried down. In this example the debit balance is carried down in the account in order to start the new period on 1 February 2008.

3 The £15 000 shown as a total in both the debit and the credit columns demonstrates that the columns balance (they do so, of course, because £7000 has been inserted in the credit column to make them balance). The totals are double-underlined in order to signify that they are a final total.

4 The balancing figure of £7000 is brought down ('b/d') in the account to start the new period on 1 February 2008. The double entry has been completed because £7000 has been debited below the line (i.e. below the £15 000 debit total), and the £7000 balancing figure credited above the line (i.e. above the £15 000 total).

Example 3.3 demonstrates how an account with a debit entry is balanced. In Example 3.4 we illustrate a similar procedure, but this time the account has a *credit* balance.

Example 3.4

## Balancing an account with a credit balance

*Scott's Account*

| | | £ | | | £ |
|---|---|---|---|---|---|
| 31.1.08 | Bank (1) | 20 000 | 15.1.08 | Purchases (1) | 10 000 |
| 31.1.08 | Balance c/d (2) | 5 000 | 20.1.08 | Purchases (1) | 15 000 |
| | (3) | 25 000 | | (3) | 25 000 |
| | | | 1.2.08 | Balance b/d (4) | 5 000 |

*Note*: The number shown after each narration relates to the tutorial notes below.

*Tutorial notes to Example 3.4*

1 Apart from the balance, there is only one debit entry in Scott's account: the bank entry of £20 000. The total credit entries amount to £25 000 (10 000 + 15 000). Scott has a *credit balance*, therefore, in his account as at 31 January 2008 of £5000 (10 000 + 15 000 – 20 000). With many more entries in the account it would not always be possible to tell immediately whether the balance was a debit one or a credit one.

2 The credit balance of £5000 at 31 January 2008 is inserted on the *debit* side of the account in order to enable the account to be balanced. The balance is then carried down (c/d) to the next period.

3 The £25 000 shown as the total for both the debit and the credit columns identifies the balancing of the account. This has been made possible because of the insertion of the £5 000 balancing figure on the debit side of the account.

4 The balancing figure of £5000 is brought down (b/d) in the account in order to start the account in the new period beginning on 1 February 2008. The double-entry has been completed because the debit entry of £5000 above the £25 000 line on the debit side equals the credit entry below the £25 000 line on the credit side.

**Activity 3.6**

Write down in you notebook what is meant by

(a) an account having a debit balance
(b) an account having a credit balance.

The next stage after balancing each account is to check that the double entry has been completed throughout the entire system. This is done by compiling what is known as a *trial balance*.

## The trial balance

A trial balance is a working paper compiled at the end of a specific accounting period. It does not form part of the double-entry process. It is simply a convenient method of checking that all the transactions and all the balances have been entered correctly in the ledger accounts, although it is also used to help prepare the profit and loss account and the balance sheet.

It lists all the debit balances and all the credit balances extracted from each of the accounts throughout the ledger system. The total of all the debit balances is then compared with the total of all the credit balances. If the two totals agree, we can be reasonably confident that the book-keeping procedures have been carried out accurately.

The preparation of a trial balance is illustrated in Example 3.5.

Example 3.5

## Edward – compilation of a trial balance

Edward started a new business on 1 January 2007. The following transactions took place during his first month in business.

2007

| | |
|---|---|
| 1.1 | Edward commenced business with £10 000 in cash. |
| 3.1 | He paid £8000 of the cash into a business bank account. |
| 6.1 | He bought a van on credit from Perkin's garage for £3000. |
| 9.1 | Edward rented shop premises for £1000 per quarter; he paid for the first quarter immediately by cheque. |
| 12.1 | He bought goods on credit from Roy Limited for £4000. |
| 15.1 | He paid shop expenses amounting to £1500 by cheque. |
| 18.1 | Edward sold goods on credit to Scott and Company for £3000. |
| 21.1 | He settled Perkin's account by cheque. |
| 24.1 | Edward received a cheque from Scott and Company for £2000; this cheque was paid immediately into the bank. |
| 27.1 | Edward sent a cheque to Roy Limited for £500. |
| 31.1 | Goods costing £3000 were purchased from Roy Limited on credit. |
| 31.1 | Cash sales for the month amounted to £2000. |

*Required*:

(a) Enter the above transactions in appropriate ledger accounts, balance off each account as at 31 January 2007, and bring down the balances as at that date.

(b) Extract a trial balance as at 31 January 2007.

**Answer to Example 3.5(a)**

*Cash Account*

| | | £ | | | £ |
|---|---|---|---|---|---|
| 1.1.07 | Capital (1) | 10 000 | 3.1.07 | Bank (2) | 8 000 |
| 31.1.07 | Sales (12) | 2 000 | 31.1.07 | Balance c/d | 4 000 |
| | | 12 000 | | | 12 000 |
| 1.2.07 | Balance b/d | 4 000 | | | |

*Capital Account*

| | | £ | | | £ |
|---|---|---|---|---|---|
| | | | 1.1.07 | Cash (1) | 10 000 |

*Bank Account*

| | | £ | | | £ |
|---|---|---|---|---|---|
| 3.1.07 | Cash (2) | 8 000 | 9.1.07 | Rent payable (4) | 1 000 |
| 24.1.07 | Scott and Company (9) | 2 000 | 15.1.07 | Shop expenses (6) | 1 500 |
| | | | 21.1.07 | Perkin's garage (8) | 3 000 |
| | | | 27.1.07 | Roy Limited (10) | 500 |
| | | | 31.1.07 | Balance c/d | 4 000 |
| | | 10 000 | | | 10 000 |
| 1.2.07 | Balance b/d | 4 000 | | | |

*Van Account*

| | | £ | | | £ |
|---|---|---|---|---|---|
| 6.1.07 | Perkin's Garage (3) | 3 000 | | | |

*Perkin's Garage Account*

| | | £ | | | £ |
|---|---|---|---|---|---|
| 21.1.07 | Bank (8) | 3 000 | 6.1.07 | Van (3) | 3 000 |

*Rent Payable Account*

| | | £ | | | £ |
|---|---|---|---|---|---|
| 9.1.07 | Bank (4) | 1 000 | | | |

*Purchases Account*

| | | £ | | | £ |
|---|---|---|---|---|---|
| 12.1.07 | Roy Limited (5) | 4 000 | | | |
| 31.1.07 | Roy Limited (11) | 3 000 | 31.1.07 | Balance c/d | 7 000 |
| | | 7 000 | | | 7 000 |
| 1.2.07 | Balance b/d | 7 000 | | | |

*Roy Limited Account*

| | | £ | | | £ |
|---|---|---|---|---|---|
| 27.1.07 | Bank (10) | 500 | 12.1.07 | Purchases (5) | 4 000 |
| 31.1.07 | Balance c/d | 6 500 | 31.1.07 | Purchases (11) | 3 000 |
| | | 7 000 | | | 7 000 |
| | | | 1.2.07 | Balance b/d | 6 500 |

*Shop Expenses Account*

| | | £ | | | £ |
|---|---|---|---|---|---|
| 15.1.07 | Bank (6) | 1 500 | | | |

*Sales Account*

| | | £ | | | £ |
|---|---|---|---|---|---|
| | | | 18.1.07 | Scott & Company (7) | 3 000 |
| 31.1.07 | Balance c/d | 5 000 | 31.1.07 | Cash (12) | 2 000 |
| | | 5 000 | | | 5 000 |
| | | | 1.2.07 | Balance b/d | 5 000 |

*Scott and Company Account*

| | | £ | | | £ |
|---|---|---|---|---|---|
| 18.1.07 | Sales (7) | 3 000 | 24.1.07 | Bank (9) | 2 000 |
| | | | 31.1.07 | Balance c/d | 1 000 |
| | | 3 000 | | | 3 000 |
| 1.2.07 | Balance b/d | 1 000 | | | |

**Tutorial notes**

1 The number shown after each narration has been inserted for tutorial guidance only in order to illustrate the insertion of each entry in the appropriate account.

2 There is no need to balance an account and carry down the balance when there is only a single entry in one account (for example, Edward's Capital Account).

3 Note that some accounts may have no balance in them at all as at 31 January 2007 (for example, Perkin's Garage Account).

**Answer to Example 3.5(b)**

**Trial Balance at 31 January 2007**

| | Dr | Cr |
|---|---|---|
| | £ | £ |
| Cash | 4 000 | |
| Capital | | 10 000 |
| Bank | 4 000 | |
| Van | 3 000 | |
| Rent payable | 1 000 | |
| Purchases | 7 000 | |
| Roy Limited | | 6 500 |
| Shop expenses | 1 500 | |
| Sales | | 5 000 |
| Scott and Company | 1 000 | |
| | 21 500 | 21 500 |

*Tutorial notes*

1. The total debit balance agrees with the total credit balance, and therefore the trial balance balances. This confirms that the transactions appear to have been entered in the books of account correctly.
2. The total amount of £21 500 shown in both the debit and credit columns of the trial balance does not have any significance, except to prove that the trial balance balances.

## Trial balance errors

A trial balance confirms that the books of account balance arithmetically. This means that the following procedures have all been carried out correctly:

- for every debit entry there appears to be a credit entry – a cardinal rule in double-entry book-keeping;
- the value for each debit and credit entry has been entered in appropriate accounts;
- the balance on each account has been calculated, extracted and entered correctly in the trial balance;
- the debit and credit columns in the trial balance are the same.

There are, however, some errors that are not disclosed by the trial balance. They are as follows.

- *Omission*: a transaction could have been completely omitted from the books of account.
- *Complete reversal of entry*: a transaction could have been entered in (say) Account A as a debit and in Account B as a credit, when it should have been entered as a credit in Account A and as a debit in Account B.
- *Principle*: a transaction may have been entered in the wrong *type* of account, e.g. the purchase of a new delivery van may have been debited to the purchases account, instead of the delivery vans account.
- *Commission*: a transaction may have been entered in the correct type of account, but in the wrong *personal* account, e.g. in Bill's account instead of in Ben's account.

- *Compensating*: an error may have been made in (say) adding the debit side of one account, and an identical error made in adding the credit side of another account; the two errors would then cancel each other out.
- *Original entry*: a transaction may have been entered incorrectly in both accounts, e.g. as £291 instead of as £921.

Such errors may only be discovered if an audit is done of the double-entry book-keeping system. They may also become apparent when the financial statements are prepared and the results are compared with previous periods. Similarly, some errors may also come to light if they affect creditor and debtor balances and suppliers and customers begin to complain about unpaid or incorrect invoices. Notwithstanding these possible errors, the compilation of a trial balance is still useful because:

- the arithmetical accuracy of the entries made in the books of account can be confirmed;
- the balance owed or owing on each account can easily be extracted;
- the preparation of the financial statements is simplified.

**Activity 3.7**

State whether each of the following errors would be discovered as a result of preparing a trial balance.

| | | |
|---|---|---|
| (a) | £342 has been entered in both ledger accounts instead of £432. | *Yes/no* |
| (b) | The debit column in Prim's account has been overstated by £50. | *Yes/no* |
| (c) | £910 has been put in Anne's account instead of Agnes's. | *Yes/no* |

## ! Questions non-accountants should ask

As a non-accountant it is highly unlikely that you will become involved in the detailed recording, extraction and summary of basic accounting information. However as accounting is used to prepare the entity's financial statements it is important that it is accurate, relevant and fairly presented.

Your particular responsibility as a senior manager in the entity will be to ensure that:

- adequate accounting records are kept;
- they are accurate;
- an appropriate profit and loss account and a balance sheet (as required by any legislation) can be prepared from such records.

At very least, the accounting records should be capable of dealing with all cash received and paid by the entity and that they contain details of all its assets and liabilities.

In order to satisfy yourself about these requirements you should ask the following questions.

- Do we use a double-entry book-keeping system?
- Is it a manual or a computerized one?
- Does the system include a cash book in which all cash and bank transactions are entered?
- Is the balance shown in the cash book checked regularly against the balance disclosed in the bank's pass sheets or statements of account?

- Is a separate account kept for each identifiable group of fixed assets, current assets and current liabilities?
- What is included in such groups?
- Is a balance calculated regularly for each of the accounts?
- How often is a trial balance prepared?
- What steps are taken to ensure that errors not disclosed in a trial balance are minimized?
- What is the system for the separation of duties affecting the recording of the accounting information and for preparing the trial balance?
- Does a senior manager (not involved with the accounting function) receive a copy of the trial balance?

## Conclusion

This book is specifically aimed at non-accountants, and in this chapter we have deliberately avoided going into too much detail about double-entry book-keeping. In your managerial role you will almost certainly be supplied with information that has been extracted from a ledger system. In order to assess its real benefit to you, we believe that it is most important that you should know something about where it has come from, what it means, and what reliability can be placed on it.

The chapter has, therefore, covered the following features of a double-entry book-keeping system:

- the accounting equation;
- the type of accounts generally used in practice;
- the meaning of the terms 'debit' and 'credit';
- the definition of the terms 'debtor' and 'creditor';
- the method of entering transactions in ledger accounts;
- the balancing of ledger accounts;
- the compilation of a trial balance.

## Key points

1. The accounting equation is represented by the formula: assets = capital + liabilities. It underpins the dual aspect rule and it forms the basis of a conventional accounting recording system.
2. An account is an explanation, a record or a history of a particular event.
3. A book of account is known as a ledger.
4. A transaction is the carrying out and the performance of any business.
5. All transactions have a twofold effect.
6. A double-entry system records that twofold effect.

7 A debit means that a transaction is received into an account.

8 A credit means that a transaction is given by an account.

9 Debits are entered on the left-hand side of an account.

10 Credits are entered on the right-hand side of an account.

11 For every debit entry there must be a credit entry.

12 Accounts are balanced periodically.

13 The accuracy of the book-keeping is tested by preparing a trial balance.

14 The trial balance does not reveal all possible book-keeping errors.

## Check your learning

1 What is the accounting equation?

2 What is the basic rule of double-entry book-keeping?

3 What is an account?

4 What is a ledger?

5 What is meant by the terms 'debit' and 'credit'?

6 What factor would indicate whether or not a new account should be opened?

7 What distinguishes a cash account from a bank account?

8 What are the following accounts used for: (a) capital, (b) trade creditors, (c) trade debtors, (d) stock, (e) sales, (f) purchases, (g) drawings?

9 What is the difference between a discounts allowed account and a discounts received account?

10 What must there be for (a) every debit, (b) every credit?

11 What is (a) a debit balance, (b) a credit balance?

12 What is a trial balance?

13 Name three main functions that it fulfils.

14 List six book-keeping errors that a trial balance does not detect.

## News story quiz

*Remember the news story at the beginning of this chapter? Go back to that story and re-read it before answering the following questions.*

The National Australia Bank (which owns the Clydesdale Bank in Scotland and the Yorkshire Bank in England) has had to admit to a $10.3 billion mistake in its 2005 annual report. It made two major errors:

- it incorrectly classified some personal loans as overdrafts;
- it overstated its lending to the construction sector.

The precise details need not concern us unduly in this chapter. Instead, we suggest that you concentrate on what apparently caused the errors – an incorrect classification and an overstatement of some loans and advances. The chief executive puts these mistakes down to 'a simple human error'.

### Questions

1 To what extent do you think that these mistakes were due to inherent flaws in the computerized (presumably) accounting recording system?

2 Do you think it likely that the classification error was caused by someone simply putting the wrong account number on some of the invoices?

3 Is it likely that the overstatement of lending to the construction industry was more a matter of judgement rather than carelessness in coding the invoices?

4 What does it say for the bank's control procedures if these mistakes were due to 'a simple human error'?

## Tutorial questions

*The answers to questions marked with an asterisk can be found in Appendix 4.*

3.1 Do you think that non-accounting managers need to know anything about double-entry book-keeping?

3.2 'My accountant has got it all wrong,' argued Freda. 'She's totally mixed up all her debits and credits.'
'But what makes you say that?' queried Dora.
'Oh! I've only to look at my bank statement to see that she's wrong,' responded Freda. 'I know I've got some money in the bank, and yet she tells me I'm in debit when she means I'm in credit.'
Is Freda right?

3.3 'Double-entry book-keeping is a waste of time and money because everything has to be recorded twice.' Discuss.

3.4* Adam has just gone into business. The following is a list of his transactions for the month of January 2007:

(a) Cash paid into the business by Adam.
(b) Goods for resale purchased on cash terms.

(c) Van bought for cash.
(d) One quarter's rent for premises paid in cash.
(e) Some goods sold on cash terms.
(f) Adam buys some office machinery for cash.

*Required*:
State which account in Adam's books of account should be debited and which account should be credited for each transaction.

**3.5*** The following is a list of Brown's transactions for February 2008:

(a) Transfer of cash to a bank account.
(b) Cash received from sale of goods.
(c) Purchase of goods paid for by cheque.
(d) Office expenses paid in cash.
(e) Cheques received from customers from sale of goods on cash terms.
(f) A motor car for use in the business paid for by cheque.

*Required*:
State which account in Brown's books of account should be debited and which account should be credited for each transaction.

**3.6** Corby is in business as a retail distributor. The following is a list of his transactions for March 2009:

1 Goods purchased from Smith on credit.
2 Corby introduces further capital in cash into the business.
3 Goods sold for cash.
4 Goods purchased for cash.
5 Cash transferred to the bank.
6 Machinery purchased, paid for in cash.

*Required*:
State which account in Corby's books of account should be debited and which account should be credited for each transaction.

**3.7** Davies buys and sells goods on cash and credit terms. The following is a list of her transactions for April 2007:

1 Capital introduced by Davies paid into the bank.
2 Goods purchased on credit terms from Swallow.
3 Goods sold to Hill for cash.
4 Cash paid for purchase of goods.
5 Dale buys goods from Davies on credit.
6 Motoring expenses paid by cheque.

*Required*:
State which account in Davies' books of account should be debited and which account should be credited for each transaction.

**3.8** The following transactions relate to Gordon's business for the month of July 2008:

1 Bought goods on credit from Watson.
2 Sold some goods for cash.
3 Sold some goods on credit to Moon.
4 Sent a cheque for half the amount owing to Watson.
5 Watson grants Gordon a cash discount.
6 Moon settles most of his account in cash.

7 Gordon allows Moon a cash discount that covers the small amount owed by Moon.
8 Gordon purchases some goods for cash.

*Required:*
State which account in Gordon's books of accounts should be debited and which account should be credited for each transaction.

**3.9** Harry started a new business on 1 January 2009. The following transactions cover his first three months in business:

1 Harry contributed an amount in cash to start the business.
2 He transferred some of the cash to a business bank account.
3 He paid an amount in advance by cheque for rental of business premises.
4 Bought goods on credit from Paul.
5 Purchased a van paying by cheque.
6 Sold some goods for cash to James.
7 Bought goods on credit from Nancy.
8 Paid motoring expenses in cash.
9 Returned some goods to Nancy.
10 Sold goods on credit to Mavis.
11 Harry withdrew some cash for personal use.
12 Bought goods from David paying in cash.
13 Mavis returns some goods.
14 Sent a cheque to Nancy.
15 Cash received from Mavis.
16 Harry receives a cash discount from Nancy.
17 Harry allows Mavis a cash discount.
18 Cheque withdrawn at the bank in order to open a petty cash account.

*Required:*
State which account in Harry's books of account should be debited and which account should be credited for each transaction.

**3.10*** The following is a list of transactions which relate to Ivan for the first month that he is in business:

| | |
|---|---|
| 1.9.07 | Started the business with £10 000 in cash. |
| 2.9.07 | Paid £8000 into a business bank account. |
| 3.9.07 | Purchased £1000 of goods in cash. |
| 10.9.07 | Bought goods costing £6000 on credit from Roy. |
| 12.9.07 | Cash sales of £3000. |
| 15.9.07 | Goods sold on credit terms to Norman for £4000. |
| 20.9.07 | Ivan settles Roy's account by cheque. |
| 30.9.07 | Cheque for £2000 received from Norman. |

*Required:*
Enter the above transactions in Ivan's ledger accounts.

**3.11*** Jones has been in business since 1 October 2008. The following is a list of her transactions for October 2008:

| | |
|---|---|
| 1.10.08 | Capital of £20 000 paid into a business bank account. |
| 2.10.08 | Van purchased on credit from Lang for £5000. |
| 6.10.08 | Goods purchased on credit from Green for £15 000. |
| 10.10.08 | Cheque drawn on the bank for £1000 in order to open a petty cash account. |
| 14.10.08 | Goods sold on credit for £6000 to Haddock. |

| | |
|---|---|
| 18.10.08 | Cash sales of £5000. |
| 20.10.08 | Cash purchases of £3000. |
| 22.10.08 | Miscellaneous expenses of £500 paid out of petty cash. |
| 25.10.08 | Lang's account settled by cheque. |
| 28.10.08 | Green allows Jones a cash discount of £500. |
| 29.10.08 | Green is sent a cheque for £10 000. |
| 30.10.08 | Haddock is allowed a cash discount of £600. |
| 31.10.08 | Haddock settles his account in cash. |

*Required*:
Enter the above transactions in Jones's ledger accounts.

**3.12** The transactions listed below relate to Ken's business for the month of November 2009:

| | | |
|---|---|---|
| 1.11.09 | Started the business with £150 000 in cash. | |
| 2.11.09 | Transferred £14 000 of the cash to a business bank account. | |
| 3.11.09 | Paid rent of £1000 by cheque. | |
| 4.11.09 | Bought goods on credit from the following suppliers: | |
| | Ace | £5000 |
| | Mace | £6000 |
| | Pace | £7000 |
| 10.11.09 | Sold goods on credit to the following customers: | |
| | Main | £2000 |
| | Pain | £3000 |
| | Vain | £4000 |
| 15.11.09 | Returned goods costing £1000 to Pace. | |
| 22.11.09 | Pain returned goods sold to him for £2000. | |
| 25.11.09 | Additional goods purchased from the following suppliers: | |
| | Ace | £3000 |
| | Mace | £4000 |
| | Pace | £5000 |
| 26.11.09 | Office expenses of £2000 paid by cheque. | |
| 27.11.09 | Cash sales for the month amounted to £5000. | |
| 28.11.09 | Purchases paid for in cash during the month amounted to £4000. | |
| 29.11.09 | Cheques sent to the following suppliers: | |
| | Ace | £4000 |
| | Mace | £5000 |
| | Pace | £6000 |
| 30.11.09 | Cheques received from the following customers: | |
| | Main | £1000 |
| | Pain | £2000 |
| | Vain | £3000 |
| 30.11.09 | The following cash discounts were claimed by Ken: | |
| | Ace | £200 |
| | Mace | £250 |
| | Pace | £300 |
| 30.11.09 | The following cash discounts were allowed by Ken: | |
| | Main | £100 |
| | Pain | £200 |
| | Vain | £400 |
| 30.11.09 | Cash transfer to the bank of £1000. | |

*Required*:
Enter the above transactions in Ken's ledger accounts.

**3.13*** The following transactions relate to Pat's business for the month of December 2007:

| | | |
|---|---|---|
| 1.12.07 | Started the business with £10 000 in cash. | |
| 2.12.07 | Bought goods on credit from the following suppliers: | |
| | Grass | £6000 |
| | Seed | £7000 |
| 10.12.07 | Sold goods on credit to the following customers: | |
| | Fog | £3000 |
| | Mist | £4000 |
| 12.12.07 | Returned goods to the following suppliers: | |
| | Grass | £1000 |
| | Seed | £2000 |
| 15.12.07 | Bought additional goods on credit from Grass for £3000 and from Seed for £4000. | |
| 20.12.07 | Sold more goods on credit to Fog for £2000 and to Mist for £3000. | |
| 24.12.07 | Paid office expenses of £5000 in cash. | |
| 29.12.07 | Received £4000 in cash from Fog and £6000 in cash from Mist. | |
| 31.12.07 | Pat paid Grass and Seed £6000 and £8000, respectively, in cash. | |

*Required:*
(a) Enter the above transactions in Pat's ledger accounts.
(b) Balance off the accounts as at 31 December 2007.
(c) Bring down the balances as at 1 January 2008.
(d) Compile a trial balance as at 31 December 2007.

**3.14*** Vale has been in business for some years. The following balances were brought forward in his books of account as at 1 January 2008:

| | £ *Dr* | £ *Cr* |
|---|---|---|
| Bank | 5 000 | |
| Capital | | 20 000 |
| Cash | 1 000 | |
| Dodd | | 2 000 |
| Fish | 6 000 | |
| Furniture | 10 000 | |
| | 22 000 | 22 000 |

During the year to 31 December 2008 the following transactions took place:

1 Goods bought from Dodd on credit for £30 000.
2 Cash sales of £20 000.
3 Cash purchases of £15 000.
4 Goods sold to Fish on credit for £50 000.
5 Cheques sent to Dodd totalling £29 000.
6 Cheques received from Fish totalling £45 000.
7 Cash received from Fish amounting to £7000.
8 Office expenses paid in cash totalling £9000.
9 Purchase of delivery van costing £12 000 paid by cheque.
10 Cash transfers to bank totalling £3000.

*Required:*
(a) Compile Vale's ledger accounts for the year 31 December 2008, balance off the accounts and bring down the balances as at 1 January 2009.
(b) Extract a trial balance as at 31 December 2008.

**3.15** Brian started in business on 1 January 2009. The following is a list of his transactions for his first month of trading:

| | |
|---|---|
| 1.1.09 | Opened a business bank account with £25 000 obtained from private resources. |
| 2.1.09 | Paid one month's rent of £2000 by cheque. |
| 3.1.09 | Bought goods costing £5000 on credit from Linda. |
| 4.1.09 | Purchased motor car from Savoy Motors for £4000 on credit. |
| 5.1.09 | Purchased goods costing £3000 on credit from Sydney. |
| 10.1.09 | Cash sales of £6000. |
| 15.1.09 | More goods costing £10 000 purchased from Linda on credit. |
| 20.1.09 | Sold goods on credit to Ann for £8000. |
| 22.1.09 | Returned £2000 of goods to Linda. |
| 23.1.09 | Paid £6000 in cash into the bank. |
| 24.1.09 | Ann returned £1000 of goods. |
| 25.1.09 | Withdrew £500 in cash from the bank to open a petty cash account. |
| 26.1.09 | Cheque received from Ann for £5500; Ann also claimed a cash discount of £500. |
| 28.1.09 | Office expenses of £250 paid out of petty cash. |
| 29.1.09 | Sent a cheque to Savoy Motors for £4000. |
| 30.1.09 | Cheques sent to Linda and Sydney for £8000 and £2000, respectively. Cash discounts were also claimed from Linda and Sydney of £700 and £100, respectively. |
| 31.1.09 | Paid by cheque another month's rent of £2000. |
| 31.1.09 | Brian introduced £5000 additional capital into the business by cheque. |

*Required*:

(a) Enter the above transactions in Brian's ledger accounts for January 2009, balance off the accounts and bring down the balances as at 1 February 2009.

(b) Compile a trial balance as at 31 January 2009.

**3.16** An accounts clerk has compiled Trent's trial balance as at 31 March 2007 as follows:

| | *Dr* | *Cr* |
|---|---|---|
| | £ | £ |
| Bank (overdrawn) | 2 000 | |
| Capital | 50 000 | |
| Discounts allowed | | 5 000 |
| Discounts received | 3 000 | |
| Dividends received | 2 000 | |
| Drawings | | 23 000 |
| Investments | | 14 000 |
| Land and buildings | 60 000 | |
| Office expenses | 18 000 | |
| Purchases | 75 000 | |
| Sales | | 250 000 |
| Suspense (unexplained balance) | | 6 000 |
| Rates | | 7 000 |
| Vans | 20 000 | |
| Van expenses | | 5 000 |
| Wages and salaries | 80 000 | |
| | 310 000 | 310 000 |

*Required*:
Compile Trent's corrected trial balance as at 31 March 2007.

3.17 Donald's transactions for the month of March 2009 are as follows:

| | £ |
|---|---|
| *Cash receipts* | |
| Capital contributed | 6 000 |
| Sales to customers | 3 000 |
| *Cash payments* | |
| Goods for sale | 4 000 |
| Stationery | 500 |
| Postage | 300 |
| Travelling | 600 |
| Wages | 2 900 |
| Transfers to bank | 500 |
| *Bank receipts* | £ |
| Receipts from trade debtors: | |
| Smelt | 3 000 |
| Tait | 9 000 |
| Ure | 5 000 |
| *Bank payments* | £ |
| Payments to trade creditors: | |
| Craig | 2 800 |
| Dobie | 5 000 |
| Elgin | 6 400 |
| Rent and rates | 3 200 |
| Electricity | 200 |
| Telephone | 100 |
| Salaries | 2 000 |
| Miscellaneous expenses | 600 |
| *Other transactions* | |
| Goods purchased from: | |
| Craig | 3 500 |
| Dobie | 7 500 |
| Elgin | 7 500 |
| Goods returned to Dobie | 400 |
| Goods sold to: | |
| Smelt | 4 000 |
| Tait | 10 000 |
| Ure | 8 000 |
| Goods returned by Ure | 900 |
| Discounts allowed: | |
| Smelt | 200 |
| Tait | 500 |
| Ure | 400 |
| Discounts received: | |
| Craig | 50 |
| Dobie | 100 |
| Elgin | 200 |

*Required*:

(a) Enter the above transactions in appropriate ledger accounts.

(b) Balance each account as at 31 March 2009.

(c) Extract a trial balance as at that date.

**Further practice questions, study material and links to relevant sites on the World Wide Web can be found on the website that accompanies this book. The site can be found at www.pearsoned.co.uk/dyson**

# Chapter 4 Sole trader accounts

**Footballers: an expensive asset?**

## Experts boot out football reforms

**By Nicholas Neveling**

Calls to reform the way in which footballers are accounted for have been dismissed by football finance experts.

A research paper, released by academics at Cass Business School last week, argued that accounting for players as intangible assets was risky and squeezing club margins. The report said that players should instead be expensed through income statements.

But PKF partner Charles Barnett said it 'did not stack up' for clubs to expense player signing, as the value of these investments was only realized after a number of years.

'If you look at Newcastle, who have signed Michael Owen, they have the right to play him and he can score goals, which will help the club to win games, attain a higher league position and gain entry to tournaments. His performance can improve income,' Barnett said.

'You wouldn't write off a printing press or a drug patent as an expense, so why should you do it for a player?'

Gilad Livne, the co-author of the reports and a senior accounting lecturer at Cass Business School, said: 'Players have a very short shelf-life compared to other assets and are also prone to the human factor. With assets such as aircraft and buildings, you know what to expect, but players are prone to injury, illness and off-pitch problems. This makes treating them as assets risky.'

It has been mandatory to treat players as intangible assets since 1998, under FRS10.

*Accountancy Age*, 8 September 2005.



*Questions relating to this news story can be found on page 73*

## About this chapter

This chapter leads on from the previous one. Towards the end of that chapter we explained how to compile a trial balance. The trial balance is used to prepare the basic financial statements. These normally consist of a trading account, a profit and loss account, and a balance sheet. In this chapter we explain how they are prepared.

**Learning objectives**

By the end of this chapter you should be able to:

- describe what accountants mean by 'profit';
- prepare a basic set of financial statement for a trading entity.

## Why this chapter is important for non-accountants

This chapter is important for non-accountants for two main reasons.

1. It will help you to distinguish between capital and revenue items. The preparation of the basic financial statements require a distinction to be made between items called capital and items called revenues. This distinction is not easy to make in practice and there may be some disagreement about what is a capital item and what is a revenue item. The distinction is important because it has an effect on the amount of profit earned during the year.
2. It will help you to distinguish between cash and profit. The profit shown in the profit and loss account does not necessarily result in an equivalent increase in cash during the period. If this point is not understood, managers may make some incorrect and unwise decisions.

## The basic financial statements

The previous chapter finished with an explanation of how to prepare a trial balance. A trial balance has two important functions:

- it enables the accuracy of book-keeping to be checked; and
- it provides the basic data for the preparation of the financial accounts.

The precise nature of such statements will depend upon whether an entity is in the profit-making sector or the non-profit making sector, and whether it is engaged in manufacturing, trading or in providing a service. In this chapter we are going to concentrate on trading entities in the profit-making sector because this type of entity will enable us to explain most of what you need to know about preparing a basic set of financial statements.

A profit-making trading entity will normally prepare a trading account, a profit and loss account, and a balance sheet (see Figure 4.1).

The trading account matches the sales income that the entity has earned from selling goods during a certain period (normally a calendar year) against what it cost to buy those goods. The difference is called the *gross profit* (it could be a *gross loss*). The profit and loss account matches the gross profit (or gross loss) plus any other income that the entity has earned during the period against all the expenses of the business. The difference is called the *net profit* (or *net loss*). Both the trading account and the profit and loss account are part of the double-entry system, so for each debit entry there has to be a credit entry somewhere else within the system.

The balance sheet is a listing of all the balances left over at the end of the accounting period that have *not* been included in either the trading account or the profit and loss account (including also the net profit/loss taken from the profit and loss account). The balance sheet is not part of the double-entry system.

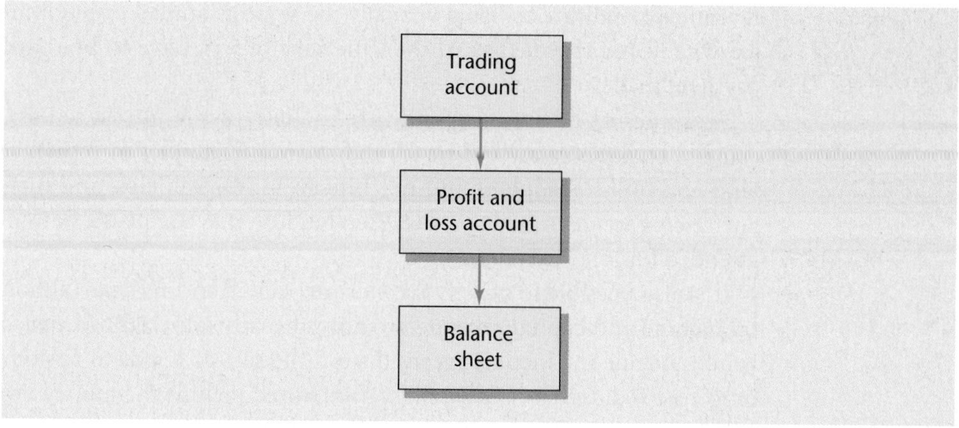


**Figure 4.1 A trading entity's basic accounts**

One very important point to note is that net profit (or net loss) is not necessarily the same as the difference between all the cash received less all the cash paid during the accounting period. We explain why in the next section.

## Cash versus profit

The owners of small businesses often try to measure the profit that it has made (i.e. how well it has done) by deducting the cash held at the end of a period from cash held at the beginning. It is then assumed that the difference represents profit (if the cash has increased) or loss (if the cash has decreased). This is *not* what accountants mean by profit.

In Chapter 2 we explained that accounts are normally prepared according to a number of accounting rules. The *realization rule*, for example, requires us to match the sales revenue for a particular period against the cost of selling those goods during the same period, while the *matching rule* requires a similar procedure to be adopted for other types of incomes and expenses. It is highly unlikely that the difference between cash received and cash paid will be the same as the difference between income and expenditure. Cash transactions may relate to earlier or later periods, whereas income and expenditure (as defined in accounting) measure the *actual* economic activity that has taken place during the accounting period. By *income* we mean something that the entity has gained during a particular period, and by *expenditure* we mean something the entity has lost during the same period.

There are a great many problems, of course, in trying to measure income and expenditure in this way, rather than on a cash receipts and cash payments basis. In calculating profit, expenditure is especially difficult to determine. For example, if the entity purchases a machine that has an estimated life of 20 years, how much of the cost should be charged against the income for Year 1 and the income for Year 20?

Accountants deal with this sort of problem by attempting to classify expenditure into capital expenditure and revenue expenditure. *Capital expenditure* is expenditure that is likely to provide a benefit to the entity for more than one accounting period, and *revenue expenditure* is expenditure that is likely to provide a benefit for only one period. As the basic financial statements are normally prepared on an annual basis, we can regard revenue expenditure as being virtually the same as annual expenditure. If a similar service is required the next year, then the service will have to be reordered and another payment made.

Examples of revenue expenditure include goods purchased for resale, electricity charges, business rates, and wages and salaries. Examples of capital expenditure include land and buildings, plant and machinery, motor vehicles, and furniture and fittings. Such items are described as *fixed assets* because they are possessions owned by the entity intended for long-term use.

It is also possible to classify *income* into *capital* and *revenue* (although the terms capital income and capital revenue are not normally adopted). *Income of a revenue nature* would include the income received from the sale of goods to customers, dividends and rents received. *Income of a capital nature* would include the money invested by the owner in the business and long-term loans (such as bank loans).

It is not always easy to distinguish between capital and revenue items and the distinction is often an arbitrary one. Some items of expenditure are particularly difficult to determine (e.g. repairs and maintenance), although most transactions fall into recognizable categories.

The distinction between capital and revenue items is very important. Accounting profit is basically the difference between revenue income and revenue expenditure (see Figure 4.2), and if capital and revenue items are not classified accurately then the accounting profit will either be overstated or understated. If it is overstated then the owner might draw too much profit out of the business or have to pay more tax. It is perhaps less serious if the profit is understated because the cash still remains in the business.

**Activity 4.1**

Are the following statements true or false?

(a) Accounting profit is normally the difference between cash received and cash paid. *True/false*

(b) Capital expenditure only provides a short-term benefit. *True/false*

(c) Fixed assets are normally written off to the trading account. *True/false*

## Preparation

In this section we explain how to prepare a set of basic financial statements.

Once you have checked that the trial balance balances, go through it line-by-line and insert against each balance the letter 'C' (for a capital item) and 'R' (for a revenue item).

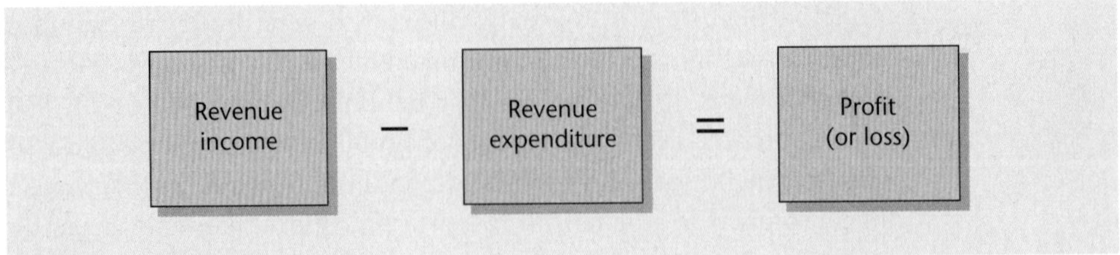


Figure 4.2 **Accounting profit**

Then transfer the R balances either to the trading account or to the profit and loss account and the C balances to the balance sheet. Of course you will have to decide how you are going to lay-out the balances and how to describe them, but fortunately there is a fairly standard format. We illustrate it in Example 4.1.

Example 4.1

## Preparation of basic financial statements

The following trial balance has been extracted from Bush's books of account as at 30 June 2008.

| *Name of account* | | *Dr* | *Cr* |
|---|---|---|---|
| | | £ | £ |
| Bank (1) | (C) | 5 000 | |
| Capital (at 1 July 2007) (2) | (C) | | 11 000 |
| Cash (3) | (C) | 1 000 | |
| Drawings (4) | (C) | 8 000 | |
| Motor vehicle at cost (5) | (C) | 6 000 | |
| Motor vehicle expenses (6) | (R) | 2 000 | |
| Office expenses (7) | (R) | 3 000 | |
| Purchases (8) | (R) | 30 000 | |
| Trade creditors (9) | (C) | | 4 000 |
| Trade debtors (10) | (C) | 10 000 | |
| Sales (11) | (R) | | 50 000 |
| | | 65 000 | 65 000 |

*Notes:*
There were no opening or closing stocks.
R = revenue items; C = Capital balances.

*Required:*
Prepare Bush's trading and profit and loss account for the year to 30 June 2008 and a balance sheet as at that date.

Answer to Example 4.1

**Bush**
**Trading and profit and loss account for the year to 30 June 2008**

| | £ | £ |
|---|---|---|
| Sales (11) | | 50 000 |
| *Less*: cost of goods sold: | | |
| Purchases (8) | | 30 000 |
| *Gross profit* | | 20 000 |
| *Less*: expenses | | |
| Motor vehicle expenses (6) | 2 000 | |
| Office expenses (7) | 3 000 | 5 000 |
| *Net profit for the year* | | 15 000 |

**Answer to Example 4.1** *continued*

**Bush**
**Balance sheet at 30 June 2008**

| | £ | £ |
|---|---|---|
| *Fixed assets* | | |
| Motor vehicles at cost (5) | | 6 000 |
| *Current assets* | | |
| Trade debtors (10) | 10 000 | |
| Bank (1) | 5 000 | |
| Cash (3) | 1 000 | |
| | 16 000 | |
| *Current liabilities* | | |
| Trade creditors (9) | 4 000 | 12 000 |
| | | 18 000 |
| *Capital* | | |
| Balance at 1 July 2007 (2) | | 11 000 |
| *Add*: Net profit for the year* | 15 000 | |
| *Less*: Drawings (4) | 8 000 | 7 000 |
| | | 18 000 |

* Obtained from the profit and loss account.
The bracketed number after each narration refers to the account number of each balance extracted from the trial balance.

*Tutorial notes*

1 Both the trading account and the profit and loss account cover a period of time. In this example it is for the year *to* (or, alternatively, *ending*) 30 June 2008. The balance sheet is prepared at a particular moment in time. It depicts the balances as they were at a specific date. In this example they are shown as at 30 June 2008.

2 The trading account, the profit and loss account, and the balance sheet are presented in what is called the *vertical* format, i.e. on a line-by-line basis starting at the top of the page and working downwards. This is in contrast to the *horizontal* format. This format lists expenditure balances in the trading and profit and loss account, and liability balances in the balance sheet on the left-hand side of the page, while income and asset balances are shown on the right-hand side. The horizontal format is now out-of-date and is rarely used. Using the vertical format, the *gross profit* of £20 000 is not only the last line in the trading account but also the first line of the profit and loss account.

3 Both the trading account and the profit and loss accounts are accounts in their own right and they form part of the double-entry system. The balance sheet is merely a list of balances left in the accounting system after the profit and loss account has been prepared. The last line of the profit and loss account shows a net profit of £15 000. This balance remains within the accounting system and so it will be carried forward to the next accounting period. It must, therefore, be included in the balance sheet, otherwise it would not balance. You will find the £15 000 towards the bottom of the balance sheet.

4 The balance sheet is divided into two main sections. The first section shows that Bush owned *net assets* worth £18 000 at 30 June 2008. It is split between *fixed assets* of £6000, i.e. those assets that are intended for long-term use in the business, and current assets, i.e. those assets that are constantly being turned over and replaced such

as stock, debtors and cash. However, *current liabilities* of £4000 have been deducted from the current assets of £16 000 to show that there was £12 000 of *net current assets*. Current liabilities are amounts owing to various parties that will be due for payment within the next 12 months.

5 The second section shows how the £18 000 of net assets has been financed, i.e. where the money has come from. There were two sources: £11 000 contributed by the owner as capital; and profit left in the business of £7000 – the £15 000 profit made for the year less £8000 taken out (in the form of cash or goods) by Bush during the year, presumably in anticipation that the entity would make a profit. Note that it is not customary to include proprietor's drawings in the profit and loss account.

6 In a more detailed example the expense section in the profit and loss account, and the fixed assets, current assets, current liabilities and capital section in the balance sheet would include many more balances. The profit and loss account balances would be grouped in sections, e.g. administration expenses, distribution costs, selling expenses. In the balance sheet, both fixed asset and current asset balances would be shown in the order of the least liquid (or realizable) assets balances being placed first, e.g. property before machinery, stocks before debtors. Similarly, current liabilities would be listed in the order of those that are going to be paid *last* being placed *first*, e.g. short-term loans would come before creditors. If there are a number of capital balances they too would be placed on 'a last should be first' basis, i.e. capital would come before retained profits.

**Activity 4.2**

In what order should the following balances be shown in a balance sheet?

(a) furniture and fittings; land; plant and machinery; property.
(b) cash; bank; insurance paid in advance; other debtors; trade debtors; stocks.
(c) bank overdraft; electricity owing; other creditors; trade creditors.

## Questions non-accountants should ask

This chapter has shown you how a simple trading and profit and loss account and a balance sheet may be prepared using the information extracted from a trial balance. When faced with such financial statements you might put the following questions to your accountants.

- What criteria have you adopted for determining whether a transaction is a capital item or a revenue item?
- Are there any such items included in the accounts where the distinction is arguable?
- How have you determined whether revenue income should or should not be included in the current trading account?

## Conclusion

In this chapter we have examined the preparation and format of a basic set of financial statements for a trading entity. In practice, once a trial balance has been balanced, a number of end-of-year adjustments would normally be made before the financial statements can be finalized. These adjustments will be examined in the next chapter.

### Key points

1. A trial balance provides the basic data for the preparation of the financial accounts.
2. The basic financial statements for a trading entity normally consist of a trading account, a profit and loss account, and a balance sheet.
3. Revenue balances are transferred to either the trading account or the profit and loss account, and capital balances to the balance sheet.
4. The trading account and the profit and loss account form part of the double-entry system. The balance sheet is merely a listing of the balances that remain in the ledger system once the trading and profit and loss accounts have been prepared.
5. The basic financial accounts are nowadays normally presented in a vertical format.

## Check your learning

*The answers to these questions can be found within the text.*

1. Suggest two reasons why this chapter is important for non-accountants.
2. Name two important functions of a trial balance.
3. What are the three financial statements that make up a set of basic accounts?
4. What are the two broad groups into which all transactions may be classified?
5. Explain why accounting profit is not the same as an increase in cash.
6. Express accounting profit in the form of a simple equation.
7. Name the two stages involved in preparing the basic accounts.
8. What term is given to the difference between sales revenue and the cost of goods sold?
9. What term is given to the difference between the total of all revenue incomes and the total of all revenue expenditures?
10. What two formats may be used for the presentation of financial statements?
11. Which format is the one now commonly used?

## News story quiz

*Remember the news story at the beginning of this chapter? Go back to that story and re-read it before answering the following questions.*

This article exposes the difficulty accountants have in deciding what is capital and what is revenue. In essence it is a conflict between the matching rule and the reliability rule.

### Questions

1 Where would you look for 'intangible assets' in a set of financial statements?

2 Do you agree with the current requirement that transfer fees and signing-on fees should be treated as an intangible asset?

3 If transfer fees and signing-on fees are not to be treated as intangible assets, how do you think that they should be dealt with in the financial statements?

4 What effect would this alternative treatment have on (a) a club's profit; and (b) on its balance sheet?

## Tutorial questions

*The answers to questions marked with an asterisk can be found in Appendix 4.*

4.1 Explain why an increase in cash during a particular accounting period does not necessarily mean that an entity has made a profit.

4.2 'The differentiation between so-called capital and revenue expenditure is quite arbitrary and unnecessary.' Discuss.

4.3 How far does a balance sheet tell users how much an entity is worth?

4.4* The following trial balance has been extracted from Ethel's books of accounts as at 31 January 2007:

| | *Dr* | *Cr* |
|---|---|---|
| | £ | £ |
| Capital | | 10 000 |
| Cash | 3 000 | |
| Creditors | | 3 000 |
| Debtors | 6 000 | |
| Office expenses | 11 000 | |
| Premises | 8 000 | |
| Purchases | 20 000 | |
| Sales | | 35 000 |
| | 48 000 | 48 000 |

*Required*:
Prepare Ethel's trading and profit and loss account for the year to 31 January 2007 and a balance sheet as at that date.

**4.5*** Marion has been in business for some years. The following trial balance has been extracted from her books of account as at 28 February 2008:

| | *Dr* | *Cr* |
|---|---|---|
| | *£000* | *£000* |
| Bank | 4 | |
| Buildings | 50 | |
| Capital | | 50 |
| Cash | 2 | |
| Creditors | | 24 |
| Debtors | 30 | |
| Drawings | 55 | |
| Heat and light | 10 | |
| Miscellaneous expenses | 25 | |
| Purchases | 200 | |
| Sales | | 400 |
| Wages and salaries | 98 | |
| | 474 | 474 |

*Required*:
Prepare Marion's trading and profit and loss account for the year to 28 February 2008 and a balance sheet as at that date.

**4.6** The following trial balance has been extracted from Jody's books of account as at 30 April 2009:

| | *Dr* | *Cr* |
|---|---|---|
| | *£000* | *£000* |
| Capital (as at 1 May 2008) | | 30 |
| Cash | 1 | |
| Electricity | 2 | |
| Maintenance | 4 | |
| Miscellaneous expenses | 7 | |
| Purchases | 40 | |
| Rent and rates | 6 | |
| Sales | | 85 |
| Vehicle (at cost) | 30 | |
| Wages | 25 | |
| | 115 | 115 |

*Required*:
Prepare Jody's trading and profit and loss account for the year to 30 April 2009 and a balance sheet as at that date.

4.7 The following trial balance has been extracted from the books of Garswood as at 31 March 2007:

| | *Dr* | *Cr* |
|---|---|---|
| | £ | £ |
| Advertising | 2 300 | |
| Bank | 300 | |
| Capital | | 55 700 |
| Cash | 100 | |
| Discounts allowed | 100 | |
| Discounts received | | 600 |
| Drawings | 17 000 | |
| Electricity | 1 300 | |
| Investments | 4 000 | |
| Investment income received | | 400 |
| Office equipment | 10 000 | |
| Other creditors | | 800 |
| Other debtors | 1 500 | |
| Machinery | 20 000 | |
| Purchases | 21 400 | |
| Purchases returns | | 1 400 |
| Sales | | 63 000 |
| Sales returns | 3 000 | |
| Stationery | 900 | |
| Trade creditors | | 5 200 |
| Trade debtors | 6 500 | |
| Wages | 38 700 | |
| | 127 100 | 127 100 |

*Required*:
Prepare Garswood's trading and profit and loss account for the year to 31 March 2007 and a balance sheet as at that date.

4.8 Pete has extracted the following trial balance from his books of account as at 31 May 2008:

| | *Dr* | *Cr* |
|---|---|---|
| | *£000* | *£000* |
| Bank | | 15 |
| Building society account | 100 | |
| Capital (as at 1 June 2007) | | 200 |
| Cash | 2 | |
| Heat, light and fuel | 18 | |
| Insurances | 10 | |
| Interest received | | 1 |
| Land and property (at cost) | 200 | |
| Long-term loan | | 50 |
| Long-term loan interest paid | 8 | |
| Motor vehicles (at cost) | 90 | |
| Motor vehicle expenses | 12 | |
| Plant and equipment (at cost) | 100 | |
| *c/f* | 540 | 266 |

| | | Dr | Cr |
|---|---|---|---|
| | | £000 | £000 |
| | b/f | 540 | 266 |
| Property maintenance | | 7 | |
| Purchases | | 300 | |
| Repairs to machinery | | 4 | |
| Rent and rates | | 65 | |
| Sales | | | 900 |
| Wages and salaries | | 250 | |
| | | 1166 | 1166 |

*Required:*
Prepare Pete's trading and profit and loss account for the year to 31 May 2008 and a balance sheet as at that date.

**Further practice questions, study material and links to relevant sites on the World Wide Web can be found on the website that accompanies this book. The site can be found at www.pearsoned.co.uk/dyson**

# Chapter 5 Last minute adjustments

## Not me, guv . . .

### Axle Group loses bearings

**Paul Rogerson**

A raft of accounting errors made public yesterday, including a near-£5m understatement of directors' pay, raises questions about the much-lauded financial turnaround of stellar entrepreneur Alan Revie's National Tyres.

The bottom line of Axle Group Holdings, formed in 2001 when Revie led a management buy-out of one of the UK's biggest fast-fit chains from German multinational Continental, was savaged in the latest trading period by reversal of the errors. These included understating boardroom remuneration in the two years immediately following the MBO by £4.9m. Directors' pay was not disclosed at all in those years, a breach of the Companies Act.

The Glasgow-based business revealed this week that its highest-paid director, most likely to be majority shareholder Revie, was paid £2.53m in calendar 2004 – a sum which would place him neck and neck with Royal Bank of Scotland chief Sir Fred Goodwin in Scotland's elite corporate pay league. This followed payments of £559,000 and £2.4m to Axle's highest-paid director in 2003 and 2002 respectively.

PricewaterhouseCoopers (PwC) succeeded rival 'big four' accountant KPMG as Axle's auditor in October 2004. PwC declined to give a clean bill of health to the 2004 group accounts, which were published this week. The firm declared that Axle 'have not kept proper accounting records' and said it did not have enough evidence to form an opinion on group losses and cash flows. In its report, the auditor also alluded to 'fundamental error in the recording of certain stocks, tangible fixed assets, directors' emoluments and releated taxes'.

The Glasgow-based team, which bought National Tyres in December 2001, has been credited with a remarkable turnaround. In the first year following the MBO, the business announced a pre-tax profit of £500,000, following a loss of £44m in 2001, through a combination of disposals, new systems, and a 20% rise in sales.

The 2004 accounts show that group sales rose to £114m from £103m in the previous 12 months. However, Axle posted a pre-tax loss for the period of £13m before amortisation of goodwill, which reduced the deficit to £3.9m. The £13m shortfall includes net exceptional charges for previous years totalling £5.5m. These charges include failing to record £4.9m in directors' pay in 2002 and 2003, and the incorrect booking of stock.

In 2003 Axle posted a loss before goodwill amortisation of £3.5m, which was turned into a surplus of £3.2m by a writeback of goodwill amounting to £6.7m.

In the annual report, Axle said its underlying trading profit had continued to improve. Asked to elaborate on the 2004 surplus, group financial director John Kemp said: 'Our main trading company, NTA (National Tyres & Autocare), returned a trading profit for the year 2004 of £1.4m and this was after exceptional costs of £700,000. This compares with £900,000 profit in 2003 and a £40m-plus loss when we bought the company.'

He added: 'Our wholesale company (Viking International) has recorded a loss of £4m in 2004, £3.2m of which relates to historic stock issues. The underlying loss of circa £800,000 has now been addressed through structural changes in the company.'

Kemp attributed accounting errors to 'valuation and obsolescence issues surrounding our stock carrying value, much of which originated within the companies before we bought them'. He added: 'It was early 2004 before we had full clarity on the issues and we have now dealt with these. KPMG were our auditors before PwC – we did not sack them – we changed as part of our corporate strategy to pull corporate, tax and audit under one roof. We have strengthened (the) accounting team and improved financial control by centralising all accounting functions in my office in Glasgow.'

*The Herald*, 12 January 2006.



*Questions relating to this news story can be found on page 91* ➡

## About this chapter

In the previous chapter we explained how the trial balance is used to prepare a set of financial statements, i.e. a trading account, a profit and loss account, and a balance account. We assumed that once the trial balance had been balanced there would be no more adjustments to make to the accounts. In practice, this would be unusual as there would normally be a number of other changes to be made to some of the balances before the financial statements can be finalized.

This chapter deals with four such changes. They are:

- an adjustment for closing stock;
- an allowance for depreciation;
- adjustments for accruals and prepayments;
- a charge for bad and doubtful debts.

Figure 5.1 shows how these changes fit into the trading account and the profit and loss account.

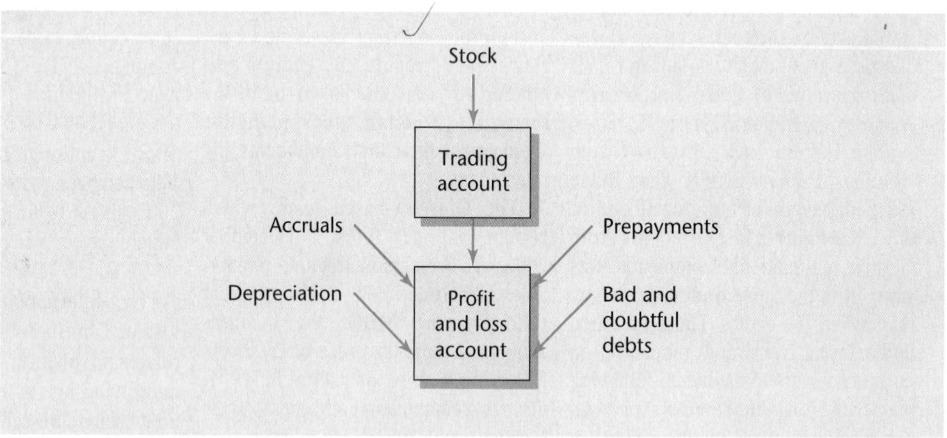


**Figure 5.1 Main adjustments**

**Learning objectives**

**By the end of this chapter you should be able to:**

- **make adjustments for stock, depreciation, accruals and prepayments, and bad and doubtful debts in a set of financial statements;**
- **prepare a set of financial statements incorporating such adjustments;**
- **list five main defects of conventional accounts.**

## Why this chapter is important for non-accountants

Your accountants will make a number of last minute adjustments to the financial statements. Such adjustments will be based, to a considerable extent, on a whole series of assumptions, estimates and guesswork and they will have a major impact on the calculation of the profit for the year, so obviously it would be unwise to leave the decisions entirely to them.

It is very important that you appreciate what each adjustment means, why it is being made, how it is has been done and the impact it has on the profit and loss account and on the balance sheet. Then you must be prepared to argue and to debate the issues that arise with your accountants. You will have a much wider perspective than your accountants and if a balanced decision is to be taken, it is important that your experience and your judgement are built into the analysis.

We start by explaining about the stock adjustment.

## Stock

It is most unlikely that all the purchases that have been made during a particular period will have been sold by the end of it and there will almost certainly be some purchases still left in the stores. In accounting terminology, purchases still on hand at the period end are referred to as *stock* (the Americans use the term *inventory*).

So when calculating the gross profit for the period it is necessary to make some allowance for closing stock, since we want to match the sales revenue earned for the period with the cost of goods sold, and not the cost of all of those goods actually purchased during the period. This means that we have to check the quantity of stock we have on hand at the end of the accounting period and then put some value on it. In practice, this is an extremely difficult exercise, and we shall be returning to it in a little more detail in Chapter 15. But we also have another problem in dealing with stock. Closing stock at the end of one period becomes the opening stock at the beginning of the next period so we also have to allow for opening stock. This means that the cost of goods sold is made up of three elements – opening stock, purchases and closing stock. Expressed as a formula:

**Cost of goods sold = (opening stock + purchases) – closing stock**

By making an adjustment for opening and closing stock, the trading account should now appear as in Example 5.1

Example 5.1

### Example of a trading account with stock adjustments

| | £ | £ |
|---|---|---|
| Sales | | 4 000 |
| *Less*: Cost of goods sold | | |
| Opening stock | 1 000 | |
| Purchases | 2 000 | |
| | 3 000 | |
| *Less*: Closing stock | 1 500 | 1 500 |
| Gross profit | | 2 500 |

**Activity 5.1**

Assume that Company A has a sales revenue of £10 000 for the year. The opening stock had a value of £2000 and during year the company made purchases of £6000. What would be the gross profit if the closing stock was valued at:

(a) £1500
(b) £2000
(c) £2500?

We now move on to the second of our last minute adjustments: depreciation.

## Depreciation

Expenditure that covers more than one accounting period is known as *capital expenditure.* Capital expenditure is not normally included in either the trading account or the profit and loss account but it would be misleading to exclude it altogether from the calculation of profit.

Expenditure on fixed assets (such as plant and machinery, motor vehicles and furniture) is necessary in order to help provide a general service to the business. The benefit received from the purchase of fixed assets must (by definition) extend beyond at least one accounting period. So the cost of the benefit provided by fixed assets ought to be charged to those accounting periods that benefit from such expenditure. The problem is in determining what charge to make. In accounting terminology, such a charge is known as *depreciation.*

There is also another reason why fixed assets should be depreciated. By *not* charging each accounting period with some of the cost of fixed assets, the level of profit will be correspondingly higher and the owner would then be able to withdraw more profit from the business. If this happens, insufficient cash may be left in it and the owner may then find it difficult to buy new fixed assets.

It is not easy to measure the benefit provided to each accounting period by some groups of fixed assets and most depreciation methods tend to be somewhat simplistic. The method most commonly adopted is known as *straight-line depreciation.* This method charges an equal amount of depreciation to each accounting period that benefits from the purchase of a fixed asset. The annual depreciation charge is calculated as follows:

$$\frac{\textbf{original cost of the asset} - \textbf{estimated residual value}}{\textbf{estimated life of the asset}}$$

You can see that in order to calculate the annual depreciation charge it is necessary to work out how long the asset is likely to last, and what it can be sold for when its useful life is ended.

It is customary to include fixed assets at their historic (i.e. original) cost in the balance sheet, but some fixed assets (such as property) may be revalued at regular intervals. If this is the case, the depreciation charge will be based on the revalued amount and not on the historic cost. It should also be noted that even if the asset is depreciated on the basis of its revalued amount there is still no guarantee that it can be replaced at that amount. A combination of inflation and obsolescence may mean that the eventual replacement cost is far in excess of either the historic cost or the revalued amount. It follows that when the fixed asset eventually comes to be replaced, the entity may still not have sufficient cash available to replace it.

**Activity 5.2**

The cost of a company's plant was £50 000. It was estimated that the plant would have a life of 20 years and that it could then be sold for £5000.

Using the straight-line method of depreciation, how much depreciation would you charge to the profit and loss account in Year 1?

The depreciation charge for the year is charged to the profit and loss account as an expense. The balance sheet would include the following details for each group of fixed assets:

**1** the historic cost (or revalued amount), i.e. the gross book value (GBV);
**2** the accumulated depreciation;
**3** the net book value (NBV).

In other words, line 1 minus line 2 = line 3.

These balance sheet requirements are illustrated in Example 5.2.

**Example 5.2**

## Balance sheet disclosure of fixed assets

| *Fixed assets* | *Cost* | *Depreciation* | *Net book value* |
|---|---|---|---|
| | £ | £ | £ |
| Buildings | 100 000 | 30 000 | 70 000 |
| Equipment | 40 000 | 25 000 | 15 000 |
| Furniture | 10 000 | 7 000 | 3 000 |
| | 150 000 | 62 000 | 88 000 |
| *Current assets* | | | |
| Stocks | | 10 000 | |
| Debtors | | 8 000 | |
| Cash | | 2 000 | |
| | | | 20 000 |
| | | | 108 000 |

The third of our last minute adjustments relates to accruals and prepayments.

# Accruals and prepayments

We will deal with accruals and prepayments separately.

## Accruals

An accrual is an amount owing for a service provided during a particular accounting period but still unpaid for at the end of it. For example, the entity may have paid the last quarter's electricity bill one week before the year end. In its accounts for that year, therefore, it needs to allow for (or *accrue*) the amount that it will owe for the electricity consumed during the last week of the year. The amount due will normally be settled in cash a few days after the year end.

The accrual will be based on an estimate of the likely cost of one week's supply of electricity, or as a proportion of the amount payable (if it has already received the invoice).

The accrual will be included in the amount charged to the profit and loss account for the period as part of the cost of the service provided. The formula is:

**(amounts paid during the year + closing accruals) – opening accruals**

The closing accruals will be shown on the balance sheet as part of the current liabilities.

**Activity 5.3**

You owed £500 to the telephone company at 31 December 2007. During the year to 31 December 2008 you paid the company £4000. At 31 December 2008 you owed the company £1000.

What amount for telephone charges would you debit to the profit and loss account for the year to 31 December 2008?

## Prepayments

A prepayment is an amount paid in cash during an accounting period for a service that will be provided in a subsequent period. For example, if a company's year end is 31 December and it buys a van halfway through 2008 and licences it for 12 months, half of the fee paid will relate to 2008 and half to 2009. It is necessary, therefore, to adjust 2008's accounts so that only half of the fee is charged in that year. The other half will eventually be charged to 2009's accounts.

Prepayments made during the year will be deducted from the amount charged to the profit and loss account. The formula is:

**(amount paid during the year + opening prepayments) – closing prepayments**

The closing prepayments will be shown in the balance sheet as part of the current assets.

**Activity 5.4**

Jill had paid £3000 in advance for insurance at 31 December 2007. During the year to 31 December 2008 she paid the insurance company £10 000. At 31 December 2007 she estimated that she had paid £2000 for insurance cover that related to the following year.

What amount for insurance charges should Jill debit to her profit and loss account for the year to 31 December 2008?

## Bad and doubtful debts

The fourth main adjustment made in finalizing the annual accounts involves making adjustments for bad debts, and provisions for bad and doubtful debts.

The realization rule allows us to claim profit for any goods that have been sold, even if the cash for them is not received until a later accounting period. This means that we are taking a risk in claiming the profit on those goods in the earlier period, even if the legal title has been passed to the customer. If the goods are not eventually paid for, we will have overestimated the profit for that earlier period. The owner might already have taken the profit out of the business (e.g. by increasing cash drawings) and it then might be too late to do anything about it.

Fortunately, there is a technique whereby we can build in an allowance for any possible *bad debts,* as they are called. This is quite a tricky operation and so we will need to explain it in two stages: firstly how to account for bad debts; and secondly how to allow for the possibility that some debts may be *doubtful.*

### Bad debts

Once it is clear that a debt is bad (i.e. it is highly unlikely it will ever be paid), then it must be written off to the profit and loss account immediately as an expense. This means that we have to charge it to the current year's profit and loss account, even though it may relate to an earlier period. It is usually impractical to change accounts once they have been finalized because the owner may have already drawn a share of the profits out of the business. This means that trade debtors on the balance sheet will be shown *after* deducting any bad debts that have been written off to the profit and loss account.

**Activity 5.5**

Gibson's trade debtors at 31 December 2007 amount to £75 000. One of the trade debtors has owed Gibson £5000 since 2001. Gibson thinks that the debtor now lives abroad in exile.

Should Gibson write off the £5000 as a bad debt to the profit and loss account for the year to 31 December 2007? If so, which account should be debited and which account should be credited? And what amount for trade debtors should be shown in Gibson's balance sheet at 31 December 2007?

### Provisions for bad and doubtful debts

The profit in future accounting periods would be severely distorted if the entity suffered a whole series of bad debts. So it seems prudent to allow for the possibility that some debts may become bad. We can do this by setting up a *provision* for bad and doubtful debts (a provision is simply an amount set aside for something that is highly likely to happen), and debiting it to a special account. In order to do so, it is necessary to estimate the likely level of bad debts. The estimate will normally be based on the experience that the entity has had in dealing with specific bad debts. In simple book-keeping exercises, the provision is usually expressed as a percentage of the outstanding trade debtors.

The procedure is illustrated in Example 5.3.

**Example 5.3**

## Accounting for bad and doubtful debts

You are presented with the following information for the year to 31 March 2008:

| | £ |
|---|---|
| Trade debtors at 1 April 2007 | 20 000 |
| Trade debtors at 31 March 2008 (including £3000 of specific bad debts) | 33 000 |
| Provision for bad and doubtful debts at 1 April 2007 | 1 000 |

*Note*: A provision for bad and doubtful debts is maintained equivalent to 5 per cent of the trade debtors as at the end of the year.

*Required*:

(a) Calculate the increase required in the bad and doubtful debts provision account for the year to 31 March 2008.

(b) Show how both the trade debtors and the provision for bad and doubtful debts account would be featured in the balance sheet at 31 March 2008.

**Answer to Example 5.3(a)**

| | £ |
|---|---|
| Trade debtors as at 31 March 2008 | 33 000 |
| *Less*: Specific bad debts to be written off to the profit and loss account for the year to 31 March 2008 | 3 000 |
| | 30 000 |
| Provision required: 5% thereof | 1 500 |
| *Less*: Provision at 1 April 2007 | 1 000 |
| Increase in the bad and doubtful debts provision account* | 500 |

* This amount will be charged to the profit and loss account for the year to 31 March 2008

***Tutorial notes***

The balance on the provision for bad and doubtful debts account will be higher at 31 March 2008 than it was at 1 April 2007. This is because the level of trade debtors is higher at the end of 2008 than it was at the end of 2007. The required increase in the provision of £500 will be *debited* to the profit and loss account. If it had been possible to reduce the provision (because of a lower level of trade debtors at the end of 2008 compared with 2007) the decrease would have been *credited* to the profit and loss account.

**Answer to Example 5.3(b)**

**Balance sheet extract at 31 March 2008**

| | £ | £ |
|---|---|---|
| *Current assets* | | |
| Trade debtors | 30 000 | |
| *Less*: Provision for bad and doubtful debts | 1 500 | |
| | | 28 500 |

As a non-accountant it is important for you to grasp just two essential points about the treatment of bad debts and doubtful debts.

- A debt should never be written off until it is absolutely certain that it is bad. Once it is written off, it is highly likely that no further attempt will ever be made to recover it.
- It is prudent to allow for the possibility of some doubtful debts. Nevertheless, it is perhaps rather a questionable decision to reduce profit by an arbitrary amount, e.g. by guessing whether it should be 3 per cent or 5 per cent of outstanding debtors. Obviously, the level that you choose can have a big effect on the profit for the period in question.

**Activity 5.6**

Watson keeps a provision for bad and doubtful debts account. It is maintained at a level of 3% of his total outstanding trade debtors as at the end of the year. The balance on the provision account at 1 January 2008 was £9000. His trade debtors at 31 December 2008 amounted to £250 000.

What balance on his provision for bad and doubtful debts does he need to carry forward as at 31 December 2008? What amount does he need to write off to the profit and loss account for that year? And will it increase or decrease his profit?

## A comprehensive example

In this section, we bring together all the material covered in this section in a comprehensive example. We cover all the basic procedures that we have outlined in this chapter as well as in the preceding one.

**Example 5.4**

### Example of basic accounting procedures

Wayne has been in business for many years. His accountant has extracted the following trial balance from his books of account as at 31 March 2008:

| | £ | £ |
|---|---|---|
| Bank | 1 200 | |
| Capital | | 33 000 |
| Cash | 300 | |
| Drawings | 6 000 | |
| Insurance | 2 000 | |
| Office expenses | 15 000 | |
| Office furniture at cost | 5 000 | |
| Office furniture: accumulated depreciation at 1 April 2007 | | 2 000 |
| Provision for bad and doubtful debts at 1 April 2007 | | 500 |
| Purchases | 55 000 | |
| Salaries | 25 000 | |
| Sales | | 100 000 |
| Stock at 1 April 2007 | 10 000 | |
| Trade creditors | | 4 000 |
| Trade debtors | 20 000 | |
| | 139 500 | 139 500 |

**Example 5.4** *continued*

*Notes*: The following additional information is to be taken into account.

1 Stock at 31 March 2008 was valued at £15 000.
2 The insurance included £500 worth of cover which related to the year to 31 March 2009.
3 Depreciation is charged on office furniture at 10 per cent per annum of its original cost (it is assumed not to have any residual value).
4 A bad debt of £1000 included in the trade debtors balance of £20 000 is to be written off.
5 The provision for bad and doubtful debts is to be maintained at a level of 5 per cent of outstanding trade debtors as at 31 March 2008, i.e. after excluding the bad debt referred to in note 4 above.
6 At 31 March 2008, there was an amount owing for salaries of £1000.

*Required*:
(a) Prepare Wayne's trading and profit and loss account for the year to 31 March 2008.
(b) Prepare a balance sheet as at that date.

**Answer to Example 5.4**

**(a)**

**Wayne**
**Trading and profit and loss account for the year to 31 March 2008**

| | £ | £ | (Source of entry) |
|---|---|---|---|
| | | 100 000 | (TB) |
| Sales | | | |
| *Less*: Cost of goods sold: | | | |
| Opening stock | 10 000 | | (TB) |
| Purchases | 55 000 | | (TB) |
| | 65 000 | | |
| *Less*: Closing stock | 15 000 | | (QN 1) |
| | | 50 000 | |
| *Gross profit* | | 50 000 | |
| *Less*: Expenses: | | | |
| Insurance (2000 – 500) | 1 500 | | (Wkg 1) |
| Office expenses | 15 000 | | (TB) |
| Depreciation: office furniture (10% × 5000) | 500 | | (Wkg 2) |
| Bad debt | 1 000 | | (QN 4) |
| Increase in provision for bad and doubtful debts | 450 | | (Wkg 3) |
| Salaries (25 000 + 1000) | 26 000 | | (Wkg 4) |
| | | 44 450 | |
| Net profit for the year | | 5 550 | |

**(b)**

**Wayne**
**Balance sheet at 31 March 2008**

| *Fixed assets* | £<br>*Cost* | £<br>*Accumulated depreciation* | £<br>*Net book value* | (Source of entry) |
|---|---|---|---|---|
| Office furniture *c/f* | 5 000 | 2 500 | 2 500 | (TB and Wkg 5) |

| | £ | £ | £ | (Source of entry) |
|---|---|---|---|---|
| b/f | 5 000 | 2 500 | 2 500 | |
| *Current assets* | | | | |
| Stock | | 15 000 | | (QN 1) |
| Trade debtors | | | | |
| (20 000 – 1000) | 19 000 | | | (Wkg 3) |
| *Less*: Provision for bad and doubtful debts | 950 | 18 050 | | (Wkg 3) |
| Prepayment | | 500 | | (QN 2) |
| Cash at bank | | 1 200 | | (TB) |
| Cash in hand | | 300 | | (TB) |
| | | 35 050 | | |
| *Less: Current liabilities* | | | | |
| Trade creditors | 4 000 | | | (TB) |
| Accrual | 1 000 | | | (QN 6) |
| | | 5 000 | 30 050 | |
| | | | 32 550 | |
| Financed by: | | | | |
| *Capital* | | | | |
| Balance at 1 April 2007 | | | 33 000 | (TB) |
| *Add*: Net profit for the year | | 5 550 | | (P&L a/c) |
| *Less*: Drawings | | 6 000 | (450) | |
| | | | 32 550 | |

Key:
TB = from trial balance;
QN = extracted straight from the question and related notes;
Wkg = workings (see below);
P&L a/c = balance obtained from the profit and loss account.

## Workings

| | £ |
|---|---|
| **1** Insurance: | |
| As per the trial balance | 2 000 |
| *Less*: Prepayment (QN 2) | 500 |
| Charge to the profit and loss account | 1 500 |
| **2** Depreciation: | |
| Office furniture at cost | 5 000 |
| Depreciation: 10% of the original cost | 500 |
| **3** Increase in provision for bad and doubtful debts: | |
| Trade debtors at 31 March 2008 | 20 000 |
| *Less*: Bad debt (QN 4) | 1 000 |
| | 19 000 |
| Provision required: 5% thereof | 950 |
| *Less*: Provision at 1 April 2007 | 500 |
| Increase in provision: charge to profit and loss | 450 |

Answer to Example 5.4 *continued*

| | |
|---|---|
| **4** Salaries: | |
| As per the question | 25 000 |
| *Add*: Accrual (QN 6) | 1 000 |
| | 26 000 |
| **5** Accumulated depreciation: | |
| Balance at 1 April 2007 (as per TB) | 2 000 |
| *Add*: Depreciation for the year (Wkg 2) | 500 |
| Accumulated depreciation at 31 March 2008 | 2 500 |

## Accounting defects

In previous sections of the book, we have emphasized that the calculation of accounting profit calls for a great deal of subjective judgement. Accounting involves much more than merely being very good at mastering some complicated arithmetical examples. So we think that it would be helpful (indeed essential) if we summarized the major defects inherent in the traditional method of calculating accounting profit.

As a non-accountant, it is most important that you appreciate one vital fact: the method that we have outlined for calculating the profit for a period results in an *estimate* of what the accountant thinks the profit should be. You must not place too much reliance on the *absolute* level of accounting profit. It can only be as accurate and as reliable as the assumptions upon which it is based. If you accept the assumptions, then you can be fairly confident that the profit figure is reliable. You will then not go too far wrong in using the information for decision-making purposes. But you must know what the assumptions are and you must support them. So we recommend that you *always question accounting information before accepting it.*

The main reasons why you should not place too much reliance on the *actual* level of accounting profit (especially if you are unsure about the assumptions upon which it is based) are summarized below.

- Goods are treated as being sold when the legal title to them changes hands and not when the customer has paid for them. In some cases, the cash for some sales may never be received.
- Goods are regarded as having been purchased when the legal title to them is transferred to the purchaser, although there are occasions when they may not be received, e.g. if a supplier goes into receivership.
- Goods that have not been sold at the period end have to be quantified and valued. This procedure involves a considerable amount of subjective judgement.
- There is no clear distinction between so-called capital and so-called revenue items.
- Estimates have to be made to allow for accruals and prepayments.
- The cost of fixed assets is apportioned between different accounting periods using methods that are fairly simplistic and highly questionable.
- Arbitrary reductions in profit are made to allow for bad and doubtful debts.
- Historic cost accounting makes no allowance for inflation. So the value of £100 (say) at 1 January 2008 is not the same as £100 at 31 December 2008. As a result profit tends to be overstated largely because of low closing stock values and low depreciation charges.

The defects of historic cost accounting as listed are serious but no one as yet has been able to suggest a better method. For the time being, therefore, all we can do is to take comfort in the old adage that 'it is better to be vaguely right than precisely wrong'.

**Activity 5.7**

Are the following statements true or false?

(a) A provision for bad and doubtful debts results in cash leaving the business. *True/false*
(b) An amount owing for rent at the end of the year is an accrual. *True/false*
(c) There is no such thing as the correct level of accounting profit. *True/false*

## Questions non-accountants should ask

It is important that as a non-accountant you should grasp the significance of this chapter. The decisions that your accountants will have taken in making a series of last minute adjustments to the financial accounts (particularly for stocks, depreciation, accruals and prepayment, and bad and doubtful debts) will have a considerable effect on the amount of profit that the entity reports for the year.

We suggest that you ask the following questions.

- Was a physical stock check done at the year end?
- What method was used to value the closing stock?
- What depreciation method has been used?
- Has historic cost been used to depreciate the fixed assets?
- If not, how has the cost of fixed assets been determined?
- How has the expected life of the assets been assessed?
- How do such lives compare with those used by our competitors?
- How have any residual values for the fixed assets been estimated?
- How have estimated values been determined for any accruals and prepayments?
- Have any bad debts been written off?
- How can we be certain that they are indeed bad?
- What basis is used to determine an appropriate level of provision for bad and doubtful debts?

## Conclusion

In this chapter, we have examined in some detail the main adjustments made to financial accounts at the end of an accounting period. You should now be in a far better position to assess the relevance and reliability of any accounting information that is presented to you.

The material that we have covered has provided a broad foundation for all the remaining chapters in this book. It is essential that before moving on to them you satisfy yourself that you really do understand the mechanics behind the preparation of a set of basic financial statements.

## Key points

1 Following the completion of the trial balance, some last minute adjustments have usually to be made to the financial statements. The main adjustments are stock, depreciation, accruals and prepayments, and bad and doubtful debts.

2 Accounting profit is merely an estimate. The method used to calculate it is highly questionable and it is subject to very many criticisms. Undue reliance should not be placed on the actual level of profit shown in the accounts. The assumptions upon which profit is based should be carefully examined and it should be viewed merely as a guide to decision making.

## Check your learning

*The answers to these questions can be found within the text.*

1 What is meant by 'stock'?

2 What is the American term for it?

3 What is meant by 'opening stock' and 'closing stock'?

4 What three items make up the closing stock?

5 To which account are opening and closing stock transferred?

6 Is opening stock shown on the balance sheet at the end of an accounting period?

7 Is closing stock shown on the balance sheet at the end of an accounting period?

8 What is depreciation?

9 Name two methods of depreciating fixed assets.

10 How are each of those methods calculated?

11 What is meant by the terms 'gross book value' and 'net book value'?

12 What amount for depreciation is shown on the balance sheet?

13 What is (a) an accrual, and (b) a prepayment?

14 Where are they normally disclosed in the profit and loss account?

15 Where are they to be found in the balance sheet?

16 What is (a) a bad debt, and (b) a doubtful debt?

17 What is a provision for bad and doubtful debts?

18 On what might the provision be based?

19 List eight reasons why the calculation of accounting profit is an arbitrary exercise.

## News story quiz

*Remember the news story at the beginning of this chapter? Go back to that story and re-read it before answering the following questions.*

This article shows that even major businesses do not necessarily keep appropriate accounting records and report properly for various transactions (such as directors' emoluments, taxes, fixed assets and stocks). As a result of having to report such deficiencies the company received a bad press. If you are still not sure why, as a non-accountant, you are required to take a course in accounting, then this story should be more than sufficient to convince you!

### Questions

1 How do you think it was possible *not* to record nearly £5m in directors' remuneration in the books of account or to disclose it in the annual accounts?

2 What do you think went wrong with the accounting system so that the auditors were not able 'to form an opinion on group losses and cash flows'?

3 What types of fundamental errors were likely to have occurred in recording 'certain stocks, tangible fixed assets, directors' emoluments and related taxes'?

4 What is meant by the phrase 'amortisation of goodwill' and 'a writeback of goodwill'?

## Tutorial questions

*The answers to questions marked with an asterisk can be found in Appendix 4.*

5.1 'Depreciation methods and rates should be prescribed by law.' Discuss.

5.2 Explain why it is quite easy to manipulate the level of gross profit when preparing a trading account.

5.3 How far is it possible for an entity to build up hidden amounts of profit (known as *secret reserves*) by making some adjustments in the profit and loss account for bad and doubtful debts?

5.4* The following information has been extracted from Lathom's books of account for the year to 30 April 2007:

| | £ |
|---|---|
| Purchases | 45 000 |
| Sales | 60 000 |
| Stock (at 1 May 2006) | 3 000 |
| Stock (at 30 April 2007) | 4 000 |

*Required*:

(a) Prepare Lathom's trading account for the year to 30 April 2007.

(b) State where the stock at 30 April 2007 would be shown on the balance sheet as at that date.

5.5 Rufford presents you with the following information for the year to 31 March 2008:

| | £ |
|---|---|
| Purchases | 48 000 |
| Purchases returns | 3 000 |
| Sales | 82 000 |
| Sales returns | 4 000 |
| Stock at 1 April 2007 | 4 000 |

He is not sure how to value the stock as at 31 March 2008. Three methods have been suggested. They all result in different closing stock values, namely:

| | £ |
|---|---|
| Method 1 | 8 000 |
| Method 2 | 16 000 |
| Method 3 | 4 000 |

*Required*:

(a) Calculate the effect on gross profit for the year to 31 March 2008 by using each of the three methods of stock valuation.

(b) State the effect on gross profit for the year to 31 March 2009 if Method 1 is used instead of Method 2.

5.6* Standish has been trading for some years. The following trial balance has been extracted from his books of account as at 31 May 2009:

| | *Dr* | *Cr* |
|---|---|---|
| | £ | £ |
| Capital | | 22 400 |
| Cash | 1 200 | |
| Creditors | | 4 300 |
| Debtors | 6 000 | |
| Drawings | 5 500 | |
| Furniture and fittings | 8 000 | |
| Heating and lighting | 1 500 | |
| Miscellaneous expenses | 6 700 | |
| Purchases | 52 000 | |
| Sales | | 79 000 |
| Stock (at 1 June 2008) | 7 000 | |
| Wages and salaries | 17 800 | |
| | 105 700 | 105 700 |

*Note*: Stock at 31 May 2009: £12 000.

*Required*:

Prepare Standish's trading and profit and loss account for the year to 31 May 2009 and a balance sheet as at that date.

**5.7** Witton commenced business on 1 July 2006. The following trial balance was extracted from his books of account as at 30 June 2007:

| | *Dr* | *Cr* |
|---|---|---|
| | £ | £ |
| Capital | | 3 000 |
| Cash | 500 | |
| Drawings | 4 000 | |
| Creditors | | 1 500 |
| Debtors | 3 000 | |
| Motor car at cost | 5 000 | |
| Office expenses | 8 000 | |
| Purchases | 14 000 | |
| Sales | | 30 000 |
| | 34 500 | 34 500 |

*Additional information*:

1 Stock at 30 June 2007: £2000.

2 The motor car is to be depreciated at a rate of 20 per cent per annum on cost; it was purchased on 1 July 2006.

*Required*:

Prepare Witton's trading and profit and loss account for the year to 30 June 2007 and a balance sheet as at that date.

**5.8** The following is an extract from Barrow's balance sheet at 31 August 2008:

| *Fixed assets* | *Cost* | *Accumulated depreciation* | *Net book value* |
|---|---|---|---|
| | £ | £ | £ |
| Land | 200 000 | – | 200 000 |
| Buildings | 150 000 | 60 000 | 90 000 |
| Plant | 55 000 | 37 500 | 17 500 |
| Vehicles | 45 000 | 28 800 | 16 200 |
| Furniture | 20 000 | 12 600 | 7 400 |
| | 470 000 | 138 900 | 331 100 |

Barrow's depreciation policy is as follows:

1 A full year's depreciation is charged in the year of acquisition, but none in the year of disposal.

2 No depreciation is charged on land.

3 Buildings are depreciated at an annual rate of 2 per cent on cost.

4 Plant is depreciated at an annual rate of 5 per cent on cost after allowing for an estimated residual value of £5000.

5 Vehicles are depreciated on a reduced balance basis at an annual rate of 40 per cent on the reduced balance, i.e. on the net book value as at the end of the previous year.

6 Furniture is depreciated on a straight-line basis at an annual rate of 10 per cent on cost after allowing for an estimated residual value of £2000.

*Additional information*:

1 During the year to 31 August 2009 new furniture was purchased for the office. It cost £3000 and it is to be depreciated on the same basis as the old furniture. Its estimated residual value is £300.

2 There were no additions to, or disposals of, any other fixed assets during the year to 31 August 2009.

*Required*:

(a) Calculate the depreciation charge for each of the fixed asset groupings for the year to 31 August 2009.

(b) Show how the fixed assets would appear in Barrow's balance sheet as at 31 August 2009.

**5.9*** Pine started business on 1 October 2008. The following is his trial balance at 30 September 2009:

| | £ | £ |
|---|---|---|
| Capital | | 6 000 |
| Cash | 400 | |
| Creditors | | 5 900 |
| Debtors | 5 000 | |
| Furniture at cost | 8 000 | |
| General expenses | 14 000 | |
| Insurance | 2 000 | |
| Purchases | 21 000 | |
| Sales | | 40 000 |
| Telephone | 1 500 | |
| | 51 900 | 51 900 |

The following information was obtained after the trial balance had been prepared:

1 Stock at 30 September 2009: £3000.

2 Furniture is to be depreciated at a rate of 15 per cent on cost.

3 At 30 September 2009, Pine owed £500 for telephone expenses, and insurance had been prepaid by £200.

*Required*:

Prepare Pine's trading and profit and loss account for the year to 30 September 2009 and a balance sheet as at that date.

**5.10** Dale has been in business for some years. The following is his trial balance at 31 October 2007:

| | | *Dr* | *Cr* |
|---|---|---|---|
| | | £ | £ |
| Bank | | 700 | |
| Capital | | | 85 000 |
| Depreciation (at 1 November 2006): | | | |
| Office equipment | | | 14 000 |
| Vehicles | | | 4 000 |
| Drawings | | 12 300 | |
| Heating and lighting | | 3 000 | |
| Office expenses | | 27 000 | |
| | *c/f* | 43 000 | 103 000 |

| | | *Dr* | *Cr* |
|---|---|---|---|
| | | £ | £ |
| | *b/f* | 43 000 | 103 000 |
| Office equipment, at cost | | 35 000 | |
| Rates | | 12 000 | |
| Purchases | | 240 000 | |
| Sales | | | 350 000 |
| Stock (at 1 November 2006) | | 20 000 | |
| Trade creditors | | | 21 000 |
| Trade debtors | | 61 000 | |
| Vehicles at cost | | 16 000 | |
| Wages and salaries | | 47 000 | |
| | | 474 000 | 474 000 |

*Additional information (not taken into account when compiling the above trial balance)*:

1 Stock at 31 October 2007: £26 000.
2 Amount owing for electricity at 31 October 2007: £1500.
3 At 31 October 2007, £2000 had been paid in advance for rates.
4 Depreciation is to be charged on the office equipment for the year to 31 October 2007 at a rate of 20 per cent on cost, and on the vehicles at a rate of 25 per cent on cost.

*Required*:
Prepare Dale's trading and profit and loss account for the year to 31 October 2007 and a balance sheet as at that date.

**5.11** The following information relates to Astley for the year to 30 November 2008:

| *Item* | *Cash paid during the year to 30 November 2008* | *As at 1 December 2007 Accruals/ Prepayments* | | *As at 30 November 2008 Accruals/ Prepayments* | |
|---|---|---|---|---|---|
| | £ | £ | £ | £ | £ |
| Electricity | 26 400 | 5 200 | – | 8 300 | – |
| Gas | 40 100 | – | – | – | 4 900 |
| Insurance | 25 000 | – | 12 000 | – | 14 000 |
| Rates | 16 000 | – | 4 000 | 6 000 | – |
| Telephone | 3 000 | 1 500 | – | – | 200 |
| Wages | 66 800 | 1 800 | – | – | – |

*Required*:
(a) Calculate the charge to the profit and loss account for the year to 30 November 2008 for each of the above items.
(b) Demonstrate what amounts for accruals and prepayments would be shown in the balance sheet as at 30 November 2008.

**5.12** Duxbury started in business on 1 January 2009. The following is his trial balance as at 31 December 2009:

| | *Dr* | *Cr* |
|---|---|---|
| | £ | £ |
| Capital | | 40 000 |
| Cash | 300 | |
| Delivery van, at cost | 20 000 | |
| Drawings | 10 600 | |
| Office expenses | 12 100 | |
| Purchases | 65 000 | |
| Sales | | 95 000 |
| Trade creditors | | 5 000 |
| Trade debtors | 32 000 | |
| | 140 000 | 140 000 |

*Additional information*:

1 Stock at 31 December 2009 was valued at £10 000.
2 At 31 December 2009 an amount of £400 was outstanding for telephone expenses, and the business rates had been prepaid by £500.
3 The delivery van is to be depreciated at a rate of 20 per cent per annum on cost.
4 Duxbury decides to set aside a provision for bad and doubtful debts equal to 5 per cent of trade debtors as at the end of the year.

*Required*:
Prepare Duxbury's trading and profit and loss account for the year to 31 December 2009 and a balance sheet as at that date.

**5.13** Beech is a retailer. Most of his sales are made on credit terms. The following information relates to the first four years that he has been in business:

| | 2007 | 2008 | 2009 | 2010 |
|---|---|---|---|---|
| Trade debtors as at 31 January: | £60 000 | £55 000 | £65 000 | £70 000 |

The trade is one that experiences a high level of bad debts. Accordingly, Beech decides to set aside a provision for bad and doubtful debts equivalent to 10 per cent of trade debtors as at the end of the year.

*Required*:
(a) Show how the provision for bad and doubtful debts would be disclosed in the respective balance sheets as at 31 January 2007, 2008, 2009 and 2010.
(b) Calculate the increase/decrease in provision for bad and doubtful debts transferred to the respective profit and loss accounts for each of the four years.

**5.14** The following is Ash's trial balance as at 31 March 2008:

| | *Dr* | *Cr* |
|---|---|---|
| | £ | £ |
| Bank | | 4 000 |
| Capital | | 20 500 |
| Depreciation (at 1 April 2007): furniture | | 3 600 |
| Drawings | 10 000 | |
| *c/f* | 10 000 | 28 100 |

| | | Dr | Cr |
|---|---|---|---|
| | | £ | £ |
| | b/f | 10 000 | 28 100 |
| Electricity | | 2 000 | |
| Furniture, at cost | | 9 000 | |
| Insurance | | 1 500 | |
| Miscellaneous expenses | | 65 800 | |
| Provision for bad and doubtful debts (at 1 April 2007) | | | 1 200 |
| Purchases | | 80 000 | |
| Sales | | | 150 000 |
| Stock (at 1 April 2007) | | 10 000 | |
| Trade creditors | | | 20 000 |
| Trade debtors | | 21 000 | |
| | | 199 300 | 199 300 |

*Additional information*:

1 Stock at 31 March 2008: £15 000.
2 At 31 March 2008 there was a specific bad debt of £6000. This was to be written off.
3 Furniture is to be depreciated at a rate of 10 per cent per annum on cost.
4 At 31 March 2008 Ash owes the electricity board £600, and £100 had been paid in advance for insurance.
5 The provision for bad and doubtful debts is to be set at 10 per cent of trade debtors as at the end of the year.

*Required*:
Prepare Ash's trading and profit and loss account for the year to 31 March 2008 and a balance sheet as at that date.

**5.15** Lime's business has had liquidity problems for some months. The following trial balance was extracted from his books of account as at 30 September 2009:

| | Dr | Cr |
|---|---|---|
| | £ | £ |
| Bank | | 15 200 |
| Capital | | 19 300 |
| Cash from sale of office equipment | | 500 |
| Depreciation (at 1 October 2008): office equipment | | 22 000 |
| Drawings | 16 000 | |
| Insurance | 1 800 | |
| Loan (long-term from Cedar) | | 50 000 |
| Loan interest | 7 500 | |
| Miscellaneous expenses | 57 700 | |
| Office equipment, at cost | 44 000 | |
| Provision for bad and doubtful debts (at 1 October 2008) | | 2 000 |
| Purchases | 320 000 | |
| Rates | 10 000 | |
| Sales | | 372 000 |
| Stock (at 1 October 2008) | 36 000 | |
| Trade creditors | | 105 000 |
| Trade debtors | 93 000 | |
| | 586 000 | 586 000 |

*Additional information*:

1 Stock at 30 September 2009: £68 000.
2 At 30 September 2009, accrual for rates of £2000 and insurance prepaid of £200.
3 Depreciation on office equipment is charged at a rate of 25 per cent on cost. During the year, office equipment costing £4000 had been sold for £500. Accumulated depreciation on this equipment amounted to £3000. Lime's depreciation policy is to charge a full year's depreciation in the year of acquisition and none in the year of disposal.
4 Specific bad debts of £13 000 are to be written off.
5 The provision for bad and doubtful debts is to be made equal to 10 per cent of outstanding trade debtors as at 30 September 2009.

*Required*:

Prepare Lime's trading, and profit and loss account for the year to 30 September 2009, and a balance sheet as at that date.

**Further practice questions, study material and links to relevant sites on the World Wide Web can be found on the website that accompanies this book. The site can be found at www.pearsoned.co.uk/dyson**

# Chapter 6 Company accounts

## Not so successful . . .

### £100m write-off for Cairn

**Nicholas Neveling**

Cairn Energy, the FTSE100 oil group, is bracing itself for a new accounting treatment that will hammer its income statement and could affect its ability to report a profit in its accounts.

In its last set of results, the Edinburgh-based group reported interim pre-tax profits of £31.2m, but analysts have prediced the change to a new accounting method for exploration could see the group write off around £100m from its profits.

In a trading update, Cairn said it would have to change its accounting for exploration from full cost accounting to the successful efforts method in order to comply with IFRIC guidance.

*Accountancy Age* brokc thc ncws last year that a number of oil companies would be forced to make write-offs because of the change, but it has emerged that Cairn will be particularly hard hit.

Full cost accounting allows companies to hold expenditure on exploration as an intangible asset. If the spend is on a dry well, then the well is grouped with successful wells and depreciated. Under successful efforts, however, all spending on dry fields has to be expensed through the income statement.

'Cairn does hold a lot of these intangible exploration assets on its balance sheet. A fair amount of these are successful but some are unsuccessful, so there is going to be an element of write-off,' said Tony Alves, oil and gas analyst at KBC Peel Hunt.

'When Cairn reported interim results for 2005, £247m of its £470m assets were intangibles, so it is quite a chunky number. I expect write-offs of at least £100m.'

Cairn, which will release a restatement incorporating the new method in February, ahead of reporting final results in March, admitted there would be a 'potentially significant impact on the income statement and balance sheet', but added that the change would have no impact on its cash flow or strategy.

*Accountancy Age*, 26 January 2006.



*Questions relating to this news story can be found on page 114*

## About this chapter

In the two previous chapters we have shown you how to prepare a set of basic financial statements for a sole trader entity. The management and organization of such entities are not normally very complex, so we have been able to cover the overall procedures without becoming too bogged down in the detail.

However, many non-accountants using this book are likely to work for a *company*. There are many different types of companies but the most common are private limited liability companies and public limited liability companies. By law, all companies have to prepare a set of annual accounts and supply a copy to their shareholders. They also have to file a copy (i.e. send) with the Registrar of Companies. This means that it is then open to inspection by the public. The amount of detail disclosed or published in company accounts (i.e. included) depends upon their type and size.

We shall be dealing with the disclosure requirements of companies in Chapters 9, 10 and 11. In this chapter we explain how to prepare a company's financial accounts for *internal* management purposes. There are no legal requirements covering the presentation and contents of financial accounts for such purposes, so a company can do more or less as it wants. Nevertheless, in order to cut down on the amount of work involved, most companies probably produce internal accounts that are similar to the ones required for external purposes, except that they are likely to be much more detailed.

**Learning objectives**

**By the end of this chapter you should be able to:**

- **explain what is meant by limited liability;**
- **distinguish between private and public companies;**
- **describe how companies are organized;**
- **prepare a basic set of financial statements for a company.**

## ! Why this chapter is important for non-accountants

This chapter is important for a non-accountant because it shows how the material covered in earlier chapters can be adapted for use in preparing company accounts. Many non-accountants work for a company while others will have some contact with one in their professional or private life.

Non-accountants should be able to do their jobs more effectively if they know something about the origin, structure and operation of companies. They will be even better placed if they can use the available accounting information to assess the past performance and future prospects of particular companies.

In order to be in a position to do so, it is necessary to know where the accounting information comes from, what it includes, how it has been summarized and any deficiencies that it may have. This can be best achieved by being able to prepare a simple set of financial statements. This chapter provides non-accountants with that opportunity.

We start our study of company accounts with an explanation of what is meant by 'limited liability'.

## Limited liability

There is a great personal risk in operating a business as a sole trader or as a partnership. If the business runs short of funds, the owners may be called upon to settle the business's debts out of their own private resources. This type of risk can have a damaging effect on the development of new businesses. So there is a need for a different type of entity that will neither make the owners bankrupt nor inhibit new developments. This need became apparent in the nineteenth century as a result of the Industrial Revolution when enormous amounts of capital were required to finance new and rapidly expanding industries such as the railways and shipbuilding.

These sorts of ventures were undertaken at great personal risk. By agreeing to become involved in them many, investors faced bankruptcy if the ventures were unsuccessful (as they often were). It became apparent that the development of industry would be hindered unless some means could be devised of restricting the personal liability of prospective investors.

So there was a need for a form of *limited liability*. In fact, the concept of limited liability was not entirely an innovation of the nineteenth century but it did not receive legal recognition until the Limited Liability Act was passed in 1855. The Act only remained in force for a few months before it was repealed and incorporated into the Joint Stock Companies Act 1856. By distinguishing between the private and public affairs of business proprietors, the 1855 Act effectively created a new form of entity. Since the 1850s Parliament has passed a number of other Companies Acts, all of which have continued to give legal recognition to the concept of limited liability.

The important point about a limited liability company is that no matter what financial difficulties it may get into, its members cannot be required to contribute more than an agreed amount of capital, so there is no risk of its members being forced into bankruptcy.

The concept of limited liability is often very difficult for business owners to understand, especially if they have formed one out of what was originally a sole trader or a partnership entity. Unlike such entities, companies are bound by some fairly severe legal operating restrictions

The legal restrictions can be somewhat burdensome but they are necessary for the protection of all those parties who might have dealings with the company (such as creditors and employees). This is because if a limited liability company runs short of funds the creditors and employees might not get paid. It is only fair, therefore, to warn all those people who might have dealings with it that they run a risk in doing business with it. So companies have to be more open about their affairs than do sole traders and partnerships.

## Structure and operation

In this section, we examine the structure and operation of limited liability companies. In order to make it easier to follow, we have broken down our examination into a number of subsections. A summary of the section is also presented in diagrammatic format in Figure 6.1.

### Share capital

Although the law recognizes that limited liability companies are separate beings with a life of their own (i.e. separate from those individuals who collectively own and manage them), it also accepts that someone has to take responsibility for promoting the company and giving it life. Only one person is required to form a private company (two for a public company), and that person (or persons) agrees to make a capital contribution by buying a number of shares. The capital of a company is known as its *share capital*. The share capital will be made up of a number of shares of a certain denomination, such as 10p, 50p or £1. Members may hold only one share, or many hundreds or thousands depending upon the total share capital of the company, the denomination of the shares and the amount that they wish to contribute.

The maximum amount of capital that the company envisages ever raising has to be stated. This is known as its *authorized share capital*, although this does not necessarily mean that it will issue shares up to that amount. In practice, it will probably only issue

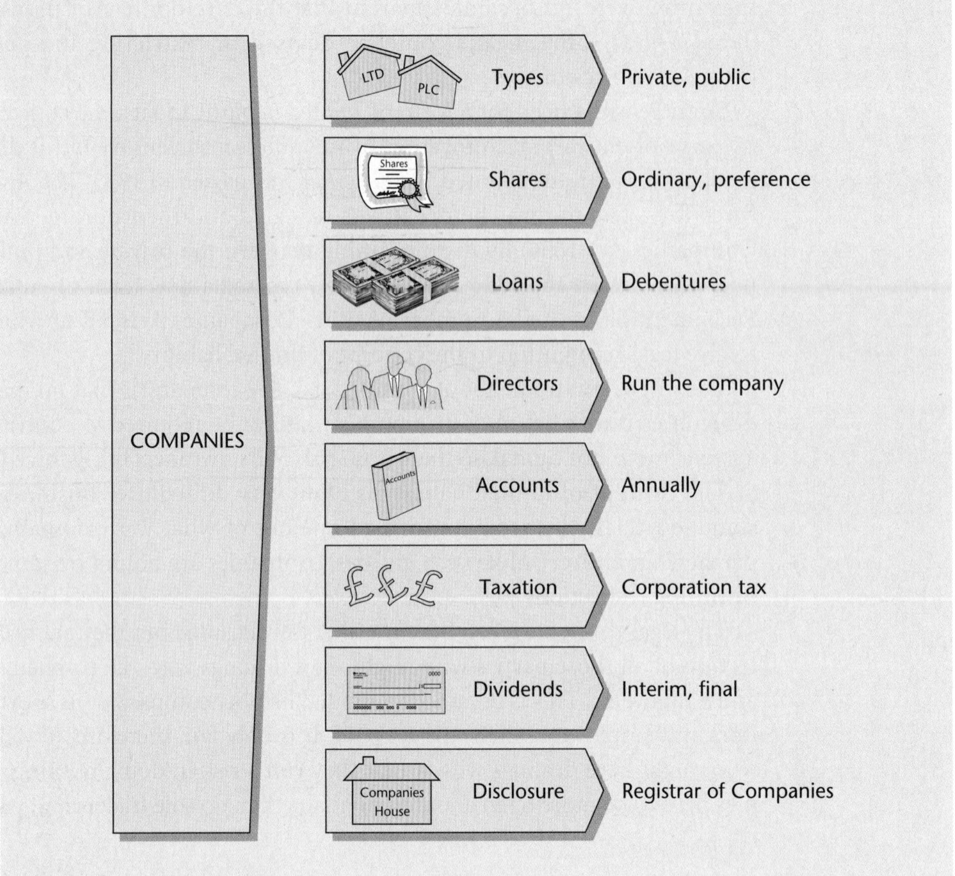


**Figure 6.1 Structure and operation of companies**

sufficient capital to meet its immediate and foreseeable requirements. The amount of share capital that it has actually issued is known as the *issued share capital.* Sometimes, when shares are issued, prospective shareholders are only required to pay for them in instalments. Once all the issued share capital has been paid for, it is described as being *fully paid.*

There are two main types of shares: *ordinary shares* and *preference shares*. Ordinary shares do not usually entitle the shareholder to any specific level of dividend. Preference shareholders are normally entitled to a fixed level of dividend and they have priority over the ordinary shareholders if the company is liquidated. Sometimes the preference shares are classed as *cumulative*; this means that if the company cannot pay its preference dividend in one year, the amount due accrues until such time as the company has the profits to pay all of the accumulated dividends.

We show the share capital structure of companies in Figure 6.2.

## Types of companies

A prospective shareholder may invest in either a public company or a private company. A *public company* must have an authorized share capital of at least £50 000, and it becomes a public company merely by stating that it is a public company. In fact, most public limited companies in the United Kingdom have their shares listed on the London Stock Exchange and so they are often referred to simply as *listed* companies.

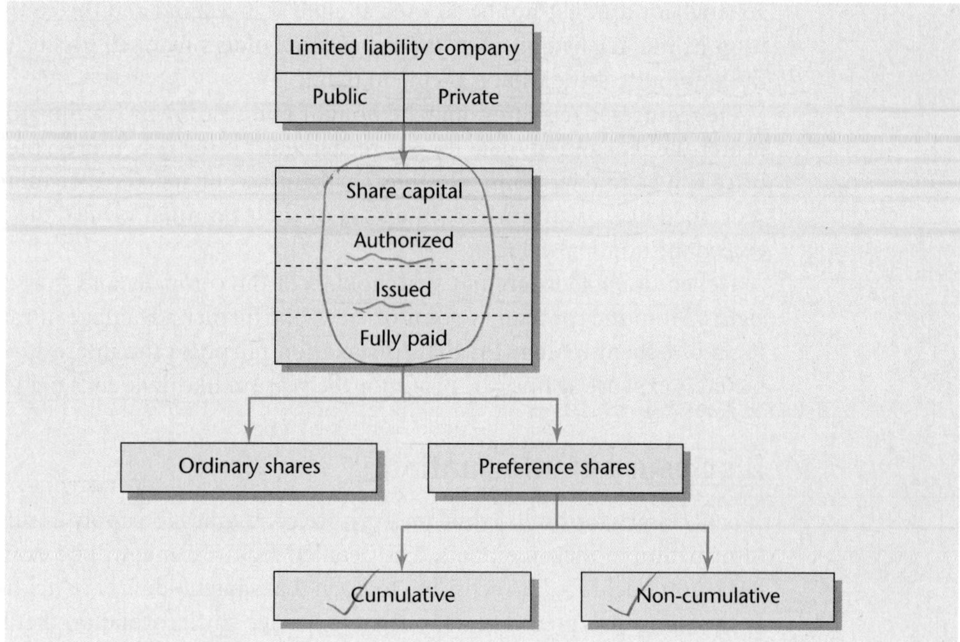


**Figure 6.2 Types of shares**

As a warning to those parties who might have dealings with them, public companies have to include the term 'public limited liability company' after their name (or its abbreviation 'plc').

Any company that does not make its shares available to the public is regarded as being a *private company*. Like public companies, private companies must also have an authorized share capital, although no minimum amount is prescribed. Otherwise, their share capital requirements are very similar to public companies.

Private companies also have to warn the public that their liability is limited. They must do so by describing themselves as 'limited liability companies', and attaching the term 'limited' after their name (or the abbreviation 'ltd').

**Activity 6.1**

Limited liability companies have to disclose some information about their operations as well as putting 'limited' ('ltd') or public limited company ('plc') after their name in order to warn the public that their liability is limited.

Do you think that such safeguards are adequate? What more can be done? How far do you think that it is fair for individuals to set up businesses under the protection of limited liability? The business may then go into liquidation and the creditors will be left without any means of getting their money back from the owners of the company. Is this acceptable if the concept of limited liability encourages new businesses to be formed?

## Loans

Besides obtaining the necessary capital from their shareholders, companies often borrow money in the form of *debentures*. A company may invite the public to loan it some money for a certain period of time (the period can be unspecified) at a certain rate of interest. A debenture loan may be secured on specific assets of the company, on its assets generally or it might not be secured at all. If it is secured and the company cannot repay it on its due repayment date, the debenture holders may sell the secured assets and use the amount to settle what is owing to them.

Debentures, like shares, may be bought and sold freely on the Stock Exchange. The nearer the redemption date for the repayment for the debentures, the closer the market price will be to their nominal value, i.e. their face, or stated paper value. If they are to be redeemed at a premium (i.e. in excess of their nominal value), the market price may exceed the nominal value.

Debenture holders are not shareholders of the company and they do not have voting rights. From the company's point of view, one further advantage of raising capital in the form of debenture loans is that for taxation purposes the interest can be charged as a business expense against the profit for the year (unlike dividends paid to shareholders).

## Disclosure of information

It is necessary for both public and private companies to supply a minimum amount of information to their members. The detailed requirements will be examined in Chapters 9–11. You might find it surprising to learn that shareholders have neither a right of access to the company's premises, nor a right to receive any information that they demand. This might not seem fair but it would clearly be difficult for a company's managers to cope with thousands of shareholders, all of whom suddenly turned up one day demanding to be let into the building in order to inspect the company's books of account.

Instead, shareholders in both private and public companies have to be supplied with an annual report containing at least the minimum amount of information required by the Companies Act 1985. The company also has to file (as it is called) a copy of the report with the Registrar of Companies. This means that on payment of a small fee the report is open to inspection by any member of the public who wants to consult it. Some companies (defined as small or medium-sized) are permitted to file an abbreviated version of their annual report with the registrar, although the full report must still be sent to their shareholders.

The disclosure requirements are shown in summary form in Figure 6.3.

## Accounts

Company accounts are very similar to those of sole traders. They do, however, tend to be more detailed and some modifications have to be made in order to comply with various legal requirements. We shall be looking at company accounts later on in the chapter.

## Directors

A limited liability company must always be regarded as a separate entity, i.e. separate from those shareholders who own it collectively and separate from anyone who works for it. This means that all those who are employed by it are its employees, no matter how senior they are. Nevertheless, someone has to take responsibility for the management of the company and so the shareholders usually delegate that responsibility to *directors.*

Directors are the most senior level of management. They are responsible for the day-to-day running of the company and they answer to the shareholders. Any remuneration paid to them as directors is charged as an expense of the business. They may also be shareholders but any payment that they receive as such is regarded as being a private matter. It should not be confused with any income that they receive as directors.

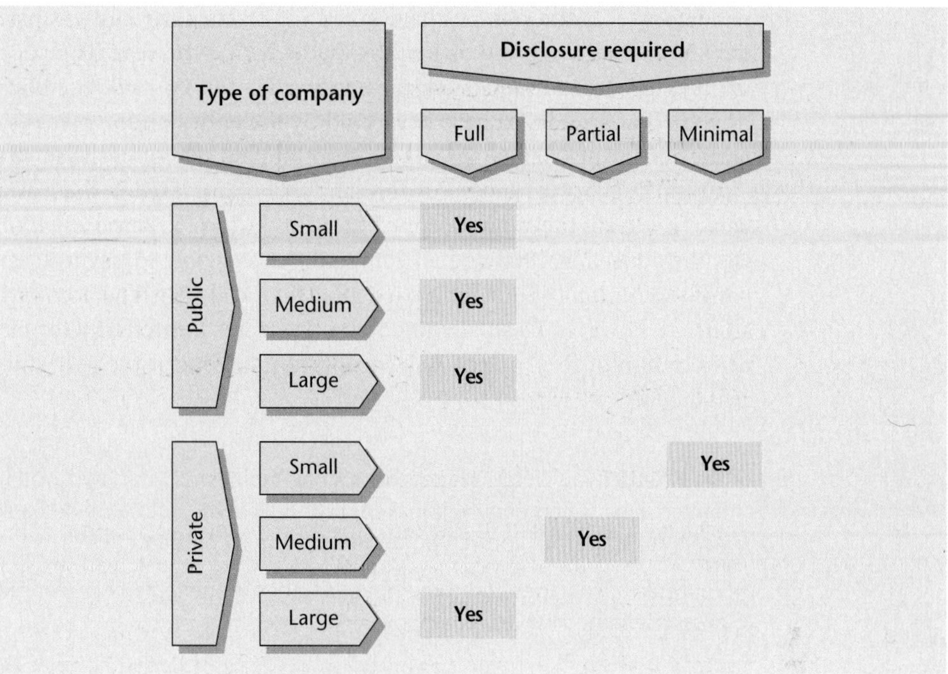


**Figure 6.3 Disclosure of information**

The distinction between employees and shareholder–employees is important, although it is one that is not always understood. This is especially the case in very small companies where both employees and shareholders may be one and the same. As we have emphasized, in law the company is regarded as being a separate entity. Even if there are just two shareholders who both work full-time for the company, the company is still treated as distinct from that of the two individuals who happen to own it. They may take decisions that appear to affect no one else except themselves but because they operate the company under the protection of limited liability, they have certain obligations as well as rights. So, they are not as free to operate the company as they would be if they ran it (say) as a partnership.

## Dividends

Profits are usually distributed to shareholders in the form of a dividend. A dividend is calculated on the basis of so many pence per share. The actual dividend will be recommended by the directors to the shareholders. It will be based on the amount of net profit earned during the year and how much profit the directors want to retain in the business.

A dividend may have been paid during the year as an *interim dividend*, i.e. a payment on account. At the year end the directors may recommend a *proposed* dividend (sometimes referred to as the *final dividend*). The proposed dividend has to be approved by the shareholders at a general meeting.

## Taxation

Taxation is another feature which clearly distinguishes a limited liability company from that of a sole trader entity.

Sole trader entities do not have tax levied on them as entities. Instead, tax is levied on the amount of profit the owner has made during the year. The tax payable is a private matter and in accordance with the entity rule, it lies outside the boundary of the entity. Any tax that appears to have been paid by the entity on the owner's behalf is treated as part of the owner's drawings (i.e. an amount paid as part of the share of the profits).

Companies are treated quite differently. They are taxed in their own right like individuals. They have their own form of taxation known as *corporation tax*. Corporation tax was introduced in 1965 and all companies are eligible to pay it. It is based on the company's accounting profit for a particular financial year. The accounting profit has to be adjusted, however, because some items are treated differently for tax purposes, e.g. the depreciation of fixed assets. Any corporation tax due at the year end is treated as a current liability.

**Activity 6.2**

Assume that you would like to start a small business of your own. You have heard that a limited liability company will make sure that you will not be made bankrupt if the business is unsuccessful and so you decide to form a company.

List three advantages and three disadvantages in the table below of running your business as a limited liability company.

| **Advantages** | **Disadvantages** |
|---|---|
| (1) | (1) |
| (2) | (2) |
| (3) | (3) |

Now that we have outlined the basic structure and operation of limited liability companies we can begin to examine company accounts in some detail. We start with the profit and loss account.

## The profit and loss account

As we suggested earlier, the preparation of a company's trading and profit and loss account is basically no different from that of sole trader entities. Almost an identical format may be adopted, and it is only after the net profit stage that some differences become apparent. Company accounts usually include what is called a *profit and loss appropriation account*. A profit and loss appropriation account comes on after the profit and loss account, although no clear dividing line is usually drawn between where the profit and loss account ends and where the appropriation account begins. An example of a company's profit and loss appropriation account is shown in Example 6.1.

Example 6.1

## A company's profit and loss appropriation account

| | £000 |
|---|---|
| Net profit for the year before taxation | 1 000 |
| Taxation | (300) |
| Net profit for the year after taxation | 700 |
| Dividends | (500) |
| Retained profit for the year | 200 |

You can see from Example 6.1, that the company's net profit for the year is appropriated (or used) in three ways:

- to pay tax;
- to pay dividends;
- for retention within the business.

Activity 6.3

Complete the following equations.

(a) ______________________ – taxation = net profit for the year after taxation.

(b) Net profit for the year after taxation – __________ = retained profit for the year.

## The balance sheet

The structure of a limited liability company's balance sheet is also very similar to that of a sole trader. The main difference arises because of the company's capital structure, although there are some other features that are not usually found in non-company balance sheets.

The main features of a company's balance sheet are shown in Example 6.2. It includes a number of tutorial notes which will help you as you work through the example.

Example 6.2

## A company's balance sheet

**Exhibitor Ltd**
**Balance sheet at 31 March 2008**

| | *£000* | *£000* | *£000* |
|---|---|---|---|
| *Fixed assets* | | | 600 |
| *Investments* (1) | | | 100 |
| *Current assets* | | 6 000 | |
| *Less*: Current liabilities | | | |
| Trade creditors | 2 950 | | |
| Accruals | 50 | | |
| Corporation tax (2) | 300 | | |
| Proposed dividend (3) | 500 | 3 800 | 2 200 |
| | | | 2 900 |

**Example 6.2** ***continued***

| Financed by: | | |
|---|---|---|
| *Capital and reserves* (4): | *Authorized* | *Issued and fully paid* |
| | *£000* | *£000* |
| Ordinary shares of £1 each (5) | 2 000 | 1 500 |
| Preference shares of £0.50 each (5) | 500 | 500 |
| | 2 500 | 2 000 |
| Capital reserves (6) | | 200 |
| Revenue reserves (7) | | 600 |
| Shareholders' funds (8) | | 2 800 |
| *Loans* (9) | | 100 |
| | | 2 900 |

*Note*: The number shown after each narration refers to the tutorial notes below.

***Tutorial notes to Example 6.2***

1 *Investments*. This item usually represents long-term investments in the shares of other companies. Short-term investments (such as money invested in bank deposit accounts) would be included in current assets. The shares may be either in public limited liability companies or in private limited companies. The market price of the investments should be stated – where this is not available a directors' valuation should be obtained.

2 *Corporation tax*. This represents the outstanding tax due on the company's profits for the year.

3 *Proposed dividend*. This will probably be due for payment very shortly after the year end, and so it will usually be shown as a current liability.

4 *Capital and reserves*. Details of the authorized, issued and fully paid-up share capital should be shown.

5 *Ordinary shares and preference shares*. Details about the different types of shares that the company has issued should be disclosed.

6 *Capital reserves*. This section may include several different reserve accounts of a capital nature, i.e. amounts that are not available for distribution to the shareholders as dividend. It might include, for example, a share premium account (an extra amount paid by shareholders in excess of the nominal value of the shares). The premium does not rank for dividend but prospective shareholders are sometimes willing to pay it if they think that the shares are particularly attractive. Another example of a capital reserve is that of an asset that has been revalued. The difference between the original cost and the revalued amount will be credited to a *revaluation* reserve account.

7 *Revenue reserves*. Revenue reserve accounts are amounts that are available for distribution to the shareholders. Any profits retained in the business and not paid out to shareholders may be included under this heading. Retained profits are normally shown separately under the heading 'profit and loss account'.

8 *Shareholders' funds*. The total amount available to shareholders at the balance sheet date is equal to the share capital originally subscribed plus all the capital and revenue reserve account balances.

9 *Loans*. The loans section of the balance sheet will include all the long-term loans obtained by the company, i.e. those loans that do not have to be repaid for at least twelve months, such as debentures and long-term bank loans.

**Activity 6.4**

State in which section of the balance sheet you are likely to find the following items.

(a) Amount owing for corporation tax.
(b) Debenture stock.
(c) Plant and machinery.
(d) Preference shares.
(e) Trade debtors.

## A comprehensive example

Example 6.3 brings together the material covered in this chapter.

**Example 6.3**

### Preparation of a company's accounts

The following information has been extracted from the books of Handy Ltd as at 31 March 2008:

| | *Dr* | *Cr* |
|---|---|---|
| | £ | £ |
| Bank | 2 000 | |
| Capital: 100 000 issued and fully paid ordinary shares of £1 each | | 100 000 |
| 50 000 issued and fully paid 8% preference shares of £1 each | | 50 000 |
| Debenture loan stock (10%: repayable 2020) | | 30 000 |
| Debenture loan stock interest | 3 000 | |
| Dividends received | | 700 |
| Dividends paid: Ordinary interim | 5 000 | |
| Preference | 4 000 | |
| Freehold land at cost | 200 000 | |
| Investments (listed: market value at 31 March 2008 was £11 000) | 10 000 | |
| Office expenses | 47 000 | |
| Motor van at cost | 15 000 | |
| Motor van: accumulated depreciation at 1 April 2007 | | 6 000 |
| Motor van expenses | 2 700 | |
| Purchases | 220 000 | |
| Retained profits at 1 April 2007 | | 9 000 |
| Sales | | 300 000 |
| Share premium account | | 10 000 |
| Stocks at cost (at 1 April 2007) | 20 000 | |
| Trade creditors | | 50 000 |
| Trade debtors | 27 000 | |
| | 555 700 | 555 700 |

*Additional information*:

1 The stocks at 31 March 2008 were valued at their historical cost of £40 000.

2 Depreciation is to be charged on the motor van at a rate of 20 per cent per annum on cost. No depreciation is to be charged on the freehold land.

Example 6.3 *continued*

3 The corporation tax for the year has been estimated to be £10 000.
4 The directors propose a final ordinary dividend of 10p per share.
5 The authorized share capital of the company is as follows:
  (a) 150 000 ordinary shares of £1 each; and
  (b) 75 000 preference shares of £1 each.

*Required*:
(a) Prepare Handy Ltd's trading and profit and loss account for the year to 31 March 2008.
(b) Prepare a balance sheet as at that date.

Answer to Example 6.3(a)

**Handy Ltd**
**Trading and profit and loss account for the year to 31 March 2008**

| | £ | £ | £ |
|---|---|---|---|
| Sales | | | 300 000 |
| *Less*: Cost of goods sold: | | | |
| Opening stocks | | 20 000 | |
| Purchases | | 220 000 | |
| | | 240 000 | |
| *Less*: Closing stocks | | 40 000 | 200 000 |
| *Gross profit* | | | 100 000 |
| *Add*: Incomes: | | | |
| Dividends received | | | 700 |
| *Less*: Expenditure: | | | 100 700 |
| Debenture loan stock interest | | 3 000 | |
| Motor van depreciation (1) | 3 000 | | |
| Motor van expenses | 2 700 | 5 700 | |
| Office expenses | | 47 000 | |
| | | | 55 700 |
| *Net profit for the year before taxation* | | | 45 000 |
| *Less*: Corporation tax (2) | | | 10 000 |
| *Net profit for the year after taxation* | | | 35 000 |
| *Less*: Dividends (3): | | | |
| Preference dividend paid (8%) | | 4 000 | |
| Interim ordinary paid (5p per share) | | 5 000 | |
| Proposed final ordinary dividend (10p per share) | | 10 000 | 19 000 |
| *Retained profit for the year* | | | 16 000 |
| *Retained profits brought forward* | | | 9 000 |
| *Retained profits carried forward* (4) | | | 25 000 |

Answer to Example 6.3(b)

**Handy Ltd Balance sheet at 31 March 2008**

| | £ | £ | £ |
|---|---|---|---|
| *Fixed assets* | *Cost* | *Accumulated depreciation* | |
| Freehold land (5) | 200 000 | – | 200 000 |
| Motor van (6) | 15 000 | 9 000 | 6 000 |
| | 215 000 | 9 000 | 206 000 |
| c/f | | | 206 000 |

| | £ | £ | £ |
|---|---|---|---|
| | b/f | | 206 000 |
| *Investments* | | | |
| At cost (market value at 31 March 2008: £11 000) (7) | | | 10 000 |
| Current assets | | | |
| Stocks at cost | | 40 000 | |
| Trade debtors | | 27 000 | |
| Bank | | 2 000 | |
| | | 69 000 | |
| *Less*: Current liabilities | | | |
| Trade creditors | 50 000 | | |
| Corporation tax (8) | 10 000 | | |
| Proposed ordinary dividend (9) | 10 000 | 70 000 | |
| Net current assets | | | (1 000) |
| | | | 215 000 |

| Financed by: | | |
|---|---|---|
| *Capital and reserves* | *Authorized* | *Issued and fully paid* |
| Ordinary shares of £1 each (10) | 150 000 | 100 000 |
| Preference shares of £1 each (10) | 75 000 | 50 000 |
| | 225 000 | 150 000 |
| Share premium account (11) | | 10 000 |
| Retained profits (12) | | 25 000 |
| Shareholders' funds (13) | | 185 000 |
| *Loans* (14) | | |
| 10% debenture stock (repayable 2020) | | 30 000 |
| | | 215 000 |

*Note*: The number shown after each narration refers to the following tutorial notes.

**Tutorial notes**

1 Depreciation has been charged on the motor van at a rate of 20 per cent per annum on cost (as instructed in question note 2).

2 Question note 3 requires £10 000 to be charged as corporation tax. Corporation tax is applied to the taxable profit and not to the accounting profit. The taxable profit has not been given in the question.

3 A proposed ordinary dividend of 10p has been included as instructed in question note 4.

4 The total retained profit of £25 000 is carried forward to the balance sheet (see tutorial note 12 below).

5 Question note 2 states that no depreciation is to be charged on the freehold land.

6 The accumulated depreciation for the motor van of £9000 is the total of the accumulated depreciation brought forward at 1 April 2007 of £6000, plus the £3000 written off to the profit and loss account for the current year (see tutorial note 1 above).

7 Note that the market value of the investments has been disclosed on the face of the balance sheet.

**Answer to Example 6.3(b)** *continued*

8 The corporation tax charged against profit (question note 3) will be due for payment in 2009. The amount due is treated as a current liability.

9 The proposed ordinary dividend will be due for payment shortly after the year end and so it is also a current liability. As the interim dividend and the preference dividend have already been paid they are not current liabilities.

10 Details of the authorized, issued and fully paid share capital should be disclosed.

11 The share premium is a capital account: it cannot be used for the payment of dividends. This account will normally remain unchanged in successive balance sheets, although there are a few highly restricted purposes for which it may be used.

12 The retained profits become part of a revenue account balance that the company could use for the payment of dividends. The total retained profits of £25 000 is the amount brought in to the balance sheet from the profit and loss account.

13 The total amount of shareholders' funds should always be shown.

14 The loans are long-term loans. Loans are not part of shareholders' funds and they should be shown in the balance sheet as a separate item.

## Questions non-accountants should ask

Many of the questions that we have suggested in previous chapters that non-accountants should ask are of relevance in this chapter. For example, the various accounting rules adopted by the accountants in preparing the company's profit and loss and balance sheet, especially those with a significant impact on revenue recognition, stock valuation, depreciation and provisions for bad and doubtful debts.

The following questions relate particularly to this chapter.

- Can our accounting records disclose with reasonable accuracy (as the 1985 Companies Act requires) our financial position at any time?
- Do the accounting records contain entries for all money received and spent?
- Do they also contain a record of all assets and all liabilities?
- Do the accounting records include a statement of the stock held at the financial year end?*
- Are there details of stocktaking from which the statement of stock has been compiled?*
- Is a record kept of all goods sold and purchased as well as all the buyers and sellers so that they can all be identified?*
- Have both the profit and loss account and the balance sheet been prepared in accordance with the requirements of the Companies Act 1985?
- Have you dealt with anything in the accounts or missed anything out that may be in conflict with the Act or with recommended practice?
- If so, can you justify it as being 'true and fair'?

* These questions are only relevant if the company deals in goods.

## Conclusion

This chapter has briefly examined the background to the legislation affecting limited liability companies. This was followed by some examples of how company accounts are prepared for *internal* purposes.

Although a great deal of information can be obtained from studying the annual accounts of a company, it is difficult to extract the most relevant and significant features. Some further guidance is needed, therefore, in how to make the best use of the financial accounting information presented to you. This will be provided in Chapters 8 and 12, but first we need to examine some other types of account. We do so in the next chapter.

## Key points

1. **The financial statements of a company are similar in format to those of sole traders.**
2. **The profits of a company are taxed separately (like an individual). The tax is based on the accounting profit for the year. Any tax due at the year end will be shown in the balance sheet as a current liability.**
3. **The net profit after tax may be paid to shareholders in the form of a dividend (although some profit may still be retained within the business). Any proposed dividend should be shown in the balance sheet as a creditor (although this does not now apply to public limited companies – see Chapter 11).**

## Check your learning

*The answers to these questions can be found within the text.*

1. What is meant by 'limited liability'?
2. When was it first incorporated into company law?
3. Why was it found necessary to do so?
4. Distinguish between the authorized, issued and fully paid share capital of a company.
5. Name two main types of shares.
6. What is the basic difference between them?
7. What are the two main types of limited liability companies?
8. What is a debenture loan?
9. What is meant by 'disclosure of information'?
10. Why do companies have to let the Registrar of Companies have certain types of information?
11. What is a director?
12. What is a dividend?

13 Name two types of dividend.

14 What name is given to the tax that a company pays on its profits?

15 Name three ways in which a company's profits are appropriated.

16 List three types of assets.

17 Name three items that may be included under the heading of 'current liabilities'.

18 Distinguish between a capital reserve and a revenue reserve.

19 What is a share premium account?

20 What is meant by 'shareholders' funds'?

21 What is the difference between a short-term loan and a long-term loan?

## News story quiz

*Remember the news story at the beginning of this chapter? Go back to that story and re-read it before answering the following questions.*

According to this article Cairn Energy plc has had to change its accounting policies in order to comply with IFRIC (International Financial Reporting Interpretations Committee) requirements. Apparently 'analysts' (who and how many?) believe that this could reduce the company's profits by around £100m.

### Questions

1 What is the effect on the profit and loss account if dry wells are grouped with 'successful-effort' wells and then the combined amount is depreciated?

2 How far do you agree with the principle of 'successful efforts' accounting that all spending on dry well costs should be 'expensed through the income statement'?

3 Is Cairn correct in arguing that the changed accounting method would have no impact on the company's cash flow?

4 Discounting the jargon, what basic accounting dilemma is this article highlighting?

## Tutorial questions

*The answers to question marked with an asterisk may be found in Appendix 4.*

6.1 'The concept of limited liability is an out-of-date nineteenth-century concept.' Discuss.

6.2 Appleton used to operate her business as a sole trader entity. She has recently converted it into a limited liability company. Appleton owns 80 per cent of the ordinary (voting) shares, the remaining 20 per cent being held by various relatives and friends. Explain to Appleton why it is now inaccurate for her to describe the company as 'her' business.

6.3 How far do you think that the information presented in a limited liability company's profit and loss account and balance sheet is useful to the owners of a small business?

**6.4*** The following balances have been extracted from the books of Margo Ltd for the year to 31 January 2007:

| | *Dr* | *Cr* |
|---|---|---|
| | *£000* | *£000* |
| Cash at bank and in hand | 5 | |
| Plant and equipment: | | |
| At cost | 70 | |
| Accumulated depreciation (at 31.1.07) | | 25 |
| Profit and loss account (at 1.2.06) | | 15 |
| Profit for the financial year (to 31.1.07) | | 10 |
| Share capital (issued and fully paid) | | 50 |
| Stocks (at 31.1.07) | 17 | |
| Trade creditors | | 12 |
| Trade debtors | 20 | |
| | 112 | 112 |

*Additional information*:

1 Corporation tax owing at 31 January 2007 is estimated to be £3000.
2 Margo Ltd's authorized share capital is £75 000 of £1 ordinary shares.
3 A dividend of 10p per share is proposed.

*Required*:
Prepare Margo Ltd's profit and loss account for the year to 31 January 2007 and a balance sheet as at that date.

**6.5*** Harry Ltd was formed in 2000. The following balances as at 28 February 2008 have been extracted from the books of account after the trading account has been compiled:

| | *Dr* | *Cr* |
|---|---|---|
| | *£000* | *£000* |
| Administration expenses | 65 | |
| Cash at bank and in hand | 10 | |
| Distribution costs | 15 | |
| Dividend paid (on preference shares) | 6 | |
| Furniture and equipment: | | |
| At cost | 60 | |
| Accumulated depreciation at 1.3.07 | | 36 |
| Gross profit for the year | | 150 |
| Ordinary share capital (shares of £1 each) | | 100 |
| Preference shares (cumulative 15% of £1 shares) | | 40 |
| Profit and loss account (at 1.3.07) | | 50 |
| Share premium account | | 20 |
| Stocks (at 28.2.08) | 130 | |
| Trade creditors | | 25 |
| Trade debtors | 135 | |
| | 421 | 421 |

*Additional information*:

1 Corporation tax owing at 28 February 2008 is estimated to be £24 000.
2 Furniture and equipment is depreciated at an annual rate of 10 per cent of cost and it is all charged against administrative expenses.

3 A dividend of 20p per ordinary share is proposed.
4 All the authorized share capital has been issued and is fully paid.

*Required*:
Prepare Harry Ltd's profit and loss account for the year to 28 February 2008 and a balance sheet as at that date.

**6.6*** The following balances have been extracted from the books of Jim Ltd as at 31 March 2008:

| | *Dr* | *Cr* |
|---|---|---|
| | *£000* | *£000* |
| Advertising | 3 | |
| Bank | 11 | |
| Creditors | | 12 |
| Debtors | 118 | |
| Furniture and fittings: | | |
| At cost | 20 | |
| Accumulated depreciation (at 1.4.07) | | 9 |
| Directors' fees | 6 | |
| Profit and loss account (at 1.4.07) | | 8 |
| Purchases | 124 | |
| Rent and rates | 10 | |
| Sales | | 270 |
| Share capital (issued and fully paid) | | 70 |
| Stock (at 1.4.07) | 16 | |
| Telephone and stationery | 5 | |
| Travelling expenses | 2 | |
| Vehicles: | | |
| At cost | 40 | |
| Accumulated depreciation (at 1.4.07) | | 10 |
| Wages and salaries | 24 | |
| | 379 | 379 |

*Additional information*:
1 Stock at 31 March 2008 was valued at £14 000.
2 Furniture and fittings, and the vehicles are depreciated at a rate of 15 per cent and 25 per cent, respectively, on cost.
3 Corporation tax owing at 31 March 2008 is estimated to be £25 000.
4 A dividend of 40p per share is proposed.
5 The company's authorized share capital is £100 000 of £1 ordinary shares.

*Required*:
(a) Prepare Jim Ltd's trading and profit and loss account for the year to 31 March 2008 and a balance sheet as at that date.
(b) Why would the business not necessarily be worth its balance sheet value as at 31 March 2008?

**6.7** The following trial balance has been extracted from Carol Ltd as at 30 April 2009:

| | *Dr* | *Cr* |
|---|---|---|
| | *£000* | *£000* |
| Advertising | 2 | |
| Bank overdraft | | 20 |
| Bank interest paid | 4 | |
| Creditors | | 80 |
| Debtors | 143 | |
| Directors' remuneration | 30 | |
| Freehold land and buildings: | | |
| At cost | 800 | |
| Accumulated depreciation at 1.5.08 | | 102 |
| General expenses | 15 | |
| Investments at cost | 30 | |
| Investment income | | 5 |
| Motor vehicles: | | |
| At cost | 36 | |
| Accumulated depreciation (at 1.5.08) | | 18 |
| Preference dividend paid | 15 | |
| Preference shares (cumulative 10% shares of £1 each) | | 150 |
| Profit and loss account (at 1.5.08) | | 100 |
| Purchases | 480 | |
| Repairs and renewals | 4 | |
| Sales | | 900 |
| Share capital (authorized, issued and fully paid ordinary shares of £1 each) | | 500 |
| Share premium account | | 25 |
| Stock (at 1.5.08) | 120 | |
| Wages and salaries | 221 | |
| | 1900 | 1900 |

*Additional information*:

1 Stock at 30 April 2009 was valued at £140 000.
2 Depreciation for the year of £28 000 is to be provided on buildings and £9000 for motor vehicles.
3 A provision of £6000 is required for the auditors' remuneration.
4 £2000 had been paid in advance for renewals.
5 Corporation tax owing at 30 April 2009 is estimated to be £60 000.
6 The directors propose an ordinary dividend of 10p per share.
7 The market value of the investments at 30 April 2009 was £35 000.

*Required*:
Prepare Carol Ltd's trading and profit and loss account for the year to 30 April 2009 and a balance sheet as at that date.

6.8 Nelson Ltd was incorporated in 2000 with an authorized share capital of 500 000 £1 ordinary shares, and 200 000 5% cumulative preference shares of £1 each. The following trial balance was extracted as at 31 May 2008:

| | *Dr* | *Cr* |
|---|---|---|
| | *£000* | *£000* |
| Administrative expenses | 257 | |
| Auditor's fees | 10 | |
| Cash at bank and in hand | 5 | |
| Creditors | | 85 |
| Debentures (12%) | | 100 |
| Debenture interest paid | 6 | |
| Debtors | 225 | |
| Directors' remuneration | 60 | |
| Dividends paid: | | |
| Ordinary interim | 20 | |
| Preference | 5 | |
| Furniture, fittings and equipment: | | |
| At cost | 200 | |
| Accumulated depreciation at 1.6.07 | | 48 |
| Investments at cost (market value at 31.5.08: £340 000) | 335 | |
| Investment income | | 22 |
| Ordinary share capital (issued and fully paid) | | 400 |
| Preference share capital | | 200 |
| Profit and loss account (at 1.6.07) | | 17 |
| Purchases | 400 | |
| Sales | | 800 |
| Share premium account | | 50 |
| Stock at 1.6.07 | 155 | |
| Wages and salaries | 44 | |
| | 1722 | 1722 |

*Additional information:*

1 Stock at 31 May 2008 was valued at £195 000.
2 Administrative expenses owing at 31 May 2008 amounted to £13 000.
3 Depreciation is to be charged on the furniture and fittings at a rate of $12\frac{1}{2}$ per cent on cost.
4 Salaries paid in advance amounted to £4000.
5 Corporation tax owing at 31.5.08 is estimated to be £8000.
6 Provision is to be made for a final ordinary dividend of 1.25p per share.

*Required:*

Prepare Nelson Ltd's trading and profit and loss account for the year to 31 May 2008 and a balance sheet as at that date.

6.9 The following trial balance has been extracted from the books of Keith Ltd as at 30 June 2008:

| | Dr | Cr |
|---|---|---|
| | £000 | £000 |
| Advertising | 30 | |
| Bank | 7 | |
| Creditors | | 69 |
| Debentures (10%) | | 70 |
| Debtors (all trade) | 300 | |
| Directors' remuneration | 55 | |
| Electricity | 28 | |
| Insurance | 17 | |
| Investments (quoted) | 28 | |
| Investment income | | 4 |
| Machinery: | | |
| At cost | 420 | |
| Accumulated depreciation at 1.7.07 | | 152 |
| Office expenses | 49 | |
| Ordinary share capital (issued and fully paid) | | 200 |
| Preference shares | | 50 |
| Preference share dividend | 4 | |
| Profit and loss account (at 1.7.07) | | 132 |
| Provision for bad and doubtful debts | | 8 |
| Purchases | 1240 | |
| Rent and rates | 75 | |
| Sales | | 2100 |
| Stock (at 1.7.07) | 134 | |
| Vehicles: | | |
| At cost | 80 | |
| Accumulated depreciation (at 1.7.07) | | 40 |
| Wages and salaries | 358 | |
| | 2825 | 2825 |

*Additional information*:

1 Stock at 30 June 2008 valued at cost amounted to £155 000.
2 Depreciation is to be provided on machinery and vehicles at a rate of 20 per cent and 25 per cent respectively on cost.
3 Provision is to be made for auditors' remuneration of £12 000.
4 Insurance paid in advance at 30 June 2008 amounted to £3000.
5 The provision for bad and doubtful debts is to be made equal to 5 per cent of outstanding trade debtors as at 30 June 2008.
6 Corporation tax owing at 30 June 2008 is estimated to be £60 000.
7 An ordinary dividend of 10p per share is proposed.
8 The investments had a market value of £30 000 at 30 June 2008.
9 The company has an authorized share capital of 600 000 ordinary shares of £0.50 each and of 50 000 8 per cent cumulative preference shares of £1 each.

*Required*:

(a) Prepare Keith Ltd's trading and profit and loss account for the year to 30 June 2008 and a balance sheet as at that date.

(b) Explain why shareholders of Keith Ltd would not necessarily have been able to sell the business for its balance sheet value as at 30 June 2008.

**Further practice questions, study material and links to relevant sites on the World Wide Web can be found on the website that accompanies this book. The site can be found at www.pearsoned.co.uk/dyson**

Chapter 7

# Other entity accounts

## Accountants to the rescue . . .

### Home Office pins Whitehall farce on IT implementation difficulties

The Home Office has responded to damning criticism of its financial management by the chairman of the government's committee of public accounts. Its finance chiefs were forced to issue a public statement after Edward Leigh censured the department for its 'spectacular failure' to produce unqualified accounts for 2004–05.

The National Audit Office (NAO) had revealed that the Home Office's accounts were in such poor shape that it couldn't confirm their fairness. An NAO spokesman told *FM* that the accounts of three other government departments had been qualified, but in the Home Office's case it was 'relatively rare for there to be so little confidence in the figures or the underlying mechanisms that we can't form an opinion on whether they are true and accurate'.

In its defence, the Home Office blamed the introduction of a new accounting system for the catalogue of errors highlighted in the audit. Problems with the implementation meant that the department was unable to reconcile its cash position. In one case it had to make adjustments of £946m to correct a £3m discrepancy. 'A great deal of work has been done over recent months to put right the problems highlighted,' it said in its statement.

Although the IT implementation was identified as the main culprit, Leigh also blamed Home Office finance chiefs for poor management accounting practice. He described the NAO report as a 'serious criticism of the department's internal financial administration and of its senior management'.

But Curtis Juman, chairman of the central government panel at the Chartered Institute of Public Finance and Accountancy, was more sympathetic. 'Having been through a similar IT implementation at the DTI, I can understand their problems,' he told *FM*. 'The Home Office is a complex department and clearly had difficulties taking all the necessary corrective action before the reporting deadlines.'

Juman believes that the Home Office's finance function is taking positive action. 'It has indicated that it intends to recruit more experienced accountants,' he said. 'But the proof of the pudding will be in next year's accounts.'

*Financial Management*, March 2006.

*Questions relating to this news story can be found on page 136*

## About this chapter

In previous chapters we have concentrated on sole trader and company entities operating in the private sector. However, we would be presenting an unbalanced view of accounting if we concentrated almost entirely on such entities. There are also many other types of entities operating in both the private and the public sectors. In some cases their accounting requirements are different from those entities that we have looked at so far. We cannot deal with them all but at least we can give you an indication of varying accounting practices that you will find in some other types of entities.

In broad terms, most entities, irrespective of their nature and the economic sector in which they operate, collect information according to conventional accounting rules and record it in a traditional (computerized) double-entry book-keeping system. The main difference is the way that they may present it. So the accounting procedures covered in this book can be easily adapted to meet these slightly different circumstances.

**Learning objectives**

**By the end of this chapter you should be able to:**

- **outline the contents of a manufacturing account;**
- **prepare a simple manufacturing account;**
- **describe the type of account required by service sector entities;**
- **compare and contrast accounts in the profit-making sector with those in the not-for-profit sector;**
- **state why accounting in the public sector may be different from that in the private sector.**

## Why this chapter is important for non-accountants

This chapter is important for non-accountants because it helps to present a more balanced and a more well-rounded appreciation of accounting and the presentation of accounting information in different types of entities.

Most accounting textbooks concentrate on looking at accounting practices in the private profit-making sector, especially those relating to manufacturing and trading entities. However, the service sector now forms a significant element in the private sector, so it would be misleading to ignore the accounting procedures in that sector. Similarly, in the not-for-profit sector there are many types of entities (such as charities and voluntary bodies) that play an important part in the life of many people. In addition, the Government has a major impact on economic life and it too has its own form of accounting, although it has recently changed and is now similar to that in the private sector.

In a book of this nature we cannot deal with every conceivable entity. In this chapter we cover just a few of them. This then gives you an indication of how basic accounting practices are used (with some modification) in other kinds of entities. You will also find that if you are involved in such entities you can adapt your accounting knowledge to suit the requirements of different entities. For example, many non-accountants will be members of various social and sporting clubs. The accounting knowledge that you have gained by working your way through this book will enable you to assess the financial position and future prospects of such entities with relative ease. Indeed, you may already have come across misleading statements prepared by club treasurers, such as calling a summary of cash received and cash paid a 'balance sheet'! Mistakes like this may not be very serious but they will certainly confuse the club members and give them a false impression of the club's assets and liabilities.

It is to be hoped that after reading this book in general and this chapter in particular, you will not make such mistakes.

## Manufacturing accounts

A manufacturing entity is an entity that purchases or obtains raw materials and converts them to a finished goods state. The finished goods are then sold to customers. Manufacturing entities are normally to be found in the private sector and they may be organized as sole traders, partnerships or companies.

Unlike the examples we have used in the previous chapters, manufacturing entities are not likely to use a *purchases* account. This is because they normally buy raw materials and then process them before they are sold as *finished goods*. So before the trading account can be compiled it is necessary to calculate the cost of converting the raw materials into finished goods. The conversion cost is called the *manufacturing cost* and it is the equivalent of a trading entity's *purchases*.

In order to calculate an entity's manufacturing cost, we need to prepare a *manufacturing account*. A manufacturing account forms part of the double-entry system and it is included in the periodic financial accounts. It normally contains only manufacturing *costs* since it is rare to have any manufacturing *incomes*.

Manufacturing costs are debited to the manufacturing account. They are usually classified into *direct* and *indirect* costs. Direct costs are those costs that can be easily and economically identified with a particular segment. A segment may be a department, a section, a product or a unit. Indirect costs are those costs that cannot be easily and economically identified with a particular segment. Indirect costs are sometimes referred to as 'overhead' or 'overheads'.

The format of the manufacturing account is straightforward. Normally, it contains two main sections comprising the direct and the indirect costs. Each section is then analysed into what are called the *elements of cost*. The elements of cost include materials, labour and other expenses.

Example 7.1 illustrates the format of a typical manufacturing account. A detailed explanation of its contents follows.

**Example 7.1**

### Format of a basic manufacturing account

| | | £000 | £000 |
|---|---|---|---|
| *Direct costs* (1) | | | |
| Direct materials (2) | | 20 | |
| Direct labour (3) | | 70 | |
| Other direct expenses (4) | | 5 | |
| Prime cost (5) | | | 95 |
| *Manufacturing overhead* (6) | | | |
| Indirect material cost (7) | | 3 | |
| Indirect labour cost (7) | | 7 | |
| Other indirect expenses (7) | | 10 | |
| *Total manufacturing overhead incurred* (8) | | | 20 |
| *Total manufacturing costs incurred* (9) | | | 115 |
| *Work-in-progress* (10) | | | |
| Opening work-in-progress | | 10 | |
| Closing work-in-progress | | (15) | (5) |
| *Manufacturing cost of goods produced* (11) | c/f | 45 | 110 |

Example 7.1 *continued*

| | | £000 | £000 |
|---|---|---|---|
| | b/f | 45 | 110 |
| *Manufacturing profit* (12) | | | 11 |
| *Market value of goods produced transferred to the trading account* (13) | | | 121 |

*Notes*:

(a) The number shown after each item refers to the tutorial notes immediately below. The amounts have been inserted purely for illustrative purposes.

(b) The term 'factory' or 'work' is sometimes substituted for the term manufacturing.

*Tutorial notes to Example 7.1*

1 *Direct costs*. The exhibit relates to a *company's* manufacturing account. It is assumed that the direct costs listed for materials, labour and other expenses relate to those expenses that have been easy to identify with the specific products manufactured by the company.

2 *Direct materials*. The charge for direct materials will be calculated as follows:

direct material cost = (opening stock of raw materials + purchases of raw materials) – closing stock of raw materials

The total of direct material cost is sometimes referred to as *materials consumed*. Direct materials will include all the raw material costs and component parts that have been easy to identify with particular products.

3 *Direct labour*. This will include all those employment costs that have been easy to identify with particular products.

4 *Other direct expenses*. Besides direct materials and direct labour costs, there are sometimes other direct expenses that are easy to identify with particular products, e.g. the cost of hiring a specific machine. Such expenses are relatively rare.

5 *Prime cost*. The total of direct material costs, direct labour costs and other direct expenses is known as prime cost.

6 *Manufacturing overhead*. Overhead refers to the total of all indirect costs, and so any manufacturing costs that are not easy to identify with specific products will be classified separately under this heading.

7 *Indirect material cost, indirect labour cost and other indirect expenses*. Manufacturing overhead will probably be shown separately under these three headings.

8 *Total manufacturing overhead incurred*. This item represents the total of indirect material cost, indirect labour cost and other indirect expenses.

9 *Total manufacturing costs incurred*. The total of prime cost and total manufacturing overhead incurred equals the total manufacturing costs incurred.

10 *Work-in-progress*. This represents the estimated cost of incomplete work that is not yet ready to be transferred to finished stock. There will usually be some opening and closing work-in-progress.

11 *Manufacturing cost of goods produced*. This equals the total manufacturing costs incurred plus (or minus) the difference between the opening and closing work-in-progress.

12 *Manufacturing profit*. The manufacturing cost of goods produced may be transferred straight to the finished goods stock account. The finished goods stock

account is the equivalent of the purchases account in a trading organization. Sometimes, however, a manufacturing profit is added to the manufacturing cost of goods produced before it is transferred to the trading account. The main purpose of this adjustment is to enable management to compare more fairly the company's total manufacturing cost (inclusive of profit) with outside prices (since such prices will also normally include some profit). The profit added to the manufacturing cost of goods produced may simply be an appropriate percentage, or it may represent the level of profit that the industry generally expects to earn. Any profit element added to the manufacturing cost (irrespective of how it is calculated) is an internal book-keeping arrangement, because the profit has not been earned or *realized* outside the business.

13 *Market value of goods produced.* As explained in note 12 above, the market value of goods produced is the amount that will be transferred (i.e. debited) to the trading account.

**Activity 7.1**

Do you think that the structure of a manufacturing account makes it easy to follow? Are you clear about the meaning of each individual item? What does the information tell you about the cost of manufacturing during the period in question?

## Construction of the account

In this section, we are going to explain how to construct a manufacturing account. We use Example 7.2 to do so.

**Example 7.2**

### Constructing a manufacturing account

The following balances, *inter alia*, have been extracted from the Wren Manufacturing Company as at 31 March 2008:

| | *Dr* |
|---|---|
| | £ |
| Carriage inwards (on raw materials) | 6 000 |
| Direct expenses | 3 000 |
| Direct wages | 25 000 |
| Factory administration | 6 000 |
| Factory heat and light | 500 |
| Factory power | 1 500 |
| Factory rent and rates | 2 000 |
| Factory supervisory costs | 5 000 |
| Purchase of raw materials | 56 000 |
| Raw materials stock (at 1 April 2007) | 4 000 |
| Work-in-progress (at 1 April 2007) | 5 000 |

*Additional information*:

1 The stock of raw materials at 31 March 2008 was valued at £6000.
2 The work-in-progress at 31 March 2008 was valued at £8000.
3 A profit loading of 50 per cent is added to the total cost of manufacture.

*Required*:
Prepare Wren's manufacturing account for the year to 31 March 2008.

Answer to Example 7.2

**Wren Manufacturing Company**
**Manufacturing account for the year to 31 March 2008**

| | £ | £ | £ |
|---|---|---|---|
| *Direct materials* | | | |
| Raw material stock at 1 April 2007 | | 4 000 | |
| Purchases | 56 000 | | |
| Carriage inwards (1) | 6 000 | 62 000 | |
| | | 66 000 | |
| *Less*: Raw material stock at 31 March 2008 | | 6 000 | |
| *Cost of materials consumed* | | | 60 000 |
| *Direct wages* | | | 25 000 |
| *Direct expenses* | | | 3 000 |
| *Prime cost* | | | 88 000 |
| *Other manufacturing costs* (2) | | | |
| Administration | | 6 000 | |
| Heat and light | | 500 | |
| Power | | 1 500 | |
| Rent and rates | | 2 000 | |
| Supervisory | | 5 000 | |
| *Total manufacturing overhead expenses* | | | 15 000 |
| | | | 103 000 |
| *Work-in-progress* | | | |
| *Add*: Work-in-progress at 1 April 2007 | | 5 000 | |
| *Less*: Work-in-progress at 31 March 2008 | | (8 000) | (3 000) |
| *Manufacturing cost of goods produced* | | | 100 000 |
| Manufacturing profit (50%) (3) | | | 50 000 |
| *Market value of goods produced* (4) | | | 150 000 |

*Tutorial notes*

1 Carriage inwards (i.e. the cost of transporting goods to the factory) is normally regarded as being part of the cost of purchases.

2 Other manufacturing costs include production overhead expenses. In practice, there would be a considerable number of other manufacturing costs.

3 A profit loading of 50 per cent has been added to the manufacturing cost (see question note 3). The manufacturing profit is a debit entry in the manufacturing account. The corresponding credit entry will eventually be made in the profit and loss account.

4 The market value of goods produced will be transferred to the finished goods stock account.

## Links with the other accounts

Example 7.2 deals with the manufacturing account in isolation. However, once the manufacturing account has been prepared it will then be linked with the trading account and the profit and loss account by transferring either the *manufacturing cost* of the goods produced or the *market value* of the goods produced to the trading account. So the manufacturing cost or the market value of the goods produced is the equivalent of 'purchases' in the trading account of a non-manufacturing entity. Apart from this minor amendment, the preparation of a trading account for a manufacturing entity is exactly the same as it is for a trading entity. This relationship is shown in outline in Figure 7.1.

## Service entity accounts

The profit-making sector is made up of a great many other types of entities beside those that may be classified as manufacturing or trading. For convenience, we will describe them as *service entities*. Unlike manufacturing or trading entities, service entities do not normally deal in physical or tangible goods. Instead they offer advice and provide assistance to their customers, clients, patients or passengers. In recent years the manufacturing sector in the United Kingdom has declined and the service sector has become much more important.

The service sector is extremely diverse, but there are a number of recognizable categories. Some of the main ones are as follows.

- *Hotels and catering.* Such entities are generally regarded as being part of the service sector, although the service they offer includes a physical or tangible element, e.g. the supply of food and drink.
- *Leisure and recreational activities.* Services included in this category include cinema, concerts and theatre productions, leisure and sports centres, and travel agencies.
- *Personal.* Examples of personal services include beauticians, hairdressing and manicuring.
- *Professional.* The more common professional services include accounting, legal and medical (including chiropody and optical).
- *Transportation.* Transportation services include the movement of goods and passengers by air, land and sea.

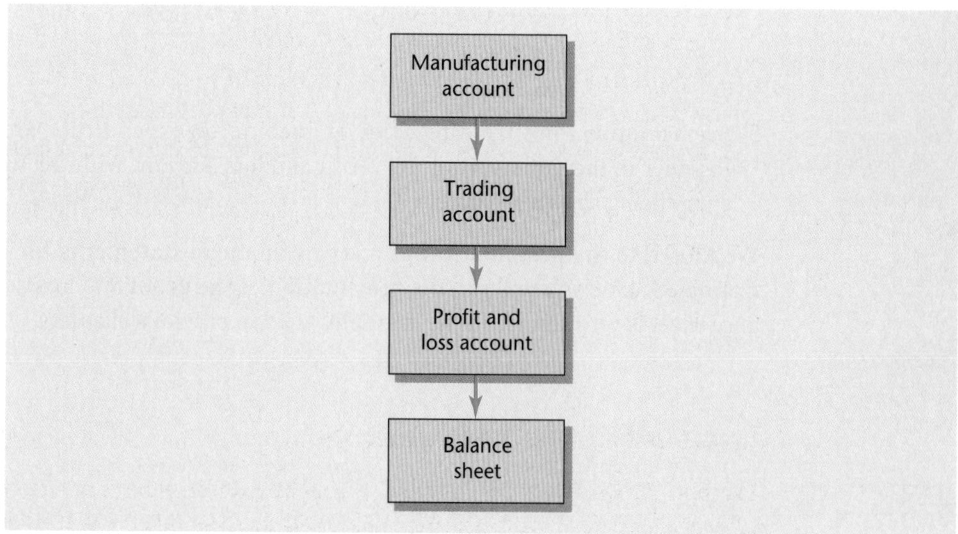


**Figure 7.1 The relationship between the main accounts**

**Activity 7.2** Think of the main street in your own town or city. List six different types of service entities.

It will be apparent from the above summary that there is an extremely wide variety of different types of service entities. This means that the accounts of different entities will also be somewhat different, e.g. the accounts of a beautician will not be identical to those of a railway company. Nevertheless, there are some basic features that are common to all service sector entities and that distinguish them from manufacturing and trading entities. These may be summarized as follows:

1 *No manufacturing and trading accounts.* Such accounts are irrelevant in service entities because such entities do not normally manufacture products or trade in tangible goods.
2 *No gross profit.* As service entities do not prepare trading accounts the calculation of gross profit is irrelevant.
3 *Primacy of the profit and loss account.* Details of the income and expenditure for a particular accounting period are shown in the profit and loss account.
4 *Format.* The format of a service-sector profit and loss account is very similar to that of a trading entity. However, sometimes specific groups of expenditure are deducted from specific groups of income, the net amount then being highlighted in the profit and loss account. For example, suppose an entity sells food for £1000 and its cost was £600. The £1000 income *could* be shown in the income section of the profit and loss account with the £600 being shown separately as an expenditure item. But, as there is a close relationship between the income and the expenditure, it is helpful to users if it is grouped as in Example 7.3.

**Example 7.3**

## Extract from the profit and loss account

| | £ | £ |
|---|---|---|
| Income from sale of food | 1 000 | |
| *Less:* cost of provision | 600 | 400 |

5 *Segmentation.* Similar categories of income or expenditure are usually grouped together in the same part of the profit and loss account with the subtotal of each category being shown separately.

We illustrate the presentation of a set of financial statements for a service entity in Example 7.4. As you will see, the presentation of the profit and loss account and the balance sheet is very similar to the examples used in previous chapters.

Example 7.4

## A service entity account

**Mei Loon: Educational training consultant**
**Profit and loss account for the year to 31 March 2009**

| | £ | £ |
|---|---|---|
| INCOME (1) | | |
| Article fees | 5 000 | |
| Author's licensing and collecting payments | 2 000 | |
| Consultation fees | 90 000 | |
| Lecture fees | 30 000 | |
| Public lending right payment | 1 000 | |
| Royalties | 20 000 | 148 000 |
| EXPENDITURE (2) | | |
| Computing | 5 000 | |
| Depreciation : equipment (3) | 2 000 | |
| : furniture (3) | 500 | |
| Heat and light | 1 000 | |
| Insurances | 600 | |
| Photocopying | 200 | |
| Postage | 100 | |
| Rates | 1 500 | |
| Secretarial | 30 000 | |
| Stationery (4) | 700 | |
| Subscriptions | 400 | |
| Travelling | 6 000 | 48 000 |
| Net profit for the year (5) | | 100 000 |

**Balance sheet at 31 March 2009**

| | £ | £ |
|---|---|---|
| FIXED ASSETS (6) | | |
| Office equipment | 10 000 | |
| *Less*: accumulated depreciation | 4 000 | 6 000 |
| Office furniture | 5 000 | |
| *Less*: accumulated depreciation | 1 500 | 3 500 |
| | | 9 500 |
| CURRENT ASSETS | | |
| Stock of stationery (7) | 200 | |
| Debtors (8) | 15 000 | |
| Prepayments (9) | 3 000 | |
| Cash at bank and in hand | 52 300 | |
| | 70 500 | |
| CURRENT LIABILITIES | | |
| Creditors (10) | 2 000 | |
| Accruals (11) | 1 000 | |
| | 3 000 | 67 500 |
| | | 77 000 |

Example 7.4 *continued*

| | £ | £ |
|---|---|---|
| CAPITAL | | |
| At 1 April 2008 (12) | | 17 000 |
| Net profit for the year (13) | 100 000 | |
| *Less*: drawings (14) | 40 000 | 60 000 |
| Balance at 31 March 2009 | | 77 000 |

*Tutorial notes to Example 7.4*

1 All six of the listed income items will have been compiled on an accruals and prepayments basis, i.e. the cash received during the period will have been adjusted for any opening and closing debtors.

2 Apart from depreciation, the expenditure items will have been adjusted for any opening or closing accruals and prepayments.

3 Mei Loon appears to be depreciating her office furniture by 10 per cent per annum on cost [(£500 ÷ £5000) × 100%], and her office equipment by 20 per cent per annum on cost [(£2000 ÷ £10 000) × 100%].

4 The stationery costs for the year have been reduced by the stock at 31 March 2009 (see note 7).

5 The net profit for the year has been added to Mei Loon's capital at 1 April 2008 (see note 12).

6 The fixed assets are shown at their gross book value less the accumulated depreciation. Sometimes additional information would be provided by inserting separate columns for the gross book value, the accumulated depreciation, and the net book value.

7 Mei Loon has valued the stock of stationery that she held at 31 March 2009 at £200.

8 The debtors entry probably represents what is owed to Mei Loon for various fees as at 31 March 2009.

9 The prepayments represent what she has paid in advance at the end of the year for various services, such as insurances or heat and light, from which she would expect to benefit in the year to 31 March 2010.

10 The creditors represent what she owes at the end of the year for various goods and services supplied during the year.

11 The accruals are similar to the creditors, but they probably relate to services such as insurances or heat and light (see note 9).

12 Mei Loon's opening capital balance is shown as £17 000. This would be composed of her original capital contribution plus previous years' profits that she had not drawn out of the business.

13 The net profit for the year is the balance on the profit and loss account.

14 Mei Loon has drawn £40 000 out of the business during the year for her own private use. Some of the £40 000 probably relates to previous years' profits that she has drawn out during the current year, along with various amounts drawn out in advance of this year's profits.

**Activity 7.3**

Referring to Example 7.4, examine Mei Loon's profit and loss account and balance sheet. What does the information tell you? How well has her consultancy done during the year to 31 March 2009? Is she likely to go bankrupt in the near future?

## Not-for-profit entity accounts

As the term suggests, not-for-profit entities are those entities whose primary objective is non-profit-making, for example voluntary associations, charities, clubs, pressure groups and societies. The main objective of such entities may be to provide leisure, social or welfare facilities for their members. It is possible that they may be involved in some trading (or even manufacturing) activities but the profit motive would not be their main consideration.

If not-for-profit entities have some manufacturing or trading activities, they will prepare manufacturing and trading accounts. The balance on the manufacturing account would be transferred to the trading account, and the balance on the trading account (i.e. the gross profit) would then be transferred to an *income and expenditure account*. An income and expenditure account is almost identical to a profit and loss account except that the title is different and the balance on the account is described as the *excess of income over expenditure* (or expenditure over income) instead of *profit* (or *loss*).

An example of an income and expenditure account and a balance sheet for a social club is shown in Example 7.5. The preparation of such accounts is very similar to that for trading entities.

Example 7.5

### A social club's accounts

**Balli Social Club**
**Income and expenditure account for the year to 31 March 2008**

| | £ | £ |
|---|---|---|
| INCOME (1) | | |
| Bar sales (2) | 60 000 | |
| *Less*: purchases | 40 000 | 20 000 |
| Building society interest | | 200 |
| Dances (2) | 1 600 | |
| Less expenses | 900 | 700 |
| Food sales (2) | 8 000 | |
| *Less*: purchases | 4 500 | 3 500 |
| Members' subscriptions | | 36 200 |
| | | 60 600 |
| EXPENDITURE (3) | | |
| Accountants' fees | 250 | |
| Depreciation: furniture and fittings | 3 900 | |
| Insurances | 600 | |
| Electricity | 1 400 | |
| Office expenses | 22 000 | |
| Rates | 2 000 | |
| Salaries and wages | 14 000 | |
| Telephone | 3 100 | |
| Travelling expenses | 13 000 | 60 250 |
| Excess of income over expenditure for the year (4) | | 350 |

**Example 7.5 continued**

**Balance sheet at 31 March 2008**

| | £ | £ | £ |
|---|---|---|---|
| | *Cost* | *Accumulated depreciation* | |
| FIXED ASSETS (5) | | | |
| Club premises | 18 000 | – | 18 000 |
| Furniture and equipment | 39 000 | 17 900 | 21 100 |
| | 57 000 | 17 900 | 39 100 |
| CURRENT ASSETS (5) | | | |
| Stocks | 1 500 | | |
| Prepayments | 200 | | |
| Members' subscriptions (in arrears) | 7 000 | | |
| Building society account | 2 700 | | |
| Cash | 5 500 | 16 900 | |
| CURRENT LIABILITIES (5) | | | |
| Trade creditors | 2 000 | | |
| Members' subscriptions (paid in advance) | 800 | | |
| Accruals | 1 250 | 4 050 | 12 850 |
| | | | 51 950 |
| ACCUMULATED FUND (6) | | | |
| Balance at 1 April 2007 (7) | | | 51 600 |
| Excess of income over expenditure for the year (8) | | | 350 |
| Balance at 31 March 2008 (9) | | | 51 950 |

***Tutorial notes to Example 7.5***

1 The income items will have been calculated on an accruals and prepayments basis.

2 Details relating to the bar, dances and food sales (and other similar activities) may require separate disclosure. If so, individual accounts would be prepared for these activities, the balance on such accounts then being transferred to the income and expenditure account.

3 Expenditure items would be calculated on an accruals and prepayments basis.

4 The balance on the account (the excess of income over expenditure for the year) is transferred to the Accumulated Fund account (see note 6).

5 Fixed assets, current assets and current liabilities are calculated and presented in exactly the same way that they are for profit-making entities.

6 The Accumulated Fund is the equivalent of the capital element in the accounting equation. The total amount of £51 950 represents what the members have invested in the club as at 31 March 2008, and what could have been paid back to them (in theory) if the club had been closed down at that date. In practice, of course, the various items on the balance sheet would not necessarily have been disposed of at their balance sheet values.

7 This was the balance in the Accumulated Fund at the beginning of the club's financial year.

8 This balance has been transferred from the income and expenditure account.

9 This is the balance in the Accumulated Fund as at the end of the club's financial year.

**Activity 7.4** Referring to Example 7.5, how satisfactory do you think the Balli Social Club's financial performance has been during the year to 31 March 2008?

## Government accounts

Another important set of entity accounts relate to the Government sector of the economy. Such accounts may generally be regarded as part of the not-for-profit service sector. There are three broad categories: central government accounts, local government accounts, and quasi-governmental accounts.

Central government accounts incorporate the results of major departments such as defence, the environment, social security and trade and industry. Until a few years ago they were prepared on a cash basis, i.e. cash received for the year was matched with cash paid during that year. The Government has now adopted what it calls *resource* accounting. This is just another term for accounts prepared on an accruals and prepayments basis.

The switch to resource accounting has been made because government services need to become more efficient, i.e. to offer a better service to the public for every pound spent. Cash accounting resulted in a lack of control of operations and projects. If a project was costing more than had been budgeted for it, for example, payments to suppliers would be delayed because this made the cash position look better.

Resource accounting has required government departments to adopt a different approach to the way that they manage their affairs. It involves setting objectives, laying down long-term and short-term plans, the tight management of funds and resources, and statutory reporting similar to that required in the private sector.

Resource accounting involves producing sets of accounts that include operating cost statements. These are similar to profit and loss accounts and balance sheets. It is claimed that they will have the following advantages:

- costs are charged to departments when they are incurred and not when they are paid for;
- distortions are removed between when goods and services are received, when they are paid and when they are consumed;
- departmental budgets are more realistic;
- it is much more difficult to disguise the overall cost of departmental activities;
- there is greater control over the safeguarding of fixed and current assets, e.g. stocks, and the monitoring of current liabilities such as creditors.

These are substantial claims. Bearing in mind the difficulties that the commercial world has in dealing with 'accruals and prepayment' accounting, it is doubtful whether resource accounting operates quite as smoothly as the Government had hoped.

**Activity 7.5** Consider the benefits listed above that the switch to resource accounting was supposed to bring to Government activities. How far do you think that they are being met? Is the absence of the profit motive in the not-for-profit sector a major difficulty?

An important part of the government sector is *local government*. Local government accounts include income and expenditure details relating to major services such as education, housing, police and social services. The annual budget (running from 1 April to 31 March) determines the amount of cash that the local authority needs to raise from its council tax payers in order to finance its projected expenditure for the forthcoming year. This is a highly political consideration and councillors are usually more concerned about the impact that a forthcoming budget may have on the electorate than about expenditure that has already been incurred.

Another part of the government sector includes *quasi-government* bodies. They include those entities that are owned by the government but operated at arm's length (i.e. indirectly) through specially appointed authorities and councils. Examples include the British Broadcasting Corporation (BBC), secondary and tertiary education colleges, the Post Office and universities. Such entities are often heavily dependent on the Government for providing a great deal of their operational income.

Overall, Government accounting generally is a highly specialist activity, although the basics are similar to the procedures used in the private sector. As it is so specialized, we will not consider it any further in this book.

### ! Questions non-accountants should ask

This chapter covers a number of different types of entity so the following questions may not be relevant in all instances.

- How has a distinction been made between 'direct cost' and 'indirect costs'?
- Why bother with manufacturing profit?
- How has the amount added for manufacturing profit been determined?
- Are there any problems in determining when income should be taken to the income and expenditure account?
- How have the depreciation rates for the fixed assets been determined?
- Should we allow for any bad debts or any doubtful ones? [A very important question in the case of social clubs.]
- What method is used to assess or calculate them?
- How have any accruals and prepayments been determined?

## Conclusion

We began this chapter by describing the nature and purpose of manufacturing accounts and demonstrating how they may be compiled. We then moved the focus away from manufacturing and trading accounts toward other types of accounts used in the service sector, the non-for-profit sector and in government.

You will have noticed that there is a great deal of similarity between manufacturing and trading accounts and the accounts of service sector entities. Manufacturing, trading and service sector entities all usually adopt an accruals and prepayments basis for preparing their financial statements and they are presented in the form of a profit and loss account (or equivalent) and a balance sheet.

The main differences are in the detail. Non-manufacturing and trading entities have few (if any) raw material stocks, work-in-progress or finished goods, and product costing is largely irrelevant. There are also a few differences in the way that information is presented in the profit and loss account (or the income and expenditure account) and the balance sheet. So if you can work your way through a manufacturing entity's accounts, you should not have too much difficulty with non-manufacturing, non-trading and service sector accounts.

## Key points

1 Entities that convert raw materials and component parts into finished goods may need to prepare a manufacturing account.

2 A manufacturing account is part of the double-entry system. Normally, it will be prepared annually along with the other main financial accounts. It usually comes before the trading account.

3 The main elements of a manufacturing account include direct materials, direct labour, direct expenses and various indirect manufacturing costs.

4 A direct cost is a cost that can be easily and economically identified with a particular department, section, product, process or unit. An indirect cost is a cost that cannot be so easily and economically identified.

5 The type of manufacturing account described in this chapter would not be necessary if an entity operated a management accounting system.

6 Service sector entities do not normally deal in physical or tangible goods or services. So they do not need to prepare a manufacturing or a trading account, their basic accounts consisting of a profit and loss account and a balance sheet. The preparation of such financial statements is similar to that required for compiling manufacturing and trading entity accounts.

7 The accounts of not-for-profit entities are very similar to those of service entities, except that the profit and loss account is referred to as an income and expenditure account.

8 Government accounts are highly specialized although their basic structure is now similar to that adopted in the private sector.

## Check your learning

*The answers to these questions can be found within the text.*

1 What is a manufacturing account?

2 What is (a) a direct cost, (b) an indirect cost?

3 What is meant by the term 'prime cost'?

4 How does an allowance for profit in the manufacturing account affect the cash position of the entity?

5 To which account is the 'market value of goods produced' transferred?

6 What is meant by the 'service sector'?

7 List five different groups of service sector entities.

8 Name four different types of businesses operating in the service sector.

9 What is meant by a 'not-for-profit' entity?

10 What terms are applied to its main financial statement?

11 Can a not-for-profit entity make profits?

12 What is the balance called that is transferred to the accumulated fund at the end of a financial period?

13 What is meant by an 'accumulated fund'?

14 What term does the Government now use to describe its method of accounting?

15 Name two types of local government activities.

16 Name two quasi-governmental entities.

## News story quiz

*Remember the news story at the beginning of this chapter? Go back to that story and re-read it before answering the following question.*

The Home Office's apparent inability to produce reliable accounts for 2004–05 attracted considerable press criticism when the Auditor General issued a 'disclaimer of opinion' in the early part of 2006. The headlines ranged from 'Home Office accused of "casual disregard" for taxpayers' cash' (the *Press Association*) to 'Home Office hauled over the coals for £180m hole in accounts' (*The Guardian*). The headline reproduced at the beginning of this chapter (from *Financial Management*, the journal of the Chartered Institute of Management Accountants) is relatively modest.

### Questions

1 What do you think is meant by the phrase '… it couldn't confirm their fairness'?

2 Would you expect auditors to report that accounts are 'true and *accurate*'?

3 Is it a reasonable excuse to argue that the Home Office could not 'reconcile its cash position' because it introduced a new computer system?

4 Do you think that it was fair of the chairman of the government's committee of public accounts to blame 'Home Office finance chiefs for 'poor management accounting practice'?

5 Do you accept that 'the proof of the pudding' in next year's accounts will really depend upon whether or not more 'experienced' accountants have been recruited?

## Tutorial questions

*The answers to questions marked with an asterisk can be found in Appendix 4.*

7.1 A direct cost has been defined as 'a cost that that can be easily and economically identified with a particular department, section product or unit'. Critically examine this definition from a non-accounting manager's perspective.

7.2 Although a manufacturing account may contain a great deal of information, how far do you think that it helps managers who are in charge of production cost centres?

7.3 It has been asserted that the main objective of a profit-making entity is to make a profit, while that of not for profit entity is to provide a service. Discuss this assertion in the context of the accounting requirements of different types of entities.

7.4* The following information relates to Megg for the year to 31 January 2007:

| | *£000* |
|---|---|
| Stocks at 1 February 2006: | |
| Raw material | 10 |
| Work-in-progress | 17 |
| Direct wages | 65 |
| Factory: Administration | 27 |
| Heat and light | 9 |
| Indirect wages | 13 |
| Purchases of raw materials | 34 |
| Stocks at 31 January 2007: | |
| Raw material | 12 |
| Work-in-progress | 14 |

*Required*:
Prepare Megg's manufacturing account for the year to 31 January 2007.

7.5* The following balances have been extracted from the books of account of Moor for the year to 28 February 2008:

| | £ |
|---|---|
| Direct wages | 50 000 |
| Factory indirect wages | 27 700 |
| Purchases of raw materials | 127 500 |
| Stocks at 1 March 2007: | |
| Raw material | 13 000 |
| Work-in-progress | 8 400 |
| Stocks at 28 February 2008: | |
| Raw material | 15 500 |
| Work-in-progress | 6 300 |

*Required*:
Prepare Moor's manufacturing account for the year to 28 February 2008.

7.6 The following balances have been extracted from the books of Stuart for the year to 31 March 2009:

| | *£000* |
|---|---|
| Administration: Factory | 230 |
| Direct wages | 330 |
| Purchases of raw materials | 1 123 |
| Stocks at 1 April 2008: | |
| Raw material | 38 |
| Work-in-progress | 29 |

| *Additional information*: | *£000* |
|---|---|
| Stocks at 31 March 2009: | |
| Raw material | 44 |
| Work-in-progress | 42 |

*Required*:
Prepare Stuart's manufacturing account for the year to 31 March 2009.

7.7 The following balances have been extracted from the books of the David and Peter Manufacturing Company as at 30 April 2008:

| | *£000* |
|---|---|
| Direct wages | 70 |
| Factory equipment: at cost | 360 |
| General factory expenses | 13 |
| Heat and light (factory $\frac{3}{4}$; general $\frac{1}{4}$) | 52 |
| Purchases of raw materials | 100 |
| Stocks at 1 May 2007: | |
| Raw material | 12 |
| Work-in-progress | 18 |
| Rent and rates (factory $\frac{2}{3}$; general $\frac{1}{3}$) | 42 |

*Additional information*:

1 Stocks at 30 April 2008:

| | *£000* |
|---|---|
| Raw material | 14 |
| Work-in-progress | 16 |

2 The factory equipment is to be depreciated at a rate of 15 per cent per annum on cost.

*Required*:
Prepare the David and Peter Manufacturing Company's manufacturing account for the year to 30 April 2008.

**Further practice questions, study material and links to relevant sites on the World Wide Web can be found on the website that accompanies this book. The site can be found at www.pearsoned.co.uk/dyson**

Chapter 8

# Cash flow statements

**Slow payers and cash flow problems . . .**

## Larger companies taking longer to pay up

Analyst study into spending patterns reveals firms take around 80 days to pay suppliers

**Laura Hailstone**

UK businesses are still taking two months to pay their bills, almost exactly the same as a year earlier, new research released this week by analyst Experian has revealed.

Based on the payment patterns of 366 633 companies, the findings showed that large companies have extended the time they take to pay their suppliers even further and take an average of 80.6 days, compared with 80.3 days a year earlier. Small companies take 59.2 days, on average, to pay their bills, while medium-sized companies now take 60.7 days, up 0.7 days on 2004. As a result, the average payment period for UK companies, irrespective of size, is 60.1 days.

Richard Lloyd, managing director of Experian's Business Information division, said 'Insolvencies in the UK last year hit their highest level since 2002. It has been proven time and again that late payment by customers plays a major part in the failure of some companies and, of course, a rapidly deteriorating payment trend is very often a warning sign that a company is in financial difficulties and heading towards insolvency.'

He continued: 'Companies owe it to their shareholders and employees to ensure that they protect themselves from customers that simply pay late and those that are suffering cash flow problems by checking the payment record of prospects and customers – even if they've been customers for years. Circumstances change and previous research by Experian has shown that up to half of bad debts come from long-standing customers.'

The slowest paying industry overall was the electricity industry, which takes an average of 69.8 days to pay its bills, while the property sector came a close second with 69.4 days.

*Accountancy Age*, 24 January 2006.



*Questions relating to this news story can be found on page 153*

## About this chapter

This chapter deals with *cash flow statements* (CFS). A CFS is a financial statement listing all the cash receipts and all the cash payments for a designated period of time. It is now considered to be one of the main financial statements along with the profit and loss account and the balance sheet. Its importance was clearly recognized in 1991 when cash flow became the subject of the very first *Financial Reporting Standard* (FRS 1).

**Learning objectives**

By the end of this chapter you should be able to:

- explain what is meant by a cash flow statement;
- describe its purpose;
- prepare a simple cash flow statement;
- outline the main structure of a cash flow statement prepared in accordance with *FRS 1*;
- identify the main causes of a change in cash flow during an accounting period.

## Why this chapter is important for non-accountants

This chapter is very important for non-accountants, especially those who are hoping to become senior managers in any entity no matter what its type or size.

No entity can survive unless it takes in more cash than it is paying out and that applies both in the short term and in the long term. So managers have to ensure on a daily basis that they have enough cash available (or they can borrow enough) to meet their debts. If they cannot then they will go bankrupt.

It follow that managers must monitor their cash position constantly and one way of doing this is for their accountants to prepare a cash flow statement (CFS) for them – preferably on a regular basis.

A CFS will not mean much to you if you do not know where the information has come from, what it means and what you should do with it. This chapter gives you the knowledge to make full use of all that it is telling you.

## The what

A cash flow statement is a financial statement that now ranks in importance alongside the profit and loss account and the balance sheet. It is a summary statement reconciling the opening cash balance plus the cash receipts less the cash payments for the period with the closing cash balance:

**opening cash + (cash receipts – cash payments) = closing cash**

Cash may include notes and coins and those bank balances that have a withdrawal period of less than three months. A simple CFS is shown below.

**Cash flow statement for the year to 31 December 2008**

| | | *£000* | *£000* |
|---|---|---|---|
| Opening cash balance | | | 10 |
| Cash receipts | | 100 | |
| Cash payments | | 95 | |
| | *c/f* | 5 | 10 |

| | | £000 | £000 |
|---|---|---|---|
| | b/f | 5 | 10 |
| Net cash receipts | | | 5 |
| Closing cash balance | | | 15 |

## The why

You might think that the profit and loss account along with the balance sheet would give you enough information to monitor an entity's cash position. There are three main reasons why this is not so.

- Purchases and sales are often made on credit terms, there may be delays in paying for services provided and some services may be paid for in advance. These factors cause a time lag between when cash is paid and when it is received.
- A number of items included in the profit and loss account do not affect the cash position, e.g. depreciation, bad debts and provisions for bad debts.
- Some transactions, such as the issue of shares and the purchase of fixed assets, are not recorded in the profit and loss account.

All of these factors mean that it is highly dangerous to assume that if an entity is making an accounting profit then it will not have any cash worries.

As a result of such factors, the profit and loss account is a mixture of a selected number of cash receipts and payments and accruals and prepayment, and the balance (the net profit) does not necessarily reflect the cash position for the period. The balance sheet does provide some information about the cash position, i.e. the balance at the end of the period, and if comparative figures are shown the opening balance as well. Even so, the *movement* of cash during the period is not disclosed.

All these considerations have meant that about 40 years ago it was recognized that there was a need for another type of financial statement – one that does show the cash position. So for sometime entities used to prepare a financial report called a *statement of source and application of funds*. Unfortunately, this statement did not show the cash position very clearly as it got mixed up with working capital movements (i.e. stocks, debtors and creditors) so in 1991 it was replaced by the very first financial reporting standard, *FRS 1*. We will examine its requirements later. In the meantime we explain how to prepare a basic cash flow statement and how to interpret it.

**Activity 8.1**

List as many items as you can think of that are normally included in a profit and loss account that have neither been debited nor credited to the cash/bank account.

Prepare a similar list for all the cash/bank items that have not been included in the profit and loss account.

## The how

Details of the cash received and cash paid required to prepare a cash flow statement could be obtained from the cash book but it is much more helpful to a general understanding of the overall financial statements if they are integrated. This involves taking the information in the profit and loss account and balance sheet and converting it into cash terms. We do this by examining the items in those statements and then adjusting them for any opening and closing creditors and debtors, accruals and prepayments, and for any non-cash and capital items. Not all items will require to be adjusted, of course, and so the procedure is not quite as complicated as it might at first appear. The relationship between the profit and loss account, the balance sheet and the cash flow statement is very close and you can see that clearly in Figure 8.1.

We now use a simple example to demonstrate how to construct a cash flow statement. The details are contained in Example 8.1.

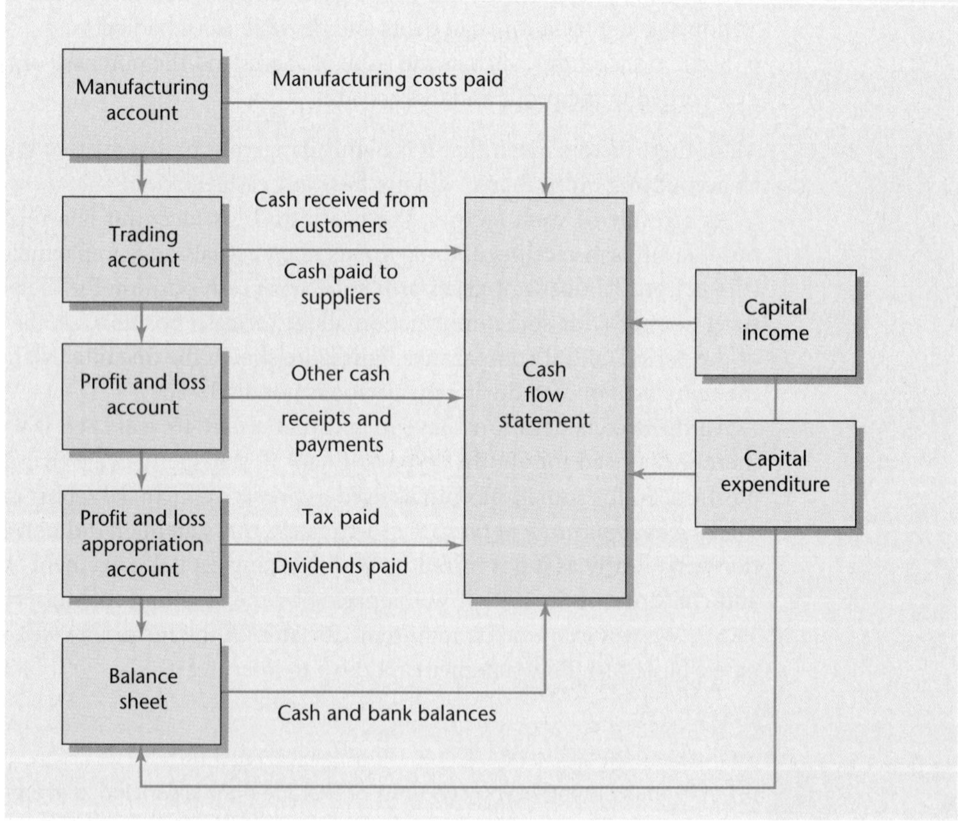


**Figure 8.1 The interrelationship between the main financial statements**

Example 8.1

## Preparation of a cash flow statement

You are presented with the following information:

**Durton Ltd**
**Trading and profit and loss account for the year to 31 December 2009**

| | £000 | £000 |
|---|---|---|
| Sales (1) | | 1 000 |
| Less: Cost of goods sold: | | |
| Opening stock (NA) | 200 | |
| Purchases (3) | 700 | |
| | 900 | |
| Less: Closing stock | 300 | 600 |
| Gross profit | | 400 |
| Operating expenses (4) | | (240) |
| Operating profit | | 160 |
| Debenture interest (5) | | (10) |
| Net profit before taxation | | 150 |
| Taxation (6) | | (50) |
| Net profit after taxation | | 100 |
| Dividends (7) | | (60) |
| Retained profit for the year | | 40 |

**Durton Ltd**
**Balance sheet at 31 December 2009**

| | 2008 | | 2009 | |
|---|---|---|---|---|
| | £000 | £000 | £000 | £000 |
| Fixed assets at cost (8) | 900 | | 1 050 | |
| *Less*: Accumulated depreciation (4) | 150 | 750 | 255 | 795 |
| *Current assets* | | | | |
| Stocks (NA) | 200 | | 300 | |
| Trade debtors (1) | 120 | | 150 | |
| Cash (NA) | 20 | | 45 | |
| | 340 | | 495 | |
| *Less*: *Current liabilities* | | | | |
| Trade creditors (3) | 70 | | 90 | |
| Taxation (4) | 40 | | 50 | |
| Proposed dividend (7) | 30 | | 60 | |
| | 140 | 200 | 200 | 295 |
| | | 950 | | 1 090 |

Example 8.1 *continued*

| | *2008* | | *2009* | |
|---|---|---|---|---|
| | *£000* | *£000* | *£000* | *£000* |
| *Capital and reserves* | | | | |
| Ordinary shares of £1 each (NA) | | 750 | | 750 |
| Profit and loss account (NA) | | 200 | | 240 |
| | | 950 | | 990 |
| *Loans* | | | | |
| Debenture stock (10%: issued 1 January 2009) (2) | | – | | 100 |
| | | 950 | | 1 090 |

*Notes*:
The bracketed number shown after each narration refers to the tutorial notes below.
NA = no adjustment necessary.

*Required*:
Prepare a cash flow statement for the year to 31 December 2009.

Answer to Example 8.1

**Durton Ltd**
**Cash flow statement for the year to 31 December 2009**

| | *£000* |
|---|---|
| *Cash receipts* | |
| Sale of goods (£1000 + £120 – £150) (1) | 970 |
| Issue of debenture stock (£100 – £0) (2) | 100 |
| | 1 070 |
| *Cash payments* | |
| Purchases of goods (£700 + £70 – £90) (3) | (680) |
| Operating expenses (£240 – (£255 – £150)) (4) | (135) |
| Debenture interest paid (5) | (10) |
| Taxation (6) | (40) |
| Dividends (7) | (30) |
| Purchases of fixed assets (£1050 – £900) (8) | (150) |
| | (1 045) |
| Increase in cash during the year (9) | 25 |
| Cash at 1 January 2009 (9) | 20 |
| Cash at 31 December 2009 (9) | 45 |

*Tutorial notes*

1 The cash received from the sale of goods has been calculated by taking the sales figure of £1 000 000, adding the opening trade debtors of £120 000, and then deducting the closing trade debtors of £150 000.

2 The issue of debenture stock equals the closing balance of £100 000 as at 31 December 2009. As there was no opening balance, all of the debenture stock must have been issued during the year.

3 The cash payments to suppliers has been calculated as follows:

Purchases + Opening trade creditors – Closing trade creditors, i.e. £700 000 + £70 000 – £90 000.

4 The other cash payments relate to the operating expenses of £240 000 less the depreciation on the fixed assets of £105 000 (i.e. the closing accumulated balance of £255 000 less the opening accumulated depreciation balance of £150 000). As there were no opening or closing debtors or creditors for operating expenses, the whole of the £135 000 must have been paid during the year.
5 This is the total amount of debenture interest paid during the year.
6 The tax paid of £40 000 represents the taxation due for payment in 2009, since the amount outstanding at 31 December 2009 of £50 000 is the same as the figure for tax shown in the profit and loss account.
7 The dividend paid is the same as the proposed dividend at 31 December 2009, because the dividends shown in the profit and loss account as £60 000 had not been paid as at that date.
8 Purchase of fixed assets equals the closing balance of £1 050 000 less the opening balance of £900 000.
9 The increase in cash during the year of £25 000 plus the opening balance of £20 000 equals the closing balance of £45 000.

Referring to Durton Ltd's balance sheet in Example 8.1, we can see that at 31 December 2008 it had a cash balance of £20 000. By 31 December 2009, the cash balance was £45 000, an increase of £25 000. Note that the retained profit for the year of £40 000 is more than the £25 000 increase in cash during the year. We do not, of course, need to prepare a CFS to find out such information but we do need some help in determining why there is a difference. A CFS provides us with the evidence. Most of the cash received for the year came from sales and much of it was spent on buying goods, but if you look at the CFS a little more closely, however, you will also see that £100 000 was raised by issuing some debenture stock and that £150 000 was incurred on purchasing some fixed assets. These items do not appear in the profit and loss account. There is probably a connection between them, i.e. the debentures might have been issued to finance the purchase of the fixed assets. Certainly, without the debentures the cash position at the end of the year would have been very different, e.g. an overdrawn amount of £55 000 (45 000 – 100 000) instead of a favourable balance of £45 000. Similarly, if the taxation balance of £50 000 and the proposed dividend of £60 000 at 31 December 2009 had had to be paid early in 2010, the cash position would have been extremely vulnerable. Durton Ltd would then have to depend on its trade debtors (£150 000 at 31 December 2009) settling their debts before it could pay its trade creditors of £90 000.

Durton's CFS is a simplified example of a company's cash flow statement. Nevertheless, it does enable the major cash items to be highlighted and to bring them to the attention of the managers and to the owners of the entity. Although it is to be hoped that the cash position of Durton was being closely monitored during the year, an annual CFS enables the year's results to be put into context.

The format that we have adopted in preparing the solution to Example 8.1 demonstrates the close relationship between the profit and loss account, the balance sheet and the CFS. The various changes that have been made are, however, somewhat difficult to trace and if it is possible a CFS should be presented in such a way that its close relationship with the profit and loss account and the balance sheet is much more apparent. The ASB has devised such a format and we can now examine it.

## *FRS 1* format

*FRS 1* was first issued in 1991 and revised in 1996. It is quite a complicated standard but we will make matters easier for you by dealing only with a CFS for single entities. We will then return to the subject in Chapter 11, when we have a brief look at a *listed* company's CFS.

*FRS 1* requires the CFS to be set out under eight main headings. These are listed in Table 8.1 together with some examples of what you might expect to find under each heading.

**Table 8.1 Structure of a cash flow statement according to *FRS 1***

| Heading[a] | Contents[b] |
|---|---|
| 1 Net cash inflow from operating activities | Operating or trading activities[c] |
| 2 Returns on investments and servicing of finance | Investment income. Interest payments on loans. Dividends paid to preference shareholders |
| 3 Taxation | Tax paid on profits |
| 4 Capital expenditure and financial investment[d] | Purchases and sales of fixed assets. Loans to other entities received and paid |
| 5 Acquisitions and disposals | Sales and purchases of other entities or of investments in them |
| 6 Equity dividends paid | Dividends paid to ordinary shareholders |
| 7 Management of liquid resources[e] | Purchases and sales of current asset investments |
| 8 Financing[e] | Receipts and payments relating to share issues and redemptions, debentures, loans and other long-term borrowings |

*Notes*:

(a) Headings may be omitted if no cash transaction has taken place either in the current period or in the previous period. They must be in the order listed. A subtotal should be included for each heading.

(b) The contents reflect only the *cash* flow for each transaction. Cash includes cash in hand, deposits repayable on demand, and overdrafts. *Cash flow* is an increase or decrease in cash during the period.

(c) *FRS 1* requires a reconciliation to be made between the operating profit and the net cash flows from operating activities.

(d) The heading 'capital expenditure' may be used if there are no cash flows relating to financial investment (such as loans).

(e) Headings 7 and 8 may be combined under one heading provided that each of their respective cash flows are shown separately and that separate subtotals are given for each heading.

*FRS 1* also requires the CFS to be accompanied by a number of notes. There are three such notes that are particularly relevant for our purposes. We summarize the requirements of each of them below.

### Note reconciling operating profit to operating cash flows

This note should show a reconciliation between the operating profit shown in the profit and loss account and the net cash flow arising from its *operating* activities. Alternatively, the information required may be presented in the form of a statement attached to the CFS (the example given in *FRS 1* shows it *preceding* the CFS).

There are two ways that the operating profit can be reconciled with the net cash flow. The *direct* method requires all the operating cash receipts (e.g. sales income) and all the operating cash expenditures (e.g. purchases and production expenses) to be listed and a balance struck between them. All the information required may be obtained from the cash book so this method appears to be simple and straightforward. However, there is no obvious relationship between cash received and cash paid and the balances shown in the profit and loss account and the balance sheet, so most entities prefer to use the second method (known as the *indirect* method) as there is a much more obvious relationship between the balances in the financial statements and the adjustments made to convert them on to a cash flow basis.

In summary you may use the following procedure for making the required reconciliation.

1 Draw up a schedule on a piece of A4 paper with one wide column for entering the narrative details and two or three columns for the monetary values.
2 Extract the operating (or trading) profit for the year from the profit and loss account and enter it on your schedule as the first line.
3 Extract the opening and closing balances for stocks, debtors, prepayments, creditors and accruals from this year's and last year's balance sheets and calculate the movement between the respective balances.
4 Decide whether the movement for each item represents an *increase* or a *decrease* in cash during the year (this is the tricky bit but Table 8.2 will help you to sort it out). Enter each of the movements on your schedule. If a particular movement has the effect of decreasing the cash, enter it in brackets.

**Table 8.2 The effect of working capital movements on cash flow**

| Item | Movement (closing balance less opening balance) | Effect on cash |
|---|---|---|
| Stocks | Increase | Down (more cash has been spent on stocks). Insert the movement in brackets |
| | Decrease | Up (less cash has been spent on stocks) |
| Trade debtors, other debtors and prepayments | Increase | Down (less cash has been received). Insert the movement in brackets |
| | Decrease | Up (more cash has been received) |
| Trade creditors, other creditors and accruals (excluding taxation payable and proposed dividends) | Increase | Up (less cash has been spent) |
| | Decrease | Down (more cash has been paid). Insert the movement in brackets |

5 Go through the profit and loss account looking for non-cash items. Some items will need to be *added* to the operating profit, e.g. losses on disposals of fixed assets, depreciation, increases in provisions for bad and doubtful debts and bad debts written off. Other items will need to be *deducted*, e.g. profits on sales of fixed assets and reductions in provisions for bad and doubtful debts. Enter them all on your schedule remembering to put deductions in brackets.
6 Now add up all the balances that you have entered on your schedule. The total amount should represent the net cash inflow (or outflow) from operating activities for the period. It then becomes the first line on your CFS.

This procedure may appear somewhat complicated at this stage but we will illustrate it shortly with a practical example.

**Activity 8.2**

State whether each of the following statements is true or false.

| | | |
|---|---|---|
| (a) | Operating activities reflect total cash inflows. | *True/false* |
| (b) | Depreciation decreases the cash position. | *True/false* |
| (c) | Tax paid decreases the tax position. | *True/false* |
| (d) | A proposed dividend increases the cash position. | *True/false* |
| (e) | A decrease in debtors increases the cash position. | *True/false* |
| (f) | An increase in creditors decreases the cash position. | *True/false* |

### Note reconciling net cash flow to movement in net debt

The second note required by *CFS 1* involves preparing a schedule reconciling the difference between the net debt at the beginning of the period and net debt at the end of it. Net debt is basically the difference between long-term loans and any cash and bank balances (net *funds* if the cash and bank balances are greater than the net debt). This note helps users of financial statements to assess the liquidity position of the company and to determine its solvency.

Such a note is quite a simple one and there are no great difficulties in preparing it. It has three main elements:

- the change in the cash for the period;
- the movement in debt during the period;
- the net debt at the end of the period.

We will come across it again in Example 8.2. It is usually shown immediately after the CFS itself.

### Note analysing changes in net debt

The third note involves analysing the changes that have taken place in the net debt position during the period. Net debt is split between cash and debt. These two elements are then analysed into:

- the balances at the beginning of the period;
- changes that happened during the period;
- the balances at the end of the period.

This note usually follows Note 2.

In the next section we explain how to prepare and present a CFS in accordance with *FRS 1* and how to present the required notes.

## An illustrative example

In order to demonstrate how a cash flow statement is compiled in accordance with *FRS 1* and how it should be presented, we are going to use the data from Example 8.1. As explained earlier, *FRS 1* gives a choice between the direct and indirect methods. We will be using the indirect method.

**Example 8.2**

## Preparation of a cash flow statement in accordance with *FRS 1*

**Durton Ltd**

**Cash flow statement for the year to 31 December 2009**

| | £000 |
|---|---|
| **Net cash inflow from operating activities** (1) | 155 |
| **Returns on investments and servicing of finance** | |
| Interest paid (7) | (10) |
| **Taxation** (8) | (40) |
| **Capital expenditure** | |
| Payments to acquire tangible fixed assets (9) | (150) |
| **Equity dividends paid** (10) | (30) |
| | (75) |
| **Management of liquid resources and financing** | |
| Issue of debenture stock (11) | 100 |
| Increase in cash (12) | 25 |

Note 1 Reconciliation of operating profit to net cash inflow from operating activities

| | £000 |
|---|---|
| Operating profit (2) | 160 |
| Depreciation (3) | 105 |
| (Increase) in stocks (4) | (100) |
| (Increase) in trade debtors (5) | (30) |
| Increase in trade creditors (6) | 20 |
| **Net cash inflow from operating activities** (1) | 155 |

Note 2 Reconciliation of net cash flow to movement in debt

| | £000 |
|---|---|
| **Increase in cash during the period** (12) | 25 |
| Cash from issuing debentures (13) | (100) |
| **Change in net debt** (14) | (75) |
| **Net funds at 1 January 2009** (15) | 20 |
| **Net debt at 31 December 2009** (16) | 55 |

Note 3 Analysis of change in net debt

| | **At 1.1.09** | **Cash flows** | **At 31.12.09** |
|---|---|---|---|
| | £000 | £000 | £000 |
| Cash | 20 (15) | 25 (12) | 45 (17) |
| Debt due after one year | – (15) | (100) (13) | (100)(13) |
| Total | 20 (15) | (75) (14) | (55)(16) |

[*Note*: the number in brackets after each amount refers to the tutorial notes.]

*Tutorial notes to Example 8.2*

1 The calculation of the net cash inflow from operating activities totalling £155 000 is shown in **Note 1** to the CFS (as required by *FRS 1*).

2 The operating profit of £160 000 has been obtained from the profit and loss account.

3 The depreciation charge has been obtained from the balance sheet. It is the difference between the accumulated depreciation of £255 000 as at 31 December 2009 and £150 000 as at 31 December 2008.

4 The increase in stocks has been obtained from the two balance sheets. It is the movement between the two balances of £300 000 and £200 000. Note that an increase in stocks is the equivalent of a *reduction* in cash because more cash will have been paid out.

5 The increase in trade debtors of £30 000 represents the movement between the opening and closing trade debtors as obtained from the two balance sheets. An increase in trade debtors represents a *reduction* in cash because less cash has been received by the entity.

6 The increase in trade creditors of £20 000 is again obtained from the balance sheets. The £20 000 represents an *increase* in cash because less cash has been paid out of the business.

7 The interest paid of £10 000 has been obtained from the profit and loss account.

8 The taxation amount of £40 000 is the balance shown on the previous year's balance sheet. As £50 000 was charged to this year's profit and loss account for taxation and this amount features on this year's balance sheet, only £40 000 must have been paid during the year.

9 The capital expenditure amount of £150 000 is the difference between the two balance sheet amounts for fixed assets, of £1 050 000 and £900 000 respectively. No further details are given. In practice, the calculation of this amount would normally be more complex.

10 The equity dividends of £30 000 represent the dividends paid out to ordinary shareholders during the year (there are no other groups of shareholders in this example). The amount has been obtained from the 2008 balance sheet. The 2009 balance sheet shows an amount of £60 000, which is the same amount as disclosed in the profit and loss account. This means that only last year's dividend has been paid during the current year. Sometimes, there would also be other payments during the year.

11 The debenture stock balance has been obtained from the 2009 balance sheet. There was no such balance at the end of 2008, and so all the debenture must have been issued during 2009, as indeed is stated in the example.

12 After making all the above adjustments to the financial accounts, the net increase in cash during 2009 is found to be £25 000.

13 See note 11 above.

14 Without the issue of the debentures, there would have been a £75 000 net outflow of cash during the year.

15 The company only had cash at 1 January 2009; it did not have any debt.

16 The entity's net debt at 31 December 2009 was £55 000, i.e. the debenture stock of £100 000 less the cash in hand of £45 000.

17 This was the cash balance at 31 December 2009, as shown in the balance sheet at that date.

Before we conclude this chapter we should mention that *FRS 1* is now no longer relevant for listed companies. Since 2005, listed companies throughout the European Union have had to prepare their financial statements in accordance with International Accounting Standard Board (IASB) requirements. We shall be returning to this subject in later chapters but you should be aware at this stage that although the IASB also requires a CFS to be published, the format is slightly different from that of *FRS 1* and its definition of cash is somewhat broader. However, you will be glad to know that it is probably easier to prepare than the ASB version.

### ! Questions non-accountants should ask

It is unlikely that as a non-accountant you will have to prepare cash flow statements. Your accountants will do that for you and present you with them from time to time. Unlike the profit and loss account and the balance sheet, a cash flow statement does not require any estimates to be made so it should be accurate. You do not need to ask questions about the way it has been compiled. You can take it at its face value.

We will assume that after studying this chapter you know where the information comes from and what it means. So what should you do with it? What questions should you ask? We suggest that the following may be appropriate.

- Why has there been an increase or a decrease in cash during the period?
- What are the main items that have caused it?
- Did we anticipate them happening?
- What caused them?
- What did we do about any likely problems?
- Are we going to be short of cash in the immediate period?
- Will the bank support an extension of our overdraft?
- Can we borrow some funds from elsewhere?
- Might we need to borrow some on a long-term basis?
- How will that affect our future profitability bearing in mind interest and repayment requirements?

## Conclusion

A cash flow statement produced using the indirect method links directly with the profit and loss account and the balance sheet. It contains some extremely useful information because it gives a lot more detail about the movement in the cash position. This is vital as it is possible for an entity to be profitable without necessarily having the cash resources to keep it going. Strict control over cash resources is absolutely essential, and a cash flow statement can help in this respect.

## Key points

1. Entities may have a long-term profitable future, but in the short term they may be short of cash. This may curb their activities, and in extreme cases they may be forced out of business.
2. To avoid this happening, owners and managers should be supplied with information about the cash movement and resources of the entity, i.e. about its liquidity. This can be done by preparing a cash flow statement.
3. A cash flow statement can be presented in any format, but most companies, apart from those listed, are expected to adopt the requirements specified in *FRS 1*. Listed companies now have to comply with an international accounting standard.
4. A cash flow statement can be presented using either the direct method or the indirect one. The indirect method is to be preferred because it can be linked more obviously to the profit and loss account and the balance sheet.

## Check your learning

*The answers to these questions can be found within the text.*

1. List five reasons why the accounting profit for a period will not necessarily result in an improvement in an entity's cash position.
2. Identify two balance sheet items that may change an entity's cash position.
3. How does depreciation affect the cash and bank balances?
4. What two methods may be used for preparing a CFS?
5. What Financial Reporting Standard covers the preparation of CFSs, and when was it issued?
6. How many headings does the standard suggest for a CFS?
7. What are they?
8. Does an *increase* in (a) stocks, (b) debtors, (c) creditors increase or decrease the cash position?
9. Does a *decrease* in (a) stocks, (b) debtors, (c) creditors increase or decrease the cash position?
10. What is (a) net debt, (b) net funds?
11. List the assumptions and estimates that have to be made when compiling a CFS.
12. How reliable is a CFS?
13. What action would you expect a manager to take on receiving a CFS based on (a) historical data, (b) forecasted data?
14. What type of companies now have to prepare a CFS under International Accounting Standard Board requirements?

## News story quiz

*Remember the news story at the beginning of this question? Go back to that story and re-read it before answering the following questions.*

This article is a useful reminder that the longer your debtors take to pay then the greater the chance that you will run into cash flow problems. According to the article large companies are taking an average of nearly 81 days to pay their suppliers, small companies almost 60 days and medium-sized companies 61 days.

### Questions

1 Why do you think that generally larger companies take much longer than small and medium-sized companies to pay their suppliers?

2 What can suppliers do to protect themselves?

3 What is the effect on (a) their accounting profit, (b) their cash flow if their customers take almost 12 weeks to pay what they owe?

4 Once they are into a regular cycle does it matter if they know that their larger customers are going to be slow payers?

## Tutorial questions

*The answers to questions marked with an asterisk can be found in Appendix 4.*

8.1 'Proprietors are more interested in cash than profit.' Discuss.

8.2 Unlike traditional financial accounting, cash flow accounting does not require the accountant to make a series of arbitrary assumptions, apportionments and estimates. How far, therefore, do you think that there is a case for abandoning traditional financial accounting?

8.3 Does a cash flow statement serve any useful purpose?

8.4* You are presented with the following information:

**Dennis Limited**
**Balance sheet at 31 January 2007**

| | *31 January 2006* | | *31 January 2007* | |
|---|---|---|---|---|
| | *£000* | *£000* | *£000* | *£000* |
| *Fixed assets* | | | | |
| Land at cost | | 600 | | 700 |
| *Current assets* | | | | |
| Stock | 100 | | 120 | |
| Debtors | 200 | | 250 | |
| Cash | 6 | | 10 | |
| c/f | 306 | 600 | 380 | 700 |

| | 31 January 2006 | | 31 January 2007 | |
|---|---|---|---|---|
| | £000 | £000 | £000 | £000 |
| b/f | 306 | 600 | 380 | 700 |
| *Less: Current liabilities* | | | | |
| Creditors | 180 | 126 | 220 | 160 |
| | | 726 | | 860 |
| *Capital and reserves* | | | | |
| Ordinary share capital | | 700 | | 800 |
| Profit and loss account | | 26 | | 60 |
| | | 726 | | 860 |

*Required:*

(a) Prepare Dennis Limited's cash flow statement for the year ended 31 January 2007.
(b) Outline what it tells the managers of Dennis Limited.

8.5* The following balance sheets have been prepared for Frank Limited:

| Balance sheets at: | 28.2.08 | | 28.2.09 | |
|---|---|---|---|---|
| | £000 | £000 | £000 | £000 |
| *Fixed assets* | | | | |
| Plant and machinery at cost | | 300 | | 300 |
| *Less:* Depreciation | | 80 | | 100 |
| | | 220 | | 200 |
| *Investments at cost* | | – | | 100 |
| *Current assets* | | | | |
| Stocks | 160 | | 190 | |
| Debtors | 220 | | 110 | |
| Bank | – | | 10 | |
| | 380 | | 310 | |
| *Less: Current liabilities* | | | | |
| Creditors | 200 | | 160 | |
| Bank overdraft | 20 | 160 | – | 150 |
| | 220 | 380 | 160 | 450 |
| *Capital and reserves* | | | | |
| Ordinary share capital | | 300 | | 300 |
| Share premium account | | 50 | | 50 |
| Profit and loss account | | 30 | | 40 |
| | | 380 | | 390 |
| Shareholders' funds | | | | |
| *Loans* | | | | |
| Debentures | | – | | 60 |
| | | 380 | | 450 |

*Additional information:*
There were no purchases or sales of plant and machinery during the year.

*Required:*

(a) Prepare Frank Limited's cash flow statement for the year ended 28 February 2009.
(b) What does it tell the managers of Frank Limited?

**8.6** You are presented with the following information:

**Starter**
**Profit and loss account for the year to 31 March 2009**

| | £ | £ |
|---|---|---|
| Sales | | 10 000 |
| Purchases | 5 000 | |
| *Less*: Closing stock | 1 000 | 4 000 |
| Gross profit | | 6 000 |
| *Less*: Depreciation | | 2 000 |
| *Net profit for the year* | | 4 000 |

**Balance sheet at 31 March 2009**

| | £ | £ |
|---|---|---|
| Van | | 10 000 |
| *Less*: Depreciation | | 2 000 |
| | | 8 000 |
| Stock | 1 000 | |
| Trade debtors | 5 000 | |
| Bank | 12 500 | |
| | 18 500 | |
| *Less*: Trade creditors | 2 500 | 16 000 |
| | | 24 000 |
| Capital | | 20 000 |
| *Add*: Net profit for the year | | 4 000 |
| | | 24 000 |

*Note*: Starter commenced business on 1 April 2008.

*Required*:
(a) Compile Starter's cash flow statement for the year ended 31 March 2009.
(b) What does it tell the owners of Starter?

**8.7** The following is a summary of Gregory Limited's accounts for the year ended 30 April 2007.

**Profit and loss account for the year ended 30 April 2007**

| | *£000* |
|---|---|
| Net profit before tax | 75 |
| Taxation | 25 |
| | 50 |
| Dividend (proposed) | 40 |
| Retained profit for the year | 10 |

**Balance sheet at 30 April 2007**

| | *30.4.06* | | *30.4.07* | |
|---|---|---|---|---|
| | *£000* | *£000* | *£000* | *£000* |
| *Fixed assets* | | | | |
| Plant at cost | | 400 | | 550 |
| *Less*: Depreciation | | 100 | | 180 |
| | *c/f* | 300 | | 370 |

| | 30.4.06 | | 30.4.07 | |
|---|---|---|---|---|
| | *£000* | *£000* | *£000* | *£000* |
| *b/f* | | 300 | | 370 |
| *Current assets* | | | | |
| Stocks | 50 | | 90 | |
| Debtors | 70 | | 50 | |
| Bank | 10 | | 2 | |
| | 130 | | 142 | |
| *Less: Current liabilities* | | | | |
| Creditors | 45 | | 55 | |
| Taxation | 18 | | 25 | |
| Proposed dividend | 35 | | 40 | |
| | 98 | 32 | 120 | 22 |
| | | 332 | | 392 |
| *Capital and reserves* | | | | |
| Ordinary share capital | | 200 | | 200 |
| Profit and loss account | | 132 | | 142 |
| | | 332 | | 342 |
| *Loans* | | – | | 50 |
| | | 332 | | 392 |

*Additional information*:
There were no sales of fixed assets during the year ended 30 April 2007.

*Required*:
(a) Prepare Gregory Limited's cash flow statement for the year ended 30 April 2007.
(b) Outline what it tells the managers of Gregory Limited.

8.8 The following summarized accounts have been prepared for Pill Limited:

**Profit and loss account for the year ended 31 May 2008**

| | *2007* | *2008* |
|---|---|---|
| | *£000* | *£000* |
| Sales | 2 400 | 3 000 |
| *Less*: Cost of goods sold | 1 600 | 2 000 |
| *Gross profit* | 800 | 1 000 |
| *Less*: Expenses: | | |
| Administrative expenses | 310 | 320 |
| Depreciation: vehicles | 55 | 60 |
| furniture | 35 | 40 |
| | 400 | 420 |
| Net profit | 400 | 580 |
| Taxation | 120 | 150 |
| | 280 | 430 |
| Dividends | 200 | 250 |
| Retained profits for the year | 80 | 180 |

**Balance sheet at 31 May 2008**

| | 31.5.07 | | 31.5.08 | |
|---|---|---|---|---|
| | £000 | £000 | £000 | £000 |
| Fixed assets | | | | |
| Vehicles at cost | 600 | | 800 | |
| *Less*: Depreciation | 200 | 400 | 260 | 540 |
| Furniture | 200 | | 250 | |
| *Less*: Depreciation | 100 | 100 | 140 | 110 |
| *Current assets* | | | | |
| Stocks | 400 | | 540 | |
| Debtors | 180 | | 200 | |
| Cash | 320 | | 120 | |
| | 900 | | 860 | |
| *Less*: Current liabilities | | | | |
| Creditors | 270 | | 300 | |
| Corporation tax | 170 | | 220 | |
| Proposed dividends | 150 | | 100 | |
| | 590 | 310 | 620 | 240 |
| | | 810 | | 890 |
| *Capital and reserves* | | | | |
| Ordinary share capital | | 500 | | 550 |
| Profit and loss account | | 120 | | 300 |
| Shareholders' funds | | 620 | | 850 |
| *Loans* | | | | |
| Debentures (10%) | | 190 | | 40 |
| | | 810 | | 890 |

*Additional information*:
There were no sales of fixed assets during the year ended 31 May 2008.

*Required*:
(a) Compile Pill Limited's cash flow statement for the year ended 31 May 2008.
(b) What does it tell the managers of Pill Limited?

**8.9** The following information relates to Brian Limited for the year ended 30 June 2009:

**Profit and loss account for the year to 30 June 2009**

| | £000 | £000 |
|---|---|---|
| Gross profit | | 230 |
| Administrative expenses | 76 | |
| Loss on sale of vehicle | 3 | |
| Increase in provision for doubtful debts | 1 | |
| Depreciation on vehicles | 35 | 115 |
| Net profit | | 115 |
| Taxation | | 65 |
| | | 50 |
| Dividends | | 25 |
| Retained profit for the year | | 25 |

**Balance sheet at 30 June 2009**

| | 2008 | | 2009 | |
|---|---|---|---|---|
| | *£000* | *£000* | *£000* | *£000* |
| *Fixed assets* | | | | |
| Vehicle at cost | | 150 | | 200 |
| *Less*: Depreciation | | 75 | | 100 |
| | | 75 | | 100 |
| *Current assets* | | | | |
| Stocks | | 60 | | 50 |
| Trade debtors | 80 | | 100 | |
| *Less*: Provision for bad and doubtful debts | 4 | 76 | 5 | 95 |
| Cash | | 6 | | 8 |
| | | 142 | | 153 |
| *Current liabilities* | | | | |
| Trade creditors | (60) | | (53) | |
| Taxation | (52) | | (65) | |
| Proposed dividend | (20) | (132) | (25) | (143) |
| | | 85 | | 110 |
| *Capital and reserves* | | | | |
| Ordinary share capital | | 75 | | 75 |
| Profit and loss account | | 10 | | 35 |
| | | 85 | | 110 |

*Additional information*:

1 The company purchased some new vehicles during 2009 for £75 000.

2 During 2009 the company also sold a vehicle for £12 000 in cash. The vehicle had originally cost £25 000, and £10 000 had been set aside for depreciation.

*Required*:

(a) Prepare a cash flow statement for Brian Limited for the year ended 30 June 2009.

(b) Outline what it tells the managers of Brian Limited.

**Further practice questions, study material and links to relevant sites on the World Wide Web can be found on the website that accompanies this book. The site can be found at www.pearsoned.co.uk/dyson**

# Case study: Preparation of financial statements

**Learning objectives**

By the end of this case study you should be able to:

- identify the accounting rules adopted in preparing a set of accounts;
- evaluate the format and presentation of such accounts;
- suggest a more meaningful way of presenting them.

**Background**

**Location** Glasgow

**Personnel** Alan Marshall: a member of the All Weather Rambling Club
Wendy Hargreaves: Treasurer, All Weather Rambling Club

**Synopsis**

Alan Marshall has recently joined the All Weather Rambling (AWR) Club based in Glasgow. A few months after joining the AWR he attended the annual general meeting.

Among the items on the agenda was the treasurer's report. Alan did not know a great deal about accounting and so he was somewhat mystified by the 'accounts' presented by the treasurer, Wendy Hargreaves. He took the opportunity to ask her a few questions but he did not understand the explanations. A copy of the accounts as presented at the meeting is shown in the appendix to this case study. They were described as a 'balance sheet' and all the information was presented on one page.

After the meeting Alan learnt that Wendy had been in post for nearly 25 years and the accounts had always been presented in that way. As long as the club had some money in the bank nobody else seemed concerned about them.

When he got home, Alan decided to write to Wendy asking for clarification about certain items contained in the 'balance sheet'. She was very helpful and she provided him with more information. He was still not satisfied that the accounts presented a clear picture of the club's financial position for the year 2007/08. He also suspected that this was probably true for the preceding year as well. Alan's questions and Wendy's answers are shown below.

A: *What is 'Mr Smith's bequest'?*
W: A legacy left by ex-chairman Arthur Smith to the club some years ago.

A: *On the left-hand side, what does the item 'Cheques not through bank' mean?*
W: Cheques that had not gone through the bank at the end of the year.

A: *On the right-hand side what do the 'Deposits' mean?*
W: The New Year deposit relates to a booking made at a youth hostel for the forthcoming New Year. The Slide Show deposit is a payment to the hotel for the room booking for the slide show in December.

A: *On the right-hand side, what does the item 'Through bank' mean?*
W: Cheques that had not gone through the bank at the beginning of the year.

A: *Were any amounts paid in 2006/07 for 2007/08?*
W: Yes – a deposit of £88 paid to the rugby club for the Christmas party held in December 2007.

A: *Did we receive any money in 2006/07 that related to 2007/08?*
W: Yes – subscriptions of £50 in total from five members.

***Required:***

(a) Identify those accounting rules that the treasurer appears to have adopted in preparing AWR's accounts and explain what each of them means.
(b) Giving your reasons, indicate what other accounting rules might be appropriate for the treasurer to adopt.
(c) Prepare the club's accounts in a format that you believe would more clearly present its financial performance and position during and at the end of the year.

## Appendix

**All Weather Rambling Club**
**Balance sheet of accounts for year 2007/08**

| | £ | | £ |
|---|---|---|---|
| **Bank balance at 13.9.07** | 4 365 | Affiliation fees | 20 |
| Subscriptions | 1 920 | Rights of Way membership | 150 |
| Donations | 5 | Mountain Hut membership | 30 |
| Profits from: | | Youth Hostel membership | 6 |
| Bus cancellation fees | 406 | Youth Hostel donation | 100 |
| Private buses | 144 | National Trust donation | 50 |
| Christmas party | 173 | | |
| Cheese and wine | 17 | **Expenses:** | |
| | | Printing and stationery | 330 |
| Mr Smith's bequest | 96 | Leaders' expenses | 16 |
| Bank interest (2007/08) | 83 | Recce expenses | 1 072 |
| **Subscriptions (2008/09)** | 30 | Postage/telephones | 6 |
| | | Secretary | 131 |
| | | Treasurer | 36 |
| | | **Sundry items:** | |
| | | Hire of halls | 285 |
| | | Insurance | 88 |
| | | General | 42 |
| | | **Deposits:** | |
| | | New Year 2008/09 | 128 |
| | | Slide show 16.12.08 | 50 |
| | | **Losses:** | |
| | | High tea | 5 |
| | | Lecture | 17 |
| | | Through bank | 297 |
| **Cheques not through bank** | 841 | **Balance in bank 23.8.08** | 5 221 |
| TOTAL | **£8 080** | TOTAL | **£8 080** |

# Case study: Accounting policies

**Learning objectives**

By the end of this case study you should be able to:

- outline the meaning of various conventional accounting policies used in preparing financial statements;
- explain the effect each policy has on the profit or loss for a particular period.

**Background**

**Location** Aberdeen

**Personnel** Clare Marshall: Potential investor
Kate Moorfield: Chartered Accountant

**Synopsis**

After leaving Birmingham University, Clare Marshall took up a marketing job in an Aberdeen oil firm. During her first five years with the company she earned a good salary and she was paid some highly satisfactory bonuses. She had managed to put a deposit down and take out a mortgage on a flat in Aberdeen, furnish it, buy a car and still have plenty of money for taking advantage of Aberdeen's amenities. She had also fallen in love with Scotland, and with a postgraduate student at Aberdeen University. So she was pretty certain that she would not be moving away from Scotland.

She had realized, however, that she might not always be earning a lot of money so she decided that she must start investing what spare cash she had. She decided that as her future probably lay in Scotland she might as well invest in the country. Clare had taken a basic course in accounting when she was at university and her job gave her some knowledge of business life around the world, but she did not know very much about suitable companies in which to invest. So she decided to collect a number of Scottish companies' annual reports and accounts. They were delivered to her flat in dribs and drabs but eventually she was able to go through them all in detail.

It was hard going. Some of the reports were long and technical (especially and rather ironically, the oil company ones). However, one of the reports was from an Edinburgh-based construction company called J. Smart & Co. (Contractors) plc. Its 2005 report was only 31 pages long, so she started to go through it without feeling too daunted. But she found even this report hard going and she wished fervently that she had listened more carefully to her accounting lecturer at university.

She got frustrated and bored, and so she decided to ring Kate Moorfield, one of the many new friends that she had made in Aberdeen. After they had discussed their respective boyfriends, Clare mentioned what she had been trying to do. Kate had recently passed her chartered accountancy examinations and she offered to go round to help Clare.

Kate was in her element. She took Clare through Smart's report pretty smartly stressing what she said were two very important points:

- the preparation of accounting statements requires a great deal of individual judgement;
- apart from their relative brevity the format and content of Smart's accounts were no different from most other public companies.

Clare was reassured about the second point but concerned about accounts apparently needing a lot of 'individual judgement'.

'OK,' said Kate, 'let's look at the accounting policies on pages 18 to 20. Rather interestingly they've called them accounting policies and *estimation* techniques. That makes my point. Apart from a few things that relate more to a construction company, they are pretty well what you will find in most reports.' Clare was beginning to feel a little less concerned.

Kate continued, 'If we go through a few of the policies, I can explain why some individual judgement is required and what impact the policies may have on the company's results.' 'How do you mean?' queried Clare, 'Are they flexible?' 'Oh yes,' replied Kate with the enthusiasm expected of a newly qualified chartered accountant. 'Not ... you don't mean, er fiddled surely?' queried Clare rather anxiously. 'Not in the fraud sense. Now don't look so concerned, I'm sure there's nothing to worry about. But in one sense, yes you're right. Depending on what accounting policies are adopted and what assumptions are made, it is possible to arrive at almost any figure for profit that you want.'

Kate may have been overstating the point and Clare's face once more began to register alarm. She was not sure that she wanted to buy shares in Smart's or indeed in any other company.

Nevertheless, Kate began to explain the company's accounting policies while Clare listened very carefully. But it wasn't long before they decided to go out for a coffee and it was several weeks later before Clare bought some shares in ... well, we'd better not say.

*Required*:

Some of Smart's accounting policies are outlined in the appendix to this case study.

(a) Explain what each of the accounting policies means.

(b) Demonstrate how the application of each these policies can affect the level of accounting profit (or loss) for a particular period.

## Appendix

**J. Smart & Co. (Contractors) plc**
**Selected accounting policies and estimation techniques**

**Accounting policies**

The accounts are prepared under the historical cost convention, modified to include the revaluation of completed investment properties, and in accordance with applicable accounting standards. The true and fair view override provisions of the Companies Act 1985 have been invoked.

**Depreciation**

Depreciation is provided on all tangible fixed assets, other than investment properties and freehold land, at rates calculated to write off the cost of each asset over its expected useful life, as follows:

| | |
|---|---|
| Freehold buildings | over 40 to 66 years |
| Plant, machinery and vehicles | 15% to $33\frac{1}{3}$% reducing balance or straight line as appropriate. |

**Stocks and work in progress**

- Stocks are valued at the lower of cost and net realizable value.
- Land held for development is included at the lower of cost and net realizable value.
- Work in progress, other than long-term contract work in progress, is valued at the lower of cost and net realizable value.
- Cost comprises direct materials on a first-in first-out basis and direct labour plus attributable overheads where appropriate.
- Net realizable value is based on estimated selling price less anticipated disposal costs.

**Long-term contracts**

Amounts recoverable on contracts which are included in debtors, are stated at cost [see accounting convention above] plus attributable profit to the extent that this is reasonably certain after making provision for maintenance costs, less any losses incurred or foreseen in bringing contracts to completion, and less amounts received as progress payments. For any contracts where receipts exceed the book value of work done, the excess is included in creditors as payments on account.

**Turnover***

Turnover, which is stated net of value added tax, represents the invoiced value of goods sold, except in the case of long-term contracts where turnover represents the sales value of work done in the year.

Profits on long-term contracts are calculated in accordance with standard accounting practice and do not relate directly to turnover. Profit on current contracts is only taken at a stage near enough to completion for that profit to be reasonably certain after making provision for contingencies, whilst provision is made for all losses incurred to the accounting date together with any further losses that are foreseen in bringing contracts to completion.

**Part of Note 2: Turnover and Profits.*

# Case study: Cash flow statements

**Learning objectives**

By the end of this case study you should be able to:

- identify the main features of a published cash flow statement;
- evaluate the main reasons for changes in the cash position of an entity.

**Background**

**Location** Sidmouth

**Personnel** Edgar Glennie: a retired aircraft engineer
James Arbuthnot: a retired chartered accountant

**Synopsis**

Edgar Glennie retired from his job as an aircraft engineer some six years ago. He now lives in Sidmouth. He spends most of his time playing bowls and worrying about his pension. The financial and political news is not good and from what he has read in the various papers at the library he thinks that he will be lucky to have much of a pension by the time he is 75.

Edgar has always been careful about money and during the last ten years before he retired he was able to buy a few shares in a number of companies. One of Edgar's investments was in Aggreko plc, a public company operating internationally supplying power, temperature control and compressed air wherever and whenever it is needed – usually in an emergency.

Edgar had recently received the company's 2005 annual report and accounts, and when he turned to the 'accounts section' on pages 59 to 108 he found that some of the information and presentation of the material was different from previous reports and accounts. Edgar had had little training in accounting but over the years he had taught himself enough to have some idea of what the accounts were telling him. Like most investors he was mainly interested in what profit the company had made and what dividends he was going to get, but he knew enough about business to realize that cash flow was also important.

So he turned to the 'Group Income Statement' on page 60, which he thought must be a new name for the 'Consolidated Profit and Loss Account'. This showed that the company had made a profit of £36.7 million in 2005 compared with £18.8 million in 2004. 'Wonderful!' Edgar intoned out aloud, 'But what's the dividend like?' He was alarmed to find that there was no mention of any dividends in the Group Income Statement, but after some searching he found some details on page 79. He couldn't quite work out what dividends he could expect so in desperation he turned back to the 'Highlights' on page 2. Apparently the dividend for 2005 was going to be 6.11p per share compared with 5.82p in 2004. 'And so it should be,' muttered Edgar, 'after making all that profit, but what about the cash position?'

He went back to 'Accounts' and the 'Group Balance Sheet' on page 61 told him that at the end of 2005 the company had 'cash and cash equivalents' (whatever they were) of £8.3 million compared with £7.9 million in 2004. So not much change there then. What had happened to all that profit? The 'Group Cash Flow Statement' on page 62 gave him the details but again he found that it was presented in a different way from what he had become used to.

By now Edgar was suspicious and a little worried. Why had the company messed around with the accounts? Why were they different? Where had all that profit gone? And where was the cash? He was so concerned that he rang James Arbuthnot, a golfing colleague. James had recently retired from being a partner in a small firm of chartered accountants, although he still acted as a consultant for his old firm.

When Edgar told him what he was worried about, James laughed and said, 'Well, old boy I don't think you need to be too bothered. These changes to the accounts since 2005 have come about because all public companies in that bl...(pardon my French) European Union have now to prepare their accounts in accordance with what are called *International Financial Reporting Standards* instead of with our own UK standards, so you can expect some differences. As far as the Group Cash Flow is concerned, I think you'll find it's not much different from the UK one. There are just three main sections instead of about eight, and there may be not as many notes. Oh! And instead of balancing just to "cash", it should balance to "cash and cash equivalents". Cash equivalents are basically just very short-term cash deposits at the bank.'

'I see,' said Edgar, trying very hard to take in all of this detailed explanation. 'Thanks James. So you don't think I've anything to worry about?' 'I shouldn't have thought so, old boy. But go through the cash flow statement again and let me know if you've still got some problems.' Edgar did just that. He did ring James – but mainly about a forthcoming golf match.

***Required:***

Aggreko's Group Cash Flow Statement for 2005 is shown in the appendix to this case study. Assume that you were James Arbuthnot and that Edgar Glennie had asked you to explain how a profit of £36.7 million for the year had resulted in 'cash and cash equivalents' increasing only from £4.9 million in 2004 to £6.0 million in 2005.

## Appendix

**Aggreko plc**
**Group cash flow statement for the year ended 31 December 2005**

| | *2005* *£ million* | *2004* *£ million* |
|---|---|---|
| **Cash flow from operating activities** | | |
| Cash generated from operations | 101.9 | 98.7 |
| Tax paid | 18.3 | 10.4 |
| Net cash generated from operating activities | 83.6 | 88.3 |
| **Cash flows from investing activities** | | |
| Purchases of property, plant and equipment (PPE) | (80.1) | (56.0) |
| Proceeds from sale of PPE | 3.8 | 3.7 |
| Purchase of intangible assets | (0.1) | (0.1) |
| Net cash used in investing activities | (76.4) | (52.4) |

| | 2005 £ million | 2004 £ million |
|---|---|---|
| **Cash flows from financing activities** | | |
| Net proceeds from issue of ordinary shares | 1.0 | 0.3 |
| Increase in long-term loans | 31.5 | 29.0 |
| Repayment of long-term loans | (19.0) | (47.0) |
| Net movement in short-term loans | 3.4 | 2.6 |
| Interest received | 0.5 | 0.3 |
| Interest paid | (4.6) | (4.2) |
| Dividends paid to shareholders | (15.7) | (15.2) |
| Purchase of treasury shares | (3.2) | (3.3) |
| Net cash used in financing activities | (6.1) | (37.5) |
| **Net increase/(decrease) in cash and cash equivalents** | 1.1 | (1.6) |
| **Cash and cash equivalents at beginning of year** | 4.9 | 6.6 |
| Exchange loss on cash and cash equivalents | – | (0.1) |
| **Cash and cash equivalents at end of year** | 6.0 | 4.9 |

**Reconciliation of net cash flow to movement in net debt**

For the year ended 31 December 2005

| | 2005 | 2004 |
|---|---|---|
| Increase in cash and cash equivalents | 1.1 | (1.6) |
| Cash (inflow)/outflow from movement in debt | (15.9) | 15.4 |
| Changes in net debt arising from cash flows | (14.8) | 13.8 |
| Exchange (losses)/gains | (6.0) | 4.0 |
| Movement in net debt in period | (20.8) | 17.8 |
| Net debt at beginning of period | (82.1) | (99.9) |
| **Net debt at end of period** | (102.9) | (82.1) |

**Cash flow from operating activities**

| | 2005 £ million | 2004 £ million |
|---|---|---|
| Profit for the year | 36.7 | 18.8 |
| Adjustments for: | | |
| Tax | 19.7 | 8.7 |
| Depreciation | 63.0 | 58.0 |
| Impairment of property, plant and equipment | – | 2.3 |
| Amortization of intangibles | 0.4 | 0.2 |
| Interest income | (0.5) | (0.3) |
| Interest expense | 4.8 | 4.2 |
| Profit on sale of property, plant and equipment (see below) | (1.1) | (1.3) |
| Share-based payments | 2.5 | 1.0 |
| Changes in working capital (excluding the effects of exchange differences on consolidation): | | |
| Increase in inventories | (9.0) | (2.6) |
| Increase in trade and other receivables | (35.9) | (11.5) |
| Increase in trade and other payables | 25.4 | 15.1 |
| Net movement in provisions for liabilities and charges | (4.2) | 5.8 |
| Increase in retirement benefit obligation | 0.1 | 0.3 |
| Cash generated from operations | 101.9 | 98.7 |

In the cash flow statement, proceeds from sale of property, plant and equipment comprise:

| | *2005* *£ million* | *2004* *£ million* |
|---|---|---|
| Net book amount | 2.7 | 2.4 |
| Profit on sale of property, plant and equipment | 1.1 | 1.3 |
| Proceeds from sale of property, plant and equipment | 3.8 | 3.7 |

*Note*:
Cash and cash equivalents at the end of 2005 were made up of:
(a) cash at bank and in hand £7.9m;
(b) short-term bank deposits £0.4m;
(c) bank overdrafts £2.3m.

# FINANCIAL REPORTING

# Part 3

In Part 3 we deal with the subject of *financial reporting*. The distinction between financial accounting (as covered in Part 2) and financial reporting is blurred. Indeed, at one time no such distinction would be made. However, financial accounting is now regarded as a rather mechanical and technical process that ends with the preparation of the profit and loss account, balance sheet and a cash flow statement. Financial reporting is more concerned with how accounting data can best be communicated to users of financial statements in accordance with legal and professional requirements.

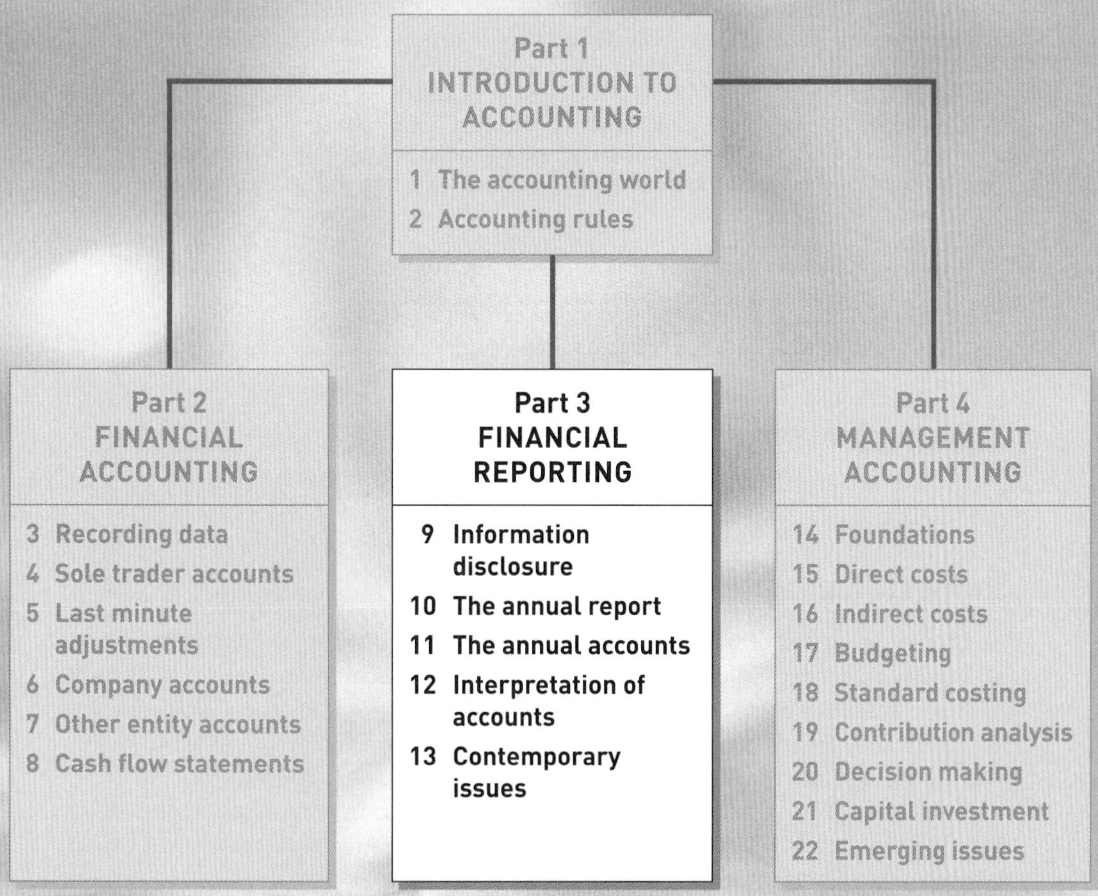

# Chapter 9 Information disclosure

## International Accounting Standards begin to bite ...

### Spirent hit hard by IFRS rules

**Nicholas Neveling**

Shares in telecommuniations company Spirent tumbled 14% last week as the company was forced to announce a significant write down as a result of new IFRS rules.

The company booked a goodwill impairment charge because of declining revenues at its service assurance division. Impairment charges are a new feature of company accounting following the introduction of IFRS. Previously, goodwill was amortised over several years on a straight-line basis.

The service assurance division provides network monitoring software, hardware and accounts for around 20% of the FTSE 250 group's sales.

Spirent said earnings at its service assurance division would decline over the rest of the year because of revenue delays on long- term contacts.

'Under IFRS the expected revenue decline in the service assurance division is likely to necessitate a further goodwill impairment at the interim stage,' the company said in a trading statement.

In addition to these revenue delays, Spirent also warned that it needed to determine the value of intangible assets it owned after acquiring rivals SwissQual and QuadTex. Spirent finance director Eric Hutchinson will now amortise these assets, with early indications suggesting the exercise will result in a further £2.5m charge.

Robert Lea, an analyst at UBS, downgraded Spirent's EPS forecasts by 34% for 2006 and 7% for 2007 following the announcement. 'Residual timing and execution risks remain on both the first half and 2006 final year outcome,' said Lea.

*Accountancy Age*, 22 June 2006.



*Questions relating to this news story can be found on page 180*

## About this chapter

This chapter is the first of three dealing with the financial reporting requirements of limited liability companies in the United Kingdom. By law such companies must disclose (i.e. make available) some information about their affairs to their shareholders and to the public. They are also bound by various so-called 'professional' requirements and for listed companies, along with some Stock Exchange ones as well.

This chapter gives you the background to these various requirements. It provides a foundation for our more detailed studies in Chapters 10 and 11 of the annual report and accounts of listed UK limited liability companies.

**Learning objectives**

By the end of this chapter you should be able to:

- explain what is meant by disclosure of information;
- list seven groups that use financial information;
- outline the main sources of authority for the disclosure of company information in the United Kingdom.

## Why this chapter is important for non-accountants

This chapter is of considerable importance for non-accountants. As a manager in a limited liability company you should know what basic legal requirements cover the disclosure of information to your shareholders and to parties external to the company. Similarly, you must be aware of other requirements both of a professional and a Stock Exchange nature that you are expected to follow. If you do not there could be serious legal consequences for the future of your company.

The chapter is also important because it provides a background and a framework for the two following chapters. These deal with the contents of a company's annual report and accounts.

## Disclosure

You might be surprised to find that there are laws requiring a company to disclose only a minimum amount of information to parties that have an interest in the company. By 'disclose' we mean to reveal something about the company's affairs. Why is this necessary? What right have those parties (whoever they are) to be given information about the company? And what information do they want?

It is perhaps even more surprising to learn that the main group that the law has in mind are *shareholders*. This seems odd. Shareholders are *owners* of the company. Surely there is no need for the law to lay down what they are entitled to? As owners are they not entitled to anything they want? As far as the last question is concerned, the answer is 'no'.

Until the second half of the twentieth century, shareholders had few rights about a company in which they had invested and they were given very little information about it. They also had no right of access to the company's premises. This is still the position today.

Why are companies required to supply only a *minimum* amount of information to their owners? Why is there no right of access? There are two possible reasons why shareholders' rights are restricted.

- *Fairness.* Large shareholders might believe that they are entitled to more information and more freedom to deal with the company than small shareholders. By treating large and small shareholders alike there is no question of one shareholder being given more favourable treatment. In practice, of course, important shareholders who visit the company's premises are likely to be received extremely warmly!
- *Practical.* Some companies are very large and they may have thousands of shareholders. It would not be practical to expect every minor piece of information to be given to shareholders. Similarly, it would be inconvenient (to say the least) if all shareholders could wander around the company' premises just when they felt like it and give instructions to the employees.

Given that shareholders are entitled to receive only certain specified information, what should they receive, how, and in what format? In the next two chapters we will be dealing with what is required currently. In recent years, the amount of information supplied has increased substantially, and it is also very hard to understand. There is little evidence to suggest, however, that more information has necessarily led to a greater understanding of company accounts among shareholders.

So far we have indicated that shareholders are the main users requiring company information, so much so that the law hardly recognizes other users. Creditors and employees are recognized to a limited extent if a company goes into liquidation but that is about all the acknowledgement that other users get.

Nevertheless, there is now an increasing recognition that other users are interested in how companies are doing. Who are they? And what information do they want? We consider the various user groups (as they are called) in the next section.

**Activity 9.1**

Do you think that shareholders in limited liability companies should be entitled to be told anything that they wish to know or to receive any information that they would like to have about a company's affairs? Why should directors be allowed to keep information away from the owners of the company? Are the reasons outlined above for restricting access and information plausible?

## User groups

The Accounting Standards Board (ASB) has identified seven main user groups. They are listed below and they are also represented pictorially in Figure 9.1

1 *Investors.* The investors' group includes both present and potential investors. Investors provide the risk capital and as shareholders they are also the owners of the company. Shareholders may be regarded as the main user group because their rights are enshrined in law.
2 *Lenders.* Lenders are groups of people who have loaned funds to the business under some formal agreement, e.g. by buying debentures in the company. It is considered that they need to be supplied with some information about the company's affairs in order to be reassured that the company will be able to continue paying interest on their debt, and that they will eventually be repaid what is owed to them.
3 *Suppliers and other trade creditors.* This group is similar to the lenders group. Suppliers and trade creditors need some information about the company in order to decide whether to sell to it. They too need some reassurance that they will be paid what they are owed.

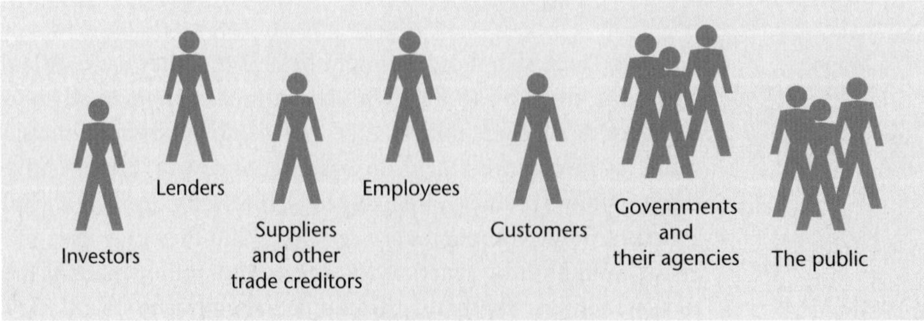


**Figure 9.1 The main users of financial statements**

*Source: Statement of Principles for Financial Reporting,* ASB 1999

4 *Employees.* Without an appropriate amount of *financial* capital, a company could not be formed, but it would also soon go out of business without the input of some *human* capital, i.e. someone to manage and operate it. It follows that employees must be an important user group of financial information. They need some assurance about the stability and profitability of the company. It could be argued that employees are hardly an *external* group since they work *within* the company. However, this does not necessarily mean that they have ready access to the type of information about the company that is of interest to them, e.g. its stability and profitability.
5 *Customers.* Customers often have a long-term involvement with a company and like many of the other groupings they too need some reassurance about its long-term future. They may, for example, have long-term warranties covering equipment that they may have purchased.
6 *Governments and their agencies.* Governments and their agencies (as the ASB puts it) are another important user group interested in a company's progress, whether this is in respect of employment prospects, the collection of taxes (such as value added tax or corporation tax) or the compilation of statistics.
7 *The public.* A company does not work in isolation and its success or otherwise does have an indirect impact on many other people with whom it comes into contact. A company that happens to be a major employer in a small town, for example, helps to generate employment outside the company itself, since other entities provide services to the company's employees and their families. So the public, in the form of the local community, has an interest in a company's performance and future prospects.

It is not generally accepted that there *are* seven such user groups. Some accountants argue, for example, that the public's interest is too remote for a company to be required to inform the local community about its affairs (although it may be good public relations to do so). Similarly, the Government can obtain all the information it wants about a company by other means, without necessarily having to establish a separate reporting system.

We now move on to a discussion of what information has to be disclosed publicly by a company. We do so in the next three sections.

**Activity 9.2**

The table below shows the ASB's seven user groups. What is the most important piece of information that you think each user group needs about a company? We have inserted one for shareholders but try to think of another important one.

| User group | Information required |
|---|---|
| 1 Investors | 1 Dividend to be paid<br>2 |
| 2 Lenders | |
| 3 Suppliers and other trade creditors | |
| 4 Employees | |
| 5 Customers | |
| 6 Governments and other agencies | |
| 7 The public | |

## Sources of authority

In the United Kingdom there are now four main sources of authority covering the disclosure of information: legal, the ASB, the IASB and the capital market. The statutory requirements are covered in an Act of Parliament (the Companies Act 1985). The ASB and IASB requirements may both be regarded as 'professional' requirements, although, as we shall see, they have semi-statutory status. The capital market requirements are determined by the London Stock Exchange. We examine the background to each of these four sources of authority below.

### Legal requirements

For well over 150 years the United Kingdom has adopted what is sometimes called a *permissive* system of financial reporting. This means that Parliament lays down a body of general accounting law but the detailed implementation of it is left to those parties who have a direct interest in financial reporting. Until recently, this meant mainly the accountancy profession but nowadays the wider business and professional community have also become involved. The permissive system is in marked contrast to the *prescriptive* system of financial reporting found in most continental European countries (such as France and Germany) and the USA. In a prescriptive system, some very detailed accounting rules and regulations are laid down in law. So there is not the same opportunity for individual interpretation of the law as there is in a permissive system.

The present British statutory requirements are contained in an Act of Parliament known as the Companies Act 1985. This Act is a consolidating measure. It includes the earlier Companies Acts of 1948, 1967, 1976, 1980 and 1981, although some provisions have been amended by the Companies Act 1989.

Companies Act legislation since 1981 has been brought about mainly by the UK's membership of the European Union, so strictly speaking, it is no longer UK law but *European* law that has set the pace and direction for change.

The statutory disclosure of information to external parties takes two main forms:

- *The annual report and accounts.* Shareholders are automatically supplied with a copy of the company's annual report and accounts, although they can opt for a summary version, but even this is still quite a detailed and technical document.
- *Filing.* The annual report and accounts has to be 'filed' with the Registrar of Companies by depositing a copy at Companies House either in Edinburgh or in Cardiff. Anyone can go along to have a look at what has been filed. 'Large' companies must file the full annual report, but 'medium' and 'small' companies may submit a modified version. The terms 'large', 'medium' and 'small' are defined in the Act but they can be amended from time-to-time by means of a 'statutory instrument'. The definitions are based on a combination of size criteria, viz. turnover, gross assets and number of employees.

### Accounting Standards Board requirements

An accounting standard is an *authoritative statement of how particular types of transactions and other events should be reflected in financial statements.* Until 1970 there were no accounting standards. Up until that time Parliament laid down what was required and the details were contained in a major Act of Parliament (the 1948 Companies Act) and a minor one (the 1967 Companies Act). There were also some additional Stock Exchange requirements for listed companies. The accountancy profession did make some recommendations but they were not mandatory.

A major change took place at the end of the 1960s. A number of questionable well-publicized mergers and takeovers took place that outraged the public because almost overnight, it seemed, reported profits were suddenly turned into losses. As a result of such activities it began to dawn on the public that there was much more to accounting than adding up a lot of figures – the figures could be fiddled! It was not generally realized at that time that working out a company's profits involves making a number of assumptions and guessing what is likely to happen. In such circumstances, of course, it was to be expected that different accountants would arrive at different profit levels. The public did not see it that way and they demanded that something be done about it!

With its reputation somewhat tarnished, the accountancy profession began to investigate what could be done. The Institute of Chartered Accountants in England and Wales (ICAEW) acted first when it formed the Accounting Standards Steering Committee (ASSC). By 1996 all six major professional accountancy bodies had become members of it (by then it had been renamed to the Accounting Standards Committee (ASC)). Its objectives were:

> *To define accounting concepts, to narrow difference of financial accounting and reporting treatment, and to codify generally accepted best practice in the public interest.*

In order to help achieve these objectives the ASC issued what were called *Statements of Standard Accounting Practice* (SSAP). SSAPs laid down the procedures for dealing with various contentious issues such as depreciation and stock valuation. Professionally qualified accountants were required to follow them. There were relatively few measures that could be taken if they didn't, but they could be disciplined by their respective professional body.

The ASC was disbanded in 1990. During its existence it had issued 25 standards but it had still failed to achieve its objectives, partly because it was slow to act and partly because its standards were too flexible. It was replaced in the same year by the Accounting Standards Board (ASB).

The ASB operates (it's still in existence) under the umbrella of the Financial Reporting Council (FRC). The FRC is a private body operating as a company limited by guarantee, i.e. it does not issue shares. It is financed by a combination of the accountancy profession, the City of London (through the London Stock Exchange and the banking and insurance communities), and the Government. Its objectives are:

- to provide support for the ASB and the Financial Review Panel (a subsidiary of the FRC responsible for examining departures from the Companies Act 1985 and applicable accounting standards);
- generally, to encourage good financial reporting.

The ASB is also a company limited by guarantee. Although it is a subsidiary of the FRC it is a totally autonomous body. It has one basic function, to issue accounting standards. These are called *Financial Reporting Standards* (FRS) but it has also adopted some ten SSAPs that still await replacement by FRSs. By the summer of 2006 the ASB had issued 29 FRSs.

What then is the legal position of FRSs and the existing SSAPs? The details are contained in the Companies Act 1989. A summary of its requirements is as follows:

- *Definition.* Accounting standards are statements of standard accounting practice issued by such body or bodies as may be prescribed by regulations.
- *References.* Reference in the Act to accounting standards relate to those that are relevant for a company's circumstances and to the accounts.
- *Compliance.* It must be stated whether the accounts have been prepared in accordance with applicable accounting standards. Reasons must be given if there are any material departures from such standards.

So it is clear that it is not a direct requirement of the Companies Act 1985 that accounts *must* by prepared in accordance with appropriate accounting standards. However, if they are not followed, reasons must be given. Furthermore, as the Secretary of State has the power to seek revision of what are called 'defective accounts and reports', it can be argued that the ASB's accounting standards have a *semi-statutory* status. As a result, if directors do not comply with the Act, they may be 'guilty of an offence and liable to a fine'.

It is unlikely that any director would be put in that position. The Companies Act 1989 has a very important clause that gives directors a great deal of room for individual judgement. We reproduce the clause below.

> *The balance sheet shall give a true and fair view of the state of affairs of the company as at the end of the financial year; and the profit and loss account shall give a true and fair view of the profit and loss of the company for the financial year.*

The phrase 'a true and fair view' (twice mentioned) has been underlined. It was first introduced in the Companies Act 1947 and it has been a feature of UK company law ever since. Indeed, it has now been incorporated into European law so it is now a statutory requirement throughout the European Union. But what does it mean?

The 1985 Companies Act requires companies to publish details of their financial performance. The Act lays down certain formats for the presentation of accounts and what should be included in them, and the various accounting standards all add to the amount of information required. This information has to be presented in such a way that it is 'true and fair'. But the Act recognizes that in some specific cases accounts may not represent a true and fair view if they follow the provisions laid down either in the Act or in accounting standards. In such an event, directors may ignore the respective statutory or professional requirement. This provision has become known as 'the true and fair view override' rule.

So directors have to decide whether by following the Act or the accounting standards their accounts would then not present a true and fair view. What have they got to go on? Not much. Although the clause has been around for nearly 60 years no company has ever been challenged in court if it has fallen back on this rule. This is because in practice it is relatively easy for them to argue that their accounts would *not* be true and fair if they followed the requirements of a particular standard since it is difficult for any external party to challenge this judgement without knowing a great deal about the company. In reality, however it can be argued that in the vast majority of cases it is accepted that accounts do represent a true and fair view if they have been prepared in accordance with the 1985 Companies Act and applicable accounting standards.

Accounting standards themselves are regarded as the most authoritative and definitive view of how certain accounting matters should be treated. They have considerable weight behind them and so no company would ignore their requirements without much discussion, not least because it might generate a great deal of unwelcome publicity. Such publicity could affect the company's share price and ultimately cause problems with the capital markets, e.g. over borrowing requirements.

## International Accounting Standards Board requirements

In 1973 a body similar to the ASSC was formed. It was originally called the International Accounting Standards Committee (IASC) but in 2001 it changed its name to the International Accounting Standards Board (IASB). The objective of the IASC was to make financial statements much more comparable *internationally*. It did so mainly by issuing *International Accounting Standards* (IASs).

The IASB has a similar remit to that of the IASC. It is a private body based in London and it is financed largely by its members. The IASB is solely responsible for setting and publishing what it calls *International Financial Reporting Standards* (IFRS). By the late summer of 2006 seven IFRSs had been issued and seven of the original 41 IASs had either been replaced by IFRSs or withdrawn. Clearly the IASB has much work to do before all the remaining IASs are eventually superseded by IFRSs.

The issues previously covered by the IASC were almost identical to those of the ASB, and there was also little difference in the accounting treatment required by either the international standards or the UK ones. So compliance with UK requirements generally meant automatic compliance with their international counterparts. The main difference was that the international standards tended to be much broader in scope than the UK ones. This was because it was thought that international accounting standards had to be much less prescriptive than national ones in order to accommodate the widely differing economic, political and social conditions in the IASB's member countries.

As a result of the similarity between the two types of standards, until recently the IASB did not play a predominant role in UK corporate reporting. This changed in 2005 when the EU made it mandatory for listed companies in the EU to comply with IASB requirements. It soon became apparent that the IASB had become a much more powerful body than it had been previously and, as far as the UK was concerned, the ASB's role in setting accounting standards had unexpectedly become much less significant.

The ASB soon accepted the inevitable and agreed that it would be unnecessarily cumbersome to have two sets of accounting standards, one for listed companies and one for non-listed companies and other types of entities. It decided, therefore, not to issue any more of its own standards unless an accounting issue arose that was specific to the UK. This is unlikely so it looks as though the ASB's future role will be mainly to safeguard British interests.

## Stock Exchange requirements

Those companies who want to sell their shares to the public have to obtain what is called a Stock Exchange listing, i.e. they need a means of marketing their shares and this can only be done through the Stock Exchange. In order to get a listing, a company has to provide a great deal of information about its history, constitution, management, financial conditions, continuing obligations and its future prospects.

Once a company is listed it has also to disclose some additional financial reporting information besides that required by the law, the ASB and the IASB. The additional information required does not now amount to very much as most of what used to be required has been incorporated into statutory and accounting standard requirements. Some examples of the extra information that is still required include:

- *Issue of reports.* Annual reports and accounts must be issued within six months of the end of the relevant financial period.
- *Directors' report.* Some additional information must be included in the directors' report. This includes reasons for departing from accounting standards, an explanation of why (if material) actual trading results differ from forecasted results, a geographic analysis of turnover, the principal country of each subsidiary and details of other companies in which the equity share is 20 per cent or more.
- *Interim reports.* Half-yearly accounts are required, although in much less detail than the annual accounts.

The above extra requirements are not particularly significant. The 1985 Companies Act and accounting standard requirements are much more onerous.

**Activity 9.3**

Do you think that interim accounts should be produced on a quarterly or a sixth-monthly basis? Would a more frequent basis be of benefit to current and prospective shareholders? How far would it be of any help to other users of accounts?

## ! Questions non-accountants should ask

The Companies Act 1985 requires directors to 'lay before the company in a general meeting copies of the company's annual accounts, the directors' report and the auditors' report on those accounts'.

We will assume that you will want to make sure that your company obeys the law and that it abides by accounting standard and Stock Exchange reporting requirements. So what questions should you ask your accountants? We suggest the following.

- Can you assure us that these accounts have been prepared fully in accordance with the Companies Act 1985?
- Have all applicable accounting standards been followed?
- Are there any relevant Stock Exchange requirements that we need to follow?
- Are there any requirements that cause a difficulty for our company?
- Do we have to follow the accounting standards on those issues?
- What effect would it have on our results if we followed them?
- Can we invoke the true and fair view override rule?
- What do the auditors think?
- If we ignore the requirements are we likely to end up in court?

## Conclusion

In this chapter, we have provided you with some background information about the external disclosure requirements relating to limited liability companies. Seven user groups of published financial information have been identified although the Companies Act 1985 concentrates almost exclusively on the investor group. Indeed, it is only in the event of liquidation of a company that two other groups (creditors and employees) are given some recognition.

In addition to statutory requirements, SSAPs and FRSs add to the amount of information to be disclosed. Listed companies are also bound by IAS, IFRSs and a few extra Stock Exchange requirements. As will be seen in the next two chapters, all these requirements mean that the amount of information supplied to shareholders in a listed company in the form of an annual report and accounts results in a document of daunting proportions.

### Key points

1. The Companies Act 1985 lays down the minimum amount of information that must be given to company shareholders.
2. This is supplemented by professional requirements issued by the ASB in the form of SSAPs and FRSs.
3. Such accounting and financial reporting standards have semi-statutory status.
4. Listed companies are bound by international accounting standards and some Stock Exchange requirements.
5. Accounts should be prepared in such a way that they represent a 'true and fair view' of the company's affairs. This is an overriding rule of the Companies Act 1985. It takes precedence over other legislative, accounting standard and Stock Exchange requirements.

## Check your learning

*The answers to these questions can be found within the text.*

1. What is meant by 'disclosure'?
2. Why do shareholders not have an automatic right to information?
3. Why do they not have a right to visit the company's premises as and when they wish?
4. List seven user groups of accounting information.
5. Name four sources of authority for the disclosure of information required by UK-listed companies.
6. What is the main piece of legislation covering such disclosure?

7 What was the ASC?

8 What did it try to do?

9 When was it abandoned?

10 What took its place?

11 What do the following initials stand for (a) FRC, (b) ASB, (c) ISAB, (d) IFRS?

12 What is the role of (a) the ASB, (b) the IASB?

13 What is meant by the 'true and fair view override rule?

14 Name three additional reporting items required by the Stock Exchange.

## News story quiz

*Remember the news story at the beginning of this chapter? Go back to that story and re-read it before answering the following questions.*

It used to be thought that international accounting standards were not as prescriptive as their UK counterparts but this article seems to suggest otherwise.

### Questions

1 What is a 'write down' and where would it have been written down to?

2 What is meant by the phrase 'The company booked a goodwill impairment charge ...'?

3 Why should IFRS requirements result in an expected revenue decline?

4 What is meant by the suggestion that 'the exercise will result in a further £2.5m charge?

5 What impact do you think that IFRS rules have had on Spirent's cash flow?

## Tutorial questions

9.1 What type of information do you think a company should disclose to its shareholders?

9.2 Should the disclosure of accounting information for companies be prescribed in detail in an Act of Parliament?

9.3 'Accounting standards should become enshrined in company law.' Discuss.

9.4 Do you think that the 'true and fair view' rule should be abandoned?

**Further practice questions, study material and links to relevant sites on the World Wide Web can be found on the website that accompanies this book. The site can be found at www.pearsoned.co.uk/dyson**

# Chapter 10 The annual report

**OFR to be or not to be . . .**

## An adequate replacement

The end of the OFR doesn't make a black day for the greens, says Timothy Copnell. But the business review fails to go far enough, argues Julian Oram

Does the decision to abolish the statutory OFR and replace it with a business review represent a backwards step in the business sector's commitment to the social and environmental agenda, both here and abroad? This is certainly the view of many commentators representing ethical investors, charities, faith groups, think tanks and academic institutions.

I don't believe that the removal of the operating and financial review requirement will have such a negative effect. The OFR may have been used by readers to gauge a company's progress on issues such as employee relations, social impacts and environment performance, but it was never intended to replace CSR reporting.

Indeed, there was no blanket OFR requirement to report on employees, the environment, and social and community issues. Rather, disclosure was required only where necessary to enable members to assess the success of strategies adopted by a company.

Does the 'so-called' scaled-down business review set a lower standard of reporting that fails the needs of investors? I don't think so. Its requirements are, in many ways, just as onerous as those promoted by the OFR. Significantly, business reviews must be prepared for all companies.

At the same time, the business review concept is not that dissimilar. Disclosure of a company's principal risks and uncertainties is still required, as are key performance indicators addressing environmental and employee matters, where necessary.

The business review requirements are silent as to social and community issues and corporate policy in relation to employees and the environment, but silence should not be interpreted as an exemption from reporting.

Finally, one has to consider the expectations of investors. The OFR legislation was crafted over seven years of rigorous debate. You can not turn the clock back simply by abolishing the OFR. Those companies that were committed to the social and environmental agenda will continue to be – and they will do so because it makes sound business sense.

*Accountancy Age*, 12 January 2006.

*Source*: Republished with permission from VNU Business Publications LTD. 2007 VNU Business Publications LTD.

*Questions relating to this news story can be found on page 195*

## About this chapter

We explained in the previous chapter that a limited liability company usually publishes an annual report and accounts. Some of the contents are statutory, i.e. required by law, some are 'professional' and some are Stock Exchange requirements, while others are voluntary, i.e. companies can decide for themselves what to put in.

The annual report and accounts of a large international company can be extremely long and highly technical. In order to make your studies a little easier we are going to cover the subject in two chapters. This chapter deals mainly with the non-statutory information normally found in an annual report. The next covers the annual accounts. These include the statutory items, especially those relating to financial matters.

We are going to confine our study to UK-listed companies. This means that their published annual reports and accounts will have to have been prepared in accordance with the Companies Act 1985 and international accounting standards. If by any chance you come across (you probably won't) the accounts of non-listed companies, you will probably find that they have been prepared in accordance with the Companies Act 1985 and UK accounting standards. As a result, the presentation, the terminology and some of the accounting methods will be slightly different from the material we have presented in both this chapter and in the next.

**Learning objectives**

**By the end of this chapter you should be able to:**

- **identify the main sections of a listed company's annual report;**
- **outline the main contents of a chairman's statement;**
- **summarize the contents of a number of other reports found in such an annual report.**

## ! Why this chapter is important for non-accountants

This chapter is important for non-accountants for the following reasons:

- you will become aware of what an annual report may contain;
- you will find out where to look for certain types of information;
- you will learn to distinguish between statutory and non-statutory information;
- you will be able to use the information contained in the annual report to help assess the company's performance and future prospects.

**Activity 1.1**

Get hold of an annual report and accounts for three UK public limited liability companies.

*Guidance*: If some of your friends or relatives have shares in a company they should automatically receive a copy of that company's report and accounts. See if they will let you have it. Otherwise select three companies and write to the company secretary. Most companies will let you have a set without any questions being asked. You may also be able to download some reports from the Internet. Choose commercial or industrial companies and avoid banking and insurance companies as they have different requirements.

*Note: It is important that you do this activity and have some annual reports and accounts available otherwise you will find it more difficult to work your way through this chapter and the next.*

## Reports covered

We shall be covering seven types of reports that you may find in a plc's annual report and accounts. These are:

- introductory material;
- the chairman's statement;
- an operating and financial review;
- the directors' report;
- a corporate governance statement;
- a remuneration report;
- some information for the company's shareholders.

The introductory material (there usually is some) and the shareholder information are not strictly reports as such but for our purposes it is convenient to categorize them in this way. The main structure of the chapter is shown in Figure 10.1.

You may well find other types of reports in some companies' published annual reports and accounts. The order of the contents may also be different from the order that we are following in this chapter so you may have to consult the list of contents at the beginning of the report (if there is one) to find what you want. The format, the style and the terminology may also vary slightly, so you have to allow for these differences as well.

With these reservations and warnings in mind we can now turn to the 'introductory material' usually found in the report section of a company's annual report and accounts.

## Introductory material

A company's annual report and accounts can be a formidable document even for those users who have some accounting knowledge. It can easily be over 50 pages long. It is usually full of jargon and technical detail and it contains a great deal of numerical analyses. The document can be very off-putting for those users who are frightened of figures. This should not apply to readers of this book because we have gradually been preparing you for what otherwise might have been an alarming experience.

**CONTENTS**

| Reports | Accounts |
|---|---|
| • Introductory material | • Consolidated income statement |
| • Chairman's statement | • Statement of recognized income and expense |
| • Operating and financial review | • Consolidated balance sheet |
| • Directors' report | • Consolidated cash flow statement |
| • Corporate governance | • Notes to the financial statements |
| • Remuneration report | • Independent auditor's report |
| • Shareholder information | • Periodic summary |

**Figure 10.1 The reports section of an annual report and accounts**

The introductory material probably tells you something about the company, along with a brief summary of the financial results for the year. For example, Devro plc's 2005 annual report and accounts makes the following statement on the inside cover of the front page (in a large font):

> Devro is one of the world's leading producers of manufactured casings for the food industry, supplying a wide range of products and technical support to manufacturers of sausages, salami, hams and other cooked meats. The group's main focus is edible collagen-based products. These are a key component of our customers' product offerings, and have been steadily replacing gut casings in markets around the world.

Unless you had heard about Devro, you might be mystified by this statement. 'Collagen' is a technical term. It is described later in the report as one of the most common forms of animal protein. You might be put off by some of the jargon, e.g. 'casings', 'key component' and 'product offerings'. Nevertheless, the statement is very eye-catching (black on a red background).

The top of that page also includes a list of the contents of the report. Opposite on page 1 is a summary of the 'Key financials'. This is a very clear, simple summary of the results for the year – so we have reproduced it for you as Figure 10.2.

Some of the information shown in Figure 10.2 will not mean much to you yet, so you can appreciate how difficult it must be for those users who have not had *any* training in accounting. Pages 2 and 3 of Devro's report give you some information about the company under the heading 'Global reach' while pages 4 and 5 tell you about 'Our product

**Devro plc** **Key financials**

| | **2005** | 2004* |
|---|---|---|
| Earnings per share (before exceptional item) | **8.7p** | 8.0p |
| Dividends per share | **4.4p** | 4.0p |
| Group revenue | **£152.5m** | £148.9m |
| Gross profit | **£47.6m** | £49.2m |
| – margin | **31.2%** | 33.0% |
| Operating profit (before exceptional item) | **£21.3m** | £20.7m** |
| – margin | **13.9%** | 13.9% |
| Exceptional item – profit on sale of land | **£6.3m** | – |
| Profit before tax | **£25.8m** | £18.0m |
| Cash generated from operations | **£28.5m** | £28.3m |
| Captial expenditure | **£16.7m** | £11.5m |
| Net debt | **£17.7m** | £25.5m |
| Gearing | **28.9%** | 47.8% |

*Prior year information has been restated to incorporate adjustments required under International Financial Reporting Standards (IFRSs).

**Including the share of the operating loss of the joint venture.

**Figure 10.2 Introductory material: an example**

*Source*: Devro plc, *Annual Report and Accounts 2005*.

applications'. The information is presented in several colours and it is accompanied by more statistics along with a number of pictures. The chairman's statement is on pages 6 and 7 but there is more introductory material on pages 8 and 9 ('Eating Wieners around the world'). The operating and financial review then follows on pages 10 to 13.

In other companies, especially those that are consumer orientated, you will usually find many more pages of publicity material promoting the company's products than is the case with Devro.

**Activity 10.2** Consult your copies of the three sets of annual report and accounts that you obtained when you completed Activity 10.1. Read through the introductory material and summarize the contents.

## Chairman's statement

Most company chairmen like to include a report or statement of their own in the annual report. There are no statutory, ASB/IASB or Stock Exchange requirements for chairmen to publish a report, so the format and content will vary from company to company.

You will probably find the chairman's statement in the first few pages of the annual report (on pages 6 to 7 in Devro's case). You can expect it to be anything from one to four pages in length. It will be largely narrative in style although it will not be entirely devoid of quantitative information. Research evidence suggests that chairmen's statements are the most widely read section of an annual report, perhaps because they are mainly narrative.

Chairmen tend to adopt an upbeat approach about the recent performance of the company and they are usually extremely optimistic about the future. You must, therefore, read their reports with a great deal of scepticism, and you should check their comments against the detailed results contained elsewhere within the overall annual report and accounts. Nevertheless, chairmen have to be careful that they do not become too optimistic. Their remarks can have a significant impact on the company's share price and they might have to answer to the Stock Exchange authorities if they publish misleading statements.

The contents of a typical chairman's statement may include the following items:

- *Results.* A summary of the company's results for the year covering turnover, pre- and post-tax profits, earnings per share and cash flow.
- *Dividend.* Details about any interim dividend paid for the year and any proposed final dividend.
- *Prospects.* A summary of how the chairman sees the general economic and political outlook and the future prospects for the company.
- *Employees.* A comment about the company's employees including any notable successes, concluding with the Board's thanks to all employees for their efforts.
- *Directors.* A similar note may be included about the Board of Directors including tributes to retiring directors.

A relatively brief chairman's statement is reproduced in Figure 10.3.

## J. Smart & Co. (Contractors) Plc

## CHAIRMAN'S REVIEW

### ACCOUNTS

Group profits for the full year at £5 458 000, which compares with profits for the previous year of £5 286 000, turned out somewhat higher than anticipated in the interim report. This is due to the recent resolution of a contractual dispute and sales of land and property concluded late on in the year.

The Board is recommending a Final Dividend of 9.50p nett making a total for the year of 12.40p nett which compares with 12.05p nett for the previous year. After waivers by members holding approximately 51% of the shares the Dividends will cost the Company £611 000.

Unappropriated profits for the year amounted to £3 398 000 which, when added to the retained profits brought forward and the surplus on the revaluation reserve, bring the consolidated capital and reserves of the Group to £87 784 000.

### TRADING ACTIVITIES

Group turnover dcreased by 26%, own work capitalised was negligible and other operating income increased by 5%. Overall Group profits increased by 3%.

Turnover and profits in contracting improved. Sales and profits in private housing declined. Sales in precast concrete manufacture decreased, although cost cutting measures substantially reduced losses in spite of continuing adverse pressure on prices.

The large industrial unit completed last year at Cardonald Business Park, Glasgow is now let. The development of small industrial units at Bilston Glen near Edinburgh is letting slowly. The office block at Glenbervie Business Park near Stirling is now completely let. Voids have increased at our large office development at Links Place, Edinburgh. An upgrading and refurbishment operation is planned for the new year.

The third phase of our joint venture development with EDI (Industrial) Ltd at A1 Industrial Estate, Edinburgh is now completely let. The fourth and last phase, part of which is pre-let, is due to commence in the current financial year. Phase three of our joint venture development with EDI at Starlaw Industrial Estate, Livingstone which is also pre-let is currently underway.

Fresh negotiations are proceeding for a pre-let Prestonfield Park, Edinburgh, our joint venture development with Walker Group.

### FUTURE PROSPECTS

During the next calendar year we anticipate commencing large industrial units for lease at Helen Street, Glasgow and Cardonald Business Park, Glasgow, and office developments at Glenbervie Business Park near Stirling and McDonald Road, Edinburgh.

The amount of contracting work in hand is again greater than last year. Over three quarters of this work has been obtained on a negotiated and/or design and construct basis and the balance by traditional competitive tender. However, future work prospects are uncertain and upward pressure on costs is mounting.

Private house sales in Edinburgh have slowed substantially and it is anticipated that revenue will again be less than last year.

Bearing in mind the foregoing it is not possible at this stage to forecast with any degree of accuracy the profit figure for the current year.

J. M. SMART
*Chairman*

*15th November 2005*

**Figure 10.3 A chairman's statement**

*Source*: J. Smart & Co. (Contractors) PLC, *Annual Report and Accounts, 2005*.

**Activity 10.3**

Referring to your three sets of annual reports and accounts, find the chairmen's statements and read through each of them carefully. Are there any items not included in the summary shown above?

List the main contents of each chairman's statement.

## Operating and financial review

An operating and financial review (OFR) may be defined as follows:

> **an exposition of a company's performance and prospects supported by both narrative and quantitative information**

In 1991 the accountancy profession and the financial community set up the 'Cadbury Committee' to examine what has come to be called 'corporate governance' (we will be returning to this topic later in the chapter). One of its suggestions was that companies should issue an OFR. The idea was taken up by the business and financial community and in 1993 the ASB issued a statement supporting the suggestion.

An OFR is not at present covered by any statute or by any accounting standard, although this may well change. The recommendation to publish one is persuasive and not mandatory. The ASB's recommendation is of relevance mainly to listed companies although other entities are encouraged to publish one.

The form and content will vary from company to company but most companies publish an OFR. It can easily be up to ten pages in length so it is not worthwhile reproducing one here. However, in order to give you an idea of what might be included there follows a summary of the possible contents.

### The operating review

- *Review.* A review of the business environment in which the company operates, any developments in the business and the impact they have had on the company's results.
- *Prospects.* The main factors affecting the company's future prospects.
- *Expansion.* Details of investments aimed at increasing future income and profits.
- *Returns.* The dividends paid to shareholders and the changes in shareholders' funds.

### The financial review

- *Capital.* Details of the capital funding of the company and of its capital structure.
- *Taxation.* Additional information about the tax items included in the accounts.
- *Cash.* Details of cash inflows and outflows.
- *Liquidity.* An assessment of the company's liquidity at the end of the period.
- *Going concern.* A statement of the company's ability to remain a going concern.

**Activity 10.4**

Consult your three annual reports and accounts. Find the pages containing the operating and financial review. Read through them carefully, taking your time over the exercise. Then summarize the contents of each OFR.

## Directors' report

The directors of the company are required to publish a report of their activities and responsibilities. This is a statutory requirement of the 1985 Companies Act [s234(1)]:

> *The directors of a company shall for each financial year prepare a report:*
>
> *(a) containing a fair review of the development of the business and its subsidiary undertakings during the financial year and of their position at the end of it; and*
>
> *(b) stating the amount (if any) which they recommend should be paid as dividend and the amount (if any) which they propose to carry to reserves.*

The Act also requires some other matters to be disclosed. For example:

- *Business review.* A fair review of the development of the business, the principal activities of the company, important events, future developments, research and development activities, dividend payments and transfers to reserves.
- *Fixed assets.* Changes to fixed assets and details of differences between book values and market values.
- *Directors.* The names of the directors and their holdings in the company's shares and debentures.
- *Political and charitable donations.* Details of amounts given for political, and charitable purposes.
- *Shares.* Details concerning the purchase of the company's owns shares.
- *Disabled persons.* Information about the employment of disabled persons.
- *Employee involvement.* Details about keeping employees informed and involved in the company's activities.
- *Employees' health, safety and welfare.* This includes what steps the company has taken to protect the employees while they are at work.

In accordance with corporate governance principles (referred to earlier), you may also find other items in a directors' report such as:

- a statement about the application of the principles in the *Combined Code on Corporate Governance* (London Stock Exchange);
- a statement of directors' responsibilities;
- details of internal financial control procedures;
- a short section explaining how the company deals with its shareholders;
- a statement confirming that the company is a going concern.

The statutory and corporate governance items required in a directors' report is quite formidable. This part of the annual report can take up many pages, perhaps between six and twelve. The directors' report for even a relatively small company like J. Smart & Co. (Contractors) plc takes up five pages and contains 22 separate items (see Figure 10.4).

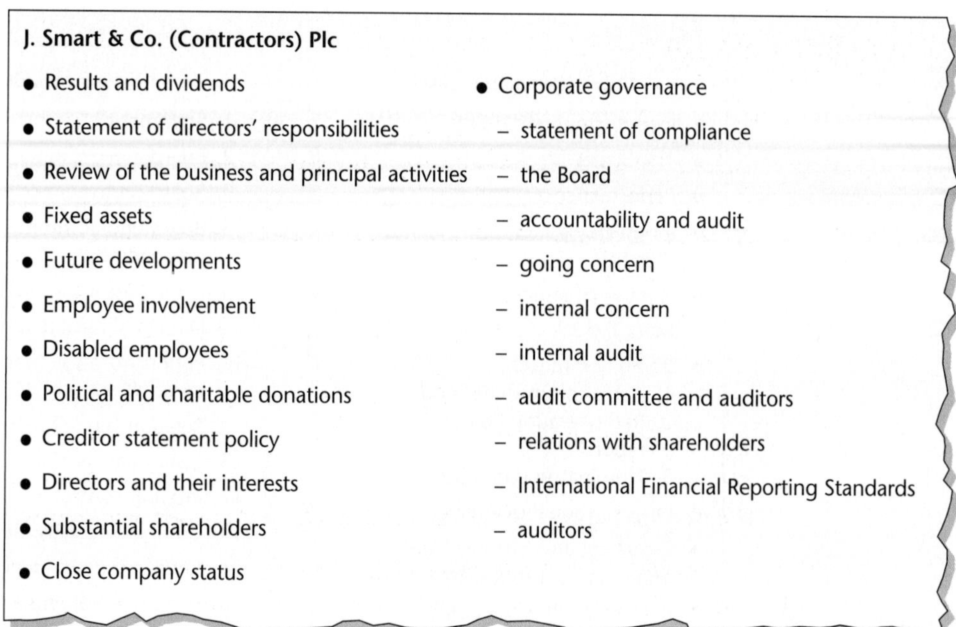

**J. Smart & Co. (Contractors) Plc**

- Results and dividends
- Statement of directors' responsibilities
- Review of the business and principal activities
- Fixed assets
- Future developments
- Employee involvement
- Disabled employees
- Political and charitable donations
- Creditor statement policy
- Directors and their interests
- Substantial shareholders
- Close company status
- Corporate governance
  - statement of compliance
  - the Board
  - accountability and audit
  - going concern
  - internal concern
  - internal audit
  - audit committee and auditors
  - relations with shareholders
  - International Financial Reporting Standards
  - auditors

**Figure 10.4 Directors' report contents: an example**

*Source*: J. Smart & Co. (Contractors) PLC, *Annual Report and Accounts, 2005.*

**Activity 10.5**

Referring to your three annual reports and accounts, read through each directors' report. Then list in three adjacent columns the headings used in each report. Try to list them so that similar headings are opposite each other. Are there any items that are only included by one company? Do the other two companies include such items elsewhere? If so, make a note of the differences.

## Corporate governance

We have already referred to the Cadbury Committee. The idea of 'corporate governance' was taken up by both the business and the financial communities, and the London Stock Exchange has also issued some guidance on the subject in its *Combined Code on Corporate Governance*. As a result you will find that many annual reports and accounts now contain frequent references to corporate governance. Such references may be scattered through the annual report and accounts, and you may find them in the OFR, the directors' report or in a separate statement.

In order to give you some idea of what a separate corporate governance statement may include, Figure 10.5 lists the headings used in two such statements, for Cairn Energy plc and for Devro plc.

As you can see from Figure 10.5 the contents of both Cairn's and Devro's corporate governance statements include some items that some companies might have included in the directors' report. There may be little disagreement about what should be disclosed

| Cairn Energy plc 2005 | Devro plc 2005 |
|---|---|
| • Introductory paragraph | 1. Statement |
| • The Board | 2. Board composition |
| • Performance evaluation | 9. Board performance evaluation |
| • Independence of non-executive directors | 3. Board and committee proceedings |
| • Hamish Grossart | 5. Report from the audit committee |
| • Mark Tyndall | 4. Directors' remuneration |
| • Board committees 1. Audit committee report 2. Remuneration committee report 3. Nominaton committee report | 10. Report from the nomination committee |
| • Organizational planning | 7. Relationship with shareholders |
| • Directors' attendance at board and board committee meetings | 13. Going concern |
| • Relations with shareholders | 12. Internal control |
| • Annual general meeting | 14. Compliance with the code |
| • Directors' responsibility statement | 6. Auditor independence |
| • Going concern | 8. Directors' training and development |
| • Internal control | 11. Financial reporting |
| • Compliance with combined code | |

*Note*: Devro presented its corporate governance statement in numbered paragraphs (as above). These have been placed wherever possible to match with Cairn's paragraph headings.

**Figure 10.5 Corporate governance statements: two examples of contents**

*Source*: Cairn Energy plc, *Annual Report and Accounts*, 2005; Devro plc, *Annual Report and Accounts*, 2005.

but there is obviously an argument about where it should go. This is a good illustration of the difficulties that users of financial statements face when there is inconsistency about the presentation of annual reports and accounts. Indeed, there is a strong case for the IASB to make the requirements prescriptive.

**Activity 10.6**

Once again turn to your collection of annual reports and accounts. Check whether they include a corporate governance statement. Read through them. Then copy the headings into adjacent columns, listing similar items on the same line opposite each other.

## Remuneration report

As part of the corporate governance requirements, companies are expected to set up a remuneration committee. Its purpose is to disclose some details about the directors' remuneration. The committee members should only include non-executive directors and they should not have a personal or financial interest in the outcome of the committee's deliberations.

The remuneration committee is then expected to submit an annual report to the shareholders, either attached to or included within the annual report and accounts. Their report should set out the remuneration policies and criteria for determining the pay of directors. It should also include the pay of each director by name, along with any information about pension entitlements and share options. This information has to be audited.

Remuneration policies are expected to be such that directors are paid a fair rate for the job, the notice attached to service contracts should be for no longer than one year, and compensation schemes should not appear to reward failure. The remuneration report has to state that recognition has been given to these principles. Any departure from them has to be explained.

The contents of the Cairn and Devro remuneration reports are shown in Figure 10.6. Cairn's remuneration report is almost nine pages long, and Devro's four.

As you can see from Figure 10.6 a remuneration report contains a great deal of information about the directors' pay (in all sorts of forms) and the arrangements that they may have to buy shares in the company. Some of it is highly technical and probably most users of accounts are only interested in the directors' basic pay. Cairn's executive directors were paid between £382 991 and £720 237 for 2005, and Devro's executive directors, between £205 000 and £336 000.

**Cairn Energy plc 2005**

- Remuneration committment and advisors
- Remuneration policy
- Basic salary and benefits
- Share options
- Long-term incentive plan
- Annual cash bonus scheme
- Pension scheme
- Service contracts
- Performance graphs
- Information subject to audit (Directors' remuneration, LTIP and other awards)

**Devro plc 2005**

- Opening paragraph
- Composition of the non-exectuive directors' remuneration committee
- Composition of the executive directors' remuneration committee
- Policy on non-executive directors' remuneration
- Policy on executive directors' remuneration
- Performance share plan
- Deferred bonus scheme
- Company pensions policy regarding executive directors
- Company policy on contracts of service
- Directors' detailed emoluments
- Directors' interests
- Compliance

*Note*: Devro's remuneration report headings have been placed wherever possible to match with Cairn's.

**Figure 10.6 Directors' remuneration reports: two examples**

*Source*: Cairn Energy plc, *Annual Report and Accounts*, 2005; Devro plc, *Annual Report and Accounts*, 2005.

**Activity 10.7**

Consult your set of three annual reports and accounts. Check whether a remuneration report is included. Work your way through each one and then list the headings in columns as in Figure 10.6. Try to put similar items on the same line. Note the ones that are specific to one company. List the reasons why you think the company has decided to disclose them.

## Shareholder information

The order and type of the various reports and statements in an annual report and accounts will vary but when you are about halfway through you should come across the financial statements. We will deal with these in the next chapter. Following the 'notes to the accounts' and possibly the audior's report you will probably come cross some miscellaneous information. For convenience we have called this 'shareholder information'.

This part of the annual report contains mainly administrative matters. It is likely to include the following information:

- notice of the annual general meeting (AGM);
- company information (names of senior staff and advisers and company addresses);
- proxy form (to be used if a shareholder cannot attend the AGM);
- shareholder information (the financial calendar, details about dividend payments and shareholder enquiries);
- list of principal companies of the group.

**Activity 10.8**

List the shareholder information contained in each of your three sets of annual reports and accounts.

Note: Such additional information may not always be towards the end of the annual report and accounts.

### ! Questions non-accountants should ask

In previous chapters we have stressed that the detailed accounting information presented to you will have been prepared by your accountants and that you are unlikely to be involved in its preparation. This chapter is different. The matters with which we have been dealing will be the responsibility of a large team of non-accountants with the assistance of the accountants. So what do you need to ask if you are involved in preparing your company's annual report? We suggest the following.

- What information is legally required and where should it be shown?
- What information is an IASB requirement and where should it go?
- What corporate governance information and other matters are we duty bound to disclose and where is the best place to put it?
- Are we sure that any statements made are in line with the financial data presented in the annual accounts?

- Do we have some evidence to justify any predictions we make about our future prospects?
- Are we presenting too much information to our shareholders and, if so, can we cut it back?
- Is the design, format and general content of the material likely to encourage users to read it?
- Do the various reports contain any jargon and, if so, can we either cut it out or reduce it?
- Are the publicity pages likely to annoy our shareholders?

## Conclusion

A company usually publishes an *annual report* and *accounts*. It then supplies a copy to each shareholder and files one with the Registrar of Companies for public inspection. In this chapter we have examined the annual *report* section of an annual report and accounts. The next chapter examines the annual *accounts* section.

In order to make our study of an annual report a little easier, we have suggested that it can be broken down into seven main sections. The first few pages usually contain some introductory material about the company, such as its objectives and a summary of the financial results for the year. In consumer-orientated companies there may also be many pages advertising the company's products. Thereafter the contents and order will vary from company to company.

Most companies include a short chairman's report summarizing the company's progress during the year and its prospects for the future. This will probably be followed by a fairly lengthy and detailed operating and financial review. This is a non-mandatory section recommended by the ASB. It is likely that the directors then present their report. A directors' report is a statutory requirement and the 1985 Companies Act lays down what must be included. These days it may also include a number of 'corporate governance' items so a directors' report probably includes much more than the information required by statute.

The annual report and accounts will almost certainly include a separate corporate governance statement, even if such matters are covered elsewhere in the document. In effect, a corporate governance statement informs readers how the company is operated and how it is managed. Again, as part of corporate governance proposals, there will also be a separate report about the remuneration paid and the terms and conditions of employment of the directors.

The annual reports are usually followed by the annual accounts (discussed in the next chapter), and the annual accounts by various items of 'shareholder information' such as company names and addresses and details of the AGM.

## Key points

1 A company's annual report and accounts contains a great many reports and statements, some of which are voluntary and some of which are mandatory. In this chapter we have dealt with annual reports. These are largely voluntary.

2 It is possible to identify seven main sections of an annual report, although the detailed content and structure varies from company to company. The size of such reports also varies depending partly on the size of the company and partly on its type, e.g. consumer-orientated companies usually include a great deal of publicity material.

3 The introductory section contains some details about the company, a summary of its financial results for the year and possibly some publicity material.

4 The specific reports that follow include a chairman's statement (not mandatory), an operating and financial review statement (recommended by the ASB), a directors' report (statutory), a corporate governance statement and a remuneration report (both required by listed companies).

5 The annual accounts will normally then be presented followed by the last few pages of the overall document containing some miscellaneous information largely for the benefit of the shareholders.

## Check your learning

*The answers to these questions can be found within the text.*

1 List three items that may be included in the introductory section of a company's annual report.

2 What mandatory requirement covers the contents of a chairman's statement?

3 List three items that will normally be included in a chairman's statement.

4 What is an operating and financial review?

5 What statutory and mandatory professional pronouncements require a review to be published?

6 List two items that may be found in the operating section and two items that may be found in the financial review section of an OFR.

7 What statutory and mandatory professional requirements require directors to submit a report to shareholders?

8 Name four items that should be included in a directors' report.

9 What is meant by 'corporate governance'?

10 What is a remuneration report?

11 How has it come about?

12 List four items that it should include.

13 What type of information will normally be included in the last few pages of an annual report?

## News story quiz

*Remember the news story at the beginning of this chapter? Go back to that story and re-read it before answering the following questions.*

On very good authority, companies were expecting that an operating and financial review statement would become a statutory requirement. And then the Government changed its mind upsetting almost everyone – whatever their views.

### Questions

1 Do you think an OFR statement should be made a statutory requirement and if so, for what type of entities?

2 Why do you think it was decided to abandon the decision to make it statutory?

3 What benefits do you think an OFR provides for the users of financial statements, and do the benefits outweigh the costs?

## Tutorial questions

10.1 'A limited liability company's annual report should be made easier to understand for the average shareholder'. Discuss.

10.2 Examine the argument that annual reports are a costly irrelevance because hardly anyone refers to them.

10.3 Should companies be banned from including non-financial data in their annual reports?

Further practice questions, study material and links to relevant sites on the World Wide Web can be found on the website that accompanies this book. The site can be found at www.pearsoned.co.uk/dyson

# Chapter 11 The annual accounts

## At least there will be no new standards . . .

### FDs and investors divided over IFRS

**Nicholas Neveling**

Finance directors and fund managers appear to be completely divided in their opinions on the implementation and usefulness of international accounting standards.

In two separate pieces of research PricewaterhouseCoopers found that while fund managers felt that IFRS had improved transparency and aided investment decisions, FDs believed the new standards had complicated accounts and placed an unnecessary drain on resources.

In a recent MORI poll of 93 FTSE 350 finance executives, PwC found that 85% of the respondents felt that IFRS had made their accounts more difficult to explain. Over a third of the finance directors (40%) said IFRS was unhelpful to the board.

The FDs also bemoaned the cost of the exercise, with some companies spending more than £1m on the transition. Other companies had to fork out at least £500 000 to implement the standards.

Kevin O'Byrne, FD of FTSE 100 group DSGI and one of the most vocal critics, summed up these feelings. 'Anything that adds cost and complexity to the business is not welcome,' he declared.

In an earlier poll of 75 fund managers, responsible for funds worth more than £2 trillion, the view on IFRS was the complete opposite.

More than 66% of the fund managers said the standards had improved company reporting, while 59% welcomed the introduction of fair value accounting. More importantly, one in three fund managers polled said they had changed investment decisions because of IFRS.

Ian Dilks, PwC's IFRS conversions leader, put the difference in opinion down to conversion fatigue among FDs.

'They [FDs] have borne the cost in terms of cash and human resources and clearly recognise there's still much more to do,' Dilks said.

Investors had been more enthusiastic about IFRS because they were 'more likely to have seen the benefits of greater disclosure and international comparability of corporate results' and didn't have to incur the costs of the transition, or struggle with the complex interpretations of the standards.

FDs will be encouraged, however, by a promise from the International Accounting Standards Board this week that it would issue no new major standards before 2009.

The standard-setter said it had announced this timeline to provide companies with a period of stability. The IASB said this would 'benefit the marketplace' without curtailing the IASB's convergence discussions with the US's Financial Accounting Standards Board.

*Accountancy Age*, 27 July 2006.



*Questions relating to this news story can be found on page 214*

## About this chapter

This chapter is a continuation of Chapter 10. There we dealt with the non-statutory reports that you will find in a listed company's annual report and accounts. In this chapter we are going to look at what may be found in its annual *accounts*, i.e. a profit and loss account, a statement of total recognized income and expense, a balance sheet, a cash flow statement, various detailed notes to the accounts, an auditor's report and a non-statutory periodic summary. Figure 11.1 may help to give you an overview of what we will be covering in this chapter.

CONTENTS

| Reports | Accounts |
|---|---|
| • Introductory material | • Consolidated income statement |
| • Chairman's statement | • Statement of recognized income and expense |
| • Operating and financial review | • Consolidated balance sheet |
| • Directors' report | • Consolidated cash flow statement |
| • Corporate governance | • Notes to the financial statements |
| • Remuneration report | • Independent auditor's report |
| • Shareholder information | • Periodic summary |

**Figure 11.1 The accounts section of an annual report and accounts**

**Learning objectives**

By the end of this chapter you should be able to:

- list the main reports and statements that are included in a listed company's published annual accounts;
- outline what each of these reports and statements contain;
- locate additional information in the notes to the accounts;
- extract meaningful and useful information about the company's performance from the various reports and statements;
- evaluate the significance of the auditor's report;
- review the company's financial performance over the medium-to-long-term using a periodic summary.

## Why this chapter is important for non-accountants

The various *reports* included in a company's published annual report and accounts are important because they provided a great deal of background information about the company and its operations. Apart from some information in the directors' report. the law does not require these reports or their contents to be disclosed. Similarly, while the various standard setting bodies may desire certain types of information to be published, they do not necessarily make it mandatory.

The annual accounts section is different – most of what it contains is required by law or by the standard-setting bodies (the main exception being a periodic summary). The information that it contains is considered vital because it tells shareholders and other users what profit the company has made, what its cash flow is like, what assets it owns and what liabilities it has incurred. Such information can provide the basis for a rigorous analysis of the company's performance in order to help assess its future prospects.

In the next chapter we shall explain how you can go about undertaking such an analysis. Accountants refer to it as 'interpreting the accountants', or as the man in the street might say, 'reading between the lines of the balance sheet'. This chapter provides you with the basic information that will enable you to interpret a set of accounts. It is important that you work your way through this chapter if you are going to be able to cope with the next one.

Of course we are not suggesting that you do this just as a book exercise. You will find that at some time in your future career you will almost certainly have to interpret a set of accounts. It may even be useful in your private life if, for example, you decide to buy some shares in a company and you want to know whether it might be a good buy or not. You won't be able to do that if its published accounts are a complete mystery to you. By the end of this chapter you will not be in that position.

**Activity 11.1**

Turn to the three sets of the annual report and accounts that you used in the previous chapter. Find out what accounts are included in each of them and then list their titles in three adjacent columns.

## Setting the scene

### International financial reporting standards

Unlike most of the earlier chapters in this book, we are dealing here with the *published* accounts of a limited liability company. And if the accounts have been published then that means that the company is *listed*, i.e. it is a public limited liability company and you can buy its shares on the Stock Exchange. We will also assume that it is incorporated in the United Kingdom. However, most of the points that we cover in this chapter are relevant even if the company is incorporated in one of the other 26 member countries of the European Union.

It is important that we make the above assumptions clear because it then follows that the company's accounts will be published under British company law (i.e. the Companies Act 1985) and in accordance with International Financial Reporting Standards (IFRS). We mentioned in Chapter 9 that from 2005 onwards listed companies in the EU are required to use IFRSs and *not* their own country's accounting standards. This means that in the UK the ASB's accounting standards no longer apply to a listed company – the IASB's programme takes precedence.

From your own point of view as a non-accountant, what difference does this make? In brief, when you are dealing with listed companies you will need to adapt some of the accounting knowledge that you have gained so far from this book so that it meets IASB requirements and not ASB ones. Fortunately, you will not need to get involved in the complex accounting changes that professionally qualified accountants have had to cope with over the last few years. However, you will need to note the following:

- the accounting treatment of certain accounting matters is different, e.g. proposed dividends at the end of a financial year are not accrued;
- the terminology used may be different, e.g. an income statement instead of a profit and loss account;
- there may be slightly different ways of presenting and sectionalizing the accounts, although almost certainly the vertical format will have been adopted.

The main requirements affecting the presentation of published accounts under the IASB programme may be found in *IAS 1* (*Presentation of Financial Statements*), *IAS 7* (*Cash Flow Statements*), *IAS 27* (*Consolidated and Separate Financial Statements*), and *IAS 28* (*Investments in Associates*). All IASs will eventually be replaced by IFRSs but the old IASs remain valid until that happens.

There are also two other matters that will be new to you when you come across a set of published accounts (although these have not come about as a result of adopting the international accounting standards' programme):

- corresponding figures for the preceding year will be disclosed;
- most published accounts are published on a *group* basis.

We deal with group accounts in a little more detail below.

## Group accounts

A group of companies is like a family. One company (say Company A) may buy shares in another company (say Company B). When Company A owns more than 50 per cent of the voting shares in Company B, B becomes a *subsidiary* of A. If A were to own more than 20 per cent but less than 50 per cent of the voting shares in B, B would be known as an *associated company* of A. In effect, B is considered to be the offspring of A. Of course B might have children of its own, say Company C and Company D. So C and D become part of the family, i.e. part of the A group of companies. An example of a group structure is shown in Figure 11.2

The main significance of these relationships is that you can expect the published accounts to be those of the *group*, i.e. in effect, as though it were one entity so that any

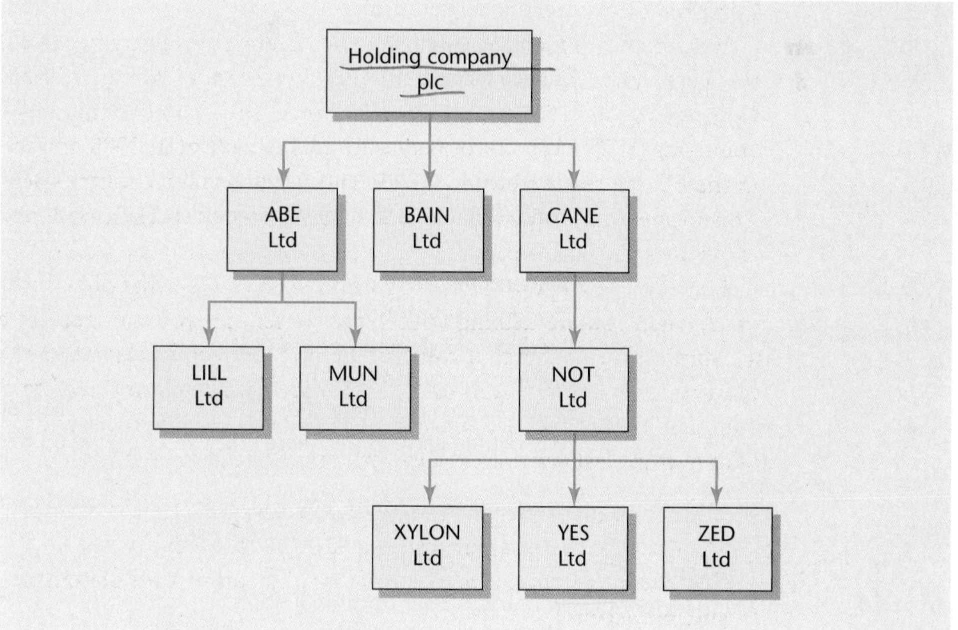


**Figure 11.2 A group of companies**

intergroup activities (such as sales between group companies or transfers of funds) are ignored. This involves adding together all the accounts of the group companies, or *consolidating* them. Using IASB terminology you can, therefore, expect a published set of accounts to include a *consolidated* income statement, a *consolidated* statement of recognized income and expense, a *consolidated* balance sheet and a *consolidated* cash flow statement. These are now considered in turn in the following sections.

## Consolidated income statement

An example of a consolidated income statement extracted from A. G. Barr plc's annual report and accounts for the year to 28 January 2006 prepared under IASB requirements is shown in Example 11.1.

### Example 11.1 A consolidated income statement

**A.G. Barr plc**
**Consolidated income statement for the year to 28 January 2006**

| | *£000* |
|---|---|
| Revenue (1) | 128 760 |
| Cost of sales (2) | 63 398 |
| Gross profit (3) | 65 362 |
| Net operating expenses (4) | 48 422 |
| Operating profit before exceptional items (5) | 16 940 |
| Exceptional items (6) | (533) |
| Operating profit (7) | 16 407 |
| Finance income (8) | 1,557 |
| Finance costs (9) | (583) |
| Profit on ordinary activities before tax (10) | 17 381 |
| Tax on profit on ordinary activities (11) | 5,128 |
| Profit attributable to equity shareholders (12) | 12 253 |
| Dividend per share paid (13) | 29.25p |
| Dividend paid (£000) (14) | 5,628 |
| Dividend per share proposed (15) | 22.00p |
| Dividend proposed (£000) (16) | 4,282 |
| Basic earnings per share (17) | 65.06p |
| Fully diluted earning per share (18) | 63.87p |

A.G. Barr plc, *Annual Report and Accounts, 2006.*

*Notes*:
1 The numbers in brackets refer to tutorial notes.
2 References to the formal notes, the notes themselves, and the Group's restated consolidated income statement for 2005 have not been reproduced in the above example.

*Tutorial notes to Example 11.1*

1 *Revenue.* Revenue is defined as the net invoiced sales value exclusive of value added tax of goods and services supplied to external customers during the year. All the revenue earned for the year was derived from the continuing operations of the group, i.e. there was no revenue from activities that ceased during the year, and all the revenue came from one business segment.

2 *Cost of sales.* These are details disclosed of what is included in this figure except that it does not include distribution costs and administration expenses (see note 4 below). As there are no further operating expenses we can assume that it includes the cost of purchasing raw materials and the production costs.

3 *Gross profit.* Gross profit is normally defined as the difference between the sales revenue and the cost of purchases (after allowing for opening and closing stocks). It is likely that production costs are also included in most published accounts.

4 *Net operating expenses.* There are only two items included in net operating expenses – distribution costs and administrative expenses. Barr discloses them separately (as is required) in a formal note to the accounts instead of on the face of the 'consolidated income statement', i.e. the group profit and loss account.

5 *Operating profit before exceptional items.* This is the profit that the company has earned during the year on its normal manufacturing and selling activities.

6 *Exceptional items.* Exceptional items are unusual items of either income or expenditure earned or incurred during the year on ordinary activities that are not expected to occur again in subsequent years. Barr's exceptional items for 2006 relate to a reorganization of its sales and logistics facilities in Scotland.

7 *Operating profit.* This is the amount of profit the company has earned for the year on all its operating activities after allowing for any exceptional items.

8 *Finance income.* Barr describes this as 'interest receivable'. It could include, for example, bank interest.

9 *Finance costs.* Finance costs include interest payable and charges relating to the cost of retirement and post-employment benefit schemes.

10 *Profit on ordinary activities before tax.* This is the amount of profit Barr made on all of its activities for the year. It is a subtotal.

11 *Tax on profit on ordinary activities.* The tax on the profit on ordinary activities is mainly corporation tax but it also includes some technical accounting adjustments affecting the taxation charge for the current year.

12 *Profit attributable to equity shareholders.* This is another subtotal. It shows what amount could be distributed to the company's shareholders if all the year's profit was paid out.

13 *Dividend per share paid.* A company would not normally pay out all that it had earned during the year. This figure shows what shareholders received in dividends during 2006 for each share that they held. It includes some dividends that relate to the previous year's results as well as something on account (an 'interim' dividend) for the current year.

14 *Dividend paid.* This is the total amount of what the company actually paid out in dividends during the year, i.e. last year's 'final' dividend plus this year's interim dividend.

15 *Dividend per share proposed.* The directors propose to pay a final dividend for this year if the shareholders give their approval. It will amount to 22.00p for every share that a shareholder holds.

16 *Dividend proposed.* This is the total cost of the proposed 'final' dividend for 2006.

*Tutorial notes to Example 11.1 continued*

17 *Basic earnings per share.* This figure is calculated by taking the profit attributable to shareholders and dividing it by the weighted average number of ordinary shares in issue during the year.

18 *Fully diluted earnings per share.* This is similar to the basic earnings per share, except that it may include an allowance for some shares that *might* be issued if the right to take them up is exercised.

Barr has presented its consolidated income statement by aggregating its expenses according to *function*, i.e. by itemizing the cost of sales, distribution costs and administrative expenses. This is known as the *operational* format and most companies adopt it. An alternative format is to aggregate expenses according to their *nature* by itemizing changes in inventories of finished goods and work in progress, raw materials and consumables, depreciation and amortization expenses, and other operating expenses. This is known as the *type of expenditure* format. The chances are that you will not come across this format very often. There is no difference in presentation between the two formats after the operating profit line.

**Activity 11.2**

Refer to your three sets of annual accounts and turn to the page that includes the consolidated income statement. Read down through the statement on a line-by-line basis. If you do not understand a particular item look it up in the 'notes to the accounts'. Compare your three statements with Example 11.1 and list any significant differences between them.

## Statement of recognized income and expense

The ASB's *FRS 3* requires relevant entities to prepare a statement called a *statement of total recognized gains and losses.* The IASB's *IAS 1* requires a similar statement which it calls a *statement of changes in equity,* but we prefer to adopt the more common term a *statement of recognized income and expense.* This statement is presented immediately following the income statement. It should include *all* the gains and losses that the company has made during the year and not just those that have been disclosed in the income statement. Gains or losses on the revaluation of property, for example, would not normally be taken to the income statement until they have been realized, i.e. only when the property has been sold. So until they are, any gains or losses should be shown in the statement of recognized income and expenses.

Other income and expense items that are not reflected in the income statement but which affect the shareholders' equity include exchange differences on the translation of foreign operations, gains on the sales of investments 'available-for-sale' and other non-realized gains and losses. You will also find that in this statement the profit for the year has been transferred to it from the income statement.

Barr's consolidated statement of recognized income and expense for 2006 is shown in Example 11.2.

Example 11.2

## A consolidated statement of recognized income and expense

**A.G. Barr plc**

**Statement of recognized income and expense for the year to 28 January 2006**

| | *£000* |
|---|---|
| Actuarial (cost)/gain recognized on defined benefit pension plans (1) | (2 235) |
| Deferred tax relating to defined benefit pension plans (1) | 671 |
| **Net (expense)/income recognized directly in equity** (1) | (1 564) |
| Profit for the period (2) | 12 253 |
| **Total recognized income and expense for the period** (3) | **10 689** |
| **Attributable to equity shareholders** (3) | **10 689** |

A.G. Barr plc, *Annual Report and Accounts, 2006.*

*Notes*:

1 The number in brackets refer to the tutorial notes.

2 Reference to the formal notes, the notes themselves and the restated 2005 results have not been reproduced in the above example.

*Tutorial notes to Example 11.2*

1 These three items relate to some highly complicated technical adjustments to the Group's pension scheme arrangements as a result of a deficit on its 'defined benefit plan'. In effect £1 564 000 is being taken out of its total retained earnings in order to cover some of the outstanding deficit.

2 This is the profit attributable to the equity shareholders obtained from the consolidated income statement (see Example 11.2, tutorial note 12).

3 The £10 689 000 is a total reflecting all the adjustments made in the Statement of recognized income and expenditure all of which is due to the equity (i.e. the ordinary) shareholders as the Group does not have any other types of shareholders. This amount is included in 'retained earnings' on the balance sheet although it is shown in detail and not as a net figure.

Activity 11.3

Look up the statement of recognized income and expense in each of your three accounts. List all the various items (there should not be many) in each statement in adjacent columns.

## Consolidated balance sheet

Most published balance sheets are now presented in the vertical format (like the other financial statements), i.e. the items are listed on a line-by-line basis from the top of the page to the bottom. It is also customary to group the items into various categories, such as fixed assets and current assets.

The IASB has adopted this approach. *IAS 1* requires current assets to be separated from non-current assets and liabilities but it does not prescribe a particular format. So you can expect variations in the way that companies do present the information that *must* be disclosed on the face of the balance sheet. Generally, however, you will probably find that most companies start with the non-current assets, followed by the current assets to arrive at *total assets.* This will then be followed in sequence by three sections listing the capital and reserves, the non-current liabilities and the current liabilities – the total of which will be described as the *total equity and liabilities.* This balance should, of course, be the same as the total assets.

Barr's consolidated balance sheet is shown in Example 11.3. We have not included the *company's* balance sheet.

Example 11.3

## A consolidated balance sheet

**A.G. Barr plc**

**Group balance sheet for the year to 28 January 2006**

| | £000 | |
|---|---|---|
| **Non-current assets** (1) | | |
| Property, plant and equipment (2) | 34 932 | |
| Deferred tax assets (3) | 5 777 | |
| | 40 709 | (4) |
| **Current assets** (5) | | |
| Inventories (6) | 8 274 | |
| Trade and other receivables (7) | 29 546 | |
| Cash at bank (8) | 31 412 | |
| Assets classified as held for sale (9) | 937 | |
| | 70 169 | (10) |
| **Total assets** (11) | 110 878 | |
| **Current liabilities** (12) | | |
| Trade and other payables (13) | 22 083 | |
| Current tax (14) | 1 962 | |
| | 24 045 | (15) |
| **Non-current liabilities** (16) | | |
| Deferred income (17) | 611 | |
| Deferred tax liabilities (18) | 5 030 | |
| Retirement benefit obligations (19) | 16 248 | |
| | 21 889 | (20) |

| **Capital and reserves attributable to equity shareholders** (21) | | |
|---|---|---|
| Called-up share capital (22) | 4865 | |
| Share premium account (23) | 905 | |
| Own shares held (24) | (4298) | |
| Share options reserve (25) | 1416 | |
| Retained earnings (26) | 62056 | |
| | 64944 | (27) |
| Total equity and liabilities | 110878 | (28) |

A.G. Barr plc, *Annual Report and Accounts, 2006.*

*Notes*:
1 The numbes in brackets refer to tutorial notes.
2 Reference to the formal notes, the notes themselves, the restated 2005 results and the Company's balance sheet have not been reproduced in the above example.

***Tutorial notes to Example 11.3***

1 This is just another term for 'fixed assets'.

2 Details of the property, plant and equipment, including the original cost, accumulated depreciation and the net book value, are shown in a one-and-a-half page detailed formal note to the accounts.

3 Deferred taxation adjustments are extremely complex. They arise basically because there is often a difference between what a company may set aside for taxation based on the accounting profit for the year and the definition of profit that the Inland Revenue uses. Often the tax due for a particular year is less than the accounting profit would indicate but sometimes it is more. In order to smooth out these fluctuations it is customary to set aside a provision for corporation tax that may be due to be paid at some time in the future. Depending on whether the company is likely either to be owed *by* or owe *to* the Inland Revenue, various 'asset' or 'liability' balances may occur within the book-keeping system. Barr has both 'deferred tax assets' and 'deferred tax' liabilities (see tutorial note 18).

4 The total net book value of all the Group's fixed assets.

5 This term is identical to the one used in previous chapters.

6 The American term for 'stocks'.

7 Trade debtors, other debtors and prepayments.

8 This includes physical cash and short-term accounts kept at the bank.

9 These assets relate to surplus land that is expected to be sold in the near future.

10 The total of all the current assets.

11 The total of all the non-current assets and current assets.

12 Another term whose definition is identical to the one used in previous chapters.

13 This item includes trade creditors, various taxes and social security costs due, and accruals.

14 No details are given about this balance. It presumably relates to some amount for corporation tax due for payment within the next twelve months as 'other taxes' have been included in the previous item.

15 The total of all the current liabilities.

*Tutorial notes to Example 11.3 continued*

16 Liabilities that do not have to be paid for at least twelve months.

17 No indication is given about what is meant by 'deferred income'. It may relate to income from some sales or other types of revenue raising activities that is expected to be received beyond the next twelve months.

18 See note 3.

19 Another complicated pension balance. It relates to the difference between the 'present value of funded obligations' and the 'fair value of plan assets'. In other words the Group's pension scheme is underfunded.

20 The total of all the non-current liabilities.

21 This group of liabilities shows in detail the source of long-term funding of the Group.

22 The amount of ordinary share capital contributed by the shareholders (there are no other types of shares).

23 The extra amount that the shareholders were prepared to pay for their shares above their nominal value. No dividend can be paid on this amount and its use is strictly limited by the Companies Act 1985.

24 A company is permitted to buy back some of its own shares. This means that, *caeteris paribus*, a higher dividend can be paid to the remaining shareholders. Notice that the amount is negative, i.e. it is a debit balance.

25 No explanation is given in the accounts about this amount but the Group is probably setting aside funds so that it can buy back more of its own shares.

26 This large amount (nearly 96% of the total capital and reserves attributable to equity shareholders) is the accumulated amount of profits built up over many years that have not been paid out to shareholders as dividends.

27 The total of all the 'capital and reserves attributable to equity shareholders' balances.

28 The total of the non-current liabilities section and the capital and reserves attributable to equity shareholders. It balances with the total assets (see note 11).

**Activity 11.4**

Referring to your set of three published accounts, work your way down each of the three consolidated balance sheets. If you do not understand what any of the items mean, consult the 'notes to the accounts'. Then compare Barr's main section headings and those in each of your three balance sheets. Note any differences in the description of the headings and the order in which they are presented. Assuming that there are some differences between them, which format do you think is the easiest to follow?

## Consolidated cash flow statement

The IASB requires companies to prepare a CFS. The details are contained in *IAS 7*. As you might expect by now, there are some differences between the UK requirement (under *FRS 1*) and *IAS 7* involving definitions, terminology and format.

Perhaps the most important difference is what is meant by 'cash'. In paragraph 2, *FRS 1* defines cash as follows:

> *cash-in-hand and deposits repayable on demand with any qualifying financial institution, less overdrafts from any qualifying institution repayable on demand.*

This is immediately followed by what is meant by 'deposits':

> *deposits are repayable on demand if they can be withdrawn at any time without notice and without penalty or if a maturity or period of notice of not more than 24 hours or one working day has been agreed.*

Before confirming that:

> *cash includes cash-in-hand and deposits denominated in foreign currencies.*

*IAS 7*'s definition of 'cash is much wider because it includes what it calls 'cash equivalents' (7.7-8): These are:

> *short-term, highly liquid investments that are readily convertible to known amounts of cash and subject to insignificant risk of changes in value.*

You should also note two other differences:

- *IAS 7* only requires cash flows to be itemized under three headings (instead of *FRS 1*'s eight) – cash flows from operating activities, cash flows from investing activities and cash flows from financing activities.
- No reconciliation of the movement in cash flows to the movement in net debt is required.

Otherwise, the preparation and format required under *IAS 7* is very similar to that of *FRS 1*. Barr's consolidated cash flow statement is shown in Example 11.4.

**Example 11.4**

## A consolidated cash flow statement

**A.G. Barr plc**
**Cash flow statement for the year ended 28 January 2006**

| | *£000* |
|---|---|
| **Operating activities** | |
| Profit on ordinary activities before tax | 17 381 |
| Interest receivable | (1 557) |
| Interest payable | 583 |
| Depreciation of property, plant and equipment | 5 756 |
| Share option costs | 299 |
| Gain on sale of property, plant and equipment | (215) |
| Government grants written back | (8) |
| **Operating cash flows before movements in working capital** | 22 239 |
| Decrease in inventories | 898 |
| Increase in receivables | (1 473) |
| **Increase in payables** | 255 |
| Decrease in retirement benefit obligations | (3 031) |

**Example 11.4** *continued*

| | |
|---|---|
| **Cash generated by operations** | 18 888 |
| Tax on profit paid | (4 876) |
| **Net cash from operating activities** | 14 012 |
| **Investing activities** | |
| Proceeds on sale of property, plant and equipment | 514 |
| Purchase of property, plant and equipment | (12 029) |
| Interest received | 1 557 |
| Interest paid | (583) |
| **Net cash used in investing activities** | (10 541) |
| **Financing activities** | |
| Purchase of own shares | (3 149) |
| Sale of own shares | 1 760 |
| Dividends paid | (5 628) |
| **Net cash used in financing activities** | (7 017) |
| **Net (decrease)/increase in cash** | (3 546) |
| **Cash at beginning of period** | 34 958 |
| **Cash at end of period** | 31 412 |

A.G. Barr plc, *Annual Report and Accounts, 2006.*

*Notes*:
The restated 2005 results and the Company's cash flow statement have not been reproduced in the above example.

**Activity 11.5**

Turn to the cash flow statements in each of your three accounts. Examine the terminology, the presentations and layout of each CFS along with Barr's. Are there any substantial differences between the four CFSs? If there are, make a note of them. Then extract the two or three most significant items in each CFS that have resulted in an increase or a decrease in cash and cash equivalents during the year.

## Notes to the financial statements

The income statement, the statement of recognized income and expense and the balance sheet are usually supported by a great deal of additional notes. These notes serve two main purposes:

- they avoid too much detail being shown on the face of the financial statements;
- they make it easier to provide some supplementary information.

Both legislative and IASB requirements specify what information *must* be disclosed on the face of the financial statements. It does not amount to much and most companies usually go well beyond what is required. Even so, the notes can stretch to many pages. Barr's 2006 accounts, for example, have three pages of notes outlining its 'accounting policies', 17 pages of 'notes to the accounts' and four pages of notes described as 'reconciliations of UK-GAAP to IFRS', a total of 24 pages. Barr is not a particularly large company, its operations are not complex and it is based largely in the UK. With a large complex international company you could expect even more pages of notes. An oil company like Cairn Energy, for example, has 38 pages of notes in its 2005 accounts.

So although most companies probably publish the minimum information required by law and by the IASB, their annual accounts still contain a great deal of detail much of which is not easy to absorb or to understand. In its 1999 *Statement of Principles for Financial Reporting* the ASB expected financial information to be *understandable*, but only if users had:

> *a reasonable knowledge of business and economic activities and accounting and a willingness to study with reasonable diligence the information provided.*

After studying the information in some financial statements (no doubt reasonably diligently) you could perhaps be forgiven if you felt that the ASB was being just a little bit too optimistic in its expectations.

## Independent auditor's report

The placement of the independent (i.e. external) auditor's report will vary from company to company. Some companies include it before the financial statements, while others include it after the 'notes to the accounts'.

By law, the external auditors are required to report to the shareholders. Their report will be short – probably no longer than one page – and unless some highly unusual events have taken place, most auditor's reports will be very similar.

Barr's independent auditor's report is reproduced in Figure 11.3. Read through it very carefully.

The following features of Barr's report are of particular interest.

1 The independent auditor has audited not only the financial statements but also parts of the director's remuneration report.
2 There is quite a long statement explaining the respective responsibilities of the directors and of the auditor.
3 The audit has been conducted on the basis of international auditing standards.
4 The auditor explains what was involved in doing the audit.
5 The auditor confirms that the group and the company's financial statements give a 'true and fair' view for the period in question.
6 This opinion is in accordance with IFRS requirements and the provision of the 1985 Companies Act.

**Activity 11.6**

Find the auditor's report in each of your three accounts. Read through them. Does the auditor state that the accounts represent a 'true and fair' view or are there any qualifications or reservations about something in the financial statements? If there are any qualifications (probably introduced by the phrase 'except for ...'), list them.

## Independent Auditor's Report to the Members of A.G. BARR plc

We have audited the group and parent company financial statements on pages 32 to 58. We have also audited the information in the Directors' Remuneration Report that is described as having been audited.

The report is made solely to the company's members, as a body, in accordance with section 235 of the Companies Act 1985. Our audit work has been undertaken so that we might state to the company's members those matters we are required to state to them in an auditor's report and for no other purpose. To the fullest extent permitted by law, we do not accept or assume responsibility to anyone other than the company and the company's members as a body, for our audit work, for this report, or for the opinions we have formed.

**Respective responsibilities of directors and auditors**
The directors' responsibilities for preparing the annual report, the Directors' Remuneration Report and the financial statements in accordance with applicable law and those International Financial Reporting Standards (IFRSs) adopted for use in the European Union are set out in the Statement of Directors' Responsibilities.

Our responsibility is to audit the financial statements and the part of the Directors' Remuneration Report to be audited in accordance with relevant legal and regulatory requirements and International Standards on Auditing (UK and Ireland).

We report to you our opinion as to whether the financial statements give a true and fair view and whether the financial statements and the part of the Directors' Remuneration Report to be audited have been properly prepared in acordance with the Companies Act 1985 and Article 4 of the IAS Regulation. We also report to you if, in our opinion, the Directors' Report is not consistent with the financial statements, if the company has not kept proper accounting records, if we have not received all the information and explanations we require for our audit, or if information specified by law regarding directors' remuneration and other transactions is not disclosed.

We review whether the Corporate Governance Statement reflects the company's compliance with the nine provisions of the 2003 FRC Combined Code specified for our review by the Listing Rules of the Financial Services Authority, and we report if it does not. We are not required to consider whether the board's statement on internal control cover all risk and controls, or form an opinion on the effectiveness of the group's corporate governance procedures of its risk and control procedures.

We read other information contained in the annual report and consider whether it is consistent with the audited financial statements. The other information comprises only the Directors' Report, the unaudited part of the Directors' Remuneration Report, the Chairman's Statement, the Operating and Financial Review and the Corporate Governance Statement. We consider the implications for our report if we become aware of any apparent misstatements or material inconsistencies with the financial statements. Our responsibilities do not extend to any other information.

**Base of audit opinion**
We consider our audit in accordance with International Standards on Auditing (UK and Ireland) issued by the Auditing Practices Board. An audit includes examination, on a test basis, of evidence relevant to the amounts and disclosures in the financial statements and the part of the Directors' Remuneration Report to be audited. It also includes an assessment of the significant estimates and judgements made by the directors in the preparation of the financial statements, and of whether the accounting policies are appropriate to the group's and company's circumstances, consistently applied and adequately disclosed.

We planned and performed our audit so as to obtain all the information and explanations which we considered necessary in order to provide us with sufficient evidence to give reasonable assurance that the financial statements and the part of the Directors' Remuneration Report to be audited are free from material misstatement, whether caused by fraud or other irregularity or error. In forming our opinion we also evaluated the overall adequacy of the presentation of information in the financial statements and the part of the Directors' Remuneration Report to be audited.

**Opinion**
In our opinion:

- the group financial statements give a true and fair view, in accordance with those IFRSs adopted for use in the European Union, of the state of the group's affairs as at 28th January, 2006 and of its profits for the year then ended;
- the parent company financial statements give a true and fair view in accordance with those IFRSs adopted for use in the European Union as applied in accordance with the provisions of the Companies Act, 1985, of the state of the parent company's affairs as at 28th January, 2006; and
- the financial statements and the part of the Directors' Remuneration Report to be audited have been properly prepared in accordance with the Companies Act 1985 and Article 4 of the IAS Regulation.

**Separate opinion in relation to IFRSs**
As explained in the acounting policies, the group in addition to complying with its legal obligation to comply with those IFRSs adopted for use in the European Union, has also complied with the IFRSs as issued by the International Accounting Standards Board.

In our opinion the group financial statements give a true and fair view, in accordance with IFRS, of the state of the group's affairs as at 28th January, 2006 and of its profit for the year then ended.

*Baker Tilly*

BAKER TILLY
REGISTERED AUDITOR
CHARTERED ACCOUNTANTS
BRECKENRIDGE HOUSE
274 SAUCHIEHALL STREET
GLASGOW G2 3EH
28TH MARCH, 2006

**Figure 11.3 An example of an independent auditor's report**

*Source*: A.G. Barr plc, Barr Soft Drinks, *Annual Report and Accounts, 2006*.

## Periodic summary

Many companies include a periodic summary, as part of their accounts, covering a period of five or even ten years. It will usually be found after the 'notes to the accounts'.

As there are no statutory or IASB requirements to produce such a summary companies are free to decide whether to publish one and, what to include in it. You will probably find, sales revenue, gross profit, profit before and after tax and dividends paid in most periodic summaries. You might also find some items extracted from the balance sheet such as fixed assets, some non-current liabilities and retained earnings.

Although periodic statements are limited in scope they can help users to assess the company's performance over a much longer period than the two years that are legally required (the current year's result and the previous one). This is a significant point because conventional financial statements prepared on an annual basis may not suit some entities whose activities are much more long-term. As a result, the preparation of financial statements on such a short-term basis may be highly misleading. Periodic summaries may help, therefore, to give a much fairer picture of the company's affairs, but there do not appear to be any current plans to make them mandatory.

Barr's 'review of trading results' (as it is described) is shown in Example 11.5.

**Example 11.5**

### A periodic summary

**A.G. Barr plc**
**Review of trading results for the five-year period 2001 to 2006**

| | Prepared under IFRS | | Prepared under UK-GAAP | | |
|---|---|---|---|---|---|
| | **2006** | 2005 | 2004 | 2003 | 2002 |
| | **£000** | £000 | £000 | £000 | £000 |
| **Revenue** | **128 760** | 127 222 | 125 235 | 120 005 | 116 261 |
| **Operating profit before exceptional items** | **16 940** | 15 629 | 13 198 | 11 873 | 10 487 |
| **Exceptional items** | **533** | – | – | – | – |
| **Operating profit after exceptional items** | **16 407** | 15 629 | 13 198 | 11 873 | 10 487 |
| Interest receivable | **1 557** | 1 288 | 599 | 340 | 253 |
| Interest payable | **(583)** | (630) | – | – | – |
| Interest | **974** | 658 | 599 | 340 | 253 |
| **Profit on ordinary activities before tax** | **17 381** | 16 287 | 13 797 | 12 213 | 10 740 |
| Tax on profit on ordinary activities | **(5 128)** | (4 585) | (4 085) | (3 693) | (3 254) |
| **Profit on ordinary activities after tax** | **12 253** | 11 702 | 9 712 | 8 520 | 7 486 |
| **Earning per share on issued share capital** | **62.96p** | 60.13p | 49.90p | 43.78p | 38.47p |
| **Dividends recognized as an appropriation in the year** | **29.25p** | 26.25p | 25.50p | 23.10p | 21.60p |

A.G. Barr plc, *Annual Report and Accounts, 2006.*

**Example 11.5 continued**

*Notes:*

1 The earnings per share on issued share capital for each period has been calculated to reflect the shares in issue at 28 January 2006.

2 Three main adjustments were required in order to restate UK-GAAP figures from 2002 to 2004 into IFRS. The first relates to share options awards and share awards, the second involves final salary pension schemes, and the third requires *disclosure* of proposed dividends at the end of the year instead of them being treated as a liability. The first two adjustments are fairly technical. The third is a change in UK accounting custom and practice.

### Questions non-accountants should ask

It is probably only at a very senior level that you would be in a position to ask questions about the company's draft annual report and accounts prepared for publication, but similar questions might apply to smaller non-listed companies.

- Are we absolutely confident that we have complied with the minimum statutory and mandatory accounting statements?
- Can we reduce the number of pages without missing out any essential information?
- Would it be possible to use different formats so that users not trained in accounting can follow them more easily?
- Can any item be left out to make it easier for users to understand?
- Could we avoid professional jargon and substitute terms that the layperson would understand?

## Conclusion

In this chapter we have examined the accounts section of a listed company's annual report and accounts. We have suggested that it is possible to group the various types of financial statements into seven major categories:

- income statement
- statement of recognized income and expense
- balance sheet
- cash flow statement
- notes to the accounts
- auditor's report
- periodic summary.

All of these statements are mandatory apart from the periodic summary because listed companies are required to prepare an annual financial statement in accordance with European company law as enacted in their own country (in the UK, the Companies Act 1985), IFRSs and with those international accounting standards not yet replaced.

Most (if not all) listed companies will form part of a group, so their financial statements will be prefaced by the term 'consolidated', or sometimes 'group'.

## Key points

1. An annual report and accounts contains a great many statements but those relating to the accounts (often referred to as the 'financial statements') may take up to about half of the entire contents.
2. The accounts section will include an income statement, a statement of recognized income and expense, a balance sheet (two if the accounts deal with a group of companies), a cash flow statement, notes to the accounts, an auditor's report and a periodic summary.
3. In the case of UK companies, the statutory and mandatory requirements are contained in the Companies Act 1985 and the accounting standards programme of the IASB. Only the periodic summary is a voluntary statement.
4. *IAS 1* specifies the format of the income statement and the balance sheet, the contents and the sectional heading. *IAS 7* covers the cash flow statement.
5. A minimum amount of information is usually shown on the face of the various statements with the remaining mandatory information being shown in notes to the accounts.

## Check your learning

*The answers to these questions can be found within the text.*

1. What is meant by 'disclosure'?
2. What is a group of companies?
3. What are consolidated accounts?
4. Which main international accounting standard covers the presentation of accounts?
5. What is meant by the 'operational' and 'type of expenditure' formats for the presentation of the income statement?
6. Can a company charge any proposed dividends to its income statement?
7. Name two items that you might find in a statement of recognized income and expense.
8. What is meant by the term 'current' and 'non-current' used in a company's balance sheet?
9. Give an example of a non-current liability.
10. What international accounting standard covers the preparation of a listed company's cash flow statement?
11. How many main headings are there in a listed company's cash flow statement?
12. Why are 'notes to the accounts' used?
13. What opinion does an independent auditor usually express about a company's financial statements?
14. What mandatory requirements cover the publication of a periodic summary statement?

## News story quiz

*Remember the news story at the beginning of this chapter? Go back to that story and re-read it before answering the following questions.*

The switch to international financial reporting standards throughout the European Union was a considerable breakthrough towards the use of such standards on a worldwide basis. As this article indicates, major changes can be costly in terms of time, money and pride – and not least in the UK which previously already had its own well-developed accounting standards programme.

### Questions

1 What objections to the introduction of IFRSs can you identify in the article?

2 What benefits do there appear to have been?

3 Why might opinion be divided between finance directors and fund managers?

4 Do you think that the switch to IFRSs has been beneficial?

5 What are your reasons for your view?

## Tutorial questions

11.1 What items could be taken out of a listed company's published income statement and its balance sheet without affecting the usefulness of such statements?

11.2 Describe what is meant by a 'qualified audit report' illustrating your answer with appropriate examples.

11.3 Suggest ten items that should be disclosed in a listed company's periodic summary statement.

**Further practice questions, study material and links to relevant sites on the World Wide Web can be found on the website that accompanies this book. The site can be found at www.pearsoned.co.uk/dyson**

Chapter 12

# Interpretation of accounts

## But exactly what is profiteering ...?

# Shell under fire as oil price boom results in UK's biggest ever profit

### CEO denies profiteering at expense of consumers Unions, activists and buyers call for windfall tax

**Terry Macalister**

Shell yesterday announced the biggest ever profits by a British company – £1.5m an hour – on the back of soaring oil prices and came under immediate attack from consumers, trade unions and green groups.

Chief executive Jeroen van der Veer insisted the company was not profiteering on the back of the UK motorist or gas consumer, saying 90% of its profits came from abroad. 'Our profits came out of 140 countries where we are. It's not true to say that all $23bn [£13bn] came out of the UK,' he said, claiming later that the UK figure was below $2.3bn.

The company also said $1.2bn had been paid to the British Treasury in tax, almost double the amount for 2004. And that was before a recent tax rise by the chancellor which had not yet kicked in, it said.

Shell plans to hand back £3bn of the £13bn profits to investors through share buybacks over the next 12 months.

The earnings were up to 30% on 2004 but shares fell 2.5% to 1956p as some figures disappointed the City. There was particular concern that Shell had only replaced up to 70% of its reserves year-on-year, while oil and gas production fell from 3.7m barrels a day to 3.5bn.

The oil group tried to head off wider criticism by saying the profits resulted from long-term investments, for instance in the North Sea. But this did not impress the trade unions.

'It is high time the government acted decisively and brought in a proper windfall tax,' said Tony Woodley, general secretary of the T&GWU. 'At a stroke a windfall tax could strengthen the Financial Assistance Scheme and put some backbone into the Pension Protection Fund.'

> **Backstory**
>
> The £13bn-plus profit reported by **Shell** catapults it above banking giant **HSBC**, which last year set a new record when it broke through the £10bn barrier for the first time in British corporate history. The two firms have been playing leapfrog, with Shell briefly taking the record a year ago with profts of £9.4bn, only to be trumped by HSBC a couple of weeks later. But the surge reported by Shell yesterday looks likely to see it retain the record this year. Though HSBC and **BP** have yet to report their 2005 figures, analysts do not expect them to top Shell's numbers.

Fellow union Amicus described the figures as 'obscene' and said it undermined the "huff and puff" of the oil industry over the November tax hike by Gordon Brown.

Meanwhile fuel poverty activists argued that Shell's profit came at the expense of one million more households falling into fuel poverty.

'Continuing domestic energy price rises will lead to a major increase in the number of households struggling to pay their bills, or paying the health and social costs of living in cold, damp homes,' said William Gillis, chief executive of National Energy Action. 'NEA urges Shell to consider gas consumers who are facing debt and cold homes this winter and to dedicate more of their profits to poor communities and practical energy saving programmes.'

Shell is a major supplier of gas to the wholesale market but Mr van der Veer was unable to say exactly how much his company had earned from this business.

The Road Haulage Association also joined in the attack on Shell, urging the government to 'take a little more' from the oil companies and use the cash to reduce fuel tax for road transport operators.

'Shell has benefited from high global prices; meanwhile road hauliers dependent on the corresponding high price of diesel can barely make ends meet,' said chief executive Roger King.

And Friends of the Earth also called for higher taxes, saying everyone else was paying the price for Shell's profits.

'Oil companies must be forced to face up to their wider responsibilities on climate change, on the environment and on human rights. Shell claims the costs are too great to protect the western Pacific whale – and yet again announced record profits,' said FoE's head of corporate accountability, Craig Bennett.

The Shell boss described the financial performance of the group as good and said it gave the company a 'solid platform' to build on during 2006. He said oil and gas production was in line with expectations, given the impact of hurricanes in the US Gulf. After a very turbulent 2004 on the back of reserved downgrades, Mr van der Veer said Shell's position was 'solid'.

*The Guardian*, 3 February 2006.



*Questions relating to this news story can be found on page 247*

## About this chapter

In this chapter we cover what accountants call the 'interpretation of accounts'. In essence, all that this means is that you dig behind the figures shown in the financial statements in order to make more sense of them and to put them into context. You will often see, for example, a newspaper screaming in large headlines that Company X has made a profit of (say) £50m. In absolute terms £50m is certainly a lot of money but what does it mean? Is it a lot compared with what it took to make it? How does it compare with previous years? And does it meet the chairman's reported expectations?

These questions cannot always be answered directly from the financial statements themselves. The figures may have to be reworked, and then they might have to be compared with other data that are closely related to them. So interpreting accounts is a type of detective work – you look for the evidence, you analyse it and then you give your verdict.

This chapter explains how you do the detective work. There are various ways of going about it but we are going to concentrate on *ratio analysis*. This is one of the most common methods used in interpreting accounts and we shall be spending a lot of time on it.

**Learning objectives**

**By the end of this chapter you should be able to:**

- **define what is meant by the 'interpretation of accounts';**
- **outline why it is needed;**
- **summarize the procedure involved in interpreting a set of accounts;**
- **explain the usefulness and importance of ratio analysis;**
- **calculate 15 main accounting ratios;**
- **explore the relationship between those ratios.**

## ! Why this chapter is important for non-accountants

For non-accountants, this chapter is one of the most important in the book. In your professional life you could rely entirely on your accountants to present you with any financial information that *they* think you might find useful. In time and with some experience you might understand most of it. The danger is that you might take the figures at their face value, just as you might when you read an eye-catching newspaper story. On 2 February 2006, for example, the *Edinburgh Evening News* had this headline in very large type:

**Shell pumps out record profits of £12.93 billion**

You could be misled by such a headline and on the basis of it take what might turn out to be a most unwise decision (e.g. buying or selling shares in Shell, or perhaps even making a takeover bid for the company!). Now nearly £13 billion pounds might be a record but how can we be certain that it is all that amazing? The short answer is that we can't unless we relate it to something else, such as what sum of money it took to earn that profit or what profit other oil companies have made. To be fair to the newspaper the article that followed the headline did give Shell's annual profits over the previous four years (described as 'Shell's annual profit haul'!).

Accountants refer to the explanation process as the *interpretation of accounts*. After working your way through the chapter you too will be able to interpret a set of accounts so that whenever you come across some financial statements (or you see a story in the newspapers) you can make much more sense of the information and you can put it into context, i.e. compare it with something meaningful. This is sometimes referred to as 'reading between the lines of the balance sheet'. We hope that by the end of the chapter you too can read between these lines, and for that matter between the lines of all the other financial statements as well. Such a skill is vital if you are to become a *really* effective and efficient manager.

## Nature and purpose

In this section we explain what accountants mean when they talk about 'interpreting a set of accounts', why such an exercise is necessary and who might have need of it.

### Definition

The verb 'to interpret' has several different meanings. Perhaps the most common is 'to convert' or 'to translate' the spoken word of one language into another, but it also has other meanings such as 'to construe', 'to define' or 'to explain'. We will use the latter meaning. Our definition of what we mean by the *interpretation of accounts* may then be expressed as follows:

> *A detailed explanation of the financial performance of an entity incorporating data and other information of a quantitative and qualitative nature extracted from both internal and external sources.*

### Limited information

By this stage of your accounting studies you will no doubt have realized that the amount of information contained in a set of accounts prepared for *internal* purposes is considerable, but even published accounts can be quite detailed. The 2005 annual report and accounts of Sig plc, for example, a supplier of specialist products to the construction industry, covers 109 pages. You would think that accounts of this length would provide you with all the information that you would ever want to know about the company but unfortunately this is not necessarily the case. There are three main reasons why this may not be so.

- *Structural.* Financial accounts are prepared on the basis of a series of accounting rules. Even financial accounts prepared for internal purposes contain a restricted amount of information (this is especially the case with published accounts). Only information that can be translated easily into quantitative financial terms is usually included, and even then some highly arbitrary assessments have to be made about the treatment of certain matters such as stock valuation, depreciation and bad debts. Financial accounts are also usually prepared on a historical basis so they may be out-of-date by the time that they become available, the details may relate at best to one or two accounting periods and probably no allowance will have been made for inflation.

- *Absolute.* The monetary figures are presented almost solely in absolute terms. For example, Sig plc's sales revenue for 2005 was £1 639 322 000 and its profit before tax was £86 811 000. Figures of this size are way above most users' comprehension so about the only thing that they can read into them is that they appear to be very large sums of money.
- *Contextual.* Even if you could understand what sales of over £1 600m and profits of £87m meant, in isolation they do not mean very much. In order to make them more meaningful they need to be related to something such as what the sales and profits were for previous years or how they compare with other similar sized companies in the same industry.

## Users

Company law concentrates almost exclusively on one user group, the shareholders – but as we explained in Chapter 9 there are many other user groups. We reproduce the seven main user groups outlined in that chapter in Table 12.1. Beside each group we have posed a question that a user in each particular group may well ask.

The questions in Table 12.1 cannot always be answered directly from the financial statements. For example, investors asking the question 'What's the dividend like?' will find that the annual report and accounts gives them the dividend per share for the current and the previous year in *absolute* amounts. Somewhere within the annual report and accounts the percentage increase may be given but that still does not really answer the question. Investors will probably want to know how their dividend relates to what they have invested in the company (what accountants call the 'yield'). As most investors probably paid different amounts for their shares, it would be impossible to show each individual shareholder's yield in the annual account so investors have to calculate it for themselves.

**Table 12.1 Users of financial accounts and their questions**

| User group | Questions asked |
|---|---|
| Customers | How do its prices compare with its competitors? |
| Employees | Has it enough money to pay my wages? |
| Governments and their agencies | Can the company pay its taxes? |
| Investors | What's the dividend like? |
| Lenders | Will I get my interest paid? |
| Public | Is the company likely to stay in business? |
| Suppliers and other creditors | Will we get paid what we are owed? |

**Activity 12.1**

Taking the seven user groups listed in Table 12.1, what other questions do you think that each user group would ask? List each user group and all the questions that you think each would ask. Then insert:

(a) where the basic information could be found in the annual report and accounts to answer each question; and

(b) what additional information would be required to answer each question fully.

## Procedure

In this section we outline the basic procedure involved in interpreting a set of accounts. The scale and nature of your investigation will clearly depend on its purpose so we can only point you in the right direction. For example, if you were working for a large international company proposing to take over a foreign company, you would need a vast amount of information and it might take months before you had completed your investigation. By contrast, if you were a private individual proposing to invest £1000 in Tesco plc, you might just spend part of Saturday morning reading what the city editor of your favourite newspaper had to say about the company (although we would recommend you to do more than that).

In essence an exercise involving the interpretation of accounts involves four main stages:

- collecting the information;
- analysing it;
- interpreting it;
- reporting on the results of your findings.

### Collecting the information

This stage involves you first conducting a fairly general review of the international economic, financial, political and social climate, and a more specific one of the *country* in which the entity operates. In broad terms, you are looking for political and social stability in the country with excellent prospects for sound and continuing economic growth. Then you should look at the particular *industry* in which it operates. Ask yourself the following questions.

- Is the government supportive of the industry?
- Is there an expanding market for its products?
- Is there sufficient land and space available for development?
- Is there a reliable infrastructure, e.g. utility supplies and a transport network?
- Are there grants and loans available for developing enterprises?
- Is there an available and trained labour force near by?

Once you have got all this macro and micro information you will need to obtain as much information about the *entity* as you can get. This will involve finding out about its history, structure, management, operations, products, markets, labour record and financial performance. These days you should be able to obtain much of this information from the Internet but don't forget about old-fashioned sources such as the company's annual and interim reports and accounts, press releases, trade circulars and analysts' reviews.

By the end of this early stage of your investigation you will probably already have a 'feel' or a strong impression about the entity but your work is not yet over. Indeed, there is still a great deal more to do.

### Analysing the information

Analysing the information involves putting together all the information you have collected and making sense of it. In this book as we are primarily concerned with the accounting aspects of business so we will concentrate on how you can begin to make sense of the *financial* information that you have collected.

The main source of such information will normally be the entity's annual report and accounts. In order to make our explanation easier to follow we will assume that we are dealing primarily with public limited liability companies (although you will find that much of what we have to say is relevant when dealing with other types of entities).

There are four main techniques that you can use in interpreting a set of financial statements: horizontal analysis, trend analysis, vertical analysis and ratio analysis. Figure 12.1 depicts a diagrammatic representation of these different types of analyses and a brief description of each one is outlined below.

1 *Horizontal analysis.* This technique involves making a line-by-line comparison of the company's accounts for each accounting period chosen for the investigation. You may

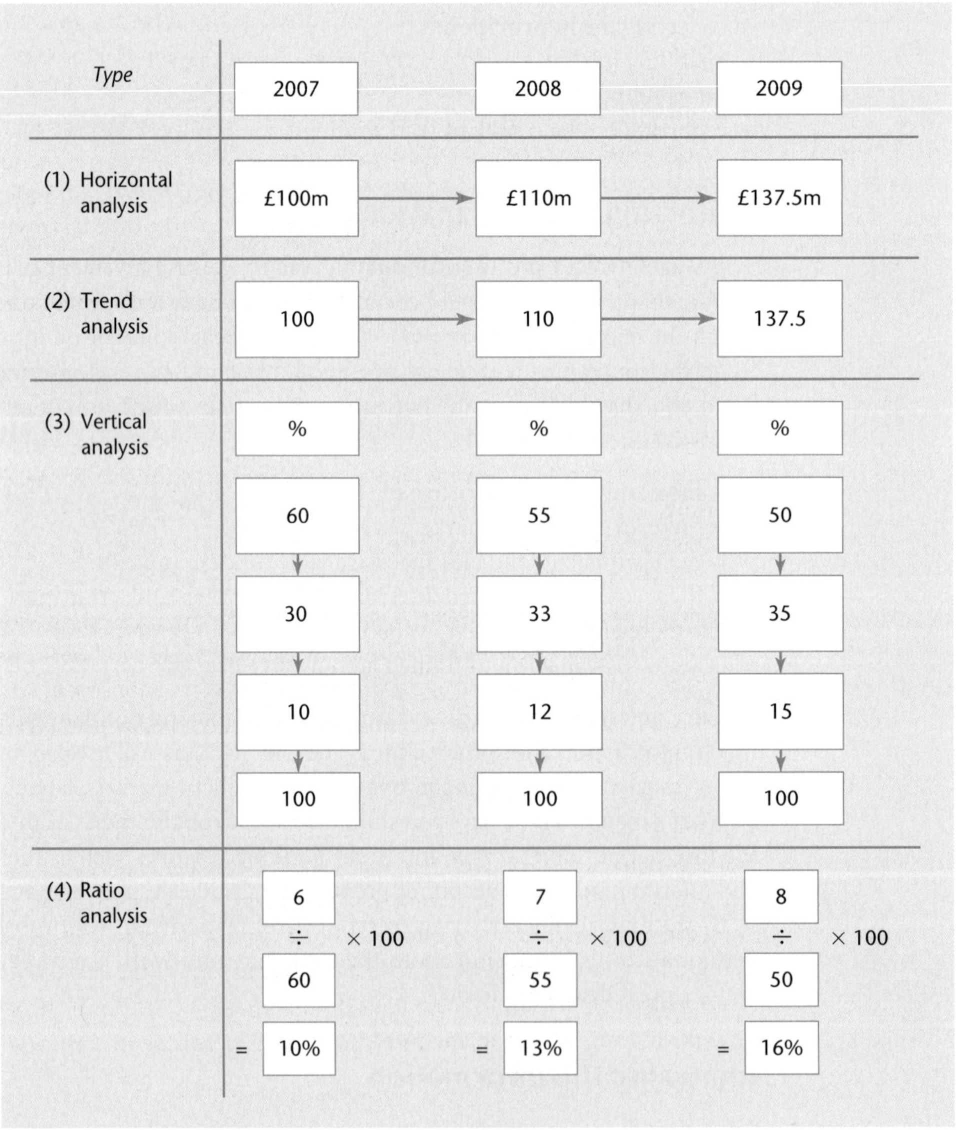


**Figure 12.1 Interpreting accounts: main analytical techniques**

have noted, for example, that the sales for the year 2007 were £100m, £110m in 2008 and £137.5m in 2009 and so on. This type of comparison across a row of figures is something that we do naturally, but such a casual observation is not very effective when we are faced with a great many detailed figures. In order to grasp what they mean and (at the very least) we would need to calculate the changes from one year to the next. Even then their significance might still be hard to take in. So we would probably have to calculate the *percentage* increases year-by-year (10% for 2008 and 25% in 2009 in the above example) and this could involve an awful lot of work with a pen, paper and a calculator (or a spreadsheet if you are into computing).

2 *Trend analysis.* This is similar to horizontal analysis except that all the figures in the first set of accounts in a series are given a base line of 100 and the subsequent sets of accounts are converted to that base line. So if the sales for 2007 were £50m, £70 for 2008 and £85m for 2009, the sales of £50m for 2007 would be given a base line of 100; the 2008 sales would then become 140 (70 × 100/50) and the 2009 sales 170 (85 × 100/50). This method enables us to grasp much more easily the changes in the absolute costs and values shown in the financial statements. For example, if we told you that the sales were £202 956 000 for 2008 and £210 161 000 in 2009 it is not difficult to calculate that they have gone up by about £7m but the figures are still too big for most of us to absorb. The changes that have taken place would be much easier to take in if they are all related to a base line of 100. In this example, the sales for 2008 would then be given a value of 100, with 103 (210 161 × 100/202 956) for 2009, an increase of about 3% (it's actually 3.6%). The figures then begin to mean something because by converting in this way they relate more to our experience of money terms and values in our everyday life.

3 *Vertical analysis.* This technique requires the figures in each financial statement (usually restricted to the profit and loss account and the balance sheet) to be expressed as a percentage of the total amount. For example, assume that a company's trade debtors were £10m in 2008 and the balance sheet total was £50m; in 2009 the trade debtors were £12m and the balance sheet total was £46m. Trade debtors would then be shown as representing 20% of the balance sheet total (10 × 100/50) in 2008 and 26% in 2009 (12 × 100/46). This would be considered quite a large increase so the reasons for it would need to be investigated in some detail. The modern practice of using lots of sectionalized accounts and subtotals means that it is not always easy to decide what *is* the total of a particular financial statement. If you come across this difficulty we suggest that you use the sales revenue figure for the total of the profit and loss account and the total of net assets (or shareholders' funds, it should be the same figure!) for the total of the balance sheet.

4 *Ratio analysis.* A ratio is simply the division of one arithmetical amount by another arithmetical amount, and then expressed as a percentage or as a factor. Ratio analysis is a most useful means of comparing one figure with another because it expresses the relationship between lots of amounts easily and simply. If the cost of sales for 2008 was £12m, for example, and the sales revenue was £20m, we would express the relationship as 60% (12 × 100/20) sales or 0.6 to 1 (12/20). Ratio analysis is such an important technique in the interpretation of accounts that we will be dealing with it in some detail later in the chapter.

**Activity 12.2**

State whether the following assertions are true or false:

(a) Ratio analysis is only one form of analysis that can be used in interpreting accounts. *True/false*

(b) Ratio analysis aims to put the financial results of an entity into perspective. *True/false*

(c) Ratio analysis helps to establish whether or not an entity is a going concern. *True/false*

## Interpreting the information

This is the third stage in a broad interpretative exercise. By this stage of your investigation you would have collected a great deal of information about the company you are investigating and you would have put that information into context by subjecting it to a whole battery of analyses. Now you have to use all the information that you have before you to interpret or to *explain* what has happened. Some of the questions you might ask yourself include the following.

- What does it tell me about the company's performance?
- Has the company done well compared with other financial periods?
- How does it compare with other companies in the same sector of the economy?
- What about the future – are the world economic, political and social circumstances favourable to trade generally?
- What are they like for this company's industry?
- How do these various circumstances apply to the region where this company does its business?

Asking and answering such questions might seem a formidable task but, like anything else, the more practice you get the easier it becomes. In any case, by the time that you come to this stage of the exercise, your initial research and your various analyses will already have given you a strong indication about the company's progress and its future prospects. You will have realized that there are a number of obvious strengths and weaknesses and a variety of positive and negative factors and trends.

When you have come to a conclusion based on the evidence and the analysis that you have framed, you have one further task – report it to whoever asked you to do the study in the first place.

## Reporting the findings

In most interpretive exercises of the type described in this chapter you will probably have to write a written report. Many people are fearful of having to commit themselves to paper and they find this part of the exercise very difficult. However, having to write something down helps you to think more clearly and logically. It may also throw up gaps in your argument, so regard this part of the exercise as more of an opportunity as opposed to a threat.

The format of your report will depend on its purpose but basically it should be broken down into three main sections. You cannot do better than follow the example of the preacher from the American south who explained the structure of his sermons this way, 'I *tells 'em what I'm going to tell 'em. I tells 'em and then I tells 'em what I told 'em*'. In other words, divide your report into three main sections. Your first section should be an *introduction* in which you outline the nature and purpose of your report, including a brief outline of its structure. The second part should contain your *discussion* section in which you present your evidence and your assessment of what the evidence means. In the third *concluding* section summarize briefly the entire study, list your conclusions and state your recommendations for the action that should now be taken.

In the next section we return to consider in much more detail one of the topics outlined earlier in the chapter: *ratio analysis*.

## Ratio analysis

For much of the rest of this chapter we are going to spend our time discussing ratio analysis in some detail. Before we begin you should note the following points.

- There are literally hundreds of ratios that we could produce but most accountants have just a few favourites.
- Always check the definition of a particular ratio you come across because, while the name may be familiar to you, the definition could be different from the one that you normally use.
- There is no standard system for grouping ratios into representative categories.
- Strictly limit the number of ratios you adopt. If you use 20 different types of ratios, for example, and you are covering a five-year period, you have 100 ratios to calculate *and* to incorporate in your analysis. That's a lot to handle!

In this book we are going to limit the number of accounting ratios that we cover to just 15. In order to simplify our discussion, we will also group them into four broad categories (although there is some overlap between them):

- liquidity ratios;
- profitability ratios;
- efficiency ratios;
- investment ratios.

A diagrammatic representation of this classification and the names of the ratios included in each grouping are shown in Figure 12.2.

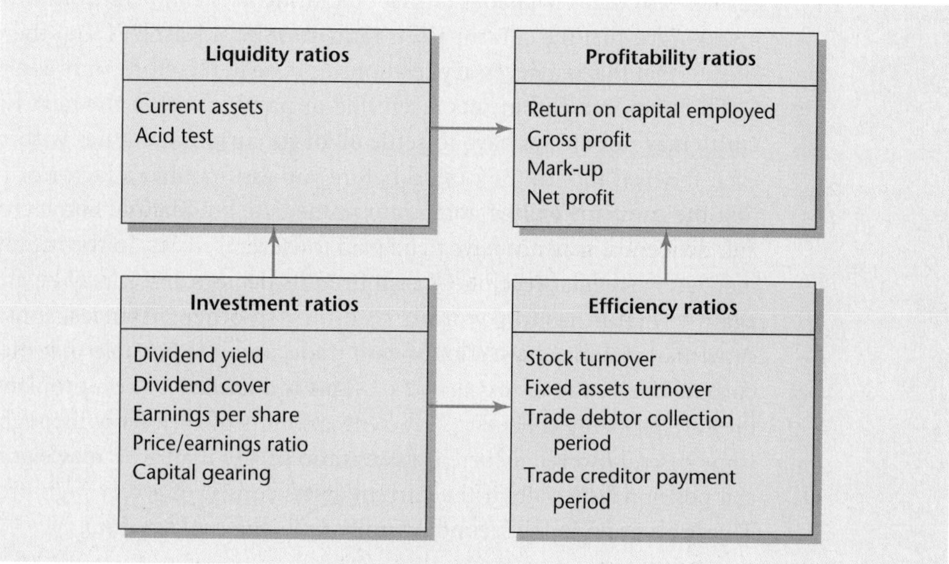


**Figure 12.2 Accounting ratios: classification**

When we have explained what these ratios mean and how they should be calculated, we will then illustrate their use in a practical example based on an actual company's published accounts. We cannot always extract the information that we need from published accounts so we may have to adapt some of our 15 ratios and some of them may not be relevant, e.g. if the company does not have any preference shares we cannot calculate a gearing ratio.

We start our detailed study with what we call *liquidity* ratios.

## Liquidity ratios

Liquidity ratios measure the extent to which assets can be turned into cash quickly. In other words, they try to assess how much cash the entity has available in the short term (this usually means within the next twelve months). For example, it is easy to extract the total amount of trade debtors and trade creditors from the balance sheet, but are they too high? We cannot really tell until we put them into context. We can do this by calculating two liquidity ratios known as the *current assets ratio* and the *acid test ratio.*

### Current assets ratio

The *current assets ratio* is calculated as follows:

$$\frac{\textbf{current assets}}{\textbf{current liabilities}}$$

It is usually expressed as a factor, e.g. 3 to 1, or 3 : 1, although you will sometimes see it expressed as a percentage, 300% in our example, i.e. $\frac{3}{1} \times 100$.

In most circumstances we can expect that current assets will be in excess of current liabilities. The current assets ratio will then be at least 1 : 1. If this is not the case, the entity may not have sufficient liquid resources (i.e. current assets that can be quickly turned into cash) available to meet its immediate financial commitments. Some textbooks argue that the current assets ratio must be at least 2 : 1, but there is no evidence to suggest that this is a necessary relationship. Use it, therefore, only as a guide.

The term 'current' means receivable or payable within the next twelve months. The entity may not always have to settle all of its current liabilities within the next week or even the next month. Be careful before you assume that a factor of (say) 1 : 2 suggests that the company will be going into immediate liquidation. Some creditors, such as tax and dividends, may not have to be paid for several weeks. In the meantime, the company may receive regular receipts of cash from its debtors and it may be able to balance these against what it has to pay to its creditors. In other instances, some entities (such as supermarkets) may have a lot of cash trade, and it is possible that they then may have a current assets ratio of less than 2 : 1. This is not likely to be a problem for them because they are probably collecting sufficient amounts of cash daily through the checkouts. In some cases, however, a current assets ratio of less than 2 : 1 may signify a serious financial position, especially if the current assets consist of a very high proportion of stocks. This leads us on to the second liquidity ratio, the *acid test ratio.*

### Acid test ratio

It may not be easy to dispose of stocks in the short term as they cannot always be quickly turned into cash. In any case, the entity would then be depriving itself of those very assets that enable it to make a trading profit. It seems sensible, therefore, to see what would happen to the current ratio if stocks were not included in the definition of current assets. This ratio is called the acid test (or quick) ratio. It is calculated as follows:

$$\frac{\text{current assets} - \text{stocks}}{\text{current liabilities}}$$

Like the current ratio, the acid test ratio is usually expressed as a factor (or occasionally as a percentage). It is probably a better measure of an entity's immediate liquidity position than the current assets ratio because it may be difficult to dispose of the stocks in the short term. Do not assume, however, that if current assets less stocks are less than current liabilities, the entity's cash position is vulnerable. As we explained above, some of the current liabilities may not be due for payment for some months. Some textbooks suggest that the acid test ratio must be at least 1 : 1, but again there is no evidence to support this assertion, so use it only as a guide.

**Activity 12.3**

Fill in the blanks in the following equations.

(a) $$\frac{\text{Current assets}}{\text{Current liabilities}} = \frac{£65\,500}{\text{------}} = 1.60$$

(b) $$\frac{\text{Current assets} - \text{------------}}{\text{Current liabilities}}$$

## Profitability ratios

Users of accounts will want to know how much profit a business has made, and then to compare it with previous periods or with other entities. The absolute level of accounting profit will not be of much help, because it needs to be related to the size of the entity and how much capital it has invested in it. There are four main profitability ratios. We examine each of them below.

### Return on capital employed ratio

The best way of assessing profitability is to calculate a ratio known as the *return on capital employed* (ROCE) ratio. It can be expressed quite simply as

$$\frac{\text{profit}}{\text{capital}} \times 100 = x\%$$

This ratio is usually expressed as a percentage, and it is one of the most important. Even so, there is no common agreement about how it should be calculated. The problem is that both 'profit' and 'capital' can be defined in several different ways. As a result, a variety of ROCE ratios can be produced merely by changing the definitions of either profit or capital. For our purposes you only need to be aware of four definitions of ROCE. They are given below:

(1)
$$\frac{\textbf{net profit before taxation}}{\textbf{average shareholders' funds}} \times 100 = x\%$$

This definition measures the pre-tax profit against what the shareholders have invested in the entity. Use it if you want to know how profitable the entity has been as a whole.

(2)
$$\frac{\textbf{net profit after taxation}}{\textbf{average shareholders' funds}} \times 100 = x\%$$

This definition is similar to the previous one except that it measures post-tax profit against the shareholders' investment in the entity. Taxation is normally regarded as an *appropriation* of profit and not as an expense. The tax payable will be based on the profit for the year and an entity has no option other than to pay it. The distinction between tax as an appropriation and tax as a profit is blurred, and some accountants prefer to use this definition as a measure of overall profitability. However, bear in mind that the taxation charge in the accounts can be subject to various accounting adjustments, so you would have to be careful using this definition in comparing one entity with another entity.

(3)
$$\frac{\textbf{net profit after taxation and preference dividends}}{\textbf{average shareholders' funds less preference dividends}} \times 100 = x\%$$

This definition should be used if you want to assess how profitable the entity has been from an *ordinary* shareholder's point of view. It measures how much profit could be distributed to ordinary shareholders as a proportion of what they have invested in the business.

(4)
$$\frac{\textbf{profit before taxation and interest}}{\textbf{average shareholders' funds plus long-terms loans}} \times 100 = x\%$$

This definition measures what profit has been earned in relation to what has been used to *finance* the entity in total. Interest is a cost of borrowing money, so it is added back to the profit made. Similarly, long-term loans are added to the shareholders' funds because that gives us the *total* financial investment in the entity. Use this definition if you want to know how profitable the entity has been in relation to what it has taken to finance it.

The above definitions use an *average* for shareholders' funds (usually a simple average, i.e. 2/(opening shareholders' funds plus closing shareholders' funds). The closing balance, however, is often used, especially if ROCE is being calculated over a fairly long period, say three to five years.

**Activity 12.4**

There are many other ways of calculating ROCE other than the four listed above. Divide a page into two broad columns. In the left-hand column list all the various levels of profit that you would find in a published profit and loss account (e.g. operating profit). In the right-hand column list all the various levels or types of capital shown in a published balance sheet (e.g. total assets). Then try to relate each definition of profit to a compatible definition of capital.

Remember that what you are trying to do is to find how much profit (however defined) has been earned for the particular level or type of capital invested. So the numerator (profit) has got to be compatible with the denominator (the capital employed).

## Gross profit ratio

The *gross profit ratio* enables us to judge how successful the entity has been at trading. It is calculated as follows:

$$\frac{\text{gross profit}}{\text{total sales revenue}} \times 100 = x\%$$

The gross profit ratio measures how much profit the entity has earned in relation to the amount of sales that it has made. The definition of gross profit does not usually cause any problems. Most entities adopt the definition we have used in this book, namely sales less the cost of goods sold [the cost of sales being (opening stock + purchase) – closing stock], and so meaningful comparisons can usually be made between different entities. However, if you are using published accounts, sales may be described as 'turnover' and the cost of sales may well include production costs (which are not usually disclosed). Be wary, therefore, if you are making comparisons between different companies.

## Mark-up ratio

The gross profit ratio complements another main trading ratio, which we will refer to, for convenience, as the *mark-up ratio*. This is calculated as follows:

$$\frac{\text{gross profit}}{\text{cost of goods sold}} \times 100 = x\%$$

Mark-up ratios measure the amount of profit added to the cost of goods sold. The cost of goods sold plus profit equals the sales revenue. The mark-up may be reduced to stimulate extra sales activity, but this will have the effect of reducing the gross profit. However, if extra goods are sold, there may be a greater volume of sales and this will help to compensate for the reduction in the mark up on each unit.

## Net profit ratio

Owners sometimes like to compare their net profit with the sales revenue. This can be expressed in the form of the *net profit ratio*, which is calculated as follows:

$$\frac{\text{net profit before taxation}}{\text{total sales revenue}} \times 100 = x\%$$

It is difficult to compare the net profit ratio for different entities fairly. Individual operating and financing arrangements vary so much that entities are bound to have different levels of expenditure, no matter how efficient one entity is compared with another. So it may only be realistic to use the net profit ratio in making *internal* comparisons. Over a period of time a pattern may emerge and it might then be possible to establish a trend. If you use the net profit ratio to make intercompany comparisons, make sure you allow for different circumstances.

In published accounts you might also want to substitute 'operating profit' or 'profit on ordinary activities before tax' for net profit.

## Efficiency ratios

Traditional accounting statements do not tell us how *efficiently* an entity has been managed, i.e. how well its resources have been looked after. Accounting profit may, to some extent, be used as a measure of efficiency. However, as we have explained in earlier chapters, it is subject to a great many arbitrary adjustments, and in this context it can be misleading. What we need to do is to make comparisons between different periods and with other similar entities.

There are very many different types of ratios that we can use to measure the efficiency of an entity, but in this book we will cover only the more common ones.

### Stock turnover ratio

The stock turnover ratio may be calculated as follows:

$$\frac{\text{cost of goods sold}}{\text{average stock}} = x \text{ times}$$

A simple average is usually used to calculate the average stock, i.e.

$$\tfrac{1}{2}(\text{opening stock} + \text{closing stock})$$

The stock turnover ratio is normally expressed as a number (e.g. 5 or 10 times) and not as a percentage. Note that there are also various other ways in which this ratio can be calculated.

Sometimes the sales revenue is substituted for the cost of goods sold. It should *not* be used if it can be avoided because the sales contain a profit loading and this can cause the ratio to become distorted. Many accountants prefer to substitute a more accurate average stock level than the simple average shown above (particularly if goods are purchased at irregular intervals). It is also quite common to compare the *closing* stock with the cost of sales in order to gain a clearer idea of the stock position at the end of the year. This may be misleading if the company's trade is seasonal or if the year end falls during a quiet period.

The greater the turnover of stock, the more efficient the entity would appear to be in purchasing and selling goods. A stock turnover of 2 times, for example, would suggest that the entity has about six months of sales in stock. In most circumstances, this would appear to be a high relative volume, whereas a stock turnover of (say) 12 times would mean that the entity had only a month's normal sales in stock.

## Fixed assets turnover ratio

Another important area to examine, from the point of view of efficiency, relates to fixed assets. Fixed assets (susch as plant and machinery) enable the business to function more efficiently, and so a high level of fixed assets ought to generate more sales. We can check this by calculating a ratio known as the fixed asset turnover ratio. This may be done as follows:

$$\frac{\textbf{total sales revenue}}{\textbf{fixed assets at net book value}} = x$$

The fixed assets turnover ratio may also be expressed as a percentage. The more times that the fixed assets are covered by the sales revenue, the greater the recovery of the investment in fixed assets.

This ratio is really only useful if it is compared with previous periods or with other entities. In isolation it does not mean very much. For example, is a turnover of 5 good and one of 4 poor? All we can suggest is that if the trend is upwards, then the investment in fixed assets is beginning to pay off, at least in terms of increased sales. Note also that the ratio can be strongly affected by the entity's depreciation policies. There is a strong argument, therefore, for taking the *gross* book value of the fixed assets, and not the *net* book value.

**Activity 12.5**

A company has a turnover of £4 000 000 for the year to 31 December 2009. At that date the gross book value of its fixed assets was £22 000 and the net book value £12 000. When measuring the efficiency with which its uses its fixed assets, is it more meaningful to use the gross book value in relation to turnover or the net book value? Give your reasons.

Gross book value ☐ Net book value ☐

Reason: ______________________________

## Trade debtor collection period ratio

Investing in fixed assets is all very well, but there is not much point in generating extra sales if the customers do not pay for them. Customers might be encouraged to buy more by a combination of lower selling prices and generous credit terms. If the debtors are slow at paying, the entity might find that it has run into cash flow problems. So it is important for it to watch the trade debtor position very carefully. We can check how successful it has been by calculating the *trade debtor collection period*. The ratio may be calculated as follows:

$$\frac{\textbf{average trade debtors}}{\textbf{total credit sales}} \times \textbf{365 days} = x \textbf{ days}$$

The average trade debtors term is usually calculated by using a simple average [i.e $\frac{1}{2}$ (opening trade debtors + closing trade debtors)]. The closing trade debtors figure is sometimes substituted for average trade debtors. This is acceptable, provided that the figure is representative of the overall period.

It is important to relate trade debtors to *credit* sales if possible, and so cash sales should be excluded from the calculation. The method shown above for calculating the ratio would relate the average trade debtors to $x$ days' sales, but it would be possible to substitute weeks or months for days. It is not customary to express the ratio as a percentage.

An acceptable debtor collection period cannot be suggested, as much depends on the type of trade in which the entity is engaged. Some entities expect settlement within 28 days of delivery of the goods or on immediate receipt of the invoice. Other entities might expect settlement within 28 days following the end of the month in which the goods were delivered. On average, this adds another 14 days (half a month) to the overall period of 28 days. If this is the case, a company would appear to be highly efficient in collecting its debts if the average debtor collection period was about 42 days – the United Kingdom experience is that the *median* debtor collection period is about 50 days.

Like most of the other ratios, it is important to establish a trend. If the trend is upwards, then it might suggest that the company's credit control procedures have begun to weaken.

**Activity 12.6**

A company's sales for 2009 were £4452 million and its trade debtors for that year were £394 million. Assuming that all the sales were made on credit terms, do you think that its debtor collection was efficient?

Yes ☐ No ☐

Reason: ______________________________

## Trade creditor payment period

A similar ratio can be calculated for the trade creditor payment period. The formula is as follows:

$$\frac{\text{average trade creditors}}{\text{total credit purchases}} \times 365 \text{ days} = x \text{ days}$$

The average trade creditors amount is usually just an average of the opening and closing balances. Many accountants use the closing balance, and you also may have to because you may not always be given the information to calculate an average balance. The trade creditors should be related to credit purchases (although this information will often not be available), and weeks or months may be substituted for the number of days. Like the trade debtor collection period, it is not usual to express this ratio as a percentage.

In published accounts you might have to calculate the purchases figure for yourself. The accounts should disclose the opening and closing stock figures and the cost of sales. By substituting them in the equation (opening stock + purchases) – closing stock = cost of sales, you can calculate the purchases. Other expenses may have been included in the cost of sales but unless these have been disclosed you will just have to accept the cost of sales figure shown in the accounts.

An upward trend in the average level of trade creditors would suggest that the entity is having some difficulty in finding the cash to pay its creditors. Indeed, it might be a sign that it is running into financial difficulties.

## Investment trends

The various ratios examined in the previous sections are probably of interest to all users of accounts, such as creditors, employees and managers, as well as to shareholders. There are some other ratios that are primarily (although not exclusively) of interest to prospective investors. These are known as *investment ratios*.

### Dividend yield

The first investment ratio that you might find useful is the *dividend yield*. It usually applies to ordinary shareholders and it may be calculated as follows:

$$\frac{\text{dividend per share}}{\text{market price per share}} \times 100 = x\,\%$$

The dividend yield measures the rate of return that an investor gets by comparing the cost of his shares with the dividend receivable (or paid). For example, if an investor buys 100 £1 ordinary shares at a market rate of 200p per share, and the dividend was 10p per share, the yield would be 5 per cent (10/200 × 100). While he may have invested £200 (100 × £2 per share), as far as the company is concerned he will be registered as holding 100 shares at a nominal value of £1 each (100 shares × £1). He would be entitled to a dividend of £10 (10p × 100 shares), but from the shareholder's individual point of view, he will only be getting a return of 5 per cent, i.e. £10 for his £200 invested.

### Dividend cover

Another useful investment ratio is called *dividend cover*. It is calculated as follows:

$$\frac{\text{net profit after taxation and preference dividend}}{\text{paid and proposed ordinary dividends}} = x \text{ times}$$

This ratio shows the number of times that the ordinary dividend could be paid out of current earnings. The dividend is usually described as being *x* times covered by the earnings. Thus, if the dividend is covered twice, the company would be paying out half of its earnings as an ordinary dividend.

### Earnings per share

Another important investment ratio is that known as *earnings per share* (EPS). This ratio enables us to put the profit into context, and to avoid looking at it in simple absolute terms. It is usually looked at from the ordinary shareholder's point of view. The following formula is used to calculate what is called the *basic* earnings per share:

$$\frac{\text{net profit (or loss) for the period less dividends and other appropriations in respect of non-equity shares}}{\text{weighted average number of ordinary shares outstanding during the period}}$$

The above definition uses the term 'non-equity shares'. Preference shares are an example of such shares.

In published accounts you will sometimes see other definitions of the EPS. The calculations involved in obtaining them are often highly complex. We recommend you to stick to the above definition, i.e. basically, net profit divided by the number of ordinary shares.

EPS enables a fair comparison to be made between one year's earnings and another by relating the earnings to something tangible, i.e. the number of shares in issue.

## Price to earnings ratio

Another common investment ratio is the *price to earnings ratio* (P/E). It is calculated as follows:

$$\frac{\textbf{market price per share}}{\textbf{earnings per share}} = x$$

The P/E ratio enables a comparison to be made between the earnings per share (as defined above) and the market price. It tells us that the market price is $x$ times the earnings. It means that it would take $x$ years before we recovered the market price paid for the shares out of the earnings (assuming that they remained at that level, and that they were all distributed). Thus the P/E ratio is a multiple of earnings. A high or low ratio can only be judged in relation to other companies in the same sector of the market.

A high P/E ratio means that the market thinks that the company's future is a good one. The shares are in demand and hence the price of the shares will be high. Of course, it would take you a long time to get your 'earnings' back (even if the company paid them all out as dividends) so the shares are probably highly priced. However, the expectation is that the company will be able to increase its earnings and pay out a higher dividend, so the shares are a good buy from that point of view.

**Activity 12.7**

At 2 June 2006, Carphone Warehouse's P/E ratio was 47.6 while Inchcape's was 2.5. Both are grouped in the 'general retailer' sector of the economy. What do these P/E ratios tell you about the market's perception of these two companies?

## Capital gearing ratio

The last ratio that we are going to consider is the *capital gearing ratio*. As outlined in Chapter 6, companies are financed out of a mixture of share capital, retained profits and loans. Loans may be long-term (such as debentures) or short-term (such as credit given by trade creditors). In addition, the company may have set aside all sorts of provisions (e.g. for taxation) which it expects to meet sometime in the future. These may also be regarded as a type of loan. From an ordinary shareholder's point of view, even preference share capital can be classed as a loan because the preference shareholders may have priority over ordinary shareholders both in respect of dividends and upon liquidation. So if a company finances itself from a high level of loans, there is obviously a higher risk in investing in it. This arises for two main reasons:

- the higher the loans, the more interest the company will have to pay, and that may affect the company's ability to pay an ordinary dividend;

- if the company cannot find the cash to repay its loans then the ordinary shareholders may not get any money back if the company goes into liquidation.

There are many different ways of calculating capital gearing. You can use either of

$$\frac{\textbf{loans}}{\textbf{shareholders' funds + loans}} \times 100 - x\,\%$$

or

$$\frac{\textbf{loans}}{\textbf{shareholders' funds}} \times 100 = x\,\%$$

It doesn't matter which formula you adopt so long as you are consistent. We prefer the first method because it tells you what proportion of a company has been *financed* by loans – a worrying sign if it is high. The second method merely shows the loans from a certain proportion of shareholder's funds (including peference shares).

Both methods require that *you* define what *you* mean by shareholders' funds and loans, and this is where it gets difficult as there are many definitions. Shareholders' funds may include:

- ordinary share capital
- preference share capital (may be classed as loans)
- share premium account
- capital reserves
- revenue reserves
- other reserves
- profit and loss account.

Loans may include:

- preference share capital (may sometimes be included in shareholders' funds)
- debentures
- loans
- overdrafts
- provisions
- accruals
- current liabilities
- other amounts due for payment.

*Note*:
In a complex group structure, you might also come across other items that could be classed as loans.

So what definition do we recommend? As we do not want to complicate the calculation of the ratio by getting involved in too much technical detail, we suggest that you go for a fairly straightforward approach and adopt the following definition of capital gearing:

$$\frac{\textbf{preference shares + long-term loans}}{\textbf{shareholders' funds + long-term loans}} \times 100 = x\,\%$$

A company that has financed itself out of a high proportion of loans (e.g. in the form of a combination of preference shares and long-term loans) is known as a highly-geared company. Conversely, a company with a low level of loans is regarded as being low-geared. Note that 'high' and 'low' in this context are relative terms. A highly-geared company is potentially a higher risk investment, as it has to earn sufficient profit to cover the interest payments and the preference dividend before it can pay out any ordinary dividend. This should not be a problem when profits are rising, but if they are falling then they may not be sufficient to cover even the preference dividend.

**Activity 12.8**

Company A has a capital gearing of 10%, Company B 40%, and Company C 60%. What effect will such gearing ratios have on each company's reported profits when they are either rising steeply or falling sharply?

| Company | Effect on profits |
|---|---|
| A | |
| B | |
| C | |

We have now defined 15 common accounting ratios. There are many others that could have been included. However, the 15 selected are enough for you to be able to interpret a set of accounts. Many of the ratios are not particularly helpful if they are used in isolation, but as part of a detailed analysis they are invaluable.

For your convenience a summary of the 15 ratios is included in an appendix at the end of this chapter. We will now show how they can be used to interpret the accounts of a public liability company.

## An illustrative example

In this section we are going to show you how to use the ratios summarized in the previous section. In order to do so we will use the published accounts of A.G. Barr plc for the year ended 28 January 2006. We used these accounts extensively in the previous chapter so much of the detail will be familiar to you. Barr is in the soft drinks industry and you may know of it as the manufacturer of one of its best known products, *Irn-Bru*.

There are considerable advantages in using *actual* accounts (rather than fictional ones) to demonstrate how to interpret accounts, but there are also some disadvantages. Actual accounts enable us to understand much more clearly what happens in the real world. It then becomes easier for you to use what you have learned in interpreting the accounts of other companies. But actual accounts are usually extremely complicated, they may contain material that relates only to that company, and they do not always include all the information you would normally be provided with in a fictitious example. For example, it would be unusual for a company to disclose the data that we need to calculate our definition of the cost of sales (opening stock + purchases – closing stock). Nevertheless, we think that the advantages outweigh the disadvantages, and fortunately Barr's accounts are relatively straightforward.

We summarize the details that we require for our purposes in Example 12.1.

Example 12.1

## Interpreting company accounts

You are provided with the following set of amended published accounts relating to A.G. Barr plc for the year to 28 January 2006.

**Consolidated Income Statement**

| | 2005 | 2006 |
|---|---|---|
| | £000 | £000 |
| Revenue | 127 222 | 128 760 |
| Cost of sales | 63 729 | 63 398 |
| Gross profit | 63 493 | 65 362 |
| Net operating expenses | 47 864 | 48 422 |
| Operating profit before exceptional items | 15 629 | 16 940 |
| Exceptional items | – | 533 |
| Operating profit | 15 629 | 16 407 |
| Finance income less finance costs | 658 | 974 |
| Profit on ordinary activities before tax | 16 287 | 17 381 |
| Tax on profit on ordinary activities | 4 585 | 5 128 |
| Profit attributable to equity shareholders | 11 702 | 12 253 |
| | | |
| Dividend per share paid | 26.25p | 29.25p |
| Dividend paid (£000) | 5 108 | 5 628 |
| Dividend per share proposed | 19.50p | 22.00p |
| Dividend proposed (£000) | 3 795 | 4 282 |
| Basic earnings per share | 62.61p | 65.06p |

**Group Balance Sheet**

| | 2005 | 2006 |
|---|---|---|
| | £000 | £000 |
| **Non-current assets** | | |
| Property, plant and equipment | 37 315 | 34 932 |
| Deferred tax assets | 5 600 | 5 777 |
| | 42 915 | 40 709 |
| **Current assets** | | |
| Inventories | 9 172 | 8 274 |
| Trade and other receivables | 20 991 | 29 546 |
| Cash at bank | 34 958 | 31 412 |
| Assets classified as held for sale | – | 937 |
| | 65 121 | 70 169 |
| **Total assets** | 108 036 | 110 878 |
| **Current liabilities** | 24 716 | 24 045 |
| **Non-current liabilities** | 22 638 | 21 889 |

Example 12.1
*continued*

**Group Balance Sheet *continued***

| | 2005 £000 | 2006 £000 |
|---|---|---|
| **Capital and reserves attributable to equity shareholders** | | |
| Called up share capital | 4 865 | 4 865 |
| Share premium account | 905 | 905 |
| Own shares held | (3 100) | (4 298) |
| Share options reserve | 826 | 1 416 |
| Retained earnings | 57 186 | 62 056 |
| | 60 682 | 64 944 |
| | 108 036 | 110 878 |

**Group Cash Flow Statement**

| | 2005 £000 | 2006 £000 |
|---|---|---|
| **Cash generated by operations** | 21 582 | 18 888 |
| Tax on profit paid | (4 433) | (4 876) |
| **Net cash from operating activities** | 17 149 | 14 012 |
| **Investing activities** | | |
| Proceeds on sale of property, plant and equipment | 215 | 514 |
| Purchase of property, plant and equipment | (2 959) | (12 029) |
| Interest received | 1 288 | 1 557 |
| Interest paid | (630) | (583) |
| **Net cash used in investing activities** | (2 086) | (10 541) |
| **Financing activities** | | |
| Purchase of own shares | (390) | (3 149) |
| Sale of own shares | 473 | 1 760 |
| Dividends paid | (5 108) | (5 628) |
| **Net cash used in financing activities** | (5 025) | (7 017) |
| **Net (decrease)/increase in cash** | 10 038 | (3 546) |
| **Cash at beginning of period** | 24 920 | 34 958 |
| **Cash at end of period** | 34 958 | 31 412 |

Additional information:

1 In order to make the question easier to understand we have omitted some of the technical detail. We have also made some insignificant changes to the presentation of the accounts.

2 These are the first consolidated accounts produced by the company using IFRSs. Some of the terminology may be slightly different from that used earlier in the book but it should not be too difficult for you to work out what it means. For example, the first line of the consolidated income statement (i.e. profit and loss account) is listed as 'revenue' rather than as 'turnover'.

3 The 'revenue' is not broken down into cash sales and credit sales, so the calculation of the trade debtor collection period will be inaccurate.

4 Barr does not state what it means by 'cost of sales' but it probably includes production costs because there is no reference to production costs anywhere else in the accounts. This means that we cannot calculate a separate cost for purchases *and* we will have to use the combined amounts for purchases and production costs. By working backwards from our formula [opening stock + (purchases + production costs) – closing stock] we have been able to calculate that the cost of purchases + production costs was £62 483 000 for 2005 and £62 500 000 for 2006.

5 Miscellaneous opening and closing balances:

| | *Opening 2005* | *Closing 2005* | *Closing 2006* |
|---|---|---|---|
| | *£000* | *£000* | *£000* |
| Property, plant and equipment accumulated depreciation | 61 144 | 64 770 | 68 523 |
| Inventories | 10 418 | 9 172 | 8 274 |
| Trade debtors | 17 839 | 18 580 | 20 243 |
| Trade creditors | 5 706 | 6 441 | 4 802 |
| Other taxes and social security | 1 909 | 1 820 | 1 911 |
| Accruals | 13 840 | 13 905 | 15 370 |
| Shareholders' funds | 53 137 | 60 682 | 64 944 |

6 The issued share capital of the company consists of 25p ordinary shares. The market price of the ordinary shares was 850p at 29 January 2005 and 958p at 28 January 2006. There were no preference shares and no long-term loans.

*Required*:

(a) Calculate appropriate liquidity, profitability, efficiency and investment ratios over the two-year period 2005 to 2006.

(b) Comment on the company's financial performance for the year to 28 January 2006.

**Answer to Example 12.1**

## (a) Significant accounting ratios

**A.G. Barr plc**

| | *2005* | *2006* |
|---|---|---|
| **Liquidity ratios** | | |
| *Current assets:* | | |
| Current assets / Current liabilities | 65 121 / 24 716 = 2.6 to 1 | 70 169 / 24 045 = 2.9 to 1 |
| *Acid test* | | |
| (Current assets – inventories) / Current liabilities | (65 121 – 9 172) / 24 716 = 2.3 to 1 | (70 169 – 8 274) / 24 045 = 2.6 to 1 |

**Answer to Example 12.1 *continued***

| | *2005* | *2006* |
|---|---|---|
| **Profitability ratios** | | |
| *Return on capital employed:* | | |
| $\frac{\text{Operating profit before exceptional items}}{\text{Average shareholders' funds}} \times 100$ | $\frac{15\,629}{56\,910^*} \times 100$ | $\frac{16\,940}{62\,813^*} \times 100$ |
| | = 27% | = 27% |
| | $\left(\frac{^*53\,137 + 60\,682}{2}\right)$ | $\left(\frac{^*60\,682 + 64\,944}{2}\right)$ |
| $\frac{\text{Profit attributable to equity shareholders}}{\text{Average shareholders' funds}}$ | $\frac{11\,702}{56\,910} \times 100$ | $\frac{12\,253}{62\,813} \times 100$ |
| | = 21% | = 20% |

*Note*: Other ROCE ratios are not relevant as the company does not have any preference shares or any long-term loans.

| | *2005* | *2006* |
|---|---|---|
| *Gross profit:* | | |
| $\frac{\text{Gross profit}}{\text{Revenue}} \times 100$ | $\frac{63\,493}{127\,222} \times 100$ | $\frac{65\,362}{128\,760} \times 100$ |
| | = 50% | = 51% |
| *Mark-up:* | | |
| $\frac{\text{Gross profit}}{\text{Cost of sales}} \times 100$ | $\frac{63\,493}{63\,729} \times 100$ | $\frac{65\,362}{63\,398} \times 100$ |
| | = 100% | = 103% |
| *Operating profit:* | | |
| $\frac{\text{Operating profit before exceptional items}}{\text{Revenue}} \times 100$ | $\frac{15\,629}{127\,222} \times 100$ | $\frac{16\,940}{128\,760} \times 100$ |
| | = 12% | = 13% |
| **Efficiency ratios** | | |
| *Stock turnover:* | | |
| $\frac{\text{Cost of sales}}{\text{Average inventories}}$ | $\frac{63\,729}{9\,795^*}$ | $\frac{63\,398}{8\,723^*}$ |
| | = 6.5 times | = 7.3 times |
| | $\left(\frac{^*10\,418 + 9\,172}{2}\right)$ | $\left(\frac{^*9\,172 + 8\,274}{2}\right)$ |
| *Fixed assets turnover:* | | |
| $\frac{\text{Revenue}}{\text{Net tangible fixed assets}}$ | $\frac{127\,222}{37\,315}$ | $\frac{128\,760}{34\,932}$ |
| | = 3.4 times | = 3.7 times |

| | *2005* | *2006* |
|---|---|---|
| $\dfrac{\text{Revenue}}{\text{Gross tangible fixed assets}}$ | $\dfrac{127\,222}{102\,085^*}$ | $\dfrac{128\,760}{103\,455^*}$ |
| | = 1.2 times | = 1.2 times |
| | (*37 315 + 61 770) | (*34 932 + 68 523) |
| *Trade debtor collection period:* | | |
| $\dfrac{\text{Average trade debtors}}{\text{Revenue}} \times 365$ | $\dfrac{18\,210^*}{127\,222} \times 365$ | $\dfrac{19\,412^*}{128\,760} \times 365$ |
| | = 53 days | = 56 days |
| | $\left(\dfrac{^*\,17\,839 + 18\,580}{2}\right)$ | $\left(\dfrac{^*\,18\,580 + 20\,243}{2}\right)$ |
| *Trade creditor payment period:* | | |
| $\dfrac{\text{Average trade creditors}}{\text{Purchases + production costs}} \times 365$ (no separate figures for purchases available) | $\dfrac{6\,074^*}{62\,483} \times 365$ | $\dfrac{5\,622^*}{62\,500} \times 365$ |
| | = 36 days | = 33 days |
| | $\left(\dfrac{^*5\,706 + 6\,441}{2}\right)$ | $\left(\dfrac{^*6\,441 + 4\,802}{2}\right)$ |

### Investment ratios

| | | |
|---|---|---|
| *Dividend yield:* | | |
| $\dfrac{\text{Dividend per share}}{\text{Market price per share}}$ | $\dfrac{26.25 \times 100}{850}$ | $\dfrac{29.25 \times 100}{958}$ |
| | = 3.1% | = 3.0% |
| *Dividend cover:* | | |
| Not relevant as there are no preference shares | – | – |
| *Basic earnings per share:* | | |
| $\dfrac{\text{Profit attributable to shareholders}}{\text{Weighted average number of ordinary shares in issue during the period}}$ | 62.61p (given) | 65.06p (given) |
| *Price/earnings ratio:* | | |
| $\dfrac{\text{Market price per share}}{\text{Earnings per share}}$ | $\dfrac{850}{62.61}$ | $\dfrac{958}{65.06}$ |
| | = 13.6 | = 14.7 |
| *Capital gearing:* | | |
| Not relevant as the company does not have any long-term borrowings | – | – |

Answer to Example 12.1 *continued*

## (b) Comments on the company's financial performance for the year to 28 January 2006

### Where to begin

Commenting on your results is perhaps the more difficult part of the exercise. The calculation of ratios is relatively straightforward if you can remember the formulae or you have them in front of you. In a complicated set of published accounts it might not always be easy to find the data you need or the information might not be exactly in the form that you would like. You will also find that even with a 100-page published annual report and accounts there will probably be some information that you would like that is either not disclosed or it is not clear what it means. Nevertheless, you will still be able to calculate or extract a considerable number of ratios and it likely that you end up with too many to handle comfortably in your analysis. So how do you go about it?

With experience you will probably develop your own method of interpreting a set of financial accounts, but until then we recommend that you examine your ratios in the following order: (1) liquidity, (2) profitability, (3) efficiency, and (4) investment.

We think that generally the liquidity ratios are the most critical and should therefore be examined first. If a company (or any other entity for that matter) does not have or is not likely to have sufficient cash to finance its day-to-day needs it cannot continue in business for very long no matter how profitable it could turn out to be in the long run. Assuming that it has no cash problems, *then* we want to know whether or not it is making a lot of money.

If a company has no cash problems and it appears to be profitable, is it as profitable as it could be? Is it making the best use of the resources that have been invested in the business? In other words, is it operating efficiently? And finally perhaps, if we are satisfied that the liquidity, profitability and efficiency indicators are positive, would we recommend an investment in the company – and what does the market have to say about it? This is the point at which we look at the company from an *investor's* perspective.

Let us now examine A.G. Barr plc's 2006 results using the above step-by-step approach. Unless stated otherwise all currency figures are in £000s.

### Liquidity

The easiest and most obvious place to start is to check the cash position at the end of the financial year. At the end of 2005 Barr had £34 958 in cash at the bank but this had dropped to £31 412 at the end of 2006, a decrease of £3 546 or 10.1%. In absolute terms these are large amounts of money but are they significant as far as Barr is concerned? There are two main points we can make here:

- the two balances represent 53.7% and 44.8%, respectively, of current assets at the end of each year;
- each balance covers much more than the *total* of current liabilities at the respective year ends (£24 716 for 2005 and £24 045 for 2006).

So although Barr had £3.5m less cash at the end of 2006 than it had at the end of 2005 there does not appear to be any liquidity problem. This assertion is supported by the two liquidity ratios that we calculated. The current assets ratio shows that there was an actual improvement in the overall liquidity position in 2006 (from 2.6 to 2.9). When we exclude inventories from the equation, the acid test ratio has also risen (from 2.3 to 2.6).

This is a very healthy position, but is it too healthy? Has Barr too much of its liquid resources in cash? Should it not be investing more of its resources in the business? Or, if it does not want to do so, why is it not paying a much higher proportion of its earnings to its shareholders? The company had £57 186 of retained earnings at the end of 2005 and £62 056 at the end of 2006, and yet it only paid out dividends totalling £5 108 and £5 628 respectively during each financial year. It appears that for these two years at least the directors could have been a great deal more generous. But perhaps it has got some massive expansion plans that it hopes to finance out of its earnings? Might this explain the £3.5m drop in the cash position at the end of 2005? Was this the start of a large capital investment programme? Perhaps the cash flow statement gives us a clue?

It is easy to get mesmerized by so many figures so how do you begin? We suggest the following approach. Firstly, do a simple horizontal analysis by calculating the increase or decrease for each line in the cash flow statement. Insert the increase or decrease for each line at the side of the statement (but make sure that each section and the final total balance). Secondly, look down the changes and highlight the three largest ones measured in absolute cash terms.

In Barr's case the three most significant changes are:

- an increase of £9 070 in the purchase of property, plant and equipment;
- a *decrease* of £2 694 in cash generated by operations;
- an increase of £2 759 in the cost of purchasing the company's own shares (buying back the company's shares means that, other things being equal, the company can pay out a higher dividend to a smaller number of shareholders).

The company is, in fact, already engaged in a major capital investment project but it would appear that it has the liquid resources to go even further.

The *overall verdict* is that the company does not appear to have any immediate liquidity problems.

### Profitability

We can be reasonably confident, therefore, that in the immediate future the company will not have any cash problems and that its future as a going concern is not in question. We now need to ask just how good it is at maximizing the return it gets on the amounts invested in the business. In other words, just how profitable is it?

We can see from the consolidated income statement that:

- its operating profit before exceptional items was £15 629 in 2005 compared with £16 940 in 2006;
- the profit on ordinary activities was £17 381 compared with £16 287;
- the profit attributable to equity shareholders was £12 253 compared with £11 702.

These are all increases and in absolute terms they are very large amounts (remember these figures are all in 'thousands'). But what did it take to achieve them? What sort of return is the company getting on the amount invested in the business?

In order to answer these questions we need once again to put the data into context and we can do so by examining the profitability ratios we calculated in answering the first part of the question.

The *operating* profit before any exceptional items (i.e. items that are not expected to recur again) are taken into account as a proportion of what the shareholders had invested in the business was 27% in both years. When other costs and incomes are taken into account, the return was 21% in 2005 and 20% in 2006. In broad terms, therefore, the company performed just as well in 2006 as it did in 2005. But is 27% (or 20%) good, bad or indifferent? This is where you perhaps have to use your instinct.

Normally you would expect an increase in profitability year-on-year but this did not happen in Barr's case in 2006. So are we happy with a return of 27% or 20% (depending on how you calculate it)? The answer to this question is almost certainly 'yes'. If you had had £1000 available in 2006 available for investment and you managed to get a return of 20% you would think that you had done very well. Why? Because you would compare the return that you could get with other returns and 20% would be far greater that you could have got by investing in (say) a bank or a building society. You might have got a higher return in another company but remember that the higher the return the greater the risk. The other points to remember, of course, are that:

Answer to Example 12.1 *continued*

- the company would not pay out all of the profit that it has made to its shareholders;
- the amount that you might have paid for your shares almost certainly would have been well in excess of their nominal value, hence reducing substantially the *yield* that you would get (see the investment section).

Nevertheless, the indicators that we have highlighted so far in Barr's case are encouraging, so what about the other ratios? The gross profit ratio in both years is round about 50% and the mark-up 100% (103% in 2006). In other words, the company sells its products at a price about double what it takes to make them. The operating profit (before exceptional items) is also steady (12% in 2005 and 13% in 2006). Normally we would want to calculate these ratios over a much longer period but we cannot do so as the data were not provided in the question and so we do not know what the gross profit and net profit trends have been.

The *overall verdict* is the company appears to be achieving and is maintaining a high level of profitability.

### Efficiency

We may be satisfied with the company's level of profitability, but is it making as much profit as it could for what has been invested? In other words, just how *efficient* are its operations?

In this exercise we have calculated four efficiency ratios: stock turnover, fixed assets turnover (on both a gross and net basis), the trade debtor collection period and the trade creditor payment period. What do they tell us and do they give an overall impression of the company's efficiency?

We must treat the stock turnover ratios that we have calculated with some caution because we think that the cost of sales includes production costs and so we do not have a separate figure for the cost of the purchases. Nevertheless, provided that we compare 2005 and 2006 on an identical basis we can read *something* into the result. The stock turnover appears to have gone up from 6.5 to 7.3, so as a proportion of its production and purchasing stock the company is turning over its stock faster in 2006 than it did in 2005.

On a net basis the fixed assets turnover has increased from 3.4 to 3.7, but on a gross basis (i.e. excluding depreciation) it has remained static at 1.2. We have no means of knowing whether these ratios are of little or no concern. Circumstances vary so much between companies (even between those in the same sector of the economy) so we do not have much to go on. All we can do is try to calculate what has happened over a longer period for this particular company – but in this exercise we don't have the information to do so.

The trade debtor collection period has increased slightly from 53 days to 56 days. This means that its debtors took longer to pay in 2006 than they did in 2005. But bear in mind that we do not have any information about credit sales so this ratio must be treated with some caution. At the moment this increase does not appear to be of great concern because, as we have seen, the company's liquidity position is very healthy. Nevertheless, this key indicator should be watched very closely because if the trade debtor collection period continues to rise then it will not be long before the company's customers are taking two months to settle their debts.

By contrast the company's trade creditor period has decreased by three days, from 36 days in 2005 to 33 days in 2006. In other words it paid its trade creditors faster in 2006 than it did in 2005. A company with a less strong liquidity position than Barr's could find that a combination of an increase in the trade debtor collection period and a decrease in the trade creditor payment causes it to have a liquidity problem. An average trade payment period of 30 days or so would normally be considered to be fairly low. It means that Barr treats its suppliers with a great deal of consideration and that the company makes every effort to settle with them very quickly. It is a sign of a company acting very responsibly. But again bear in mind that we do not have the information to calculate the ratio *accurately*, i.e. by just using purchases and not purchases plus production costs.

The *overall verdict* seems to be that we have insufficient information to be absolutely confident that Barr is operating at maximum efficiency. There are one or two areas where we need more information before we can be too categorical but we have no reason to believe that the company is doing anything other that striving to improve its performance.

### Investment

We must stress that in this exercise we do not intend to advise whether or not you should invest in this company! However, for the purpose of this exercise let us assume that you are interested in the company as a potential investment. What then is the overall picture? We have seen that the company liquidity and profitability both appear to be highly satisfactory, while its efficiency is, at the very least, satisfactory. From a combined liquidity, profitability and efficiency point of view an existing shareholder should be reasonably happy with the performance of the company, although remember that most shareholders are primarily interested in the dividends that they are getting or are likely to get.

Viewed from this perspective, shareholders will be pleased that there was an increase in the dividend paid from 26.25p per share in 2005 to 29.25p in 2006, an increase of 11.4%. Even so, in recent years, at least, the directors do not seem to have been particularly generous in distributing to shareholders what profits the company has made. Note that the company's retained earnings in 2005 represent 94.2% of shareholders' funds and 95.6% in 2006! The dividends paid in 2005 and 2006 appear, therefore, extremely modest when compared with what could have been paid out. Nevertheless, the dividends paid out do represent 42% and 45% of the basic earnings per share for 2005 and 2006, respectively, which on a year-by-year basis is not an unreasonable proportion. The yield (based on the market price of the company's shares at the end of the two financial years) was about 3%. This was not out of line with what could have been obtained by investing in other similar public companies. The P/E ratio was 13.6 and 14.7 for 2005 and 2006, respectively, meaning that in theory you would have to wait a fairly long time before the company's earnings per share covered what you might have paid for them. However, a rising P/E ratio indicates that the market has confidence in the future of the company so the increase in this ratio in 2006 is very encouraging.

The *overall verdict* is that the investment ratios confirm the favourable analysis that we have put forward when dealing with the liquidity, profitability and investment ratios.

### Summary

Based on just two years' data and with the limited amount of information that we have in this exercise, Barr appears to be in a favourable liquid position, earning a comfortable profit and operating reasonably efficiently. It retains a high proportion of its profits and is cautious about paying out a high dividend that, perhaps in a more difficult economic climate, it may not be able to sustain. Nevertheless, judged by its P/E ratio the market appears to view the company highly favourably.

The company has clearly performed very well in the last two years during a relatively prosperous economic period. However, you should remember that Barr operates in the soft drinks industry and if there is ever a downturn in the economy then the industry may suffer unduly from lower consumer spending. Soft drinks are not an absolutely essential commodity and some families may choose to economize on this product if they really do have to cut back on what they spend. So in a more detailed analysis than we have done here we would want to include a general assessment of the general national and international economic and political climate and a specific one for the UK soft drinks industry.

We suggest that you now have a go at doing Exercise 12.1 on your own without looking at the suggested solution. If you cannot remember the formulae for the accounting ratios, you can refer to the summary provided at the end of the chapter.

### Questions non-accountants should ask

As far as this chapter is concerned, there are two situations in which you might find yourself: either with a set of financial accounts that will have been interpreted for you, or some that you might have to interpret for yourself. Irrespective of which situation you find yourself in, you might find it useful to ask the following questions.

- How reliable is the basic accounting information underpinning this information in front of me?
- Have consistent accounting policies been adopted throughout the period covered?
- If not, has each year's results been adjusted on to the same accounting basis?
- Were there any unusual items in any year that may have distorted a comparative analysis?
- Was the rate of inflation significant in any year covered by the report?
- If so, should the basic accounting data be adjusted to allow for it?
- What are the three or four most significant changes in these accounts during the period they cover?
- Are there any apparent causal links between them, such as greater efficiency resulting in a higher level of profitability or higher profits causing cash flow problems?
- What are the most important factors that this report tells me about the entity's progress during the period in question and its prospects for the future?

## Conclusion

This chapter has explained how you can examine the financial performance of an entity over a certain period of time. If a detailed examination is required it may be necessary to examine the general business environment and economic sector in which the entity operates. Much information will also be collected about the entity itself. One of the main sources of information will be its annual report and accounts (especially if it is a company).

While a great deal of information may be found in the annual accounts, that information has to be put into context as the absolute numbers disclosed in the accounts are often large but do not mean much in isolation and are often difficult to understand. This means that the accounts need to be analysed. There are four main types of analysis:

- horizontal analysis, involving a line-by-line inspection across the various time periods;
- trend analysis, in which all the data are indexed to a base of 100;
- vertical analysis, where each period's data is expressed as a percentage of a total;
- ratio analysis, which requires a comparison to be made of one item with another item expressing the relationship as either a percentage or a factor.

All of these four types of analyses rely primarily on the accounting data, which itself is subject to a number of reservations, such as the accounting policies and the methods used in preparing the accounts. These reservations must be allowed for when interpreting a set of accounts, especially when a comparison is made with other entities since accounting policies and methods vary between companies.

Ratio analysis is the most important of the four types of analyses. There are literally hundreds of ratios that could be calculated, plus some highly specialist ones that relate to particular industries. In this chapter we have selected just 15 common but important ratios and grouped them under four headings:

- liquidity ratios, which help to decide whether an entity has enough cash to continue as a going concern;
- profitability ratios, which measure the profit an entity has made;
- efficiency ratios, which ratios show how well the entity has used its resources;
- investment ratios, which help to consider the investment potential of an entity.

Irrespective of the category into which they fall, ratios should only be regarded as a signpost: in themselves they do not actually *interpret* the accounts for you. They are merely an arithmetical device that points you in the right direction and help you to assess what *has* happened and to predict what *might* happen. They provide you with the evidence, but you have to use that evidence to come to a verdict.

## Key points

1. The interpretation of accounts involves examining financial accounts in some detail so as to be able to explain what has happened and to predict what is likely to happen.
2. The examination can be undertaken by using a number of techniques, such as horizontal analysis, trend analysis, vertical analysis and ratio analysis.
3. Ratio analysis is a common method of interpreting accounts. It involves comparing one item in the accounts with another closely related item. Ratios are normally expressed in the form of a percentage or a factor. There are literally hundreds of recognized accounting ratios (excluding those that relate to specific industries) and we have restricted our study to just 15.
4. Not all of the ratios covered in this chapter will be relevant for non-manufacturing, non-trading or not-for-profit entities. It is necessary to be selective in your choice of ratios.
5. When one item is related to another item in the form of a ratio, it is necessary to make sure that there is a close and logical correlation between the two items.
6. In the case of some ratios, different definitions can be adopted. This applies particularly to ROCE and capital gearing. In other cases, sometimes only year-end balances are used and not an annual average. This applies especially to ratios relating to stocks, debtors and creditors.
7. Assessing trends and calculating ratios is not the same as interpreting a set of financial accounts. Interpretation involves using a wide range of information sources as well as the incorporation of various types of analyses into a cohesive appraisal of an entity's past performance and its future prospects.

## Check your learning

*The answers to these questions can be found within the text.*

1 What is meant by the term 'interpretation of accounts'?

2 Give three reasons why the absolute data shown in financial accounts may need to be interpreted.

3 List the users of accounts and suggest one piece of information that each user group may require from a set of financial accounts.

4 What is the difference between (a) horizontal analysis, (b) trend analysis?

5 What is vertical analysis?

6 What is (a) a ratio, (b) ratio analysis?

7 What four main categories may be used for classifying accounting ratios?

8 What does 'ROCE' mean and how may it be calculated?

9 What is the difference between the gross profit ratio and the mark-up ratio?

10 Why might it be misleading to compare the net profit ratio of one entity with that of another entity?

11 Why is liquidity important, and what two ratios may be used for assessing it?

12 How would you assess whether stock turnover and fixed asset turnover ratios were good or bad?

13 What is meant by the 'trade debtor collection period'. Is a 60-day period worrying?

14 What is meant by the 'trade creditor payment period'. Is a 100-day period worrying?

15 Which two investment ratios take market prices into account?

16 Explain why there may be a difference between the dividend payable and its yield.

17 What is meant by 'EPS' and where might you find it in a set of published accounts?

18 What is the P/E ratio, and what is its importance?

19 What is capital gearing and how might it be calculated?

20 What is a possible link between the following ratios: (a) profitability and efficiency; (b) profitability and liquidity; (c) profitability and investment, and (d) efficiency and liquidity?

21 Outline the main steps you would take if you were asked to appraise the financial performance of a company using its annual report and accounts.

## News story quiz

*Remember the news story at the beginning of this chapter? Go back to that story and re-read it before answering the following questions.*

Shell's 2005 results were covered extensively and somewhat sensationally in the press. The main point to bear in mind is that while £13 billion pounds is undoubtedly a lot of money, and that apparently it may be a record, we still have not have much else to go on.

### Questions

1 How meaningful is to you as a newspaper reader to be informed that Shell made a profit of £1.5 million an hour?

2 How far does the article enable you to put the £13 billion profit ($23bn) into context?

3 Is the chief executive justified in appearing to claim that the $23bn was acceptable since apparently 90% of it was earned outside the UK?

4 Can you be certain that Shell was 'profiteering', and if so, what do you think should be done about it?

## Tutorial questions

*The answers to questions marked with an asterisk may be found in Appendix 4.*

12.1 'Accounting ratios are only as good as the data on which they are based.' Discuss.

12.2 How far do you accept the argument that the return on capital employed ratio can give a misleading impression of an entity's profitability?

12.3 Is ratio analysis useful in understanding how an entity has performed?

12.4* The following information has been extracted from the books of account of Betty for the year to 31 January 2008:

**Trading and profit and loss account for the year to 31 January 2008**

| | *£000* | *£000* |
|---|---|---|
| Sales (all credit) | | 100 |
| *Less*: Cost of goods sold: | | |
| Opening stock | 15 | |
| Purchases | 65 | |
| | 80 | |
| *Less*: Closing stock | 10 | 70 |
| *Gross profit* | | 30 |
| Administrative expenses | | 16 |
| *Net profit* | | 14 |

**Balance sheet at 31 January 2008**

| | £000 | £000 |
|---|---|---|
| *Fixed assets* (net book value) | | 29 |
| *Current assets* | | |
| Stock | 10 | |
| Trade debtors | 12 | |
| Cash | 3 | |
| | 25 | |
| *Less: Current liabilities* | | |
| Trade creditors | 6 | 19 |
| | | 48 |
| *Financed by:* | | |
| Capital at 1 February 2007 | | 40 |
| *Add:* Net profit | 14 | |
| *Less:* Drawings | 6 | 8 |
| | | 48 |

*Required*:
Calculate the following accounting ratios:
(a) gross profit
(b) net profit
(c) return on capital employed
(d) current ratio
(e) acid test
(f) stock turnover
(g) debtor collection period.

12.5* You are presented with the following summarized accounts:

**James Ltd**
**Profit and loss account for the year to 28 February 2009**

| | £000 |
|---|---|
| Sales (all credit) | 1 200 |
| Cost of sales | 600 |
| *Gross profit* | 600 |
| Administrative expenses | (500) |
| Debenture interest payable | (10) |
| Profit on ordinary activities | 90 |
| Taxation | (30) |
| | 60 |
| Dividends | (40) |
| Retained profit for the year | 20 |

**James Ltd**
**Balance sheet at 28 February 2009**

| | £000 | £000 | £000 |
|---|---|---|---|
| *Fixed assets* (net book value) | | | 685 |
| *Current assets* | | | |
| Stock | | 75 | |
| Trade debtors | | 200 | |
| | | 275 | |
| *Less: Current liabilities* | | | |
| Trade creditors | 160 | | |
| Bank overdraft | 10 | | |
| Taxation | 30 | | |
| Proposed dividend | 40 | 240 | 35 |
| | | | 720 |
| *Capital and reserves* | | | |
| Ordinary share capital | | | 600 |
| Profit and loss account | | | 20 |
| *Shareholders' funds* | | | 620 |
| *Loans:* | | | |
| 10% debentures | | | 100 |
| | | | 720 |

*Required*:
Calculate the following accounting ratios
(a) return on capital employed
(b) gross profit
(c) mark-up
(d) net profit
(e) acid test
(f) fixed assets turnover
(g) debtor collection period
(h) capital gearing.

12.6 You are presented with the following information relating to three companies:

**Profit and loss accounts for the year to 31 March 2006**

| | *Mark Limited* £000 | *Luke Limited* £000 | *John Limited* £000 |
|---|---|---|---|
| Profit before tax | 64 | 22 | 55 |

**Balance sheet (extracts) at 31 March 2006**

| | *Mark Limited* | *Luke Limited* | *John Limited* |
|---|---|---|---|
| | *£000* | *£000* | *£000* |
| *Capital and reserves* | | | |
| Ordinary share capital of £1 each | 100 | 177 | 60 |
| Cumulative 15% preference shares of £1 each | – | 20 | 10 |
| Share premium account | – | 70 | 20 |
| Profit and loss account | 150 | 60 | 200 |
| *Shareholders' funds* | 250 | 327 | 290 |
| *Loans* | | | |
| 10% debentures | – | – | 100 |
| | 250 | 327 | 390 |

*Required*:
Calculate the following accounting ratios:
(a) return on capital employed
(b) capital gearing.

12.7 The following information relates to Helena Limited:

**Trading account year to 30 April**

| | *2004* | *2005* | *2006* | *2007* | *2008* | *2009* |
|---|---|---|---|---|---|---|
| | *£000* | *£000* | *£000* | *£000* | *£000* | *£000* |
| Sales (all credit) | – | 130 | 150 | 190 | 210 | 320 |
| *Less*: Cost of goods sold: | | | | | | |
| Opening stock | – | 20 | 30 | 30 | 35 | 40 |
| Purchases (all in credit terms) | – | 110 | 110 | 135 | 145 | 305 |
| | – | 130 | 140 | 165 | 180 | 345 |
| *Less*: Closing stock | – | 30 | 30 | 35 | 40 | 100 |
| | – | 100 | 110 | 130 | 140 | 245 |
| Gross profit | – | 30 | 40 | 60 | 70 | 75 |
| Trade debtors at 30 April | 40 | 45 | 40 | 70 | 100 | 150 |
| Trade creditors at 30 April | 20 | 20 | 25 | 25 | 30 | 60 |

*Required*:
Calculate the following accounting ratios for each of the five years from 30 April 2005 to 2009 inclusive:
(a) gross profit
(b) mark-up
(c) stock turnover
(d) trade debtor collection period
(e) trade creditor payment period.

12.8 You are presented with the following information relating to Hedge public limited company for the year to 31 May 2008:

1 The company has an issued and fully paid share capital of £500 000 ordinary shares of £1 each. There are no preference shares.
2 The market price of the shares at 31 May 2008 was £3.50.
3 The net profit after taxation for the year to 31 May 2008 was £70 000.
4 The directors are proposing a dividend of 7p per share for the year to 31 May 2008.

*Required:*
Calculate the following accounting ratios:
(a) dividend yield
(b) dividend cover
(c) earnings per share
(d) price/earnings ratio.

12.9 The following information relates to Style Limited for the two years to 30 June 2008 and 2009 respectively:

**Trading and profit and loss accounts for the years**

| | *2008* | | *2009* | |
|---|---|---|---|---|
| | *£000* | *£000* | *£000* | *£000* |
| Sales (all credit) | | 1 500 | | 1 900 |
| *Less*: Cost of goods sold: | | | | |
| Opening stock | 80 | | 100 | |
| Purchases (all on credit terms) | 995 | | 1 400 | |
| | 1 075 | | 1 500 | |
| *Less*: Closing stock | 100 | 975 | 200 | 1 300 |
| *Gross profit* | | 525 | | 600 |
| *Less*: Expenses | | 420 | | 495 |
| *Net profit* | | 105 | | 105 |

**Balance sheet at 30 June**

| | *2008* | | *2009* | |
|---|---|---|---|---|
| | *£000* | *£000* | *£000* | *£000* |
| *Fixed assets* (net book value) | | 685 | | 420 |
| *Current assets* | | | | |
| Stock | 100 | | 200 | |
| Trade debtors | 375 | | 800 | |
| Bank | 25 | | – | |
| | 500 | | 1 000 | |
| *Less: Current liabilities* | | | | |
| Bank overdraft | – | | 10 | |
| Trade creditors | 80 | | 200 | |
| | 80 | 420 | 210 | 790 |
| | | 1 105 | | 1 210 |
| *Capital and reserves* | | | | |
| Ordinary share capital | | 900 | | 900 |
| Profit and loss account | | 205 | | 310 |
| *Shareholders' funds* | | 1 105 | | 1 210 |

*Required*:

(a) Calculate the following accounting ratios for the two years 2008 and 2009 respectively:
 1 gross profit
 2 mark-up
 3 net profit
 4 return on capital employed
 5 stock turnover
 6 current ratio
 7 acid test
 8 trade debtor collection period
 9 trade creditor payment period.

(b) Comment on the company's performance for the year to 30 June 2009.

**Further practice questions, study material and links to relevant sites on the World Wide Web can be found on the website that accompanies this book. The site can be found at www.pearsoned.co.uk/dyson**

# Appendix: Summary of the main ratios

## Liquidity ratios

$$\text{Current assets ratio} = \frac{\text{current assets}}{\text{current liabilities}}$$

$$\text{Acid test ratio} = \frac{\text{current assets} - \text{stocks}}{\text{current liabilities}}$$

## Profitability ratios

$$\text{ROCE} = \frac{\text{net profit before taxation}}{\text{average shareholders' funds}} \times 100$$

$$\text{ROCE} = \frac{\text{net profit after taxation}}{\text{average shareholders' funds}} \times 100$$

$$\text{ROCE} = \frac{\text{net profit after taxation and preference dividends}}{\text{average shareholders' funds less preference shares}} \times 100$$

$$\text{ROCE} = \frac{\text{profit before taxation and interest}}{\text{average shareholders' funds} + \text{long-term loans}} \times 100$$

$$\text{Gross profit ratio} = \frac{\text{gross profit}}{\text{total sales revenue}} \times 100$$

$$\text{Mark-up ratio} = \frac{\text{gross profit}}{\text{cost of goods sold}} \times 100$$

$$\text{Net profit ratio} = \frac{\text{net profit before taxation}}{\text{total sales revenue}} \times 100$$

## Efficiency ratios

$$\text{Stock turnover} = \frac{\text{cost of goods sold}}{\text{average stock}}$$

$$\text{Fixed assets turnover} = \frac{\text{total sales revenue}}{\text{fixed assets at net book value}}$$

$$\text{Trade debtor collection period} = \frac{\text{average trade debtors}}{\text{total credit sales}} \times 365 \text{ days}$$

$$\text{Trade creditor payment period} = \frac{\text{average trade creditors}}{\text{total credit purchases}} \times 365 \text{ days}$$

### Investment ratios

$$\text{Dividend yield} = \frac{\text{dividend per share}}{\text{market price per share}} \times 100$$

$$\text{Dividend cover} = \frac{\text{net profit after taxation and preference dividend}}{\text{paid and proposed ordinary dividends}}$$

$$\text{Earnings per share} = \frac{\text{net profit (or loss) for the period less dividends and other appropriations in respect of non-equity shares}}{\text{weighted average number of shares in issue during the period}}$$

$$\text{Price/earnings ratio} = \frac{\text{market price per share}}{\text{earnings per share}}$$

$$\text{Capital gearing} = \frac{\text{preference shares + long-term loans}}{\text{shareholders' funds + long-term loans}} \times 100$$

# Chapter 13 Contemporary issues

**Not everyone is happy ...**

## ASB faces fierce opposition over approach to standards

**Dismay and disappointment over US bias and lack of influence, writes Paul Grant**

Opposition to the reporting regime for UK and international financial standards has reached a new level with the ASB being told to reconsider its approach.

Significant opposition was raised to initial proposals at a public meeting held by the UK Accounting Standards Board.

Andy Simmonds, technical partner at Deloitte and member of the Urgent Issues Task Force, said he had been 'sadly disappointed' with the direction IFRS had taken. He argued that the standards had been 'steered towards US GAAP', and that the board did not seem to listen to any constituents other than the US.

Richard Martin, head of financial reporting at ACCA, reflected the view of many when he argued that, for the ASB to have any influence on the direction of international standards, it would have to get involved at a very early stage. 'At the exposure draft stage it is already too late,' he said.

Key accounting figures from the profession, business and academia, who attended the meeting, raised concerns over the IASB's plan to converge with US GAAP.

Professor Stella Fearnley of Portsmouth University said that, apart from the small number of companies with a US listing, the benefits to the rest from the project were not clear. She added that many of those with a listing were currently trying to exit the market.

A large proportion of the meeting's attendees favoured the introduction of a system that would see full IFRS remain for all the public interest entities, while the rest would adopt the standard to come out of the IASB's SME project, or a version of the current FRSSE.

A similar number wanted to see the introduction of a third tier of companies, between those using full IFRS and the SME standard, which would use a scaled-down version of international standards.

There is no timescale for the ASB to produce a concrete plan, but chairman Ian Mackintosh said: 'We need to finalise the strategy pretty soon.'

*Accountancy Age*, 26 January 2006.



*Questions relating to this news story can be found on page 268*

## About this chapter

In this chapter we look ahead over the next five years or so to see what major issues are likely to arise in financial accounting and reporting practices. We identify four such issues that we think will be of particular interest and relevance to non-accountants. There will be, of course, many other problems that affect the accountancy profession but as these are likely to be highly technical, they are not of immediate concern to non-specialists. The four issues that we are going to discuss in this chapter are:

- pending legal changes;
- the increasing internationalization of financial reporting;
- the problem of 'accounting scandals';
- the determination of revenue in financial reporting.

**Learning objectives**

**By the end of this chapter you should be able to:**

- **summarize the proposed legal changes to UK financial accounting and reporting;**
- **predict the impact of international accounting standards on UK financial reporting;**
- **assess the effect that accounting scandals have on the accountancy profession;**
- **describe the difficulties of apportioning revenue to specific accounting periods.**

## Why this chapter is important for non-accountants

Accounting is a dynamic discipline. It has to be in order to cope with a rapidly changing world. New problems and new issues arise and some way has to be found of dealing with them as quickly as possible. There may then be a need to report them to interested parties, and, if there is, how and in what form should the report take?

Accountants are expected to take a lead on the reporting issues because this is their expertise but non-accountants should also be heavily involved because the impact of many issues is far too wide-ranging to be left to just one group of specialists. For example, a decision to write-off goodwill to the profit and loss account instead of leaving it on the balance sheet can have a significant effect on a company's reported profit, the dividend it pays and on its share price.

It is as a result of such consequences that non-accountants need to know what new accounting and reporting issues are currently under discussion in the business, economic, financial and political worlds and what proposals are being suggested to deal with them. Space does not allow us to deal with all of them in this book but we can give you an indication of some of the changes that are likely to take place in the next five to ten years. We have chosen four of the major ones but you are encouraged to read the business and financial press regularly to keep up with emerging issues in financial reporting.

In summary, then, we suggest that this chapter is particularly important for non-accountants for the following reasons.

- To be briefed about the general business environment in which accounting operates both nationally and internationally.
- To be informed about some contemporary issues in financial accounting and reporting.
- To advise your senior manager of any changes that may affect your own responsibilities.
- To take an active part in any debate on the effect of any proposed financial reporting changes affecting your own entity.

## Overview

We cannot be absolutely certain what changes will take place in financial accounting and reporting over the next few years. Some changes that appear highly likely at the moment may be abandoned altogether, while others may be radically amended or at the very least delayed well into the long term. We can, however, be reasonably confident of two broad changes:

- sometime during the next five years (short of a political earthquake) there will be a new Companies Act;
- within ten years or so international accounting standards will have replaced most of the UK standards.

In the next two sections we look at the statutory and accounting standards changes that are likely to take place. There then follows a section dealing with what we have called 'accounting scandals', or to use a less emotive term 'accounting irregularities'. The last main section of the chapter deals with the highly complex and contentious issue of revenue recognition. Indeed, many so-called accounting irregularities have arisen largely because of the difficulty in determining *when* it is prudent to transfer revenue incomes to the profit and loss account.

We now turn to the first of the four contemporary financial reporting issues that we are going to discuss, the changes to statutory requirements.

## Statutory changes

In Chapter 9 we explained that British company law is based on the 1985 Companies Act as amended by the 1989 Companies Act. The 1985 Act consolidated the Companies Acts of 1948, 1967, 1976, 1980 and 1981. The 1967 and 1976 Acts were relatively slim, so you can see that Parliament deals with company law issues only at infrequent and long intervals. This trend has continued into recent times. It is now nearly twenty years since the last Companies Act was passed, although it does look now as though there is another well on its way.

It will have taken its time. As long ago as 1998 the Company Law Review Steering Group started to look at what could be done to improve UK company law but it was not until November 2005 that a bill was finally introduced into the House of Lords. It reached the House of Commons in May 2006 and by the end of July 2006 it had completed its Commons Committee stage. So in the autumn of 2006 it looked as though it would not be long before there was a new Companies Act on the statute book.

The bill is long and complex and it deals with company law generally, not just with matters that relate largely to accounting. We summarize below those matters that are of particular relevance to users of this book but remember that they are just a *summary*. We have also not necessarily extracted the actual wording of the bill and before it becomes an Act, some clauses might be amended or dropped altogether.

- A quoted company is defined, *inter alia*, as a company that is 'officially listed in an EEA state'. An 'unquoted company' is one that is not quoted!
- Every company must keep adequate accounting records (the bill explains what is meant by 'adequate') and every officer of the company who does not do so commits an offence.

- Company directors must not approve accounts if they do not give 'a true and fair view'. So this requirement once again receives statutory backing.
- International accounting standards also receive statutory recognition. Company accounts can be prepared in accordance with either the Act (as it will become) or with IASs, while group accounts must be prepared in accordance with IASs.
- The company's directors have to approve the annual accounts, they must be signed by a director of the company on behalf of the board and the signature must be on the balance sheet.
- The directors must prepare a directors' report and, *inter alia*, it must contain a business review. The business review takes the place of the operating and financial review. The OFR was expected to become mandatory but rather unexpectedly the Government changed its mind, allegedly because of the extra burden and cost that might be placed on companies.
- The directors of quoted companies have to prepare a directors' remuneration report. The bill lays down what it should contain, how it should be set out and what sections should be audited.
- Companies may supply summarized financial statements (SFS) to those shareholders who want them instead of the detailed annual report and accounts. The bill spells out what SFSs should contain.
- Quoted companies have to make their annual report and accounts and their preliminary results available on the Internet.
- The statutory accounts must be accompanied by an auditor's report.
- The bill defines what is meant by 'publishing'. A document is regarded as being published if a company 'publishes (sic), issues or circulates it or otherwise makes it available for public inspection in a manner calculated to invite members of the public generally, or any class of members of the public, to read it'.
- Public companies must file their accounts with the Registrar of Companies within six months of their year end. Private companies are allowed nine months.
- The bill gives a general definition of accounting standards. 'Accounting standards', it states, 'means statements of standard accounting practice issued by such body or bodies as may be prescribed by regulations'. So if an Inter-galactic Accounting Standards Board comes along in the next 25 years, the Act will be able to accommodate it.

The accounts and reports section of the bill is contained in 58 pages and has 97 clauses (some of which are short and some long) and it is estimated that it will replace about two-thirds of the 1985 Companies Act. One of the most interesting developments, at least from our point of view, is the specific incorporation into law of international accounting standards. And it is to that subject that we now turn.

**Activity 13.1**

Log on to the Internet for an update on the progress of this bill (you might try **www.dti.gov.uk**). If the bill has been enacted try searching for a summary of its provisions, but confine your search to the part covering 'accounts and reports'. Compare the above summary with the provisions of the new Act.

## Accounting standards

The requirement for EU-listed companies to adopt international accounting standards from 2005 onwards and the enactment of that into British company law has, of course, dealt a body blow to the work of the UK Accounting Standards Board. For over 30 years the ASB and its predecessor bodies have struggled to narrow the differences in accounting treatment between entities, and there were signs in recent years that the ASB was having some success.

When the ASB was faced with much of its work being replaced by IASB requirements it could have decided to continue formulating and issuing accounting standards applicable only to non-listed UK companies and other entities. It has not chosen to do so. Instead it intends to substitute international accounting standards in place of the equivalent UK standards. It is unlikely that this will be achieved in less than five years, and it could take a great deal longer. So you can expect that for some time a number of ASB accounting standards will still be of relevance for many UK entities. But what about the longer term?

In an Exposure Draft issued in 2005, the ASB outlined what it expected its future role to be. It indicated that it would have five main activities:

- to contribute to the work of the IASB (this was considered to be its most significant activity);
- to influence EU policy on the development of accounting standards;
- to achieve 'convergence' between UK and IFRS standards;
- to improve 'other aspects' of UK accounting standards;
- to improve communications between companies and investors.

ASB Exposure Draft, *Accounting Standard-setting in a Changing Environment: The Role of the Accounting Standards Board*, 2005.

In effect, therefore, the ASB sees itself becoming largely a lobbying organization for promoting UK interests in international accounting standard-setting matters. It clearly expects that the IASB will become the predominant accounting standards-setting body in the world and this will almost certainly be the case if convergence (as it is called) can be achieved with the US accounting standards body, the Financial Accounting Standards Board (FASB). The IASB has been working with the FASB for some time with the aim of achieving convergence but so far the negotiations have proved unsuccessful. At least they have not broken down and it is probably only a matter of time before there is some agreement between the two bodies.

It will be a remarkable achievement. International accounting standards were meant to narrow accounting practices throughout the world. However, it was recognized that if they were to be generally accepted then they could not be too prescriptive as they had to allow for widely differing economic, financial, political and social conditions among the IASB's member countries. Now that the IASB has become a much more powerful body (as a result of the EU's requirement for EU-listed companies) it will be interesting to see whether future standards become much more prescriptive, and if they do how the poorer countries cope with some very tight (and costly) reporting requirements.

The UK has been accustomed to working with fairly prescriptive accounting standards for quite some time so it should not have a problem if new international accounting standards are tightened up. Indeed, because of the UK's experience the ASB will have an extremely powerful voice in future international accounting standard setting. So by 2015 (say) the ASB may no longer be setting its own standards but it will have become heavily involved in formulating and promoting the best accounting practices throughout the world.

**Activity 13.2**

On a scale of 1 to 5 (1 = highly unlikely; 5 = very likely) how likely do you think that by 2015 (a) the ASB will have been disbanded altogether, (b) the US-GAAP (generally accepted accounting principles) will have converged with the IASB-GAAP?

(a) ASB disbanded

1 ☐ 2 ☐ 3 ☐ 4 ☐ 5 ☐

(b) US-IASB convergence

1 ☐ 2 ☐ 3 ☐ 4 ☐ 5 ☐

We now move on to examine the controversial topic referred to by the popular press as 'accounting scandals' – a feature of corporate life that accounting standard-setting bodies (such as the ASB and the IASB) have been doing their best to eliminate.

## Accounting scandals

In the early 2000s there was a whole series of what came to be known as 'accounting scandals'. In more recent times there have been fewer of them although there is still the occasional press article highlighting yet another. What are accounting scandals and what causes them?

### Definition

A 'scandal' is an event that causes great concern, annoyance and indignation, and which brings those concerned with it into disrepute. So an *accounting* scandal is something to do with the discipline of accounting that causes such a reaction among those who get to hear about it. The most obvious example is when a company reports that it has made a profit in one particular period and then later it has to admit that it really made a loss. When asked why it made such an error, there is often a press release stating that it was caused by an 'accounting error'. This is similar to the familiar excuse of blaming 'the computer' but, to be fair, genuine accounting errors can and do happen. How and why?

### Causes

We can distinguish three main causes that give rise to an accounting scandals: mistakes, frauds, matters of opinion. We will deal with each of these in turn.

- *Mistakes.* All of us make mistakes from time-to-time, i.e. we do something or we get something wrong. This may happen unintentionally because we are incompetent, careless or ignorant. Sometimes a deliberate mistake is made perhaps because someone is malicious, or to cover up a fraud or theft, or perhaps they just want to promote a cause. Many mistakes, whether deliberate or intentional, are not significant but the major ones (such as unintentionally overvaluing stocks) may have an impact on a company's financial results. If the mistake is not discovered until after the accounts are published then all the company can do is apologize, correct the mistake and promise that it will never happen again. Of course, the mistake *ought* to have been picked up by the company's control system (and perhaps by the auditors) but it is amazing how the most glaring errors can go unspotted. And so another 'accounting irregularity' is reported in the financial press.

- *Fraud.* Someone who engages in fraud is deliberately attempting to deceive, and it is usually for personal gain. Fraud is a criminal offence and it cannot be condoned no matter what the circumstances. But it can and does occur and no matter how sophisticated a company's control system may be, someone who is determined to commit a fraud will do so. When it is discovered, again all the company can do is to apologize and promise that its control system has been tightened up. Someone is bound to argue that the external auditors ought to have spotted the fraud but this is not necessarily the case. You will remember that their job is to confirm that the financial statements represent a true and fair view. It is only if their audit tests have not been rigorous or if they showed up some problem that was not tackled that they would be guilty of malpractice.
- *Matters of opinion.* As you now know from working your way through the earlier chapters of this book, accounting is not simply an exercise in basic arithmetic. It involves a great deal more than adding figures together and making the occasional subtraction. Indeed, it requires, above all else, *judgement* because in many situations assumptions and estimates have to be made about what to do, e.g. in valuing stock and depreciating fixed assets. These are two basic examples but they can have a substantial effect on the eventual profit that a company reports to its shareholders. A cautious accountant will select accounting policies that will tend to understate profits (in case circumstances turn out to be worse than anticipated) whereas a more optimistic accountant will take decisions that tend to overstate profits. There may be no right or wrong answers, so if their judgement turns out to be hopelessly wrong then it might result in a major restatement of the accounts. With major policy decisions, of course, the Board should have been heavily involved but they often blame it on an 'accounting irregularity' as though it were nothing to do with them.

But why were there so many apparent accounting irregularities at the beginning of the twenty-first century? There were many causes but perhaps one of the main ones was the development of new industries, especially in electronics and information technology. These new developments were often pioneered by brilliant young entrepreneurs who were well rewarded for their inventiveness. The rewards came in the form of high salaries, even higher bonuses and generous share options. Share options meant that they could buy the shares when they were cheap and sell them when the price rose as the company boomed. Unfortunately, the bubble burst for many of these companies. As such industries became more and more competitive, it became harder to maintain the sales momentum and keep up the profits. That affected the share price and, hence, the opportunity for the young entrepreneurs to sell the share options at a high price.

So they began to look around for other ways of 'increasing' sales. They found their answer in the accountants' fairly loose definition of 'revenue'. The contracts that they signed with their customers (especially those involving service agreements) could be interpreted very flexibly. In some cases this meant that it was possible to justify taking future incomes to the current profit and loss account at a much earlier stage than was perhaps always prudent. This meant, of course, that in future years there was less income to claim unless the sales momentum was kept up. But it didn't as the market became very competitive. Profits began to fall, the share price followed suit and the young entrepreneurs' bonuses and share options were no longer quite as generous as they had been. Worse was to follow. A drop in sales income meant that there was less cash coming into the business. The inevitable happened – and often very quickly – the business went into liquidation. And another 'accounting scandal' hit the headlines.

So where were the auditors? We now turn to their role in financial reporting.

## Auditors

Auditors are usually qualified accountants who specialize in auditing work and who are employed by a firm of chartered or certified accountants. Most firms of accountants are very small and they don't have either the staff or the experience to audit large listed companies. Indeed, in the UK there are probably only about four firms of accountants capable of doing a very large audit, certainly for a large international group of companies.

There is no evidence to suggest that auditors in the UK colluded in the type of practices mentioned in the previous section, although they were undoubtedly placed in a very difficult position. This was partly due to their role in company auditing and partly because they had little guidance on what accounting practices the new industries should adopt.

The law states that shareholders appoint the auditors of the company. In practice they cannot do so because it is impossible for them all to get together and vote on the merits of the various firms. So it is usually left to the directors to select a firm and put the name forward to the shareholders at a general meeting for their formal approval. As it is rare for the shareholders to vote against the directors' recommendation, the auditors are well aware that if they fall out with the directors they are likely to lose the audit. Auditors are not, therefore, as independent as is sometimes believed.

The auditors' independence may also be compromised because of a number of other factors:

- They may become heavily dependent on the fee earned for a particular audit.
- The staff generally, and the partner in charge particularly, may become too friendly with the directors.
- It is common for staff to leave an audit firm and take up a full-time position with the client company.
- Audit firms often do lucrative non-audit work for the company, such as management consultancy and tax advice.

All these factors are of very real concern because they could compromise the audit firm's independence. So if an accounting scandal does occur then the auditors may be accused of not doing anything about it because they were in the directors' pockets.

This may be so in some cases but a more likely cause is the *expectations gap* that we referred to in Chapter 1, i.e. the public think that the auditors are there to do one job, whereas in reality they are there to do another. Their job is primarily to confirm that the accounts represent a true and fair view and not to discover if there has been any fraud.

So what about the questionable accounting practices that some companies might have been adopting? At the time, of course, it was not necessarily obvious that questionable accounting practices *were* being adopted. For example, as we shall see in the next section, it is often difficult to know how much revenue income to take to the profit and loss account and when to take it. So the directors would have had to convince the auditors that what they were doing was fair and reasonable. With hindsight we now know the policies adopted were often far too imprudent but it was not obvious at the time. These industries were very new and the future looked promising. But no one had much experience of how they should operate and there were certainly no detailed accounting guidelines. In any case, it was not unusual for companies to take some profit on account before a job had been finally completed, e.g. in long-term construction work.

In order to try to justify what happened, all we can suggest is that directors and auditors were ultimately faced with a conflict between two of the accounting rules that we outlined in Chapter 2 – neutrality and prudence. Ten years on, it appears that there was, perhaps, far too much neutrality and not enough prudence.

**Activity 13.3**

(a) Should an independent body appoint company auditors? *yes/no*

If so, what type of independent body should it be?

(b) Should auditors be allowed to do other work in addition to auditing for their clients? *yes/no*

(c) Should auditors be allowed to take up full-time employment with a former client? *yes/no*

(d) Should auditors be allowed to do an audit for only a limited period? *yes/no*

If so, for how long?

Three years ☐ Five years ☐ Other ☐

Before we leave the subject of accounting scandals it would be appropriate to discuss once such scandal that did become a major cause *célèbre*: Enron.

## Enron

One of the most infamous accounting scandals in recent times involved a major American company called Enron. Originally a natural gas supplier, it converted itself into one of the largest energy trading companies in the world, so much so that its turnover rose from $40 billion in 1999 to $101 billion in 2000. Before the end of 2001 it had collapsed. A number of the former company's officers have been before the courts on fraud charges and some of them have been found guilty. Fraud clearly played a part in its collapse but the company also engaged in some apparently questionable accounting practices. These are of particular interest to us in this chapter.

US accounting principles allowed the company to keep what are called 'special purpose entities' (SPE) from being disclosed in the balance sheet. It would appear that these entities were allegedly being used to conceal from the market some very large losses made by the company as well as to provide large fees for Enron executives. Although the auditors were in some doubt about the way that the SPEs had been treated they did not disclose their misgivings to the shareholders. Enron's subsequent decline and fall was sudden and swift and it took their auditors down with it.

The demise of such a high-profile company, the sheer amount of money it appeared to generate, its contacts in the business, financial and political world, and the fall of a renowned international firm of auditors helped to generate a huge amount of adverse publicity that continues to this day. It also means that any other company that gets into financial trouble is immediately subject to a similar amount of scrutiny. This gives the impression that what it did is typical of all companies.

But could an *Enron* happen in the UK? Many observers think that this would be impossible because of the difference between UK and US accounting practices.

The US uses a *rule-book* system of preparing accounts. This means that companies have to follow a great number of rules when preparing a set of financial statements. It follows that if a particular action is not covered by the rules then it is permissible, i.e. you can do what you like. By contrast the UK uses a *principles* approach. Basically, Parliament lays down some general laws covering accounting practice (including the recognition now given to accounting standards) but there is an overriding requirement that the accounts should represent a 'true and fair view'. Effectively, therefore, accounts are prepared on the basis of whether they look right for that *particular* entity and not whether they are in accordance with a series of rules.

This gives British (and now European) financial reporting great flexibility but there is a danger of being able to hide behind the 'true and fair' rule. This is because it is quite easy to argue that maybe some unusual accounting practices are appropriate in *this* case (i.e. perhaps the argument that the now defunct IT companies used). Such decisions would be a matter of judgement based on a sound knowledge of the actual circumstances – in reality, very few outsiders would be in a position to know.

No doubt on occasions the true and fair override does get abused and it would perhaps be going too far to suggest that because the UK uses a principles approach to financial reporting, an Enron-type scenario could not happen here. Fraudsters and rogues know no national boundaries, and indeed the UK has had its share of accounting irregularities as a result of the actions of such miscreants. It would be *less* provocative, therefore, to argue that perhaps an Enron-type accounting scandal is less likely to happen in the UK than in the US.

**Activity 13.4**

Over the last few years you may not have heard as much about accounting scandals as once was the case but you will almost certainly know about Enron. What impact has this had on your perceptions of accountants? Complete the following table using a scale of 1 to 5 (1 = very low; 5 = very high).

| *Quality* | *Before starting Chapter 1* | *At this stage in the book* |
|---|---|---|
| Boring | ☐ | ☐ |
| Honest | ☐ | ☐ |
| Meticulous | ☐ | ☐ |
| Pedantic | ☐ | ☐ |
| Reliable | ☐ | ☐ |
| Selfless | ☐ | ☐ |
| Trustworthy | ☐ | ☐ |

We now move on to examine in a little more detail the problem we touched on earlier, that of revenue recognition.

## Revenue recognition

The IASB believes that the definition of *revenue* and how to *account* for it are among the most difficult and contentious issues in accounting practice today. The problem is currently undergoing intensive investigation by the IASB, partly because of the crucial role that revenue plays in the calculation of accounting profit and partly because it appears to have been at the centre of so many accounting scandals.

In order to disentangle this problem we need to establish what we mean by 'revenue'. As it happens, there is an international accounting standard dealing with revenue recognition (*IAS 18*):

> *The gross inflow of economic benefits (cash, receivables and other assets) arising from the ordinary operating activities of an enterprise (such as sales of goods, sales of services, interest, royalties and dividends.*

So what is meant by 'recognition'? Basically, it is the point at which it is appropriate to transfer revenue to the profit and loss account. The IASB explains it as follows:

> *Revenue should be recognized if the customer must accept performance to date. That is, the contract's legal remedy for breach is, or is like, specific performance, or in the event of cancellation, the customer is obliged to pay damages reflecting performance to date.*
>
> IASB Update, *Revenue Recognition*, July 2006.

It might be relatively easy to define 'revenue' and 'recognition' on paper but there is still a great deal of room for manoeuvre when it comes to deciding what is meant by 'must' in the phrase 'the customer must accept performance to date'. There is no UK accounting standard that deals specifically with revenue recognition. *FRS 5* does deal indirectly with the issues involved and more guidance is also given in an ASB Exposure Draft issued in February 2003 called *Amendment to FRS 5, Reporting the Substance of Transactions: Revenue Recognition ED.* Otherwise, although the ASB did issue a discussion paper in 2000, it was not taken any further and it was decided to wait for a new international accounting standard on the subject.

The issue is so important and so complex that the IASB is now working on a joint project with the US FASB with the objective of eventually publishing an accounting standard that will be acceptable to both IASB members and to the FASB. Notwithstanding the definitions we have given above for 'revenue' and 'recognition', the two bodies are not finding it easy to come up with acceptable and workable recommendations and the project has been much delayed. Although it began in 2002, it appears unlikely that a standard will be in place before 2009.

We will now explore the problem in a little more depth. How can we go about deciding how much income should be recognized in any one accounting period? This question gives rise to what is called the 'timing problem'. There are three possible approaches.

- *The critical events approach.* This approach recognizes the income when the most critical event in the operating cycle has occurred – for example (a) when the production process has been completed; (b) when a sale has been made; (c) when the goods or services have been delivered; (d) when they have been paid for. Clearly, (a) is highly risky as the goods may never be sold, while (d) is an extremely prudent approach.
- *The accretion approach.* Here income is recognized during the production process – for example with long-term contract work some profit may be taken as the contract nears completion. This approach means taking some risk and it can go horribly wrong if some major unexpected problem is encountered.

- *The revenue allocation approach.* This approach is a combination of the *critical events* approach and the *accretion* approach. It involves taking some of the income in stages – for example some income at the time a sale is agreed, some when the product is handed over and the rest at the end of the warranty period. By its very nature, this is a compromise approach and it is still fraught with difficulties because the various stages have to be identified. This is not always easy (as was discovered in the new electronics and IT industries) and an arbitrary decision has then to be made about the precise proportion of the income to be taken at the various stages.

There is clearly no simple solution to the problem of revenue recognition and it is difficult to see how IASB and FASB will be able to come up with an accounting standard that will be acceptable on a worldwide basis suitable for all types of entities. So we wait the arrival of the new standard with interest, but not with a great deal of confidence that the outcome will be very satisfactory.

**Activity 13.5**

A building has now been under construction for three years. It is expected to be completed in two years. The agreed contract price is £500 000. The costs to date are £300 000 and it is expected that another £100 000 will be spent on the building before it is completed.

What profit would you recognize in the profit and loss account for Year 3?

### ! Questions non-accountants should ask

Allowing for changes that *may* have taken place since the book was published, you might like to pose the following questions.

- What changes do we have to make to our accounting and financial reporting practices in order to comply with the new Companies Act?
- Are we required to adopt IFRSs, and if so what new ones are likely to affect us?
- Can we honestly argue that the information presented in our financial statements is relevant, reliable, comparable and material – as well as being understandable?
- Are we sure that our methods of determining revenue income can be wholly justified?

## Conclusion

This chapter has concentrated on some financial reporting issues that are likely to be of considerable importance in the next five to ten years. A new Companies Act will have replaced much of the Companies Act 1985 and a good part of it will require changes to the way in which companies prepare and present accounts. The new Act will be supported by new IFRSs and amendments to old IASs. These standards will be of great consequence and significance to listed companies but they will also become increasingly important for large non-listed companies, and eventually for other types and sizes of reporting entities. When this happens the ASB will have become largely a lobbying organization.

There still will be a number of so-called accounting scandals from time-to-time as some unscrupulous company directors find ingenious ways to bypass the legal and accounting standard requirements. Revenue recognition will, however, become much less of a problem when a new IFRS is issued even though there will still probably be a number of loopholes.

## Key points

1 A new Companies Act should be on the statute book by 2007/08. This will require some changes to accounting practice and financial reporting.

2 IFRSs will gradually take over from UK standards but in the short term they are not likely to have a direct effect on non-listed companies and other entities.

3 The ASB will become primarily a lobbying organization.

4 As the new regulatory regime begins to bite there will be fewer reported cases of accounting irregularities but it will be difficult to eliminate then altogether.

5 A new IFRS on revenue recognition will reduce considerably the number of cases of financial statements having to be restated because of over-optimistic assumptions about the sales and other incomes.

## Check your learning

*The answers to these questions can be found within the text.*

1 How many Companies Acts have there been since the Second World War?

2 What is the status of accounting standards in the new Companies Act?

3 What do the following initials mean: (a) FRC, (b) ASB, (c) IASC, (d) IASB, (e) FRS, (f) IAS, (g) IFRS?

4 Where is the IASB based?

5 What are the two names for accounting standards associated with the IASB?

6 What type of UK companies are required to adopt international accounting standards?

7 What is meant by an 'accounting scandal'?

8 How does it differ from an accounting regularity?

9 Are accounting scandals and accounting irregularities unlawful?

10 What has caused so many accounting irregularities in recent years?

11 What responsibilities have auditors for them?

12 Why might external auditors not be completely independent?

13 What is meant by the 'expectations gap'?

14 How might it be bridged?

15 What is meant by revenue?

16 What is meant by 'revenue recognition'?

17 What accounting standard deals specifically with revenue recognition?

18 What is the FASB?

19 What are the three approaches that may be adopted to deal with the timing problem associated with revenue recognition?

20 What is the IASB doing to deal with this problem?

## News story quiz

*Remember the news story at the beginning of this chapter? Go back to that story and re-read it before answering the following questions.*

The switch to international accounting standards was an enormous one for anybody connected with the financial reporting of listed companies. As this article shows, it was also highly controversial and its aftermath somewhat contentious.

### Questions

1 Do you think that, with increasing internationalization, IASB standards are likely to become more US-orientated?

2 Why should there be concern over alleged closer IASB and US generally accepted accounting principles convergence?

3 How could the ASB get involved with international accounting standards setting 'at a very early stage'?

4 What difficulties would 'non-public interest entities' have in adopting IASB accounting standards instead of ASB ones?

## Tutorial questions

13.1 Comment on those aspects of the Government's reform of company law that relate to accounting and financial reporting.

13.2 Should the IASB work towards either *harmonizing* or *standardizing* accounting policies on a worldwide basis?

13.3 Examine the respective role and responsibilities of the various parties that may have been implicated in a number of recent accounting scandals.

13.4 Explain why revenue recognition is a major problem in accounting practice.

Further practice questions, study material and links to relevant sites on the World Wide Web can be found on the website that accompanies this book. The site can be found at www.pearsoned.co.uk/dyson

# Case study: The communication of financial information

**Learning objectives**

After preparing this case study you should be able to:

- identify significant features in a company's profit and loss account, balance sheet and cash flow statement;
- describe the financial performance of a company using the above statements;
- prepare a chairman's report based on the information extracted from the profit and loss account, balance sheet and cash flow statement, and from other sources.

**Background**

**Location** Moodiesburn, Scotland

**Company** Devro plc

**Synopsis**

Devro plc is a Scottish-based company with its headquarters at Moodiesburn near Glasgow. It produces the casings (i.e. 'skins') for the manufacture of products such as sausages, salami and hams. The casings incorporate *collagen* – a common form of animal protein. The collagen is then transformed into edible casings by what is claimed to be a highly sophisticated processing technology. The company regards itself as the world's leading provider of collagen products. As well as operating in Scotland it has production plants in Australia, the Czech Republic and the United States of America.

The average monthly number of persons employed by the group during the year was as follows:

| | *2005* | *2004* |
|---|---|---|
| **By employee category** | *Number* | *Number* |
| Operations and engineering | 1 853 | 1 800 |
| Sales and marketing | 96 | 98 |
| Distribution | 29 | 30 |
| Administration | 119 | 118 |
| Research and development | 103 | 106 |
| | 2 200 | 2 152 |

During the year Mr P.J.E. Mocatta retired from the Board of Directors while Mr P.A.J. Neep joined it. The company also sadly lost through death Mr J.A. Napier, a non-executive director.

The majority of the company's major markets showed increases in sterling revenue during 2005, although the trading environment was softer in the second half of the year and especially towards the end when there was a significant downturn. The UK market was somewhat subdued but there was excellent growth in continental Europe. In the Americas, sterling revenue increased by almost 3% while sales in Latin America were down on the year before. Revenue in Asia/Pacific increased by 3.5%.

Real productivity gains in manufacturing and tight cost controls helped to offset significant rises in energy costs (an extra £2m compared with 2004); the greatest impact was in the UK (amounting to £1.3m of the increase).

The company spent £16.7m on capital expenditure in 2005 (2004: £11.5m), £7.4m of which was incurred in the Czech Republic on plant installation.

The appendix to this case study includes Devro plc's consolidated income statement, the group balance sheet and the group cash flow statement for the year ended 31 December 2005.

*Required*:

Based on the above information and that contained in the appendix, draft a chairman's statement covering the year to 31 December 2005.

*Note*:

In order to minimize the amount of data presented in this case study, the statements of recognized income and notes to the financial statements have all been excluded from the appendix.

## Appendix

**Devro plc**
**Consolidated income statement for the year ended 31 December 2005**

| | *2005* | *2004* |
|---|---|---|
| | *£000* | *£000* |
| **Revenue** (continuing operations) | 152518 | 148938 |
| **Operating profit** (continuing operations) | 27600 | 20948 |
| **Analysed as:** | | |
| Operating profit before exceptional item | 21256 | 20948 |
| Exceptional item | 6344 | – |
| Operating profit | 27600 | 20948 |
| Finance income | 351 | 862 |
| Finance expense | (2165) | (3587) |
| Share of post-tax loss of joint venture | – | (184) |
| **Profit before tax** | 25786 | 18039 |
| Taxation | (7091) | (5157) |
| **Profit for the year** | 18695 | 12882 |
| **Attributable to:** | | |
| Equity holders | 18651 | 12882 |
| Minority interest | 44 | – |
| | 18695 | 12882 |
| **Earnings per share** | | |
| – Basic | 11.5p | 8.0p |
| – Diluted | 11.4p | 7.9p |

*Note*:

The directors propose a final dividend in respect of the financial year ended 31 December 2005 of 3.025 pence per share, which will absorb an estimated £4 893 000 of shareholders' funds. It will be paid on 17 May 2006 to shareholders who are on the register at close of business on 18 April 2006.

**Group balance sheet at 31 December 2005**

| | *2005* | *2004* |
|---|---|---|
| | *£000* | *£000* |
| **Assets** | | |
| **Non-current assets** | | |
| Goodwill | 177 | 177 |
| Other intangible assets | 901 | 809 |
| Property, plant and equipment | 101 357 | 92 380 |
| Deferred tax assets | 16 500 | 13 700 |
| Other receivables | 171 | – |
| | 119 106 | 107 066 |
| **Current assets** | | |
| Inventories | 21 056 | 19 766 |
| Current tax assets | 870 | 160 |
| Trade and other receivables | 20 218 | 19 735 |
| Financial assets | 541 | – |
| Cash and cash equivalents | 11 243 | 11 010 |
| | 53 928 | 50 671 |
| **Liabilities** | | |
| **Current liabilities** | | |
| Financial liabilities | | |
| – Borrowings | 895 | 1 661 |
| – Derivative financial instruments | 132 | – |
| Trade and other payables | 21 450 | 18 697 |
| Current tax liabilities | 3 571 | 2 916 |
| | 26 048 | 23 274 |
| **Net current assets/ (liabilities)** | 27 880 | 27 397 |
| **Non-current liabilities** | | |
| Financial liabilities | | |
| – Borrowings | 28 068 | 34 815 |
| Deferred tax liabilities | 15 406 | 14 555 |
| Retirement benefit obligation | 41 985 | 31 580 |
| Other non-current liabilities | 165 | 217 |
| | 85 624 | 81 167 |
| **Net assets** | 61 362 | 53 296 |
| **Equity** | | |
| **Capital and reserves attributable to equity holders** | | |
| Ordinary shares | 16 176 | 16 133 |
| Share premium | 5 471 | 5 194 |
| Other reserves | 49 681 | 46 448 |
| Retained (losses)/earnings | (9 966) | (14 435) |
| **Total shareholders' equity** | 61 362 | 53 340 |
| Minority interest – equity | – | (44) |
| **Total equity** | 61 362 | 53 296 |

## Group cash flow statement for the year ended 31 December 2005

| | *2005* | *2004* |
|---|---|---|
| | *£000* | *£000* |
| **Cash flows from operating activities** | | |
| Cash generated from operations | 28 521 | 28 281 |
| Interest received | 357 | 861 |
| Interest paid | (2 218) | (4 029) |
| Tax (paid)/received | (6 434) | (4 998) |
| Net cash from operating activities | 20 226 | 20 115 |
| **Cash flows from investing activities** | | |
| Purchase of property, plant and equipment | (14 962) | (11 325) |
| Proceeds from sale of land | 7 305 | – |
| Proceeds from sale of other property, plant and equipment | 94 | 97 |
| Purchase of intangible assets | (338) | (151) |
| Payments to former minority shareholders of Cutisin a.s. | (13) | (1 744) |
| Cash balances of joint venture acquired | – | 126 |
| Net cash (used in)/generated from investing activities | (7 914) | (12 997) |
| **Cash flows from financing activities** | | |
| Issue of ordinary share capital | 320 | 429 |
| Net repayments under the loan facility | (7 697) | (2 822) |
| Payments under finance leases | (41) | (70) |
| Dividends paid to shareholders | (6 639) | (5 831) |
| Net cash used in financing activities | (14 057) | (8 294) |
| **Net decrease in cash and cash equivalents** | (1 745) | (1 176) |
| Cash and cash equivalents at beginning of year | 11 010 | 12 828 |
| Exchange gains/(losses) on cash and cash equivalents | 1 978 | (642) |
| **Net cash and cash equivalents at end of year** | 11 243 | 11 010 |

# Case study

# Interpretation of accounts

**Learning objectives**

**After preparing this case study you should be able to:**

- **evaluate a set of financial statements for a public limited company;**
- **identify the main changes in the company's financial position over a period of time;**
- **summarize the information contained within such statements.**

**Background**

**Location** Scotland

**Company** Robert Wiseman Dairies PLC

**Synopsis**

Robert Wiseman Dairies is a public limited company. Its head office is in East Kilbride near Glasgow. The group's revenue and profits arise wholly from the processing and distribution of liquid milk and associated products. It operates entirely within the UK with five major processing dairies at Aberdeen, East Kilbride, Glasgow, Manchester and Droitwich Spa. The average number of persons employed by the group during 2006 (excluding executive directors and key management personnel) was 3760 (3281 on production and distribution, and 479 on administration).

The company was originally a small family business. In recent years it has expanded rapidly. It has done this partly by natural growth and partly through acquiring other companies. It became a public company in 1994.

The appendix to this case study shows some data extracted from the Group's annual report and accounts for 2002, 2003, 2004, 2005 and 2006.

*Required*:

Analyse the company's financial performance for the five years 2002 to 2006 inclusive.

## Appendix

**Robert Wiseman Dairies PLC**
**Five year financial statement summary**

| | UK GAAP | | | IFRS | |
|---|---|---|---|---|---|
| **For the year ended** | *30.3.02* | *29.3.03* | *3.4.04* | *2.4.05* | *1.4.06* |
| | *£000* | *£000* | *£000* | *£000* | *£000* |
| **Income statement** | | | | | |
| Revenue | 371 056 | 390 982 | 474 514 | 489 168 | 568 564 |
| Cost of sales | (287 267) | (295 747) | (361 250) | (373 400) | (429 883) |
| Gross profit | 83 789 | 95 235 | 113 264 | 115 768 | 138 681 |
| Operating profit | 18 842 | 25 109 | 30 347 | 25 077 | 27 495 |
| Profit before tax | 16 534 | 22 803 | 28 918 | 25 221 | 26 726 |
| Profit for the year | 11 574 | 15 738 | 19 953 | 21 551 | 18 450 |
| **Balance sheet** | | | | | |
| Property, plant and equipment | 136 690 | 142 095 | 144 071 | 146 228 | 150 119 |
| Inventories | 5,114 | 5 804 | 6 304 | 6 826 | 7 037 |
| Trade debtors | 27 269 | 25 949 | 32 909 | 32 237 | 39 876 |
| Cash at bank and in hand | 3 286 | 5 581 | 16 431 | 8 317 | N/A |
| Cash and cash equivalents | N/A | N/A | N/A | 8 317 | 4 732 |
| Current assets | 38 199 | 40 180 | 59 356 | 49 851 | 56 328 |
| Trade creditors | (36 368) | (38 706) | (36 709) | (38 321) | (44 803) |
| Current liabilities | (63 330) | (69 326) | (83 340) | (67 889) | (76 170) |
| Total equity | 77 660 | 89 287 | 103 893 | 114 069 | 119 258 |
| **Cash flow statement** | | | | | |
| Operating activities | N/A | N/A | N/A | 31 424 | 36 010 |
| Investing activities | N/A | N/A | N/A | (18 953) | (23 871) |
| Financing activities | N/A | N/A | N/A | (20 585) | (15 724) |
| Net increase/(decrease) in cash and cash equivalents | N/A | N/A | N/A | (8,114) | (3 585) |
| Cash and cash equivalents at start of year | N/A | N/A | N/A | 16 431 | 8 317 |
| Cash and cash equivalents at end of year | N/A | N/A | N/A | 8 317 | 4 732 |
| **Statistics** | | | | | |
| Average credit period taken on sale of goods | N/D | N/D | N/D | 28 | 28 |
| Average credit period taken for trade purchases | N/D | N/D | N/D | 35 | 35 |
| Basic earnings per share (p) | 14.56p | 20.15p | 25.78p | 28.38p | 25.35p |
| Dividends per share (p) | 4.85p | 5.75p | 7.25p | 8.00p | 9.00p |
| Market price per share (p) | 115.5p | 176.0p | 265.0p | 269.5p | 312.0p |

*Note:*

*N/A = not available or not applicable; N/D = not disclosed*

*Notes:*

1 The accounts for 2002, 2003 and 2004 have been prepared using UK generally accepted accounting principles, i.e. a combination of legislation under the Companies Act 1985 and ASB requirements. The accounts for 2005 and 2006 have been prepared using IFRS 'as adopted for use in the European Union'. The data for 2002, 2003 and 2004, therefore, are not strictly comparable with data for 2005 and 2006, although there is no indication in the 2006 financial statements of any significant differences.

2 The cash flow information for 2002, 2003 and 2005 has not been reproduced because of the different formats used by *FRS 1* and *IAS 7*. In particular, *FRS 1* shows the 'cash 'balances at the beginning and end of each year while *IAS 7* shows 'cash and cash equivalents'. Note 32 to the financial statements states that 'Cash and cash equivalents (which are presented as a single class of assets on the face of the balance sheet) comprise cash at bank and other short-term highly liquid investments with a maturity of three months or less.'

3 Details of the cost of sales are not disclosed in the accounts.

4 During 2004 the company '. . . witnessed significant changes in the dairy industry, particularly in relation to certain of the major retailers making decisions about their supply arrangements for liquid milk. During the financial year we announced significant increased contracts with Sainsbury's commencing in January, and with Tesco commencing in April, and these more than compensated for the loss of ASDA.' (Chairman's statement)

5 Additional information may be obtained by logging on to www.wiseman-dairies.co.uk

# MANAGEMENT ACCOUNTING

# Part 4

Part 4 deals with management accounting. Chapter 14 provides a foundation for a study of the subject. Chapters 15 and 16 deal with some basic costing accounting matters, Chapters 17 and 18 with planning and control procedures, and Chapters 19, 20 and 21 with some decision-making issues. Finally, Chapter 22 reviews some emerging issues in management accounting.

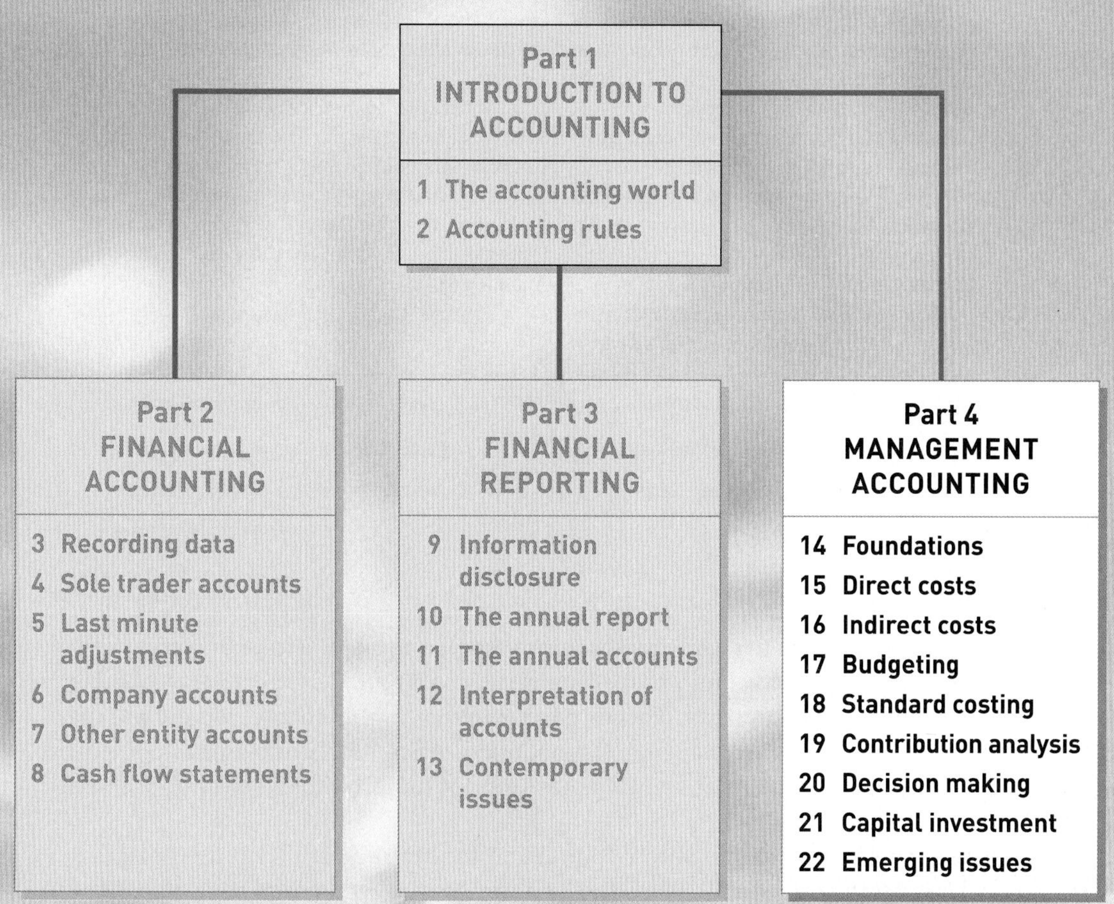

# Chapter 14 Foundations

**Which comes first . . .?**

## NHS told to put finances ahead of medicine

**Health secretary Patricia Hewitt to call for financial control ahead of clinical objectives at NHS**

**Kevin Reed**

Health secretary Patricia Hewitt is expected to call for the NHS to put financial management at the head of its agenda, ahead of clinical objectives.

Hewitt is expected to say that financial management must have a higher priority than clinical objectives in a bid to clear financial deficits crippling the health service.

But as part of a new regime, health trusts will be paid through performance.

She will issue the 'business arrangements' manual explaining how NHS finances should be controlled for 2006/2007 on Thursday, according to the *The Guardian*.

At the weekend, details of restructuring at the top of the Department of Health emerged. Finance director Richard Douglas became directly accountable to NHS chief executive Sir Nigel Crisp.

John Bacon, director of delivery who oversaw financial management, heads up a team to handle changes to the health service in London.

Last week *Accountancy Age* revealed that KPMG had been called to investigate the dire financial straits of 81 NHS trusts, primary care trusts and strategic health authorities; a figure described as 'worrying' by Conservative shadow health secretary Andrew Lansley.

*Accountancy Age*, 23 January 2006.



*Questions relating to this news story can be found on page 288*

## About this chapter

The first three parts of this book have concentrated on financial accounting and financial reporting. In Part 4 we turn to management accounting. Management accounting is one of the most important branches of accounting. In this chapter we outline the nature and purpose of management accounting, trace its historical development, describe its main functions and examine the impact it has on the behaviour of those coming into contact with it.

The chapter provides you with a foundation for the subject which then makes it easier for you to deal with the nine other chapters that cover management accounting in some depth.

**Learning objectives**

By the end of this chapter, you should be able to:

- describe the nature and purpose of management accounting;
- trace its historical development;
- outline the six main functions of management accounting;
- assess its impact on human behaviour.

## Why this chapter is important for non-accountants

The previous chapters in this book covered mainly financial accounting and financial reporting. It is logical to start a study of accounting in this way because financial accounting practices have strongly influenced the development of management accounting.

Nevertheless, until you become a senior manager it is unlikely that you will be involved to any extent in the financial accounting and reporting requirements of an entity. This is not the case with management accounting. Even as a junior manager you are likely to have to provide information for management accounting purposes and to receive reports of your departmental or sectional performance.

At the very least, therefore, it is helpful to know what that information is for and what the various reports mean, especially when you are asked to act on them. It also suggests that almost all employees in an entity should know something about management accounting if they want to be good at their jobs.

It follows that this chapter is, in particular, very important for non-accountants. It tells you a great deal about management accounting: what it is, how it developed, what it involves and its impact on human behaviour. In other words, it provides the background for a detailed study of management accounting.

## Nature and purpose

Accounting is a specialized service function involving the collection, recording, storage and summary of data (primarily of a financial nature), and the communication of information to interested parties. It has six main branches, the two most prominent being financial accounting and management accounting. *Financial accounting* deals mainly with information normally required by parties that are *external* to an entity, e.g. shareholders or government departments. *Management accounting* has a similar role, except that the information supplied is normally for parties *within* an entity, e.g. management.

In Chapter 1 we gave you CIMA's definition of management accounting. For convenience, we will repeat it here.

> *Management accounting is the application of the principles of accounting and financial management to create, protect, preserve and increase value for the stakeholders of for-profit and not-for-profit enterprises in the public and private sectors. (CIMA, Official Terminology, 2005)*

It should be noted that financial accounting is also not necessarily concerned exclusively with financial information, it is of great interest to various internal managerial parties such as the board of directors and divisional directors. Similarly, management accounting is not restricted solely to the supply of management information and it may be of relevance to some external parties, for example the Government. Nevertheless, there are differences between management accounting and financial accounting and they may be summarized as follows.

- *Non-mandatory*: there are no statutory or mandatory professional requirements covering management accounting.
- *Data*: more quantitative data are normally incorporated into a management accounting system.
- *Qualitative data*: management accounting information increasingly includes a great deal of qualitative data.
- *Non-monetary*: data that cannot be translated into monetary terms is incorporated into management accounting reports.
- *Forecasted and planned*: data of both a historic and a forecasted or planned nature is of considerable importance and relevance in management accounting.
- *Users*: management accounting is primarily concerned with providing information for use *within* an entity.

Unlike financial accountants, therefore, management accountants have considerably more freedom in providing information that meets the specific requirements of interested parties. The main party will normally be the entity's managers.

**Activity 14.1**

The above section has provided you with some idea of what management accountants do. But *how* can they help you do a better job? Jot down what help you think that they could give you.

## Historical review

Until the eighteenth century Britain was primarily an agrarian society and there were comparatively few recognizable industrial entities. Furthermore, most entities (of whatever type) were relatively small and they were largely financed and managed by individuals or their families. As a result, it was largely unnecessary to have formal documentary systems for planning, control and reporting purposes because the entities were small enough for the owners to assess these considerations for themselves on a day-to-day basis.

During the eighteenth century, Britain became the first country in the world to undergo an industrial revolution. In just a short period of time it changed from a predominantly agricultural society to an industrial one, and by the late nineteenth century it had become a major industrial power in the world. There were two specific consequences of this development. Firstly, the new industrial enterprises needed large amounts of capital. This could not be provided by just a few individuals. Capital had to be sought from 'investors' whose interest in the enterprise was largely financial.

Such investments were extremely risky and there was the strong possibility of personal bankruptcy. So Parliament intervened and introduced the concept of *limited liability* into company law. Secondly, the new enterprises needed specialist staff to operate and manage them. Such staff had often to be recruited from outside the immediate family circle.

These two consequences resulted in the ownership of the enterprise often being divorced from its management. So through a number of Companies Acts passed in the nineteenth and twentieth centuries, Parliament decided that shareholders in limited liability companies should have a right to receive a minimum amount of information annually, and that auditors should be appointed to report to shareholders on the information presented to them by the company's management.

The complexity, scale and size of the new industrial enterprises meant that it was difficult for professional managers to exercise control on the basis of personal knowledge and casual observation. It became necessary to supply them with information that was written down. At first this revolved round the statutory annual accounts, but it soon became clear that such accounts were produced too late, too infrequently and in too little detail for effective day-to-day managerial control. As a consequence, during the period from 1850 to about 1900, a more detailed recording and reporting system gradually evolved. We now refer to this as a cost *accounting system*. Its main purposes were to provide sufficient information for the valuation of closing stock, work-in-progress and finished goods, and for calculating the costs of individual products. In the early days it was common for financial accounting systems and cost accounting systems to run side-by-side but they eventually merged when it became clear that they used much of the same basic data.

The main developments in management accounting occurred in the United States at the beginning of the twentieth century. By 1925 most of the practices and techniques used today were established. Indeed, between 1925 and 1980 few new developments in management accounting took place. The position has changed somewhat during the last 30 years or so, and many new ideas have been put forward. Some of them have been incorporated into practice, albeit mainly by large companies.

The new management accounting techniques were rapidly developed and practised fairly widely in the United States from the beginning of the twentieth century. Progress was much slower in Britain. Apart from the largest industrial companies, the application of management accounting did not become common until about 1970. Even now, there is evidence that many smaller entities still depend on what is sometimes called 'back of the envelope' exercises for managerial planning and control purposes. It should also be noted that over the same period, manufacturing industry in many industrial nations has given way to service industries. This means that many of the traditional management accounting issues, such as stock control and pricing, standard costing and product costing are of much less significance than they once were. Nevertheless, they are still of some considerable relevance and we will be covering them in subsequent chapters.

**Activity 14.2**

Write down two reasons why, following the Industrial Revolution, it became apparent that accounting, as practised previously, was not geared to working out the cost of individual products.

## Main functions

The overall role of a management accountant is to provide information for management purposes. Six specific functions can be readily identified: planning, control, cost accounting, decision making, financial management, and auditing.

The interrelationship of these functions is shown in Figure 14.1 and we outline them briefly in the rest of this section.

### Planning

Planning can be classified into two broad groupings: long-term and short-term.

#### Long-term planning

Long-term planning is commonly called *strategic planning* or *corporate planning*. We will refer to it as 'strategic planning' because this appears to be the most widely used term. *Strategy* is a military term meaning the ability to plan and organize manoeuvres in such a way that the enemy is put at a disadvantage. Over the last 20 years, strategic planning has become an important managerial function in both profit-making and not-for-profit entities. In essence, it involves working out what the entity wants to achieve in the long term (i.e. beyond a calendar year) and how it intends to achieve it.

There are six basic steps involved in preparing a strategic plan. A summary is shown in Table 14.1.

Strategic planning is not specifically a management accounting function. The senior management of the entity will probably set up a multidisciplined strategic planning team that may include a management accountant. The management accountant's major role will be to collect data and to provide information (mainly of a financial nature) required by the team.

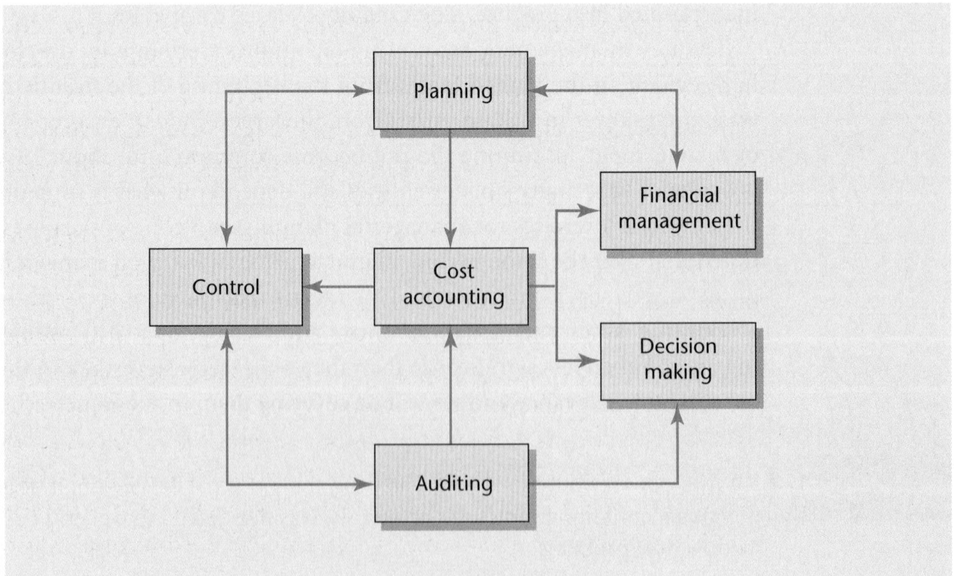


**Figure 14.1 Management accounting: main functions**

**Table 14.1 Steps in preparing a strategic plan**

| Step | Action | Question to be asked |
|---|---|---|
| 1 | Establish the entity's objective (e.g. to earn a minimum of 20% on capital employed) | *'Where do we want to be in x years' time?'* |
| 2 | Assess the entity's current position | *'Where are we now?'* |
| 3 | Evaluate the external factors (economic, financial, political and social) that will apply during the period of the plan | *'What is the outside world likely to be like?'* |
| 4 | Specify the differences between the current position and the required future one | *'What gaps are there between where we are now and where we want to be?'* |
| 5 | Conduct a SWOT analysis | *'What are our strengths, weaknesses, opportunities and threats?'* |
| 6 | Put the strategic plan together | *'What do we have to do to get towards where we want to go?'* |

### Short-term planning

Accountants normally refer to short-term planning as *budgeting*, the 'short term' being regarded as being a period of up to a calendar year. Budgeting is covered in Chapter 17.

## Control

A clear plan of what an entity wants to do and how it intends to get there is clearly preferable to having no plan at all. Otherwise the entity will just drift. However, an additional benefit of planning is that it can also form part of the control mechanism of the entity. What management accountants do is to measure what has actually happened over a certain period of time and then compare it with what was planned to happen. Any apparent significant differences (or *variances* as they are called) are investigated, and if they are not acceptable then action is taken to ensure that future actual events will meet the agreed plan. It may be found, for example, that the actual price paid for some raw materials was £5 per kilo when the plan allowed for a payment of only £4.50 per kilo. Why was there a variance? Was it poor planning? Was it impossible to estimate the actual price more accurately? Was it inefficient purchasing? Were higher-quality materials purchased and if so, was there less wastage?

Not all variances are unwelcome. For instance, 1000 units might have been sold when the plan only allowed for sales of 950 units. The reasons for this variance should still be investigated, and if this *favourable* trend were deemed likely to continue then it would be necessary to ensure that additional resources (e.g. production, administration, distribution, and finance) were made available to meet higher expected levels of sales.

Note that it would be the responsibility of the management accountants to coordinate the investigation of any variances and report back to the senior management of the entity. *It would not be the management accountant's responsibility to take any disciplinary action if a variance had been caused by inefficient management.* This is a point that is not always understood by those employees who come into contact with management accountants!

Further aspects of control are covered in Chapters 17 and 18.

**Activity 14.3**

Planning involves working out want you want to happen. Control involves (a) looking at what has happened, then (b) taking action if the actual events are different from the planned events. But the control element happens after the events. So how can they be controlled?

Write down reasons why trying to control events after they have happened may be of some benefit.

## Cost accounting

Historically, cost accounting has been the main function of management accounting. It is now much less significant, and other functions, such as the provision of information for decision making, have become much more important. The cost accounting function involves the collection of the entity's ongoing costs and revenues, the recording of them in a double-entry book-keeping system (a task that these days is normally done by computer), the balancing of the 'books' and the extraction of information as and when required by management. Cost accounting also involves the calculation of *actual costs* of products and services for stock valuation, control and decision-making purposes.

We deal with cost accounting in Chapter 15.

## Decision making

The provision of information for decision making is now one of the major functions of management accountants. Although actual costs collected in the cost accounting records may provide some guidance, decision-making information usually requires dealing with anticipated or expected future costs and revenues and it may include data that would not normally be incorporated in a traditional accounting ledger system.

Most decisions are of a special or 'one-off' nature and they may involve much ingenuity in obtaining information that is of assistance to managers in considering a particular decision. Note that it is the managers themselves who will (and should) take the decision, not the management accountants.

Various aspects of decision making are covered in Chapters 19, 20 and 21.

## Financial management

The financial management function associated with management accounting generally is again one that has become much more significant in recent years. Indeed, financial management has almost become a discipline in its own right. Its main purpose is to seek out the funds necessary to meet the planning requirements of the entity, to make sure that they are available when required and that they are used efficiently and effectively.

Financial management is not covered in any depth in this book, although we do return briefly to it in Chapter 21.

## Auditing

Auditing involves the checking and verification of accounting information and accounting reports. There are two main types of audit: external and internal.

External auditing may be regarded as part of the financial accounting function, while internal auditing is more of a management accounting responsibility. External auditors work for an outside entity, while internal auditors are employees of the entity itself and they are answerable to its management. In practice external and internal auditors work closely together. Internal auditors' remit may also be extended to assessing the effectiveness and efficiency of management systems generally, instead of concentrating almost exclusively on the cost and financial records.

The management accountant's involvement in auditing is not considered any further in this book.

## Behavioural considerations

The collection of data and the supply of information are not neutral activities. They have an impact on those who are involved in supplying and receiving such material. The impact can be strongly negative and it can adversely affect the quality of the data or information. In turn, this may cause management to make some erroneous decisions because of unreliable data and biased information. This is a feature of the job that accountants are now trained to recognize, i.e. the *behavioural impact* that *they* may have on other employees. What relevance has this for non-accountants?

Much of the information collected and stored in a financial accounting system is backed by legislation and neither accountants nor non-accountants can ignore what is required regardless of their own personal views. The legal position puts financial accountants in a powerful position because, if necessary, they can *demand* what they want from other employees.

Management accountants cannot make such demands as there are no statutory requirements to produce management accounts. Their power, as such, comes from the close working relationship that they have with the directors and other senior managers. There is no doubt that in practice this is an extremely powerful position.

However, irrespective of the source of the power that accountants may have in making demands on other employees, modern thinking suggests that it is unwise to exercise it too obviously. Accountants are now taught that they have a much better chance of obtaining what they want when they want it by working *with* other employees rather than by ordering them around.

This approach to dealing with other staff works best, of course, if it is reciprocated. So as a non-accountant you too should regard accountants more as friends rather than as enemies, i.e. try to work with them rather than against them. Some non-accountants may find this hard to do especially if they have had some unfortunate confrontations with accountants in the past. However, remember that it is usually better to talk than to fight (*jaw jaw, rather than war war*) and that accountants are basically employed to provide a service for other employees.

So in return for cooperating fully with your accountants and getting the service that you want and that they can provide, what approach can you expect them to adopt? We suggest that their behaviour should be as follows:

- *Cooperative.* Management accountants should treat you as an equal and they should make it obvious that your contribution is just as valuable as their own.
- *Non-autocratic.* Management accountants should not adopt an autocratic, condescending and superior attitude when dealing with other employees.
- *Diplomatic.* Management accountants should be courteous, patient, polite and tactful when dealing with others.

- *Informative.* You are entitled to a detailed explanation of why, what and when some information is required and in what form it should be presented.
- *Helpful.* Management accountants should be prepared to help you in digging out the information that they want from you.
- *Considerate.* You should be given a realistic amount of time to provide any information that is required, taking into account your other responsibilities.
- *Courteous.* Management accountants should not imply that you may be subject to disciplinary action if you do not comply with their requests.
- *Instructive.* You should receive some guidance in the operation of the various management accounting systems that relate to your particular responsibilities.

In practice, the above requirements may be somewhat idealistic. Sometimes, for example, senior managers do not encourage a participative approach and they may not always be willing to provide appropriate training courses. The management accountants in the entity then have a responsibility to point out to the senior managers that the planning and control systems that operate in such an environment are not likely to be particularly successful.

It must also not be forgotten that the relationship between management accountants and non-accountants is not one-sided and that non-accountants have an equal responsibility to be cooperative. Clearly, management accountants will find it difficult to work with staff who adopt a resentful or surly manner and who try to make life difficult for them.

**Activity 14.4**

Suppose, as a departmental manager, you received an e-mail from the chief management accountant that included the following statement:

> *I wish to inform you that you overran your budget by £10 000 for March 2008. Please inform me immediately what you intend to do about this overspend. Furthermore, I will need to know why you allowed this gross piece of mismanagement to happen.*

Jot down what your feelings would be if you had received such an e-mail. Then re-write the above using a more tactful tone.

## Questions non-accountants should ask

Some entities do not involve their employees in providing information for management. A system is imposed on them and they are expected to do just as they are told. However, experience suggests that such an approach does not work. It is much better to involve staff in the detailed implementation and operation of information systems. What approach does *your* own organization take? We suggest that you ask the following questions (but remember to be tactful!).

- Who wants this information?
- What is it for?
- What's going to happen to it?
- Will I get some feedback?
- What will I be expected to do about it?
- May I suggest some changes?
- How can I help to improve what is done?

## Conclusion

This chapter has provided a foundation for a more detailed study of management accounting. Management accounting is one of the six main branches of accounting. Its main purpose is to supply information to management for use in planning and controlling an entity, and in decision making. It grew out of the simple financial accounting systems used in the late nineteenth century when it became apparent that they could not provide managers with the day-to-day information that they needed, e.g. for use in stock control and for product costing purposes. In the early part of the twentieth century management accounting came to be recognized as a useful planning and control mechanism. More recently it has become an integral part of overall managerial decision making. The discipline now has six main recognizable functions: planning, control, cost accounting, decision making, financial management and auditing.

There are no statutory or mandatory professional requirements that govern the practice of management accounting. Nevertheless, management accounting techniques are now regarded as being of considerable benefit in assisting an entity to achieve its longer-term objectives. As a result, management accountants tend to hold senior positions in most entities and they may wield considerable power and influence. However, their work can be largely ineffective and the quality of the information that they provide poor if they do not receive the wholehearted support of their fellow employees. Unless this is forthcoming, the eventual decisions taken by management, based on the information provided by the management accountants, may possibly lead to problems in the running of the entity.

## Key points

1. Management accounting is one of the six main branches of accounting.
2. Its main purpose is to collect data and provide information for use in planning and control, and for decision making.
3. Management accounting evolved in the late nineteenth century out of the simple financial accounting systems used at the time when more detailed information was needed for stock control and for production costing purposes.
4. It began to be used as a planning and control technique in the early part of the twentieth century.
5. In more recent years, management accounting techniques have become incorporated into managerial decision making.
6. Six main functions of modern management accounting can now be recognized: planning, control, cost accounting, decision making, financial management and auditing.
7. Management accounting practices can have a negative impact on both the providers and the users of information if management accountants adopt an autocratic and non-participative attitude.
8. A negative approach to management accounting requirements may result in poor-quality information and erroneous decision making.

## Check your learning

*The answers to these questions can be found within the text.*

1 What is meant by 'management accounting'?

2 List six ways in which it is different from financial accounting.

3 Suggest two reasons why in pre-industrial times there was no need for entities to have a management accounting system.

4 For what purposes did nineteenth century managers need a more detailed costing system?

5 What is meant by 'strategic planning'?

6 How does it differ from budgeting?

7 What are the six steps involved in preparing a strategic plan?

8 What is meant by 'control'?

9 Describe briefly the nature of cost accounting.

10 What is meant by 'decision making'?

11 What is the main purpose of financial management?

12 To what extent are management accountants involved in auditing?

13 Why should management accountants be aware of the behavioural impact of information supply?

## News story quiz

*Remember the news story at the beginning of this chapter? Go back to that story and re-read it before answering the following questions.*

We have emphasized in this book that accountants are employed to provide a service for the management of an entity and that accounting systems should not hinder the objectives of an entity. So this is a very strange story. It appears that financial management in the National Health Service is going to take precedence over clinical considerations. Surely this is a classic case of the putting the cart before the horse?

### Questions

1 Do you think that in future accountants are going to become more important than doctors in the running of the National Health Service?

2 What do you think the Health Secretary means by 'financial management'?

3 Do you think that she really does mean to put financial management ahead of clinical objectives?

4 In what ways could an emphasis on financial control actually increase the resources available for clinical needs?

## Tutorial questions

*The answers to questions marked with an asterisk can be found in Appendix 4.*

14.1 Examine the usefulness of management accounting in a service-based economy.

14.2 The first step in preparing a strategic plan is to specify the entity's goals. Formulate three possible objectives for (a) a manufacturing entity, (b) a national charity involved in animal welfare.

14.3 Assess the importance of taking into account behavioural considerations when operating a management accounting system from the point of view of (a) the management accountant; and (b) a senior departmental manager.

14.4* Distinguish between financial accounting and management accounting.

14.5* Describe the role of a management accountant in a large manufacturing entity.

14.6 Outline the main steps involved in preparing a strategic plan.

14.7 What is the difference between 'planning' and 'control'?

14.8 'Management accountants hold an extremely powerful position in an entity, and this enables them to influence most of the decisions.' How far do you think that this assertion is likely to be true in practice?

**Further practice questions, study material and links to relevant sites on the World Wide Web can be found on the website that accompanies this book. The site can be found at www.pearsoned.co.uk/dyson**

# Chapter 15 Direct costs

## The end of the pricing problem?

### Drinks supplier improves supply chain efficiency

**Planning software to maximise manufacturing cycles**

**Miya Knights**

Drinks supply company Kingsland Wines and Spirits is installing manufacturing planning software designed to achieve same-day ordering and delivery.

The company, which manufactures own-brand alcohol for most of the major UK supermarkets, wanted to reduce orders that rely on manual, spreadsheet-based forecasting methods, and to react much more quickly to changes in customer demand.

Tim Horton, Kingsland chief information officer, says the planning software will automate demand forecasting to ensure that enough raw materials are ordered, reducing the safety stocks held on-site to deal with spikes in demand.

'We need to plan our production around very long manufacturing lead times because, regardless of demand, once the raw materials come in we can only flow liquids through the business at a certain rate,' said Horton.

Kindsland will use software from supplier Geac and an IBM iSeries server to deliver the extra computing capacity and performance needed for the just-in-time manufacturing procedures.

'The system will answer three questions: what is needed, when it is needed and where it is needed,' said Horton. 'It will improve supply chain efficiency.'

*Computing*, 26 January 2006.



*Questions relating to this news story can be found on page 302*

## About this chapter

In the previous chapter we explained something about the nature and purpose of management accounting, why and how it developed as a separate branch of accounting, and what its main functions are today. One such function is *cost accounting*.

Cost accounting involves collecting detailed financial data about products and services, and the recording of that data. The data may then be extracted from the books of account, summarized and presented to the management of an entity. The managers will use the information presented to them for planning and control purposes. The information may take various forms depending on what it is to be used for. At the very least, managers are usually interested in knowing the profit or loss made by individual products or services. For convenience, we will call this process *product costing*.

Following the Industrial Revolution, the new type of managers in the nineteenth century attempted to base their selling prices on what products had cost to make. Unfortunately, the financial accounting systems at that time could not provide the information required so a separate branch of accounting called *cost accounting* slowly began to develop. In the twentieth century cost accounting has been subsumed into a much broader branch of accounting generally referred to as *management accounting*.

Even so, accountants still cost products using a technique that has hardly changed in over 100 years. This technique is generally known as *absorption costing*. In broad terms, absorption costing involves the following procedure:

- isolate those costs that can be easily identified with a particular product;
- apportion the non-indentifiable costs.

Accountants describe the first stage as *allocating* the direct costs, and the second as *absorbing* the indirect costs. In this chapter we cover the first stage, and in the next chapter the second stage.

**Learning objectives**

**By the end of this chapter, you should be able to:**

- **identify material, labour and other direct costs;**
- **describe three important methods of charging direct material costs to production;**
- **calculate prime costs.**

## Why this chapter is important for non-accountants

This is the first of two chapters covering the subject of cost accounting. As a non-accountant you may be puzzled why you need to know *anything* about cost accounting. It might seem reasonable to assume that you can safely leave that subject to your accountants. We do not think so.

There are two broad reasons why we hold this view. In order to be a really successful manager we think that you need to know something about cost accounting firstly to achieve greater control over the resources for which you are responsible, and secondly to make better decisions. But there is also another reason that is specific to the content of this chapter. The treatment of what accountants call *direct material* costs requires a decision to be made about the price at which materials should be charged to production. If managers get the pricing decision wrong it can have some serious and often adverse consequences for the survival of the company. So it is far too important a decision for you to delegate it entirely to your accountants.

The accountants will usually supply you with all the cost and financial information that you need but you will be in a much better position to assess its reliability and usefulness if you are familiar with its source, the assumptions made in preparing it and the methods used to compile it.

# Responsibility accounting

A cost accounting system will normally be based on a system of what accountants call 'responsibility accounting'. *Responsibility accounting* contains the following features:

- *Segments*. The entity is broken down into separate identifiable segments. Such segments are known as 'responsibility centres'. There are three main types:

- *Cost centres.* A cost centre is a clearly defined area of responsibility under the overall control of a designated individual to which the costs directly associated with the specified area are charged. There are two main types of costs centres: *production* cost centres where products are manufactured or processed, e.g. a machining department or an assembly area; and *service* cost centres where a service is provided to other cost centres, e.g. the personnel department or the canteen. Cost centres can take a number of forms such as a department, a production line, a machine, a product or a sales area.
- *Profit centres.* A profit centre is similar to a cost centre except that both costs and revenues associated with the centre are charged to it. It is then possible to calculate the profit or loss for each profit centre. The oil division of a large chemical company is an example of a profit centre.
- *Investment centres.* An investment centre is similar to a profit centre except that it is also responsible for all the major investment decisions that relate to that centre. A division of a large multinational company is an example of an investment centre.

- *Boundaries.* The boundaries of each segment will be clearly established.
- *Control.* A manager will be put in charge of each separate segment.
- *Authorization.* Segmental managers will be given the independence to run their segments as autonomously as possible.

The identification of different segments within an entity means that the cost accounting system can be so organized that the costs and revenues associated with each segment can be similarly identified. This means that it is then possible to make segmental managers solely responsible for planning, budgeting and controlling all their segment's activities and for making any decisions that affect it. They will also, of course, be held responsible for whatever does or does not happen within it.

**Activity 15.1**

What are your first thoughts about responsibility accounting? Do you think that it is possible to divide a complex organization into neat little segments? Is it realistic to say to someone 'you're in complete charge of that segment'?

How much autonomy do you think a cost centre manager can really be given? Base your answer on the following scale.

*No autonomy* *Complete autonomy*

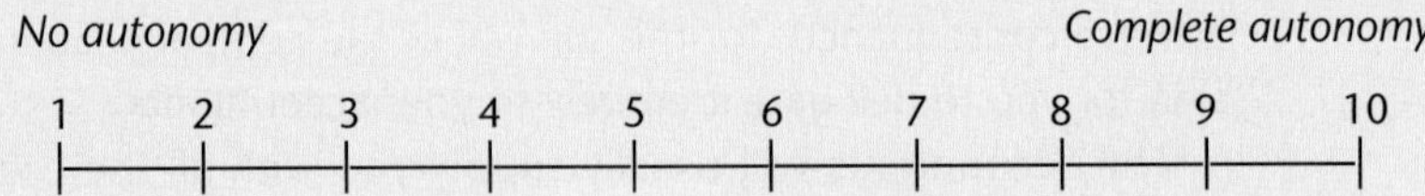


## Classification of costs

The establishment of a responsibility accounting system enables costs and revenues to be easily identified on a segmental basis – from now on we will now refer to all responsibility centres simply as 'cost centres'.

In practice, it is not always easy to identify each cost with a particular cost centre because there are some costs that are so general and so basic that no one manager has control over them. One example is that relating to business rates. Business rates are a form of local property tax. They are levied on a property as a whole and they do not relate directly to any particular cost centre.

**Activity 15.2** Specify which cost centre you think should be charged with the cost of a company's business rates.

Costs that are easily and economically identifiable with a particular segment are known as *direct costs*. So if it is possible to identify all the costs of the entity with particular cost centres then, by definition, *all* costs must be direct costs. While this may be true at the cost centre level it is usually not true at the product or unit level. Some costs will certainly be easy to identify with particular units (classed as *direct unit costs*) but there will be other costs (classed *as indirect unit costs*) where it is much more difficult, e.g. the canteen costs or the wages department. In what way, therefore, can you charge some of the indirect costs to individual units? In practice, it is not easy but we explain how it might be done in the next chapter.

Irrespective of whether costs are classified into the direct or indirect categories, we also need to have some idea of their nature, so management accountants usually break costs down into their *elements*, i.e. whether they are material costs, labour costs or other types of costs. The *elements of cost* are shown in diagrammatic form in Figure 15.1. This breakdown is similar to the one we adopted for manufacturing accounts in Chapter 7.

There are two particular points to note about Figure 15.1. Firstly, in a competitive market, selling price can rarely be determined on a 'cost-plus' basis, i.e. total cost of sales plus a profit loading. If the entity's prices are higher than its competitors, then it is not likely to sell very many units. However, if its selling prices are lower than its competitors, then it might sell many units but the profit on each unit may be low. Even so its competitors are likely to bring down their prices very quickly. So when the market largely determines selling prices, it is vital that the entity's total costs are controlled and monitored strictly so that the gap between its total sales revenue and its total cost of sales (i.e. its profit) is as wide as possible.

Secondly, the classification shown will not necessarily be relevant for all entities. For example, an entity in the service sector (such as insurance broker) is not likely to have any direct or indirect production costs.

Figure 15.1 is based on what is called *total absorption costing*. This is a method whereby *all* costs of the entity are charged to (or absorbed into) particular products irrespective of their nature. If only production costs are absorbed into product costs, the system is referred to simply as absorption costing.

There is also another important costing method known as *marginal* costing. This method involves classifying costs into their fixed and variable elements. Fixed costs are those that do not change irrespective of how many units are produced (i.e. the output). Variable costs are those costs that do change and change directly proportionally to the number of units produced. We shall be dealing with marginal costing in Chapter 19.

We can now begin our detailed study of direct costs. We start with direct materials.

## Direct materials

Materials consist of raw materials and component parts. Raw materials are those basic ingredients that are incorporated into the production of a product, such as flour, sugar, and raisins used in making cakes. Component parts include miscellaneous ready-made goods or parts that are purchased (or manufactured specially) for insertion into a main product, e.g. a car radiator.

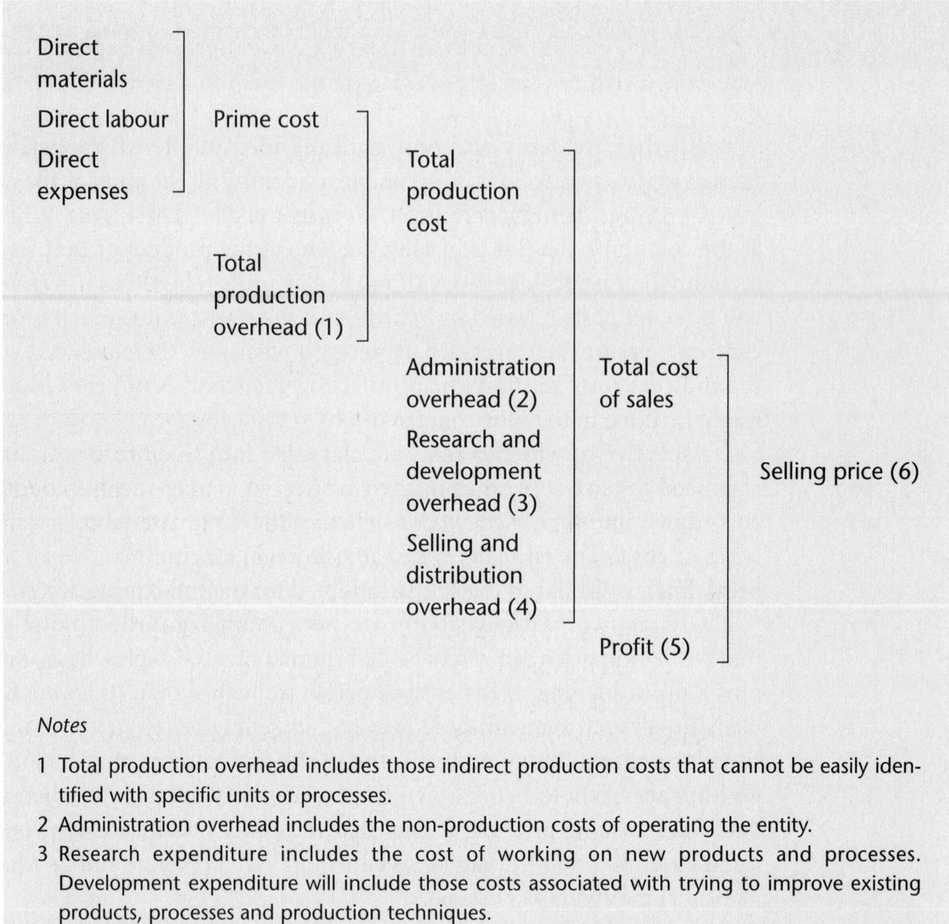


*Notes*

1 Total production overhead includes those indirect production costs that cannot be easily identified with specific units or processes.
2 Administration overhead includes the non-production costs of operating the entity.
3 Research expenditure includes the cost of working on new products and processes. Development expenditure will include those costs associated with trying to improve existing products, processes and production techniques.
4 Selling and distribution overhead includes the cost of promoting the entity's products and services and the cost of delivering them to its customers or clients.
5 A profit loading may be added to the total cost of sales in order to arrive at the unit's selling price.
6 In this chapter we only go as far as the prime cost level.

**Figure 15.1 The elements of cost**

As we discussed earlier, a direct cost is one that can be easily and economically identified with a particular segment, such as a cost centre or a particular product. However, there is a problem when relating this definition to materials. It might be easy and economic to identify them *physically* with a particular segment but it does not necessarily follow that it is then easy to attach a cost to them. There are two main problems. Firstly *size*. We might be able to identify a few screws used in assembling a chair, for example, but it would not be worthwhile costing them separately because their relative value is so small. Such costs would, therefore, be classified as *indirect* material costs. Secondly, *timing*. Materials may have been purchased at different times and at different prices. Thus it might not be possible to know whether 1000 kg of material held in stock had been purchased at £1, £2 or £3 per kilo. This problem applies particularly when materials that are purchased in separate batches are stored in the same containers, e.g. grains and liquids.

In such circumstances, it is necessary to determine an appropriate pricing method. Many such methods are available. However, as the price of materials charged to production also affects the value of closing stock, regard has to be had to the financial reporting requirements of the entity. In management accounting we are not bound by any statutory or mandatory professional requirements, and so we are perfectly free to adopt any stock valuation method we wish. Unfortunately, if the chosen method is not acceptable for financial reporting purposes, we would have to revalue the closing stock for the annual accounts. This may be a very expensive exercise. We would, therefore, normally adopt a pricing method for issuing materials to production and for valuing closing stocks that is suitable for both the annual accounts and for management accounting purposes. This means adopting the requirements contained in *SSAP 9* (Stocks and long-term contracts). There are four preferred methods. We summarize them below. They are also shown in diagrammatic format in Figure 15.2.

- *Unit cost.* The unit cost is the cost of purchasing identifiable units of stocks. If it is possible to identify the specific cost of materials issued to production, then no particular pricing problem arises and we would obviously use this method.
- *First-in, first-out (FIFO).* This method adopts the first price at which materials have been purchased. We consider it in more detail below.
- *Average cost.* An average cost may be calculated by dividing the total value of materials in stock by the total quantity. There are a number of acceptable averaging methods but we will be using the *continuous weighted average* (CWA) cost method.
- *Standard cost.* This method involves estimating what materials are likely to cost in the future. Instead of the actual price, the *estimated* or *planned* cost is then used to charge out the cost of materials to production. The standard cost method is usually adopted as part of a standard costing system. We shall not be considering it any further in this chapter because we will be dealing with standard costing in Chapter 18.

**Activity 15.3**

Assuming that you do not know the specific unit price of some materials, which method would you use to price them? Tick the appropriate box below and insert the main reason for your choice.

FIFO ☐ Average cost ☐ Standard cost ☐

Main reason:

________________________________________

________________________________________

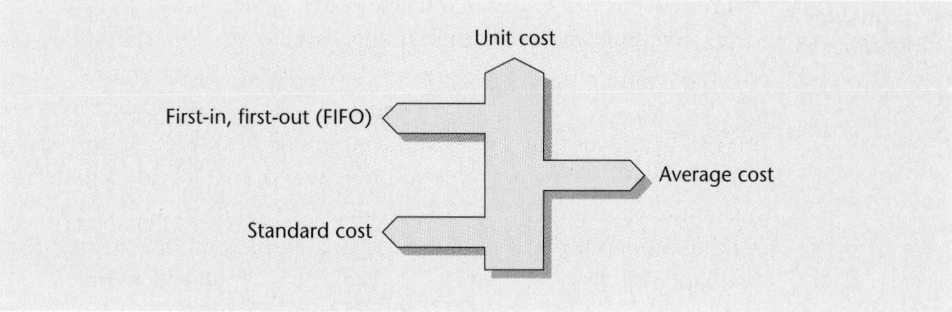

**Figure 15.2 Direct material costing methods**

## First-in, first-out

It is sensible to issue the oldest stock to production first, followed by the next oldest and so on, and this should be done wherever possible. This method of storekeeping means that old stock is not kept in store for very long, thus avoiding the possibility of deterioration or obsolescence. However, some materials may be stored in such a way that they become a mixture of old and new stock and it is then not possible to identify each separate purchase, e.g. grains and liquids. Nevertheless, in pricing the issue of stock to production it would still seem appropriate to follow the first-in, first-out procedure and charge production with the oldest price first, followed by the next oldest price and so on.

FIFO is a very common method used in charging out materials to production. The procedure is as follows:

1 Start with the price paid for the oldest material in stock, and charge any issues to production at that price.
2 Once all of the goods originally purchased at that price have been issued, use the next-oldest price until all of that stock has been issued.
3 The third-oldest price will be used next, then the fourth oldest, and so on.

The use of the FIFO pricing method is illustrated in Example 15.1.

**Example 15.1**

### The FIFO pricing method of charging direct materials to production

The following information relates to the receipts and issue of a certain material into stock during January 2009:

| *Date* | *Receipts into stores* | | | *Issue to production* |
|---|---|---|---|---|
| | *Quantity units* | *Price £* | *Value £* | *Quantity units* |
| 1.1.09 | 100 | 10 | 1 000 | |
| 10.1.09 | 150 | 11 | 1 650 | |
| 15.1.09 | | | | 125 |
| 20.1.09 | 50 | 12 | 600 | |
| 31.1.09 | | | | 150 |

*Required*:
Using the FIFO method of pricing the issue of goods to production, calculate:
(a) the issue prices at which goods will be charged to production;
(b) the closing stock value at 31 January 2009.

**Answer to Example 15.1**

(a) The issue price of goods to production:

| *Date of issue* | *Tutorial note* | *Units* | *Calculation* | *£* |
|---|---|---|---|---|
| 5.1.09 | (1) | 100 | units × £10 = | 1 000 |
| | (2) | 25 | units × £11 = | 275 |
| | | 125 | | 1 275 |
| 31.1.09 | (3) | 125 | units × £11 = | 1 375 |
| | (4) | 25 | units × £12 = | 300 |
| | | 150 | | 1 675 |

**(b)** Closing stock:

| | |
|---|---|
| 25 units × £12 = | 300 |
| Check: | |
| Total receipts (£1000 + £1650 + £600) | 3250 |
| Total issues (£1275 + £1675) | 2950 |
| Closing stock | 300 |

*Tutorial notes*

1 The goods received on 1 January 2009 are now assumed to have all been issued.
2 This leaves 125 units in stock out of the goods received on 10 January 2009.
3 All the goods purchased on 10 January 2009 are assumed to have been issued.
4 There are now 25 units left in stock out of the goods purchased on 20 January 2009.

Although Example 15.1 is a simple one, it can be seen that if the amount of material issued to production includes a number of batches purchased at different prices, the FIFO method involves using a considerable number of different prices.

The advantages and disadvantages of the FIFO method may be summarized as follows.

*Advantages*

- The method is logical.
- It appears to match the physical issue of materials to production.
- The closing stock value is closer to the current economic value.
- The stores ledger account is arithmetically self-balancing and there are no adjustments that have to be written off to the profit and loss account.
- It meets the requirements of *SSAP 9.*
- It is acceptable for UK tax purposes.

*Disadvantages*

- It is arithmetically cumbersome.
- The cost of production relates to out-of-date prices.

## Continuous weighted average

In order to avoid the detailed arithmetical calculations involved in using the FIFO method, it is possible to substitute an *average* pricing method. There are a number of different types but we are going to use the continuous weighted average (CWA) method.

This method may require frequent changes to be made to the issue prices depending on the number of orders purchased. Although it appears very complicated, it is the easiest one to use *provided* that the receipts and issues of goods are recorded in a stores ledger account. An example of a manual stores ledger account is shown in Figure 15.3.

You will note from Figure 15.3 that the stores ledger account shows both the quantity and the value of the stock in store at any one time. The CWA price is obtained by dividing the total value of the stock by the total quantity. A new price will be struck each time new purchases are taken into stock.

The method is illustrated in Example 15.2. We use the same data as in Example 15.1 but we have taken the opportunity to present a little more information, so that we can explain more clearly how a CWA price is calculated.

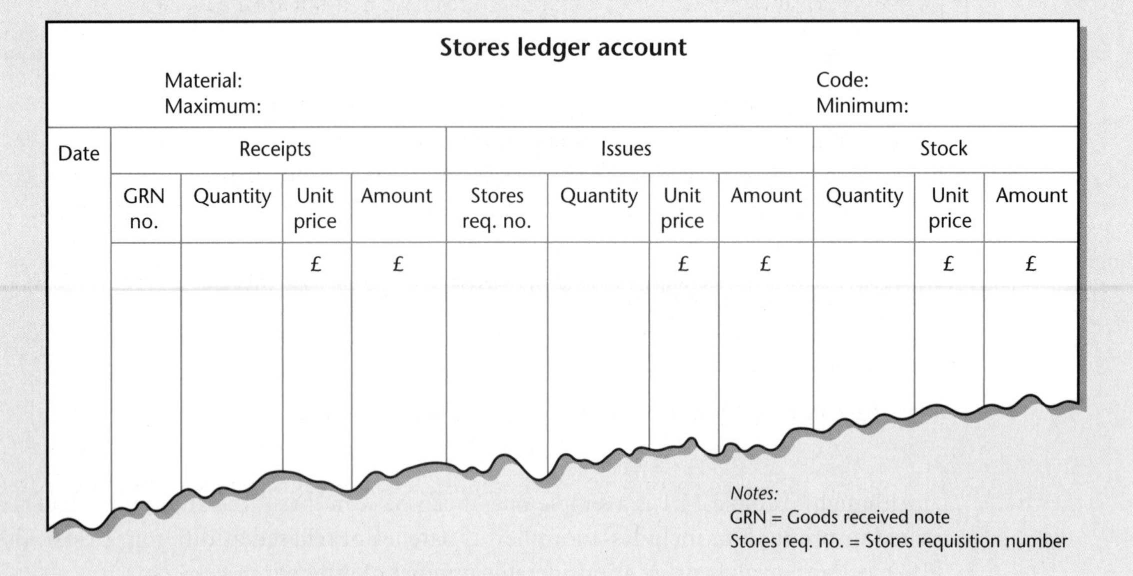

| Date | Receipts | | | | Issues | | | | Stock | | |
|---|---|---|---|---|---|---|---|---|---|---|---|
| | GRN no. | Quantity | Unit price | Amount | Stores req. no. | Quantity | Unit price | Amount | Quantity | Unit price | Amount |
| | | | £ | £ | | | £ | £ | | £ | £ |

Stores ledger account

Material: Code:
Maximum: Minimum:

*Notes:*
GRN = Goods received note
Stores req. no. = Stores requisition number

**Figure 15.3 Example of a stores ledger account**

**Example 15.2**

## The CWA pricing method of charging direct materials to production

You are presented with the following information relating to the receipt and issue of a certain material into stock during January 2009:

| *Date* | *Receipts into stores* | | | *Issues to production* | | | *Stock balance* | |
|---|---|---|---|---|---|---|---|---|
| | *Quantity units* | *Price £* | *Value £* | *Quantity units* | *Price £* | *Value £* | *Quantity units* | *Value £* |
| 1.1.09 | 100 | 10 | 1 000 | | | | 100 | 1 000 |
| 10.1.09 | 150 | 11 | 1 650 | | | | 250 | 2 650 |
| 15.1.09 | | | | 125 | 10.60 | 1 325 | 125 | 1 325 |
| 20.1.09 | 50 | 12 | 600 | | | | 175 | 1 925 |
| 31.1.09 | | | | 150 | 11.00 | 1 650 | 25 | 275 |

*Note*:
The company uses the continuous weighted average method of pricing the issue of goods to production.

*Required*:
Check that the prices of goods issued to production during January 2009 have been calculated correctly.

**Answer to Example 15.2**

The issue prices of goods to production during January 2009 using the continuous weighted average method have been calculated as follows:

$$15.1.09 \quad \frac{\text{Total stock value at 10.1.09}}{\text{Total quantity in stock at 10.1.09}} = \frac{2650}{250} = \underline{\underline{£10.60}}$$

$$25.1.09 \quad \frac{\text{Total stock value at 20.1.09}}{\text{Total quantity in stock at 20.1.09}} = \frac{1925}{175} = \underline{\underline{£11.00}}$$

The main advantages and disadvantages of the CWA method are as follows.

*Advantages*

- The CWA is easy to calculate, especially if a stores ledger account is used.
- Prices relating to previous periods are taken into account.
- The price of goods purchased is related to the quantities purchased.
- The method results in a price that is not distorted either by low or high prices, or by small or large quantity purchases.
- A new price is calculated as recent purchases are taken into stock, and so the price is updated regularly.

*Disadvantages*

- A CWA price tends to lag behind current economic prices.
- The CWA price may not relate to any actual price paid.
- It is sometimes necessary to write-off any arithmetical adjustments in the stock ledger account to the profit and loss account.

We now move on to have a look at the other main type of direct cost, labour.

## Direct labour

Labour costs include the cost of employees' salaries, wages, bonuses, and the employer's national insurance and pension fund contributions. Wherever it is economically viable to do so, we will aim to charge labour costs to specific units. If this is not possible they will have to be treated as indirect costs.

The identification and pricing of direct labour is much easier than with direct materials. Basically, the procedure is as follows.

1 Employees working on specific units are required to keep a record of how many hours they spend on each unit.
2 The total hours worked on each unit is multiplied by the appropriate hourly rate.
3 A percentage amount is added to the total to allow for the employer's other labour costs, e.g. national insurance, pension fund contributions and holiday pay.
4 The total amount is then charged directly to that unit.

The procedure is illustrated in Example 15.3.

**Example 15.3**

### The charging of direct labour cost to production

Alex and Will are the two employees working on Unit X. Alex is paid £10 an hour and Will £5. Both men are required to keep record of how much time they spend on each job they do. Alex spent 10 hours and Will 20 when working on Unit X. The employer has estimated that it costs him an extra 20 per cent on top of what he pays them to meet his contributions towards national insurance, pension contributions and holiday pay.

*Required*:
Calculate the direct labour cost of producing Unit X.

**Answer to Example 15.3**

Calculation of the direct labour cost:

| | *Hours* | | *Rate per hour* | | *Total* |
|---|---|---|---|---|---|
| | | | £ | | £ |
| Alex | 10 | × | 10 | = | 100 |
| Will | 20 | × | 5 | = | 100 |
| | | | | | 200 |
| Employer's costs (20%) | | | | | 40 |
| Total direct labour cost | | | | | 240 |

It should be made clear that in practice it is by no means easy to obtain an accurate estimate of the direct labour cost of one unit. Indeed, if it is very difficult to do so, then it will probably not be worthwhile. In those cases where there is no doubt that employees were working on a particular unit (as in Example 15.3) we depend on them keeping an accurate record. If you have ever had to do this in your own job you will know that this is difficult, especially if you are frequently being switched from one job to another, or you spend lots of time chatting in the corridor!

Even if it is difficult, it is important that management should emphasize to employees just how important it is to keep an accurate record of their time. Labour costs may form a high proportion of total cost (especially in service industries) and so tight control is important. This is especially the case if tender prices are based on total unit cost. A high cost could mean that the company fails to get a contract, whereas too low a cost diminishes profit.

## Other direct costs

Apart from material and labour costs, there may be other types of costs that can be economically identified with specific units. These are, however, relatively rare because unlike materials and labour it is usually difficult to trace a direct physical link to specific units unless, for example, some specialist plant is hired to work on one particular job. It would then be possible to charge the hire cost specifically to that job.

Irrespective of the difficulties of identifying other expenses with production, it is important to make every effort do so. Otherwise, the indirect charge just becomes bigger and bigger, and that then causes even greater problems when calculating the total cost of a specific unit.

### ! Questions non-accountants should ask

We suggest that you put the following questions to your management accountants.

- What is included in material costs?
- What criteria do you use for determining whether the costs are direct or indirect?
- What method do you use for charging them out to production?
- How do you determine whether labour costs are direct or indirect?
- What system is used to ensure that time spent on specific jobs is recorded accurately?

- Are there any other costs that could be classified as direct?
- What are they?
- What criteria can we use for classifying them as such?

## Conclusion

Responsibility accounting is a management control system that involves dividing an entity into segments and placing each segment under the control of a designated manager. Three main types of segments may be identified: cost centres (responsible for costs only), profit centres (responsible for costs and revenues) and investment centres (responsible for costs, revenues and investment decisions). All costs and revenues are then assigned to a specific responsibility centre.

A direct cost is a cost that can be easily and economically identified with a specific cost centre. Some direct costs can then be identified with specific units or products. Those that cannot be so identified are known as *indirect* costs.

Costs are usually classified into elements of cost. By building the costs up in layers it is possible to determine a selling price, although market conditions have also to be taken into account.

Direct material costs include raw materials and component parts. If the cost of materials used in a particular product is known then there is no problem in charging them out to products. The unit cost will be used. Otherwise, a pricing method has to be devised. The methods recommended are the first-in, first-out method, an averaging method or the standard cost method.

Direct labour costs are those costs that can be easily and economically identified with specific products. They are charged out on the basis of hours worked and the hourly rate paid plus an allowance for employer's employment costs, such as national insurance, pension contributions and holiday pay.

There may be other direct costs but these are relatively rare.

## Key points

1 Product costing has three main purposes: stock valuation, the planning and controlling of costs, and the determination of selling prices.

2 The procedure involves isolating those costs that are easy and economic to identify with specific units. Such costs are described as *direct costs*. Those costs that are not easy or economic to identify with specific costs are known as *indirect costs*. The total of indirect costs is known as *overhead* (or *overheads*).

3 Some material costs can be physically identified with specific units and their cost ascertained easily. In cases where it is difficult to isolate the cost of material charged to production, e.g. where batches of materials are purchased at different prices and where they are stored collectively, an estimated price has to be determined. There are four acceptable methods for pricing materials: unit cost, first-in, first-out, average cost, and standard cost. The average cost method recommended in this book is known as the *continuous weighted average* (CWA) cost method.

4 Wherever possible, labour costs should be charged directly to specific units. Employees will need to keep time sheets that record the hours they have spent working on specific jobs. The amount charged to a particular unit will then be the time spent working on that unit multiplied by the respective hourly wage rate.

5 Some other services may also be identifiable with specific units, e.g. the hire of a machine for a particular contract. The cost of such services should be charged directly to production if it can be easily and economically determined.

## Check your learning

*The answers to these questions can be found within the text.*

1 What is meant by 'responsibility accounting'?

2 What is (a) a cost centre, (b) a profit centre, (c) an investment centre?

3 What is (a) a direct cost, (b) an indirect cost?

4 What is meant by the 'elements of cost'?

5 What is meant by 'prime cost'?

6 What are direct materials?

7 What four methods may be used for charging them out to production?

8 What is meant by 'direct labour'?

9 How is it collected and charged out to production?

10 Give an example of a direct cost other than materials or labour.

## News story quiz

*Remember the news story at the beginning of the chapter? Go back to that story and re-read it before answering the following questions.*

This article reports that Kingsland Wines and Spirits are installing a 'just-in-time' (JIT) manufacturing system. At its simplest, this means that the company will only start the manufacturing process when it has a firm order from a customer.

### Questions

1 What effect will a JIT system have on the company's stocks of (a) raw materials, (b) finished goods?

2 What problem issues might arise when it gets an unexpected and urgent order from a customer?

3 What method should be used for pricing raw materials to production under a JIT system?

4 How can Kingsland reduce its long manufacturing lead times?

## Tutorial questions

*The answers to questions marked with an asterisk can be found in Appendix 4.*

**15.1** Examine the argument that an arbitrary pricing system used to charge direct materials to production leads to erroneous product costing.

**15.2*** The following stocks were taken into stores as follows:

1.1.09 1000 units @ £20 per unit.
15.1.09 500 units @ £25 per unit.

There were no opening stocks.

On 31.1.09 1250 units were issued to production.

*Required*:
Calculate the amount that would be charged to production on 31 January 2009 for the issue of material on that date using each of the following methods of material pricing:

(a) FIFO (first-in, first-out)
(b) continuous weighted average.

**15.3*** The following information relates to material ST 2:

| | | *Units* | *Unit price* | *Value* |
|---|---|---|---|---|
| | | | £ | £ |
| 1.2.07 | Opening stock | 500 | 1.00 | 500 |
| 10.2.07 | Receipts | 200 | 1.10 | 220 |
| 12.2.07 | Receipts | 100 | 1.12 | 112 |
| 17.2.07 | Issues | 400 | – | – |
| 25.2.07 | Receipts | 300 | 1.15 | 345 |
| 27.2.07 | Issues | 250 | – | – |

*Required*:
Calculate the value of closing stock at 28 February 2007 assuming that the continuous weighted average method of pricing materials to production has been adopted.

**15.4** You are presented with the following information for Trusty Limited:

| *2008* | *Purchases (units)* | *Unit cost* £ | *Issues to production (units)* |
|---|---|---|---|
| 1 January | 2 000 | 10 | |
| 31 January | | | 1 600 |
| 1 February | 2 400 | 11 | |
| 28 February | | | 2 600 |
| 1 March | 1 600 | 12 | |
| 31 March | | | 1 000 |

*Note*: There was no opening stock.

*Required*:
Calculate the value of closing stock at 31 March 2008 using each of the following methods of pricing the issue of materials to production:

(a) FIFO (first-in, first-out)
(b) continuous weighted average.

15.5 The following information relates to Steed Limited for the year to 31 May 2009:

| | £ |
|---|---|
| Sales | 500 000 |
| Purchases | 440 000 |
| Opening stock | 40 000 |

Closing stock value using the following pricing methods:

| | |
|---|---|
| FIFO (first-in, first-out) | 90 000 |
| Continuous weighted average | 79 950 |

*Required*:
Calculate Steed Limited's gross profit for the year to 31 May 2009 using each of the above closing stock values.

15.6 Iron Limited is a small manufacturing company. During the year to 31 December 2009 it has taken into stock and issued to production the following items of raw material, known as XY1:

| *Date 2009* | *Receipts into stock* | | | *Issues to production* |
|---|---|---|---|---|
| | *Quantity (litres)* | *Price per unit* | *Total value* | *Quantity (litres)* |
| | | £ | £ | |
| January | 200 | 2.00 | 400 | |
| February | | | | 100 |
| April | 500 | 3.00 | 1 500 | |
| May | | | | 300 |
| June | 800 | 4.00 | 3 200 | |
| July | | | | 400 |
| October | 900 | 5.00 | 4 500 | |
| December | | | | 1 400 |

*Notes*:

1 There were no opening stocks of raw materials XY1.

2 The other costs involved in converting raw material XY1 into the finished product (marketed as Carcleen) amounted to £7000.

3 Sales of Carcleen for the year to 31 December 2009 amounted to £20 000.

*Required*:

(a) Illustrate the following methods of pricing the issue of materials to production:
  1 first-in, first-out (FIFO)
  2 continuous weighted average.

(b) Calculate the gross profit for the year using each of the above methods of pricing the issue of materials to production.

**Further practice questions, study material and links to relevant sites on the World Wide Web can be found on the website that accompanies this book. The site can be found at www.pearsoned.co.uk/dyson**

Chapter 16

# Indirect costs

**And increasing overheads too . . .**

## Rise in profit warnings blamed on poor sales

**Report by Ernst & Young shows low sales and natural disasters lead to rapid rise in profit warnings and a slew of insolvencies**

Profit warnings rose nearly 25% in 2005 compared with the previous 12 months, Ernst & Young has reported.

Almost half of the highest rise since 2001 was blamed on lower sales, with difficult trading conditions and increasing costs and overheads – and natural disasters – also given as factors.

Profit warnings averaged 95 per quarter compared with 65 in 2004, the audit firm's research found.

In the final quarter of 2005, the highest number of warnings were in the support services sector, with 16 warnings, six of which came from recruitment companies.

However, general retailers were also in trouble with nine warnings adding to the woes of Allders, Allsports, Furnitureland, Kookai and Unwins, which all went into administration in 2005. All up, it was a tough year for retailers, with 35 profit warnings that accounted for 12% of the sector.

The engineering, insurance, and software and computer services sectors also had seven warnings each.

Indeed, the insurance sector had its worst year on record, both in terms of claims and warnings, thanks to a record number of natural disasters including hurricanes Katerina, Rita and Wilma. This led to 15 profit warnings being issued during the year – seven during the last quarter – which compares with only eight warnings issued in the whole of 2004.

Keith McGregor, corporate restructuring partner at Ernst & Young said the conditions on the high street were likely to remain difficult this year: 'The first quarter of 2006 is likely to see a similar warnings picture, possibly with a heavier bias toward retailers, in particular, the higher-end, clothing and electrical suppliers.

'With rents and employee costs on the rise and no opportunity to increase prices, all retailers will be looking to manage out costs and increase volumes.'

*Accountancy Age*, 16 January 2006.



*Questions relating to this news story can be found on page 324*

## About this chapter

This is the second of two chapters in Part 4 that deal with *cost accounting*. We have split our study of cost accounting into two parts because the subject is too big to deal with in one. Chapter 15 dealt with direct costs and this chapter covers indirect costs. By the end of the chapter we will have been able to show you how accountants have traditionally gone about calculating product costs. In recent years the traditional method has been severely criticized, so before we finish the chapter we will outline a relatively new technique for dealing with indirect costs (or overheads). This technique is called *activity-based costing* and its proponents make great claims for it.

**Learning objectives**

By the end of this chapter, you should be able to:

- outline the nature of indirect production and non-production costs;
- calculate unit costs using absorption costing;
- assess its usefulness;
- explain what is meant by activity-based costing;
- summarize its advantages and disadvantages.

## Why this chapter is important for non-accountants

In the previous chapter we suggested that you needed to know something about cost accounting for three main reasons:

- to achieve greater control over what you are employed to manage;
- to make better decisions;
- to get involved in the material pricing decision.

The first two reasons hold good for this chapter, but there is another reason that relates directly to the contents of this chapter.

The treatment of indirect costs in product costing involves some fairly questionable procedures and there is much controversy in accounting circles about their usefulness and reliability. So you should not leave it to the accountants to decide what to do. As a non-accountant and manager you have to get stuck right into the debate but you cannot do that if you don't know what the accountants are talking about.

This chapter will enable you to talk to accountants at their level and enable *you* to decide what is best for *your* department when it comes to dealing with the 'overheads'.

## Production overhead

In the previous chapter we suggested that if management accounting is going to be used as part of a control system, it is necessary for all costs within an entity to become the direct responsibility of a designated cost centre manager. In this section we will examine how the *production* overhead gets charged to specific units. It is quite a complicated procedure, and so we will take you through it in stages. Three main stages may be identified:

- allocation
- apportionment
- absorption.

The overall flow of costs in an absorption costing system is also shown diagrammatically in Figure 16.1. The figure shows the terms associated with the technique and also how costs are absorbed into a unit.

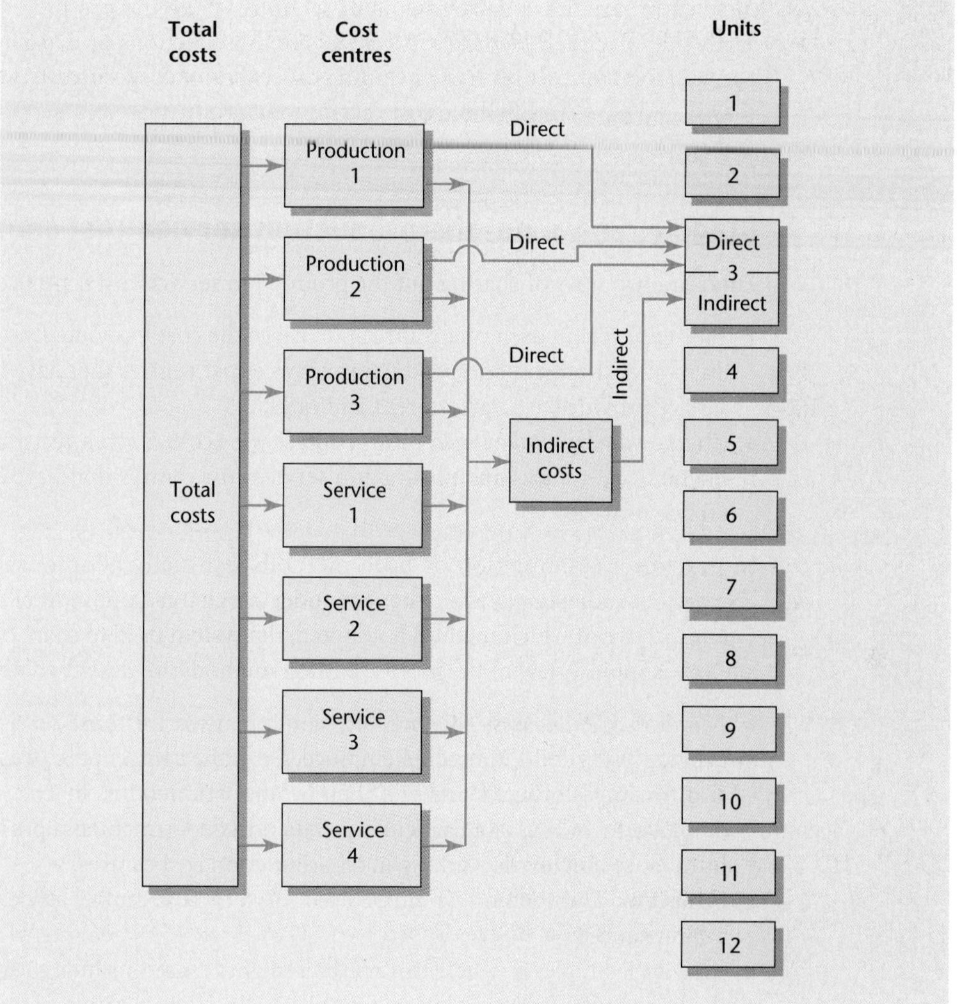


Figure 16.1 **Flow of costs in an absorption costing system**

## Stage 1: Allocate all costs to specific cost centres

*Allocation* is the process of charging the entire cost of an item to a cost centre (or a cost unit) without needing to apportion it or share it out in any way. It is essential that all costs are first allocated to a cost centre because they then become the responsibility of the manager of that centre. Some costs may be difficult to identify with a particular cost centre because they can be associated with a number of cost centres, e.g. factory rent or business rates. Nevertheless, such costs should be charged to a specific cost centre and not a 'general' or a 'sundry' one (even though the relationship may be largely nominal). This requirement is very important because if it is not strictly applied then some costs will not be monitored and they will just spiral out of control.

Once all the costs have been allocated to a cost centre, we then classify the cost centres into two broad categories: *production* cost centres and *service* cost centres. Production cost centres are those departments or sections where the product is manufactured or partly manufactured. *Service* cost centres are those sections or departments that provide a service to other cost centres (including other service cost centres).

Once we have classified the cost centres into 'production' and 'service' we can move on to Stage 2.

## Stage 2: Share out the production service cost centre costs

There are two ways of sharing out the production service cost centre costs.

- Take *each* cost in each cost centre and charge the cost individually to all the other production cost centres and production service cost centres that have benefited from the service provided, e.g. factory rent and rates.
- Charge out the *total* of each production service cost centre's costs to all the other production cost centres and production service cost centres that have benefited from the service provided.

In practice a combination of both methods is usually adopted, i.e. some costs are charged out individually while the remainder are charged out in total.

Irrespective of which method is adopted, the system used to share out the costs is usually very simple. A few of the more common methods are described below.

- *Numbers of employees.* This method would be used for those service cost centres that provide a service to individual employees, e.g. the canteen, the personnel department, and the wages office. Costs will then be apportioned on the basis of the number of employees working in a particular production department as a proportion of the total number of employees working in all production cost centres.
- *Floor area.* This method would be used for such cost centres as cleaning and building maintenance.
- *Activity.* Examples of where this method might be used include the drawings office (on the basis of drawings made), materials handling (based on the number of requisitions processed) and the transport department (on the basis of vehicle operating hours).

A problem arises in dealing with the apportionment of service cost-centre costs when service cost centres provide a service for each other. The wages office, for example, will probably provide a service for the canteen staff, and in turn the canteen staff may provide a service for the wages staff. Before the service cost-centre costs can be apportioned among the production cost centres, therefore, the service cost-centre costs have to be charged out to each other.

Unfortunately, the problem becomes a circular because it is not possible to charge some of the canteen costs to the wages office until the canteen has been charged with some of the costs of the wages office. Similarly, it is not possible to charge out the wages office costs until part of the canteen costs have been charged to the wages office. The problem is shown in diagrammatic form in Figure 16.2. The treatment of *reciprocal service costs* (as they are called) can become an involved and time-consuming process unless a clear policy decision is taken about their treatment. There are three main ways of dealing with this problem.

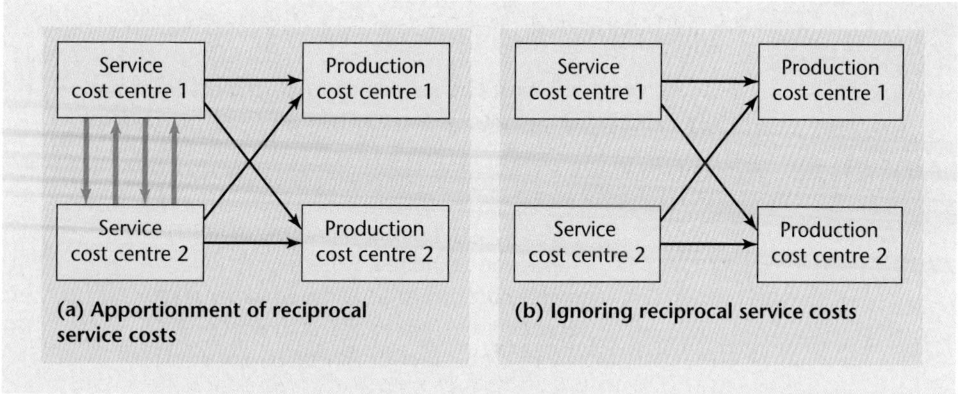


**Figure 16.2 Service cost centre reciprocal costs**

- *Ignore interdepartmental service costs.* If this method is adopted, the respective service cost-centre costs are only apportioned among the production cost centres. Any servicing that the service cost centres provide for each other is ignored.
- *Specified order of closure.* This method requires the service cost-centre costs to be closed off in some specified order and apportioned among the production cost centres and the remaining service cost centres. As the service cost centres are gradually closed off, there will eventually be only one service cost centre left. Its costs will then be apportioned among the production cost centres. Some order of closure has to be specified, and this may be quite arbitrary. It may be based, for example, on those centres that provide a service for the largest number of other service cost centres, or it could be based on the cost centres with the highest or the lowest cost in them prior to any interdepartmental servicing. It could also be based on an estimate of the benefit received by the other centres.
- *Mathematical apportionment.* Each service cost centre's total cost is apportioned among production cost centres and other service cost centres on the basis of the estimated benefit provided. The effect is that additional amounts keep being charged back to a particular service cost centre as further apportionment takes place. It can take a very long time before there is no more cost to charge out to any of the service cost centres. But when that point is reached, all the service cost-centre costs will then have been charged to the production cost centres. This method involves a great deal of exhaustive arithmetical apportionment. It is also very time-consuming, especially when there are a great many service cost centres. Although it is possible to carry out the calculations manually, it is more easily done by computer.

In choosing one of the above methods, it should be remembered that they all depend on an *estimate* of how much benefit one department receives from another. Such an estimate amounts to no more than an informed guess. It seems unnecessary, therefore, to build an involved arithmetical exercise on the basis of some highly questionable assumptions. We would suggest that in most circumstances interdepartmental servicing charging may be ignored.

We have covered some fairly complicated procedures in dealing with Stages 1 and 2. So, before moving on to Stage 3, we use Example 16.1 to illustrate the procedure.

**Example 16.1**

## Charging overhead to cost centres

You are provided with the following indirect cost information relating to the New Manufacturing Company Limited for the year to 31 March 2009:

| | £ |
|---|---|
| *Cost centre*: | |
| Production 1: indirect expenses (to units) | 24 000 |
| Production 2: indirect expenses (to units) | 15 000 |
| Service cost centre A: allocated expenses | 20 000 |
| Service cost centre B: allocated expenses | 8 000 |
| Service cost centre C: allocated expenses | 3 000 |

*Additional information*:
The estimated benefit provided by the three service cost centres to the other cost centres is as follows:

Service cost centre A: Production 1 50%; Production 2 30%; Service cost centre B 10%; Service cost centre C 10%.
Service cost centre B: Production 1 70%; Production 2 20%; Service cost centre C 10%.
Service cost centre C: Production 1 50%; Production 2 50%.

*Required*:
Calculate the total amount of overhead to be charged to cost centre units for both Production cost centre 1 and Production cost centre 2 for the year to 31 March 2009.

**Answer to Example 16.1**

**New Manufacturing Co. Ltd**
**Overhead distribution schedule for the year to 31 March 2009**

| *Cost centre* | *Production* | | *Service* | | |
|---|---|---|---|---|---|
| | *1* | *2* | *A* | *B* | C |
| | £ | £ | £ | £ | £ |
| Allocated indirect expenses | 24 000 | 15 000 | 20 000 | 8 000 | 3 000 |
| Apportion service cost-centre costs: | | | | | |
| A (50 : 30 : 10 : 10) | 10 000 | 6 000 | (20 000) | 2 000 | 2 000 |
| B (70 : 20 : 0 : 10) | 7 000 | 2 000 | – | (10 000) | 1 000 |
| C (50 : 50 : 0 : 0) | 3 000 | 3 000 | – | – | (6 000) |
| Total overhead to be absorbed by specific units | 44 000 | 26 000 | – | – | – |

*Tutorial notes*

1 Units passing through Production cost centre 1 will have to share total overhead expenditure amounting to £44 000. Units passing through Production cost centre 2 will have to share total overhead expenditure amounting to £26 000. The number of units passing through both departments may be the same. They might be assembled, for example, in cost centre 1 and packed in cost centre 2.

2 The total amount of overhead to be shared amongst the units is £70 000 (44 000 + 26 000) or (£24 000 + 15 000 + 20 000 + 8000 + 3000). The total amount of overhead originally collected in each of the five cost centres does not change.

3 This exhibit involves some interdepartmental reapportionment of service cost-centre costs. However, no problem arises because of the way in which the question requires the respective service cost-centre costs to be apportioned.

4 The objective of apportioning service cost-centre costs is to share them out among the production cost centres so that they can be included in the cost of specific units.

We can now move on to examine stage 3 of the absorption process.

## Stage 3: Absorb the production overhead

Once all the indirect costs have been collected in the production cost centres, the next step is to charge the total amount to specific units. This procedure is known as *absorption*.

The method of absorbing overhead into units is normally a simple one. Accountants recommend a single factor, preferably one related as closely as possible to the movement of overhead. In other words, an attempt is made to choose a factor that directly correlates with the amount of overhead expenditure incurred. Needless to say, like so much else in accounting, there is no obvious factor to choose!

There are six main methods that can be used for absorbing production overhead. All six adopt the same basic equation:

$$\text{Cost centre overhead absorption rate} = \frac{\text{total cost centre overhead}}{\text{total cost centre activity}}$$

A different absorption rate will be calculated for each production cost centre, and so by the time that a unit has passed through various production cost centres it may have been charged with a share of overhead from a number of production cost centres.

The six main absorption methods follow.

### Specific units

$$\text{Absorption rate} = \frac{\text{total cost centre overhead}}{\text{number of units processed in the cost centre}}$$

This method is the simplest to operate. The same rate is applied to each unit and so it is only suitable if the units are identical.

### Direct materials cost

$$\text{Absorption rate} = \frac{\text{total cost centre overhead}}{\text{cost centre total direct material costs}} \times 100$$

The direct material cost of each unit is then multiplied by the absorption rate.

It is unlikely that there will normally be a strong relationship between the direct material cost and the level of overheads. There might be some special cases, but they are probably quite unusual, e.g. where a company uses a high level of precious metals and its overheads strongly reflect the cost of safeguarding those materials.

### Direct labour cost

$$\text{Absorption rate} = \frac{\text{total cost centre overhead}}{\text{cost centre total direct labour costs}} \times 100$$

The direct labour cost of each unit is then multiplied by the absorption rate.

Overheads tend to relate to the amount of time that a unit spends in production, and so this method may be particularly suitable since the direct labour cost is a combination of hours worked and rates paid. It may not be appropriate, however, where the total direct labour cost consists of a relatively low level of hours worked and of a high labour rate per hour, because the cost will not then relate very closely to time spent in production.

### Prime cost

$$\text{Absorption rate} = \frac{\text{total cost centre overhead}}{\text{prime cost}} \times 100$$

The prime cost of each unit is then multiplied by the absorption rate. This method assumes that there is a close relationship between prime cost and overheads.

As there is probably no close relationship between either direct materials or direct labour and overheads, it is unlikely that there will be much of a correlation between prime cost and overheads. So the prime cost method tends to combine the disadvantages of both the direct materials cost and the direct labour cost methods without having any real advantages of its own.

### Direct labour hours

$$\text{Absorption rate} = \frac{\text{total cost centre overhead}}{\text{cost centre total direct labour hours}}$$

The direct labour hours of each unit are then multiplied by the absorption rate.

This method is highly acceptable, especially in those cost centres that are labour intensive, because time spent in production is related to the cost of overhead incurred.

### Machine hours

$$\text{Absorption rate} = \frac{\text{total cost centre overhead}}{\text{cost centre total machine hours}}$$

The total machine hours used by each unit is then multiplied by the absorption rate.

This is a most appropriate method to use in those departments that are machine intensive. There is probably quite a strong correlation between the amount of machine time that a unit takes to produce and the amount of overhead incurred.

The various absorption methods are illustrated in Example 16.2.

**Activity 16.1**

Think of all the costs of running a factory. Apart from direct material and direct labour costs, what other costs are likely to be involved? List three of them and then attach to each one the main factor that is likely to cause them either to increase or to decrease.

**Example 16.2**

## Calculation of overhead absorption rates

Old Limited is a manufacturing company. The following information relates to the assembling department for the year to 30 June 2009:

| | *Assembling department* |
|---|---|
| | *Total* |
| | *£000* |
| Direct material cost incurred | 400 |
| Direct labour incurred | 200 |
| Total factory overhead incurred | 100 |
| Number of units produced | 10 000 |
| Direct labour hours worked | 50 000 |
| Machine hours used | 80 000 |

*Required*:
Calculate the overhead absorption rates for the assembling department using each of the following methods:
(a) specific units
(b) direct material cost
(c) direct labour cost
(d) prime cost
(e) direct labour hours
(f) machine hours.

**Answer to Example 16.2**

(a) Specific units:

$$\text{OAR} = \frac{\text{TCCO}}{\text{Number of units}} = \frac{£100\,000}{10\,000} = \underline{\underline{£10.00 \text{ per unit}}}$$

(b) Direct material cost:

$$\text{OAR} = \frac{\text{TCCO}}{\text{Direct material cost}} \times 100 = \frac{£100\,000}{400\,000} \times 100 = \underline{\underline{25\%}}$$

(c) Direct labour cost:

$$\text{OAR} = \frac{\text{TCCO}}{\text{Direct labour cost}} \times 100 = \frac{£100\,000}{200\,000} \times 100 = \underline{\underline{50\%}}$$

(d) Prime cost:

$$\text{OAR} = \frac{\text{TCCO}}{\text{Prime cost}} \times 100 = \frac{£100\,000}{400\,000 + 200\,000} \times 100 = \underline{\underline{16.67\%}}$$

(e) Direct labour hours:

$$\text{OAR} = \frac{\text{TCCO}}{\text{Direct labour hours}} = \frac{£100\,000}{50\,000} = \underline{\underline{£2.00 \text{ per direct labour hour}}}$$

(f) Machine hours:

$$\text{OAR} = \frac{\text{TCCO}}{\text{Machine hours}} = \frac{£100\,000}{80\,000} = \underline{\underline{£1.25 \text{ per machine hour}}}$$

Example 16.2 illustrates the six absorption methods outlined in the text. In practice, only one absorption method would normally be chosen for each production cost centre, although different production cost centres may adopt different methods, e.g. one may choose a direct labour-hour rate and another may adopt a machine-hour rate.

The most appropriate absorption rate method will depend on individual circumstances. A careful study would have to be made of the correlation between (a) direct materials, direct labour, other direct expenses, direct labour hours and machine hours; and (b) total overhead expenditure. However, it is generally accepted that overhead tends to move with time, so the longer a unit spends in production the more overhead it will incur.

So if this is the case, labour-intensive cost centres should use the direct labour hour method, while machine-intensive departments should use the machine hour method.

## A comprehensive example

At this stage it will be useful to illustrate overhead absorption in the form of a comprehensive example, although that does not mean that we are going to use hundreds of costs centres! The example chosen uses the minimum amount of information for us to demonstrate the principles of overhead absorption.

**Example 16.3**

### Overhead absorption

Oldham Limited is a small manufacturing company producing a variety of pumps for the oil industry. It operates from one factory that is geographically separated from its head office. The components for the pumps are assembled in the assembling department; they are then passed to the finishing department, where they are painted and packed. There are three service cost centres: administration, stores and work study.

The following costs were collected for the year to 30 June 2009:

| *Allocated cost-centre overhead costs:* | *£000* |
|---|---|
| Administration | 70 |
| Assembling | 25 |
| Finishing | 9 |
| Stores | 8 |
| Work study | 18 |

*Additional information*:

1 The allocated cost-centre overhead costs are all considered to be indirect costs as far as specific units are concerned.

2 During the year to 30 June 2009, 35 000 machine hours were worked in the assembling department, and 60 000 direct labour hours in the finishing department.

3 The average number of employees working in each department during the year to 30 June 2009 was as follows:

| | |
|---|---|
| Administration | 15 |
| Assembling | 25 |
| Finishing | 40 |
| Stores | 2 |
| Work study | 3 |
| | 85 |

4 During the year to 30 June 2009, the stores received 15 000 requisitions from the assembling department, and 10 000 requisitions from the finishing department. The stores department did not provide a service for any other department.
5 The work study department carried out 2000 chargeable hours for the assembling department, and 1000 chargeable hours for the finishing department.
6 One special pump (code named MEA 6) was produced during the year to 30 June 2009. It took 10 machine hours of assembling time, and 15 direct labour hours were worked on it in the finishing department. Its total direct costs (materials and labour) amounted to £100.

*Required:*
(a) Calculate an appropriate absorption rate for:
  (i) the assembling department,
  (ii) the finishing department.
(b) Calculate the total factory cost of the special MEA 6 pump.

**Answer to Example 16.3(a)**

**Oldham Ltd**
**Overhead distribution schedule for the year to 30 June 2009**

| | *Production* | | *Service* | | |
|---|---|---|---|---|---|
| *Cost centre* | *Assembling* | *Finishing* | *Adminis-tration* | *Stores* | *Work study* |
| | *£000* | *£000* | *£000* | *£000* | *£000* |
| Allocated overhead costs (1) | 25 | 9 | 70 | 8 | 18 |
| Production | | | | | |
| Apportion administration: | | | | | |
| 25 : 40 : 2 : 3 (2) | 25 | 40 | (70) | 2 | 3 |
| Apportion stores: 3 : 2 (3) | 6 | 4 | – | (10) | – |
| Apportion work study: 2 : 1 (4) | 14 | 7 | – | – | (21) |
| Total overhead to be absorbed | 70 | 60 | – | – | – |

**Tutorial notes**

1 The allocated overhead costs were given in the question.
2 Administration costs have been apportioned on the basis of employees. Details were given in the question. There were 85 employees in the factory, but 15 of them were employed in the administration department. Administration costs have, therefore, been apportioned on a total of 70 employees, or £1000 per employee. The administration department is the only service department to provide a service for the other service departments, so no problem of interdepartmental servicing arises.
3 The stores costs have been apportioned on the number of requisitions made by the two production cost centres, that is 15 000 + 10 000 = 25 000, or 3 to 2.
4 The work study costs have been apportioned on the basis of chargeable hours, i.e. 2000 + 1000 = 3000, or 2 to 1.

*Calculation of chargeable rates:*

1 Assembling department:

$$\frac{\text{TCCO}}{\text{Total machine hours}} = \frac{£70\,000}{35\,000} = £2.00 \text{ per machine hour}$$

2 Finishing department:

$$\frac{\text{TCCO}}{\text{Total direct labour hours}} = \frac{£60\,000}{60\,000} = £1.00 \text{ per direct labour hour}$$

It would seem appropriate to absorb the assembling department's overhead on the basis of machine hours because it appears to be a machine-intensive department. The finishing department appears more labour intensive, and so its overhead will be absorbed on that basis.

Answer to Example 16.3(b)

**MEA 6: Calculation of total factory cost**

| | £ | £ |
|---|---|---|
| Direct costs (as given in note 6) | | 100 |
| *Add*: factory overhead: | | |
| Assembling department (10 machine hours × £2.00 per MH) | 20 | |
| Finishing department (15 direct labour hours × £1.00 per DLH) | 15 | 35 |
| Total factory cost | | 135 |

We suggest that you now have a go at doing Example 16.3 without looking at the answer.

## Non-production overhead

In the previous section we concentrated on the apportionment and absorption of *production* overheads. Most companies will, however, incur expenditure on activities that are not directly connected with production activities. For example, there could be selling and distribution costs, research and development costs, and head office administrative expenses. How should these types of costs be absorbed into unit cost?

Before this question can be answered, it is necessary to find out *why* we should want to apportion them. There are three possible reasons:

- *Control.* The more that an entity's costs are broken down, the easier it is to monitor them. It follows that just as there is an argument for having a detailed system of responsibility accounting at cost-centre level, so there is an argument for having a similar system at unit-cost level. However, in the case of non-production expenses this argument is not a very strong one.

  The relationship between units produced and non-production overhead is usually so remote that no meaningful estimate of the benefit received can be made. So the apportionment of non-production overhead is merely an arithmetical exercise, and no manager could be expected to take responsibility for costs charged to their cost centre in this way. From a control point of view, therefore, the exercise is not very helpful.
- *Selling price.* In some cases, it might be necessary to add to the production cost of a specific unit a proportion of non-production overhead in order to determine a selling price that covers all costs and allows a margin for profit. This system of fixing selling prices may apply in some industries, e.g. in tendering for long-term contracts or in estimating decorating costs. In most cases, however, selling prices are determined by the market and companies are not usually in a position to fix their selling prices based on cost with a percentage added on for profit (known as cost-plus pricing).
- *Stock valuation.* You might think that we need to include non-production overheads in valuing stocks but as *SSAP 9* does not permit them to be included they are usually ignored, even in mangement accounting. This is largely because much more work will be involved if the management accounts had to be altered to suit the requirements of the financial accounts.

It is obvious from the above summary that there are few benefits to be gained by charging a proportion of non-production overhead to specific cost units. In theory, the exercise is attractive because it would be both interesting and useful to know the *actual* cost of each unit produced. In practice, however, it is impossible to arrive at any such cost, and so it seems pointless becoming engaged in a purely spurious arithmetical exercise.

The only real case for apportioning non-production overhead applies where selling prices can be based on cost. What can be done in those situations? There is still no magic formula and an arbitrary estimate has still to be made. The easiest method is simply to add a percentage to the total production cost, perhaps based on this relationship between non-production overhead and total cost. This is bound to be a somewhat questionable method, since there can be no close relationship between production and non-production activities. It follows that the company's tendering or selling-price policy should not be too rigid if it is based on this type of cost-plus pricing.

**Activity 16.2**

You are a manager in a company that manufactures consumer products. Market prices are competitive and you need to keep down your costs. Do you think that charging non-production overhead to unit costs serves any purpose in this context? Tick the box below as appropriate and then give your reasons.

Yes ☐ No ☐

Why? ______________________________

## Predetermined absorption rates

An absorption rate can be calculated on a historical basis (i.e. after the event), or it can be predetermined (i.e. calculated in advance).

As we have argued, there is no close correlation between fixed overhead and any particular measure of activity: it can only be apportioned on what seems to be a reasonable basis. However, if we know the total actual overhead incurred, we can make sure that it is all charged to specific units, even if we are not sure of the relationship that it has with any particular unit.

In order to do so we need to know the *actual cost of overheads* and the *actual activity level* (whether measured in machine hours, direct labour hours or on some other basis). In other words, we can only make the calculation when we know *what* has happened.

The adoption of *historical* absorption rates is not usually very practicable. We have to wait until the actual period is over before an absorption rate can be calculated, the products costed and the customers invoiced. It is therefore, preferable to use what is known as a *predetermined absorption rate.*

This involves estimating the overhead likely to be incurred and the direct labour hours (or machine hours) that are expected to be worked. If one or other of these estimates turns out to be inaccurate then we would have either undercharged our customers (if the rate was too low), or overcharged them (if the rate was too high).

This situation could be very serious for a company. Low selling prices caused by using a low absorption rate could have made the company's products very competitive, but there is not much point in selling a lot of units if they are being sold at a loss. Similarly, a high absorption rate may result in a high selling price. Each unit may then make a large profit, but not enough units may be sold to enable the company to make an overall profit.

The difference between the actual overhead incurred and the total overhead charged to production (calculated on a predetermined basis) gives rise to what is known as a *variance.* If the actual overhead incurred is in excess of the amount charged out, the variance will be *adverse,* i.e. the profit will be less than expected. However, if the total

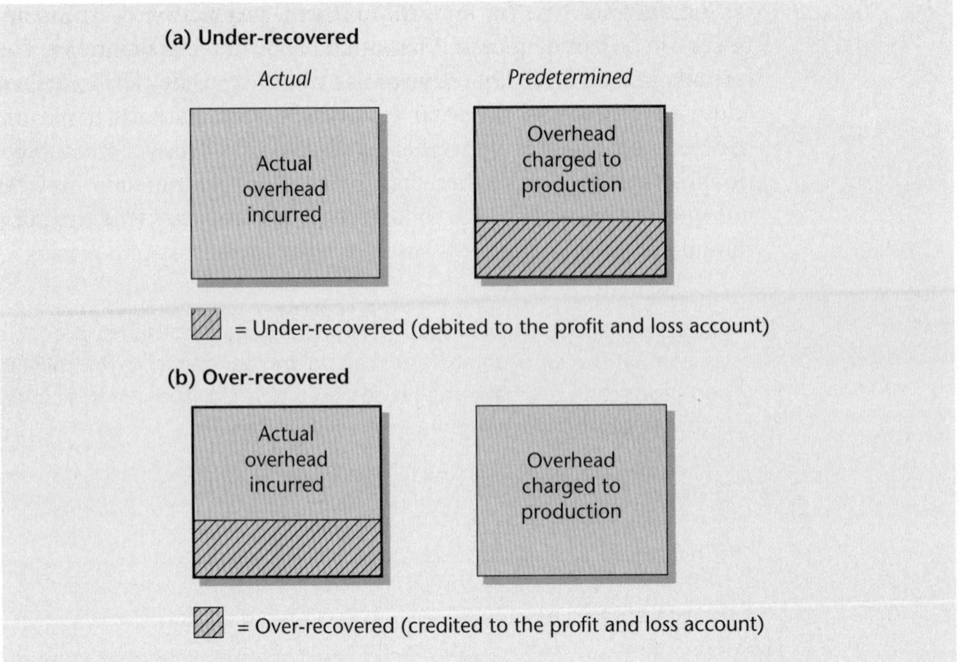


**Figure 16.3 The under- and over-recovery of overhead by using predetermined rates**

overhead charged to production is less than was estimated then the variance will be *favourable*. The effect of this procedure is shown in diagrammatic form in Figure 16.3. Other things being equal, a favourable variance gives rise to a higher profit, and an adverse variance results in a lower profit.

It is a cardinal rule in costing that variances should be written off to the profit and loss account at the end of the costing period in which they were incurred. It is not considered fair to burden the next period's accounts with the previous period's mistakes. In other words, we should start off the new accounting period with a clean sheet.

Throughout the preceding sections we have clearly expressed many reservations about the way in which accountants have traditionally dealt with overheads. In recent years, dissatisfaction about overhead absorption has become widespread, and now a different technique called *activity-based costing* is being advocated. We review it briefly in the next section.

## Activity-based costing

As we have seen, the calculation of product costs involves identifying the *direct costs* of a product and then adding (or absorbing) a proportion of the *indirect costs* (i.e. the overheads) to the total of the direct costs.

This was the method used for most of the twentieth century. It was only in the 1980s that it began to be apparent that the traditional method of absorbing overhead was inappropriate in an advanced manufacturing environment. As the traditional method involves calculating the total cost of overheads in a particular cost centre and charging them out to particular units on a time basis, the total cost is *averaged* among those units that flow through that particular cost centre. The assumption behind this procedure is that the more time that a unit spends in production, the more overhead it will incur. Such an assumption means, of course, that no distinction is made between fixed and variable overhead. It also means that, irrespective of whether a particular unit causes a certain cost to arise in a cost centre, it is still charged with a proportion of that cost.

We will use an example to illustrate this point. The details are contained in Example 16.4.

Example 16.4

### Overhead absorption: the unfairness of the traditional approach

In Jasmine Ltd's production cost centre 1, two units are produced: Unit A and Unit B, the total overhead cost being £1000. This is made up of two costs: (1) machine set-up costs of £800; and (2) inspection costs of £200. Overhead is absorbed on the basis of direct labour hours. The total direct labour hours (DLH) amount to 200. Unit A requires 150 DLH and Unit B 50 DLH.

The machinery for Unit A only needs to be set up once, whereas Unit B requires nine set-ups. Unit A and Unit B both require two inspections each.

*Required*:

(a) Calculate the total overhead to be charged to Unit A and to Unit B using:
   (i) the traditional method of absorbing overhead
   (ii) a fairer method based on set-up and inspection costs

(b) Prepare a table comparing the two methods.

Answer to Example 16.4

**(a) (i) The traditional method**

The absorption rate is £5 per direct labour hour (£1000 total overhead ÷ 200 direct labour hours). As Unit A has 150 direct labour hours spent on it, it will absorb £750 (150 DLH × £5) of overhead. Unit B has 50 direct labour hours spent on it; it will, therefore, absorb £250 of overhead (50 DLH × £5).

**(a) (ii) A fairer method**

Each set-up costs £80 [£800 ÷ 10 (1 set-up for A + 9 set-ups for B)] and each inspection costs £50 [£200 ÷ 4 (2 inspections for A + 2 inspections for B)]. The total overhead charged to Unit A, therefore, would be £180: £80 for set-up costs (1 set-up × £80) plus £100 inspection costs (2 inspections × £50). Unit B would be charged a total of £820: £720 of set-up costs (9 set-ups × £80) and £100 inspection costs (2 inspections × £50). The fairer method illustrated here is known as *activity-based costing*.

**(b) Comparing the two methods**

The table below compares the two approaches to overhead absorption:

**Jasmine Limited**

| *Product* | *Overhead absorbed on a traditional basis* | *Overhead absorbed on an activity basis* |
|---|---|---|
| | £ | £ |
| A | 750 | 180 |
| B | 250 | 820 |
| Total | 1 000 | 1 000 |

Example 16.4 illustrates the potential unfairness of the traditional method of absorbing overhead. As the method *averages* the total cost among particular units, those units that do not benefit from a particular activity bear a disproportionate amount of the total cost. In the above example, Unit A should only be charged £180 of overhead (compared with £750 under the traditional method), whereas Unit B should be charged £820 (compared with £250 under the traditional method).

It follows that if the eventual selling price is based on cost, the traditional method would grossly inflate Unit A's selling price and deflate Unit B's selling price. Unit A's selling price would probably be highly uncompetitive and only a few units might be sold. Unit B's selling price would probably be highly competitive. So a great many units of Unit B might be sold, but the total sales revenue may not be sufficient to recover all the overhead costs.

In order to illustrate the principles behind activity-based costing, we have made reference to just one cost centre. However, in practice overheads for the whole of the entity (including both manufacturing and non-manufacturing overheads) would be dealt with collectively. They would then be allocated to *cost pools*, i.e. similar areas of activity. It is estimated that even in the largest entities a total of about 30 cost pools is the maximum number that it is practicable to handle. This means that some costs may be allocated to a cost pool where there is only a distance relationship between some of the costs. In other words, like the traditional method of absorbing overheads, activity-based costing also involves some averaging of costs.

Once the overheads have all been allocated to an appropriate cost pool, a *cost driver* for each pool is selected. A cost driver is the main cause of the costs attached to that pool. Once again, some approximation is necessary because some costs collected in that pool may only have a loose connection with the selected driver. By dividing the total cost in a particular cost pool by the cost driver, an overhead cost per driver can be calculated. For example, suppose the total overhead cost collected in a particular cost pool totalled £1000 and the costs in that pool were driven by the number of material requisitions (say 200), the cost driver rate would be £5 per material requisition (£1000 cost ÷ 200 material requisitions).

The final stage is to charge an appropriate amount of overhead to each unit benefiting from the service provided by the various cost pools. So if a particular unit required 10 material requisitions and the cost driver rate was £5 per material requisition, it would be charged £50 (£5 per material requisition × 10 requisitions). Of course, it may benefit from the services provided by a number of other cost pools, so it would collect a share of overhead from each of them as well.

The above procedures are illustrated in Example 16.5.

**Example 16.5**

## Activity-based costing (ABC)

Shish Limited has recently introduced an ABC system. The following details relate to the month of March 2009.

1 Four cost pools have been identified: parts, maintenance, stores and administration.
2 The cost drivers that were identified with each cost pool are: total number of parts, maintenance hours, number of material requisitions and number of employees.
3 Costs and activities during March 2009 were:

| *Cost pool* | *Total overhead* | *Activity* | *Quantity* |
|---|---|---|---|
| | £000 | | |
| Parts | 10 000 | Number of parts | 500 |
| Maintenance | 18 000 | Number of maintenance hours | 600 |
| Stores | 10 000 | Number of material requisitions | 20 |
| Administration | 2 000 | Number of employees | 40 |

4 In March 2009, 500 units of Product X3 were produced. This production run required 100 parts and 200 maintenance hours; 6 material requisitions were made and 10 employees worked on the units.

*Required*:
Using ABC, calculate the total amount of overhead absorbed by each unit of Product X3.

**Answer to Example 16.5**

**Shish Ltd**

| *Cost pool* | *Overhead* | *Cost driver* | *Cost driver rate* | *Usage by Product X3* | *Overhead cost charged to Product X3* |
|---|---|---|---|---|---|
| (1) | (2) | (3) | (4) | (5) | (6) |
| | £000 | | £ | | £ |
| Parts | 10 000 | 500 parts | 20 | 100 parts | 2 000 |
| Maintenance | 18 000 | 600 hours | 30 | 200 hours | 6 000 |
| Stores | 10 000 | 20 requisitions | 500 | 6 requisitions | 3 000 |
| Administration | 2 000 | 40 employees | 50 | 10 employees | 500 |
| Total overhead to be absorbed by Product X3 | | | | | 11 500 |

1 Column (4) has been obtained by dividing the data in column (2) by the data in column (3).

2 The data in column (6) has been obtained by multiplying the data in column (4) by the data in column (5).

3 The total amount of £11 500 shown in column (6) is the total amount of overhead to be absorbed by Product X3.

*Solution*
The total amount of overhead to be absorbed by each unit of Product X3 will be £23 (£11 500 ÷ 500 units).

Activity-based costing is an attempt to absorb overhead on the demands that a particular unit in production makes of the various resources that it uses before it is completed and becomes part of the 'finished stock'. In traditional overhead absorption costing, a unit is charged with the *average* charge for overheads irrespective of what proportion relates to that specific unit. This means that some units are charged with more than their fair share of overheads, while others are perhaps charged with much less.

There is no difference in principle between ABC and traditional overhead absorption costing. ABC simply looks for a closer relationship between individual activities and the relationship that they have with specific units of production, while the traditional method adopts a more general approach. However, ABC does not require any distinction to be made between production overhead and non-production overhead – an issue that is largely ignored in traditional overhead absorption.

### Questions non-accountants should ask

The topic covered in this chapter is one that should encourage non-accountants to ask some very searching questions. We suggest that you use the following as a starting point.

- Have you had any problems in identifying some costs with particular cost centres?
- If so, which?
- How did you decide which cost centre to charge them to?
- What methods have you used to charge service cost-centre costs to production cost centres?
- Have you ignored any interservice cost-centre charging?
- If not, how have you dealt with the problem?
- What activity bases have you used to absorb overheads into product costs?
- Have you worked out absorption rates on a historical or a predetermined basis?
- What have you done about non-production overheads?
- Is there a case for switching to activity-based costing?

## Conclusion

In this chapter we have continued our study of cost accounting that began in Chapter 15. In it we have explained how production overheads are absorbed into product costs. In summary, the procedure is as follows.

1 Allocate all costs to appropriate cost centres.
2 Distinguish between production and service cost centres.
3 Examine the individual costs in each production service cost centre and, where possible, apportion them on some equitable basis to other cost centres.
4 Apportion the total of any remaining service cost centre costs either (1) to production cost centres or (2) to production cost centres as well as other service cost centres. If (2), continue to reapportion the service cost centre costs until they have all been charged to production cost centres.
5 Select an absorption method based on either the number of units flowing through a particular cost centre or on the time a unit spends in the cost centre. Time spent is to be related to direct labour cost, direct labour hours or machine hours.
6 Divide the total overhead in each production cost centre by the selected absorption factor.
7 Charge each unit with its share of overhead (e.g. direct labour hours or machine hours × the absorption rate).
8 Add the amount calculated to the total direct cost of that unit.

It is also necessary to determine whether the above procedure should be done on a historical or a predetermined basis, and whether non-production overheads should also be absorbed into product cost.

The above method has been in use for well over 100 years. Some academics and practitioners do not believe that it is suitable for modern manufacturing methods. In recent years a new method called *activity-based costing* has been adopted by some large companies. ABC is similar to traditional overhead absorption costing except that both production and non-production overheads are assigned to one of a number of identifiable cost pools. The main factor that causes those overheads to be incurred (known as a *cost driver*) is identified and a cost driver rate calculated (the pool overhead divided by the cost driver). Products are then charged with their share of each of the cost pool overheads.

## Key points

1. In order to charge unit costs with a share of production overheads, *all* costs should first be identified with a specific cost centre.
2. Some cost centres provide a service to other cost centres. These are known as *service cost centres*. The various costs collected in the service costs centres should be shared out on an apportionment basis among the other cost centres. Some costs collected in the service cost centres may be apportioned separately; otherwise, the *total service cost-centre cost* will be apportioned. An element of cross-charging arises when the service centres provide services for each other. This can be resolved either by ignoring any cross-charging, apportioning the total of the service centre costs in some specified order, or by mathematical apportionment.
3. Once the production cost centres have received their share of the service centre costs, an absorption rate for each production cost centre should be calculated. The traditional method is to take the total of each production cost centre's indirect cost (i.e. its overhead) and divide it either by the actual (or planned) direct labour hours, or by the machine hours actually worked (or planned to be worked) in that particular cost centre.
4. The absorption rate calculated for each production cost centre is used to charge each unit passing through that cost centre with a share of the production overhead.
5. The total production cost of a particular unit can then be calculated as follows:

   direct materials cost + direct labour cost + direct expenses +
   share of production overhead = total production cost.
6. The absorption of non-production overhead (head office adminstration expenses, selling and distribution costs, and research development costs) is not recommended, except when it may be required for pricing purposes.
7. Absorption rates will normally be predetermined, i.e. they will be based on planned costs and anticipated activity levels.
8. The under-absorption or over-absorption of overhead should be written off to the profit and loss account in the period when it was incurred.
9. In recent years a new way of dealing with the absorption of overheads called *activity-based costing* has been suggested. ABC involves charging overheads to common cost pools, identifying what main factor drives the costs in each of the respective pools, and then calculating a cost driver rate. Units are then charged with their share of each of the pool costs.

## Check your learning

*The answers to these questions can be found within the text.*

1 What is (a) a production cost centre, (b) a service cost centre?

2 What do the terms 'allocate', 'apportion' and 'absorb' mean?

3 Suggest three ways that service cost centre-costs may be charged to other cost centres.

4 What is meant by 'reciprocal service costs'?

5 Indicate three ways to deal with them.

6 What is the basic formula for absorbing production overheads into product costs?

7 List six methods of how this may be done.

8 What is non-production overhead?

9 How should it be absorbed into product costs?

10 What is a predetermined absorption rate?

11 What is meant by 'under-' and 'over-recovery of overhead'?

12 What do the initials 'ABC' mean?

13 What is a cost pool and a cost driver?

14 How does ABC differ from traditional absorption costing?

## News story quiz

*Remember the news story at the beginning of this chapter? Go back to that story and re-read it before answering the following questions.*

This is a very gloomy report suggesting that if sales fall and natural disasters occur then company profits are almost certain to be vulnerable. But from this chapter's perspective one reason given in the report for more profit warnings in 2005 than in 2004 was 'increasing costs and overheads'. It is suggested that there will be no opportunity to raise selling prices, so with rising employee costs companies will have to 'manage costs' and 'increase volumes'.

### Questions

1 What do you think is meant by the phrase 'manage our costs'?

2 How can 'volumes' be increased if trading conditions are difficult?

3 What can the retail trade do to control an overhead such as rents?

4 What do you think is the main overhead in each of the following sectors: (a) engineering, (b) general retailers, (c) insurance, (d) software and computer services?

5 How should each of these types of overhead be absorbed into product costs?

## Tutorial questions

*The answers to questions marked with an asterisk may be found in Appendix 4.*

**16.1** 'Arithmetical precision for precision's sake.' How far is this statement true of the traditional methods used in absorbing overheads into product costs?

**16.2** Has total absorption costing any relevance in a service industry?

**16.3** Some non-accountants believe that the technique of overhead absorption was devised simply to provide jobs for accountants. How far do you agree?

**16.4** How should reciprocal service costs be dealt with when calculating product costs?

**16.5** Assess the usefulness of activity-based costing in managerial decision making.

**16.6*** Scar Limited has two production departments and one service department. The following information relates to January 2009:

| | | £ |
|---|---|---|
| Allocated expenses: | | |
| Production department: | A | 65 000 |
| | B | 35 000 |
| Service department | | 50 000 |

The allocated expenses shown above are all indirect expenses as far as individual units are concerned.

The benefit provided by the service department is shared among the production departments A and B in the proportion 60 : 40.

*Required:*
Calculate the amount of overhead to be charged to specific units for both production department A and production department B.

**16.7*** Bank Limited has several production departments. In the assembly department it has been estimated that £250 000 of overhead should be charged to that particular department. It now wants to charge a customer for a specific order. The relevant data are:

| | *Assembly department* | *Specific unit* |
|---|---|---|
| Number of units | 50 000 | – |
| Direct material cost (£) | 500 000 | 8.00 |
| Direct labour cost (£) | 1 000 000 | 30.00 |
| Prime cost (£) | 1 530 000 | 40.00 |
| Direct labour hours | 100 000 | 3.5 |
| Machine hours | 25 000 | 0.75 |

The accountant is not sure which overhead absorption rate to adopt.

*Required:*
Calculate the overhead to be absorbed by a specific unit passing through the assembly department using each of the following overhead absorption rate methods:
(a) specific units
(b) percentage of direct material cost
(c) percentage of direct labour cost
(d) percentage of prime cost
(e) direct labour hours
(f) machine hours.

16.8 The following information relates to the activities of the production department of Clough Limited for the month of March 2009:

| | *Production department* | *Order number 123* |
|---|---|---|
| Direct materials consumed (£) | 120 000 | 20 |
| Direct wages (£) | 180 000 | 25 |
| Overhead chargeable (£) | 150 000 | |
| Direct labour hours worked | 30 000 | 5 |
| Machine hours operated | 10 000 | 2 |

The company adds a margin of 50 per cent to the total production cost of specific units in order to cover administration expenses and to provide a profit.

*Required:*

(a) Calculate the total selling price of order number 123 if overhead is absorbed using the following methods of overhead absorption:
direct labour hours;
machine hours.

(b) State which of the two methods you would recommend for the production department.

16.9 Burns Limited has three production departments (processing, assembly and finishing) and two service departments (administration and work study). The following information relates to April 2009:

| | £ |
|---|---|
| *Direct material* | |
| Processing | 100 000 |
| Assembling | 30 000 |
| Finishing | 20 000 |
| *Direct labour* | |
| Processing (£4 × 100 000 hours) | 400 000 |
| Assembling (£5 × 30 000 hours) | 150 000 |
| Finishing (£7 × 10 000 hours) + (£5 × 10 000 hours) | 120 000 |
| Administration | 65 000 |
| Work study | 33 000 |
| *Other allocated costs* | |
| Processing | 15 000 |
| Assembling | 20 000 |
| Finishing | 10 000 |
| Administration | 35 000 |
| Work study | 12 000 |

Apportionment of costs:

| | *Process* % | *Assembling* % | *Finishing* % | *Work study* % |
|---|---|---|---|---|
| Administration | 50 | 30 | 15 | 5 |
| Work study | 70 | 20 | 10 | – |

Total machine hours: Processing 25 000

All units produced in the factory pass through the three production departments before they are put into stock. Overhead is absorbed in the processing department on the basis of machine hours, on the basis of direct labour hours in the assembling department, and on the basis of the direct labour cost in the finishing department.

The following details relate to unit XP6:

| | £ | £ |
|---|---|---|
| *Direct materials* | | |
| Processing | 15 | |
| Assembling | 6 | |
| Finishing | 1 | 22 |
| *Direct labour* | | |
| Processing (2 hours) | 8 | |
| Assembling (1 hour) | 5 | |
| Finishing [(1 hour × £7) + (1 hour × £5)] | 12 | 25 |
| Prime cost | | 47 |

XP6: Number of machine hours in the processing department = 6

*Required:*
Calculate the total cost of producing unit XP6.

16.10 Outlane Limited's overhead budget for a certain period is as follows:

| | £000 |
|---|---|
| Administration | 100 |
| Depreciation of machinery | 80 |
| Employer's national insurance | 10 |
| Heating and lighting | 15 |
| Holiday pay | 20 |
| Indirect labour cost | 10 |
| Insurance: machinery | 40 |
| property | 11 |
| Machine maintenance | 42 |
| Power | 230 |
| Rent and rates | 55 |
| Supervision | 50 |
| | 663 |

The company has four production departments: L, M, N and O. The following information relates to each department.

| *Department* | *L* | *M* | *N* | *O* |
|---|---|---|---|---|
| Total number of employees | 400 | 300 | 200 | 100 |
| Number of indirect workers | 20 | 15 | 10 | 5 |
| Floor space (square metres) | 2000 | 1500 | 1000 | 1000 |
| Kilowatt hours' power consumption | 30000 | 50000 | 90000 | 60000 |
| Machine maintenance hours | 500 | 400 | 300 | 200 |
| Machine running hours | 92000 | 38000 | 165000 | 27000 |
| Capital cost of machines (£) | 110000 | 40000 | 50000 | 200000 |
| Depreciation rate of machines (on cost) | 20% | 20% | 20% | 20% |
| Cubic capacity | 60000 | 30000 | 10000 | 50000 |

Previously, the company has absorbed overhead on the basis of 100 per cent of the direct labour cost. It has now decided to change to a separate machine-hour rate for each department.

The company has been involved in two main contracts during the period, the details of which are as follows:

| *Department* | *Contract 1: Direct labour hours and machine hours* | *Contract 2: Direct labour hours and machine hours* |
|---|---|---|
| L | 60 | 20 |
| M | 30 | 10 |
| N | 10 | 10 |
| O | – | 60 |
| | 100 | 100 |

Direct labour cost per hour in both departments was £3.00.

*Required:*

(a) Calculate the overhead to be absorbed by both contract 1 and contract 2 using the direct labour cost method.

(b) Calculate the overhead to be absorbed using a machine hour rate for each department.

**Further practice questions, study material and links to relevant sites on the World Wide Web can be found on the website that accompanies this book. The site can be found at www.pearsoned.co.uk/dyson**

# Chapter 17 Budgeting

## Budgeting moves into the 21st century . . .

### Joseph signs up Cognos to cut out spreadsheets

Selects enterprise planning technology for better budgeting and planning

Cognos, the world leader in business intelligence and corporate performance management (CPM), has announced that international clothing retailer, Joseph, is investing in Cognos enterprise planning technology to improve budgeting and planning processes across its business. Although this has yet to be quantified, it is estimated that the company will cut its current budgeting and planning process by at least 25% of the time currently taken.

The solution, which will be rolled out by Cognos partner Tahola, a retail solutions specialist, will be used by the finance team to prepare annual, quarterly and monthly reports and rolling forecasts into sales figures, retail trends and profit margins.

Currently, the finance team at Joseph relies on spreadsheet applications to manage its budgeting and planning. The company takes a bottom up approach, from store level upwards, resulting in a very cumbersome and complex process. Any subsequent changes to the data can slow the whole procedure down even further and result in inaccuracies in the final reports.

'By implementing Cognos Planning we'll be able to do away with the complex spreadsheet system that we use at present and prepare budgets and forecasts more quickly and more accurately than before – an absolute must in the fast moving retail sector,' explained Kathleen Starkey, finance director at Joseph. 'For the first time, we'll be able to truly integrate profit and loss (P&L), balance sheet and cash flow information leading to better business management all round.'

'Working with Tahola we've found a partner with an excellent track record in retail and one that really understands our business. The team demonstrated a real dedication to making the project happen,' Starkey added.

'Joseph was struggling with the same problems that many retailers face, namely the inflexibility of Excel as an enterprise planning and forecasting tool. Cognos Planning will resolve all of those issues whilst providing "what-if" facilities to easily test many different scenarios. We look forward to working with the team at Joseph,' commented Geoff McClure, managing director of Tahola Ltd.

'Our technology will give the finance team at Joseph a much better insight into sales information, trends and margins, enabling the company as a whole to improve its budgeting and planning practices,' said Graham Walter, vice-president of Cognos UK, Middle East and South Africa.

*Lewis Virtual Press Room*, 1 February 2006.

*Questions relating to this news story can be found on page 345*

## About this chapter

This chapter tells you something about the nature and purpose of a budget – it outlines the various types of budgets, how they all fit together and how they may be used to keep a tight control of an entity's operations. It also explains that budgets and budgetary control are not neutral techniques. They have an impact on human behaviour and this has to be taken into account when using them.

**Learning objectives**

By the end of this chapter, you should be able to:

- describe the nature and purpose of budgeting and budgetary control;
- list the steps involved in operating a budgetary control system;
- describe the difference between fixed and flexible budgets;
- outline the behavioural consequences of a budgetary control system.

## Why this chapter is important for non-accountants

The more knowledge that you have as a manager, the more influence you will be able to exert – and that applies particularly to budgeting. So this chapter is important for non-accountants for the following reasons.

- Your job will probably involve you in supplying information for budgetary purposes. It is easier to supply what is needed if you know what it is for and how it will be used.
- You are likely to have to prepare a budget for your department. Obviously, it is easier to do this if you have had some training in how to do it.
- You may be supplied with various reports that show your budgeted results against actual results. You may then be asked what you are going to do to correct any variance. The impact that the 'request' will have on you will depend on a number of factors, such as how familiar you are with the way that the information has been compiled, what inherent deficiencies it may have and what reliability you can place on it.

Budgeting is not a process that is of interest only to accountants. It should involve the whole entity. As a manger you will find that if you throw yourself wholeheartedly into the process you will be able to do your job more effectively.

## Budgeting and budgetary control

We start our analysis by establishing what we mean by a 'budget' and 'budgetary control'.

### Budget

The term *budget* is usually well understood by the layman. Many people, for example, budget for their own household expenses even if it is only by making a rough comparison between next month's salary and the next month's expenditure. Such a budget may not be very detailed but it contains all the main features of a budget.

- *Policies.* A budget is based on the policies needed to fulfil the objectives of the entity.
- *Data.* It is usually expressed in monetary terms.
- *Documentation.* It is usually written down.
- *Period.* It relates to a future period of time.

Most entities will usually prepare a considerable number of budgets. A manufacturing entity, for example, would normally prepare sales, production and administration budgets. These budgets would then be combined into an overall budget known as a *master budget*. This will include a budgeted profit and loss account, a budgeted balance sheet and a budgeted cash flow statement.

Once a master budget has been prepared, it will be examined closely to see whether the overall plan can be accommodated. It might be the case, for example, that the sales budget indicates a large increase in sales. This will have required the production budgets to be prepared on the basis of this extra sales demand. The cash budget, however, might show that the entity could not finance the extra sales and production activity out of its budgeted cash resources, so additional financing arrangements will have to be made because obviously no entity would normally turn down the opportunity of increasing its sales.

Budgets are useful because they encourage managers to examine what they have done in relation to what they *could* do. However, the full benefits of a budgeting system only became apparent when it is used for *control* purposes. This involves making a constant comparison between the actual results and the budgeted results, and then taking any necessary corrective action. This procedure is called 'budgetary control'.

**Activity 17.1** Write down three reasons why we prepare budgets.

## Budgetary control

When the actual results for a period are compared with the budgeted results and it is seen that there are material (or significant) differences (called variances) then corrective action must be taken to ensure that future results will conform to the budget. This is the essence of budgetary control. It has several important features.

- *Responsibilities*. Managerial responsibilities are clearly defined.
- *Action plan*. Individual budgets lay down a detailed plan of action for a particular sphere of responsibility.
- *Adherence*. Managers have a responsibility to adhere to their budgets once the budgets have been approved.
- *Monitoring*. The actual performance is monitored constantly and compared with the budgeted results.
- *Correction*. Corrective action is taken if the actual results differ significantly from the budget.
- *Approval*. Departures from the budget are only permitted if they have been approved by senior management.
- *Variances*. Those that are unaccounted for are subject to individual investigation.

Any variance that occurs should be investigated carefully. The current actual performance will be immediately brought back into line with the budget if it is considered necessary. Sometimes the budget itself will be changed, e.g. if there is an unexpected increase in sales. Such changes may, of course, have an effect on the other budgets and so cannot be done in isolation.

Now that we have outlined the nature and purpose of budgeting and budgetary control, we are in a position to investigate how the system works.

## Procedure

The budget *procedure* starts with an examination of the entity's objectives. These may be very simple. They may include, for example, an overall wish to maximize profits, to foster better relations with customers, or to improve the working conditions of employees. Once an entity has decided on its overall objectives, it is in a position to formulate some detailed plans.

These will probably start with a *forecast*. There is a technical difference between a forecast and a budget. A forecast is a prediction of what is *likely* to happen, whereas a budget is a carefully prepared plan of what *should* happen.

In order to guide you through the budgeting process, we will examine each stage individually (as depicted in Figure 17.1). To make the process easier to understand we will assume that we are dealing with a manufacturing company in the private sector. The procedure is similar in service sector entities but somewhat different in the public sector.

### The budget period

The main budget period is usually based on a calendar year. It could be shorter or longer depending on the nature of the product cycle. The fashion industry, for example, may adopt a short budget period of less than a year, while the construction industry may opt for a five-year period. Irrespective of the industry, however, a calendar year is usually a convenient period to choose as the base period because it fits in with financial accounting requirements.

Besides determining the main budget period, it is also necessary to prepare budgets for much shorter periods. These are required for budgetary control purposes in order to compare the actual results with the budgeted results on a frequent basis. The sub-budget periods for some activities may need to be very short if very tight control is to be exercised over them, e.g. the cash budget may need to be compiled on a weekly basis. In contrast, the administration budget may need to be prepared only quarterly.

### Administration

The budget procedure may be administered by a special budget committee, or it may be supervised by the accounting function. It will be necessary for the budget committee to lay down general guidelines in accordance with the company's objectives, and to ensure that individual departments do not operate completely independently. The production

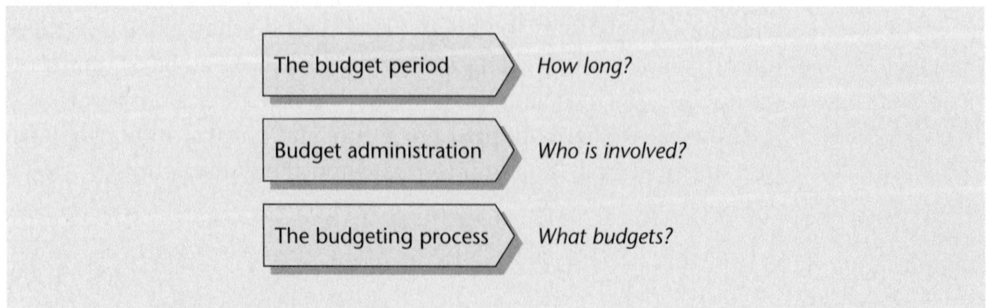


**Figure 17.1 The budgeting procedure**

department, for example, will need to know what the company is budgeting to sell so that it can prepare its own budget on the basis of those sales. However, the detailed production budget must still remain the entire responsibility of the production manager.

This procedure is in line with the concept of responsibility accounting (see Chapter 15). If the control procedure is to work properly, managers must be given responsibility for clearly defined areas of activity, such as their particular cost centre. They are then fully answerable for all that goes on there. Unless managers are given complete authority to act within clearly defined guidelines, they cannot be expected to account for something for which they are not responsible. This means that, as far as budgets are concerned, managers must help prepare, amend and approve their own cost centre's budget if the budgetary control system is to work.

**Activity 17.2**

A budget can act as a measure against which actual performance can be matched. However, some experts argue that when a measure becomes a target ('you must meet your budget') it becomes meaningless. To what extent do you think that budgeting is a waste of time? Mark your response on a scale like the one below.

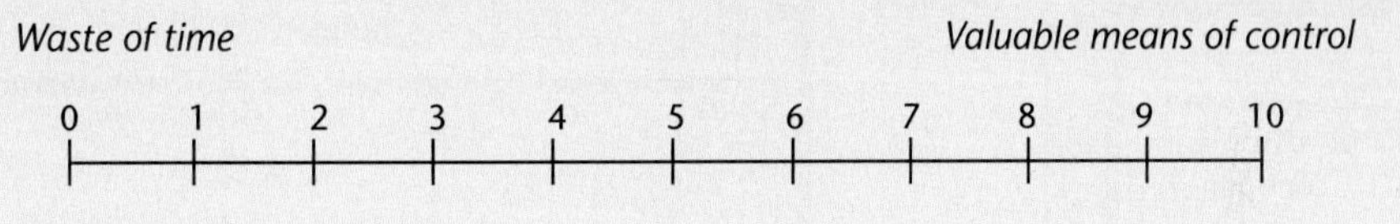


## The budgeting process

The budgeting process is illustrated in Figure 17.2. Study this very carefully, noting how the various budgets fit together.

Later in this chapter we shall be using a quantitative example to illustrate the budgeting process. For the moment, however, it will be sufficient to give a brief description.

In commercial organizations, the first budget to be prepared is usually the sales budget. Once the sales for the budget period (and for each sub-budget period) have been determined, the next stage is to calculate the effect on production. This will then enable an agreed level of activity to be determined. The *level of activity* may be expressed in so many units, or as a percentage of the theoretical productive capacity of the entity. Once it has been established then departmental managers can be instructed to prepare their budgets on the basis of the required level of activity.

Let us assume, for example, that 1000 units can be sold for a particular budget period. The production department manager will need this information in order to prepare his budget. This does not necessarily mean that he will budget for a production level of 1000 units because he will also have to allow for the budgeted level of opening and closing stocks.

The budgeted production level will then be translated into how much material and labour will be required to meet that particular level. Similarly, it will be necessary to prepare overhead budgets. Much of the general overhead expenditure of the company (such as factory administrative costs, head office costs and research and development expenditure) will be fixed and it will not be affected by the activity level. One type of overhead that may be affected by the activity level is the sales and distribution overhead budget because an increase in the number of units sold, for example, may involve additional delivery costs.

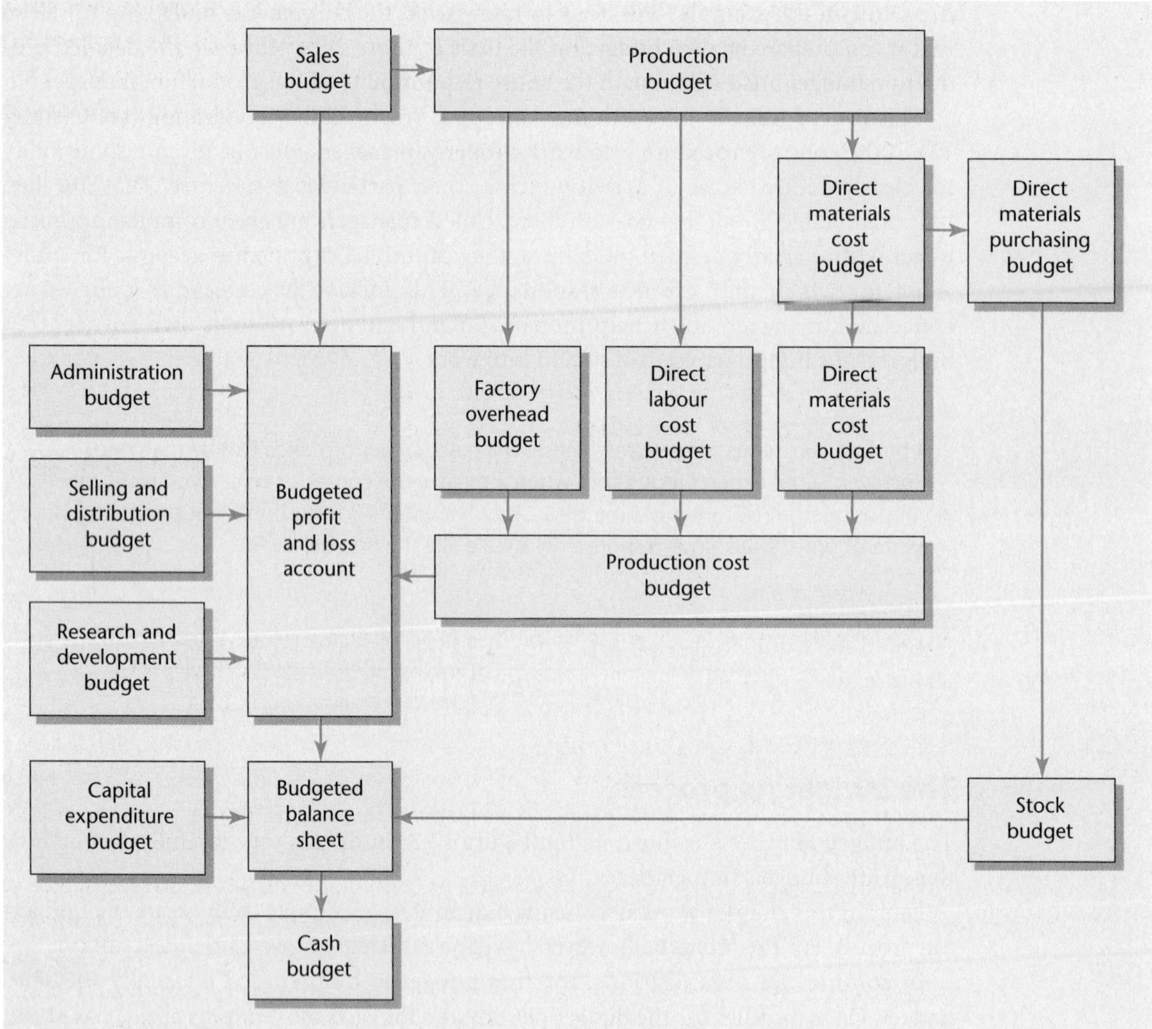


**Figure 17.2 The interrelationship of budgets**

Not all entities start the budget process with sales. A local authority is a good example. It usually prepares a budget on the basis of what it is likely to spend. The total budgeted expenditure is then compared with the total amount of council tax (after allowing for grants and other income) needed to cover it. If the political cost of an increase in council tax appears to be too high then the council will require a reduction in the budgeted expenditure. Once the budget has been set, and the tax has been levied on that basis, departments have to work within the budgets laid down. However, since the budget will have been prepared on an estimate of the actual expenditure for the last two or three months of the old financial year, account has to be taken of any a surplus or shortfall expected in the current year. If the estimate eventually proves excessive, the local authority will have overtaxed. This means that it has got some additional funds available to cushion the current year's expenditure. Of course, if it has undertaxed for any balance brought forward, departments might have to start cutting back on what they thought they could spend.

This process is quite different in the private sector because the budgeted sales effectively determine all the other budgets. In a local authority it is the expenditure budgets that determine what the council tax should be, and it is only the control exercised by central government and by the local authority itself that places a ceiling on what is spent.

## Functional budgets

A budget prepared for a particular department, cost centre or any other responsibility centre is known as a *functional budget*. Once all the functional budgets have been prepared, they are combined into the *master budget*. The master budget is, in effect, a consolidated budgeted profit and loss account, a budgeted balance sheet and a budgeted cash flow statement.

An initial draft of the master budget may not be acceptable to the senior management of the company. This may be because it cannot cope with that particular budgeted level of activity, e.g. as a result of production or cash constraints. Indeed, one of the most important budgets is the *cash budget*. The cash budget translates all the other functional budgets (including that for capital expenditure) into cash terms. It will show in detail the pattern of cash inputs and outputs for the main budget period, as well as for each sub-budget period. If it shows that the company will have difficulty in financing a particular budgeted level of activity (or if there is going to be a period when cash is exceptionally tight), the management will have an opportunity to seek out alternative sources of finance.

This latter point illustrates the importance of being aware of future commitments, so that something can be done in advance if there are likely to be constraints (irrespective of their nature). The master budget usually takes so long to prepare, however, that by the time it has been completed it will be almost impossible to make major alterations, although IT developments are now making this less of a difficulty. It is then tempting for senior management to make changes to the functional budgets without referring them back to individual cost-centre managers. It is most unwise to make changes in this way, because it is then difficult to use such budgets for control purposes. If managers have not agreed to the changes, they will argue that they can hardly take responsibility for budgets that have been imposed on them.

In the next section we use a comprehensive example to illustrate how all the functional budgets fit together.

## A comprehensive example

Clearly, it would be very difficult to observe the basic procedures involved in the preparation of functional budgets if we used an extremely detailed example, and so Example 17.1 cuts out all the incidental information. As a result, it only illustrates the main procedures but this will still enable you to see how all the budgets fit together.

Example 17.1

## Preparation of functional budgets

Sefton Limited manufactures one product known as EC2. The following information relates to the preparation of the budget for the year to 31 March 2009:

1 Sales budget details for product EC2:
   Expected selling price per unit: £100.
   Expected sales in units: 10 000.
   All sales are on credit terms.
2 EC2 requires 5 units of raw material E and 10 units of raw material C. E is expected to cost £3 per unit, and C £4 per unit. All goods are purchased on credit terms.
3 Two departments are involved in producing EC2: machining and assembly. The following information is relevant:

| | *Direct labour per unit of product (hours)* | *Direct labour rate per hour* £ |
|---|---|---|
| Machining | 1.00 | 6 |
| Assembling | 0.50 | 8 |

4 The finished production overhead costs are expected to amount to £100 000.
5 At 1 April 2008, 800 units of EC2 are expected to be in stock at a value of £52 000, 4500 units of raw material E at a value of £13 500, and 12 000 units of raw materials at a value of £48 000. Stocks of both finished goods and raw materials are planned to be 10 per cent above the expected opening stock levels as at 1 April 2008.
6 Administration, selling and distribution overhead is expected to amount to £150 000.
7 Other relevant information:
   (a) Opening trade debtors are expected to be £80 000. Closing trade debtors are expected to amount to 15 per cent of the total sales for the year.
   (b) Opening trade creditors are expected to be £28 000. Closing trade creditors are expected to amount to 10 per cent of the purchases for the year.
   (c) All other expenses will be paid in cash during the year.
   (d) Other balances at 1 April 2008 are expected to be as follows:

| | £ | £ |
|---|---|---|
| Share capital: ordinary shares | | 225 000 |
| Retained profits | | 17 500 |
| Proposed dividend | | 75 000 |
| Fixed assets at cost | 250 000 | |
| *Less*: Accumulated depreciation | 100 000 | |
| | | 150 000 |
| Cash at bank and in hand | | 2 000 |

8 Capital expenditure will amount to £50 000, payable in cash on 1 April 2008.
9 Fixed assets are depreciated on a straight-line basis at a rate of 20 per cent per annum on cost.

*Required*:
As far as the information permits, prepare all the relevant budgets for Sefton Limited for the year to 31 March 2009.

**Answer to Example 17.1**

Even with a much simplified budgeting exercise, there is clearly a great deal of work involved in preparing the budgets. To make it easier for you to understand what is happening, the procedure will be outlined step by step.

### Step 1: Prepare the sales budget

| *Units of EC2* | | *Selling price per unit* | | *Total sales value* |
|---|---|---|---|---|
| | | £ | | £ |
| 10 000 | × | 100 | = | 1 000 000 |

### Step 2: Prepare the production budget

| | | *Units* |
|---|---|---|
| Sales of EC2 | | 10 000 |
| Less: Opening stock | | 800 |
| | | 9 200 |
| *Add*: Desired closing stock (opening stock + 10%) | | 880 |
| Production required | = | 10 080 |

### Step 3: Prepare the direct materials usage budget

Direct materials:

| | | |
|---|---|---|
| E: 5 units × 10 080 | = | 50 400 units |
| C: 10 units × 10 080 | = | 100 800 units |

### Step 4: Prepare the direct materials purchases budget

| Direct materials: | = | *E* | *C* |
|---|---|---|---|
| | | *(units)* | *(units)* |
| Usage (as per Step 3) | | 50 400 | 100 800 |
| Less: Opening stock | | 4 500 | 12 000 |
| | | 45 900 | 88 800 |
| *Add*: Desired closing stock (opening stock + 10%) | | 4 950 | 13 200 |
| | | 50 850 | 102 000 |
| | | × £3 | × £4 |
| Direct material purchases | | = £152 550 | = £408 000 |

### Step 5: Prepare the direct labour budget

| | | *Machining* | | *Assembling* |
|---|---|---|---|---|
| Production units (as per Step 2) | | 10 080 | | 10 080 |
| × direct labour hours required | | × 1 DLH | | × 0.50 DLH |
| | | 10 080 DLH | | 5 040 DLH |
| × direct labour rate per hour | | × £6 | | × £8 |
| Direct labour cost | = | £60 480 | = | £40 320 |

### Step 6: Prepare the fixed production overhead budget

| | |
|---|---|
| Given: | £100 000 |

**Answer to Example 17.1** *continued*

### Step 7: Calculate the value of the closing raw material stock

| *Raw material* | *Closing stock** *(units)* | | *Cost per unit* £ | | *Total value* £ |
|---|---|---|---|---|---|
| E | 4950 | × | 3 | = | 14850 |
| C | 13200 | × | 4 | = | 52800 |
| | | | | | 67650 |

*Derived from Step 4.

### Step 8: Calculate the value of the closing finished stock

| | £ | | £ |
|---|---|---|---|
| Unit cost: | | | |
| Direct material E: 5 units × £3 per unit | 15 | | |
| Direct material C: 10 units × £4 per unit | 40 | | 55 |
| Direct labour for machining: 1 hour × £6 per DLH | 6 | | |
| Direct labour for assembling: 0.50 hours × £8 per DLH | 4 | | 10 |
| Total direct cost | | = | 65 |
| × units in stock | | | × 880 |
| Closing stock value | | = | 57200 |

### Step 9: Prepare the administration, selling and distribution budget

Given: £150000

### Step 10: Prepare the capital expenditure budget

Given: £50000

### Step 11: Calculate the cost of goods sold

| | £ |
|---|---|
| Opening stock (given) | 52000 |
| Manufacturing cost: | |
| Production units (Step 2) × total direct cost (Step 3) = 10080 × £65 | 655200 |
| | 707200 |
| *Less*: Closing stock (Step 8: 880 units × £65) | 57200 |
| Cost of goods sold (10000 units) | = 650000 |
| (or 10000 units × total direct costs of £65 per unit) | |

### Step 12: Prepare the cash budget

| | £ | | £ |
|---|---|---|---|
| Receipts | | | |
| *Cash from debtors*: | | | |
| Opening debtors | 80000 | | |
| Sales | 1000000 | | |
| | 1080000 | | |
| *Less*: Closing debtors (15% × £1000000) | 150000 | c/f | 930000 |

| | | b/f | £ | £ |
|---|---|---|---|---|
| | | | | 930 000 |
| *Payments* | | | | |
| *Cash payments to creditors:* | | | | |
| Opening creditors | | | 28 000 | |
| Purchases [Step 4: (£152 550 + 408 000)] | | | 560 550 | |
| | | | 588 550 | |
| Less: Closing creditors (£560 550 × 10%) | | | 56 055 | 532 495 |
| Wages (Step 5: £60 480 + 40 320) | | | | 100 800 |
| Fixed production overhead | | | | 100 000 |
| Administration, selling and distribution overhead | | | | 150 000 |
| Capital expenditure | | | | 50 000 |
| Dividend paid for 2008 | | | | 75 000 |
| | | | | 1 008 295 |
| | | | | £ |
| Net receipts | | | | (78 295) |
| *Add*: Opening cash | | | | 2 000 |
| Budgeted closing cash balance (overdrawn) | | | | (76 295) |

### Step 13: Prepare the budgeted profit and loss account

| | £ | £ |
|---|---|---|
| Sales (Step 1) | | 1 000 000 |
| *Less*: Variable cost of sales (Step 8: 10 000 × £65) | | 650 000 |
| Gross margin | | 350 000 |
| *Less*: Fixed production overhead (Step 6) | 100 000 | |
| Depreciation [(£250 000 + 50 000) × 20%] | 60 000 | 160 000 |
| Production margin | | 190 000 |
| *Less*: Administration, selling and distribution Overhead (Step 9) | | 150 000 |
| Budgeted net profit | | 40 000 |

### Step 14: Prepare the budgeted balance sheet

| | £ | £ | £ |
|---|---|---|---|
| *Fixed assets* (at cost) | | | 300 000 |
| *Less*: Accumulated depreciation | | | 160 000 |
| | | | 140 000 |
| *Current assets* | | | |
| Raw materials (Step 7) | | 67 650 | |
| Finished stock (Step 8) | | 57 200 | |
| Trade debtors (15% × £1 000 000) | | 150 000 | |
| | | 274 850 | |
| *Less*: *Current liabilities* | | | |
| Trade creditors | | | |
| [Step 4: 10% × (£152 550 + 408 000)] | 56 055 | | |
| Bank overdraft (Step 12) | 76 295 | 132 350 | 142 500 |
| | | | 282 500 |
| Financed by: | | | |
| *Share capital* | | | |
| Ordinary shares | | | 225 000 |
| Retained profits (£17 500 + 40 000) | | | 57 500 |
| | | | 282 500 |

We suggest that you now have a go at Example 17.1 without looking at the answer.

## Fixed and flexible budgets

The master budget becomes the detailed plan for future action that everyone is expected to work towards. However, some entities only use the budgeting process as a *planning* exercise. Once the master budget has been agreed, there may be no attempt to use it as a control technique. So the budget may be virtually ignored and it may not be compared with the actual results. If this is the case, then the company is not getting the best out of the budgeting system.

As was suggested earlier, budgets are particularly useful if they are also used as a means of control. The control is achieved if the actual performance is compared with the budgeted performance. Significant variances should then be investigated and any necessary corrective action taken.

The constant comparison of the actual results with the budgeted results may be done either on a *fixed budget* basis or a *flexible budget basis.* A fixed budget basis means that the actual results for a particular period are compared with the original budgets. This is as you would expect because the budget is a measure (you would get some very misleading results if you used an elastic ruler to measure distances!) Similarly, an elastic-type budget might also give some highly unreliable results. In some cases, however, a variable measure is used in budgeting in order to allow for certain circumstances that might have taken place *since* the budgets were prepared. Accountants call this *flexing* the budget. A flexible budget is an original budget that has been amended to take account of the *actual* level of activity.

This procedure might appear somewhat contradictory. Is changing a budget once it has been agreed not similar to using an elastic ruler to measure distances? 'Not really' is the short answer as sometimes a fixed budget can be misleading.

As we explained earlier, in order to prepare their budgets, some managers (especially production managers) will need to be given the budgeted level of activity. This means that such budgets will be based on a given level of activity. If, however, the *actual* level of activity is greater (or less) than the budgeted level, managers will have to allow for more (or less) expenditure on materials, labour and other expenses.

Suppose, for example, that a manager has prepared his budget on the basis of an anticipated level of activity of 70 per cent of the plant capacity. The company turns out to be much busier than expected and it achieves an actual level of activity of 80 per cent. The production manager is likely to have spent more on materials, labour and other expenses than he originally thought. If the actual performance is then compared with the budget (i.e. on a fixed budget basis), it will look as though he had spent a great deal more than he had anticipated. And, of course, he has, although *some* of it, at least, must have been beyond his control. So it is considered only fair to allow for those costs for which he is not responsible.

Hence the need to flex the budget, i.e. revise it on the basis of what it would have been if the manager had budgeted for an activity of 80 per cent instead of 70 per cent. The other assumptions and calculations made at the time the budget was prepared (such as material prices and wage rates) would not be amended.

If a company operates a flexible budget system, the budgets may be prepared on the basis of a wide range of possible activity levels. This is a time-consuming method, and managers would be very lucky if they prepared one that happened to be identical to the *actual* level of activity. The best method is to wait until the actual level of activity is known before the budget is flexed.

We illustrate how to operate a flexible budgeting procedure in Example 17.2.

**Example 17.2**

## Flexible budget procedure

The following information had been prepared for Carp Limited for the year to 30 June 2009.

| | *Budget* | *Actual* |
|---|---|---|
| *Level of activity* | *50%* | *60%* |
| | £ | £ |
| Costs: | | |
| Direct materials | 50 000 | 61 000 |
| Direct labour | 100 000 | 118 000 |
| Variable overhead | 10 000 | 14 000 |
| Total variable cost | 160 000 | 193 000 |
| Fixed overhead | 40 000 | 42 000 |
| Total costs | 200 000 | 235 000 |

*Required*:
Prepare a flexed budget operating statement for Carp Limited for the year to 30 June 2009.

**Answer to Example 17.2**

**Carp Ltd**
**Flexed budget operating statement for the year 30 June 2009**

| | *Fixed budget* | *Flexed budget* | *Actual costs* | *Variance (col. 2 less col. 3) favourable/ (adverse)* |
|---|---|---|---|---|
| *Activity level* | *50%* | *60%* | *60%* | |
| | £ | £ | £ | £ |
| Direct materials | 50 000 | 60 000 | 61 000 | (1 000) |
| Direct labour | 100 000 | 120 000 | 118 000 | 2 000 |
| Variable overhead | 10 000 | 12 000 | 14 000 | (2 000) |
| Total variable costs | 160 000 | 192 000 | 193 000 | (1 000) |
| Fixed overhead | 40 000 | 40 000 | 42 000 | (2 000) |
| Total costs | 200 000 | 232 000 | 235 000 | (3 000) |

*Tutorial notes*

1 All the budgeted *variable* costs have been flexed by 20% because the actual activity was 60% compared with a budgeted level of 50%, i.e. a 20% increase

$$\left(\frac{60\% - 50\%}{50\%} \times 100\right)$$

2 The budgeted fixed costs are not flexed because, by definition, they should not change with activity.

3 Instead of using the total fixed budget cost of £200 000, the total flexed budget costs of £232 000 can be compared more fairly with the total actual cost of £235 000.

**Answer to Example 17.2** *continued*

4 Note that the terms 'favourable' and 'adverse' (as applied to variances) mean favourable or adverse to profit. In other words, profit will be either greater (if a variance is favourable) or less (if it is adverse) than the budgeted profit.

5 The reasons for the variances between the actual costs and the flexed budget will need to be investigated. The flexed budget shows that, even allowing for the increased activity, the actual costs were in excess of the budget allowance.

6 Similarly, it will be necessary to investigate why the actual activity was higher than the budgeted activity. It could have been caused by inefficient budgeting, or by quite an unexpected increase in sales activity. While this would normally be welcome, it might place a strain on the productive and financial resources of the entity. If the increase is likely to be permanent, management will need to make immediate arrangements to accommodate the new level of activity.

## Behavioural consequences

Budgeting and budgetary control systems are not neutral. They have an impact on people causing them to react favourably, unfavourably or with indifference.

If managers react favourably then their budgets are likely to be accurate and relevant. Similarly, any information provided for them will be received with interest and it will be taken seriously. As a result, any necessary corrective action required will be pursued with some vigour.

Managers who react unfavourably, or with indifference may prepare budgets that are inaccurate or irrelevant, and then under considerable protest. Obviously, such managers are not likely to take seriously any subsequent information they are given that is based on data that they know to be suspect or to take any 'corrective action' unless they are forced to.

For the budgeting and budgetary control systems to work effectively, a number of important elements must be present.

- *Consultation.* Managers must be consulted about any proposal to install a budgeting or a budgetary control system.
- *Education and training.* Managers must undergo some education and training so that they are fully aware of the relevance and importance of budgeting and budgetary control systems and the part that the managers are expected to play in them.
- *Involvement.* Managers must be directly involved in what is installed in their own responsibility centre.
- *Participative.* Managers should prepare their own budgets (subject to some general guidelines) instead of having them imposed on them. Imposed budgets (as they are called) usually mean that managers do not take them seriously and they will then disclaim responsibility for any variances that may have occurred.
- *Disciplinary action.* Managers should not be disciplined for any variances (especially if a budget has been imposed) unless they are obviously guilty of negligence. Budgetary control is a means of finding out *why* a variance occurred. It is not supposed to be a means of catching managers out and a vehicle for disciplining them.

As far as the last point is concerned, if managers believe that the budgeting or budgetary control system operates against them rather than for them, they are likely to undermine it. This may take the form of *dysfunctional behaviour*, i.e. behaviour that may be in their own interest but not in the best interests of the company. They may, for example, act aggressively, become uncooperative, blame other managers, build a great deal of slack (i.e. tolerance) into their budgets, make decisions on a short-term basis or avoid making them altogether, and spend money unnecessarily up to the budget level that they have been given.

All of these points emphasize the importance of consulting managers and involving them fully in both the installation and operation of budgeting and budgetary control systems. If this is not the case, experience suggests that such systems will not work.

**Activity 17.3**

As a departmental manager you budgeted to spend £10 000 in 2010. You spent £9000. You budgeted to spend £12 000 in 2011 but you were told you could only spend £11 000 as you had 'over-budgeted in 2010'. What is likely to happen when you come to prepare your budget for 2012?

### ! Questions non-accountants should ask

This is a most important chapter for non-accountants because you are likely to be involved in the budgetary process no matter what junior or senior position you hold. If your entity uses an imposed budgetary control system you may not have as much freedom to ask questions but you might want to point out as diplomatically as you can that there are problems with such systems. You might like to put the following questions to your accountants and senior mangers.

- How far is the time spent on preparing budgets cost effective?
- Do you think that budgets prepared for a calendar year is too long a period?
- Should those costs and revenues that relate to a longer timescale be apportioned to sub-budget periods?
- Is it appropriate to compare actual events with fixed budgets?
- Why can't I be responsible for preparing my own department's budget?
- Why do you alter my budget after I have prepared it?
- Do you expect me to be responsible for any variances that are outside my control?
- Is it fair to punish me and my staff when we were not responsible either for the budget or for what went wrong with it?

## Conclusion

The full benefits of budgeting can only be gained if it is combined with a budgetary control system. The preparation of budgets is a valuable exercise in itself because it forces management to look ahead to what *might* happen, rather than to look back at what *did* happen. However, it is even more valuable if it is also used as a form of control.

Budgetary control enables actual results to be measured frequently against an agreed budget (or plan). Departures from that budget can then be quickly spotted, and steps taken to correct any unwelcome trends. However, the comparison of actual results with a fixed budget may not be particularly helpful if the actual level of activity is different from that budgeted. It is advisable, therefore, to compare actual results with a flexed budget.

As so many functional budgets are based on the budgeted level of activity, it is vital that it is calculated as accurately as possible, since an error in estimating the level of activity could affect all the company's financial and operational activities. So it is important that any difference between the actual and the budgeted level of activity is investigated carefully.

Budgeting and budgetary control systems may be resented by managers and they might then react to the systems in such a way to protect their own position. This may not be of benefit to the entity as a whole.

## Key points

1. **A budget is a short-term plan.**
2. **Budgetary control is a cost control method that enables actual results to be compared with the budget, thereby enabling any necessary corrective action to be taken.**
3. **The preparation of budgets will be undertaken by a budget team.**
4. **Managers must be responsible for producing their own functional budgets.**
5. **Functional budgets are combined to form a master budget.**
6. **A fixed budget system compares actual results with the original budgets.**
7. **In a flexed budget system, the budget may be flexed (or amended) to bring it into line with the actual level of activity.**
8. **A budgeting and budgetary control system is not neutral. It may cause managers to act in a way that is not in the best interests of the entity.**

## Check your learning

1. What is a budget?
2. List its essential features.
3. What is meant by 'budgetary control'?
4. List its essential features.
5. What is a variance?
6. What is a forecast?
7. How long is a normal budgeting period?
8. What is a sub-budget period?
9. What administration procedures does a budgeting system require?

10 In a commercial organization, which budget is normally the first to be prepared?

11 What initial criterion is given to production managers before they begin to prepare their budgets?

12 What is meant by a 'functional budget'?

13 List six common functional budgets.

14 What is meant by a 'fixed budget'?

15 What is meant by a 'flexible budget'?

16 Why is it desirable to prepare one?

17 List five desirable behavioural elements necessary to ensure a budgeting system is effective.

## News story quiz

*Remember the news story at the beginning of this chapter? Go back to that story and re-read it before answering the following questions.*

This article shows that budgeting and budgetary control procedures may be considerably improved and made more effective by abandoning spreadsheets and incorporating advanced information technology techniques into the process.

### Questions

1 How may a 'bottom-up approach' to budgeting and planning, as described in the article, result in a cumbersome and complex process?

2 How do you think spreadsheets currently help Joseph in the budgeting and planning process?

3 What main benefits is Joseph expecting from its investment in 'enterprise planning technology'?

## Tutorial questions

*The answers to questions marked with an asterisk can be found in Appendix 4.*

17.1 The Head of Department of Business and Management at Birch College has been told by the Vice Principal (Resources) that his departmental budget for the next academic year is £150 000. What comment would you make about the system of budgeting used at Birch College?

17.2 Suppose that when all the individual budgets at Sparks plc are put together there is a shortfall of resources needed to support them. The Board suggests that all departmental budgets should be reduced by 15 per cent. As the company's Chief Accountant, how would you respond to the Board's suggestion?

17.3 Does a fixed budget serve any useful purpose?

**17.4** 'It is impossible to introduce a budgetary control system into a hospital because if someone's life needs saving it has to be saved irrespective of the cost.' How far do you agree with this statement?

**17.5*** The following information has been prepared for Tom Limited for the six months to 30 September 2008:

**Budgeted production levels for product X**

| | *Units* |
|---|---|
| April | 140 |
| May | 280 |
| June | 700 |
| July | 380 |
| August | 300 |
| September | 240 |

Product X uses two units of component A6 and three units of component B9. At 1 April 2008 there were expected to be 100 units of A6 in stock, and 200 units of B9. The desired closing stock levels of each component were as follows:

| *Month end 2008* | *A6 (units)* | *B9 (units)* |
|---|---|---|
| 30 April | 110 | 250 |
| 31 May | 220 | 630 |
| 30 June | 560 | 340 |
| 31 July | 300 | 300 |
| 31 August | 240 | 200 |
| 30 September | 200 | 180 |

During the six months to 30 September 2008, component A6 was expected to be purchased at a cost of £5 per unit, and component B9 at a cost of £10 per unit.

*Required*:
Prepare the following budgets for each of the six months to 30 September 2008:
(a) direct materials usage budget;
(b) direct materials purchase budget.

**17.6*** Don Limited has one major product that requires two types of direct labour to produce it. The following data refer to certain budget proposals for the three months to 31 August 2009:

| *Month* | *Production units* |
|---|---|
| 30.6.09 | 600 |
| 31.7.09 | 700 |
| 31.8.09 | 650 |

Direct labour hours required per unit:

| | *Hours* | *Budgeted rate per hour* £ |
|---|---|---|
| Production | 3 | 4 |
| Finishing | 2 | 8 |

*Required*:
Prepare the direct labour cost budget for each of the three months to 31 August 2009.

**17.7** Gorse Limited manufactures one product. The budgeted sales for period 6 are for 10 000 units at a selling price of £100 per unit. Other details are as follows:

1 Two components are used in the manufacture of each unit:

| *Component* | *Number* | *Unit cost of each component* |
|---|---|---|
| | | £ |
| XY | 5 | 1 |
| WZ | 3 | 0.50 |

2 Stocks at the beginning of the period are expected to be as follows:
4000 units of finished goods at a unit cost of £52.50.
Component XY: 16 000 units at a unit cost of £1.
Component WZ: 9600 units at a unit cost of £0.50.

3 Two grades of employees are used in the manufacture of each unit:

| *Employee* | *Hours per unit* | *Labour rate per hour* |
|---|---|---|
| | | £ |
| Production | 4 | 5 |
| Finishing | 2 | 7 |

4 Factory overhead is absorbed into unit costs on the basis of direct labour hours. The budgeted factory overhead for the period is estimated to be £96 000.

5 The administration, selling and distribution overhead for the period has been budgeted at £275 000.

6 The company plans a reduction of 50 per cent in the quantity of finished stock at the end of period 6, and an increase of 25 per cent in the quantity of each component.

*Required*:
Prepare the following budgets for period 6:
(a) sales
(b) production quantity
(c) materials usage
(d) materials purchase
(e) direct labour
(f) the budgeted profit and loss account.

**17.8** Avsar Limited has extracted the following budgeting details for the year to 30 September 2010:

1 Sales: 4000 units of V at £500 per unit
7000 units of R at £300 per unit

2 Materials usage (units):

| | *Raw material* | | |
|---|---|---|---|
| | *O1* | *I2* | *L3* |
| V | 11 | 9 | 12 |
| R | 15 | 1 | 10 |

3 Raw material costs (per unit):

| | £ |
|---|---|
| O1 | 8 |
| I2 | 6 |
| L3 | 3 |

4 Raw material stocks:

| | *Units* | | |
|---|---|---|---|
| | *O1* | *I2* | *L3* |
| At 1 October 2009 | 1300 | 1400 | 400 |
| At 30 September 2010 | 1400 | 1000 | 200 |

5 Finished stocks:

| | *Units* | |
|---|---|---|
| | *V* | *R* |
| At 1 October 2009 | 110 | 90 |
| At 30 September 2010 | 120 | 150 |

6 Direct labour:

| | *Product* | |
|---|---|---|
| | *V* | *R* |
| Budgeted hours per unit | 10 | 8 |
| Budgeted hourly rate (£) | 12 | 6 |

7 Variable overhead:

| | *Product* | |
|---|---|---|
| | *V* | *R* |
| Budgeted hourly rate (£) | 10 | 5 |

8 Fixed overhead: £193 160 (to be absorbed on the basis of direct labour hours).

*Required*:

(a) Prepare the following budgets:
- (i) sales;
- (ii) production units;
- (iii) materials usage;
- (iv) materials purchase; and
- (v) production cost.

(b) Calculate the total budgeted profit for the year to 30 September 2010.

17.9 The following budget information relates to Flossy Limited for the three months to 31 March 2010:

1 **Budgeted profit and loss accounts:**

| *Month* | *31.1.10* | *28.2.10* | *31.3.10* |
|---|---|---|---|
| | £000 | £000 | £000 |
| Sales (all on credit) | 2 000 | 3 000 | 2 500 |
| Cost of sales | 1 200 | 1 800 | 1 500 |
| *Gross profit* | 800 | 1 200 | 1 000 |
| Depreciation | (100) | (100) | (100) |
| Other expenses | (450) | (500) | (600) |
| | (550) | (600) | (700) |
| Net profit | 250 | 600 | 300 |

2 **Budgeted balance sheets:**

| *Budgeted balances* | *31.12.09* | *31.1.10* | *28.2.10* | *31.3.10* |
|---|---|---|---|---|
| | £000 | £000 | £000 | £000 |
| *Current assets:* | | | | |
| Stocks | 100 | 120 | 150 | 150 |
| Debtors | 200 | 300 | 350 | 400 |
| Short-term investments | 60 | – | 40 | 30 |
| *Current liabilities:* | | | | |
| Trade creditors | 110 | 180 | 160 | 150 |
| Other creditors | 50 | 50 | 50 | 50 |
| Taxation | 150 | – | – | – |
| Dividends | 200 | – | – | – |

3 Capital expenditure to be incurred on 20 February 2010 is expected to amount to £470 000.

4 Sales of plant and equipment on 15 March 2010 is expected to raise £30 000 in cash.

5 The cash at bank and in hand on 1 January 2010 is expected to be £15 000.

*Required:*
Prepare Flossy Limited's cash budget for each of the three months during the quarter ending 31 March 2010.

17.10 Chimes Limited has prepared a flexible budget for one of its factories for the year to 30 June 2009. The details are as follows:

| *% of production capacity* | *30%* | *40%* | *50%* | *60%* |
|---|---|---|---|---|
| | *£000* | *£000* | *£000* | *£000* |
| Direct materials | 42 | 56 | 70 | 84 |
| Direct labour | 18 | 24 | 30 | 36 |
| Factory overhead | 22 | 26 | 30 | 34 |
| Administration overhead | 17 | 20 | 23 | 26 |
| Selling and distribution overhead | 12 | 14 | 16 | 18 |
| | 111 | 140 | 169 | 198 |

*Additional information*:

1 The company only expects to operate at a capacity of 45%. At that capacity, the sales revenue has been budgeted at a level of £135 500.
2 Variable costs per unit are not expected to change, irrespective of the level of activity.
3 Fixed costs are also not likely to change, irrespective of the level of activity.

*Required*:
Prepare a flexible budget for the year to 30 June 2009 based on an activity level of 45%.

**Further practice questions, study material and links to relevant sites on the World Wide Web can be found on the website that accompanies this book. The site can be found at www.pearsoned.co.uk/dyson**

# Chapter 18 Standard costing

**Perhaps the 21st century dawns for standard costing . . .**

## Sage readies integrated software for SMEs

**New software due to be delivered to customers in May**

**Roger Howorth**

Newcastle-based, accounting software developer, Sage has revealed more details about Sage 1000, its new integrated software suite for medium-sized business, due to be delivered to customers in May.

David Pinches, director of accounts and enterprise resource planning (ERP) at Sage, said the new suite includes all the components needed to run firms with a turnover of between £10m and £500m.

'It's generic product that's applicable across a wide range of industries,' Pinches said. 'It has all the core requirements for a mid-market firm, like an accounting system and operations management, including sales order processing, procurement, warehousing and inventory of goods.' Additional modules are available to handle specialist requirements, such as general manufacturing and build-to-order manufacturing, he added.

Pinches said more and more medium-sized firms are using such integrated suites. 'The days of deploying standalone accounting, customer relationship management [CRM] and manufacturing systems are eroding fast in the mid-market. These companies want to manage their processes across the entire business, not at a departmental level,' he added.

Other elements in Sage 1000 include sales management tools for both field and office-based sales teams, and a module to manage sales campaigns, including lead management and sales forecasting. A customer support module includes tools for service-level targets and the logging of enquiries.

'Full reporting is available throughout the suite, either using dashboards or grid-oriented reporting,' Pinches said. 'There's also a self-service web module, so a company can expose selected information to trading partners.'

The software runs on Windows Server systems and requires Microsoft SQL Server. Clients connect to the suite via Internet Explorer.

The price of the suite has yet to be confirmed, but Pinches said it would be competitive for the mid-market. He noted that other products in this sector cost between £1000 and £4000 per suite.

*Accountancy Age*, 21 February 2006.



*Questions relating to this news story can be found on page 370*

## About this chapter

This chapter examines *standard costing*, another planning and control technique used in management accounting. Like budgeting and budgetary control, standard costing involves estimating future sales revenue and product costs. But standard costing goes into much more detail: the total *budgeted* cost is broken down into the elements of cost (direct materials, direct labour, variable overhead and fixed overhead) and these costs are then compared with the *actual* cost of those elements. The difference between the standard cost and the *actual* cost is known as a variance. Each variance is then analysed into a volume variance and a price variance. Significant variances are then investigated and immediate action is taken to correct any unexpected or unwelcome ones. The difference between budgeted sales and actual sales can also be analysed into volume and price variances. In addition, both production volume and sales volume variances can be further analysed into sub-variances.

Standard costing is of particular relevance in manufacturing industry where specific products or processes are produced and where all three elements of cost (materials, labour and overheads) are relevant. It is of less relevance in non-manufacturing entities and few such entities use the technique.

**Learning objectives**

**By the end of this chapter, you should be able to:**

- **describe the nature, purpose and importance of standard costing and variance analysis;**
- **identify the main steps involved in implementing and operating a standard-costing system;**
- **calculate three standard-costing performance measures;**
- **calculate sales, direct materials, direct labour, variable overhead and fixed overhead variances;**
- **prepare a standard-cost operating statement.**

## Why this chapter is important for non-accountants

Standard costing is an important management accounting planning and control technique in manufacturing companies and you may need to know what it is and how it works if you are to become a really effective and self-aware manager. So this chapter is important for three reasons:

- you may be required to provide information for standard-costing purposes;
- you may be presented with standard costing operating statements;
- you may be asked what action you propose to take in order to control those areas that show significant variances.

# Operation

The operation of a standard-costing system requires virtually everyone in an entity to be involved in it. This is because the system depends on the supply of a vast amount of information from every cost centre throughout the entity, and the personnel who are best placed to supply it are those who work in the cost centre. It is not, however, a one-way process. Once the information has been processed it is fed back to those people who supplied it originally. They are then supposed to use that information to help ensure that their particular cost centre sticks to the agreed plan.

So if a standard-costing system is to work properly it is vital that it is fully supported by those people it is supposed to help. If they do not think that it is of any benefit to them they are then likely to behave in two ways:

- the information that they supply is likely to be inaccurate and incomplete – this means that the various plans and standard costs based on that information will be unreliable;
- they will ignore any subsequent reports given to them because they will be perfectly aware that they are unreliable.

If this is how they behave then the system might as well be abandoned because it will not result in the effective planning and control of the entity.

The motto for the entity's senior management is then:

**Make sure your employees are fully with you if you want to install a standard costing system.**

Of course, this motto is probably true for all planning and control systems.

## Definitions

There are four important standard-costing terms you need to be familar with:

1 ***Standard:*** *the amount or level set for the performance of a particular activity.*
2 ***Standard cost:*** *the planned cost for a particular level of activity.*
3 ***Variance:*** *the difference between the standard (or planned) cost and the actual cost.*
4 ***Variance analysis:*** *an investigation into and an explanation of why variances occurred.*

## Uses

We can identify four main purposes of standard costing.

- *Stock valuation.* The standard-cost method of stock valuation is the expected or planned price that the entity expects to pay for its materials. Its advantages are that it is simple to use and it can remain stable for some time. The main difficulties are in establishing a standard cost and in coping with significant differences between the actual costs and the standard costs.
- *Control.* By comparing frequently and in detail actual costs against the standard costs swift action can be taken to correct any departures from what was planned.
- *Performance measurement.* Standard costing provides information that enables an entity to determine if it is meeting its objectives.
- *Pricing.* The information provided by a standard-costing system helps entities to set their selling prices.

## Types of entities

Standard costing is really only appropriate for certain types of entities. It is particularly suitable for manufacturing entities where it is possible to analyse the cost of particular units or processes into materials, labour and overheads. It is also probably only cost-effective in larger entities because of the vast amount of information that it both demands and generates.

## The standard-costing period

The standard-costing period will usually be the same as that for the main budget and sub-budget periods. Short periods are preferred so that the actual results can be compared frequently with the standard results. Corrective action can then be taken quickly before it is too late to do anything about any unexpected trends. Short standard-costing periods may also be necessary where market or production conditions are subject to frequent changes or where it is particularly difficult to prepare long-term plans, e.g. in the fashion industry.

## Types of standard

The preparation of standard costs requires great care and attention. As each element of cost is subject to detailed arithmetical analysis, it is important that the initial information is accurate. Indeed, the information produced by a standard-costing system will be virtually worthless if subsequent analyses reveal that variances were caused by inefficient budgeting or standard setting.

In preparing standard costs, management will need to be informed of the level of activity to be used in preparing the standard costs, i.e. whether the entity will need to operate at, say, 80 per cent or 90 per cent of its theoretical capacity. An activity level should be chosen that is capable of being achieved. It would be possible to choose a standard that was ideal, i.e. one that represented a performance that could be achieved only under the most favourable of conditions. Such a standard would, however, be unrealistic, because it is rare for ideal conditions to prevail. An ideal standard is a standard that is attainable under the most favourable conditions and where no allowance is made for normal losses, waste and machine downtime.

A much more realistic standard is called an *attainable* standard. Such a standard is one that the entity can expect to achieve in reasonably efficient working conditions. In other words, it is accepted that some delays and inefficiencies (such as normal losses, waste and machine downtime) will occur, but it is also assumed that management will attempt to minimize them.

You may also come across the term *basic* cost standards. These are standards that are left unchanged over long periods of time. This enables some consistency to be achieved in comparing actual results with the same standards over a substantial period of time, but the standards may become so out of date that meaningful comparisons are not possible.

**Activity 18.1**

Your company bases its standard costs on an ideal level, i.e. no allowance is made for losses and the standard costs can only be achieved in entirely favourable conditions. As a cost centre manager, what would your reaction be when you received a report showing that your centre had a number of large unwelcome variances? What would you do about such variances?

## Information required

The information needed to operate a standard-costing system is considerable. The main requirements are as follows.

- *Direct materials*: types, quantities and price.
- *Direct labour*: grades, numbers and rates of pay.
- *Variable overhead*: the total variable overhead cost analysed into various categories, such as employee and general support costs.
- *Fixed overhead*: the total fixed overhead, also analysed into various categories such as employee costs, building costs and general administration expenses.

The above summary shows that the standard cost of a particular unit comprises four elements: direct materials, direct labour, variable overhead and fixed overhead. In turn, each element comprises two factors, namely quantity and price. We can now show you how the standard cost of a specific unit is built up. We do so in Example 18.1.

Example 18.1

### Calculation of the total standard cost of a specific unit using absorption costing

| | £ |
|---|---|
| • Direct materials | |
| Quantity × price (2 units × £5) | 10 |
| • Direct labour | |
| Hours × hourly rate (5 hours × £10) | 50 |
| • Variable overhead | |
| Hours × variable overhead absorption rate per hour (5 hours × £6) | 30 |
| • Fixed overhead | |
| Hours × fixed overhead absorption rate per hour (5 hours × £3) | 15 |
| Total standard cost per unit | 105 |

*Note*: The example is based on fictitous data. It assumes that the unit cost is calculated on the basis of standard absorption costing. This is the most common method of standard costing. It is also possible to adopt a system of standard *marginal* costing (see Chapter 19).

## Standard hours and the absorption of overhead

Standard absorption costing requires overhead to be absorbed on the basis of *standard* hours, whereas in a non-standard costing system it is absorbed on the basis of *actual* hours. A standard hour represents the amount of work that should be performed in an hour assuming that it is done in standard conditions, i.e. in *planned* conditions. Each unit is given a standard time of so many hours in which the work should be done. It is against that standard that the actual hours will be compared.

In order to calculate the standard overhead cost of a unit, the standard overhead absorption rate for the period is multiplied by the number of *standard* (not actual) hours that the unit should have taken to produce. The absorption of overhead by multiplying the standard absorption rate by the standard hours is a significant departure from the approach adopted in a non-standard costing system. This is a most important point and you should make sure that you understand it before moving on.

## Sales variances

Some companies also use sales variances, although this is not common. If sales variances are used, the difference between the actual sales revenue and the standard revenue is analysed into a number of sub-variances, such as price and quantity. A detailed analysis of the budgeted sales is needed in order to obtain the following information:

- the range and number of each product to be sold;
- the selling price of each product;
- the respective periods in which sales are to take place.

## Performance measures

Management may find it useful if some performance measures are extracted from the standard costing data. Such measures pinpoint the level of efficiency of the entity, help managers to spot unfavourable trends and enable them to take immediate corrective action. There are three specific performance measures that we are going to cover in this chapter: the efficiency ratio, the capacity ratio and the production volume ratio. They are shown in diagrammatic form in Figure 18.1.

Referring to Figure 18.1, the actual hours are those direct labour hours actually worked. The budgeted direct labour hours are those that were expected or planned to be worked. The standard direct labour hours of production for the actual activity measure the output produced in standard direct labour hours. If, for example, each unit produced *should have* taken five hours and 100 units were produced, the total standard direct labour hours for the actual activity would be 500 (5 DLH × 100). The budget might have been planned on the basis of 120 units, in which case the total budgeted labour hours would have been 600 (5 DLH × 120).

We explain how to calculate the three performance measures below. Direct labour hours are used in the formulae but in a machine-intensive cost centre machine hours would be used.

### The efficiency ratio

This compares the total standard (or allowed) hours of units produced with the total actual hours taken to produce those units. It is calculated as follows:

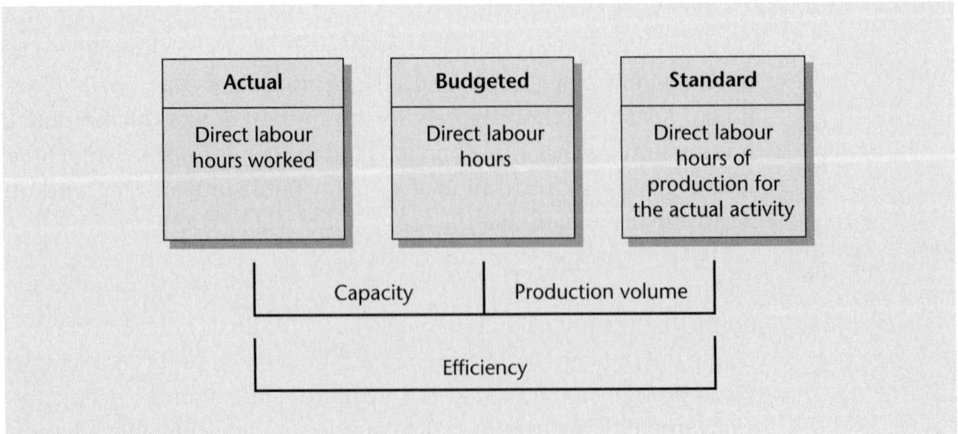


**Figure 18.1 Three performance measures**

$$\frac{\text{standard hours produced}}{\text{actual direct labour hours worked}} \times 100$$

*Note*:
The standard hours produced = the standard direct labour hours of production for the *actual* activity.

The efficiency ratio enables management to check whether the company has produced the units in more or less time than had been allowed.

### The capacity ratio

This compares the total actual hours worked with the total budgeted hours. It is calculated as follows:

$$\frac{\text{actual direct labour hours worked}}{\text{budgeted direct labour hours}} \times 100$$

The capacity ratio enables management to ascertain whether all of the budgeted hours (i.e. all the hours *planned* to be worked) were used to produce the actual units.

### The production volume ratio

This compares the total allowed hours for the work actually produced with the total budgeted hours. It is calculated as follows:

$$\frac{\text{standard hours produced}}{\text{budgeted direct labour hours}} \times 100$$

The production volume ratio enables management to compare the work produced (measured in terms of standard hours) with the budgeted hours of work. This ratio gives management some information about how effective the company has been in using the budgeted hours.

Example 18.2 shows how to calculate these three ratios.

**Example 18.2**

## Calculation of efficiency, capacity and production volume ratios

The following information relates to the Frost Production Company Limited for the year to 31 March 2008:

1 Budgeted direct labour hours: 1000
2 Budgeted units: 100
3 Actual direct labour hours worked: 800
4 Actual units produced: 90

*Required*:
Calculate the following performance ratios:
(a) the efficiency ratio
(b) the capacity ratio
(c) the production volume ratio.

**Answer to Example 18.2**

**(a) The efficiency ratio:**

$$\frac{\text{Standard hours produced}}{\text{Actual direct labour hours worked}} \times 100 = \frac{900^*}{800} \times 100 = \underline{112.5\%}$$

* Each unit is allowed 10 standard hours (1000 hours/100 units). Since 90 units were produced, the total standard hours of production must equal 900.

It would appear that the company has been more efficient in producing the goods than was expected. It was allowed 900 hours to do so, but it produced them in only 800 hours.

**(b) The capacity ratio:**

$$\frac{\text{Actual direct labour hours worked}}{\text{Budgeted hours}} \times 100 = \frac{800}{1000} \times 100 = \underline{80\%}$$

All of the time planned to be available (the capacity) was not utilized, either because it was not possible to work 1000 direct labour hours, or because the company did not undertake as much work as it could have done.

**(c) The production volume ratio:**

$$\frac{\text{Standard hours produced}}{\text{Budgeted hours}} \times 100 = \frac{900^*}{1000} \times 100 = \underline{90\%}$$

* As calculated for the efficiency ratio.

It appears that if 90 units had been produced in standard conditions, another 100 hours would have been available (10 units × 10 hours). In fact, since the 90 units only took 800 hours to produce, at least another 20 units $\left(\frac{1000 - 800}{10}\right)$ could have been produced in standard conditions.

**Comments on the results**

The budget allowed for 100 units to be produced and each unit was expected to take 10 direct labour hours to complete, a total budgeted activity of 1000 direct labour hours. However, only 90 units were actually produced. If these units had been produced in standard time, they should have taken 900 hours (90 units × 10 direct labour hours). These are the standard hours produced. The 90 units were completed in 800 actual hours. It appears, therefore, that the units were produced more efficiently than had been expected. The management will still need, of course, to investigate why only 90 units were produced and not the 100 expected in the budget.

We have now covered the operation of a standard-costing system. In the next section we will examine how standard cost variances may be calculated and whether they may be viewed as being either favourable or unfavourable.

## Cost variances

### Structure

The difference between actual costs and standard costs may result in two main variances: price and quantity. These variances may either be favourable (F) to profit, or adverse (A). This means that the actual prices paid or costs incurred can be more than anticipated (adverse to profit), or less than anticipated (favourable to profit). Similarly, the quantities used in production can result in more being used (adverse to profit) or less than expected (favourable to profit).

The basic standard production cost variances are shown in diagrammatic form in Figure 18.2. We explain how to calculate them below.

#### Direct materials

1 **Total** = (actual cost per unit × actual quantity used) – (standard cost per unit × standard quantity for actual production)
2 **Price** = (actual cost per unit – standard cost per unit) × total actual quantity used
3 **Usage** = (total actual quantity used – standard quantity for actual production) × standard cost

These relationships are shown in Figure 18.3.

#### Direct labour

1 **Total** = (actual hourly rate × actual hours) – (standard hourly rate × standard hours for actual production)
2 **Rate** = (actual hourly rate – standard hourly rate) × actual hours worked
3 **Efficiency** = (actual hours worked – standard hours for actual production) × standard hourly rate

These relationships are shown in Figure 18.4.

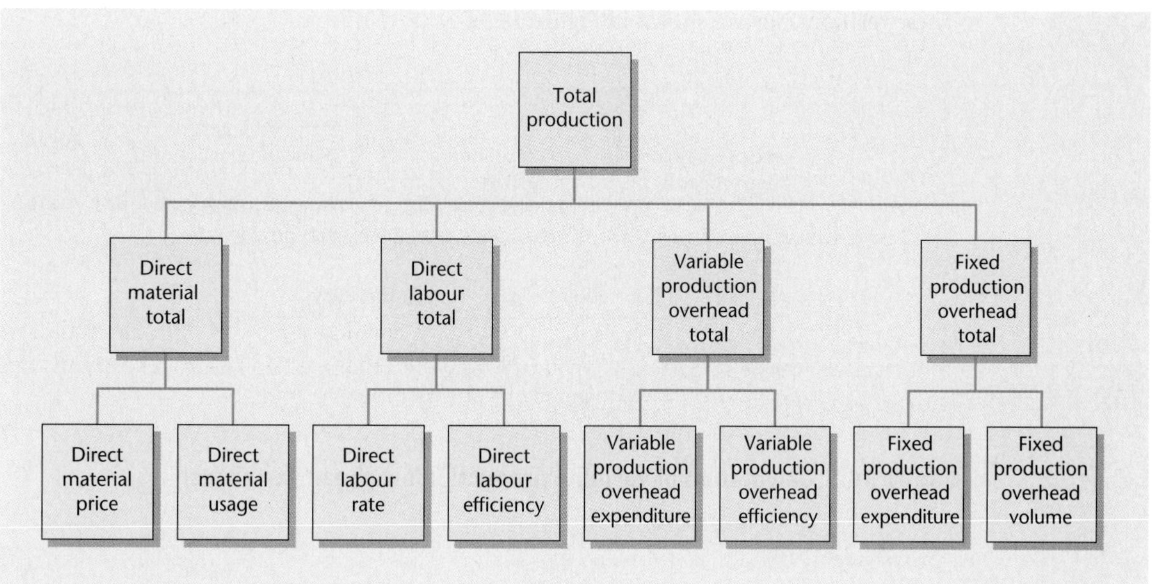


**Figure 18.2 Main standard production cost variances**

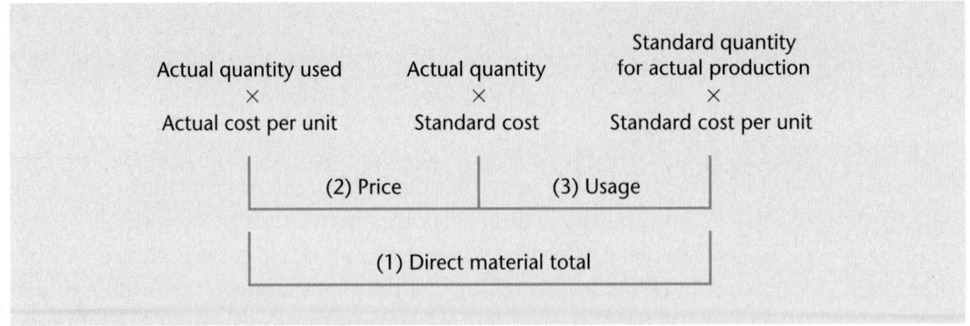


**Figure 18.3 Calculation of direct material cost variances**

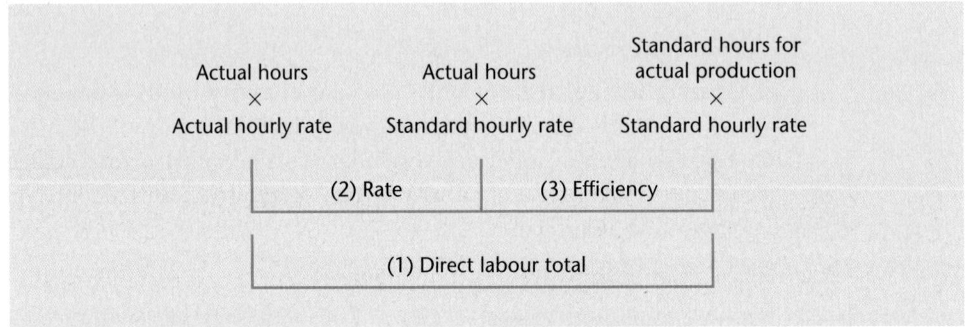


**Figure 18.4 Calculation of direct labour cost variances**

### Variable production overhead

1. **Total** = actual variable overhead – [standard hours for actual production × variable production overhead absorption rate (VOAR)]
2. **Expenditure** = actual variable overhead – (actual hours worked × VOAR)
3. **Efficiency** = (standard hours for actual production – actual hours worked) × VOAR

These relationships are shown in Figure 18.5.

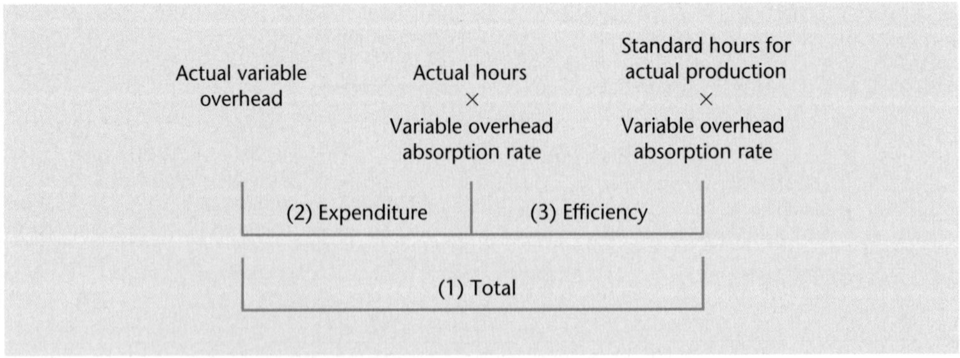


**Figure 18.5 Calculation of variable production overhead variances**

### Fixed production overhead

1 **Total** = actual fixed overhead – [standard hours of production × fixed overhead absorption rate (FOAR)]
2 **Expenditure** = actual fixed overhead – budgeted fixed expenditure
3 **Volume** = budgeted fixed overhead expenditure – (standard hours for actual production × FOAR)

These variances are shown in Figure 18.6.

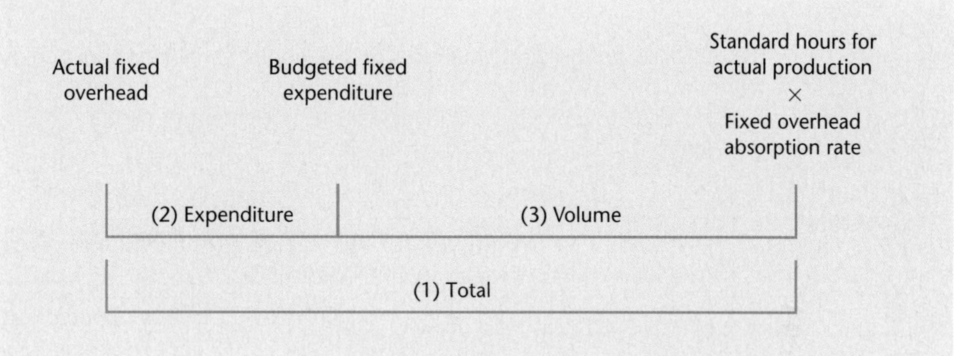


Figure 18.6 **Calculation of fixed production overhead variances**

## A comprehensive example

We will now use a comprehensive example to illustrate the main cost variances. The details are contained in Example 18.3.

**Example 18.3**

### Calculation of the main cost variances

The following information has been extracted from the records of the Frost Production Company Limited for the year to 31 March 2008:

| *Budgeted costs per unit:* | £ |
|---|---|
| Direct materials (15 kilograms × £2 per kilogram) | 30 |
| Direct labour (10 hours × £4 per direct labour hour) | 40 |
| Variable overhead (10 hours × £1 per direct labour hour) | 10 |
| Fixed overhead (10 hours × £2 per direct labour hour) | 20 |
| Total budgeted cost per unit | 100 |

The following budgeted data are also relevant:

1 The budgeted production level was 100 units.
2 The total standard direct labour hours amounted to 1000.
3 The total budgeted variable overhead was estimated to be £1000.
4 The total budgeted fixed overhead was £2000.
5 The company absorbs both fixed and variable overhead on the basis of direct labour hours.

**Example 18.3 continued**

| *Actual costs*: | £ |
|---|---|
| Direct materials | 2 100 |
| Direct labour | 4 000 |
| Variable overhead | 1 000 |
| Fixed overhead | 1 600 |
| Total actual costs | 8 700 |

*Note*: 90 units were produced in 800 actual hours, and the total actual quantity of direct materials consumed was 1400 kilograms.

*Required*:
(a) Calculate the direct materials, direct labour, variable production overhead and fixed production overhead total cost variances.
(b) Calculate the detailed variances for each element of cost.

**Answer to Example 18.3(a)**

In answering part (a) of this question we need to summarize the total variance for each element of cost for the actual 90 units produced:

| | *Actual costs* | *Total standard cost for actual production* | *Variance* |
|---|---|---|---|
| | £ | £ | £ |
| Direct materials | 2 100 | 2 700 (1) | 600 (F) |
| Direct labour | 4 000 | 3 600 (2) | 400 (A) |
| Variable production overhead | 1 000 | 900 (3) | 100 (A) |
| Fixed production overhead | 1 600 | 1 800 (4) | 200 (F) |
| Total | 8 700 | 9 000 | 300 (F) |

*Notes*:
(a) F = favourable to profit; A = adverse to profit.
(b) The numbers in brackets refer to the tutorial notes below.

*Tutorial notes*

1 The standard cost of direct material for actual production = the actual units produced × the standard direct material cost per unit, i.e. 90 × £30 = £2700.

2 The standard cost of direct labour for actual production = the actual units produced × standard direct labour cost per unit, i.e. 90 × £40 = £3600.

3 The standard variable cost for actual performance = the actual units produced × variable overhead absorption rate per unit, i.e. 90 × £10 = £900.

4 The fixed overhead cost for the actual performance = the actual units produced × fixed overhead absorption rate, i.e. 90 × £20 = £1800.

*Comments on the answers to Example 18.3(a)*

Example 18.3(a) shows that the total actual cost of producing the 90 units was £300 less than the budget allowance. An investigation would need to be made in order to find out why only 90 units were produced when the company had budgeted for 100. Although the 90 units have cost £300 less than expected, a number of other variances have contributed to the total variance. So assuming that these variances are considered significant, they would need to be carefully investigated in order to find out what caused them.

As a result of calculating variances for each element of cost, it becomes much easier for management to investigate why the actual production cost was £300 less than expected. However, by analysing the variances into their major causes, the accountant can provide even greater guidance. This is illustrated in part (b) of the example.

**Answer to Example 18.3(b)**

In answering part (b) of Example 18.3, we will deal with each element of cost in turn. As we do so we will take the opportunity to comment on the results.

### Direct materials

**1 Price** = (actual cost per unit – standard cost per unit) × total actual quantity used

∴ the price variance = (£1.50 – 2.00) × 1400 (kg) = £700 (F)

The actual price per unit was £1.50 (£2100/1400) and the standard price was £2.00 per unit. There was, therefore, a total saving (as far as the price of the materials was concerned) of £700 (£0.50 × 1400). This was favourable (F) to profit.

**2 Usage** = (total actual quantity used – standard quantity for actual production) × standard cost

∴ the usage variance = (1400 – 1350) × £2.00 = £100 (A)

In producing 90 units, Frost should have used 1350 kilograms (90 × 15 kg) instead of the 1400 kilograms actually used. If this extra usage is valued at the standard cost (the difference between the actual price and the standard cost has already been allowed for), there is an adverse usage variance of £100 (50 (kg) × £2.00).

**3 Total** = price + usage:

∴ the total direct materials variance = £700 (F) + £100 (A) = £600 (F)

The £600 favourable total variance was calculated earlier in answering part (a) of the question. This variance might have arisen because Frost purchased cheaper materials. If this were the case then it probably resulted in a greater wastage of materials, perhaps because the materials were of an inferior quality.

### Direct labour

**1 Rate** = (actual hourly rate – standard hourly rate) × actual hours worked

∴ the rate variance = (£5.00 – £4.00) × 800 DLH = £800 (A)

The actual hourly rate is £5.00 per direct labour hour (£4000/800) compared with the standard rate per hour of £4. Every extra actual hour worked, therefore, resulted in an adverse variance of £1, or £800 in total (£1 × 800).

**2 Efficiency** = (actual hours worked – standard hours for actual production) × standard hourly rate.

∴ the efficiency variance = (800 – 900) × £4.00 = £400 (F)

The actual hours worked were 800. However, 900 hours would be the allowance for the 90 units actually produced (90 × 10 DLH). If these hours were valued at the standard hourly rate (differences between the actual rate and the standard rate having already been allowed for when calculating the rate variance), a favourable variance of £400 arises. The favourable efficiency variance has arisen because the 90 units took less time to produce than the budget allowed for.

**3 Total** = rate + efficiency

∴ the total direct labour variance = £800 (A) + £400 (F) = £400 (A)

**Answer to Example 18.3(b)** *continued*

The £400 adverse total variance was calculated earlier in answering part (a) of the question. It arises because the company paid more per direct labour hour than had been budgeted, although this was offset to some extent by the units being produced in less time than the budgeted allowance. This variance could have been caused by using a higher grade of labour than had been intended. Unfortunately, the higher labour rate per hour was not completely offset by greater efficiency.

### Variable production overhead

1 **Expenditure** = actual variable overhead – (actual hours worked × variable production overhead absorption rate)

∴ the expenditure variance = £1000 – (800 × £1.00) = £200 (A)

2 **Efficiency** = (standard hours for actual production – actual hours worked) × variable production overhead absorption rate

∴ the efficiency variance = (900 – 800) × £1.00 = £100 (F)

3 **Total** = expenditure + efficiency

∴ the total variable production overhead variance = £200 (A) + £100 (F) = £100 (A)

The adverse variance of £100 (A) arises because the variable overhead absorption rate was calculated on the basis of a budgeted cost of £10 per unit. In fact the absorption rate ought to have been £11.11 per unit (£1000/90) because the total actual variable cost was £1000. There would, of course, be no variable production overhead cost for the ten units that were not produced. The £100 adverse total variance was calculated earlier in answering part (a) of the example.

### Fixed production overhead

1 **Expenditure** = actual fixed overhead – budgeted fixed expenditure

∴ the expenditure variance = £1600 – £2000 = £400 (F)

The actual expenditure was £400 less than the budgeted expenditure. This means that the fixed production overhead absorption rate was £400 higher than it needed to have been if there had not been any other fixed overhead variances.

2 **Volume** = budgeted fixed overhead – (standard hours of production × fixed production overhead absorption rate)

∴ the volume variance = £2000 – (900 × £2.00) = £200 (A)

As a result of producing fewer units than expected, £200 less overhead has been absorbed into production.

3 The fixed production overhead total variance was calculated earlier in answering part (a) of the question. The simplified formula is as follows:

Total = expenditure + volume

= £400 (F) + £200 (A) = £200 (F)

As the actual activity was less than the budgeted activity, only £1800 of fixed overhead was absorbed into production instead of the £2000 expected in the budget. However, the actual expenditure was only £1600 so the overestimate of expenditure compensated for the overestimate of activity.

## Sales variances

In an *absorption* costing system, a total sales variance would be classified into a selling price variance and a sales volume profit variance (see Figure 18.7).

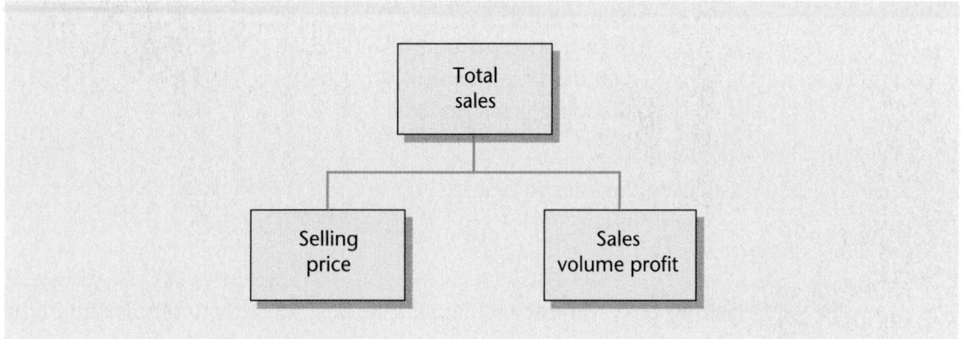


Figure 18.7 **Main sales variances**

The formulae are outlined below and are also shown in diagrammatic form in Figure 18.8.

1 **Total sales variance** = [actual sales revenue – (actual sales quantity × standard cost per unit)] – (budgeted quantity × standard profit per unit)

2 **Selling price variance** = [actual sales revenue – (actual sales quantity × standard cost per unit)] – (actual quantity × standard profit per unit)

An alternative formula for the calculation of the selling price variance is as follows: (actual selling price per unit – standard selling price per unit) × actual sales quantity.

3 **Sales volume profit variance** = (actual quantity – budgeted quantity) × standard profit per unit

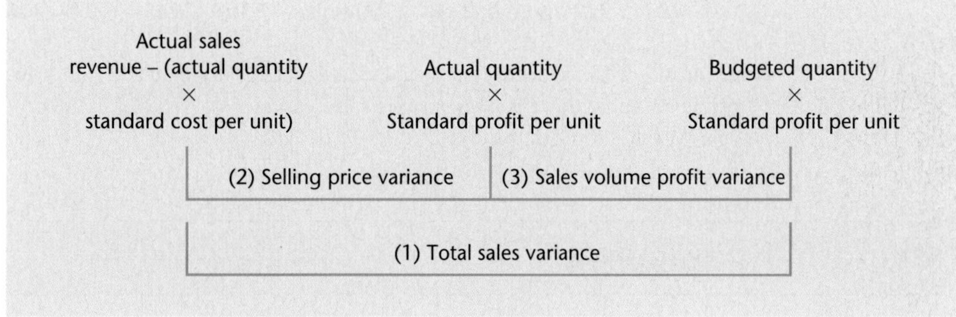


Figure 18.8 **Calculation of sales profit variances**

The use of sales variance formulae is illustrated in Example 18.4.

Example 18.4

### Calculating sales variances

The following data relate to Frozen Limited for the year to 31 July 2008:

| | *Budget/standard* | *Actual* |
|---|---|---|
| Sales (units) | 100 | 90 |
| Selling price per unit | £10 | £10.50 |
| Standard cost per unit | £7 | – |
| Standard profit per unit | £3 | |

*Required*:
Calculate the sales variances.

Answer to Example 18.4

**Selling price variance** = [actual sales revenue – (actual sales quantity × standard cost per unit)] – (actual quantity × standard profit per unit)

= [£945 – (90 units × £7)] – (90 units × £3) = (£945 – 630) – 270 = £45 (F)

The actual selling price per unit was £0.50 more than the standard selling price (£10.50–10.00) and so the variance is favourable. Other things being equal, the profit would be £45 higher than budgeted *for the actual number of units sold*.

**Sales volume profit variance** = (actual quantity – budgeted quantity) × standard profit per unit

The standard profit is £3 per unit.

(90 units – 100 units) = 10 × £3 = £30 (A)

The sales volume profit variance is £30 adverse because only 90 units were sold instead of the budgeted amount of 100 units. As a result, £30 less profit was made.

**Total sales variance** = [actual sales revenue – (actual sales quantity × standard cost per unit)] – (budgeted quantity × standard profit per unit)

The actual sales revenue = £945 (90 units × £10.50).

[£945 – (90 units × £7)] – (100 units × £3) = (£945 – 630) – 300 = £15 (F)

When the £45 favourable selling price is set off against the £30 adverse sales volume profit variance, there is a favourable sales variance of £15 (£45 – 30).

## Operating statements

Once all the variances have been calculated, they may usefully be summarized in the form of an operating statement. There is no standardized format for such a statement but the one shown in Example 18.5 is suitable for our purposes.

Example 18.5

## Preparation of a standard cost operating statement

Example 18.3 gave some information relating to the Frost Production Company Limited for the year to 31 March 2008. The cost data used in that example will now be used in this, along with some additional information that is required.

*Additional information*:

1 Assume that the budgeted sales were 100 units at a selling price of £150 per unit.
2 90 units were sold at £160 per unit.

*Required*:
Prepare a standard cost operating statement for the year to 31 March 2008.

Answer to Example 18.5

Frost Production Company Limited. Standard cost operating statement for the year to 31 March 2008:

| | | | £ |
|---|---|---|---|
| Budgeted sales (100 × £150) | | | 15 000 |
| Budgeted cost of sales (100 × £100) | | | 10 000 |
| Budgeted profit | | | 5 000 |
| Sales volume profit variance (1) | | | (500) |
| Budgeted profit from actual sales | | | 4 500 |
| Variances: (2) | (F) | (A) | |
| | £ | £ | |
| Sales price (3) | 900 | | |
| Direct materials usage | | 100 | |
| Direct materials price | 700 | | |
| Direct labour efficiency | 400 | | |
| Direct labour rate | | 800 | |
| Variable overhead efficiency | 100 | | |
| Variable overhead expenditure | | 200 | |
| Fixed overhead volume | | 200 | |
| Fixed overhead expenditure | 400 | | |
| | 2 500 | 1 300 | 1 200 |
| *Actual profit* | | | 5 700 |

*Tutorial notes*

1 **Sales volume profit variance** = (actual quantity – budgeted quantity) × standard profit per unit
= (90 – 100) × £50 = £500 (A)

2 Details of the cost variances were shown in the answer to Example 18.3.

3 **Selling price variance** = (actual selling price per unit – standard selling price per unit) × actual sales quantity
= (£160 – £150) × 90 = £900 (F)

The format used in Example 18.5 is particularly helpful because it shows the link between the budgeted profit and the actual profit. This means that management can trace the main causes of sales and cost variances. In practice, the statement would also show the details for each product.

The operating profit statement will help management to decide where to begin an investigation into the causes of the respective variances. It is unlikely that they will all be investigated. It may be company policy, for example, to investigate only those variances that are particularly significant, irrespective of whether they are favourable or adverse. In other words, only *exceptional* variances would be investigated. A policy decision would then have to be taken on what was meant by 'exceptional'.

### Questions non-accountants should ask

The calculation of standard cost variances is a complex arithmetical exercise. As a non-accountant it is unlikely that you will have to calculate variances but it is important for you to have some idea of how it is done so that you are in a stronger position to find out what happened. You can then take any necessary corrective action.

So what questions should you ask? We suggest that you can use the following as a basis for any subsequent investigation.

- Was the given level of activity accurate?
- Was the standard set realistic?
- Is there anything unusual about the actual events?
- Is the measure (i.e. the standard) reliable?
- Are there any particular variances that stand out?
- Are there any that are the main cause of any total variance?
- Is there a linkage between variances, e.g. between a favourable price variance and an unfavourable quantity/volume variance?
- Are there any factors that could not possibly have been seen at the time that the standards were prepared?

## Conclusion

We have come to the end of a complex chapter. You may have found that it has been extremely difficult to understand just how standard cost variances are calculated. Fortunately, it is unlikely that, as a non-accountant, you will ever have to calculate them for yourself. It is sufficient for your purposes to understand their meaning and to have some idea of the arithmetical foundation on which they are based.

Your job will usually be to investigate the causes of the variances and to take necessary action. A standard costing system is supposed to help managers to plan and control the entity much more tightly than can be achieved in the absence of such a system but it can only be of real benefit if it is actually used by managers.

## Key points

1 A standard cost is the planned cost of a particular unit or process.

2 Standard costs are usually based on what is reasonably attainable.

3 Actual costs are compared with standard costs.

4 Corrective action is taken if there are any unplanned trends.

5 Three performance measures used in standard costing are the efficiency ratio, the capacity ratio and the production volume ratio.

6 Variance analysis is an arithmetical exercise that enables differences between actual and standard costs to be broken down into the elements of cost.

7 The degree of analysis will vary, but usually a total cost variance will be analysed into direct material, direct labour, variable overhead and fixed overhead variances and sub-analysed into quantity and expenditure variances.

8 Sales variances may also be calculated, the total sales variance being analysed into a selling price variance and a sales volume profit variance.

9 The variances help in tracing the main causes of differences between actual and budgeted results but they do not *explain* what has actually happened – they are merely the starting point for a more detailed investigation.

## Check your learning

1 Explain what is meant by the following terms: (a) a standard, (b) a standard cost, (c) a variance, (d) variance analysis.

2 List four uses of standard costing.

3 What type of entities might benefit from a standard costing system?

4 How long should a standard costing period be?

5 What is (a) a basic standard, (b) an attainable standard, (c) an ideal standard?

6 Name four types of information required for a standard costing system.

7 What is meant by 'a standard hour'?

8 Name three standard cost performance measures.

9 What are their respective formulae?

10 Complete the following equations:

(a) direct materials total = _________ + _________

(b) direct labour total = _________ + _________

(c) variable production overhead total = _________ + _________

(d) fixed production overhead total = _________ + _________

11 What is (a) an adverse variance, (b) a favourable variance?

12 Complete this equation: total sales variance = __________ + __________

13 Complete this statement: a standard cost operating statement links the budgeted profit to the __________ __________ for the period.

## News story quiz

*Remember the news story at the beginning of this chapter? Go back to that story and re-read it before answering the following questions.*

Standard costing has been around since the early twentieth century and, like many other management accounting techniques that have been around a long time, it has hardly changed. This article suggests that with the rapid developments that are now taking place in information technology this particular sleeping giant is about to wake up.

### Questions

1 What effect would the sales management tools described in this article have on the traditional method of preparing sales budgets?

2 What impact would this have on the compilation of the standard cost of those sales?

3 How would you see the reporting of sales and cost variances changing as a result of the use of integrated software suites that were able 'to manage processes across the entire business'?

4 Do you think developments in IT are likely to make standard costing become much more widely adopted?

## Tutorial questions

*The answers to questions marked with an asterix can be found in Appendix 4.*

18.1 Is it likely that a standard-costing system is of any relevance in a service industry?

18.2 'Standard costing is all about number crunching, and for someone on the shop floor it has absolutely no relevance.' Do you agree with this statement?

18.3 'Sales variance calculations are just another example of accountants playing around with numbers.' Discuss.

18.4* You are presented with the following information for X Limited:

Standard price per unit: £10.
Standard quantity for actual production: 5 units.
Actual price per unit: £12.
Actual quantity: 6 units.

*Required:*
Calculate the following variances:

(a) direct material total variance
(b) direct material price variance
(c) direct material usage variance.

**18.5** The following information relates to Malcolm Limited:

Budgeted production: 100 units.
Unit specification (direct materials): 50 kilograms × £5 per kilogram = £250.
Actual production: 120 units.
Direct materials used: 5400 kilograms at a total cost of £32 400.

*Required*:
Calculate the following variances:

(a) direct material total
(b) direct material price
(c) direct material usage.

**18.6*** The following information relates to Bruce Limited:

Actual hours: 1000.
Actual wage rate per hour: £6.50.
Standard hours for actual production: 900.
Standard wage rate per hour: £6.00.

*Required*:
Calculate the following variances:

(a) direct labour total
(b) direct labour rate
(c) direct labour efficiency.

**18.7** You are presented with the following information for Duncan Limited:

Budgeted production: 1000 units.
Actual production: 1200 units.
Standard specification for one unit: 10 hours at £8 per direct labour hour.
Actual direct labour cost: £97 200 in 10 800 actual hours.

*Required*:
Calculate the following variances:

(a) direct labour total
(b) direct labour rate
(c) direct labour efficiency.

**18.8*** The following overhead budget has been prepared for Anthea Limited:

Actual fixed overhead: £150 000.
Budgeted fixed overhead: £135 000.
Fixed overhead absorption rate per hour: £15.
Actual hours worked: 10 000.
Standard hours of production: 8000.

*Required*:
Calculate the following fixed production overhead variances:

(a) total
(b) expenditure
(c) volume.

18.9* Using the data contained in the previous question, calculate the following performance measures:

(a) efficiency ratio
(b) capacity ratio
(c) production volume ratio.

18.10 The following information relates to Osprey Limited:

Budgeted production: 500 units.
Standard hours per unit: 10.
Actual production: 600 units.
Budgeted fixed overhead: £125 000.
Actual fixed overhead: £120 000.
Actual hours worked: 4900.

*Required:*
Calculate the following fixed production overhead variances:

(a) total
(b) expenditure
(c) volume.

18.11 Using the data from the previous question, calculate the following performance measures:

(a) efficiency ratio
(b) capacity ratio
(c) production volume ratio.

18.12* Milton Limited has produced the following information:

Total actual sales: £99 000.
Actual quantity sold: 9000 units.
Budgeted selling price per unit: £10.
Standard cost per unit: £7.
Total budgeted units: 10 000 units.

*Required:*
Calculate:

(a) the selling price variance
(b) the sales volume profit variance
(c) the sales variance in total.

18.13 You are presented with the following budgeted information for Doe Limited:

| | |
|---|---|
| Sales units | 100 |
| *Per unit:* | £ |
| Selling price | 30 |
| Cost | (20) |
| *Profit* | 10 |
| | |
| Actual sales | 120 units |
| Actual selling price per unit | £28 |

*Required:*
Calculate the sales variances.

18.14 The budgeted selling price and standard cost of a unit manufactured by Smillie Limited is as follows:

| | £ |
|---|---|
| Selling price | 30 |
| Direct materials (2.5 kilos) | 5 |
| Direct labour (2 hours) | 12 |
| Fixed production overhead | 8 |
| | 25 |
| Budgeted profit | 5 |

Total budgeted sales: 400 units

During the period to 31 December 2009, the actual sales and production details for Smillie were as follows:

| | £ |
|---|---|
| Sales (420 units) | 13 440 |
| Direct materials (1260 kilos) | 2 268 |
| Direct labour (800 hours) | 5 200 |
| Fixed production overhead | 3 300 |
| | 10 768 |
| Profit | 2 672 |

*Required*:

(a) Prepare a standard cost operating statement for the period to 31 December 2009 incorporating as many variances as the data permit.

(b) Explain what the statement tells the managers of Smillie Limited.

18.15 Mean Limited manufactures a single product, and the following information relates to the actual selling price and actual cost of the product for the four weeks to 31 March 2009:

| | *£000* |
|---|---|
| Sales (50 000 units) | 2 250 |
| Direct materials (240 000 litres) | 528 |
| Direct labour (250 000 hours) | 1 375 |
| Variable production overhead | 245 |
| Fixed production overhead | 650 |
| | 2 798 |
| Loss | (548) |

The budgeted selling price and standard cost of each unit was as follows:

| | £ |
|---|---|
| Selling price | 55 |
| Direct materials (5 litres) | 10 |
| Direct labour (4 hours) | 20 |
| Variable production overhead | 5 |
| Fixed production overhead | 15 |
| | 50 |
| Budgeted profit | 5 |

Total budgeted production: 40 000 units.

*Required*:

(a) Prepare a standard cost operating statement for the four weeks to 31 March 2009 incorporating as many variances as the data permit.

(b) Explain how the statement may help the managers of Mean Limited to control the business more effectively.

**Further practice questions, study material and links to relevant sites on the World Wide Web can be found on the website that accompanies this book. The site can be found at www.pearsoned.co.uk/dyson**

# Chapter 19 Contribution analysis

**It depends what you mean . . .**

## Queen's Flight costs were 'ten times higher'

**NAO calculation reveals true cost of MPs' trips**

The addition of fixed costs as calculated by the National Audit Office (in a 2001 report) have pushed up the cost of Tony Blair and his ministers using the royal flight on trips to the EU by ten times the original amount.

The PM's 22 trips to Brussels between 2002 and 2004 was originally said to be £32 421, but including the NAO's calculation this goes up to £283 953.

Gordon Brown's total of 38 trips add up to £28 000, but with fixed costs soar to £264 000, while Margaret Beckett the Environment Secretary's 23 flights total £210 000.

According to *The Times*, the MoD said that the NAO report had recommended using the lower figure.

*Accountancy Age*, 21 April 2006.



*Questions relating to this news story can be found on page 395*

## About this chapter

In the previous two chapters we have been concerned with the planning and control functions of management accounting. We now turn our attention to another important function of management accounting, *decision making*. In this chapter we explore a basic technique of decision making known as *contribution analysis*.

Contribution analysis is based on the premise that in almost any decision-making situation some costs are irrelevant, that is they are not affected by the decision. They can, therefore, be ignored. In such circumstances management should concentrate on the *contribution* that a project may make. Contribution (C) is the difference between the sales revenue (S) of a project and the variable or extra costs (V) incurred by investing in that project. Other things being equal, as long as S – V results in C being positive then management should go ahead or continue with the project. A positive C means that something is left over to make a *contribution* to the fixed (or remaining) costs (F) of the entity. If the fixed costs have already been covered by other projects then the contribution increases the entity's profit.

**Learning objectives**

By the end of this chapter, you should be able to:

- explain why absorption costing may be inappropriate in decision making;
- describe the difference between a fixed cost and a variable cost;
- use contribution analysis in managerial decision making;
- assess the usefulness of contribution analysis in problem solving.

## Why this chapter is important for non-accountants

Of all the chapters in this book this is the most relevant and vital for non-accountants. Why? Whatever job you are doing and at whatever level, you will be required to make or to take decisions. Many of those decision will be straightforward day-to-day ones such as, '*Do we order a week's or a month's supply of paper towels?*' Other decisions will be more significant and long-term, for example '*Should we increase our selling prices?*' or '*Do we buy this other company?*'

While there is a cost implication in these sorts of decisions, it is unlikely that you would have to do the detailed calculations for yourself. Your accountants will do this for you and then present you with the results. However, in order to make sense of the information and to take an informed decision you need to know where the information has come from and how it has been compiled.

This is a valid point irrespective of the particular issue but it is especially valid for specific one-off decision making. If such decisions are based on absorbed costs you might make a spectacularly wrong decision because it would not be based on the project's *relevant* costs, i.e. it should include only those costs that are likely to be affected by that particular decision.

This chapter will help you to appreciate more clearly the nature of relevant costs and their importance in managerial decision making. As a result, you will be able take more soundly based decisions and be more confident about their eventual outcome.

# Marginal costing

Chapters 15 and 16 dealt with cost accounting. The costing method described in some detail in those chapters is known as *absorption costing*. The ultimate aim of absorption costing is to charge out all the costs of an entity to individual units of production. The method involves identifying the *direct costs* of specific units and then absorbing a share of the *indirect costs* into each unit. Indirect costs are normally absorbed on the basis of direct labour hours or machine hours. Assuming that an overhead absorption rate is predetermined – i.e. calculated in advance – this method involves estimating the total amount of overhead likely to be incurred and the total amount of direct labour hours or machine hours expected to be worked. So the absorption rate could be affected by the total cost of the overhead, the hours worked or by a combination of cost and hours.

The total of the indirect costs (the overhead) is likely to be made up of a combination of costs that will change depending on how many units a department produces, and those costs that are not affected by the number of units produced. Costs that change with activity are known as *variable costs*. It is usually assumed that variable costs vary directly with activity, e.g. if 1 kg costs £1, then 2 kg will cost £2, 3 kg will cost £3 and so on. Those costs that do not change with activity are known as *fixed costs*.

As we argued in Chapters 15 and 16, if we are attempting to work out the total cost of manufacturing particular units, or if we want to value our stocks, it is appropriate to use absorption costing. Most cost book-keeping systems are based on this method of costing but absorption costing is not normally appropriate in decision making as the fixed element inherent in most costs may not be affected by a particular decision.

Suppose that a manager is costing a particular journey that a member of staff is proposing to make to visit a client. The staff member has a car that is already taxed and insured, so the main cost of the journey will be for petrol, although the car may depreciate slightly more quickly and it may require a service sooner. The tax and insurance costs will not be affected by one particular journey: they are *fixed costs*, no matter how many extra journeys are undertaken. The manager is, therefore, only interested in the *extra* cost of using the car to visit the client and he can then compare the cost of using the car with the cost of the bus, the train or going by air. Note that cost alone would not necessarily be the determining factor in practice; non-quantifiable factors such as comfort, convenience, fatigue and time would also be important considerations.

The extra cost of making the journey is sometimes described as the *marginal cost*. Hence the technique used in the above example is commonly referred to as *marginal costing*. Economists also use the term 'marginal cost' to describe the extra cost of making an additional unit (as with the extra cost of a particular journey). When dealing with production activities, however, units are more likely to be produced in batches. It would then be more appropriate to substitute the term *incremental costing* and refer to the *incremental cost*, meaning the extra cost of producing a batch of units. As the terms 'marginal costing' and 'marginal cost' are so widely used, however, we will do the same.

The application of marginal costing revolves round the concept of what is known as *contribution*. We explore this concept in the next section.

**Activity 19.1**

A business college has recently considered starting some extra evening classes on basic computing. The college runs other courses during the evening. The proposed course fee has been based on the lecturer's fee and the cost of heat, light, caretaking and other expenses incurred solely as a result of running the extra classes. However, the principal has insisted that a 25% loading be added to the fee to go towards the college's day-to-day running costs. This is in accordance with the college's normal costing procedures.

Give reasons why the principal's requirement may be inappropriate when costing the proposed evening class lectures.

## Contribution

In order to illustrate what is meant by 'contribution' we will use a series of equations. The first is straightforward:

$$\textbf{sales revenue} - \textbf{total costs} = \textbf{profit (or loss)} \qquad (1)$$

The second equation is based on the assumption that total costs can be analysed into variable costs and fixed costs:

$$\textbf{total costs} = \textbf{variable costs} + \textbf{fixed costs} \qquad (2)$$

By substituting equation 2 into equation 1 we can derive equation 3:

$$\text{sales revenue} - (\text{variable costs} + \text{fixed costs}) = \text{profit (or loss)} \quad (3)$$

By rearranging equation 3 we can derive the following equation:

$$\text{sales revenue} - \text{variable costs} = \text{fixed costs} + \text{profit (or loss)} \quad (4)$$

Equation 4 is known as the *marginal cost equation*. Let us simplify it and substitute symbols for words, namely sales revenue = $S$, variable costs = $V$, fixed costs = $F$, and profit = $P$ (or loss = $L$). The equation now reads as follows:

$$S - V = F + P \quad (5)$$

But where does contribution fit into all of this? Contribution (C) *is the difference between the sales revenue and the variable costs of that sales revenue.* Hence, in equation form:

$$S - V = C \quad (6)$$

Contribution can also be looked at from another point of view. If we substitute $C$ for $(S - V)$ in Equation 5, the result will be:

$$C = F + P \quad (7)$$

In other words, contribution can be regarded as being either the difference between the sales revenue and the variable costs of that sales revenue or the total of fixed cost plus profit.

What do these relationships mean in practice and what is their importance? The meaning is reasonably straightforward. If an entity makes a contribution, it means that it has generated a certain amount of sales revenue and the variable cost of making those sales is less than the total sales revenue ($S - V = C$). Hence there is a balance left over that can go towards contributing towards the fixed costs ($C - F$); any remaining balance must be the profit ($C - F = P$). Alternatively, if the contribution is insufficient to cover the fixed costs, the entity will have made a loss: $C - F = L$.

The importance of the relationships described above in equation format is important for two main reasons. First, fixed costs can often be ignored when taking a particular decision because, by definition, fixed costs will not change irrespective of whatever decision is taken. This means that any cost and revenue analysis is made much simpler. Second, managers can concentrate on decisions that will maximize the contribution, since every additional £1 of contribution is an extra amount that goes toward covering the fixed costs. Once the fixed costs have been covered then every extra £1 of contribution is an extra £1 of profit.

**Activity 19.2**

Company M's annual sales were £100 000, its variable costs £40 000 and its fixed costs £50 000.

Calculate the profit for the year using the marginal cost equation.

## Assumptions

The marginal cost technique used in contribution analysis is, of course, based on a number of assumptions. They may be summarized as follows:

- total costs can be split between fixed costs and variable costs;
- fixed costs remain constant irrespective of the level of activity;
- fixed costs do not bear any relationship to specific units;
- variable costs vary in direct proportion to activity.

The reliability of the technique depends very heavily on being able to distinguish between fixed and variable costs. Some costs may be semi-variable, i.e. they may consist of both a fixed and variable element. Electricity costs and telephone charges, for example, both contain a fixed rental element plus a variable charge. The variable charge depends on the units consumed or the number of telephone calls made. Such costs are relatively easy to analyse into their fixed and variable elements.

In practice, it may be difficult to split other costs into their fixed and variable components. The management accountants may need the help of engineers and work study specialists in determining whether a particular cost is fixed or variable. They may also have to draw on a number of graphical and statistical techniques. These techniques are somewhat advanced and beyond this book, so for our purposes we will assume that we can analyse costs into their fixed and variable components.

**Activity 19.3**

Re-read the assumptions summarized above. Do you think that these assumptions are reasonable? Rank them in the order of how far you think that they are generally valid (1 = the most valid; 2 = the next most valid, and so on).

## Format

In applying the marginal cost technique, the cost data are usually arranged in a vertical format on a line-by-line basis. The order of the data reflects the marginal cost equation ($S - V = F + P$). This format enables the attention of managers to be directed towards the contribution that may arise from any particular decision. This is now called *contribution analysis*. The basic procedure is illustrated in Example 19.1.

**Example 19.1**

### A typical marginal cost statement

| | | *Product* | | | |
|---|---|---|---|---|---|
| | *Symbol* | *A* | *B* | *C* | *Total* |
| | | *£000* | *£000* | *£000* | *£000* |
| Sales revenue (1) | *S* | 100 | 70 | 20 | 190 |
| *Less*: variable costs of sales (2) | *V* | 30 | 32 | 18 | 80 |
| Contribution (3) | C | 70 | 38 | 2 | 110 |
| *Less*: fixed costs (4) | *F* | | | | 60 |
| Profit (5) | *P* | | | | 50 |

**Example 19.1** *continued*

*Notes:*

- The number in brackets after each item description refers to the tutorial notes below.
- The marginal cost equation is represented in the 'symbol' column, i.e. $S - V = C$; $C = F + P$; and thereby $S - V = F + P$.

*Tutorial notes*

1 The total sales revenue would normally be analysed into different product groupings. In this example there are three products: A, B and C.

2 The variable costs include direct materials, direct labour costs, other direct costs and variable overheads. Variable costs are assumed to vary *in direct proportion* to activity. Direct costs will normally be the same as variable costs, but in some cases this will not be so. A machine operator's salary, for example, may be fixed under a guaranteed annual wage agreement. It is a direct cost in respect of the machine but it is also a fixed cost because it will not vary with the number of units produced.

3 As stated above, the term *contribution* is used to describe the difference between the sales revenue and the variable cost of those sales. A positive contribution helps to pay for the fixed costs.

4 The fixed costs include all the other costs that do not vary in direct proportion to the sales revenue. Fixed costs are assumed to remain constant over a period of time. They do not bear any relationship to the units produced or the sales achieved. So it is not possible to apportion them to individual products. The *total* of the fixed costs can only be deducted from the *total contribution*.

5 The total contribution less the fixed costs gives the profit (if the balance is positive) or a loss (if the balance is negative).

Managers supplied with information similar to that contained in Example 19.1 may subject the information to a series of 'What if?' questions such as the following.

- What would the profit be if we increased the selling price of product A, B or C?
- What would be the effect if we reduced the selling price of product A, B or C?
- What would be the effect if we eliminated one or more of the products?
- What would happen if we changed the quality of any of the products so that the variable cost of each product either increased or decreased?
- Would any of the above decisions have an impact on fixed costs?

**Activity 19.4**

Rearrange the following data in a marginal cost format.

Annual rent £3000; direct labour £20 000; direct material £10 000; sales £75 000; staff salaries £47 000.

## Application

As we have seen, the basic assumptions used in marginal costing are somewhat simplistic. In practice, they would probably only be regarded as appropriate when a particular decision was first considered. Thereafter, each of the various assumptions would be rigorously tested and they would be subject to a number of searching questions, such as: 'If we change the selling price of this product, will it affect the sales of the other products?' 'Will variable costs always remain in direct proportion to activity?' or 'Will fixed costs remain fixed irrespective of the level of activity?'

We will now use a simple example to illustrate the application of the technique. The details are shown in Example 19.2. This illustrates the effect of a change in variable costs on contribution.

Example 19.2

## Changes in the variable cost

| | One unit | Proportion | 100 units | 1000 units |
|---|---|---|---|---|
| | £ | % | £ | £ |
| Sales revenue | 10 | 100 | 1000 | 10 000 |
| *Less*: variable costs | 5 | 50 | 500 | 5 000 |
| Contribution | 5 | 50 | 500 | 5 000 |

*Tutorial notes to Example 19.2*

1 The selling price per unit is £10, and the variable cost per unit is £5 (50 per cent of the selling price). The contribution, therefore, is also £5 per unit (50 per cent of the selling price).

2 These relationships are assumed to hold good no matter how many units are sold. So if 100 units are sold the contribution will be £500; if 1000 units are sold there will be a contribution of £5000, i.e. the contribution is assumed to remain at 50 per cent of the sales revenue.

3 The fixed costs are ignored because it is assumed that they will *not* change as the level of activity changes.

Every extra unit sold will increase the profit by £5 per unit *once the fixed costs have been covered* – an important qualification. This point is illustrated in Example 19.3.

Example 19.3

## Changes in profit at varying levels of activity

| *Activity (units)* | 1000 | 2000 | 3000 | 4000 | 5000 |
|---|---|---|---|---|---|
| | £ | £ | £ | £ | £ |
| Sales | 10 000 | 20 000 | 30 000 | 40 000 | 50 000 |
| *Less*: variable costs | 5 000 | 10 000 | 15 000 | 20 000 | 25 000 |
| Contribution | 5 000 | 10 000 | 15 000 | 20 000 | 25 000 |
| *Less*: fixed costs | 10 000 | 10 000 | 10 000 | 10 000 | 10 000 |
| Profit/(Loss) | (5 000) | – | 5 000 | 10 000 | 15 000 |

*Tutorial notes to Example 19.3*

1 The exhibit illustrates five levels of activity: 1000 units, 2000 units, 3000 units, 4000 units and 5000 units.

2 The variable costs remain directly proportional to activity at all levels, i.e. 50 per cent. The contribution is, therefore, 50 per cent (100% – 50%). The contribution per unit may be obtained by dividing the contribution at any level of activity level by the activity at that level, e.g. at an activity level of 1000 units the contribution per unit is £5 (£5000 ÷ 1000).

3 The fixed costs do not change, irrespective of the level of activity.

4 The contribution needed to cover the fixed costs is £10 000. As each unit makes a contribution of £5, the total number of units needed to be sold in order to break even (i.e. to reach a point where sales revenue equals the total of both the variable and the fixed costs) will be 2000 (£10 000 ÷ £5).

5 When *more than* 2000 are sold, the increased contribution results in an increase in profit. Thus, for instance when 3000 units are sold instead of 2000, the increased contribution is £5000 (£15 000 – 10 000); the increased profit is also £5000 (£5000 – 0). Similarly, when 4000 units are sold instead of 3000, the increased contribution is another £5000 (£20 000 – 15 000) and the increased profit is also £5000 (£10 000 – 5000). Finally, when 5000 units are sold instead of 4000 units, the increased contribution is once more £5000 (£25 000 – 20 000), as is the increased profit (£15 000 – 10 000).

*Tutorial notes to Example 19.3 continued*

6 The relationship between contribution and sales is known (rather confusingly) as the *profit/volume* (or P/V) ratio. Note that it does not mean *profit* in relationship to sales but the *contribution* in relationship to sales.

7 Assuming that the P/V ratio does not change, we can quickly calculate the profit at any level of sales. All we need to do is to multiply the P/V ratio by the sales revenue and then deduct the fixed costs. The balance will then equal the profit at that level of sales. It is also easy to accommodate any possible change in fixed costs as the activity level moves above or below a certain range.

Example 19.2 and Example 19.3 are simple examples but we hope that they demonstrate just how useful contribution analysis can be in managerial decision making. While the basic assumptions may be somewhat simplistic, they can readily be adapted to suit more complex problems.

**Activity 19.5**

You are presented with the following data: number of units sold 5000, sales revenue £50 000, variable costs £25 000, fixed costs £10 000.

If the company wanted to make the same amount of profit, how many units would have to be sold if the fixed costs rose to £15 000?

## Charts and graphs

Contribution analysis lends itself to the presentation of information in a pictorial format. Indeed, the $S - V = F + P$ relationship is often easier to appreciate when it is reported to managers graphically.

The most common format is in the form of what is called a *break-even chart.* A break-even chart is illustrated in Example 19.4. The chart is based on the data used in Example 19.3.

Example 19.4 shows quite clearly the relationships that are assumed to exist when the marginal costing technique is adopted. Sales revenue, total costs and fixed costs are all assumed to be linear, so they are all drawn as straight lines. Note also the following points.

- When no units are sold, the sales revenue line runs from the origin up to £50 000 when 5000 units are sold. It may then continue as a straight line beyond that point.
- The total cost line is made up of both the fixed costs and the variable costs. When there is no activity the total costs will be equal to the fixed costs, so the total cost line runs from the fixed cost point of £10 000 up to £35 000 when 5000 units are sold. It may then continue beyond that point.
- The fixed cost line is drawn from the £10 000 point as a straight line parallel to the $x$ axis irrespective of the number of units sold.

In practice, the above relationships are not likely to hold good over the range of activity indicated in the example. They are usually assumed to remain valid over only a small range of activity. This is known as the *relevant range.* In this example the relevant range may be from (say) 1000 to 3000 units. Above or below these levels the selling prices, the variable costs and the fixed costs may all change.

While this point might appear to create some difficulty, it should be appreciated that wide fluctuations in activity are not normally experienced. It is usually quite reasonable to assume that the entity will be operating in a fairly narrow range of activity and that

Example 19.4

## A break even chart

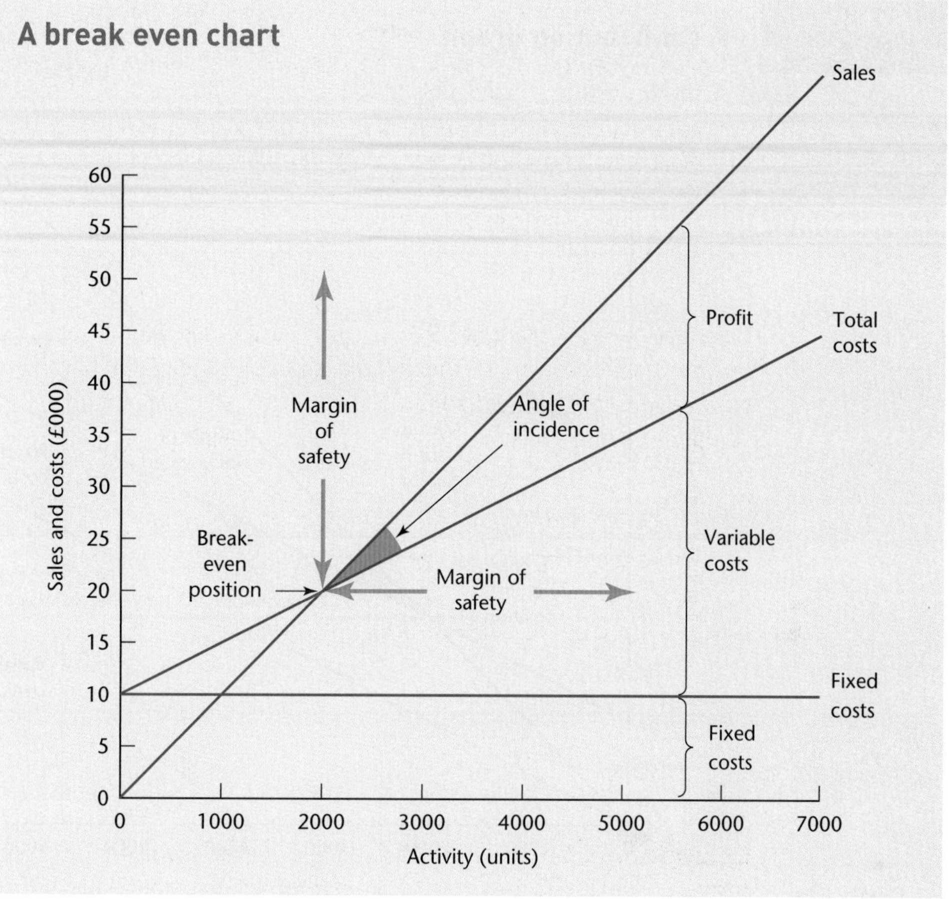


*Tutorial notes to Example 19.4*

1 The total costs line is a combination of the fixed costs and the variable costs. So it ranges from a total cost of £10 000 (fixed costs only) at a nil level of activity, to £35 000 when the activity level is 5000 units (fixed costs of £10 000 + variable costs of £25 000).

2 The angle of incidence is the angle formed between the sales line and the total cost line. The wider the angle, the greater the amount of profit. A wide angle of incidence and a wide margin of safety (see note 3) indicates a highly profitable position.

3 The margin of safety is the distance between the sales achieved and the sales level needed to break even. It can be measured either in units (along the *x* axis of the graph) or in sales revenue terms (along the *y* axis).

4 Activity (measured along the *x* axis) may be measured either in units or as a percentage of the theoretical maximum level of activity, or in terms of sales revenue.

the various relationships will be linear. It must also be remembered that the information is meant to be only a *guide* to managerial decision making and that it is impossible to be absolutely precise.

You will see that the break-even chart shown in Example 19.4 does not show a separate variable cost line. This may be somewhat confusing, and so sometimes the information is presented in the form of a *contribution graph*. A contribution graph based on the data used in Example 19.4 is illustrated in Example 19.5. Can you spot the differences between the two examples?

Example 19.5

## A contribution graph

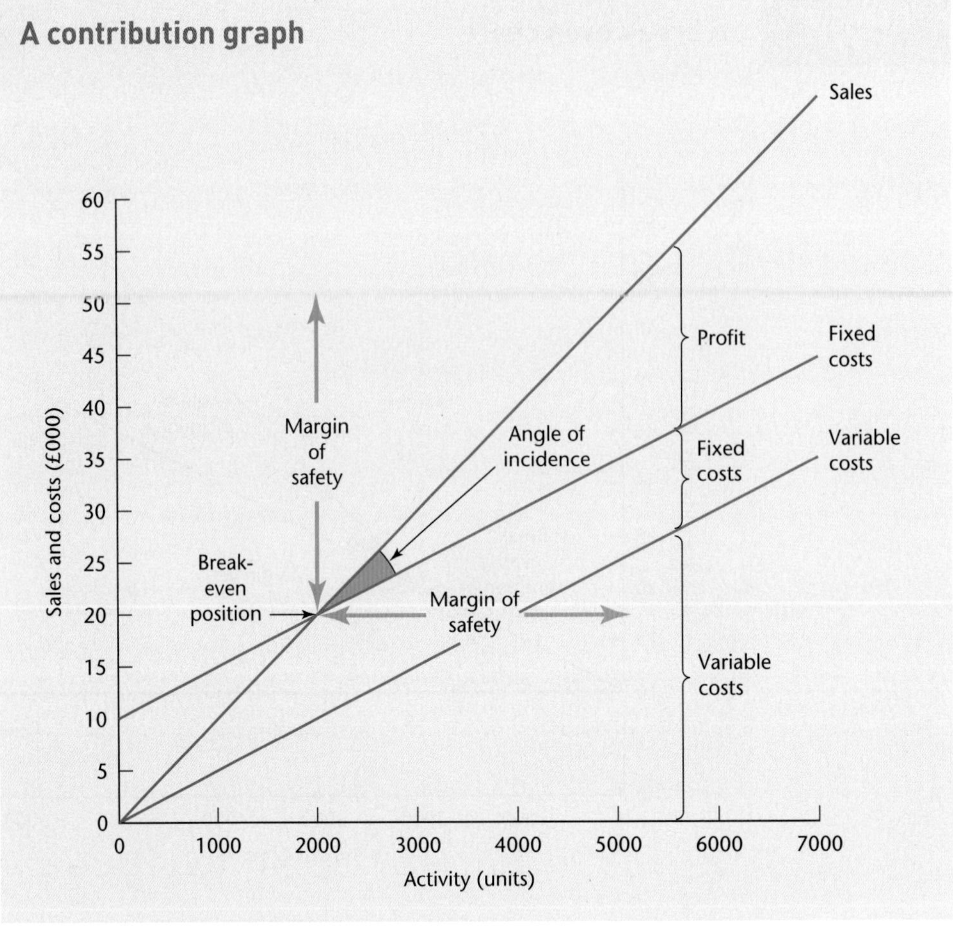


- The contribution graph shows the variable cost line ranging from the origin when there is no activity to £25 000 when 5000 units are sold. It then continues beyond that point in a straight line.
- The fixed cost line is drawn parallel to the variable cost line, i.e. higher up the *y* axis. As the fixed costs are assumed to remain fixed irrespective of the level of activity, the fixed cost line runs from £10 000 when there is no activity to £35 000 when 5000 units are sold. It is then continued as a straight line beyond that point.
- The fixed cost line also serves as the total cost line.

Apart from the above differences, the break-even chart and the contribution graph are identical. Which one should you adopt? There is no specific guidance that we can give since the decision is one largely of personal preference. The break-even chart is more common, but the contribution chart is probably more helpful since the fixed and the variable cost lines are shown separately.

One problem with both the break-even chart and the contribution graph is that neither shows the *actual amount of profit or loss* at varying levels of activity. So, if you wanted to know what the profit was when (say) 4000 units were sold, you would have to use a ruler to measure the distance between the sales line and the total cost line. This is not very satisfactory so in order to get over this problem we can use a *profit/volume chart* (or graph).

A profit/volume chart shows the effect of a change in activity on profit. An example of such a chart is shown in Example 19.6. It is based on the data used in Example 19.3.

Example 19.6

## A profit/volume chart

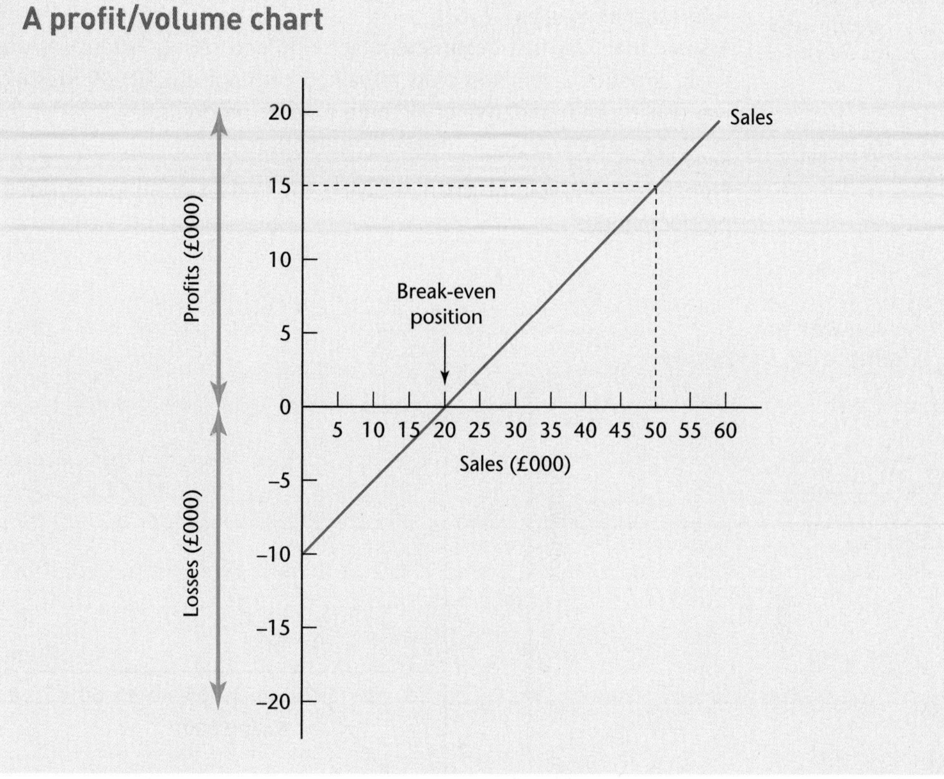


*Tutorial notes to Example 19.6*

1. The *x* axis can be represented either in terms of units, as a percentage of the activity level or in terms of sales revenue.
2. The *y* axis represents profits (positive amounts) or losses (negative amounts).
3. With sales at a level of £50 000, the profit is £15 000. The sales line cuts the *x* axis at the break-even position of £20 000 sales. If there are no sales, the loss equals the fixed costs of £10 000.

As you can see from Example 19.6 the profit/volume chart only shows the entity's *total* profit or loss. It does not show the profit or loss made on individual products.

It is possible to show the impact of individual products on profits on the chart, although the result is somewhat simplistic. We do so in Example 19.7.

Example 19.7

## Tilsy Limited

You are presented with the following information.

| *Product* | *A* | *B* | *C* | *Total* |
|---|---|---|---|---|
| | £ | £ | £ | £ |
| Sales | 5 000 | 20 000 | 25 000 | 50 000 |
| Less: variable costs | 3 000 | 10 000 | 12 000 | 25 000 |
| Contribution | 2 000 | 10 000 | 13 000 | 25 000 |
| Less: fixed costs | | | | 10 000 |
| Profit | | | | 15 000 |

**Example 19.7 continued**

*Additional information*:
Assume that Tilsy first began manufacturing and selling Product A, then Product B, and finally Product C. Its fixed costs remained constant at £10 000 irrespective of whether it was dealing with one, two or all three of these products.

*Required*:
Prepare a profit/volume chart showing the impact on its profit/(loss) of the individual product ranges.

**Answer to Example 19.7**

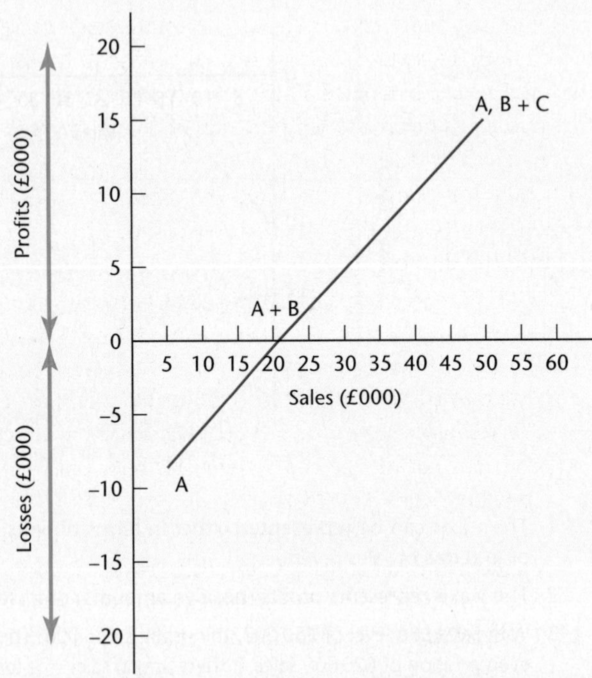


1 If Product A is the first product, the company makes a loss of £8000 (£2000 – 10 000). Once Product B is introduced a profit of £2000 is made (£10 000 – 8 000). Then when Product C is added the profit becomes £15 000 (£2000 + 13 000).
2 It would be possible to plot the three product ranges in a different order, e.g. Product B, then Product C, then Product A; or possibly Product C, then Product A, then Product B.
3 The disclosure of the impact of individual products on profit is useful because it can highlight the performance of a poorly performing product. Product A does make a small contribution of £2000 (£5000 – 3000) but this is not sufficient to off-set the fixed costs of £10 000. It is only when Product B is introduced that the company begins to make a profit. The chart shows this fairly clearly.

**Activity 19.6**

On a scale of 1 to 5, how useful do you think that the following diagrams are to management (5 = very useful; 1 = not at all useful)?

(a) a break-even chart ☐

(b) a contribution graph ☐

(c) a profit/volume chart ☐

## Criticisms

The assumptions adopted in preparing marginal cost statements and their use in contribution analysis lead to a number of important reservations about the technique. The main ones are as follows.

- *Cost classification.* Costs cannot be easily divided into fixed and variable categories.
- *Variable costs.* Variable costs do not necessarily vary in direct proportion to sales revenue at all levels of activity. The cost of direct materials, for example, may change if supplies are limited in availability or if they are bought in bulk. It is also questionable whether direct labour should be treated as a variable cost (as is often the case) since current legislative practice makes it difficult to dismiss employees at short notice.
- *Fixed costs.* Fixed costs are unlikely to remain constant over a wide range of activity. There is a good chance that they will change both beyond and below a fairly narrow range. They may perhaps move in 'steps', so that between an activity level of 0 and 999 units, for example, the fixed costs may be £10 000, be £12 000 between an activity level of 1000 and 2999 units, be £15 000 between an activity level of 3000 and 5000 units, and so on.
- *Time period.* The determination of the time period over which the relationship between the fixed and variable costs may hold good is difficult to determine. In the very short term (say a day), all costs may be fixed. In the long term (say five years), all costs may be variable as the entity could go out of business.
- *Complementary products.* A specific decision affecting one product may affect other products. For example, a garage sells both petrol and oil. A decision to stop selling oil may affect sales of petrol.
- *Cost recovery.* It may be unwise to exclude fixed costs altogether from the analysis. In the medium-to-long term an entity must recover all of its costs. Decisions cannot be taken purely in terms of the impact that they may have on contribution.
- *Diagrammatic presentations.* Break-even charts, contribution graphs and profit/volume charts are somewhat simplistic. The sales of individual products are considered in total and it is assumed that any change made to one product will have a proportionate effect on all the other products.
- *Non-cost factors.* Decisions cannot be taken purely on the basis of cost. Sometimes factors that cannot be easily quantified and costed are more important, e.g. comfort, convenience, loyalty, reliability or speed.
- *Behavioural factors.* In practice, behavioural factors also have to be considered. Individuals do not always act rationally and an actual behaviour pattern may be quite different from what was expected. A decrease in the selling price of a product, for example, may reduce the quantity of good purchased because it is *perceived* to be of poor quality.

The factors listed above are all fairly severe criticisms of the marginal costing technique and its use in contribution analysis. Nevertheless, experience suggests that it has still a useful part to play in managerial decision making, provided that the basis on which the information is built is understood, its apparent arithmetical precision is not regarded as a guarantee of absolute certainty and non-cost factors are also taken into account.

With these reservations in mind, we can now move on to look at the technique in a little more detail. Before we do so, however, it would be useful to summarize the main formulae so that it will be easier for you to refer back to them when dealing with the various examples.

**Activity 19.7**

Re-read the criticisms outlined above. Judging them from a non-accountant's point of view, select the three most significant weaknesses of the marginal costing approach and summarize them.

## Formulae

Earlier in the chapter we explained that marginal costing revolves around the assumption that total costs can be classified into fixed and variable costs. This then led us on to an explanation of what we called the *marginal cost equation*, i.e. $S - V = F + P$. This equation can be used as the basis for a number of other simple equations that are useful in contribution analysis. The main ones are summarized below.

| | *Abbreviation:* |
|---|---|
| • Sales – variable cost of sales = contribution | $S - V = C$ |
| • Contribution – fixed costs = profit/(loss) | $C - F = P/(L)$ |
| • Break-even (B/E) point = contribution – fixed costs | $C - F$ |
| • B/E in sales value terms = $\dfrac{\text{fixed costs} \times \text{sales}}{\text{contribution}}$ | $\dfrac{F \times S}{C}$ |
| • B/E in units = $\dfrac{\text{fixed costs}}{\text{contribution per unit}}$ | $\dfrac{F}{C \text{ per unit}}$ |
| • Margin of safety (M/S) in sales value terms = $\dfrac{\text{profit} \times \text{sales}}{\text{contribution}}$ | $\dfrac{P \times S}{C}$ |
| • M/S in units = $\dfrac{\text{profit}}{\text{contribution per unit}}$ | $\dfrac{P}{C \text{ per unit}}$ |

Example 19.8 illustrates the use of some of these formulae.

**Example 19.8**

### The use of the marginal cost formulae

The following information relates to Happy Limited for the year to 30 June 2009.

*Number of units sold*: 10 000

| | *Per unit* | *Total* |
|---|---|---|
| | *£* | *£000* |
| Sales | 30 | 300 |
| *Less*: Variable costs | 18 | 180 |
| Contribution | 12 | 120 |
| *Less*: Fixed costs | | 24 |
| Profit | | 96 |

*Required*:
In value and unit terms, calculate the following:
(a) the break-even position
(b) the margin of safety.

**Answer to Example 19.8**

(a) Break-even position in value terms:

$$\frac{F \times S}{C} = \frac{£24\,000 \times 300\,000}{120\,000} = \underline{£60\,000}$$

Break-even in units:

$$\frac{F}{C \text{ per unit}} = \frac{£24\,000}{12} = \underline{2000 \text{ units}}$$

(b) Margin of safety in value terms:

$$\frac{P \times S}{C} = \frac{£96\,000 \times 300\,000}{120\,000} = \underline{£240\,000}$$

Margin of safety in units:

$$\frac{P}{C \text{ per unit}} = \frac{£96\,000}{12} = \underline{8000 \text{ units}}$$

*Tutorial note*

Note the relationship between the sales revenue and the margin of safety. The sales revenue is £300 000 and £60 000 of sales revenue is required to break even. The margin of safety is, therefore, £240 000 (£300 000 – 60 000).

**Activity 19.8**

Using the data in Example 19.8 prepare (a) a break-even chart; and (b) a profit/volume chart.

It would now be helpful to incorporate the principles behind contribution analysis into a simple example. Example 19.9 outlines a typical problem that a board of directors might well face.

**Example 19.9**

## Marginal costing

Looking ahead to the financial year ending 31 March 2009, the directors of Problems Limited are faced with a budgeted loss of £10 000. This is based on the following data.

*Budgeted number of units*: 10 000

| | *£000* |
|---|---|
| Sales revenue | 100 |
| *Less*: Variable costs | 80 |
| Contribution | 20 |
| *Less*: Fixed costs | 30 |
| Budgeted loss | (10) |

The directors would like to aim for a profit of £20 000 for the year to 31 March 2009. Various proposals have been put forward, none of which require a change in the budgeted level of fixed costs. These proposals are as follows:

1 Reduce the selling price of each unit by 10 per cent.
2 Increase the selling price of each unit by 10 per cent.
3 Stimulate sales by improving the quality of the product, which would increase the variable cost of the unit by £1.50 per unit.

Example 19.9 *continued*

*Required*:

(a) For each proposal calculate:
   (i) the break-even position in units in value terms;
   (ii) the number of units required to be sold in order to meet the profit target.

(b) State which proposal you think should be adopted.

Answer to Example 19.9

**Problems Limited**

**(a) (i) and (ii)**

| *Workings*: | £ |
|---|---|
| Profit target | 20 000 |
| Fixed costs | 30 000 |
| Total contribution required | 50 000 |

The budgeted selling price per unit is £10 (£100 000/10 000). The budgeted variable cost per unit is £8 (£80 000/10 000).

The budgeted outlook compared with each proposal may be summarized as follows:

| *Per unit*: | *Budgeted position* | *Proposal* 1 | *Proposal* 2 | *Proposal* 3 |
|---|---|---|---|---|
| | £ | £ | £ | £ |
| Selling price | 10 | 9 | 11 | 10.00 |
| *Less*: Variable costs | 8 | 8 | 8 | 9.50 |
| (a) Unit contribution | 2 | 1 | 3 | 0.50 |
| (b) Total contribution required to break even (= fixed costs) | £30 000 | £30 000 | £30 000 | £30 000 |
| (c) Total contribution required to meet the profit target | £50 000 | £50 000 | £50 000 | £50 000 |
| Number of units to break even [(b)/(a)] | 15 000 | 30 000 | 10 000 | 60 000 |
| Number of units to meet the profit target [(c)/(a)] | 25 000 | 50 000 | 16 667 | 100 000 |

**(b) Comments**

1 By continuing with the present budget proposals, the company would need to sell 15 000 units to break even, or 25 000 units to meet the profit target. So in order to break even the company needs to increase its unit sales by 50% $\left(\frac{£15\,000 - 10\,000}{10\,000} \times 100\right)$ and by 150% $\left(\frac{£25\,000 - 10\,000}{10\,000} \times 100\right)$ to meet the profit target.

2 A reduction in selling price of 10% per unit would require unit sales to increase by 200% $\left(\frac{£30\,000 - 10\,000}{10\,000} \times 100\right)$ in order to break even and by 400% $\left(\frac{£50\,000 - 10\,000}{10\,000} \times 100\right)$ to meet the profit target.

**Answer to Example 19.9** *continued*

3 By increasing the selling price of each unit by 10%, the company would only have to sell at the budgeted level to break even, but its unit sales would have to increase by 66.7% $\left(\frac{£16\,667 - 10\,000}{10\,000} \times 100\right)$ to meet the profit target.

4 By improving the product at an increased variable cost of £1.50 per unit, the company would require a 500% $\left(\frac{£60\,000 - 10\,000}{10\,000} \times 100\right)$ increase in unit sales to break even, or a 900% $\left(\frac{£100\,000 - 10\,000}{10\,000} \times 100\right)$ increase to meet the profit target.

**Conclusion**

It would appear that increasing the selling price by 10% would be a more practical solution for the company to adopt. In the short run, at least, it will break even and there is the possibility that sales could be sufficient to make a small profit. In the long run this proposal has a much better chance of meeting the profit target than do the other proposals. Some extra stimulus would be needed, however, to lift sales to this level over such a relatively short period of time. It is not clear why an increase in price would increase sales, unless the product is one that only sells at a comparatively high price, such as cosmetics and patent medicines. It must also be questioned whether the cost relationships will remain as indicated in the example over such a large increase in activity. In particular, it is unlikely that the fixed costs will remain entirely fixed if there were to be a 66.7% increase in sales.

## Limiting factors

When optional decisions are being considered, the aim will always be to maximize contribution because the greater the contribution then the more chance there is of covering the fixed costs and of making a profit. When managers are faced with a choice, therefore, between (say) producing product A at a contribution of £10 per unit or of producing product B at a contribution of £20 per unit, they would normally choose product B. Sometimes, however, it may not be possible to produce unlimited quantities of product B because there could be limits on how many units could either be sold or produced. Such limits are known as *limiting factors* (or key factors).

Limiting factors may arise for a number of reasons. It may not be possible, for example, to sell more than a certain number of units, there may be production restraints (such as shortages of raw materials, skilled labour or factory space), or the company may not be able to finance the anticipated rate of expansion.

If there is a product that cannot be produced and sold in unlimited quantities, then it is necessary to follow a simple rule in order to decide which product to concentrate on producing. The rule can be summarized:

**choose the work that provides the maximum contribution per unit of limiting factor employed.**

This sounds very complicated but it is easy to apply in practice. In outline, the procedure is as follows (we will assume that direct labour hours are in short supply).

1 Calculate the contribution made by each product.
2 Divide the contribution that each product makes by the number of direct labour hours used in making each product.
3 This gives the contribution per direct labour hour employed (i.e. the limiting factor).
4 Select the project that gives the highest contribution per unit of limiting factor.

So, if we had to choose between two jobs (say) A and B, we would convert A's contribution and B's contribution into the amount of contribution earned for every direct labour hour worked on A and on B respectively. We would then opt for the job that earned the most contribution per direct labour hour. The technique is illustrated in Example 19.10.

**Example 19.10**

### Application of key factors

Quays Limited manufactures a product for which there is a shortage of the raw material known as PX. During the year to 31 March 2009, only 1000 kilograms of PX will be available. PX is used by Quays in manufacturing both product 8 and product 9. The following information is relevant:

| *Per unit:* | *Product 8* | *Product 9* |
|---|---|---|
| | £ | £ |
| Selling price | 300 | 150 |
| *Less:* Variable costs | 200 | 100 |
| *Contribution* | 100 | 50 |
| P/V ratio $\left(\frac{£100}{300} \times 100\right)$ and $\left(\frac{£50}{150} \times 100\right)$ | $33\frac{1}{3}$ | $33\frac{1}{3}$ |
| Kilograms of PX required | 5 | 2 |

*Required:*
State which product Quays Limited should concentrate on producing.

**Answer to Example 19.10**

| | *Product 8* | *Product 9* |
|---|---|---|
| | £ | £ |
| Contribution per unit | 100 | 50 |
| | ÷ | ÷ |
| Limiting factor per unit (kg) | 5 | 2 |
| Contribution per kilogram | = 20 | = 25 |

*Decision*:
Quays should concentrate on product 9 because it gives the highest contribution per unit of limiting factor.

*Check*:
Maximum contribution of product 8:

200 units (1000kg/5) × contribution per unit = 200 × £100 = £20 000

Maximum contribution of product 9:

500 units (1000kg/2) × contribution per unit = 500 × £50 = £25 000

In Example 19.10 it was assumed that there was only one limiting factor, but there could be many more. This situation is illustrated in Example 19.11. The basic data are the same as for Example 19.10.

Example 19.11

## Marginal costing using two key factors

*Information*:

1 Assume now that it is not possible for Quays Limited to sell more than 400 units of product 9.
2 The company would aim to sell all of the 400 units because product 9's contribution per unit of limiting factor is greater than product 8's. The total contribution would then be £20 000 (400 × £50).
3 The 400 units would consume 800 units of raw materials (400 × 2 kilograms), leaving 200 (1000 – 800) kilograms for use in producing product 8.
4 Product 8 requires 5 kilograms per unit of raw materials, so 40 units (200kg ÷ 5kg) could be completed at a total contribution of £4000 (40 × £100).

*Summary of the position*:

| | *Product 8* | *Product 9* | *Total* |
|---|---|---|---|
| Units sold | 40 | 400 | |
| Raw materials (kilograms used) | 200 | 800 | 1 000 |
| Contribution per unit (£) | 100 | 50 | |
| Total contribution (£) | 4 000 | 20 000 | 24 000 |

*Note*: The £24 000 total contribution compares with the contribution of £25 000 that the company could have made if there were no limiting factors affecting the sales of product 9.

Activity 19.9

A few examples of limiting factors are given in the text. Make a list of them. Now think about the concept. An entity will choose to make and sell as many units as it can of those products that make the highest contribution per unit of limiting factor. What other specific factors (think of finance, land, labour, management, materials and premises) might stop it from doing so? Add them to your list.

## ! Questions non-accountants should ask

When you have a specific decision to take as a manager, it is almost certain that your accountants will do the detailed calculative work for you. They are likely to present you with a summary of their results and their recommendations.

We will assume that you have asked them for some guidance on a specific decision that you have to take. What should you ask them when you receive the information? The following questions are suggested, although you will, of course, need to adapt them depending on the circumstances.

- Where have you got the basic data from?
- What estimates have you had to make in adapting the original data?

- Has the information been compiled on a contribution basis?
- If not, why not? What other method have you used? Why is the contribution approach not appropriate in this case?
- If the contribution approach has been used, how have the variable costs been separated from the fixed costs?
- Have you assumed that variable costs move in direct proportion to sales revenue?
- Over what timescale are the fixed costs fixed?
- Over what time period will the various cost relationships last?
- What impact will your recommendations have on other aspects of the business?
- What non-quantifiable factors have you been able to take into account?
- What non-quantifiable factors have been ignored?
- Generally, how reliable is the information that you have given me?
- What confidence can I have in it?
- Is there anything else that I should know?

## Conclusion

Contribution analysis is particularly useful in short-term decision making, but it is of less value when decisions have to be viewed over the long term. The system revolves around two main assumptions:

- some costs remain fixed, irrespective of the level of activity;
- other costs vary in direct proportion to sales.

These assumptions are not valid over the long term but provided that they are used with caution then they can be adopted usefully in the short term.

It should also be remembered that the technique is only a *guide* to decision making and that non-cost factors have to be taken into account.

In the next chapter we use contribution analysis to deal with other managerial problems.

### Key points

1. Total cost can be analysed into fixed costs and variable costs.
2. Fixed costs are assumed to be unrelated to activity. They may be ignored in making short-term managerial decisions.
3. A company will aim to maximize the *contribution* that each unit makes to profit.
4. The various relationships between costs can be expressed in the form of an equation: $S - V = F + P$, where $S$ = sales, $V$ = variable costs, $F$ = fixed costs and $P$ = profit.
5. It may not always be possible to maximize unit contribution because materials, labour, finance or other factors may be in short supply.
6. In the long run, fixed costs cannot be ignored.

## Check your learning

*The answers to these questions can be found within the text.*

1 What system of costing is normally used for the costing of products and for stock valuation purposes?

2 Why is this system not suitable for specific decision making?

3 What is meant by 'decision making'?

4 What term is given to the extra cost of a phenomenon?

5 What is meant by 'incremental costing'?

6 What is (a) a fixed cost, (b) a variable cost?

7 What is meant by the term 'contribution'?

8 What is the marginal cost equation?

9 List four main assumptions that underpin marginal costing.

10 What is a break-even chart?

11 What is meant by the terms (a) 'break-even', (b) 'angle of incidence', (c) 'margin of safety'?

12 What is a contribution graph?

13 What is a profit/volume chart?

14 List six assumptions that are adopted when preparing a marginal cost statement.

15 What is the formula for calculating (a) the break-even position in sales value terms, (b) the break-even position in units, (c) the margin of safety in sales value terms, (d) the margin of safety in units?

16 What is meant by a 'limiting factor'?

17 Give three examples of limiting factors.

18 State the rule that is used when activity is restricted by the presence of a limiting factor.

## News story quiz

*Remember that news story at the beginning of this chapter? Go back to that story and re-read it before answering the following questions.*

This is an interesting article apparently illustrating the marginal cost technique. It would appear that the National Audit Office does recognize the distinction between fixed costs and variable costs, but it is not clear how they have been able to do this for royal flight on an *individual* basis.

### Questions

1 How far do you agree with the article's subtitle that it will have been possible for the NAO to have calculated the 'true'cost of MPs' trips?

2 How do you think the NAO has been able to isolate the fixed costs associated with each of the Prime Minister's, the Chancellor of the Exchequer's and the Environment Secretary's trips on the royal flight?

3 By attaching the fixed costs to each flight is it fair to describe them as 'fixed'?

4 In what circumstances would it be possible to charge the so-called fixed costs to each flight?

## Tutorial questions

*The answers to questions marked with an asterisk can be found in Appendix 4.*

19.1 'It has been suggested that although contribution analysis is fine in theory, fixed costs cannot be ignored in practice.' Discuss this statement.

19.2 'Contribution analysis described in textbooks is too simplistic and is of little relevance to management.' How far do you agree with this statement?

19.3 Do break-even charts and profit graphs help management to make more meaningful decisions?

19.4* The following information relates to Pole Limited for the year to 31 January 2009.

| | *£000* |
|---|---|
| Administration expenses: | |
| Fixed | 30 |
| Variable | 7 |
| Semi-variable (fixed 80%, variable 20%) | 20 |
| Materials: | |
| Direct | 60 |
| Indirect | 5 |
| Production overhead (all fixed) | 40 |
| Research and development expenditure: | |
| Fixed | 60 |
| Variable | 15 |
| Semi-variable (fixed 50%, variable 50%) | 10 |
| Sales | 450 |
| Selling and distribution expenditure: | |
| Fixed | 80 |
| Variable | 4 |
| Semi-variable (fixed 70%, variable 30%) | 30 |
| Wages: | |
| Direct | 26 |
| Indirect | 13 |

*Required*:
Using the above information, compile a contribution analysis statement for Pole Limited for the year to 31 January 2009.

**19.5*** You are presented with the following information for Giles Limited for the year to 28 February 2009:

| | *£000* |
|---|---|
| Fixed costs | 150 |
| Variable costs | 300 |
| Sales (50 000 units) | 500 |

*Required:*
(a) Calculate the following:
  (i) the break-even point in value terms and in units
  (ii) the margin of safety in value terms and in units.
(b) Prepare a break-even chart.

**19.6** The following information applies to Ayre Limited for the two years to 31 March 2008 and 2009, respectively:

| *Year* | *Sales* | *Profits* |
|---|---|---|
| | *£000* | *£000* |
| 31.3.2008 | 750 | 100 |
| 31.3.2009 | 1 000 | 250 |

*Required:*
Assuming that the cost relationships had remained as given in the question, calculate the company's profit if the sales for the year to 31 March 2009 had reached the budgeted level of £1 200 000.

**19.7** The following information relates to Carter Limited for the year to 30 April 2009:

| | |
|---|---|
| Units sold: 50 000 | |
| Selling price per unit | £40 |
| Net profit per unit | £9 |
| Profit/volume ratio | 40% |

During 2010 the company would like to increase its sales substantially, but to do so it would have to reduce the selling price per unit by 20 per cent. The variable cost per unit will not change, but because of the increased activity the company will have to invest in new machinery which will increase the fixed costs by £30 000 per annum.

*Required:*
Given the new conditions, calculate how many units the company will need to sell in 2010 in order to make the same amount of profit as it did in 2009.

**19.8** Puzzled Limited would like to increase its sales during the year to 31 May 2009. To do so, it has several mutually exclusive options open to it:

- reduce the selling price per unit by 15 per cent;
- improve the product resulting in an increase in the variable cost per unit of £1.30;
- spend £15 000 on an advertising campaign;
- improve factory efficiency by purchasing more machinery at a fixed extra annual cost of £22 500.

During the year to 31 May 2008, the company sold 20 000 units. The cost details were as follows:

| | *£000* |
|---|---|
| Sales | 200 |
| Variable costs | 150 |
| Contribution | 50 |
| Fixed costs | 40 |
| Profit | 10 |

These cost relationships are expected to hold in 2009.

*Required*:
State which option you would recommend and why.

19.9 The following information relates to Mere's budget for the year to 31 December 2009:

| | *Product* | | | |
|---|---|---|---|---|
| | *K* | *L* | *M* | *Total* |
| | *£000* | *£000* | *£000* | *£000* |
| Sales | 700 | 400 | 250 | 1350 |
| Direct materials | 210 | 60 | 30 | 300 |
| Direct labour | 100 | 200 | 200 | 500 |
| Variable overhead | 90 | 60 | 50 | 200 |
| Fixed overhead | 20 | 40 | 40 | 100 |
| | 420 | 360 | 320 | 1100 |
| Profit/(loss) | 280 | 40 | (70) | 250 |
| Budgeted sales (units) | 140 | 20 | 25 | |

*Note*: Fixed overheads are apportioned on the basis of direct labour hours.

The directors are worried about the loss that product M is budgeted to make and various suggestions have been made to counteract the loss, viz.:

- stop selling product M;
- increase M's selling price by 20 per cent;
- reduce M's selling price by 10 per cent;
- reduce its costs by purchasing a new machine costing £350 000, thereby decreasing the direct labour cost by £100 000 (the machine would have a life of five years; its residual value would be nil).

*Required*:
Evaluate each of these proposals.

**Further practice questions, study material and links to relevant sites on the World Wide Web can be found on the website that accompanies this book. The site can be found at www.pearsoned.co.uk/dyson**

# Chapter 20 Decision making

## How do you price a new product . . .?

### Picture messaging still too expensive

**Four times the cost of an SMS is silly money, say users**

**Iain Thomson**

The relatively high prices charged by network operators for MMS messages is holding back market growth, according to new research from analyst firm Informa Telecoms & Media.

Operators are currently charging four times as much to send an MMS compared to a text message.

'Pricing is fundamental to the success of MMS. Subscribers are still unwilling to pay the comparatively higher tariffs for MMS and, until the price ratio with SMS narrows, traffic volumes will remain low,' said Kester Mann, senior research analyst at Informa Telecoms & Media.

'Interoperability, ease of use, handset penetration and service development are other important factors, but pricing will remain key in the long term.'

Although MMS traffic quadrupled in 2005, only three operators recorded more than 100 million MMS messages sent. This compares to 30 billion text messages in the UK alone last year.

China Mobile, the world's largest operator, recorded total SMS traffic of 62.8 billion in the third quarter of 2005, 800 times higher than its MMS traffic of 78.6 million messages.

*Accountancy Age*, 13 January 2006.



*Questions relating to this news story can be found on page 416*

## About this chapter

In the previous chapter we suggested that the use of absorption costing in most decision-making situations may lead to some unwise decisions. We suggested that a contribution approach using marginal costing would normally be more appropriate. Marginal costing involves classifying costs on a fixed/variable basis, instead of as in absorption costing on a direct/indirect basis. There are, however, other ways of classifying costs and we outline some of them in this chapter.

The chapter also uses our overall knowledge of management accounting to examine some specific decision-making situations. We cover four main types of decisions:

- those that involve determining whether to close or shut down a plant or a factory;
- those that involve deciding whether we supply or make our own materials and components;
- those that involve determining what price to charge for our goods and services;
- those that involve deciding what price to charge for one-off or special orders.

**Learning objectives**

By the end of this chapter, you should be able to:

- outline the nature of decision making;
- list six ways of classifying costs for decision-making purposes;
- incorporate cost and financial data into specific decision-making situations.

## Why this chapter is important for non-accountants

The previous chapter was one of the most important in the book and this one is also very important. It tells you a little more about decision making and the classification of costs. It then uses some numerical examples to illustrate the particular direction that various decisions should take.

The chapter is heavily biased towards helping you as a non-accountant to make and take effective decisions. This means that it is *essential* if you are to become an all-round first-class manager.

## Nature and purpose

We start our examination of this important topic by examining the nature and purpose of decision making.

The term *decision* will be familiar to you in your everyday life. It means coming to a conclusion about a particular issue, e.g. deciding when to get up in the morning, whether to have tea or coffee for breakfast, or choosing between a holiday and buying some new clothes. Similarly, in a managerial context, decisions have to be taken about whether or not to sell in particular markets, buy some new machinery or spend more money on research.

Management accountants will be involved in collecting data and supplying information for such decisions. While the information that they supply will be primarily of a financial nature, they will highlight other considerations that need to be taken into account before a decision is made. The eventual decision will rest with the segmental manager concerned. It may well be that non-cost factors turn out to be more important than measurable financial considerations. For example, an entity may buy components from an external supplier because they are cheaper. But what happens if the supplier becomes unreliable? It might then be worth the extra cost of manufacturing the components internally in order to avoid the risk of any disruption to normal production.

The information required for decision-making purposes tends to be more wide-ranging and less constrained than that used in cost accounting. Its main characteristics are summarized below and are also shown in Figure 20.1.

- *Forward looking*. While historical data may be used as a guide, information for decision making is much more concerned with what *will* happen rather than with what *did* happen. As so much of the information required is concerned with the future, considerable initiative and intuitive judgement is required in being able to obtain it.
- *One-off decisions*. Decision making often involves dealing with a problem that is unique. So a solution has to be geared towards dealing with that particular problem.
- *Data availability*. While some of the data required for decision making may be extracted from the cost accounting system, much of what is required may have to be specially obtained.

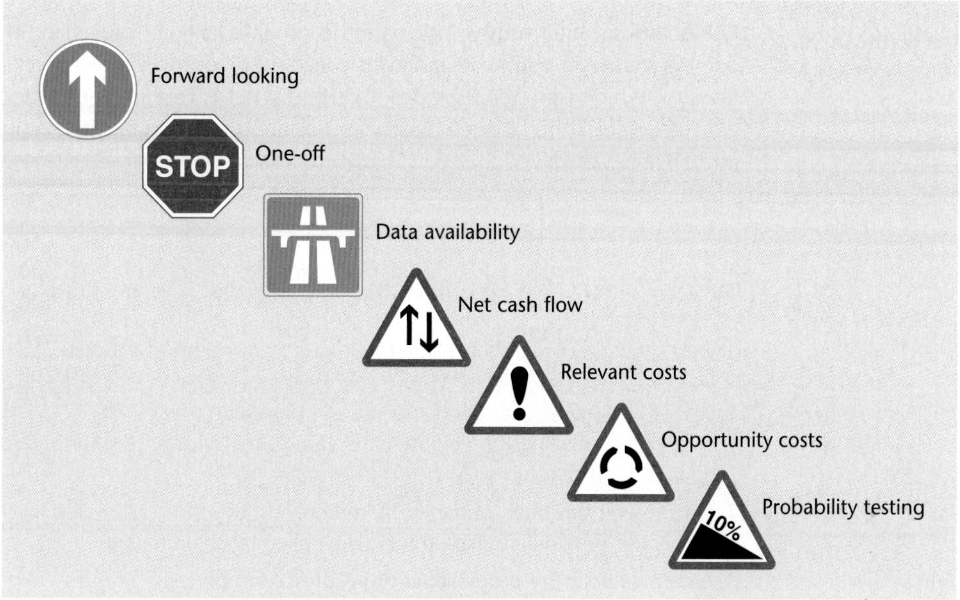


**Figure 20.1 The nature of decision making**

- *Net cash flow approach.* Managers will be concerned with the impact that a decision may have on the expected net cash flow of a particular project (i.e. future cash receipts less future cash expenditure). The calculation of periodic profit and loss based on accruals and prepayments will be largely irrelevant.
- *Relevant costs.* Costs and revenues that are not affected by a decision are excluded from the analysis. For example, fixed costs would normally be ignored because they are not likely to change.
- *Opportunity costs.* Those benefits that would be foregone or lost as a result of taking a particular decision are known as opportunity costs. They form an important part of any decision-making analysis. You may decide, for example, to look after your own garden yourself instead of doing some paid overtime. The opportunity cost would be the wages or salary you lose by not working overtime less the amount you save by not employing a gardener.
- *Probability testing.* Much of the information used in problem solving is speculative because it relates to the future and so it is advisable to carry out some probability testing. This is an extremely complex area and it goes beyond this book. In broad terms it involves calculating the *expected value* of a particular project or proposal. The basic idea is demonstrate in Example 20.1.

Example 20.1

## Probability testing

Company X sells one product codenamed A1. The marketing department has estimated that the sales of A1 for a forthcoming budget period could be £1000, £1500 or £2000. On further investigation it would appear that there is a 70 per cent chance that the sales will be £1000, a 20 per cent chance that the sales will be £1500 and a 10 per cent chance that the sales will be £2000.

*Required*:
Calculate the expected value of sales for product A1 during the forthcoming budget period.

**Answer to Example 20.1**

The question requires us to calculate the expected value of the sales of A1 for the forthcoming period. It might be easier for you to think of the expected value as the *weighted average*, which perhaps provides a clue to what is required. In order to calculate the expected values the budgeted sales figures are multiplied by their respective chances or probabilities. Thus:

| *Budgeted sales* (1) | *Probability* (2) | *Expected value* (3) |
|---|---|---|
| £ | % | £ |
| 1 000 | 70 | 700 |
| 1 500 | 20 | 300 |
| 2 000 | 10 | 200 |
| | 100 | 1 200 |

*Tutorial notes*

1 The expected value (or weighted average) of the sales for the forthcoming budget period is £1200 as per column (3).

2 The answer has been obtained by multiplying the three estimated levels of sales by their respective probabilities (column (1) multiplied by column (2)).

3 In this exhibit, the probabilities are expressed in percentage terms. When combined they should always total 100 per cent. Note that sometimes they are expressed in decimal terms; they should then total 1.0, in our example 0.7 + 0.2 + 0.1 = 1.0

4 The probabilities are estimates. They may be made partly on past experience, partly on an investigation of the market and partly on instinct. In other words they might be better described as 'guesstimates'.

5 Does the solution make sense? The expected value is £1200; this is £200 more than the lowest level of sales of £1000; the probability of this level being achieved is 70 per cent. So the chance of the sales being at least £1000 is quite high. By contrast, there is only a 20 per cent probability that the sales could be as high as £1500 and only a 10 per cent chance that they could reach £2000. It seems reasonable to assume, therefore, that the sales are likely to be nearer £1000 than £1500. So £1200 appears to be a reasonable compromise.

## Cost classification

As we have demonstrated in previous chapters, costs and revenues may be classified into various categories depending upon the purpose for which they are going to be used. In cost accounting, information is required mainly for product costing and stock valuation purposes, and so the most important category is the distinction between direct costs and indirect ones.

A direct/indirect cost classification is not normally appropriate in decision making. The preferred classification is that relating to fixed and variable costs but you will come across other cost classifications. We show the main ones used in decision making in Figure 20.2 along with a brief explanation of them below.

### Fixed and variable costs

We covered such costs in the previous chapter. Fixed costs are those that are likely to remain unchanged irrespective of the level of activity. Variable costs are those that move directly proportional to activity – one unit results in £1 of variable cost, two units results in £2 of variable cost, three units in £3 of variable cost and so on.

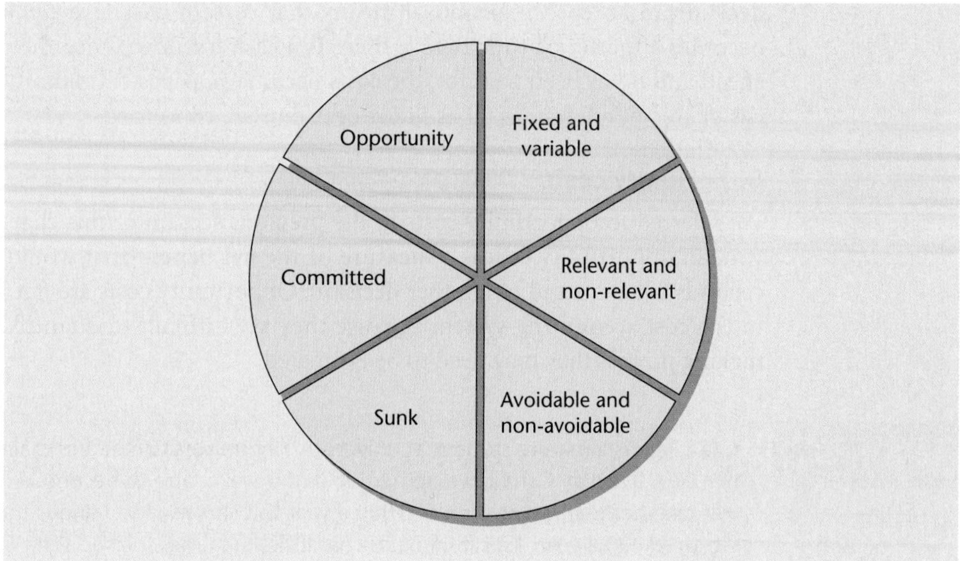


**Figure 20.2 Cost classification**

In theory, those costs classified as 'fixed' will remain the same irrespective of whether the entity is completely inactive or if it is operating at full capacity. In practice, fixed costs tend to remain fixed only over a relatively small range of activity range and only in the short term.

The assumption that fixed costs remain unchanged means that they do not normally need to be taken into account. In other words, they can be ignored because they will not be affected by the decision and they are not relevant in any consideration of the issues.

### Relevant and non-relevant costs

Relevant costs are those future costs that are likely to be affected by a particular decision. It follows that non-relevant costs are those that are *not* likely to be affected by the decision. This means that non-relevant costs can be excluded from any cost analysis, e.g. fixed costs although they are not always irrelevant.

### Avoidable and non-avoidable costs

Avoidable costs are those that may be saved by not taking a particular decision. Non-avoidable costs will still be incurred if the decision is taken. Avoidable and non-avoidable costs are very similar to relevant and non-relevant costs and sometimes the terms are used synonymously.

### Sunk costs

Sunk costs are those that have already been incurred as a result of a previous decision. So they are not relevant as far as future decisions are concerned and they can be excluded from any decision-making analysis.

### Committed costs

A committed cost arises out of a decision that has previously been taken, although the event has not yet taken place. For example, a proposal to increase the capacity of a factory from 1000 to 1500 units per annum will result in increased capital expenditure. A decision to accept the proposal means that certain costs are *committed* and it only becomes a matter of time before there is a cash outflow. Once the proposal has gone ahead and it has been paid for, the costs become *sunk* costs. Committed costs (like sunk costs) are not relevant as far as *future* decisions are concerned.

### Opportunity costs

We referred to opportunity costs in the previous section of this chapter. Just to remind you, an opportunity cost is a measure of the net benefit that would be lost if one decision is taken instead of another decision. Opportunity costs are not normally recorded in the cost accounting system because they are difficult to quantify, so in a decision-making process they may need to be estimated.

**Activity 20.1**

Carla Friar is a mature student at university. Her university fees and maintenance cost her £7000 a year. Carla gave up her job in a travel centre to become a full-time student. Her take-home pay was then £20 000 a year but she also lost various travel concessions worth £1000 a year. As a student she has little free time, she socializes infrequently and so she does not spend much. This saves her about £2000 a year but, of course, she misses her friends and her nights out.

What factors do you think that Carla should take into account if she tried to work out the opportunity cost of becoming a student?

## Types of decisions

We now turn to some specific decisions that managers may have to take. They are shown in diagrammatic format in Figure 20.3. The figure is followed by an explanation of each decision. The purchase of capital assets is another important decision that managers have to take but we leave this topic to the next chapter as we need more space to discuss it.

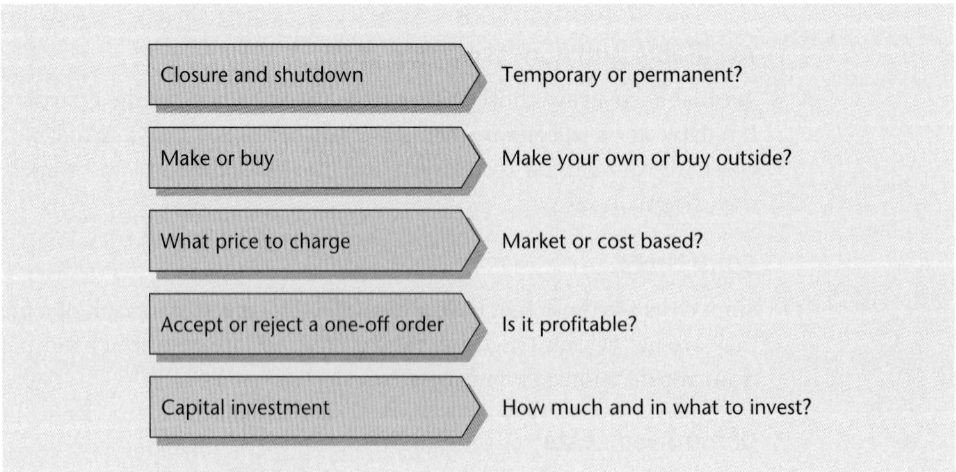


Figure 20.3 **Types of decisions**

## Closure and shutdown decision

A common problem that managers may face from time to time is whether to close some segment of the enterprise, such as a product, a service, a department or even an entire factory. This is a *closure* decision, the assumption being that the closure would be permanent. A similar decision may have to be taken in respect of a temporary closure. This is known as a *shutdown* decision.

A closure decision sometimes needs to be taken because a segment within the overall entity may have become unprofitable, out of date or unfashionable and therefore no future is seen for it. A decision to close a segment of an entity temporarily would be taken when the segment's problems are likely to be overcome in the near future. So a segment may be unprofitable at the moment but is expected to recover in (say) a year's time.

Closure and shutdown decisions are often required because a segment is regarded as being 'unprofitable'. The definition of 'unprofitable' has to be looked at very closely. A product, for example, may not be making a *profit* but it may be making a *contribution* towards the fixed costs of the company. Should it be abandoned? Great care would need to be taken before such a decision was taken. The abandonment of one product may have an impact on the sales of other products in such circumstances, it may even be beneficial to sell the product below its variable cost (at least in the short term).

Closure and shutdown decisions are not easy to make because they often require staff to be made redundant. They cannot be determined purely on narrow cost grounds, as other wide-ranging factors may need to be considered. We illustrate a relatively straightforward closure decision in Example 20.2.

**Example 20.2**

### A closure decision

Vera Limited has three main product lines: 1, 2 and 3. The company uses an absorption costing system, and the following information relates to the budget for the year 2009.

| *Product line* | *1* | *2* | *3* | *Total* |
|---|---|---|---|---|
| Budgeted sales (units) | 10 000 | 4 000 | 6 000 | |
| | *£000* | *£000* | *£000* | *£000* |
| Sales revenue | 300 | 200 | 150 | 650 |
| Direct materials | 100 | 40 | 60 | 200 |
| Direct labour | 50 | 70 | 80 | 200 |
| Production overhead | 75 | 30 | 35 | 140 |
| Non-production overhead | 15 | 10 | 5 | 30 |
| | 240 | 150 | 180 | 570 |
| Profit (Loss) | 60 | 50 | (30) | 80 |

*Additional information*:

1 Both direct materials and direct labour are considered to be variable costs.
2 The total production overhead of £140 000 consists of £40 000 variable costs and £100 000 fixed costs. Variable production overheads are absorbed on the basis of 20 per cent of the direct labour costs.
3 The non-production overhead of £30 000 is entirely fixed.
4 Assume that there will be no opening or closing stock.

*Required*:
Determine whether product line 3 should be closed.

**Answer to Example 20.2**

**Points**

1 The first step in determining whether to recommend a closure of product line 3 is to calculate the *contribution* that each product line makes.
2 In order to do so, it is necessary to rearrange the data given in the question in a marginal cost format, i.e. separate the fixed costs from the variable costs.
3 If product line 3 makes a contribution then other factors will have to be taken into account before an eventual decision can be made.

**Calculations**

| *Product line* | *1* | *2* | *3* | *Total* |
|---|---|---|---|---|
| Budgeted sales (units) | 10 000 | 4 000 | 6 000 | |
| | *£000* | *£000* | *£000* | *£000* |
| Sales revenue | 300 | 200 | 150 | 650 |
| *Less*: Variable costs: | | | | |
| Direct materials | 100 | 40 | 60 | 200 |
| Direct labour | 50 | 70 | 80 | 200 |
| Variable production overhead (question note 2: 20% of direct labour cost) | 10 | 14 | 16 | 40 |
| | 160 | 124 | 156 | 440 |
| Contribution | 140 | 76 | (6) | 210 |
| *Less*: Fixed costs: | | | | |
| Production overheads (£140 – 40) | | | | (100) |
| Non-production overheads (See question note 3) | | | | (30) |
| Profit | | | | 80 |

**Observations**

It would appear that product line 3 neither makes a profit nor contributes towards the fixed costs. Should it be closed? Before such a decision is taken a number of other factors would have to be considered. These are as follows.

- Are the budgeted figures accurate? Have they been checked? How reliable are the budgeted data?
- What method has been used to identify the direct material costs that each product line uses? Is it appropriate for all three product lines?
- The question states that direct labour is a variable cost. Is direct labour really a variable cost? Is the assessment of its cost accurate and realistic?
- Variable production overheads are absorbed on a very broad basis related to direct labour costs. Does this method fairly reflect product line 3's use of variable overheads?
- Product line 3 appears to result in only a small negative contribution. Can this be made positive by perhaps a small increase in the unit selling price or by the more efficient use of direct materials and direct labour?
- Assuming that the cost data supplied are both fair and accurate, would the closure of product line 3 affect sales for the other two product lines or the overall variable costs?
- If closure of product line 3 is recommended, should it be closed permanently or temporarily? More information is needed of its prospects beyond 2009.

**The decision**

Clearly, without more information it is impossible to come to a firm conclusion. Assuming that the cost accounting procedures are both accurate and fair, it would appear that *on purely financial grounds*, product line 3 should be closed. However, until we have more information we cannot put this forward as a conclusive recommendation.

## Make or buy decisions

Make or buy decisions require management to determine whether to manufacture internally or purchase externally. Should a car company, for example, manufacture its own components or purchase them from specialist suppliers? Similarly, should a glass manufacturer concentrate on producing glass and purchase its packaging and safety equipment externally? In local government should a housing department employ its own joiners or contract outside firms to do the necessary work? In modern parlance these types of decisions ar known as 'outsourcing'.

The theory beyond make or buy decisions revolves round the argument that entities should do what they are best at doing and employ others to undertake the peripheral activities. In other words, they should concentrate on their main objective and contract out (or 'privatize', in the case of governmental activities) all other essential activities.

A decision to contract out may often be taken simply because it appears to be cheaper to do so. This may be an unwise decision. There could be vital non-financial and non-quantifiable factors that are just as important as cost. For example, it may not be possible to obtain exactly what the company wants, or there could be delays in receiving some vital supplies. Both of these difficulties could cause a breakdown or hold-up to the company's own production. This might ultimately prove to be more expensive than manufacturing internally. So when deciding to make or buy, *all* factors should be built into the analysis, even though it may be difficult to quantify some of them.

A simple make or buy decision is illustrated in Example 20.3.

Example 20.3

### A make or buy decision

Zam Limited uses an important component in one of its products. An estimate of the cost of making one unit of the component internally is as follows.

| | £ |
|---|---|
| Direct materials | 5 |
| Direct labour | 4 |
| Variable overhead | 3 |
| Total variable cost | 12 |

*Additional information*:

1 Fixed costs specifically associated with manufacturing the components are estimated to be £8000 per month.

2 The number of components normally required is 1000 per month.

An outside manufacturer has offered to supply the components at a cost of £18 per component. Should the components be manufactured internally or purchased externally?

*Required*:

Determine whether Zam Limited should purchase the components from the outside supplier.

**Answer to Example 20.3**

**Points**

Assuming that the cost data given in the question are accurate, the first step in answering the question is to calculate the cost of manufacturing the components internally. Although the variable cost of each unit is given, there are some fixed costs directly associated with manufacturing internally and these have to be taken into account.

The fixed costs cause us a problem because the monthly activity levels may vary. However, we can only work on the data given in the question, i.e. 1000 units per month.

**Calculations**

Total cost of manufacturing internally 1000 units per month of the component:

| | £ |
|---|---|
| Total variable cost (1000 units × £12) | 12 000 |
| Associated fixed costs | 8 000 |
| Total cost | 20 000 |
| Total unit cost (£20 000 ÷ 1000) | £20 |

*Tutorial notes*

1 Assuming that Zam Limited requires 1000 units per month, it would be cheaper to obtain them from the external supplier (£20 compared with £18 per component).

2 The above assumption is based on purchases of 1000 units. The more units required, the cheaper they would be to manufacture internally. In order to match the external price, the fixed costs can be no more than £6 per unit (the external purchase price of £18 less the internal variable cost of £12 per unit). If the fixed costs were to be limited to £6 per unit, the company would need to manufacture 1334 units (£8000 ÷ £6). The total cost would then be the same as the external cost (£24 000), but it would involve a one-third increase in the activity level.

3 The cost data should be checked carefully (especially the estimated associated fixed costs) and the monthly activity level reviewed. It might then be possible to put forward a tentative recommendation.

**The decision**

Given the data provided in the question, it would be cheaper to purchase the components externally. This would free some resources within Zam Limited enabling it to concentrate on manufacturing its main product.

However, there are a number of other considerations that need to be taken into account. In particular the following questions would need to be asked.

- How accurate are the cost data?
- How variable is the monthly activity level?
- Is the external supplier's component exactly suited to the company's purposes?
- How reliable is the proposed supplier?
- Are there other suppliers who could be used in an emergency and at what cost?
- What control could be exercised over the quality of the components received?
- How firm is the quoted price of £18 per component, and for what period will that price be maintained?
- How easy would it be to switch back to internal manufacturing if the supplier proved unreliable?

It follows that much more information (largely of a non-cost nature) would be required before a conclusive decision could be taken.

## Pricing decisions

A very important decision that managers have to make in both the profit-making sector and the not-for-profit sector is that relating to pricing. Supermarkets, for example, have to price their goods, while local authorities have to decide what to charge for adult education, leisure centres and meals on wheels.

Two types of pricing decisions can be distinguished. The first relates to the prices charged to customers or clients external to the entity. We will refer to this type as *external* pricing. The second type relates to prices charged by one part of an entity to another part, such as when components are supplied by one segment to another segment. This type of pricing is known as *transfer* pricing. We will deal with each type separately.

### External pricing

External selling prices may be based either on market prices or on cost – see Figure 20.4. We will deal first with market-based prices.

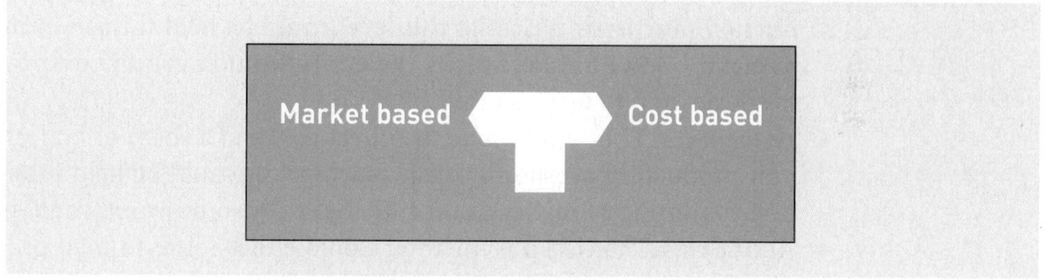


**Figure 20.4 External pricing decisions**

#### *Market-based pricing*

Many goods and services are sold in highly competitive markets. This means that there may be many suppliers offering identical or near-identical products and they will be competing fiercely in respect of price, quality, reliability and service. If the demand for a product is *elastic*, then the lower the price the more units that will be sold. The opposite also applies and higher prices will result in fewer goods being sold. The demand for most everyday items of food, for example, is elastic.

It follows that when demand is elastic it is unlikely that individual sellers can determine their own selling prices. So within narrow limits, they will have to base their selling prices on what is being charged in the market. Otherwise if they charge more than the market price their sales will be reduced. If they charge less than the market then their sales will increase but the market will quickly adjust to a lower level of selling prices.

Where market conditions largely determine a supplier's selling prices, it is particularly important to ensure that tight control is exercised over costs. Otherwise the gap between total sales revenue and total costs (i.e. the profit) will be insufficient to ensure an adequate return on capital employed.

In some cases the demand for goods is *inelastic* – i.e. price has little or no effect on the number of units sold. The demand for writing paper and stationery, for example, tends to be inelastic, perhaps because it is an infrequent purchase and it is not a significant element in most people's budgets. So when the demand for goods is inelastic, suppliers have much more freedom in determining their own selling prices and they may then base them on cost.

### *Cost-based pricing*

There are a number of cost-based pricing methods. We summarize the main ones below and the circumstances in which they are most likely to be used.

- *Below variable cost.* This price would be used:
  - when an entity was trying to establish a new product on the market;
  - when an attempt was being made to drive out competitors;
  - as a loss leader (i.e. to encourage other goods to be bought).

  A price at this level could only be sustained for a very short period (unless it is used as a loss leader) since each unit sold would not be covering its variable cost.
- *At variable cost.* Variable cost prices may be used:
  - to launch a new product;
  - to drive out competition;
  - in difficult trading conditions;
  - as a loss leader. Price could be held for some time but ultimately some contribution will be needed to cover the fixed costs.
- *At total production cost.* This will include the unit's direct costs and a share of the production overheads. Prices at this level could be held for some time (perhaps when demand is low) but eventually the entity would need to cover its non-production overheads and to make a profit.
- *At total cost.* This will include the direct cost and a share of both the production and non-production overheads. Again, such prices could be held for a very long period, perhaps during a long recession, but eventually some profit would need to be earned.
- *At cost plus.* The cost-plus method would either relate to total production cost or to total cost. The 'plus' element would be an addition to the cost to allow for non-production overhead and profit (in the case of total production cost) and for profit alone (in the case of total cost). In the long run, cost-plus prices are the only option for a profit-making entity. However, if prices are based entirely on cost then inefficiencies may be automatically built into the pricing system and this could lead to uncompetitiveness.

## Transfer pricing

In large entities it is quite common for one segment to trade with another segment. So what is 'revenue' to one segment will be 'expenditure' to the other. This means that when the results of all the various segments are consolidated, the revenue recorded in one segment's books of account will cancel out the expenditure in the other segment's books. Does it matter, therefore, what prices are charged for internal transfers?

The answer is 'Yes it does' because some segments (particularly if they are divisions of companies) are given a great deal of autonomy. They may have the authority, for example, to purchase goods and services from outside the entity. They almost certainly will do so if the price and service offered externally appears to be superior to any internal offer and this may cause them to suboptimize, i.e. to act in *their* own best interest, although it may not be in the best interests of the entity as a whole.

Let us suppose that segment A fixes its transfer price on a cost-plus basis, say at £10 per unit. Segment B finds that it can purchase an identical unit externally at £8 per unit. Segment B is very likely to accept the external offer. But segment A's costs may be based on *absorbed costs.* The *extra cost* (i.e. the variable cost) of meeting segment B's order may be much less than the external price of £8 per unit. In these circumstances it may not be beneficial for the *entity as a whole* for segment B to purchase the units from an outside supplier.

It follows that a transfer price should to be set at a level that will encourage a supplying segment to trade internally and to discourage a receiving segment to buy its goods externally. There are various transfer-pricing methods that can be adopted (see Figure 20.5) and we review the main ones below.

- *At market prices.* If there are identical or similar goods and services offered externally, transfer prices based on market prices will neither encourage nor discourage supplying or receiving segments to trade externally.
- *At adjusted market prices.* Market prices may be reduced in recognition of the lower costs attached to internal trading, e.g. advertising, administration and financing costs. This method encourages segments to trade with each other.
- *At total cost or total cost plus.* A transfer price based on total cost will include the direct costs plus a share of both production and non-production overhead. Total cost-plus methods allow for some profit. The main problems attached to the total-cost methods is that they build inefficiencies into the transfer price (as there is no incentive to control costs) and they therefore encourage suboptimization.
- *At variable cost or variable cost plus.* The variable cost method does not encourage a supplying segment to trade internally as no incentive is built into the transfer price, but a percentage addition may provide some incentive since it enables some contribution to be made towards fixed costs. However, transfer prices based on variable costs may be very attractive to *receiving* segments as the transfer price normally compares favourably with the external price.
- *Negotiated prices.* This method involves striking a bargain between the supplying and receiving segments based on a combination of market price and costs. As long as the discussions are mutually determined this method can be highly successful.
- *Opportunity costs.* This method may be somewhat impractical, but if the costs can be quantified it is the ideal one to adopt. A transfer price based on the opportunity cost comprises two elements: first, the standard variable cost in the supplying segment, and second the entity's opportunity cost resulting from the transaction. It is the second element that is the hardest to determine.

**Activity 20.2**

What is the best way out of the transfer price dilemma? Should it be based on market prices or on costs? Suppose as a manager you have the freedom to negotiate your own transfer prices with other divisional managers. Summarize the arguments that you would use in any ensuing discussions.

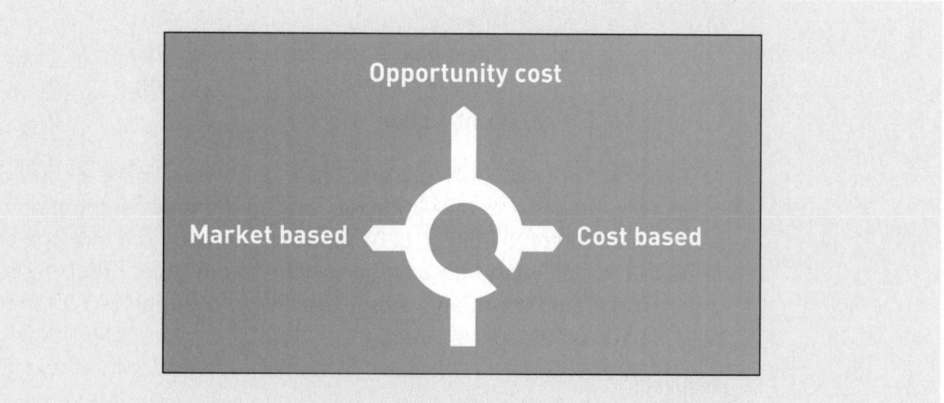


**Figure 20.5 Transfer pricing decisions**

## Special orders

On some occasions an entity may be asked to undertake an order beyond its normal trading arrangement and to quote a price for it. Such arrangements are known as *special orders.* The potential customer or client would normally expect to pay a lower price than the entity ordinarily charges, as well as possibly receiving some favourable treatment. What pricing policy should the entity adopt when asked to quote for a special order?

Much will depend on whether the entity has some surplus capacity or not. If this is the case, it may be prepared to quote a price below variable cost if it wants to avoid a possible shutdown. However, the minimum price that it would *normally* be willing to accept would be equal to the incremental (or extra) cost of fulfilling the order.

The incremental cost involved may be the equivalent of the variable cost. Prices based at or below the variable cost would be extremely competitive, thereby helping to ensure that the customer accepted the quotation. The work gained would then absorb some of the entity's surplus capacity and help to keep its workforce occupied. There is also the possibility that the customer may place future orders at prices that would enable the entity to make a profit on them. But there is then the danger that in the meantime more profitable work has to be rejected because the entity cannot cope with both the special order and the additional work.

A price in excess of the variable cost would make a contribution towards fixed costs and this would clearly be the preferred option. The quoted price would have to be judged very finely because the higher the price the greater the risk that the customer would reject the quotation. So the decision would involve trying to determine what other suppliers are likely to charge and what terms they would offer.

An indication of the difficulties associated with determining whether a special order should be accepted is demonstrated in Example 20.4.

**Example 20.4**

### A special order

Amber Limited has been asked by a customer to supply a specially designed product. The customer has indicated that he would be willing to pay a maximum price of £100 per unit. The cost details are as follows.

| *Unit cost* | £ | £ |
|---|---|---|
| Contract price | | 100 |
| *Less*: Variable costs | | |
| Direct materials | 40 | |
| Direct labour (2 hours) | 30 | |
| Variable overhead | 10 | 80 |
| Contribution | | 20 |

At a contract price of £100 per unit, each unit would make a contribution of £20. The customer is prepared to take 400 units, and so the total contribution towards fixed costs would be £8000 (400 units × £20). However, Amber has a shortage of direct labour and some of the staff would have to be switched from other orders to work on the special order. This would mean an average loss in contribution of £8 for every direct labour hour worked on the special order.

*Required*:
Determine whether Amber Limited should accept the special order.

**Answer to Example 20.4**

In order to determine whether Amber Limited should accept the special order, the extra contribution should be compared with the loss of contribution by having to switch the workforce from other orders. The calculations are as follows.

| | £ |
|---|---|
| Total contribution from the special order (400 units × £20 per unit) | 8 000 |
| *Less*: the opportunity cost of the normal contribution foregone | |
| [800 direct labour hours (400 units × 2 DLH) × £8 per unit] | 6 400 |
| Extra contribution | 1 600 |

***Tutorial notes***

Before coming to a decision, the following points should also be considered. You will see that they range well beyond simple cost factors.

1 The costings relating to the special order should be carefully checked.

2 The customer should be asked to confirm in writing that it would be willing to pay a selling price of £100 per unit.

3 Determine whether the customer is likely to place additional orders for the product or not.

4 Check that the *average* contribution of £8 per direct labour hour, obtained from other orders, applies to the workforce that would be switched to the special order, i.e. is the contribution from the other orders that would be lost more or less than £8 per direct labour hour?

5 Is it possible that new staff could be recruited to work on the special order?

6 Is more profitable work likely to come along in the meantime? Would it mean that it could not be accepted during the progress of the order?

**Recommendation**

Assuming that the points raised in the above notes are satisfied, then the recommendation would be to accept the special order at a price of £100 per unit. This would mean that Amber's total contribution would be increased by £1600.

The management accountant's main role in dealing with special orders would be to supply historical and projected cost data of the financial consequences of particular options. The eventual decision would be taken by senior management using a wide range of quantitative and qualitative information. The type of questions asked would be similar to some of the issues covered in the tutorial notes in the solution to Example 20.4.

## ! Questions non-accountants should ask

The questions that you should put to your accountants about any specific decision-making problem will revolve round the robustness of the data that they have used and any non-quantitative factors they have incorporated into their recommendations. You could use the following as a guide.

- Where have you got the data from?
- How reliable are the basic facts?
- What assumptions have you adopted?
- Have you included only relevant costs?
- Have you tested the results on a probability basis?
- What non-quantitative factors have you been able to identify?
- Is it possible to put any monetary value on them?
- Do you think that we should go ahead with this proposal?

## Conclusion

An important function of the management accountant in the twenty-first century is to assist in managerial decision making. In such a role, the primary task of the accountant is to provide managers with financial and non-financial information in order to help them make more effective decisions. Although the information provided may include much historical data, decision making often means dealing with future events, so the information provided consists of a great deal of speculative material. This means that the management accountant needs to exercise considerable skill and judgement in collecting information that is both accurate and relevant for a particular purpose. Non-relevant information can be ignored as it only obscures the broader picture.

The significance of including only relevant data is seen when managers have to make special decisions, such as whether to close or shut down a segment of an entity, make or provide goods and services internally instead of obtaining them from an outside supplier, determine a selling price for the entity's goods and services, or whether to accept a special order and at what price. These are all-important and complex decisions and managers need reliable information before they can make them.

### Key points

1. Decision making involves having to resolve an outcome for a specific problem.
2. The information required relates to the future, it is specific to the problem, it may have to be collected specially for the task and it is geared towards estimating the future net cash flows of particular outcomes.
3. The information provided to management should include only relevant costs and revenues, with an estimate of any opportunity costs.
4. The data used in a management accounting information report should be subject to some probability testing.
5. The terms 'fixed and variable costs', 'relevant and non-relevant costs', 'avoidable and non-avoidable costs', 'sunk costs', 'committed costs' and 'opportunity costs' are all of special significance in decision making.
6. Closure and shutdown decisions should be based on the contribution earned or likely to be earned on the segment under consideration and compared with the likely closure or shutdown costs.
7. Generally it is more profitable to make goods or to provide services internally than to obtain them externally if their variable cost is less than or equal to external prices.
8. The pricing of goods and services for selling externally will normally be determined by the market price for similar goods and services. In some cases, however, selling prices can be based on cost. Depending on market conditions, the cost could be at or below variable cost, the absorbed or the total absorbed cost, with or without an addition for profit.

9 The internal transfer of goods and services should be based on market price or adjusted market price. Where this is not possible, any price at or in excess of the variable cost should be acceptable.

10 The ideal transfer price is one that is based on the standard variable cost in the supplying segment plus the entity's opportunity cost resulting from the transaction.

11 Special orders should be priced so that they cover their variable cost. There may be some circumstances when it is acceptable to price them below variable cost but this can only be a short-term solution. Any price in excess of variable costs helps to cover the entity's fixed costs.

12 Cost and financial factors are only part of the decision-making process. There are other factors of a non-financial and non-quantifiable nature (such as behavioural factors) that must be taken into account.

## Check your learning

1 Define what is meant by a 'decision'.

2 List seven main characteristics of decision-making data.

3 Identify six ways of classifying costs.

4 What is an opportunity cost?

5 What is meant by a 'closure' or a 'shutdown' decision?

6 What is meant by a 'make or buy' decision?

7 What is meant by a 'pricing' decision?

8 What are the two main types of pricing decisions?

9 What is meant by a 'market' price?

10 List six cost-based pricing methods.

11 What is the basic problem in determining pricing between segments within the same entity?

12 How might it be resolved?

13 What is meant by a 'special order'?

14 How does it differ from the general pricing problem?

## News story quiz

*Remember the news story at the beginning of this chapter? Go back to that story and re-read it before answering the following questions.*

This article helps to emphasize one of the main points made in this chapter – it is very difficult in practice to decide what your selling prices should be, and if you get it wrong you will be in trouble. The article also assumes that readers are familiar with the jargon of the IT world.

### Questions

1 What do the initials MMS and SMS mean?

2 Why do you think MMS network operators have fixed their prices at up to four times the level of text messages?

3 How do you think they arrived at such prices?

4 What recognition do they appear to have given to other factors in fixing their prices?

5 Could it be the product itself, and neither the price nor the other factors mentioned in the article that is holding back the growth in MSS messages?

## Tutorial questions

*The answers to questions marked with an asterisk can be found in Appendix 4.*

20.1 This chapter has emphasized that it is managers that make decisions and not management accountants. How far do you agree with this assertion?

20.2 Many of the solutions to the problems posed in this chapter depend on being able to isolate the variable cost associated with a particular decision. In practice, is it realistic to expect that such costs can be readily identified and measured?

20.3 Assume that you were an IT manager in a large entity, and that the services that you provide are made available to both internal and external parties. Specify how you would go about negotiating an appropriate fee for services sought by other departments within the entity.

20.4* Micro Limited has some spare capacity. It is now considering whether it should accept a special contract to use some of the spare capacity. However, this contract will use some specialist direct labour that is in short supply. The following details relate to the proposed contract:

| | *£000* |
|---|---|
| Contract price | 50 |
| Variable costs: | |
| Direct materials | 10 |
| Direct labour | 30 |

In order to complete the contract, 4000 direct labour hours would be required. The company's budget for the year during which the contract would be undertaken is as follows:

| | £000 |
|---|---|
| Sales | 750 |
| Variable costs | (500) |
| Contribution | 250 |
| Fixed costs | (230) |
| Profit | 20 |

There would be 50 000 direct labour hours available during the year.

*Required:*
Determine whether the special contract should be accepted.

**20.5*** Temple Limited has been offered two new contracts, the details of which are as follows:

| *Contract* | *(1)* | *(2)* |
|---|---|---|
| | *£000* | *£000* |
| Contract price | 1 000 | 2 100 |
| Direct materials | 300 | 600 |
| Direct labour | 300 | 750 |
| Variable overhead | 100 | 250 |
| Fixed overhead | 100 | 200 |
| | 800 | 1 800 |
| Profit | 200 | 300 |
| Direct materials required (kilos) | 50 000 | 100 000 |
| Direct labour hours required | 10 000 | 25 000 |

*Note:*

The fixed overhead has been apportioned on the basis of direct labour cost. Temple is a one-product firm. Its budgeted cost per unit for its normal work for the year to 31 December 2009 is summarized below.

| | £ |
|---|---|
| Sales | 6 000 |
| Direct materials (100 kilos) | 700 |
| Direct labour (200 hours) | 3 000 |
| Variable overhead | 300 |
| Fixed overhead | 1 000 |
| | 5 000 |
| Profit | 1 000 |

The company would only have the capacity to accept one of the new contracts. Unfortunately, materials suitable for use in all of its work are in short supply and the company has estimated that only 200 000 kilos would be available during the year to December 2009. Even more worrying is the shortage of skilled labour, only 100 000 direct labour hours are expected to be available during the year. The good news is that there may be an upturn in the market for its normal contract work.

*Required*:
Calculate

(a) the contribution per unit of each limiting factor for
  (i) the company's normal work
  (ii) Contract 1
  (iii) Contract 2.
(b) The company's maximum contribution for the year to 31 December 2009, assuming that it accepts either Contract 1 or Contract 2.

**20.6** Agra Limited has been asked to quote a price for a special contract. The details are as follows:

1 The specification required a quotation for 100 000 units.
2 The direct costs per unit for the order would be: materials £3, labour £15, distribution £12.
3 Additional production and non-production overhead would amount to £500 000, although £100 000 could be saved if the order was for less than 100 000 units.
4 Agra's normal profit margin is 20 per cent of total cost.

*Required*:
Recommend a minimum selling price if the order was for:
(a) 100 000 units
(b) 80 000 units.

**20.7** Foo Limited has been asked to quote for a special order. The details are as follows:

1 Prices are to be quoted at order levels of 50 000, 100 000 and 150 000 units respectively. Foo has some surplus capacity and it could deal with up to 160 000 units.
2 Each unit would cost £2 for direct materials, and £12 for direct labour.
3 Foo normally absorbs production and non-production overhead on the basis of 200 per cent and 100 per cent respectively of the direct labour cost.
4 Distribution costs are expected to be £10 per unit.
5 Foo's normal profit margin is 20 per cent of the total cost. However, it is prepared to reduce this margin to 15 per cent if the order is for 100 000 units, and to 10 per cent for an order of 150 000 units.
6 The additional non-production overhead associated with this contract would be £200 000, although this would be cut by £25 000 if the output dropped below 100 000 units.

*Required*:
Suggest
(a) a selling price per unit that Foo Limited might charge if the contract was for 50 000, 100 000 and 150 000 units, respectively
(b) the profit that it could expect to make at these levels.

**20.8** Bamboo Limited is a highly specialist firm of central heating suppliers operating exclusively in the textiles industry. It has recently been asked to tender for a contract for a prospective customer. The following details relate to the proposed contract.

1 Materials:
- £20 000 of materials would need to be purchased.
- £10 000 of materials would need to be transferred from another contract (these materials would need to be replaced).
- Some obsolete stock would be used. The stock had originally cost £18 000. Its current disposable value is £4000.

2 The contract would involve labour costs of £60 000, of which £30 000 would be incurred regardless of whether the contract was undertaken.
3 The production manager will have to work several evenings a week during the progress of the contract. He is paid a salary of £30 000 per year, and on successful completion of the contract he would receive a bonus of £5000.
4 Additional administrative expenses incurred in undertaking the contract are estimated to be £1000.
5 The company absorbs its fixed overheads at a rate of £10 per machine hour. The contract will require 2000 machine hours.

*Required*:
Calculate the minimum contract price that would be acceptable to Bamboo Limited.

20.9 Dynasty Limited has been involved in a research project (code named DNY) for a number of months. There is some doubt as to whether the project should be completed. If it is, then it is expected that DNY will require another 12 months' work. The following information relates to the project.

1 Costs incurred to date are £500 000.
2 Sales proceeds if the project continues will be £600 000.
3 Direct material costs amount to £200 000. The type of material required for DNY had already been purchased for another project, and it would cost £20 000 to dispose of it.
4 Direct labour costs have come to £150 000. The direct labour used on DNY is highly skilled and it is not easy to recruit the type of staff required. In order to undertake DNY, some staff would have to be transferred from other projects. This would mean that there was a total loss in contribution from such projects of £350 000.
5 Research staff costs amount to £200 000. The staff would be made redundant at the end of project DNY at a cost of £115 000. If they were to be made redundant now, there would be a cost of £100 000.
6 The company can invest surplus cash at a rate of return of 10 per cent per annum.
7 Non-production overhead budgeted to be apportioned to DNY for the forthcoming 12 months amounts to £60 000.

*Required*:
Determine whether or not the DNY project should continue.

**Further practice questions, study material and links to relevant sites on the World Wide Web can be found on the website that accompanies this book. The site can be found at www.pearsoned.co.uk/dyson**

Chapter 21

# Capital investment

**The funds need to be there . . .**

## Sage acquires US firm for £184m

### Sage splashes the cash on US merchant payment processing business

Sage has begun the New Year with an acquisition, purchasing US-based merchant services business Verus for £184m, paid in cash.

Verus serves 101 000 SMEs in the US, including speciality retailers, petrol stations, restaurants and car dealerships.

The business posted a £12m operating profit for 2005, on £36m revenues.

Sage expects that a demand for linking payment processing services with back-office accounting software provides a 'long-term revenue opportunity' for the business.

'Acquiring Verus expands our business management solutions into a new and growing market, where SMEs are showing clear demand for more automation of their business processes,' said Sage chief executive Paul Walker.

The acquisition should be completed by the end of the month, subject to regulatory approval.

Sage's share price currently stands at three-quarters of a per cent up since trading began this morning, to 259.5p from 257.5p.

The FTSE100 giant announced in November that it had a potential £500m 'war chest' for acquisitions.

*Accountancy Age*, 9 January 2006.



*Questions relating to this news story can be found on page 440*

## About this chapter

This is the third chapter in Part 4 of the book dealing with management accounting decision making. It explains how various calculation techniques can help management select a particular investment. Accountants call this exercise *capital investment appraisal.* The chapter also explores the main sources of short-, medium- and long-term finance available for the financing of a project once it has been selected.

**Learning objectives**

By the end of this chapter, you should be able to:

- describe what is meant by capital investment appraisal;
- identify five capital investment appraisal techniques;
- incorporate such techniques into quantitative examples;
- recognize the significance of such techniques;
- list the main sources of financing capital investment projects.

## Why this chapter is important for non-accountants

As a junior manager you may be involved in capital investment decisions. At this stage of your career not much money will be involved and all you might be doing is deciding which one of two filing cabinets your section should buy. As you become more senior, the projects will become bigger and perhaps cost millions of pounds. You will have to decide which to go for and how it should be financed.

Such decision making will involve a consideration of various projects on both a quantitative and a qualitative basis. Your accountants will process the numbers for you, and they may use one of the techniques discussed in this chapter. They will then present you with the results. It is extremely unlikely that you will be involved in the detailed number crunching but in order to make a decision about which project you should select you will need to question your accountants about their recommendations.

You will not be able to do so with any confidence unless you have some knowledge of their methods. This chapter provides you with the basic material. After studying it you will be in a much better position to make your own capital investment decisions and not just do what your accountants tell you to do.

## Background

Accountants make a distinction between *capital* expenditure and *revenue* expenditure. Expenditure of a capital nature provides a benefit to an entity for more than a year. Revenue expenditure does so for only one year and it has to be renewed if the benefit is to be continued.

Besides its long-term nature some other features of capital expenditure may be distinguished. They include the following:

- its purpose is to help the entity to achieve its long-term objectives;
- it will often involve huge sums of money being spent on major projects;
- it may have a considerable impact on how many staff the entity employs and how they react;
- the benefits may be spread over very many years;
- it is difficult to assess precisely what those benefits will be.

All entities would find it difficult to survive if they did not invest in some form of capital expenditure from time to time, and they certainly would not be able to grow and to develop. Plant and machinery will begin to wear out and become obsolete, for example, while in the longer term buildings will need to be replaced. In addition many entities have to set aside resources for projects that do not relate directly to their main business, such as the provision of leisure and social facilities for their employees.

All entities, public or private, usually have to select from a long list of possible capital investment projects because they certainly will not have either the time or the resources to do them all at once. So which should they choose? And how should they be financed? We answer these questions in the next section.

## Main methods

In this section we are going to examine the main methods used in capital investment (CI) appraisal. We will assume that we are dealing mainly with profit-making entities. Such entities will expect all their projects to make a profit except for those undertaken on health, social and welfare grounds (these types of project are difficult to assess). There are five main techniques that accountants can use in CI appraisal. They are shown in diagrammatic form in Figure 21.1 and we examine each of them in the following subsections.

### Payback

The payback method is an attempt to estimate how long it would take before a project begins to pay for itself. For example, if a company was going to spend £300 000 on purchasing some new plant, the accountant would calculate how many years it would take before £300 000 had been paid back in cash. The recovery of an investment in a project is

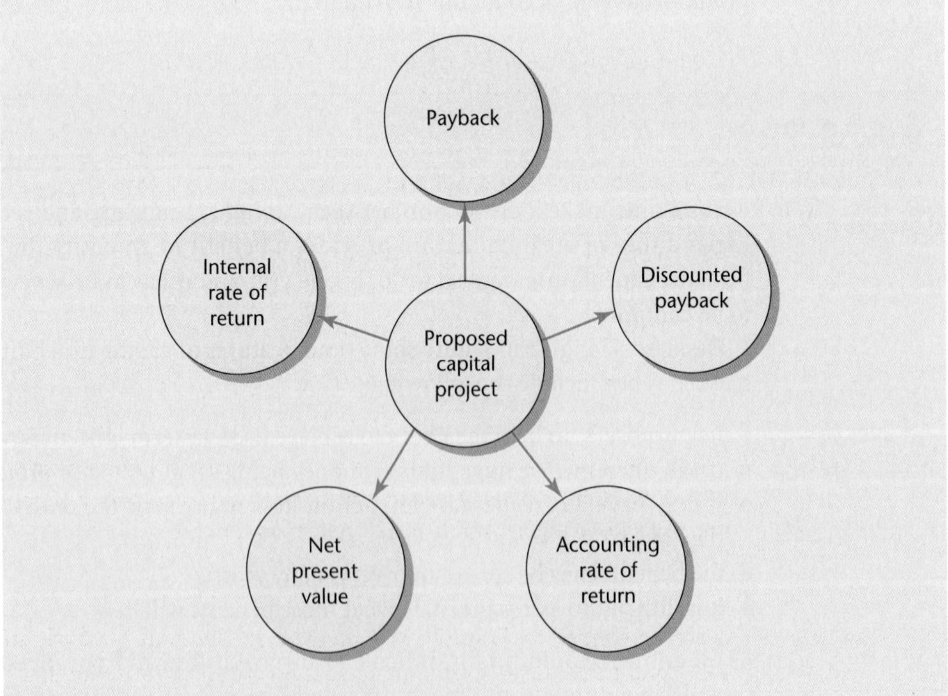


**Figure 21.1 Capital investment appraisal methods**

usually measured in terms of *net cash flow*. This is the difference between cash received and cash paid during a defined period of time. In order to adopt this method the following information is required:

- the total cost of the investment;
- the amount of cash instalments to be paid back on the investment;
- the accounting periods in which the instalments will be paid;
- the cash receipts and any other cash payments connected with the project;
- the accounting periods in which they fall.

As the payback measures the rate of recovery of the original investment in terms of net cash flow, it follows that non-cash items (such as depreciation and profits and losses on sales of fixed assets) are not taken into account.

The payback method is illustrated in Example 21.1.

**Example 21.1**

## The payback method

Miln Limited is considering investing in some new machinery. The following information has been prepared to support the project:

| | | £000 | £000 |
|---|---|---|---|
| Cost of machinery | | | 20 |
| Expected net cash flow: | | | |
| Year | 1 | 1 | |
| | 2 | 4 | |
| | 3 | 5 | |
| | 4 | 10 | |
| | 5 | 10 | 30 |
| Net profitability | | | 10 |

*Required*:
Calculate the prospective investment's payback period.

**Answer to Example 21.1**

The payback period is as follows:

| | | | £000 |
|---|---|---|---|
| Cumulative net cash flow: | | | |
| Year | 1 | | 1 |
| | 2 | (£1 000 + £4 000) | 5 |
| | 3 | (£5 000 + £5 000) | 10 |
| | 4 | (£10 000 + £10 000) | 20 |
| | 5 | (£20 000 + £10 000) | 30 |

Thus, the investment will have paid for itself at the end of the fourth year. At that stage £20 000 will have been received back from the project in terms of net cash flow and that sum would be equal to the original cost of the project.

As can be seen from Example 21.1 the payback method is a fairly straightforward technique, but it does have several disadvantages. These are as follows:

- An estimate has to be made of the amount and the timing of cash instalments due to be paid on an original investment.
- It is difficult to calculate the net cash flows and the period in which they will be received.
- There is a danger that projects with the shortest payback periods may be chosen even if they are not as profitable as projects with a longer payback period. The payback method only measures cash flow, it does not measure profitability.
- The total amount of the overall investment is ignored and comparisons made between different projects may result in misleading conclusions. A project with an initial investment of £10 000 may have a shorter payback period than one with an initial investment of £100 000, although in the long run the larger investment may prove more profitable.
- The technique ignores any net cash flows received after the payback period.
- The timing of the cash flows is not taken into account: £1 received now is preferable to £1 received in five years' time. So a project with a short payback period may recover most of its investment towards the end of its payback period while another project with a longer payback period may recover most of the original investment in the first few years. There is clearly less risk in accepting a project that recovers most of its cost very quickly than in accepting one where the benefits are deferred.

Irrespective of these disadvantages, the payback method has something to be said for it. While it may appear to be rather simplistic, it does help managers to compare projects and to think in terms of how long it takes before a project has recovered its original cost.

## Discounted payback

The simple payback method ignores the timing of net cash receipts but this problem can be overcome by *discounting* the net cash receipts. You will probably be familiar with discounting in your everyday life. You know, for example, that if you put £91 into the building society and the rate of interest is 10% per annum, your original investment will be worth about £100 [£91 + £9 (10% × £91)] at the end of the year. We could look at this example from another point of view. Assuming a rate of interest of 10% per annum, what amount of money do you have to invest in the building society in order to have £100 at the end of the year? The answer is, of course, £91 (ignoring the odd 10p). In other words, £91 received now is about the same as £100 received in a year's time. This is what is meant by *discounting*. The procedure is as follows:

1 Calculate the future net cash flows.
2 Select an appropriate rate of interest.
3 Multiply the net cash flows by a discount factor.

The discount factor will depend on the cost of borrowing money. In the case of the building society example above, the discount factor is based on a rate of interest of 10%. The factor itself is 0.9091, i.e. £100 × 0.9091 = £90.91. To check: take the £90.91 and add the year's interest, i.e. £90.91 × 10% = £9.091 + £90.91 = £100.00. You will not have to calculate discount factors as they are readily available in tables. We include one in Appendix 2 on page 468 of this book.

In order to confirm that you understand the point about discounting, turn to Appendix 2. Look along the top line for the appropriate rate of interest: in our case it is 10%. Work down the 10% column until you come to the line opposite the year (shown in the left-hand column) in which the cash would be received. In our example, the cash is going to be received in one year's time, so it is not necessary to go further than the first line. The present value of £1 receivable in a year's time is, therefore, £0.9091, or £90.91 if £100 is to be received in a year's time.

**Activity 21.1**

Assuming a rate of interest of 15% per annum, what is the present value of £200 receivable in two years' time?

We can now show you how the discounted payback method works. We do so in Example 21.2.

**Example 21.2**

## The discounted payback method

Newland City Council has investigated the possibility of investing in a new project, and the following information has been obtained:

| | *£000* | *£000* |
|---|---|---|
| Total cost of project | | 500 |
| Expected net cash flows: | | |
| Year 1 | 20 | |
| 2 | 50 | |
| 3 | 100 | |
| 4 | 200 | |
| 5 | 300 | |
| 6 | 30 | 700 |
| Net return | | 200 |

*Required*:
Assuming a rate of interest of 8%, calculate the project's overall return using the following methods:
(a) payback
(b) discounted payback.

**Answer to Example 21.2**

### (a) Payback method

| *Year* | *Net cash flow* | *Cumulative net cash flow* |
|---|---|---|
| | *£000* | *£000* |
| 0 | (500) | (500) |
| 1 | 20 | (480) |
| 2 | 50 | (430) |
| 3 | 100 | (330) |
| 4 | 200 | (130) |
| 5 | 300 | 170 |
| 6 | 30 | 200 |

*Calculation*
After 4 years the total cash flows received = £370 000 (£20 000 + 50 000 + 100 000 + 200 000). The £130 000 still necessary to equal the original cost of the investment (£500 000 − 370 000) will be met part way through Year 5, i.e. (£130 000 ÷ 300 000) × 12 months = 5.2 months. So the payback period is about 4 years and 5 months (41 months), assuming that the net cash flows accrue evenly throughout the year.

Answer to Example 21.2 *continued*

**(b) Discounted payback**

| *Year* | *Net cash flow* | *Discount factors* | *Present value at 8% [Column (2) × Column (3)]* | *Cumulative present value* |
|---|---|---|---|---|
| (1) | (2) | (3) | (4) | (5) |
| | *£000* | | *£000* | *£000* |
| 0 | (500) | 1.0 | (500) | (500) |
| 1 | 20 | 0.9259 | 19 | (481) |
| 2 | 50 | 0.8573 | 43 | (438) |
| 3 | 100 | 0.7938 | 79 | (359) |
| 4 | 200 | 0.7350 | 147 | (212) |
| 5 | 300 | 0.6806 | 204 | (8) |
| 6 | 30 | 0.6302 | 19 | 11 |

*Calculation*

Using the discounted payback method, the project would recover all of its original cost during Year 6. Assuming that the net cash flows accrue evenly, this would be about the end of the fifth month because (£8000 ÷ 19 000) × 12 months = 5.1 months. So the discounted payback period is about 5 years 5 months (65 months).

The discounted payback method has the following advantages.

- It is relatively easy to understand.
- It is not too difficult to compute.
- It focuses on the cash recovery of an investment.
- It allows for the fact that cash received now may be worth more than cash receivable in the future.
- It takes more of the net cash flows into account than is the case with the simple payback method because the discounted payback period is always longer than the simple payback method.
- It enables a clear-cut decision to be taken, since a project is acceptable if the discounted net cash flow throughout its life exceeds the cost of the original investment.

However, like the simple payback method, it has some disadvantages.

- It is sometimes difficult to estimate the amount and timing of instalments due to be paid on the original investment.
- It is difficult to estimate the amount and timing of future net cash receipts and other payments.
- It is not easy to determine an appropriate rate of interest.
- Net cash flows received after the payback period are ignored.

Irrespective of these disadvantages, the discounted payback method can be usefully and readily adopted by those entities that do not employ staff specially trained in capital investment appraisal techniques.

## Accounting rate of return

The *accounting rate of return* (ARR) method attempts to compare the *profit* of a project with the capital invested in it. It is usually expressed as a percentage. The formula is as follows:

$$\text{ARR} = \frac{\text{profit}}{\text{capital employed}} \times 100$$

Two important problems arise from this definition.

- *The definition of profit.* Normally, the average annual net profit earned by a project would be used. However, as explained in earlier chapters, accounting profit can be subject to a number of different assumptions and distortions (e.g. depreciation, taxation and inflation) and so it is relatively easy to arrive at different profit levels depending on the accounting policies adopted. The most common definition is to take profit before interest and taxation. The profit included in the equation would then be a simple average of the profit that the project earns over its entire life.
- *The definition of capital employed.* The capital employed could be either the initial capital employed in the project or the average capital employed over its life.

So, depending on the definitions adopted, the ARR may be calculated in one of two ways:

- Using the original capital employed:

$$\text{ARR} = \frac{\textbf{average annual net profit before interest and taxation}}{\textbf{initial capital employed on the project}} \times 100$$

- Using the average capital employed:

$$\text{ARR} = \frac{\textbf{average annual net profit before interest and taxation}}{\textbf{average annual capital employed on the project *}} \times 100$$

$$\text{*} \frac{\text{Initial capital employed} + \text{residual value}}{2}$$

The two methods are illustrated in Example 21.3.

**Example 21.3**

## The accounting rate of return method

Bridge Limited is considering investing in a new project, the details of which are as follows:

| *Project life* | | *5 years* |
|---|---|---|
| | *£000* | *£000* |
| Project cost | | 50 |
| Estimated net profit: | | |
| Year 1 | 12 | |
| 2 | 18 | |
| 3 | 30 | |
| 4 | 25 | |
| 5 | 5 | |
| Total net profit | 90 | |

The estimated residual value of the project at the end of Year 5 is £10 000.

*Required*:
Calculate the accounting rate of return of the proposed new project:
(a) the original capital employed
(b) the average capital employed.

**Answer to Example 21.3**

The accounting rate of return would be calculated as follows:

(a) *Using the initial capital employed*:

$$\frac{\text{Average annual net profits}}{\text{Cost of the investment}} \times 100$$

Average annual net profits = £18 000 (£90 000/5)

$$\therefore \text{Accounting rate of return} = \frac{£18\,000}{50\,000} \times 100 = \underline{36\%}$$

(b) *Using the average capital employed*:

$$\frac{\text{Average annual net profits}}{\text{Average capital employed}} \times 100$$

$$= \frac{£18\,000}{\frac{1}{2}(£50\,000 + 10\,000)} \times 100 = \underline{60\%}$$

Like the payback and discounted payback methods, the accounting rate of return method has several advantages and disadvantages.

*Advantages*

- The method is compatible with a similar accounting ratio used in financial accounting.
- It is relatively easy to understand.
- It is not difficult to compute.
- It draws attention to the notion of overall profit.

*Disadvantages*

- Net profit can be subject to different definitions, e.g. it might or it might not include the depreciation on the project.
- It is not always clear whether the original cost of the investment should be used, or whether it is more appropriate to substitute an average for the amount of capital invested in the project.
- The use of a residual value in calculating the average amount of capital employed means that the higher the residual value, the lower the ARR. For example, with no residual value, the ARR on a project costing £100 000 and an average net profit of £50 000 would be 100%, i.e.:

  $$\frac{£50\,000}{\frac{1}{2} \times (100\,000 + 0)} \times 100 = \underline{100\%}$$

  With a residual value of (say) £10 000, the ARR would be 90.9%, i.e.:

  $$\frac{£50\,000}{\frac{1}{2} \times (100\,000 + 10\,000)} \times 100 = \underline{90.9\%}$$

  The estimation of residual values is very difficult but it can make all the difference between one project and another.
- The method gives no guidance on what is an acceptable rate of return.

- The benefit of earning a high proportion of the total profit in the early years of the project is not allowed for.
- The method does not take into account the time value of money.

Irrespective of these disadvantages, the ARR method may be suitable where very similar short-term projects are being considered.

## Net present value

Unlike the payback and ARR capital investment appraisal methods, the net present value (NPV) method does take into account the time value of money. In summary the procedure is as follows. (The procedure is also demonstrated in Example 21.4).

1 Calculate the annual net cash flows expected to arise from the project.
2 Select an appropriate rate of interest, or required rate of return.
3 Obtain the discount factors appropriate to the chosen rate of interest or rate of return.
4 Multiply the annual net cash flow by the appropriate discount factors.
5 Add together the present values for each of the net cash flows.
6 Compare the total net present value with the initial outlay.
7 Accept the project if the total NPV is positive.

Example 21.4

### The net present value method

Rage Limited is considering two capital investment projects. The details are outlined as follows:

| Project | 1 | 2 |
|---|---|---|
| Estimated life | 3 years | 5 years |
| Commencement date | 1.1.01 | 1.1.01 |
| | £000 | £000 |
| Project cost at year 1 | 100 | 100 |

Estimated net cash flows:

| Year: | 1 | 2 |
|---|---|---|
| 1 | 20 | 10 |
| 2 | 80 | 40 |
| 3 | 40 | 40 |
| 4 | – | 40 |
| 5 | – | 20 |
| | 140 | 150 |

The company expects a rate of return of 10% per annum on its capital employed.

*Required*:
Using the net present value method of project appraisal, assess which project would be more profitable.

**Answer to Example 21.4**

**Rage Ltd**

Project appraisal:

| | Project 1 | | | Project 2 | | |
|---|---|---|---|---|---|---|
| *Year* | *Net cash flow* | *Discount factor* | *Present value* | *Net cash flow* | *Discount factor* | *Present value* |
| (1) | (2) | (3) | (4) | (5) | (6) | (7) |
| | £ | 10% | £ | £ | 10% | £ |
| 1 | 20000 | 0.9091 | 18182 | 10000 | 0.9091 | 9091 |
| 2 | 80000 | 0.8264 | 66112 | 40000 | 0.8264 | 33056 |
| 3 | 40000 | 0.7513 | 30052 | 40000 | 0.7513 | 30052 |
| 4 | – | – | – | 40000 | 0.6830 | 27320 |
| 5 | – | – | – | 20000 | 0.6209 | 12418 |
| Total present value | | | 114346 | | | 111937 |
| Less: Initial cost | | | 100000 | | | 100000 |
| *Net present value* | | | 14346 | | | 11937 |

*Tutorial notes*

1 The net cash flows and the discount factor of 10% (i.e. the rate of return) were given in the question.

2 The discount factors may be obtained from the discount table in Appendix 2.

3 Column (4) has been calculated by multiplying column (2) by column (3).

4 Column (7) has been calculated by multiplying column (5) by column 6.

Both projects have a positive NPV, but project 1 will probably be chosen in preference to project 2 because it has a higher NPV, even though its total net cash flow of £140000 is less than the total net cash flow of £150000 for project 2.

The advantages and disadvantages of the NPV method are as follows:

*Advantages*

- The use of net cash flows emphasizes the importance of liquidity.
- Different accounting policies are not relevant as they do not affect the calculation of the net cash flows.
- The time value of money is taken into account.
- It is easy to compare the NPV of different projects and to reject projects that do not have an acceptable NPV.

*Disadvantages*

- Some difficulties may be incurred in estimating the initial cost of the project and the time periods in which instalments must be paid back (although this is a common problem in CI appraisal).
- It is difficult to estimate accurately the net cash flow for each year of the project's life. This is a difficulty that is again common to most other methods of project appraisal.
- It is not easy to select an appropriate rate of interest. The rate of interest is sometimes referred to as the *cost of capital*, i.e. the cost of financing an investment. One rate that could be chosen is that rate which the company could earn if it decided to invest the funds outside the business (the external rate of interest). Alternatively, an internal rate of interest could be chosen. This rate would be based on an estimate of what return the company expects to earn on its existing investments. In the long run, if the internal rate

of return is lower than the external rate, then it would appear more profitable to liquidate the company and invest the funds elsewhere. A local authority does not have the same difficulty because it would probably use a rate of interest set by central government.

NPV is considered to be a highly acceptable method of CI appraisal. It takes into account the timing of the net cash flows, the project's profitability and the return of the original investment. However, a project would not necessarily be accepted just because it had an acceptable NPV as non-financial factors have to be allowed for. In some cases less profitable projects (or even projects with a negative NPV) may go ahead, for example if they are concerned with employee safety or welfare.

## Internal rate of return

The internal rate of return (IRR) method is also based on discounting. It is very similar to the NPV method, except that instead of discounting the expected net cash flows by a *predetermined* rate of return, it estimates what rate of return is required in order to ensure that the total NPV equals the total initial cost.

In theory, a rate of return that is lower than the entity's required rate of return would be rejected but in practice the IRR would only be one factor to be taken into account in deciding whether to go ahead with the project. The method is illustrated in Example 21.5.

**Example 21.5**

### The internal rate of return method

Bruce Limited is considering whether to invest £50 000 in a new project. The project's expected net cash flows would be as follows:

| *Year* | *£000* |
|---|---|
| 1 | 7 |
| 2 | 25 |
| 3 | 30 |
| 4 | 5 |

*Required:*
Calculate the internal rate of return for the proposed new project.

**Answer to Example 21.5**

**Bruce Ltd**

Calculation of the internal rate of return:

**Step 1: Select two discount factors**

The first step is to select two discount factors, and then calculate the NPV of the project using both factors. The two factors usually have to be chosen quite arbitrarily but they should preferably cover a narrow range. One of the factors should produce a *positive* NPV, and the other factor a *negative* NPV. As far as this question is concerned, factors of 10% and 15% will be chosen to illustrate the method. In practice, you may have to try various factors before you come across two that are suitable for giving a positive and a negative result.

**Answer to Example 21.5 *continued***

| *Year* | *Net cash flow* | *Discount factors* | | *Present value* | |
|---|---|---|---|---|---|
| (1) | (2) | (3) | (4) | (5) | (6) |
| | | 10% | 15% | 10% | 15% |
| | £ | | | £ | £ |
| 1 | 7000 | 0.9091 | 0.8696 | 6364 | 6087 |
| 2 | 25000 | 0.8264 | 0.7561 | 20660 | 18903 |
| 3 | 30000 | 0.7513 | 0.6575 | 22539 | 19725 |
| 4 | 5000 | 0.6830 | 0.5718 | 3415 | 2859 |
| Total present values | | | | 52978 | 47574 |
| Initial cost | | | | 50000 | 50000 |
| *Net present value* | | | | 2978 | (2426) |

*Notes:*

1 Column (2) has been obtained from the question.

2 Columns (3) and (4) are based on the arbitary selection of two interest rates of 10% and 15% respectively. The discount factors may be found in Appendix 2.

3 Column (5) has been calculated by multiplying column (2) by column (3).

4 Column (6) has been calculated by multiplying column (2) by column (4).

The project is expected to cost £50000. If the company expects a rate of return of 10%, the project will be accepted because the NPV is positive. However, if the required rate of return is 15% it will not be accepted because its NPV is negative. The maximum rate of return that will ensure a *positive* rate of return must, therefore, lie somewhere between 10% and 15%, so the next step is to calculate the rate of return at which the project would just pay for itself.

### Step 2: Calculate the specific break-even rate of return

To do this, it is necessary to interpolate between the rates used in Step 1. This can be done by using the following formula:

$$\text{IRR} = \text{positive rate} + \left( \frac{\text{positive NPV}}{\text{positive NPV} + \text{negative NPV*}} \times \text{range of rates} \right)$$

*Ignore the negative sign and add the positive NPV to the negative NPV.

So in our example:

$$\begin{aligned} \text{IRR} &= 10\% + \left( \frac{2978}{(2978 + 2426)} \times (15\% - 10\%) \right) \\ &= 10\% + (0.5511 \times 5) \\ &= 10\% + 2.76\% \\ &= \underline{\underline{12.76\%}} \end{aligned}$$

The project will be profitable provided that the company does not require a rate of return in excess of about 13%. Note that the method of calculation used above does not give the precise rate of return (because the formula is only an approximation), but it is adequate enough for decision-making purposes.

Example 21.5 shows that the IRR method is similar to the NPV method in two respects:

- the initial cost of the project has to be estimated as well as the future net cash flows of the project;
- the net cash flows are then discounted to their net present value using discount tables.

The main difference between the two methods is that the IRR method requires a rate of return to be estimated in order to give an NPV equal to the initial cost of the investment. The main difficulty arises in deciding which two rates of return to use so that one will give a positive NPV and the other will give a negative NPV. You will find that you may have to have many attempts before you arrive at two suitable rates!

The advantages and disadvantages of the IRR method may be summarized as follows.

*Advantages*

- The emphasis is placed on liquidity.
- Attention is given to the timing of net cash flows.
- An appropriate rate of return does not have to be calculated.
- The method gives a clear percentage return on an investment.

*Disadvantages*

- It is not easy to understand.
- It is difficult to determine two rates within a narrow range.
- The method gives only an approximate rate of return.
- In complex CI situations, the method can give some misleading results – e.g. if there are negative net cash flows in subsequent years and where there are mutually exclusive projects.

As a non-accountant, you do not need to be too worried about the details of such technicalities. All you need to know is that in practice the IRR method has to be used with some caution.

## Selecting a method

Of the five capital investment appraisal methods we have covered, which one is the most appropriate?

We consider it important that the time value of money is taken into account in a CI appraisal since the profitability of a future project may be grossly optimistic if such a concept is ignored. The discounted payback method, the net present value method and the internal rate of return method all meet this requirement.

The internal rate of return method involves some complex calculations, although the overall result is relatively easy to understand. Nonetheless, it may be a little too sophisticated for most entities. The discounted payback method is simple to understand and is intuitively appealing. Its main disadvantage is that net cash flow received after the payback period may be ignored. Almost by default, therefore, the net present value method would appear to be the most favoured method. The main difficulty with the NPV method is the selection of a suitable rate of return for a particular project. So great care needs to be taken before accepting or rejecting a project based on the NPV method because it is highly dependent on the arbitrary determination of a specified rate of return.

## Net cash flow

Four of the capital investment appraisal methods that we have covered in this chapter require the calculation of a project's net cash flow (payback, discounted payback, NPV and IRR). This is obviously not an easy task because it requires making a great many assumptions and estimates of what might happen in the future – possibly for very many years ahead. There are two issues in particular that can cause a problem: the impact of inflation on future net cash flows and the treatment of taxation. We discuss each of these problems below.

### Inflation

In simple terms, inflation means that in (say) a year's time £1 received *then* will not buy the same amount of goods and services as £1 received *now* (see Figure 21.2). So if we calculate future net cash flow on the basis of the currency's value *now* we are, in effect, allowing for receiving less cash in the future. Or to put it another way, we should estimate our future net cash flows on the basis of what it will take to purchase the equivalent of £1 of goods and services now. For example, if prices have risen by 10 per cent in a year, you will need to spend £1.10 in a year's time to buy exactly the same goods and services as you could today for £1.

There are two ways of allowing for inflation in capital investment appraisal: indexing and adjustment of the rate of return. Brief explanations of both are given below.

- *Indexing.* Future net cash flows may be indexed using a recognized price index. For example, assume that the net cash flow arising from a particular project will be £100 in Year 1, £150 in Year 2 and £200 in Year 3. The relevant current price index at the beginning of Year 1 is 100 but the index is expected to rise to an average level of 120 for Year 1, 140 for Year 2 and 175 for Year 3. In order to compare the net cash flows over the next three years more fairly, they need to be put on the same price base. If they are indexed, Year 1's net cash flow becomes £83 [(£100 × 100) ÷ 120]; Year 2's net cash flow becomes £107 [(£150 × 100) ÷ 140]; and Year 3's net cash flow becomes £114 [(£200 × 100) ÷ 175]. The adjusted future net cash flows of £83, £107 and £114 for Years 1, 2 and 3 respectively will then be incorporated into a CI exercise and discounted at the entity's cost of capital.
- *Adjusting the rate of return.* Instead of indexing, we could select a higher rate of return. The easiest approach would be to add the expected rate of inflation to the entity's cost of capital. So with inflation at a rate of 5% per annum and a required rate of return of

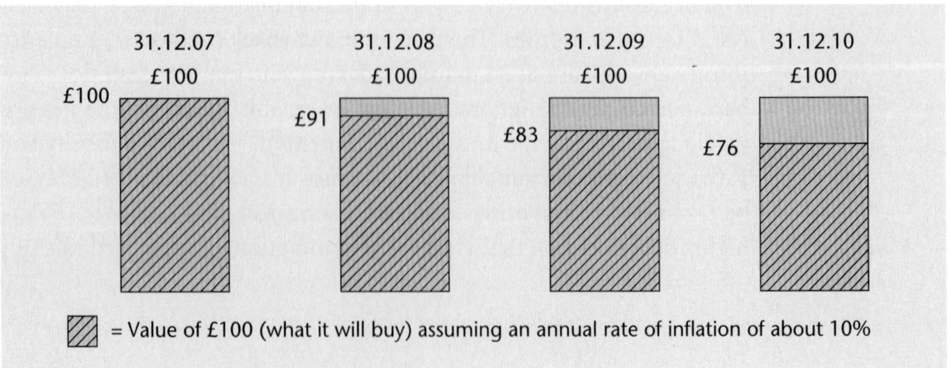


**Figure 21.2 The impact of inflation**

10%, £100 receivable in 12 months would be discounted at a rate of return of 15%, i.e. £86.96 [(£100 × 100) ÷ 115, or using discount tables £100 × 0.8696].

### Taxation

Corporation tax is based on the *accounting profit* for the year. In order to calculate the amount of *tax payable* for the year, the accounting profit is adjusted for those items that are not allowable against tax, e.g. depreciation. There are also tax concessions that are not included in the calculation of accounting profit. Capital allowances, for example, are a tax allowance given when fixed assets are purchased. In essence, they are the equivalent of a depreciation allowance. Sometimes up to 100% capital allowances are given, so that the entire cost of purchase can be deducted from the profit in the year that a fixed asset was purchased. This means that in the year that a fixed asset is purchased, other things being equal, the amount of corporation tax will be low, although in later years it will probably be higher.

So in estimating future net cash flows it is necessary to estimate what changes are likely to take place in the taxation system, what allowances will be available, what effect any changes will have on the amount of corporation tax payable and in what periods tax will have to be paid. Needless to say, the forecasting of such events is enormously difficult!

## Sources of finance

Once a decision has been taken to invest in a particular project it is then necessary to search out a suitable method of financing it. There are a considerable number of available sources, although they vary depending on what type of entity is involved. Central and local government, for example, are heavily dependent on current tax receipts for financing capital investment projects, while charities rely on loans and grants. In this section we will concentrate on the sources of finance available to companies.

The sources of finance available to companies depend on the time period involved. For convenience, we will break our discussion down into the short term, the medium term, and the long term. The various sources of finance are shown in diagrammatic format in Figure 21.3 and we discuss each of them below.

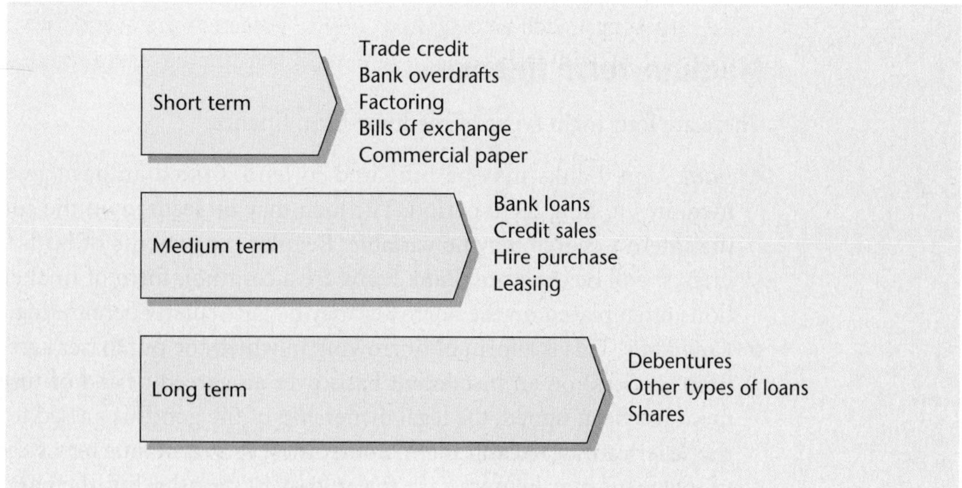


**Figure 21.3 Sources of finance**

## Short-term finance

There are five major sources of short-term finance.

- *Trade credit.* This is a form of financing common in all companies (and for all other entities). An entity purchases goods and services from suppliers and agrees to pay for them some days or weeks after they have been delivered. This method is so common that sometimes discounts are given for prompt payment. By delaying the payment of creditors, the entity's immediate cash needs are less strained and it may be able to finance projects that otherwise could not be considered. However, it is clearly only a temporary method of financing projects (particularly long-term ones). The entity is also highly vulnerable to pressure from its creditors. This method often operates in tandem with a demand for debtors to settle their accounts promptly.
- *Bank overdraft.* This is a form of loan where the bank's customer is allowed to draw out more from the bank than has been deposited. An entity's overdraft may have to be secured by a *floating charge.* This means that the bank has a general claim on any of the entity's assets if the entity cannot repay the overdraft. There is usually an upper limit, the amount overdrawn can usually be called in at any time and the interest charge may be high. The main advantages of an overdraft are that it is flexible and that interest is normally only charged on the outstanding balance on a daily basis.
- *Factoring.* Factoring relates to an entity's debtors. There are two types of factoring:
  - recourse factoring, where an entity obtains a loan based on the amount of its debtor balances;
  - non-recourse factoring, where the debtor balances are sold to a factor and the factor then takes responsibility for dealing with them.

  Factoring is a convenient way of obtaining ready cash, but either the interest rate on the loan or the discount on the invoices may be high.
- *Bill of exchange.* This is simply an invoice that has been endorsed (i.e. accepted) by a merchant bank. It can then be sold by the legal holder to obtain immediate finance. The interest charged depends on the creditworthiness of the parties involved, and if a company has a poor reputation then it will expect to pay more interest.
- *Commercial paper.* This is a form of short-term borrowing used by large listed companies. It is a bearer document, i.e. a person to whom the document is payable without naming that person. The minimum amount permitted is £100 000. This form of borrowing is not appropriate for many entities.

## Medium-term finance

There are four main types of medium-term finance.

- *Bank loan.* Banks may be prepared to lend a fixed amount to a customer over a medium- to long-term period. The loan may be secured on the company's assets and the interest charge may be variable. Regular repayments of both the capital and the interest will be expected. Bank loans are a common form of financing but the restrictions often placed on the borrower may be particularly demanding.
- *Credit sale.* This is a form of borrowing in which the purchaser agrees to pay for goods (and services) on an instalment basis over an agreed period of time. Once the agreement has been signed, the legal ownership of the goods is passed to the purchaser and the seller cannot reclaim them. Sometimes, very generous terms can be arranged, e.g. no payment may be necessary for at least 12 months, but the basic cost of the goods may be far higher than other suppliers are charging.

- *Hire purchase.* HP is similar to a credit sale except that the seller remains the legal owner of the goods until all payments due have been completed. An immediate deposit may be necessary, followed by a series of regular instalments. Once the goods have been paid for the ownership passes to the purchaser. HP is usually an expensive method of financing the purchase of fixed assets.
- *Leasing.* This is a form of renting. A fixed asset (such as a car or a printing press) remains legally in the ownership of the lessor. In the case of some leases, the asset may never actually be returned. In effect, the lessee becomes the *de facto* owner. Leasing can be expensive, although if the lessor passes on what can sometimes be some very generous tax allowances it can be a reasonably economic method of financing projects.

## Long-term finance

Long-term finance can generally be obtained from three main sources.

- *Debentures.* These are formal long-term loans made to a company; they may be for a certain period or open-ended. Debentures are usually secured on all or some of an entity's assets. Interest is payable but because it is allowable against corporation tax debentures can be an economic method of financing specific projects.
- *Other types of loans*:
  - *Loan capital* is a form of borrowing in which investors are paid a regular amount of interest and their capital is eventually repaid. The investors are creditors of the entity but they have no voting rights.
  - *Unsecured loan stock* is similar to debenture stock except that there is no security for the loan. The interest rate tends to be higher than that on debenture stock because of the greater risk.
  - *Convertible unsecured loan stock* gives stockholders the right to convert their stock into ordinary shares at specified dates.
  - *Eurobond loan capital* can be obtained by borrowing overseas in the 'Euro' market. The loans are usually unsecured and they are redeemed at their face value on a certain date. Interest is normally paid annually. The rate depends partly on the size of the loan and partly on the particular issuer.
- *Shares.* Expansion of the company could be financed by increasing the number of ordinary shares available, either on the open market or to existing shareholders in the form of a *rights issue.* An increase in an entity's ordinary share capital dilutes the holding of existing shareholders and all shareholders will expect to receive increasing amounts of dividend. Alternatively, new or additional preference shares could be offered; preference shareholders would have an automatic right to a certain percentage level of dividend, and so the issue of preference shares limits the amount of dividend available to ordinary shareholders.

**Activity 21.2**

You are in a small business as (a) a sole trader, (b) a partnership, and (c) a limited liability company. You wish to purchase some new machinery costing £50 000.
In each case, which main form of financing the project would you prefer?

(a) ______________________________

(b) ______________________________

(c) ______________________________

## Questions non-accountants should ask

Capital investment appraisal is a most important decision-making function. The selection of a particular project and the most appropriate means of financing it are difficult decisions to make. As a senior manager, you will receive some expert advice on what you can do. Ultimately, the final decision will be one for you. As far as the financial data are concerned, what questions should you put before your accountants? We suggest that the following may provide a framework for some detailed questioning.

- What capital appraisal method have you used?
- Why did you select that one?
- What problems have you encountered in calculating the net cash flow (or estimated net profit)?
- What allowances have you made for inflation and taxation?
- What rate of return have you used and why?
- What qualitative factors do you think should be taken into account?
- Are you able to put a monetary cost or value on them?

## Conclusion

CI appraisal is a complex and time-consuming exercise. It is not possible to be totally accurate in determining the viability of individual projects but a valid comparison can usually be made between them.

Managers tend to be very enthusiastic about their own sphere of responsibility. As a result a marketing manager may be *sure* that additional sales will be possible, a production director may be *certain* that a new machine will pay for itself quickly, and the data processing manager may be *convinced* that a new high-powered computer is essential.

In helping management to choose between such competing projects, the accountant's role is to try to assess their costs and to compare them with the possible benefits. Once a choice has been made, he then has to ensure that the necessary finance will be available for them. CI appraisal should not be used as a means of blocking new projects. It is no different from all the other accounting techniques. It is meant to provide additional guidance to management and ultimately it is the responsibility of management to ensure that other factors are taken into account.

## Key points

1 Capital investment appraisal forms part of the budgeting process.

2 There are five main methods of determining the viability of a project:
   - payback
   - discounted payback
   - accounting rate of return
   - net present value
   - internal rate of return.

3 All the methods listed above have their advantages and disadvantages, but the recommended methods are discounted payback and net present value.

4 Capital expenditure may be financed by a variety of sources. Sources of short-term finance for entities include trade credit, bank overdrafts, factoring, bills of exchange and commercial paper. Medium-term sources include bank loans, credit sales, hire purchase and leasing. Long-term sources include debentures and other types of loans, and share issues.

## Check your learning

*The answers to these questions can be found within the text.*

1 What is the distinction between capital and revenue expenditure?

2 List five characteristics associated with capital expenditure.

3 What is meant by 'net cash flow'?

4 What is the payback method of capital investment appraisal?

5 What information is needed to adopt it?

6 List four disadvantages of the payback method.

7 What is the discounted payback method of capital investment appraisal?

8 What is meant by 'discounting'?

9 What does a discount factor depend on?

10 List four advantages and four disadvantages of the discounted payback method.

11 What is the accounting rate of return method of capital investment appraisal?

12 What formula should be used in adopting it?

13 And how should (a) the numerator and (b) the denominator be determined?

14 List three advantages and three disadvantages of the accounting rate of return method.

15 What is the net present value method of capital investment appraisal?

16 Outline seven steps needed to adopt it.

17 List three advantages and three disadvantages of the method.

18 What is the internal rate of return method of capital investment appraisal?

19 What is its basic objective?

20 What formula is used to determine the required rate of return?

21 List three advantages and three disadvantages of the method.

22 How may (a) inflation, (b) taxation be allowed for in capital investment appraisal?

23 List three main sources of (a) short-term finance, (b) medium-term finance and (c) long-term finance.

## News story quiz

*Remember the news story at the beginning of this chapter? Go back to that story and re-read it before answering the following questions.*

This article shows clearly that some capital investment projects involve very large sums of money and that the decision making involved can be extremely complex.

### Questions

1 How do you think Sage had managed to built up its 'war chest' of £500m?

2 Why do you think that Sage thought that this acquisition was justified?

3 What comments would you make about the payback time for the acquisition of Verus?

4 What does it tell you about Sage's investment strategy?

## Tutorial questions

*The answers to questions marked with an asterisk can be found in Appendix 4.*

21.1 'In capital expenditure appraisal, management cannot cope with any technique that is more advanced than payback.' How far do you think that this assertion is likely to be true?

21.2 'All capital expenditure techniques are irrelevant because:
(a) they cannot estimate accurately future cash flows;
(b) it is difficult to select an appropriate discount rate.'
Discuss.

21.3 Do any of the traditional capital investment appraisal techniques help in determining social and welfare capital expenditure proposals?

21.4 'We can all dream up new capital expenditure proposals', asserted the Managing Director, 'but where is the money coming from?' How might the proposals be financed?

21.5* Buchan Enterprises is considering investing in a new machine. The machine will be purchased on 1 January in Year 1 at a cost of £50 000. It is estimated that it will last for five years, and it will then be sold at the end of the year for £2000 in cash. The respective net cash flows estimated to be received by the company as a result of purchasing the machine during each year of its life are as follows:

| *Year* | £ | |
|---|---|---|
| 1 | 8 000 | (excluding the initial cost) |
| 2 | 16 000 | |
| 3 | 40 000 | |
| 4 | 45 000 | |
| 5 | 35 000 | (exclusive of the project's sale proceeds) |

The company's cost of capital is 12%.

*Required*:
Calculate:
(a) the payback period for the project
(b) its discounted payback period.

**21.6*** Lender Limited is considering investing in a new project. It is estimated that it will cost £100 000 to implement, and that the expected net profit after tax will be as follows:

| *Year* | £ |
|---|---|
| 1 | 18 000 |
| 2 | 47 000 |
| 3 | 65 000 |
| 4 | 65 000 |
| 5 | 30 000 |

No residual value is expected.

*Required:*
Calculate the accounting rate of return of the proposed project.

**21.7*** The following net cash flows relate to Lockhart Limited in connection with a certain project that has an initial cost of £2 500 000:

| *Year* | *Net cash flow* | |
|---|---|---|
| | *£000* | |
| 1 | 800 | (excluding the initial cost) |
| 2 | 850 | |
| 3 | 830 | |
| 4 | 1 200 | |
| 5 | 700 | |

The company's required rate of return is 15%.

*Required:*
Calculate the net present value of the project.

**21.8** Moffat District Council has calculated the following net cash flows for a proposed project costing £1 450 000:

| *Year* | *Net cash flow* | |
|---|---|---|
| | *£000* | |
| 1 | 230 | (excluding the initial cost) |
| 2 | 370 | |
| 3 | 600 | |
| 4 | 420 | |
| 5 | 110 | |

*Required:*
Calculate the internal rate of return generated by the project.

21.9 Prospect Limited is considering investing in some new plant. The plant would cost £1 000 000 to implement. It would last five years and it would then be sold for £50 000. The relevant profit and loss accounts for each year during the life of the project are as follows:

| Year to 31 March | *1* | *2* | *3* | *4* | *5* |
|---|---|---|---|---|---|
| | *£000* | *£000* | *£000* | *£000* | *£000* |
| Sales | 2 000 | 2 400 | 2 800 | 2 900 | 2 000 |
| *Less:* Cost of goods sold | | | | | |
| Opening stock | – | 200 | 300 | 550 | 350 |
| Purchases | 1 600 | 1 790 | 2 220 | 1 960 | 1 110 |
| | 1 600 | 1 990 | 2 520 | 2 510 | 1 460 |
| *Less:* Closing stock | 200 | 300 | 550 | 350 | 50 |
| | 1 400 | 1 690 | 1 970 | 2 160 | 1 410 |
| Gross profit | 600 | 710 | 830 | 740 | 590 |
| *Less:* Expenses | 210 | 220 | 240 | 250 | 300 |
| Depreciation | 190 | 190 | 190 | 190 | 190 |
| | 400 | 410 | 430 | 440 | 490 |
| Net profit | 200 | 300 | 400 | 300 | 100 |
| Taxation | 40 | 70 | 100 | 100 | 10 |
| Retained profits | 160 | 230 | 300 | 200 | 90 |

*Additional information:*

1 All sales are made and all purchases are obtained on credit terms.

2 Outstanding trade debtors and trade creditors at the end of each year are expected to be as follows:

| *Year* | *Trade debtors* | *Trade creditors* |
|---|---|---|
| | *£000* | *£000* |
| 1 | 200 | 250 |
| 2 | 240 | 270 |
| 3 | 300 | 330 |
| 4 | 320 | 300 |
| 5 | 400 | 150 |

3 Expenses would all be paid in cash during each year in question.

4 Taxation would be paid on 1 January following each year end.

5 Half the plant would be paid for in cash on 1 April Year 0, and the remaining half (also in cash) on 1 January Year 1. The resale value of £50 000 will be received in cash on 31 March Year 6.

*Required:*

Calculate the annual net cash flow arising from the purchase of this new plant.

**21.10** Nicol Limited is considering investing in a new machine. The machine would cost £500 000. It would have a life of five years and a nil residual value. The company uses the straight-line method of depreciation.

It is expected that the machine will earn the following extra profits for the company during its expected life:

| *Year* | *Profits* |
|---|---|
| | *£000* |
| 1 | 200 |
| 2 | 120 |
| 3 | 120 |
| 4 | 100 |
| 5 | 60 |

The above profits also represent the extra net cash flows expected to be generated by the machine (i.e. they exclude the machine's initial cost and the annual depreciation charge). The company's cost of capital is 18%.

*Required:*
(a) Calculate:
  (i) the machine's payback period; and
  (ii) its net present value.
(b) Advise management as to whether the new machine should be purchased.

**21.11** Hewie Limited has some capital available for investment and is considering two projects, only one of which can be financed. The details are as follows:

| | *Project* | |
|---|---|---|
| | *(1)* | *(2)* |
| Expected life (years) | 4 | 3 |
| | *£000* | *£000* |
| Initial cost | 600 | 500 |
| Expected net cash flows (excluding the initial cost) | | |
| Year | | |
| 1 | 10 | 250 |
| 2 | 200 | 250 |
| 3 | 400 | 50 |
| 4 | 50 | – |
| Residual value | Nil | Nil |

*Required:*
Advise management on which project to accept.

21.12 Marsh Limited has investigated the possibility of investing in a new machine. The following data have been extracted from the report relating to the project:

Cost of machine on 1 January Year 6: £500 000.
Life: four years to 31 December Year 9.
Estimated scrap value: Nil.
Depreciation method: Straight-line.

| *Year* | *Accounting profit after tax* | *Net cash flows* | |
|---|---|---|---|
| | *£000* | *£000* | |
| 6 | 100 | 50 | (excluding the initial cost) |
| 7 | 250 | 200 | |
| 8 | 250 | 225 | |
| 9 | 200 | 225 | |
| 10 | – | 100 | |

The company's required rate of return is 15%.

*Required:*
Calculate the return the machine would make using the following investment appraisal methods:
(a) payback
(b) accounting rate of return
(c) net present value
(d) internal rate of return.

**Further practice questions, study material and links to relevant sites on the World Wide Web can be found on the website that accompanies this book. The site can be found at www.pearsoned.co.uk/dyson**

# Chapter 22 Emerging issues

## Management accounting: slow to change . . .

### Health warning issued on fads in management accounting

S. Heaphy

'Managers need to be wary of the side-effects of fad-like tools and practices within management accounting', said Professor Joan Luft, at the CIMA Visiting Professor Lecture 2006 held at CIMA's Headquarters on January 26.

The last 20 years have seen vigorous innovation and debate in management accounting, generating new techniques typically intended to improve profitability, which they often do. Such tools have included activity-based costing and strategic performance measurement systems such as scorecards.

However, Professor Luft suggested that overall evidence of the tools' success is mixed:

'Many management accounting innovations are appealing because they promise insights into organisational complexity – they are intended to shed light on important and ill-understood processes like strategy implementation and creation of customer value. But because they tackle complex issues they are vulnerable to the side effects of tactics used to simplify what ultimately remain complex situations and the judgement biases that result from them.'

'Regardless of whether organisations initially rate innovations as successful, there is evidence to suggest that views can easily change over time. "Flavour of the month" techniques can be swiftly abandoned, and formerly abandoned techniques are often revisited because the problems they were intended to resolve still remain'.

Professor Luft proposed that if innovative tools were to continue to be used, managers should be aware of the simplifying tactics and their consequences in order to make the tools more effective by guarding against their side effects.

*Accountingnet.ie*, 31 January 2006.

*Questions relating to this news story can be found on page 459*

## About this chapter

In this chapter, the last in the book, we deal with some emerging issues in management accounting. The basic management accounting techniques have hardly changed in over 100 years and although some new ones were introduced as the twentieth century progressed, there were few changes until about 1980. Since that time management accounting practices have begun to be reviewed and reconsidered as a result of major developments in the commercial and industrial world.

This chapter explores some of the changes that have taken place in the business environment towards the end of the twentieth century and the impact that such changes are beginning to have on management accounting practice. We then review some of the ideas that have emerged for bringing management accounting up to date to meet the requirements of business in the twenty-first century.

**Learning objectives**

By the end of this chapter, you should be able to:

- review the changes in the business environment during the last 30 years;
- explain why changes in the commercial and industrial environment have affected traditional management accounting practice;
- consider the usefulness of a number of emerging developments in management accounting, viz. activity-based management, better and beyond budgeting, environmental management accounting, performance measurement and strategic management accounting.

## Why this chapter is important for non-accountants

This chapter is important for non-accountants for the following reasons.

- You will be able to judge the value of any management accounting information presented to you if you have some knowledge of its historical development.
- You will be able to contribute to any debate that involves examining whether or not traditional management accounting practices have a place in the new business environment.
- You will be able to question your accountants on the proposals that they may have for introducing new management accounting techniques into your own entity.
- You will be able to determine whether the management accounting function could be reorganized in order to provide a better service for management.

## The business environment

The Second World War had a profound effect on the financial, economic, political and social life of the United Kingdom. The country had to be rebuilt. A great deal of damage had been done to the infrastructure, there had been a lack of investment in its traditional industries, and the UK found it difficult to compete with the emerging countries in overseas markets. Many of these countries had a large labour force and the UK found that they could sell their goods much more cheaply than it could. Furthermore, as they were able to create entirely new businesses it was much easier to introduce new ways of doing things. By contrast, the UK had an industrial base rooted in the nineteenth century with a backward rather than a forward looking approach to business.

The main country that heralded the new business era was Japan. Prior to the Second World War, Japan had been a relatively unknown and somewhat primitive country. The impact of the war required it to be almost completely rebuilt and modernized without having the benefit of many indigenous raw materials. Japan's leaders realized that it could only survive if it sold high-quality low-cost products to the rest of the world. It had to start from an almost zero industrial base, but progress was helped by the close family traditions of Japanese culture and society. It took some time but eventually Japan was able to introduce the most modern practices into its industrial life.

These practices enabled the Japanese to be flexible in offering high-quality and reliable competitive products to its customers and deliver them on time. A detailed discussion of the managerial philosophy and various production techniques used by the Japanese is beyond this book, but the following significant developments were pioneered in Japan.

- *Advanced manufacturing technology (AMT).* AMT production incorporates highly automated and highly computerized methods of design and operation. It enables machines to be easily and cheaply adapted for short production runs, thereby enabling the specific requirements of individuals to be met.
- *Just-in-time (JIT) production.* Traditional plant and machinery was often time-consuming and expensive to convert if it needed to be switched from one product to another. Once the plant and machinery was set up, therefore, long production runs were the norm. This meant that goods were often manufactured for stock (resulting in heavy storage and finance costs). By contrast, AMT leads to an overall JIT philosophy in which an attempt is made to manufacture goods only when they have been specifically ordered by a customer. The JIT approach has implications for management accountants. As goods are only manufactured when ordered, raw materials and components are similarly purchased only when they are required for a particular order. So no stock pricing problem arises and stock control becomes less of an issue, since stock levels will, by definition, be kept to a minimum.
- *Total quality management (TQM).* Another approach that the Japanese have incorporated into their production methods is TQM. The basic concept reflects two other concepts:
  - *Getting it right the first time* – whatever task is being undertaken, it should be done correctly the first time that it is attempted. This means that there should then be savings on internal failure costs, e.g. no wastage, reworking, re-inspections, downgrading or discounted prices. There will also be savings on external costs, such as repairs, handling, legal expenses, lost sales and warranties. There could, however, be additional preventive costs – e.g. planning, training and operating the system – as well as appraisal costs, such as administration, audit and inspection.
  - *The quality of the output should reflect its specification* – in this context, the concept of 'quality' should not be confused with the feeling of 'luxury'. A small mass-produced car, for example, may be regarded as a quality product (because its performance meets its specification) in exactly the same way that we equate a luxury car (such as a Rolls-Royce) with quality.

**Activity 22.1**

Do you think that a just-in-time production system avoids the type of materials pricing problem discussed in Chapter 15? List the reasons why it may do and why it may not.

The industrial changes that had taken place in Japan were observed by other countries (especially the United States) and the new developments have now been widely adopted in many countries, including the UK. Even so they tend to be found mainly in large international companies rather than in small domestic ones, although TQM in particular is an approach that can be adopted by all types of entities.

Other changes that have taken place since the end of the Second World War are more general. Among those particularly affecting the UK are the following developments.

- *Decline of manufacturing industry.* Traditional extractive and heavy manufacturing industries (such as coal mining, iron and steel, shipbuilding and car manufacturing) are now much less important, and in some cases non-existent. Those manufacturing industries that do still exist are much less labour intensive than they used to be and labour costs themselves can no longer be regarded as a variable cost.

- *Growth of service industries.* There has been a growth of service industries such as finance services, entertainment, information supply and tourism. Service industries do not generally employ the thousands of employees that manufacturing industries used to employ. The service sector now forms a major part of the economy of the UK.
- *Organization change.* Another noticeable development that has taken place in recent years in both the profit-making and not-for-profit sectors is the move to *outsourcing* or *privatization*. This means that entities now concentrate to a considerable extent on developing their core activities. Everything else is bought in and supplied from outside the entity, e.g. firms that build bathrooms and kitchens may subcontract electricians, joiners and plumbers to do the basic work on a job-by-job basis. Similarly, an industrial company may employ an outside organization to look after its payroll.
- *Automation and computerization.* Production processes and administrative backup is now intensively automated and computerized. Indeed, the impact of computerization has been phenomenal. Most employees now have a personal computer on their desk giving them ready access to a vast internal and external data bank. This means that if they need (say) a report on a particular issue they can download it immediately without waiting for the accountants to do it for them.

## Changes in management accounting

The developments that have taken (and are still taking) place in business life in recent years have also begun to have an effect on management practices. However, as we mentioned in Chapter 14, during the period 1920 to 1980 management accounting changed very little and there were very few new developments. Since 1980 the pace has quickened and many entities have incorporated new ideas into their reporting procedures. Such changes have been largely in medium- and large-scale industrial entities. The pace has been much less obvious in smaller service-based and not-for-profit entities.

We should not expect, therefore, a *revolution* to take place in management accounting practices over the next few years. We can expect more of a slow *evolutionary* process and it might take at least another 30 years before nineteenth-century management accounting practices gradually become extinct.

What changes can we expect? Although the pace will be slow, we suggest the following.

- The collection, recording, extraction and summary of data for information purposes will be performed electronically. This function will no longer be serviced by a large army of management accountants.
- As JIT procedures become dominant, stock control, materials pricing and stock valuation will become relatively insignificant tasks.
- Product costing involving the use of more sophisticated overhead absorption techniques will still be important, but it will become a relatively routine task as the basic data will be processed by computer.
- Budgeting and budgetary control procedures will also become much more computerized and they will be capable of being subject to a variety of different possible outcomes.
- Standard costing is likely to become less significant in a TQM environment but if it does survive it will be possible to produce different standard costs for a variety of different outcomes.

- Management accountants will become more like general managers specializing in the financial implications of decision making, using a wide variety of both internal and *external* data.
- Management accountants will constantly be having to develop and incorporate new techniques in order to cope with a commercial and industrial world that will be subject to rapid change.

It follows that if the above changes take place, future non-accountants are likely to meet a very different type of management accountant from the one that they are familiar with today. Tomorrow's management accountant will be much more of a team player, less bound to arithmetical recording of past events and more involved in taking highly informed decisions about future events.

Taking into account the changing business environment and the need for management accounting to adapt to such changes, which of the newer *techniques* can we see management accountants developing over the next few years? We review some of the possibilities in the following five sections, but remember that progress is likely to be evolutionary rather than revolutionary.

**Activity 22.2**

By this stage of the book you should have a good knowledge of the purpose of management accounting and the techniques used. List three changes that you would like to see incorporated into management accounting practice.

## Activity-based management

Activity-based management (ABM) is sometimes referred to as activity-based cost management (ABCM). In Chapter 16 we introduced you to the topic of activity-based costing (ABC). ABC deals with overheads. ABM covers *all* activities.

CIMA distinguishes between two types of ABM: *operational and strategic.* It defines each of them as follows.

> ***Operational ABM.*** *Actions, based on activity driver analysis, that increase efficiency, lower costs and/or improve asset utilization.*
>
> ***Strategic ABM.*** *Actions, based on activity-based cost analysis, that aim to change the demand for activities so as to improve profitability.*
> *(CIMA Official Terminology, 2005)*

By identifying the *activities* and the factors that drive them it is much easier to control an entity's costs. The traditional method of controlling costs is to organize an entity into cost centres, put managers in charge of each cost centre, allocate the cost of operating them and then require the managers to control their respective cost centre costs. It is argued that this method works because it recognizes that it is the activities that go on in a cost centre that cause the costs and not the cost centres themselves. So if you control the activities, you control the costs. This argument is very similar to that used to promote ABC. The major difference is that ABM deals with *all* costs whereas ABC is concerned only with overheads. How does ABM work? Basically, it is a four-stage process.

1 The various *activities* that take place throughout the entity are indentified.
2 The costs in separate activity cost pools are collected.
3 The main cause of each activity's cost is traced, i.e. the cost driver is identified.
4 The total cost in each cost pool and each element of cost is divided by the cost driver.

This procedure enables managers to know how much each activity costs to deliver and how much is incurred on each element of cost.

The determination of *what is an activity* is the key to achieving an effective ABM system. So in order to explain what is meant by an 'activity' we will use the example of *purchasing*.

Traditionally, a company would have a separate purchasing department. Its main costs would be salaries and wages, IT support, telephone costs, travel and stationery. However, purchasing may involve using the services of many other departments, such as accounting, credit control, customer care, finance and the legal department. As a result, some of the purchasing function costs are hidden in other departmental costs. An ABM approach would attempt to trace the total cost of operating the purchasing function, no matter where the various activities took place. This means that a more accurate cost for purchasing can be established.

The same procedure can be applied to other activities. This means that the entity becomes much more aware of the *real* cost of its various activities and it can then take much more effective control of them – activities can be better managed (or even eliminated), more accurate product costs are established and much more realistic selling prices can be determined.

Like all other techniques, of course, there are problems involved in operating an ABM system. The most obvious is that it is difficult to delineate a number of activities across a complex and large organization and to manage them. The method also cuts across traditional department and management lines and staff can become confused because they do not know which manager they should report to.

**Activity 22.3**

What do you think the reaction of the staff would be if a company switched from being organized on departmental lines to being based on activities so that staff worked in multi-disciplinary teams? List the likely reactions.

## Better and beyond budgeting

Budgeting has probably been practised in one form or another since man developed a rudimentary accounting system, but the main development came during and after the Industrial Revolution. The procedures then remained relatively unchanged until the 1980s when, like many other management accounting techniques, developments in information technology opened up new opportunities.

Traditional budgeting techniques were restrained by time and resources. As a result it was not practical to produce a number of budgets based on different assumptions (such as varying levels of activity) more than once a year. Moreover, once *the* budget had been finalized it had to stand because it would have taken too long to go back and start all over again. This meant that sometimes arbitrary decisions were taken to make overall adjustments to the budget, (e.g. 'knock 10 per cent off everybody's budget') thereby becoming of less use as a meaningful control mechanism.

All this meant that it was usually not possible to prepare frequent budgets so *the* budget had to be based on one level of activity, it took a long time to compile and it could be out of date by the time it was supposed to be used to control costs. The speed at which computers can work and the amount of data that they can process has meant that these restrictions no longer apply. It is not surprising, therefore, that a great deal of thought has been given to how budgeting can be made more effective in a highly technological world.

Two possible approaches have been identified by management accountants. One centres round a *better* budgeting approach and the other advocates a *beyond* budgeting approach. Unfortunately, these terms are not well defined and they are sometimes regarded as being synonymous. Let us try to distinguish between them.

A *better* budgeting approach involves adopting the traditional method of preparing budgets and of using them for control purposes in exactly the same way that they have always been used. However, by using the available information technology it is now possible to:

- prepare budgets more frequently than once a year;
- prepare a number of budgets according to different assumptions and scenarios;
- amend the budgets on an on-going basis as and when circumstances require.

The *beyond* budgeting approach is defined by CIMA as:

> *Idea that companies need to move beyond budgeting because of the inherent flaws in budgeting especially when used to set incentive contracts. It is argued that a range of techniques, such as rolling forecasts and market-related targets, can take the place of traditional budgets. (CIMA, Official Terminology, 2005)*

The beyond budgeting approach, therefore, reflects a view that the world is very different from what it used to be. It is not just information technology that has changed but the nature of industries, the way that they are managed and operated, and the attitude of their employees. These changes have to be reflected in the way that the budgetary process is organized and in the fact that it has to go much further than the better budgeting supporters would advocate. So what does that require? Some of the features of a beyond budgeting approach are listed below.

- The budgetary process may be merged with the financial reporting procedures.
- The budget period will normally be much shorter than a calendar year.
- Budgets will be prepared on a rolling basis, e.g. the last period's budget is dropped and the next period's budget added as each period ends.
- There will be greater emphasis on what should happen in the future rather than on what happened in the past.
- Budgets will be less detailed.
- They will incorporate external data relating to the entity's competitors.
- Non-financial performance measures will be incorporated into managerial reports.
- Managers will have greater autonomy during the preparation of their budgets and be much more responsible for meeting them.
- A reward system will be in operation for those departmental staff who meet the targets expected of them.

The above summary reflects generally the changes that are taking place in advanced industrial countries, i.e. rapid technological change and development, less authoritarian management, and a planning and control system that reward staff rather than punish them.

**Activity 22.4**

Identify one crucial factor that, in your view, makes the entire traditional budgeting process ineffective in controlling the costs and revenues of an entity. Give reasons for your choice.

Factor: ______________________________

Reasons: ______________________________

## Environmental management accounting

CIMA offers us a useful definition of what is a growing and important subject. It defines environmental management accounting as

> *Identification, collection, analysis and use of two types of information for internal decision making: physical information on the use, flows and rates of energy, water and materials (including wastes); and monetary information on environment-related costs, earnings and savings (EMARIC). (CIMA, Official Terminology, 2005)*

There has been a worldwide movement in recent years seeking 'to protect the environment'. The movement covers a wide spectrum: climate change and the depletion of natural resources (e.g. farms, forests, gas, oil, minerals, water and wildlife). The issues involved are of great concern to everyone, especially to young people, and pressure has been brought to bear on those entities and those individuals who appear to be the major perpetrators of the misuse of natural resources.

This movement has not gone unnoticed in accounting circles and a number of professional accountancy bodies have begun to take an interest in the subject by setting up working parties and publishing a number of documents and reports on environmental change. There now appears to be a strong belief among many accountants that entities ought to report on the impact that they are having on the environment, e.g. on the costs and benefits that their operations have on society. The costs will include their consumption of finite resources and the pollution that they may cause to the air, the rivers and the sea while the benefits include the jobs that they provide and the contribution that they make towards the growth of the economy.

The collection, recording and reporting of such costs is well suited to the accountancy profession, although it goes beyond the traditional confines of financial reporting. Nevertheless, the ASB has given considerable backing to companies to publish in their operating and financial review (although it is not a mandatory statement) information about environmental matters. While the ASB's encouragement relates to the annual report and accounts, the details required have an impact on the company's management accountants because they will have to collect and collate much of the required financial and non-financial information.

In order to illustrate the type of environmental matters that you might find in a company's annual report and account, Figure 22.1 shows what Devro plc included in its 2005 *Corporate and social report.*

## Environmental update

Environment issues continue to be a high priority within the group, which is committed to achieving compliance with regulations, permits and consent limits in its various activities. In addition, with a philosophy of continuous improvement in all areas of the business, improvements in environmental performance are expected.

The group's operating plants continue to make improvements to their operations with respect to the environment and some of the key projects undertaken this year are outlined below.

- **Scotland**
  The programme of energy-saving projects continued and, as a result, both our plants are on target to meet the next climate change levy milestone in 2006.

  55 tonnes of cardboard, office paper, plastics and polythene have been recycled in 2005. Following successful pilot tests, large-scale composting trials with gel and casing waste are being carried out at the Scottish Water composting site at Deerdykes.

- **United States**
  Through joint efforts with a major fertilizer manufacturer, the South Carolina facility recycled approximately three thousand tonnes of liquid ammonium sulphate, to be used as fertilizer feedstock. In total, waste minimization efforts have allowed the plant to hold the increase in total land-filled waste to 1%, while increasing overall collagen gel production to 6%.

  Investments in upgraded controls, an improved fuel delivery system and an improved ash removal system for the wood boiler have resulted in a 50% reduction in the opacity of the emissions compared to 2004, thus meeting the goal set by the air regulatory agency.

- **Australia**
  During 2005 our Australian facility has focused on improving the performance and reliability of its effluent treatment through primary screening and upgraded computer and control systems.

- **Czech Republic**
  The group's Czech plants are certified to the Environmental and Quality Management System Standard ISO 14001.

  The Czech facilities have continued to focus on waste recycling to reduce the impact of waste disposal. At the Jilemnice plant, process improvements in the shirring area have yielded a 15% reduction in waste.

**Figure 22.1 A company's environmental report**

*Source*: Devro plc, *Annual Report and Accounts, 2005*.

You will note from Figure 22.1 that there are no financial details included in this particular environmental report and that much of the information is technical. It appears that various improvements were made in 2005 compared with 2004 but we have not been provided with the means to assess their significance. This point emphasizes just how important it is that such reports should provide the reader with some meaningful and comparable information.

**Activity 22.5**

Do you think that environmental matters should be included in an entity's management accounting system? Complete the questionnaire below.

(a) Environment costs and benefits can be easily recognized. *Yes/no*

(b) They can be easily quantified. *Yes/no*

(c) It is possible to put a monetary value on them. *Yes/no*

(d) Non-financial measures only should be used. *Yes/no*

## Performance measurement

CIMA defines performance measurement as:

> *Process of assessing the proficiency with which a reporting entity succeeds, by the economic acquisition of resources and their efficient and effective deployment, in achieving its objectives. (CIMA, Official Terminology, 2005)*

CIMA points out that 'performance measures may be based on non-financial as well as on financial information'. It defines non-financial performance measures as:

> *Measures of performance based on non-financial information that may originate in and be used by operating departments to monitor and control their activities without any accounting input. (CIMA, Official Terminology, 2005)*

Both financial accounting and management accounting have traditionally concentrated on collecting and reporting on *financial* information. As a result data that could not be quantified and valued in monetary terms were usually ignored, and so not reported either to shareholders or managers. This meant that an exercise involving the interpretation of accounts, for example, was also largely confined to financial data.

This rather narrow approach to reporting the performance of an entity is slowly changing. There are a number of reasons why this is happening.

- Users are now much more aware that financial information is narrow in scope.
- They are also aware that it is compiled on the basis of a number of arguable assumptions, assertions and estimates.
- It is largely based on past performance.
- It does not take into account other aspects of the entity's activities.
- It does not provide the information that managers need for decision making and control.

As a result of the above factors there is now a gradual development towards widening the type of reports submitted to managers incorporating:

- a wide range of statistics and ratios ('metrics') to cover all aspects of the entity;
- non-financial data;
- metrics relating to the entity's market competitors.

Setting targets and using financial and non-financial metrics for comparison purposes is known as *benchmarking*. The CIMA definition is:

> *Establishment, through data gathering, of targets and comparators that permit relative levels of performance (and particularly areas of underperformance) to be identified. (CIMA, Official Terminology, 2005)*

CIMA argue that the 'adoption of identified best practices should improve performance'. It then goes on to itemize four types of benchmarking:

- *Internal*: Internal benchmarking involves making comparisons between operating units or functions within the same industry.
- *Functional*: Functional benchmarking involves making comparisons with the best external practitioners, irrespective of the industry in which they operate.
- *Competitive*: Competitive benchmarking involves collecting information about the entity's direct competitors.
- *Strategic*. Strategic benchmarking is a form of competitive benchmarking that deals with strategy and organizational change.

Even in the smallest entity it would be possible to identify hundreds of internal and external financial and non-financial performance measures that might help the managers to do a better job. However, it is important to avoid overloading managers with too much information and they should be supplied only with those metrics that are really useful to them. But what is provided should give a *balanced* view of the entity's progress.

Kaplan and Norton, two American academics, have become well known for their work in promoting the concept that managers should be presented with a limited *balanced* set of performance measures. In a series of articles [see, for example, R.S. Kaplin, and D.P. Norton (1992) 'The balanced scorecard: measures that drive performance', *Harvard Business Review*, Jan–Feb, pp. 71–80.] they outlined a device that they called a 'balanced scorecard'. They described this simply as being 'a set of measures that gives top managers a fast but comprehensive view of the business'. The model that they suggested had four perspectives which answered four basic questions:

- *Financial*: how do we look to shareholders?
- *Internal business perspective*: what must we excel at?
- *Innovation and learning*: can we continue to improve value?
- *Customer*: how do customers see us?

There have been many management accounting fads and fancies brought forward in recent years, although few of them have stood the test of time. The balance scorecard concept is not primarily a management accounting technique, although it does include a financial perspective. Nevertheless, during the period when management accountants been repositioning themselves as all-round members of the management team (and not just as accountants), the balanced scorecard seems to have become quite widely accepted as a useful means of enhancing performance. We would not argue that it has yet become as significant as (say) marginal costing in its impact but it looks as though it has some potential.

**Activity 22.6**

'Financial performance measures are too misleading for managerial decision making. They should be replaced with non-financial measures.' Do you agree with this statement?

Agree ☐ Disagree ☐

What approach would you support?

Financial performance measures only ☐

Non-financial performance measure only ☐

A combination of the two ☐

*Reasons*: ______________________________________

______________________________________

______________________________________

## Strategic management accounting

CIMA's definition of strategic management accounting (SMA) is:

> *Form of management accounting in which emphasis is placed on information which relates to factors external to the entity, as well as non-financial information and internally generated information. (CIMA, Official Terminology, 2005)*

SMA has begun to develop as a separate branch of management accounting during the last 25 years, although it is not yet well developed. SMA supports the move to a more strategic approach to managerial decision making.

The objective of SMA is to supply information to management for strategic decision-making purposes, incorporating both internal and external data of both a financial and non-financial nature. So in order to support a particular decision, or a proposal of a long-term nature, a management accountant would not restrict the data collected either to that available within the entity or to that primarily related to costs and revenues. The external information would include financial and non-financial data relating to the entity's competitors because their long-term plans are likely to have a significant impact on what the entity itself proposes to do.

The procedures available for external data collection are extremely speculative. Indeed, they cannot be anything else because obviously the entity's competitors would wish to keep their plans as confidential as possible. However, some information should be available from such published sources as annual reports and accounts, trade circulars, press releases and newspaper and journal articles. It has also been suggested that several rather unorthodox sources may be available, such as information from former employees of competitor companies or from visiting suppliers' representatives. In other words, management accountants may need to undertake a certain amount of detective work in order to obtain the data that they need!

In taking on this role, the main aim of the management accountants would be to compile competitors' plans in the form of financial statements similar to those of their own entity. The strategic planning team should then be able to make comparisons between sets of internal and external financial statements (including non-financial data) and, if need be, adjust their own strategic plan.

SMA should be of considerable assistance to the strategic planning team and it has the potential to be of considerable importance and relevance to non-accountants. But it is a long way from being widely accepted – or even understood.

**Activity 22.7**

Apart from obtaining external data, what main factor sets strategic management accounting apart from traditional management accounting?

## Questions non-accountants should ask

This chapter has indicated some of the changes that management accounting may undergo over the next five to ten years. You might like to check what changes your own entity is experiencing or envisaging. Try asking the following questions.

- Should we reallocate our management accountants to operating units, involve them more in strategic decision making, and just keep a small centralized accounting unit?
- Should managers access what reports they want from their PCs instead of leaving it to the management accountants to report to them?
- How satisfied are we that absorption costing is appropriate for our business?
- Should we move over to an ABM approach?
- Is it time to revise our budgeting and budgetary control system?
- Could both financial and non-financial indicators be incorporated into management reports?
- Can we use a balanced scorecard approach?
- Should we incorporate environmental costs and benefits into our internal decision-making projects and reports?
- Do we use strategic management accounting techniques in our performance measurement?

## Conclusion

Part 4 of this book has dealt with management accounting. Most of the chapters in this part have concentrated on traditional management accounting techniques and their usefulness for managers. However, most of those techniques originated in the late nineteenth and early twentieth centuries. They were devised to cope with a growing industrial nation at a time when companies concentrated on expanding output. Apart from their shareholders, little regard was given even to their customers, still less to their employees and the local community.

Great changes have taken place in economic activity since the Second World War ended in 1945. The main ones first took place in the Far East. These emerging countries were not bound by past practices. They were able to build up their industries using different organizational structures and new production methods. Increasing automation and development in information technology hastened the changes that were taking place. And, of course, labour was relatively cheap compared with the 'old world'.

All of this resulted in the decline of old industries in countries like the UK. Indeed, the UK found it impossible to compete with these emerging nations. The result was that by the end of the twentieth century the UK had very little manufacturing industry and its economy was largely serviced based.

These changes in the business environment have begun to have a significant impact on management accounting practices. Until 1980 there had been little movement but change became necessary as the 'old world' began to realize that it too had to accept some fundamental changes to business life. Orders were hard to get, customers were more demanding, prices were competitive, costs had to be controlled more rigorously, goods and services had to be of the highest quality and an efficient aftercare service was vital.

Traditional management techniques could not cope with these requirements so they also had to change. Perhaps the most significant of these changes has been a move towards *activity-based costing* (see Chapter 16) subsequently extended to *activity-based management*. Even so, only large industrial companies have taken much interest in either ABC or ABM and much work still needs to be done in encouraging medium and small industrial entities and many service entities of their usefulness.

There are also some other techniques that are not necessarily new but which are beginning to receive some attention. There is a call, for example, for 'better' or 'beyond' budgeting and for the incorporation of financial and non-financial indicators as well as internal and external data into performance measurement, as the development of strategic management accounting illustrates. Irrespective of the type or size of industry, most entities now recognize that they must give some attention to environmental matters and some companies are now publishing their own environmental report on a voluntary basis.

We should not expect major changes to take place in management accounting practice very quickly, or indeed on any extensive scale. Such developments take a great deal of time to become known and to become accepted. Progress will be slow and it will certainly be evolutionary rather than revolutionary.

## Key points

1. Management accounting developed as a main branch of accounting towards the end of the nineteenth century.
2. By 1925 most management accounting techniques used today were in place and there was little further development until about 1980.
3. The decline of old industries in the Western world and the emergence of new economies in the Far East (particularly Japan), the introduction of new management philosophies (such as total quality management and just-in-time procedures), and new technologically based industries have together necessitated the development of more relevant management accounting techniques.
4. We can expect a slow movement towards incorporating relatively new management accounting techniques into practice over the next few years. Activity-based management will probably become more widespread. Better and beyond budgeting procedures will be devised, and managers will be supplied with more financial and non-financial performance indicators. As a result strategic management accounting will gradually become an important brand of management accounting.
5. Greater attention will also be given to environmental accounting.

## Check your learning

*The answers to these questions can be found within the text.*

1. What were the main causes of industrial change after the Second World War?
2. What do the following initials mean: AMT, JIT, TQM?
3. List four major causes of the change in the UK economic environment over the last 30 years.
4. Identify four implications for management accounting of such changes.
5. What do the initials ABM and ABCM stand for?
6. What is the difference between ABC and ABM?
7. Name the four stages involved in an ABM exercise.
8. What is meant by 'better budgeting' and 'beyond budgeting'?
9. List five ways in which the traditional budgeting process could be improved.
10. What is environmental management accounting?
11. What is meant by 'performance measurement'?
12. What two indicators are used to classify performance measures?
13. What is meant by a 'balanced scorecard'?
14. List the four perspectives into which a balanced scorecard may be classified.
15. What is meant by 'strategic management accounting'?
16. What is the main factor that distinguishes it clearly from traditional management accounting?

## News story quiz

*Remember the news story at the beginning of this chapter? Go back to that story and re-read it before answering the following questions.*

University lecturers are expected to do some research but it is not always easy for accounting lecturers to find a topic that is publishable – at least in the academic journals and thereby lead to promotion. So when anything new comes along (like ABC) there is a tendency to jump on the bandwagon. This press release, therefore, is a timely warning particularly to management accountants working in academia of the dangers of getting carried away by the need for them 'to publish or perish'.

### Questions

1. Can you identify any topics covered in this chapter that you think are of little practical benefit? If so, what are they?
2. Do you think that the professor is correct in arguing that ABC and scorecards have improved profitability? If so, how?
3. What is she implying when she says that '…they are vulnerable to the side effects of tactics used to simplify what ultimately remain complex situations and the judgement biases that result from them'?
4. What do you think causes 'flavour of the month' techniques to be abandoned?

## Tutorial questions

22.1 'Activity-based management is fine in theory but impossible in practice'.

Discuss.

22.2 How far do you think that short budget forecasts would be more useful than budgets tied in with the traditional annual financial reporting system?

22.3 Do you think that environmental management accounting is of any benefit to a company?

22.4 'Ugh!' snorted the chairman when confronting the chief accountant. 'Strategic management accounting is another of those techniques dreamed up by you and your mates to keep you in a job.' Could the chairman have a point?

**Further practice questions, study material and links to relevant sites on the World Wide Web can be found on the website that accompanies this book. The site can be found at www.pearsoned.co.uk/dyson**

# Case study

# Fixed and flexible budgets

**Learning objectives**

**After preparing this case study you should be able to:**

- **distinguish between fixed and flexible budgets;**
- **evaluate a budgetary control variance report;**
- **indicate what action should be taken to deal with any reported variances.**

## Background

**Location:** Larkhill, Central Scotland

**Company:** Larkhill Products Limited

**Personnel:** Robert Jordan, Product Manager
Dave Ellis, Management Accountant

## Synopsis

Robert Jordan recently joined Larkhill Products Limited as a product manager. The company manufactures, distributes and sells a range of popular card games. At the end of his first month in post, Robert received the following statement from the management accountant.

**Larkhill Products Limited**
**Monthly variance report: January 2009**

| | *Original budget* | | *Flexed budget* | *Actual* | *Quantity variance* | *Price variance* | *Total variance* |
|---|---|---|---|---|---|---|---|
| | *Per unit* | *Units* | *Units* | *Units* | | | |
| Sales volume | | 20 000 | 18 000 | 18 000 | | | 2 000 (A) |
| Production volume | | 20 000 | 18 000 | 18 500 | | | 1 500 (A) |
| | *£* | *£000* | *£000* | *£000* | *£000* | *£000* | *£000* |
| Sales | 40 | 800 | 720 | 648 | – | 72(A) | 72(A) |
| Direct material | 18 | 360 | 324 | 360 | 45(F) | 81(A) | 36(A) |
| Direct labour | 12* | 240 | 216 | 270 | 90(F) | 144(A) | 54(A) |
| | 30 | 600 | 540 | 630 | 135(F) | 225(A) | 90(A) |
| Contribution | 10 | 200 | 180 | 18 | | | 162(A) |
| Fixed costs | | 150 | 150 | 140 | | 10(F) | (10)(F) |
| Profit/(loss) | | 50 | 30 | (122) | 135(F) | 287(A) | 152(A) |

*3 DLH × £4.

Robert left school at the age of 18 with a couple of GCE Advanced Level passes. He had started his career promoting double glazing for a local company before moving into selling central heating systems. He was good at persuading people to buy what he was selling and for the first ten years of his career he rarely stayed in one job for longer than two years. His ability and experience enabled him to gain promotion to more senior positions in sales and marketing.

He was never interested in going to college or university and he was far too busy to think of studying part-time for a professional qualification. So when he joined Larkhill he knew a great deal about selling, but little about the other functional activities of the company, e.g. accounting, distribution, human relations and production. His interview had not been handled particularly well, but Robert was good at dealing with people so he had been able to give the impression that he had a wide knowledge of business.

Robert panicked when he received the management accountant's statement. What was it? What did it mean? What as he supposed to do with it? Dare he ask anybody to help him?

After thinking about the problem overnight he decided to tackle it head on. The next morning he telephoned Dave Ellis, the management accountant. Robert was very authoritative and at the same time apologetic. 'Sorry about this Dave', he wheedled, 'as you know, I'm new here and my other companies had different ways of doing things. I'd appreciate it if you would do me a position paper about the monthly variance report.' He then indicated in more detail what he wanted. Dave agreed to supply him with some more information.

Robert was pretty sure that he had not convinced Dave about the reason why he wanted a 'position paper'. Nevertheless, he was confident that charm and warm words would see him through an embarrassing problem – as it always had.

***Required***:

Prepare an explanation for Robert Jordan explaining what the monthly variance report means and what action he should take over it.

# Case study Standard cost operating statements

**Learning objectives**

After preparing this case study you should be able to:

- describe the nature and purpose of a standard cost operating statement;
- evaluate the information presented in such a statement;
- suggest ways in which that information may be enhanced.

**Background**

**Location:** Burnley, Lancashire

**Company:** Amber Textiles Limited

**Personnel:** Ted Finch, Managing Director

**Synopsis**

Amber Textiles Limited is a small textile processing company based in Burnley in Lancashire. It is one of the few remaining such companies in the United Kingdom but it too is struggling to survive as a result of intense competition from the Far East.

The board of directors has been well aware for some time that if the company is to continue in business, it must retain its customer base by being extremely competitive. There is little scope to increase selling prices and so costs have to be controlled extremely tightly.

The Board has done everything possible to control the company's costs. For example, it recently introduced an 'information for management' (IFM) system. The system involves using budgets for control purposes but it also produces standard costs for each of the company's main product lines. A firm of management consultants installed the system with the assistance of the company's small accounting staff.

The new IFM system seemed to involve an awful lot of paper work and Ted Finch, the managing director, was struggling to cope with the sheer volume of reports that mysteriously appeared on his desk almost every day. By profession, Ted was a textile engineer. He had little training in numerical analysis and none related to accounting.

One morning, shortly after the new system was up and running, he found the following statement on his desk.

**Amber Textiles Limited**
**Standard Cost Operating Statement**

*Period: Four weeks to 31 March 2009*

| | £ | £ | £ |
|---|---|---|---|
| **Budgeted sales** | | | 700 000 |
| Budgeted cost of sales | | | (490 000) |
| | | | 210 000 |
| Sales volume profit variance | | | 17 600 |
| Budgeted profit from actual sales | | | 227 600 |
| Variances | Favourable | Adverse | |
| Sales price | | 20 000 | |
| Direct material price | 6 700 | | |
| Direct material usage | 15 400 | | |
| Direct labour rate | | 17 600 | |
| Direct labour efficiency | 20 800 | | |
| Variable production overhead expenditure | | 3 140 | |
| Variable production overhead efficiency | 2 600 | | |
| Fixed production overhead expenditure | | 30 000 | |
| Fixed production overhead volume | 12 000 | | |
| | 57 500 | 70 740 | (13 240) |
| **Actual profit** | | | 214 360 |

Ted studied the statement carefully. What was it? How had it been produced? What did it mean? What was he supposed to do with it?

He was still somewhat puzzled after studying it for some time so he decided to telephone the management consultants responsible for installing the IFM system. They referred him to a manual that they had prepared, a copy of which lay untouched on Ted's bookshelf. Sure enough, the manual contained an explanation and an example of a 'standard costing operating statement'.

After studying the relevant section, Ted felt a little more confident about what he was supposed to do with the statement that he had received. Nevertheless, he thought that it might be useful to take some advice. So he contacted his chief accountant and asked him to prepare a written report dealing with the specific standard cost operating statement for the four weeks to 31 March 2009. He stressed that he wanted to know precisely what action he should take (if any) to deal with its contents.

***Required:***

(a) Prepare the section of an *Information for Management* manual dealing with standard cost operating statements. The section should include an outline of the nature and purpose of such a statement, an explanation of its contents and the action management should take on receiving it.

(b) With regard to the specific standard cost operating statement for the four weeks to 31 March 2009, prepare a report explaining what the data means, what interrelationship there may be among the variances, and what specific action Ted Finch might expect his line managers to take in dealing with it.

(c) Outline what additional information might be useful to include in a standard cost operating statement.

# Case study Pricing

**Learning objectives**

After preparing this case study you should be able to:

- distinguish between an absorption costing approach and a marginal costing approach;
- prepare a quotation for a customer using a number of different costing approaches;
- identify a number of other factors that must be considered when preparing a quotation.

**Background**

**Location:** Dewsbury, West Yorkshire

**Company:** Pennine Heating Systems Limited

**Personnel:** Ali Shah, Managing Director
Hugh Rodgers, Production Manager

**Synopsis**

Pennine Heating Systems Limited is a small heating and ventilation system company located in Dewsbury in West Yorkshire. It provides customer-designed systems for small businesses. The systems are designed, manufactured and installed specially for each customer. This means that each individual contract has to be priced separately.

The company had expanded rapidly in recent years, but as it had done so its overhead costs had continued to increase. The managing director, Ali Shah, had always insisted that contracts should be priced on an absorption cost basis. This was not a problem in the early days of the company. There was then a considerable demand for what Pennine Systems was able to offer and customers almost always accepted whatever was quoted.

More recently, however, the demand for heating and ventilation systems had become less strong, competitors had come into the market, the national economy was in recession and customers were much more conscious about their costs than they used to be when the economy was expanding.

So while Pennine's reputation was good it had to be particularly sensitive about the price that it charged for its orders. Indeed, Ali sensed that the company was beginning to lose some business because its quotations were too high. He wondered whether he should review the pricing system in order to make sure that the company attracted sufficient business.

Ali was reminded of what he had intended to do late one Friday night when a request for a quotation landed on his desk. On the Monday, he asked Hugh Rodgers, his production manager to cost and price it. He had the results on the Wednesday morning. Hugh's calculations were as follows.

| | £ |
|---|---|
| Direct materials | 14 000 |
| Direct labour | 41 500 |
| Prime cost | 55 500 |
| Factory overhead | 11 100 |
| Factory cost of production | 66 600 |
| Administration overhead | 6 660 |
| Selling and distribution overhead | 9 990 |
| Total operating cost | 83 250 |
| Profit | 16 650 |
| Suggested contract price | 99 900* |

*say £100 000.

*Note*:

Factory overhead, administration overhead, and selling and distribution overhead is added to the factory cost of production at rates of 20%, 10% and 15% respectively. A profit loading of 20% is added to the total operating cost.

Ali suspected that a contract price of £100 000 may be too high to gain the contract but he wondered whether the company could afford to accept a much lower price. He asked Hugh to conduct an intensive investigation of the cost build-up and other matters relating to the contract. Hugh did so and he discovered, *inter alia*, the following information.

1 All the overheads include a share of the fixed costs of the company. 75% of the factory overhead, 80% of the administration overhead, and 60% of the selling and distribution overhead are fixed costs.
2 Hugh has been informed privately that a number of other companies have been asked to quote for the contract and that three other companies are being considered at contract prices of £70 000, £75 000 and £95 000 respectively.

*Required*:

(a) Advise Ali Shah what price Pennine Heating Systems Limited should quote for the contract.
(b) Outline what factors other than price Ali should take into account before offering a firm quotation.

# Appendix 1 Further reading

This book contains sufficient material for most first-year modules in accounting for non-accounting students. Some students may require additional information, however, and it may be necessary for them to consult other books when attempting exercises set by their tutors.

There are many very good accounting books available for *accounting* students, but they usually go into considerable technical detail. *Non-accounting* students must use them with caution otherwise they will find themselves completely lost. In any case, non-accounting students do not need to process vast amounts of highly technical data. It is sufficient for their purpose if they have an understanding of where accounting information comes from, why it is prepared in that way, what it means and what reliance can be placed on it.

Bearing these points in mind, the following books are worth considering.

## Financial accounting

Elliott, B. and Elliott, J. (2007) *Financial Accounting and Reporting*, 11th edn, Financial Times/Prentice Hall, Harlow. This is an excellent textbook that is now into its eleventh edition. It should be a very useful reference book for non-accounting students.

Holmes, G. and Sugden, A. (2005) *Interpreting Company Reports and Accounts*, 9th edn, Financial Times/Prentice Hall, Harlow. A well-established text that deals with company financial reporting in some detail.

Wood, F. and Sangster, A. (2005) *Business Accounting*, Volumes 1 and 2, 10th edn, Financial Times/Prentice Hall, Harlow. Wood is the master accounting-textbook writer. His books can be recommended with absolute confidence.

## Management accounting

Arnold, J. and Turley, S (1996) *Accounting for Management Decisions*, 3rd edn, Financial Times Prentice Hall, Harlow. This book is aimed at first- and second-year undergraduate and professional courses. Non-accounting students should be able to follow it without too much difficulty.

Ashton, D., Hopper, T. and Scapen, R.W. (eds) (1995) *Issues in Management Accounting*, 2nd edn, Prentice-Hall Europe, Harlow. This book will be useful for those students who are interested in current developments in management accounting. However, be warned! It is written in an academic style and some of the chapters are very hard going. It is also now somewhat dated.

Drury, C. (2000) *Management and Cost Accounting*, 6th edn, Business Press Thomson Learning EMEA, London. This book has become the established British text on management accounting. It is a big book in every sense of the word. Non-accounting students should only use it for reference.

Horngren, C.T. (2006) *Cost Accounting: A Managerial Emphasis.* 12th edn, Prentice Hall, Harlow. Horngren is a long-established American text. It will be of benefit to non-accounting students mainly for reference purposes.

# Appendix 2 Discount table

## Present value of £1 received after *n* years discounted at *i* %

| *i* / *n* | 1 | 2 | 3 | 4 | 5 | 6 | 7 | 8 | 9 | 10 |
|---|---|---|---|---|---|---|---|---|---|---|
| 1 | 0.9901 | 0.9804 | 0.9709 | 0.9615 | 0.9524 | 0.9434 | 0.9346 | 0.9259 | 0.9174 | 0.9091 |
| 2 | 0.9803 | 0.9612 | 0.9426 | 0.9246 | 0.9070 | 0.8900 | 0.8734 | 0.8573 | 0.8417 | 0.8264 |
| 3 | 0.9706 | 0.9423 | 0.9151 | 0.8890 | 0.8638 | 0.8396 | 0.8163 | 0.7938 | 0.7722 | 0.7513 |
| 4 | 0.9610 | 0.9238 | 0.8885 | 0.8548 | 0.8227 | 0.7921 | 0.7629 | 0.7350 | 0.7084 | 0.6830 |
| 5 | 0.9515 | 0.9057 | 0.8626 | 0.8219 | 0.7835 | 0.7473 | 0.7130 | 0.6806 | 0.6499 | 0.6209 |
| 6 | 0.9420 | 0.8880 | 0.8375 | 0.7903 | 0.7462 | 0.7050 | 0.6663 | 0.6302 | 0.5963 | 0.5645 |

| *i* / *n* | 11 | 12 | 13 | 14 | 15 | 16 | 17 | 18 | 19 | 20 |
|---|---|---|---|---|---|---|---|---|---|---|
| 1 | 0.9009 | 0.8929 | 0.8850 | 0.8772 | 0.8696 | 0.8621 | 0.8547 | 0.8475 | 0.8403 | 0.8333 |
| 2 | 0.8116 | 0.7929 | 0.7831 | 0.7695 | 0.7561 | 0.7432 | 0.7305 | 0.7182 | 0.7062 | 0.6944 |
| 3 | 0.7312 | 0.7118 | 0.6931 | 0.6750 | 0.6575 | 0.6407 | 0.6244 | 0.6086 | 0.5934 | 0.5787 |
| 4 | 0.6587 | 0.6355 | 0.6133 | 0.5921 | 0.5718 | 0.5523 | 0.5337 | 0.5158 | 0.4987 | 0.4823 |
| 5 | 0.5935 | 0.5674 | 0.5428 | 0.5194 | 0.4972 | 0.4761 | 0.4561 | 0.4371 | 0.4190 | 0.4019 |
| 6 | 0.5346 | 0.5066 | 0.4803 | 0.4556 | 0.4323 | 0.4104 | 0.3898 | 0.3704 | 0.3521 | 0.3349 |

# Appendix 3 Answers to activities

## Chapter 1

1.2 (a) account (b) double-entry book-keeping (c) profit (d) entity (e) Industrial Revolution.

1.3 (a) false (b) false (c) true (d) true (e) false.

1.4 The AAT. It is not a chartered body and it is not considered to be one of the six major professional accountancy bodies.

1.5

| *Type of entity* | *Advantage* | *Disadvantage* |
|---|---|---|
| Sole trader | The owner has total control of the business | It may be difficult to obtain sufficient finance |
| Partnership | The management of the business is shared | If the business is unsuccessful the partners may go bankrupt |
| Limited liability company | The liability of the owners is restricted | Certain financial information about the company has to be disclosed publicly |

1.6 Broadcasting: quasi-governmental.
Famine relief: social organization.
Postal deliveries: quasi-governmental.
Social services: local government.
Work and pensions: central government.

## Chapter 2

2.2 *Advantages*
Easy to compare this year's events with those that happened a year ago.
Annual comparisons are commonly made in other spheres and therefore acceptable.
A year reflects the normal climatic seasonal pattern.

*Disadvantages*
It is an artificial period of time.
It is either too short or too long for certain types of businesses.
Some of the information included in the annual accounts could be well over 12 months old by the time it is reported and it may by then be out of date.

2.3 Revenue should only be recognized when there is a high possibility that it will exceed the costs to date plus costs to be incurred. Even then only a proportion of the anticipated profit should be taken before the contract has been completed. Subject to these provisos, there may be a case for taking some profit towards the end of 2009.

## Chapter 3

3.1 (a) Assets = capital + liabilities. (b) Twice.

3.2 (a) A record or a history of a certain event.
(b) A book in which a number of accounts are kept (a book of account).
(c) To receive something or the value received.
(d) To give something or the value given.

3.3 (a) Cash account; sales account.
(b) Rent paid account; bank account.
(c) Wages account; cash account.
(d) Purchases account; bank account.
(e) Ford's account; sales account.

3.4 The entries are on the wrong side.

3.5

| *Debit* | *Credit* |
|---|---|
| (a) Suppliers | Cash |
| (b) Office rent | Bank |
| (c) Cash | Sales |
| (d) Bank | Dividends received |

3.6 A debit balance on an account means that the total on the debit side is greater than the total on the credit side. A credit balance is the opposite.

3.7 (a) no (b) yes (c) no.

## Chapter 4

4.1 (a) false (b) false (c) false.

4.2 (a) Land; property; plant and machinery; furniture and fittings.
(b) Stocks; trade debtors; other debtors; insurance paid in advance; bank; cash.
(c) Bank overdraft; trade creditors; other creditors; electricity owing.

## Chapter 5

5.1 (a) £3 500 [£10 000 less (2 000 + 6 000 – 1 500)]
(b) £4 000 [£10 000 less (2 000 + 6 000 – 2 000)]
(c) £4 500 [£10 000 less (2 000 + 6 000 – 2 500)]

5.2 £2 250 (£50 000 – 5 000 = 45 000 ÷ 20)

5.3 £4 500 [£4 000 + 1 000 – 500]

5.4 £11 000 [£3 000 + 10 000 – 2 000]

5.5 Probably yes. Debit the profit and loss account and credit Gibson's account. £70 000 (£75 000 – 5 000).

5.6 £1 500 [£9 000 – (250 000 × 3%)]. It will increase his profit by £1 500.

5.7 (a) false (b) true (c) true.

## Chapter 6

6.2 *Advantages*
Free from personal bankrupcy
The business carries on in perpetuity
Gives some status in the community.
*Disadvantages*
Formal accounting records to be kept
The Companies Act 1985 accounting requirements apply
Disclosure of information to the public.

6.3 (a) net profit for the year before taxation (b) dividends.

6.4 (a) current liabilities (b) loans (c) fixed assets (d) capital (e) current assets.

## Chapter 8

8.2 (a) false (b) false (c) true (d) false (e) true (f) false.

## Chapter 12

12.2 (a) true (b) true (c) true.

12.4 (a) £40 938 (b) stocks.

12.8

| *Company* | *Effect* |
|---|---|
| A | Not much |
| B | Considerable |
| C | Highly significant |

## Chapter 13

13.5 The expected profit on the contract is now £100 000 [£500 000 – (300 000 +100 000)]. Depending upon a review of the expected outcome, it might be appropriate to claim some profit on account. One way would be to apporption the expected profit on the basis of costs incurred to date as a proportion of the total cost. This would give a profit of £75 000 for Year 3 (£100 000 × 300 000/400 000). However, as the contract is only 60% through it life, some accountants might reduce this by an arbitrary factor of 2/3. The profit taken would then be £50 000 (£75 000 × 2/3). This is a normal accounting approach to the problem of revenue/profit recognition on contract work. But notice how judgemental the whole exercise appears to be.

## Chapter 19

19.2 S – V = F + P so £100 000 – 40 000 = 50 000 + 10 000, i.e. P = £10 000

19.4

| | £000 | £000 |
|---|---|---|
| Sales | | 75 |
| Less: variable costs | | |
| Direct material | 10 | |
| Direct labour | 20 | 30 |
| | | 45 |
| Less: fixed costs | | |
| Staff salaries | 47 | |
| Rent | 3 | 50 |
| Loss | | (5) |

19.5 The contribution per unit is £5 (£50 000 – 25 000/5 000) so another 1 000 units would have to be sold.

19.8 (a) Break-even chart

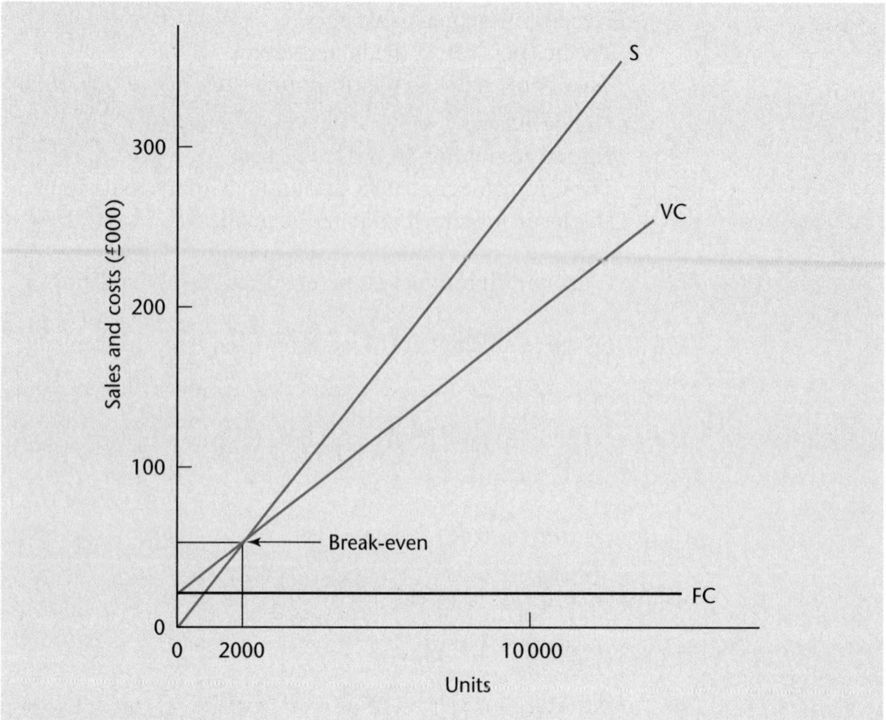


(b) Profit/volume graph

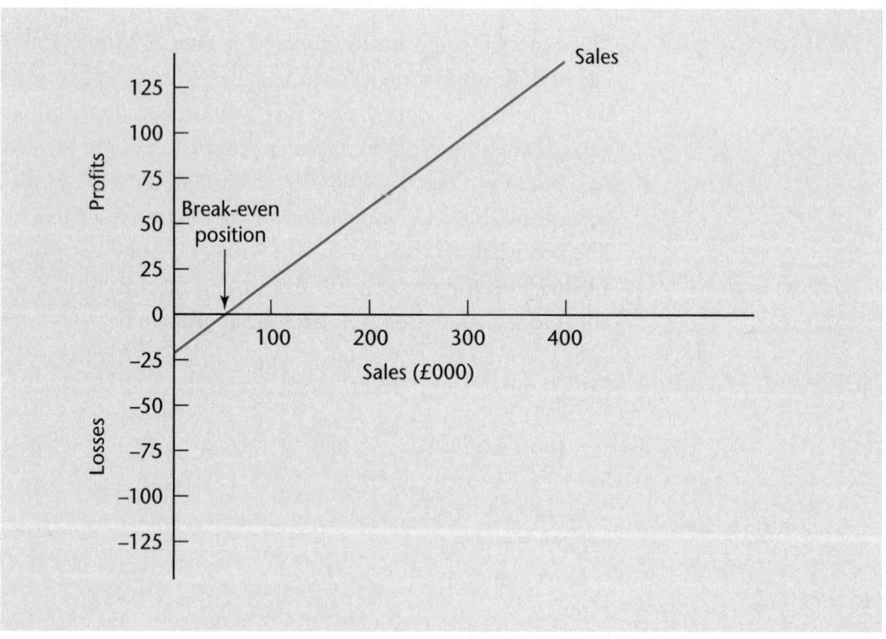


Chapter 21 21.1 £151.22 (£200 × 0.7561)

# Appendix 4 Answers to tutorial questions

## Chapter 1

1.4 Accountants collect a great deal of information about an entity's activities and then translate it into monetary terms – a language that everyone understands. The information that is collected can help non-accountants to do their job more effectively because it provides them with better guidance on which to make decisions. Any eventual decision is still theirs. Futhermore, all managers must be aware of the statutory accounting obligations to which their organization has to adhere if they are to avoid taking part in unlawful acts.

1.5 To collect and store detailed information about an entity's activities.
To abstract and summarize information in the most effective way for the requirements of a specified user or group of users.

1.6 None. The preparation of management accounts is for the entity to decide whether they serve a useful purpose.

1.8 Statutory obligations are contained in the Companies Act 1985. In addition, listed companies have to abide by certain Stock Exchange requirements, and qualified accountants are also bound by a great many mandatory professional requirements.

## Chapter 2

2.4
(a) Matching
(b) Historic cost
(c) Quantitative
(d) Periodicity
(e) Reliability
(f) Going-concern

2.5
(a) Relevance
(b) Entity
(c) Comparability
(d) Materiality
(e) Historic cost
(f) Realization

2.6
(a) Entity
(b) Reliability
(c) Periodicity
(d) Reliability
(e) Dual aspect
(f) Realization

Chapter 3

3.4 Adam's books of account:

| *Account* | |
|---|---|
| *Debit* | *Credit* |
| (a) Cash | Capital |
| (b) Purchases | Cash |
| (c) Van | Cash |
| (d) Rent | Cash |
| (e) Cash | Sales |
| (f) Office machinery | Cash |

3.5 Brown's books of account:

| *Account* | |
|---|---|
| *Debit* | *Credit* |
| (a) Bank | Cash |
| (b) Cash | Sales |
| (c) Purchases | Bank |
| (d) Office expenses | Cash |
| (e) Bank | Sales |
| (f) Motor car | Bank |

3.10 Ivan's ledger accounts:

*Cash Account*

| | | £ | | | £ |
|---|---|---|---|---|---|
| 1.9.07 | Capital | 10 000 | 2.9.07 | Bank | 8 000 |
| 12.9.07 | Cash | 3 000 | 3.9.07 | Purchases | 1 000 |

*Capital Account*

| | | £ | | | £ |
|---|---|---|---|---|---|
| | | | 1.9.07 | Cash | 10 000 |

*Bank Account*

| | | £ | | | £ |
|---|---|---|---|---|---|
| 2.9.07 | Cash | 8 000 | 20.9.07 | Roy | 6 000 |
| 30.9.07 | Norman | 2 000 | | | |

*Purchases Account*

| | | £ | | | £ |
|---|---|---|---|---|---|
| 3.9.07 | Cash | 1 000 | | | |
| 10.9.07 | Roy | 6 000 | | | |

*Roy's Account*

| | | £ | | | £ |
|---|---|---|---|---|---|
| 20.9.07 | Bank | 6 000 | 10.9.07 | Purchases | 6 000 |

*Sales Account*

| | | £ | | | £ |
|---|---|---|---|---|---|
| | | | 12.9.07 | Cash | 3 000 |
| | | | 15.9.07 | Norman | 4 000 |

*Norman*

| | | £ | | | £ |
|---|---|---|---|---|---|
| 15.9.07 | Sales | 4 000 | 30.9.07 | Bank | 2 000 |

**3.11** Jones's ledger accounts:

*Bank Account*

| | | £ | | | £ |
|---|---|---|---|---|---|
| 1.10.08 | Capital | 20 000 | 10.10.08 | Petty cash | 1 000 |
| | | | 25.10.08 | Lang | 5 000 |
| | | | 29.10.08 | Green | 10 000 |

*Capital Account*

| | | £ | | | £ |
|---|---|---|---|---|---|
| | | | 1.10.08 | Bank | 20 000 |

*Van Account*

| | | £ | | | £ |
|---|---|---|---|---|---|
| 2.10.08 | Lang | 5 000 | | | |

*Lang's Account*

| | | £ | | | £ |
|---|---|---|---|---|---|
| 25.10.08 | Bank | 5 000 | 2.10.08 | Van | 5 000 |

*Purchases Account*

| | | £ | | | £ |
|---|---|---|---|---|---|
| 6.10.08 | Green | 15 000 | | | |
| 20.10.08 | Cash | 3 000 | | | |

*Green's Account*

| | | £ | | | £ |
|---|---|---|---|---|---|
| 28.10.08 | Discounts received | 500 | 6.10.08 | Purchases | 15 000 |
| 29.10.08 | Bank | 10 000 | | | |

*Petty Cash Account*

| | | £ | | | £ |
|---|---|---|---|---|---|
| 10.10.08 | Bank | 1 000 | 22.10.08 | Miscellaneous expenses | 500 |

*Sales*

| | | £ | | | £ |
|---|---|---|---|---|---|
| | | | 14.10.08 | Haddock | 6 000 |
| | | | 18.10.08 | Cash | 5 000 |

*Haddock*

| | | £ | | | £ |
|---|---|---|---|---|---|
| 14.10.08 | Sales | 6 000 | 30.10.08 | Discounts allowed | 600 |
| | | | 31.10.08 | Cash | 5 400 |

*Cash Account*

| | | £ | | | £ |
|---|---|---|---|---|---|
| 18.10.08 | Sales | 5 000 | 20.10.08 | Purchases | 3 000 |
| 31.10.08 | Haddock | 5 400 | | | |

*Miscellaneous Expenses*

| | | £ | | | £ |
|---|---|---|---|---|---|
| 22.10.08 | Petty cash | 500 | | | |

*Discounts Received Account*

| | | £ | | | £ |
|---|---|---|---|---|---|
| | | | 28.10.08 | Green | 500 |

*Discounts Allowed Account*

| | | £ | | | £ |
|---|---|---|---|---|---|
| 30.10.08 | Haddock | 600 | | | |

**3.13** (a), (b) and (c) Pat's ledger accounts:

*Cash Account*

| | | £ | | | £ |
|---|---|---|---|---|---|
| 1.12.07 | Capital | 10000 | 24.12.07 | Office expenses | 5000 |
| 29.12.07 | Fog | 4000 | 31.12.07 | Grass | 6000 |
| 29.12.07 | Mist | 6000 | 31.12.07 | Seed | 8000 |
| | | | 31.12.07 | Balance c/d | 1000 |
| | | 20000 | | | 20000 |
| 1.1.08 | Balance b/d | 1000 | | | |

*Capital Account*

| | | £ | | | £ |
|---|---|---|---|---|---|
| | | | 1.12.07 | Cash | 10000 |

*Purchases Account*

| | | £ | | | £ |
|---|---|---|---|---|---|
| 2.12.07 | Grass | 6000 | | | |
| 2.12.07 | Seed | 7000 | | | |
| 15.12.07 | Grass | 3000 | | | |
| 15.12.07 | Seed | 4000 | 31.12.07 | Balance c/d | 20000 |
| | | 20000 | | | 20000 |
| 1.01.08 | Balance b/d | 20000 | | | |

*Grass's Account*

| | | £ | | | £ |
|---|---|---|---|---|---|
| 12.12.07 | Purchases returned | 1000 | 2.12.07 | Purchases | 6000 |
| 31.12.07 | Cash | 6000 | 15.12.07 | Purchases | 3000 |
| 31.12.07 | Balance c/d | 2000 | | | |
| | | 9000 | | | 9000 |
| | | | 1.1.08 | Balance b/d | 2000 |

*Seed's Account*

| | | £ | | | £ |
|---|---|---|---|---|---|
| 12.12.07 | Purchases returned | 2000 | 2.12.07 | Purchases | 7000 |
| 31.12.07 | Cash | 8000 | 15.12.07 | Purchases | 4000 |
| 31.12.07 | Balance c/d | 1000 | | | |
| | | 11000 | | | 11000 |
| | | | 1.1.08 | Balance b/d | 1000 |

*Sales Account*

| | | £ | | | £ |
|---|---|---|---|---|---|
| | | | 10.12.07 | Fog | 3000 |
| | | | 10.12.07 | Mist | 4000 |
| | | | 20.12.07 | Fog | 2000 |
| 31.12.07 | Balance c/d | 12000 | 20.12.07 | Mist | 3000 |
| | | 12000 | | | 12000 |
| | | | 1.1.08 | Balance b/d | 12000 |

*Fog's Account*

| | | £ | | | £ |
|---|---|---|---|---|---|
| 10.12.07 | Sales | 3 000 | 29.12.07 | Cash | 4 000 |
| 20.12.07 | Sales | 2 000 | 31.12.07 | Balance c/d | 1 000 |
| | | 5 000 | | | 5 000 |
| 1.1.08 | Balance b/d | 1 000 | | | |

*Mist's Account*

| | | £ | | | £ |
|---|---|---|---|---|---|
| 10.12.07 | Sales | 4 000 | 29.12.07 | Cash | 6 000 |
| 20.12.07 | Sales | 3 000 | 31.12.07 | Balance c/d | 1 000 |
| | | 7 000 | | | 7 000 |
| 1.1.08 | Balance b/d | 1 000 | | | |

*Purchases Returned Account*

| | | £ | | | £ |
|---|---|---|---|---|---|
| | | | 12.12.07 | Grass | 1 000 |
| 31.12.07 | Balance c/d | 3 000 | 12.12.07 | Seed | 2 000 |
| | | 3 000 | | | 3 000 |
| | | | 1.1.08 | Balance b/d | 3 000 |

*Office Expenses Account*

| | | £ | | | £ |
|---|---|---|---|---|---|
| 24.12.07 | Cash | 5 000 | | | |

***Tutorial note***
It is unnecessary to balance off an account and bring down the balance if there is only a single entry in it.

(d) Pat's trial balance:

**Pat**
**Trial balance at 31 December 2007**

| | £ *Dr* | £ *Cr* |
|---|---|---|
| Cash | 1 000 | |
| Capital | | 10 000 |
| Purchases | 20 000 | |
| Grass | | 2 000 |
| Seed | | 1 000 |
| Sales | | 12 000 |
| Fog | 1 000 | |
| Mist | 1 000 | |
| Purchases returned | | 3 000 |
| Office expenses | 5 000 | |
| | 28 000 | 28 000 |

3.14 (a) Vale's books of account:

*Bank Account*

| | | £ | | | £ |
|---|---|---|---|---|---|
| 1.1.08 | Balance b/d | 5000 | 31.12.08 | Dodd | 29000 |
| 31.12.08 | Fish | 45000 | 31.12.08 | Delivery van | 12000 |
| 31.12.08 | Cash | 3000 | 31.12.08 | Balance c/d | 12000 |
| | | 53000 | | | 53000 |
| 1.1.09 | Balance b/d | 12000 | | | |

*Capital Account*

| | | £ | | | £ |
|---|---|---|---|---|---|
| | | | 1.1.08 | Balance b/d | 20000 |

*Cash Account*

| | | £ | | | £ |
|---|---|---|---|---|---|
| 1.1.08 | Balance b/d | 1000 | 31.12.08 | Purchases | 15000 |
| 31.12.08 | Sales | 20000 | 31.12.08 | Office expenses | 9000 |
| 31.12.08 | Fish | 7000 | 31.12.08 | Bank | 3000 |
| | | | 31.12.08 | Balance c/d | 1000 |
| | | 28000 | | | 28000 |
| 1.1.09 | Balance b/d | 1000 | | | |

*Dodd's Account*

| | | £ | | | £ |
|---|---|---|---|---|---|
| 31.12.08 | Bank | 29000 | 1.1.08 | Balance b/d | 2000 |
| 31.12.08 | Balance c/d | 3000 | 31.12.08 | Purchases | 30000 |
| | | 32000 | | | 32000 |
| | | | 1.1.09 | Balance b/d | 3000 |

*Fish's Account*

| | | £ | | | £ |
|---|---|---|---|---|---|
| 1.1.08 | Balance b/d | 6000 | 31.12.08 | Bank | 45000 |
| 31.12.08 | Sales | 50000 | 31.12.08 | Cash | 7000 |
| | | | 31.12.08 | Balance c/d | 4000 |
| | | 56000 | | | 56000 |
| 1.1.09 | Balance b/d | 4000 | | | |

*Furniture Account*

| | | £ | | | £ |
|---|---|---|---|---|---|
| 1.1.08 | Balance b/d | 10000 | | | |

*Purchases Account*

| | | £ | | | £ |
|---|---|---|---|---|---|
| 31.12.08 | Dodd | 30000 | | | |
| 31.12.08 | Cash | 15000 | 31.12.08 | Balance c/d | 45000 |
| | | 45000 | | | 45000 |
| 1.1.09 | Balance b/d | 45000 | | | |

*Sales Account*

| | | £ | | | £ |
|---|---|---|---|---|---|
| | | | 31.12.08 | Cash | 20000 |
| 31.12.08 | Balance c/d | 70000 | 31.12.08 | Fish | 50000 |
| | | 70000 | | | 70000 |
| | | | 1.1.09 | Balance b/d | 70000 |

*Office Expenses Account*

| | | £ | | | £ |
|---|---|---|---|---|---|
| 31.12.08 | Cash | 9000 | | | |

*Delivery Van Account*

| | | £ | | | £ |
|---|---|---|---|---|---|
| 31.12.08 | Bank | 12000 | | | |

(b) Vale's trial balance:

**Vale**
**Trial balance at 31 December 2008**

| | *Dr* | *Cr* |
|---|---|---|
| | £ | £ |
| Bank | 12000 | |
| Capital | | 20000 |
| Cash | 1000 | |
| Dodd | | 3000 |
| Fish | 4000 | |
| Furniture | 10000 | |
| Purchases | 45000 | |
| Sales | | 70000 |
| Office expenses | 9000 | |
| Delivery van | 12000 | |
| | 93000 | 93000 |

Chapter 4 4.4 Ethel's accounts:

**Ethel**
**Trading, profit and loss account for the year to 31 January 2007**

| | £ |
|---|---|
| Sales | 35000 |
| *Less*: Purchases | 20000 |
| *Gross profit* | 15000 |
| *Less*: Expenses: | |
| Office expenses | 11000 |
| *Net profit* | 4000 |

**Ethel**
**Balance sheet at 31 January 2007**

| | | |
|---|---|---|
| *Fixed assets* | £ | £ |
| Premises | | 8 000 |
| *Current assets* | | |
| Debtors | 6 000 | |
| Cash | 3 000 | |
| | 9 000 | |
| *Less*: Current liabilities | | |
| Creditors | 3 000 | 6 000 |
| | | 14 000 |
| Financed by: | | |
| *Capital* | | |
| Balance at 1 February 2000 | | 10 000 |
| Net profit for the year | | 4 000 |
| | | 14 000 |

4.5 Marion's accounts:

**Marion**
**Trading, profit and loss account for the year to 28 February 2008**

| | £000 | £000 |
|---|---|---|
| Sales | | 400 |
| *Less*: Purchases | | 200 |
| *Gross profit* | | 200 |
| *Less*: Expenses: | | |
| Heat and light | 10 | |
| Miscellaneous expenses | 25 | |
| Wages and salaries | 98 | 133 |
| *Net profit* | | 67 |

**Marion**
**Balance sheet at 28 February 2008**

| | | |
|---|---|---|
| *Fixed assets* | *£000* | *£000* |
| Buildings | | 50 |
| *Current assets* | | |
| Debtors | 30 | |
| Bank | 4 | |
| Cash | 2 | |
| | 36 | |
| *Less: Current liabilities* | | |
| Creditors | 24 | 12 |
| | | 62 |

| | £000 | £000 |
|---|---|---|
| Financed by: | | |
| *Capital* | | |
| Balance at 1 March 2001 | | 50 |
| Net profit for the year | 67 | |
| *Less*: Drawings | 55 | 12 |
| | | 62 |

Chapter 5

5.4 (a) Lathom's trading account:

**Lathom**
**Trading account for the year to 30 April 2007**

| | £ | £ |
|---|---|---|
| Sales | | 60 000 |
| *Less*: Cost of goods sold: | | |
| Opening stock | 3 000 | |
| Purchases | 45 000 | |
| | 48 000 | |
| *Less*: Closing stock | 4 000 | 44 000 |
| Gross profit | | 16 000 |

(b) The stock would be shown under current assets, normally as the first item.

5.6 Standish's accounts:

**Standish**
**Trading, profit and loss account for the year to 31 May 2009**

| | £ | £ |
|---|---|---|
| Sales | | 79 000 |
| *Less*: Cost of goods sold: | | |
| Opening stock | 7 000 | |
| Purchases | 52 000 | |
| | 59 000 | |
| *Less*: Closing stock | 12 000 | 47 000 |
| *Gross profit* | | 32 000 |
| *Less*: Expenses: | | |
| Heating and lighting | 1 500 | |
| Miscellaneous | 6 700 | |
| Wages and salaries | 17 800 | 26 000 |
| *Net profit* | | 6 000 |

**Standish**
**Balance sheet at 31 May 2009**

| | £ | £ |
|---|---|---|
| *Fixed assets* | | |
| Furniture and fittings | | 8 000 |
| *Current assets* | | |
| Stock | 12 000 | |
| Debtors | 6 000 | |
| Cash | 1 200 | |
| | 19 200 | |
| *Less: Current liabilities* | | |
| Creditors | 4 300 | 14 900 |
| | | 22 900 |
| Financed by: | | |
| *Capital* | | |
| Balance at 1 June 2008 | | 22 400 |
| Net profit for the year | 6 000 | |
| *Less*: Drawings | 5 500 | 500 |
| | | 22 900 |

5.9 Pine's accounts:

**Pine**
**Trading, profit and loss account for the year to 30 September 2009**

| | £ | £ |
|---|---|---|
| Sales | | 40 000 |
| *Less*: Cost of goods sold: | | |
| Purchases | 21 000 | |
| *Less*: Closing stock | 3 000 | 18 000 |
| *Gross profit* | | 22 000 |
| *Less*: Expenses: | | |
| Depreciation: furniture (15% × £8 000) | 1 200 | |
| General expenses | 14 000 | |
| Insurance (£2 000 – 200) | 1 800 | |
| Telephone (£1 500 + 500) | 2 000 | 19 000 |
| Net profit | | 3 000 |

**Pine**
**Balance sheet at 30 September 2009**

| | £ | £ | £ |
|---|---|---|---|
| *Fixed assets* | | | |
| Furniture | | | 8 000 |
| *Less*: Depreciation | | | 1 200 |
| | | *c/f* | 6 800 |

| | £ | £ | £ |
|---|---|---|---|
| | | b/f | 6800 |
| *Current assets* | | | |
| Stock | | 3000 | |
| Debtors | | 5000 | |
| Prepayments | | 200 | |
| Cash | | 400 | |
| | | 8600 | |
| *Less: Current liabilities* | | | |
| Creditors | 5900 | | |
| Accrual | 500 | 6400 | 2200 |
| | | | 9000 |
| Financed by: | | | |
| *Capital* | | | |
| At 1 October 2008 | | | 6000 |
| Net profit for the year | | | 3000 |
| | | | 9000 |

Chapter 6

6.4 Margo Ltd's accounts:

**Margo Limited**
**Profit and loss account for the year to 31 January 2007**

| | £000 |
|---|---|
| Profit for the financial year | 10 |
| Tax on profit | 3 |
| Profit after tax | 7 |
| Proposed dividend (10p × £50) | 5 |
| Retained profit for the year | 2 |

**Margo Limited**
**Balance sheet at 31 January 2007**

| | £000 | £000 | £000 |
|---|---|---|---|
| *Fixed assets* | | | |
| Plant and equipment at cost | | | 70 |
| *Less*: Accumulated depreciation | | | 25 |
| | | | 45 |
| *Current assets* | | | |
| Stocks | | 17 | |
| Trade debtors | | 20 | |
| Cash at bank and in hand | | 5 | |
| | c/f | 42 | 45 |

**Margo Limited**
**Balance sheet at 31 January 2006**

| | £000 | £000 | £000 |
|---|---|---|---|
| | | b/f 42 | 45 |
| *Less: Current liabilities* | | | |
| Trade creditors | 12 | | |
| Taxation | 3 | | |
| Proposed dividend | 5 | 20 | 22 |
| | | | 67 |

| *Capital and reserves* | *Authorized* | *Issued and fully paid* |
|---|---|---|
| | £000 | £000 |
| Share capital (ordinary shares of £1 each) | 75 | 50 |
| Profit and loss account (£15 + 2) | | 17 |
| | | 67 |

6.5 Harry Ltd's accounts:

**Harry Limited**
**Profit and loss account for the year to 28 February 2008**

| | £000 | £000 |
|---|---|---|
| Gross profit for the year | | 150 |
| Administration expenses [£65 + (10% × £60)] | 71 | |
| Distribution costs | 15 | 86 |
| Profit for the year | | 64 |
| Taxation | | 24 |
| Profit after tax | | 40 |
| Dividends: Ordinary proposed | 20 | |
| Preference paid | 6 | 26 |
| Retained profit for the year | | 14 |

**Harry Limited**
**Balance sheet at 28 February 2008**

| | £000 | £000 | £000 |
|---|---|---|---|
| *Fixed assets* | | | |
| Furniture and equipment at cost | | | 60 |
| *Less:* Accumulated depreciation | | | 42 |
| | | | 18 |
| *Current assets* | | | |
| Stocks | | 130 | |
| Trade debtors | | 135 | |
| Cash at bank and in hand | | 10 | |
| | | c/f 275 | 18 |

| | £000 | £000 | £000 |
|---|---|---|---|
| | | b/f 275 | 18 |
| *Less: Current liabilities* | | | |
| Trade creditors | 25 | | |
| Taxation | 24 | | |
| Proposed dividend | 20 | 69 | 206 |
| | | | 224 |

| *Capital and reserves* | *Authorized, issued and fully paid* |
|---|---|
| | £000 |
| Ordinary shares of £1 each | 100 |
| Cumulative 15% preference shares of £1 each | 40 |
| Share premium account | 20 |
| Profit and loss account (£50 + 14) | 64 |
| | 224 |

6.6 Jim Ltd's accounts:

(a)

**Jim Limited**
**Trading and profit and loss account for the year to 31 March 2008**

| | £000 | £000 | £000 |
|---|---|---|---|
| Sales | | | 270 |
| *Less*: Cost of goods sold: | | | |
| Opening stock | | 16 | |
| Purchases | | 124 | |
| | | 140 | |
| *Less*: Closing stock | | 14 | 126 |
| *Gross profit* | | | 144 |
| *Less*: Expenses: | | | |
| Advertising | | 3 | |
| Depreciation: furniture | | | |
| and fittings (15% × £20) | 3 | | |
| vehicles (25% × £40) | 10 | 13 | |
| Directors' fees | | 6 | |
| Rent and rates | | 10 | |
| Telephone and stationery | | 5 | |
| Travelling | | 2 | |
| Wages and salaries | | 24 | 63 |
| *Net profit* | | | 81 |
| Corporation tax | | | 25 |
| Net profit after tax | | | 56 |
| Proposed dividend | | | 28 |
| *Retained profit for the year* | | | 28 |

**Jim Limited**
**Balance sheet at 31 March 2008**

| | *Cost* | *Depreciation* | *Net book value* |
|---|---|---|---|
| | *£000* | *£000* | *£000* |
| *Fixed assets* | | | |
| Vehicles | 40 | 20 | 20 |
| Furniture and fittings | 20 | 12 | 8 |
| | 60 | 32 | 28 |
| *Current assets* | | | |
| Stocks | | 14 | |
| Debtors | | 118 | |
| Bank | | 11 | |
| | | 143 | |
| *Less: Current liabilities* | | | |
| Creditors | 12 | | |
| Taxation | 25 | | |
| Proposed dividend | 28 | 65 | 78 |
| | | | 106 |

| | *Authorized* | *Issued and fully paid* |
|---|---|---|
| | £000 | £000 |
| Capital and reserves | | |
| Ordinary shares of £1 each | 100 | 70 |
| Profit and loss account (£8 + 28) | | 36 |
| | | 106 |

(b) According to Jim Limited's balance sheet as at 31 March 2008 the value of the business was £106 000. This is misleading. Under the historic cost convention the balance sheet is merely a statement listing all the balances left in the double-entry book-keeping system after the preparation of the profit and loss account.

It would be relatively easy, for example, to amend the balance of £106 000 by adjusting the method used for calculating depreciation and for valuing stocks. Furthermore, when a business is liquidated it does not necessarily mean that the balances shown in the balance sheet for other items (e.g. fixed assets, debtors and creditors) will be realized at their balance sheet amounts. There will also be costs associated with the liquidation of the business.

Chapter 7

7.4 Megg's accounts:

**Megg**
**Manufacturing account for the year to 31 January 2007**

| | £000 | £000 |
|---|---|---|
| Direct materials: | | |
| Stock at 1 February 2006 | 10 | |
| Purchases | 34 | |
| | 44 | |
| *Less*: Stock at 31 January 2007 | 12 | |
| Materials consumed | | 32 |
| Direct wages | | 65 |
| Prime cost | | 97 |
| Factory overhead expenses: | | |
| Administration | 27 | |
| Heat and light | 9 | |
| Indirect wages | 13 | 49 |
| | | 146 |
| Work-in-progress at 1 February 2006 | 17 | |
| *Less*: Work-in-progress at 31 January 2007 | 14 | 3 |
| *Manufacturing cost of goods produced* | | 149 |

7.5 Moor's accounts:

**Moor**
**Manufacturing account for the year to 28 February 2008**

| | £ | £ |
|---|---|---|
| Direct materials: | | |
| Stock at 1 March 2007 | 13 000 | |
| Purchases | 127 500 | |
| | 140 500 | |
| *Less*: Stock at 28 February 2008 | 15 500 | 125 000 |
| Direct wages | | 50 000 |
| Prime cost | | 175 000 |
| Factory overheads | | 27 700 |
| | | 202 700 |
| Work-in-progress at 1 March 2007 | 8 400 | |
| *Less*: Work-in-progress at 28 February 2008 | 6 300 | 2 100 |
| *Manufacturing cost of goods produced* | | 204 800 |

Chapter 8

8.4 Dennis Ltd's accounts:

(a)

**Dennis Limited**
**Cash flow statement for the year ended 31 January 2007**

| | £000 | £000 |
|---|---|---|
| *Net cash inflow from operating activities* | | 4 |
| *Capital expenditure* | | |
| Payments to acquire tangible fixed assets | | (100) |
| | | (96) |
| *Management of liquid resource and financing* | | |
| Issue of ordinary share capital | | 100 |
| *Increase in cash* | | 4 |

Reconciliation of operating profit to net cash inflow from operating activities

| | £000 |
|---|---|
| Operating profit (£60 – 26) | 34 |
| Increase in stocks | (20) |
| Increase in debtors | (50) |
| Increase in creditors | 40 |
| Net cash inflow from operating activities | 4 |

(b) Dennis Limited generated £4000 cash from its operating activities during the year to 31 January 2007. It also increased its cash position by that amount during the year. However, it did invest £100 000 in purchasing some tangible fixed assets during the year, but this appeared to be paid for out of issuing another £100 000 of ordinary shares.

The cash from operating activities seems low. Its probably needs to examine its stock policy and its debtor collection arrangements because both stocks and debtors increased during the year. Its creditors also increased. Taken together, these changes might indicate that it is beginning to run into cash flow problems.

8.5 Frank Ltd's accounts:

**Frank Limited**
**Cash flow statement for the year ended 28 February 2009**

| | £000 | £000 |
|---|---|---|
| *Net cash inflow from operating activities* | | 70 |
| *Management of liquid resources and financing* | | |
| Issue of debenture loan | | 60 |
| Purchase of investments | | (100) |
| *Increase in cash* | | 30 |

Reconciliation of operating profit to net cash inflow from operating activities

| | £000 |
|---|---|
| Operating profit (£40 – 30) | 10 |
| Depreciation charges | 20 |
| Increase in stocks | (30) |
| Decrease in debtors | 110 |
| Decrease in creditors | (40) |
| Net cash inflow from operating activities | 70 |

No details of debenture interest were given in the question.

Reconciliation of net cash flow to movement in net debt:

| | £000 | £000 |
|---|---|---|
| Increase in cash in the period | 30 | |
| Cash inflow from increase in debt | (60) | (30) |
| Net debt at 1.3.08 | | (20) |
| Net debt at 28.2.09 | | (50) |

Analysis of changes in net debt:

| | At 1.3.08 | Cash flows | At 28.2.09 |
|---|---|---|---|
| | £000 | £000 | £000 |
| Cash at bank | (20) | 30 | 10 |
| Debt due after 1 year | – | (60) | (60) |
| Total | (20) | (30) | (50) |

(b) The cash flow statement for the year ended 28 February 2009 tells the managers of Frank Limited that the company increased its cash position by £30 000 during the year. Its operating activities generated £70 000 in cash. This was supplemented by issuing £60 000 of debenture stock making the total increase in cash £130 000. However, £100 000 of cash was used to purchase some investments.

More tests would need to be done but on the limited evidence available, the company's cash position as at the end of the year looked healthy.

Chapter 12

12.4 **Betty**

**Accounting ratios year to 31 January 2008:**

(a) Gross profit ratio:

$$\frac{\text{Gross profit}}{\text{Total sales revenue}} \times 100 = \frac{30}{100} \times 100 = \underline{\underline{30\%}}$$

(b) Net profit ratio:

$$\frac{\text{Net profit}}{\text{Sales}} \times 100 = \frac{14}{100} \times 100 = \underline{\underline{14\%}}$$

(c) Return on capital employed:

$$\frac{\text{Net profit}}{\text{Average capital}} \times 100 = \frac{14}{\frac{1}{2}(40 + 48)} \times 100 = \underline{\underline{31.8\%}}$$

$$or \quad \frac{\text{Net profit}}{\text{capital}} \times 100 = \frac{14}{48} \times 100 = \underline{\underline{29.2\%}}$$

(d) Current ratio:

$$\frac{\text{Current assets}}{\text{Current liabilities}} = \frac{25}{6} = \underline{\underline{4.2 \text{ to } 1}}$$

(e) Acid test:

$$\frac{\text{Current assets} - \text{stock}}{\text{Current liabilities}} = \frac{25 - 10}{6} = \underline{\underline{2.5 \text{ to } 1}}$$

(f) Stock turnover:

$$\frac{\text{Cost of goods sold}}{\text{Average stock}} = \frac{70}{\frac{1}{2}(15 + 10)} = \underline{\underline{5.6 \text{ times}}}$$

(g) Debtor collection period:

$$\frac{\text{Trade debtors}}{\text{Credit sales}} \times 365 = \frac{12}{100} \times 365 = \underline{\underline{44 \text{ days}}} \text{ (rounded up)}$$

12.5 **James Limited**

**Accounting ratios year to 28 February 2009:**

(a) Return on capital employed:

$$\frac{\text{Net profit before taxation and dividends}}{\text{Average shareholders' funds}} \times 100 = \frac{90}{\frac{1}{2}(600 + 620)} \times 100 = \underline{\underline{14.8\%}}$$

$$\textit{or } \frac{\text{net profit before taxation and dividends}}{\text{shareholders' funds}} \times 100 = \frac{90}{620} \times 100 = \underline{\underline{14.5\%}}$$

(b) Gross profit:

$$\frac{\text{Gross profit}}{\text{Sales}} \times 100 = \frac{600}{1200} \times 100 = \underline{\underline{50\%}}$$

(c) Mark-up:

$$\frac{\text{Gross profit}}{\text{Cost of goods sold}} \times 100 = \frac{600}{600} \times 100 = \underline{\underline{100\%}}$$

(d) Net profit:

$$\frac{\text{Net profit before taxation and dividends}}{\text{Sales}} \times 100 = \frac{90}{1200} \times 100 = \underline{\underline{7.5\%}}$$

(e) Acid test:

$$\frac{\text{Current assets} - \text{stock}}{\text{Current liabilities}} = \frac{275 - 75}{240} \times 100 = \underline{\underline{0.83 \text{ to } 1}}$$

(f) Fixed assets turnover:

$$\frac{\text{Sales}}{\text{Fixed assets (NBV)}} = \frac{1200}{685} = \underline{\underline{1.75 \text{ times}}}$$

(g) Debtor collection period:

$$\frac{\text{Trade debtors}}{\text{Credit sales}} \times 365 = \frac{200}{1200} \times 365 = \underline{\underline{61 \text{ days}}} \text{ (rounded up)}$$

(h) Capital gearing:

$$\frac{\text{Long-term loans}}{\text{Shareholders' funds and long-term loans}} \times 100 = \frac{100}{720} \times 100 = \underline{\underline{13.9\%}}$$

## Chapter 14

14.4 The main function of *accounting* is to collect quantifiable data, translate it into monetary terms, store the information and extract and summarize it in a format convenient for those parties who require such information.

Financial accounting and management accounting are two important branches of accounting. The main difference between them is that financial accounting specializes in supplying information to parties *external* to an entity, such as shareholders or governmental departments. Management accounting information is mainly directed at the supply of information to parties *internal* to an entity, such as the entity's directors and managers.

14.5 A management accountant employed by a large manufacturing entity will be involved in the collecting and storing of data (largely, although not exclusively, of a financial nature) and the supply of information to management for planning, control and decision-making purposes. Increasingly, a management accountant is seen to be an integral member of an entity's management team responsible for advice on all financial matters.

Depending on seniority, the management accountant may be involved in some routine and basic duties such as the processing of data and the calculation of product costs and the valuation of stocks. At a more senior level, the role may be much more concerned with advising on the financial impact of a wide variety of managerial decisions, such as whether to close down a product line or determining the selling price of a new product.

## Chapter 15

15.2 Charge to production:

(a) FIFO:

| | | £ |
|---|---|---|
| 1000 units | @ £20 = | 20 000 |
| 250 units | @ £25 = | 6 250 |
| Charge to production | | 26 250 |

(b) Continuous weighted average:

| *Date* | *Units* | | *Value* |
|---|---|---|---|
| | | | £ |
| 1.1.06 | 1 000 | @ £20 | 20 000 |
| 15.1.06 | 500 | @ £25 | 12 500 |
| | 1 500 | | 32 500 |

$$\text{Average} = \frac{£32\,500}{1\,500} = £21.67$$

Charge to production on 31.1.09 = 1 250 × £21.67 = £27 088

**15.3** Value of closing stock

**Material ST 2**

| | *Stock* | *Units* | *Total stock value* £ | *Average unit price* £ |
|---|---|---|---|---|
| 1.2.07 | Opening | 500 | 500 | 1.00 |
| 10.2.07 | Receipts | 200 | 220 | |
| | | 700 | 720 | 1.03 |
| 12.2.07 | Receipts | 100 | 112 | |
| | | 800 | 832 | 1.04 |
| 17.2.07 | Issues | (400) | (416) | |
| 25.2.07 | Receipts | 300 | 345 | |
| | | 700 | 761 | 1.09 |
| 27.2.07 | Issues | (250) | (273) | |
| 28.0.07 | *Closing stock* | 450 | 488 | |

## Chapter 16

**16.6** Scar Ltd's overhead:
**Scar Limited**
**Overhead apportionment January 2009:**

| | *Production Department* | | *Service Department* |
|---|---|---|---|
| | A | B | |
| | £000 | £000 | £000 |
| Allocated expenses | 65 | 35 | 50 |
| Apportionment of service department's expenses in the ratio 60 : 40 | 30 | 20 | (50) |
| Overhead to be charged | 95 | 55 | – |

**16.7** Bank Ltd's overhead:

**Bank Limited**
**Assembly department – overhead absorption methods:**

(a) Specific units:

$$\frac{\text{Total cost centre overhead}}{\text{Number of units}} = \frac{£250\,000}{50\,000} = £5 \text{ per unit}$$

(b) Direct materials:

$$\frac{\text{Total cost centre overhead}}{\text{Direct materials}} \times 100 = \frac{£250\,000}{500\,000} \times 100 = 50\%$$

Therefore 50% of £8 = <u>£4 per unit</u>

(c) Direct labour:

$$\frac{\text{Total cost centre overhead}}{\text{Direct labour}} \times 100 = \frac{£250\,000}{1\,000\,000} \times 100 = 25\%$$

Therefore 25% of £30 = <u>£7.50 per unit</u>

(d) Prime cost:

$$\frac{\text{Total cost centre overhead}}{\text{Prime cost}} \times 100 = \frac{£250\,000}{1\,530\,000} \times 100 = 16.34\%$$

Therefore 16.34% of £40 = <u>£6.54 per unit</u>

(e) Direct labour hours:

$$\frac{\text{Total cost centre overhead}}{\text{Direct labour hours}} = \frac{£250\,000}{100\,000} = £2.50 \text{ per direct labour hour}$$

Therefore £2.50 of 3.5 DLH = <u>£8.75 per unit</u>

(f) Machine hours:

$$\frac{\text{Total cost centre overhead}}{\text{Machine hours}} = \frac{£250\,000}{25\,000} = £10 \text{ per machine hour}$$

Therefore £10 of 0.75 = <u>£7.50 per unit</u>

Chapter 17 **17.5** Direct labour cost budget for Tom Ltd:

**TOM LIMITED**

**(a) Direct materials usage budget:**

| | *Number of units* | | | | | | |
|---|---|---|---|---|---|---|---|
| *Month* | *30.4.08* | *31.5.08* | *30.6.08* | *31.7.08* | *31.8.08* | *30.9.08* | *Six months to 30.9.08* |
| Component: | | | | | | | |
| A6 (2 units for X) | 280 | 560 | 1 400 | 760 | 600 | 480 | 4 080 |
| B9 (3 units for X) | 420 | 840 | 2 100 | 1 140 | 900 | 720 | 6 120 |

**(b) Direct materials purchase budget:**

| | | | | | | | |
|---|---|---|---|---|---|---|---|
| *Component A6* | | | | | | | |
| Material usage (as above) | 280 | 560 | 1 400 | 760 | 600 | 480 | 4 080 |
| *Add*: Desired closing stock | 110 | 220 | 560 | 300 | 240 | 200 | 200 |
| | 390 | 780 | 1 960 | 1 060 | 840 | 680 | 4 280 |
| *Less*: Opening stock | 100 | 110 | 220 | 560 | 300 | 240 | 100 |
| Purchases (units) × | 290 | 670 | 1 740 | 500 | 540 | 440 | 4 180 |
| Price per unit = | £5 | £5 | £5 | £5 | £5 | £5 | £5 |
| Total purchases | £1 450 | £3 350 | £8 700 | £2 500 | £2 700 | £2 200 | £20 900 |
| *Component B9* | | | | | | | |
| Material usage (as above) | 420 | 840 | 2 100 | 1 140 | 900 | 720 | 6 120 |
| *Add*: Desired closing stock | 250 | 630 | 340 | 300 | 200 | 180 | 180 |
| | 670 | 1 470 | 2 440 | 1 440 | 1 100 | 900 | 6 300 |
| *Less*: Opening stock | 200 | 250 | 630 | 340 | 300 | 200 | 200 |
| Purchases (units) | 470 | 1 220 | 1 810 | 1 100 | 800 | 700 | 6 100 |
| Price per unit | £10 | £10 | £10 | £10 | £10 | £10 | £10 |
| Total purchases | £4 700 | £12 200 | £18 100 | £11 000 | £8 000 | £7 000 | £61 000 |

**17.6** Direct labour budget for Don Ltd:

**Don Limited**

**Direct labour cost budget:**

| | | *Quarter* | | |
|---|---|---|---|---|
| | 30.6.09 | 31.7.09 | 31.8.09 | *Three months to 31.8.09* |
| Grade: | | | | |
| *Production* (units) × | 600 | 700 | 650 | 1 950 |
| Direct labour hours per unit = | 3 | 3 | 3 | 3 |
| Total direct labour hours | 1 800 | 2 100 | 1 950 | 5 850 |
| Budgeted rate per hour (£) × | 4 | 4 | 4 | 4 |
| Production cost (£) = *c/f* | 7 200 | 8 400 | 7 800 | 23 400 |

| | | Quarter | | |
|---|---|---|---|---|
| | 30.6.09 | 31.7.09 | 31.8.09 | *Three months to 31.8.09* |
| Production cost (£) = *b/f* | 7200 | 8400 | 7800 | 23400 |
| *Finishing* (units) | 600 | 700 | 650 | 1950 |
| Direct labour hours per unit × | 2 | 2 | 2 | 2 |
| Total direct labour hours = | 1200 | 1400 | 1300 | 3900 |
| Budgeted rate per hour (£) × | 8 | 8 | 8 | 8 |
| Finishing cost (£) = | 9600 | 11200 | 10400 | 31200 |
| Total budgeted direct labour cost (£) | 16800 | 19600 | 18200 | 54600 |

Chapter 18

**18.4 Variances for X Ltd:**

(a) Direct materials total variance:

| | £ | |
|---|---|---|
| Actual price per unit × actual quantity = £12 × 6 units | 72 | |
| *Less*: Standard price per unit × standard quantity for actual production = £10 × 5 units | 50 | |
| | 22 | (A) |

(b) Direct materials price variance:
(Actual price – standard price) × actual quantity
= (£12 – 10) × 6 units — £12 (A)

(c) Direct materials usage variance:
(Actual quantity – standard quantity) × standard price = (6 – 5 units) × £10 — £10 (A)

**18.6 Variances for Bruce Ltd:**

(a) Direct labour total variance:

| | £ | |
|---|---|---|
| Actual hours × actual hourly rate = 1000 hrs × £6.50 | 6 500 | |
| *Less*: Standard hours for actual production × standard hourly rate = 900 hrs × £6.00 | 5400 | |
| | £1 100 | (A) |

(b) Direct labour rate variance:
(Actual hourly – standard hourly rate)
× actual hours = (£6.50 – 6.00) × 1000 hrs — £500 (A)

(c) Direct labour efficiency variance:
(Actual hours – standard hours for actual production)
× standard hourly rate = (1000 hrs – 900) × £6.00 — £600 (A)

**18.8 Overhead variances for Anthea Ltd:**

(a) Fixed production overhead total variance:

| | £ | |
|---|---|---|
| Actual fixed overhead | 150 000 | |
| *Less*: Standard hours of production × fixed production overhead absorption rate = (8000 hrs × £15) | 120 000 | |
| | £30 000 | (A) |

(b) Fixed production overhead expenditure variance:
Actual fixed overhead – budgeted fixed overhead = (£150 000 – 135 000) £15 000 (A)

(c) Fixed production overhead volume variance:
Budgeted fixed overhead – (standard hours of production × fixed production overhead absorption rate) = [£135 000 – (8000 × £15)] £15 000 (A)

**18.9 Performance measures for Anthea Ltd:**

Performance measures:

(a) Efficiency ratio:

$$\frac{\text{SHP}}{\text{Actual hours}} \times 100 = \frac{8000}{10\,000} \times 100 = \underline{\underline{80\%}}$$

(b) Capacity ratio:

$$\frac{\text{Actual hours}}{\text{Budgeted hours*}} \times 100 = \frac{10\,000}{9000} \times 100 = \underline{\underline{111.1\%}}$$

(c) Production volume ratio:

$$\frac{\text{SHP}}{\text{Budgeted hours*}} \times 100 = \frac{8000}{9000} \times 100 = \underline{\underline{88.9\%}}$$

$$^{*}\frac{135\,000}{15}$$

**18.12 Selling price variance for Milton Ltd:**

(a) Selling price variance:

[Actual sales revenue – (actual quantity × standard cost per unit)] – (actual quantity × standard profit per unit) = [£99 000 – (9000 × £7)] – (9000 × £3*) = £9000 (F)

* £10 – 3

(b) Sales volume profit variance:

(Actual quantity – budgeted quantity) × standard profit = (9000 units – 10 000) × £3 £3000 (A)

(c) Sales variances = £9000 (F) + 3000 (A) = £6000 (F)

Chapter 19

**19.4** Contribution analysis for Pole Ltd:

**Pole Limited**
**Marginal cost statement for the year to 31 January 2009**

| | £000 | £000 |
|---|---|---|
| Sales | | 450 |
| *Less*: Variable costs: | | |
| Direct materials | 60 | |
| Direct wages | 26 | |
| Administration expenses: variable (£7 + 4) | 11 | |
| Research and development expenditure: variable (£15 + 5) | 20 | |
| Selling and distribution expenditure: variable (£4 + 9) | 13 | 130 |
| | | 320 |
| *Contribution* | | |
| *Less*: Fixed costs: | | |
| Administration expenses (£30 + 16) | 46 | |
| Materials: indirect | 5 | |
| Production overhead | 40 | |
| Research and development expenditure (£60 + 5) | 65 | |
| Selling and distribution expenditure (£80 + 21) | 101 | |
| Wages: indirect | 13 | 270 |
| *Profit* | | 50 |

**19.5** Break-even chart for Giles Ltd:

**Giles Limited**

(a) (i) *Break-even point*:
In value terms:

$$\frac{\text{Fixed costs} \times \text{sales}}{\text{Contribution}} = \frac{£150\,000 \times 500}{(500 - 300)} = £375\,000$$

In units:

| | £ |
|---|---|
| Selling price per unit (£500 ÷ 50) | 10 |
| *Less*: Variable cost per unit (£300 ÷ 50) | 6 |
| Contribution per unit | 4 |

$$\frac{\text{Fixed costs}}{\text{Contribution per unit}} = \frac{£150\,000}{4} = 37\,500 \text{ units}$$

(ii) *Margin of safety*:
In value terms:

$$\frac{\text{Profit} \times \text{sales}}{\text{Contribution}} = \frac{£50\,000 \times 500}{200} = £125\,000$$

In units:

$$\frac{\text{Profit}}{\text{Contribution per unit}} = \frac{£50\,000}{4} = 12\,500 \text{ units}$$

(b) *Break-even chart*:

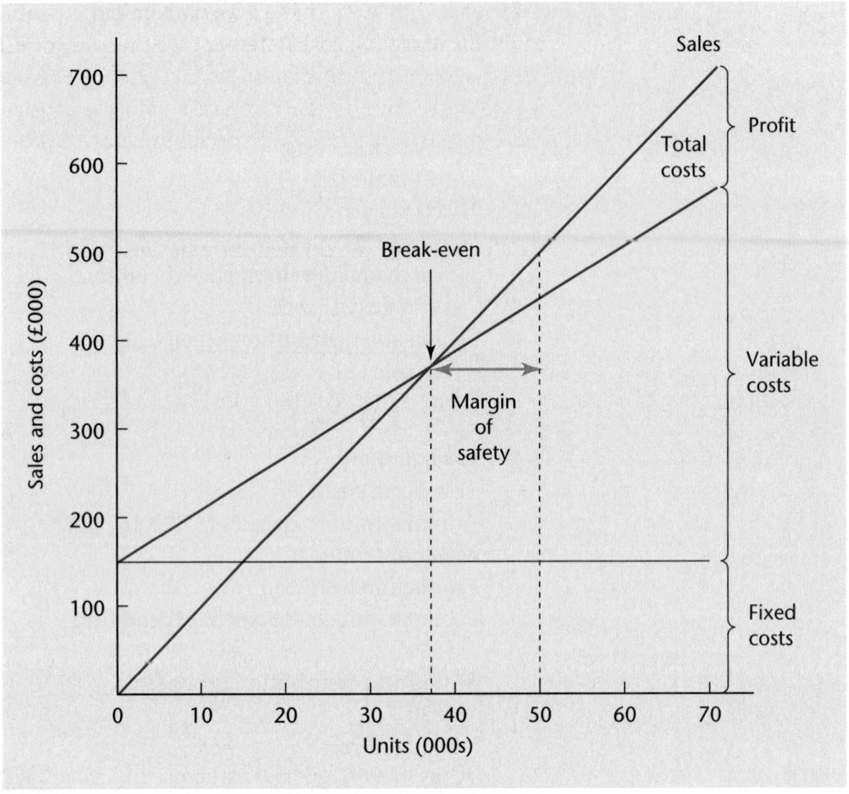


Chapter 20

**20.4 A special contract for Micro Ltd:**

Budgeted contribution per unit of limiting factor for the year:

$$\frac{£250\,000}{50\,000} = \underline{\underline{£5 \text{ per direct labour hour}}}$$

Contribution per unit of limiting factor for the special contract:

| | £ | £ |
|---|---|---|
| Contract price | | 50 000 |
| *Less*: Variable costs: | | |
| Direct materials | 10 000 | |
| Direct labour | 30 000 | 40 000 |
| Contribution | | 10 000 |

Therefore contribution per unit of limiting factor:

$$\frac{£10\,000}{4\,000 \text{ DLH}} = \underline{\underline{£2.50 \text{ per direct labour hour}}}$$

*Conclusion*:
The special contract earns less contribution per unit of limiting factor than does the *average* of ordinary budgeted work. It may be profitable to accept the contract if either it displaces less profitable work or surplus direct labour hours are available. A careful assessment should be undertaken to ascertain whether much more profitable work would be found than is the case with the contract if it will displace other more profitable contracts that could arise in the near future.

**20.5** Contributions for Temple Ltd:

(a) **Calculation of the contribution per unit of limiting factor**

(i) Normal work:

| | £ |
|---|---|
| Sales | 6 000 |
| Direct materials (100 kilos) | 700 |
| Direct labour (200 hours) | 3 000 |
| Variable overhead | 300 |
| | 4 000 |
| Contribution | 2 000 |

*Contribution per unit of key factor*:

Direct materials: $\frac{£2000}{100 \text{ kilos}} = £20 \text{ per kilo}$

Direct labour: $\frac{£2000}{200 \text{ direct labour hours}} = £10 \text{ per direct labour hour}$

(ii) and (iii) Calculation of the contribution per unit of limiting factor for each of the proposed two new contracts:

| | Contract 1 | Contract 2 |
|---|---|---|
| | £000 | £000 |
| Contract price | 1 000 | 2 100 |
| *Less*: Variable costs | | |
| Direct materials | 300 | 600 |
| Direct labour | 300 | 750 |
| Variable overhead | 100 | 250 |
| | 700 | 1 600 |
| Contribution | 300 | 500 |
| *Contribution per unit of key factor*: | | |
| Direct materials | £300 / 50 kilos | £500 / 100 kilos |
| = | £6 per kilo | £5 per kilo |
| Direct labour | £300 / 10 DLH | £500 / 25 DLH |
| = | £30 per DLH | £20 per DLH |

*Summary of contribution per unit of limiting factor*:

| | Direct materials | Direct labour |
|---|---|---|
| | £ | £ |
| Normal work | 20 | 10 |
| Contract 1 | 6 | 5 |
| Contract 2 | 30 | 20 |

(b) **Calculation of the total maximum contribution**

*Contract 1*

If Contract 1 is accepted, it will earn a total contribution of £300 000. This will leave 150 000 kilos of direct material available for its normal work (200 000 kilos maximum available, less the 50 000 used on Contract 1). This means that 1 500 units of ordinary work could be undertaken (150 000 kilos divided by 100 kilos per unit).

However, Contract 1 will absorb 10 000 direct labour hours, leaving 90 000 DLH available (100 000 DLH less 10 000 DLH). As each unit of ordinary work uses 200 DLH, the maximum number of units that could be undertaken is 450 (90 000 DLH divided by 200 DLH). Thus the maximum number of units of ordinary work that could be undertaken if Contract 1 is accepted is 450 and NOT 1500 units if direct materials were the only limiting factor. As each unit makes a contribution of £2000, the total contribution would be £900 000 (450 units × £2000).

The total maximum contribution, if Contract 1 is accepted, is therefore, £1 200 000 (£300 000 + 900 000).

*Contract 2*

If Contract 2 is accepted, only 100 000 kilos of direct materials will be available for ordinary work (200 000 kilos maximum available less 100 000 required for Contract 2). This means that only 1000 normal jobs could be undertaken (100 000 kilos divided by 100 kilos required per unit).

Contract 2 would absorb 25 000 direct labour hours, leaving 75 000 available for normal work (100 000 maximum DLH less the 25 000 DLH used by Contract 2). As each unit of normal work takes 200 hours, only 375 units could be made (75 000 DLH divided by 200 DLH per unit). Thus if this contract is accepted, 375 is the maximum number of normal jobs that could be undertaken. This would give a total contribution of £750 000 (375 units multiplied by £2000 of contribution per unit).

If Contract 2 is accepted, the total maximum contribution would be £1 250 000, i.e. Contract 2's contribution of £500 000 plus the contribution of £750 000 from the normal work.

*The decision*

Accept Contract 2 because the maximum total contribution would be £1 250 000 compared with the £1 200 000 if Contract 1 was accepted.

*Tutorial notes*

1 The various cost relationships are assumed to remain unchanged at all levels of activity.
2 Fixed costs will not be affected irrespective of which contract is accepted.
3 The market for Temple's normal sales is assumed to be flexible.
4 Contract 2 will absorb one-half of the available direct materials and one-quarter of the available direct labour hours. Would the company want to commit such resources to work that may be uncertain and unreliable and that could have an adverse impact on its normal customers?

Chapter 21

21.5 **Payback for Buchan Enterprises:**

(a) Payback period:

| *Year* | *Investment outlay* | *Cash inflow* | *Net cash flow* | *Cumulative cash flow* |
|---|---|---|---|---|
| | £ | £ | £ | £ |
| 1 | (50 000) | 8 000 | (42 000) | (42 000) |
| 2 | – | 16 000 | 16 000 | (26 000) |
| 3 | – | 40 000 | 40 000 | 14 000 |
| 4 | – | 45 000 | 45 000 | 59 000 |
| 5 | – | 37 000 | 37 000 | 96 000 |

Net cash flow becomes positive in Year 3. Assuming the net cash flow accrues evenly, it becomes positive during August: (26/40 × 12) = 7.8 months. The payback period, therefore, is about 2 years 8 months.

(b) Discounted payback period:

| *Year* | *Net cash flow* | *Discount factor @ 12%* | *Discounted net cash flow* | *Cumulative net cash flow* |
|---|---|---|---|---|
| | £ | | £ | £ |
| 0 | (50 000) | 1.0000 | (50 000) | (50 000) |
| 1 | 8 000 | 0.8929 | 7 143 | (42 857) |
| 2 | 16 000 | 0.7929 | 12 686 | (30 171) |
| 3 | 40 000 | 0.7118 | 28 472 | (1 699) |
| 4 | 45 000 | 0.6355 | 28 598 | 26 899 |
| 5 | 37 000 | 0.5674 | 20 994 | 47 893 |

Discounted net cash flow becomes positive in Year 4. Assuming the net cash flow accrues evenly throughout the year, it becomes positive in January of Year 4 (1 699/28 598 × 12 = 0.7). Discounted payback period therefore equals 3 years 1 month. This value is in contrast with the payback method, where the net cash flow becomes positive in August of Year 3 (i.e. 2 years 8 months).

21.6 **Lender Ltd's accounting rate of return:**

$$\text{Accounting rate of return (APR)} = \frac{\text{average annual net profit after tax}}{\text{cost of the investment}} \times 100\%$$

$$= \frac{\frac{1}{5}(£18\,000 + 47\,000 + 65\,000 + 65\,000 + 30\,000)}{100\,000} \times 100\%$$

$$= \frac{45\,000}{100\,000} \times 100\%$$

$$= \underline{\underline{45\%}}$$

*Note*: Based on the average investment, the ARR

$$= \frac{£45\,000}{\frac{1}{2}(100\,000 + 0)} \times 100\%$$

$$= \underline{\underline{90\%}}$$

**21.7 Net present value for a Lockhart project:**

Net present value:

| *Year* | *Net cash flow £000* | *Discount factor @15%* | *Present value £000* |
|---|---|---|---|
| 1 | 800 | 0.8696 | 696 |
| 2 | 850 | 0.7561 | 643 |
| 3 | 830 | 0.6575 | 546 |
| 4 | 1 200 | 0.5718 | 686 |
| 5 | 700 | 0.4972 | 348 |
| Total present value | | | 2 919 |
| Initial cost | | | 2 500 |
| *Net present value* | | | 419 |

# Index